VBSCRIPT INTERACTIVE COURSE

NOEL JERKE, MICHAEL HATMAKER, JONNY ANDERSON

WAITE GROUP PRESS™

A Division of

Sams Publishing

Corte Madera, C

PUBLISHER • Mitchell Waite
ASSOCIATE PUBLISHER • Charles Drucker

ACQUISITIONS MANAGER • Jill Pisoni

EDITORIAL DIRECTOR • John Crudo
PROJECT EDITOR • Kurt Stephan
DEVELOPMENTAL EDITOR • Russ Jacobs
TECHNICAL EDITOR • Steve Peschka
SOFTWARE SPECIALIST • Dan Scherf
CD-ROM TESTER • Ken Cox
COPY EDITOR • Ann Longknife/Creative Solutions

PRODUCTION DIRECTOR • Julianne Ososke
PRODUCTION MANAGER • Cecile Kaufman
SENIOR DESIGNER • Sestina Quarequio
DESIGNERS • Karen Johnston, Jil Weil
PRODUCTION EDITOR • Sally St. Lawrence
PRODUCTION SUPERVISORS • Brad Chinn, Charlotte Clapp
PRODUCTION • Jeanne Clark, Ayanna Lacey, Polly Lavrick, Lisa Pletka, Mary Ellen Stephenson
INDEXERS • Chris Barrick, Ginny Bess
ILLUSTRATIONS • Daniel Harris, Dennis Sheehan
CHAPTER OPENER ILLUSTRATION • © Steven Hunt/Image Bank
COVER ILLUSTRATION • Robert Dougherty

Printed in the United States of America
97 98 99 • 10 9 8 7 6 5 4 3 2 1

Library of Congress Cataloging-in-Publication Data
Jerke, Noel.
    VBScript interactive course / Noel Jerke, Michael Hatmaker, Jonny Anderson.
      p.   cm.
    Includes index.
    ISBN 1-57169-046-8
    1. Microsoft Visual Basic. 2. VBScript (Computer program language) I. Hatmaker, Michael.
    II. Anderson, Jonny, 1968- III. Title.
    QA76.73.B3J473   1997
    005.2'762--dc21
                                                     96-45244
                                                    CIP

www.waite.com/ezone
eZone Guided Tour

The Interactive Course title in your hands provides you with an unprecedented training system. The book itself is everything you're used to from Waite Group Press: thorough, hands-on coverage of an important cutting-edge product. There is far more, however, to the Interactive Course than the pages you are now holding. Using your Internet connection, you also get access to the eZone, where you'll find dedicated services designed to assist you through the book and make sure you really understand the subject.

FREE TUTORS, TESTING, CERTIFICATION, AND RESOURCES

The eZone provides a host of online services and resources designed to help you work through this book. If you get hung up with a particular lesson, all you have to do is ask an online mentor, a live expert in the subject you're studying. A mailing list lets you exchange ideas and hints with others taking the same course. A resource page links you to the hottest related web sites, and a monthly newsletter keeps you up to date with eZone enhancements and industry developments.

You'll also be able to work toward a certificate of completion. You can take lesson quizzes online, receive an immediate grade, and track your progress through the course. The chapters are available online, too, so that you can refer to them when you need to. Once you've finished the course with a passing grade, you can print a personalized certificate of completion, suitable for framing.

Best of all, there's no additional cost for all of these services. They are included in the price of the book. Once you journey into the eZone, you'll never want to go back to traditional book learning.

EXPLORING THE EZONE

You'll find the eZone on the World Wide Web. Fire up your Web browser and enter the following site:

`http://www.waite.com/ezone`

From there, click the eZone icon and you're on your way.

> **NOTE**
>
> If your browser does not support frames, or if you prefer frameless pages, click the *No Frames* link. Your browser must also support "cookies." Interactive Course titles that come with a CD include a copy of Microsoft's Internet Explorer browser (version 3.01), which supports frames and cookie technology. These books include an appendix to help you with browser installation, setup, and operation.

Navigating the eZone

When you enter the eZone, the eZone home page, shown in Figure 1, appears.

As you can see in Figure 1, the screen is divided into three frames. The eZone icon in the top left frame is always visible. This icon is a link back to the eZone home page. No matter where you are, you can always find your way home by clicking this icon. Beneath the eZone icon is a navigation frame containing several icons. Each of these icons links to an area of the eZone. You'll learn about each of these areas as you read through this guide.

The largest frame on the page is the main frame. This is where you'll find the information. Scroll down this frame and you'll see text-based links to the eZone areas. Keep going and you'll find the latest eZone news and information, updated regularly. Be sure to check out this information each time you enter the eZone.

Start Here

Click the *Start Here* icon in the navigation frame. This takes you to the Getting Started page where you'll find different sets of instructions. Your options are:

```
I am a GUEST and visiting the EZONE.
I HAVE the EZONE BOOK and I am ready to start the course.
I want to BUY an EZONE COURSE and get my Book.
```

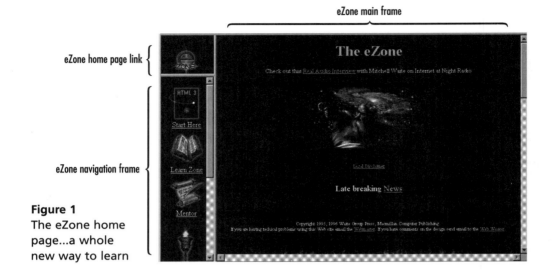

eZone main frame

eZone home page link

eZone navigation frame

Figure 1
The eZone home
page...a whole
new way to learn

Clicking these options provides instructions for how to sign on as a guest, register for a course for which you have a book, or sign up for a course and order the corresponding book.

In the next couple of pages, you'll see how to explore the eZone as a guest, register yourself, enroll in a course, and take advantage of the many service areas provided at no additional charge.

Signing on as a Guest

On your first visit to the eZone, consider signing on as a guest, even if you have a book and are anxious to get started. Signing on as guest lets you roam the eZone and familiarize yourself with its various areas and features before setting any options. You can view the first chapter of any available course and take the quizzes for that chapter (although Guests' scores aren't saved).

You can ask support questions, view the latest news, and even view the FAQs for a course. Until you register, you can't ask the mentors any questions, sign up for the eZone newsletter, or access the resource links page, but there's still plenty of stuff to check out as a Guest.

To explore the eZone as a Guest, click the *Learn* icon in the navigation frame or on the word 'Learn' at the bottom of the main frame. The first time you do this, the registration form appears. As a guest, you can ignore this form.

Just click the *Guest* link, and the Course Matrix appears. From here, you can navigate the eZone in the same manner as registered course members. Remember, however, that access for Guests is limited.

THE INITIATION ZONE

Once you're comfortable navigating the eZone, we know you'll be anxious to start learning and taking advantage of this cutting edge training system.

The first thing you have to do is create an entry for yourself in the eZone records by registering. Click the *Initiation* icon in the navigation frame or on the *Initiate* link at the bottom of the main frame, and you move into the Initiate zone, shown in Figure 2.

Initiate (Register)

You want the *Initiate (Register)* option to start the registration process. Click the *Register* link and a registration form appears.

NOTE

You don't need a book to register in the eZone. In fact, by registering before you get your hands on an Interactive Course book, you can enroll in the course as soon as you possess the book. You can save a little time by skipping the steps of creating your eZone password and ID.

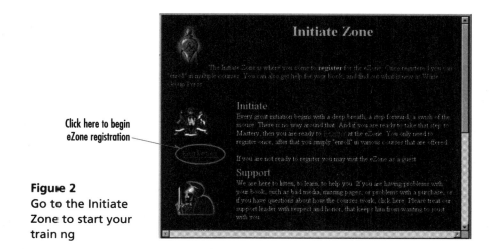

Click here to begin eZone registration

Figure 2
Go to the Initiate Zone to start your training

You need to fill out the registration form completely. Click inside each text box, then type in the appropriate information; pressing the (TAB) key cycles you through these text fields. In addition to a little information about yourself, you'll need to enter:

`Requested User ID` — Type the name you'd like to use online.
`Password (5-8 Characters)` — Type the password you'd like to use online.
`Password (Verify)` — Retype your selected password, to be sure it's properly recorded.

Once you've supplied all the information, click the *Register* button to submit the form to the eZone's data banks. A confirming message lets you know that you've successfully registered. Registration is important. If you don't register, you can't take advantage of the full power of the eZone.

Entering the eZone as a Registered User

Once you've registered, you'll use your unique ID and password to enter the eZone. Next time you enter the eZone, you need only click the *Learn Zone* icon in the navigation frame or the *Learn* link in the main frame. A simple two-line form pops up, allowing you to type in the user ID and password you created when you registered.

THE LEARN ZONE

Now that you're registered, it's time to get down to business. Much of the course work is done in the Learn Zone, shown in Figure 3. To get here, click the *Learn* icon in the navigation frame.

The Course Matrix

When you enter the Learn Zone, you'll see lists of courses and certification programs. This is called the Course Matrix, and it provides a way to select the various eZone courses. Under each discipline—such as Web Designer, Business, or Code Master—is a list of core courses. To select a course using the Course Matrix, click the desired course (titles in underlined white letters are currently available). In a moment, a three-columned Chapters Grid appears.

Verification

The first time you select a specific course, you must enroll. You'll need a copy of the book to do so. You will be asked to provide a specific word from the book. This verifies that you have the proper book for the selected course. The verification process uses the familiar page-line-word formula; in other words, you'll need to locate and enter a word from a specified line of text on a specified page of your book. Click your mouse in the text box and type the specified word to verify that you have the course book.

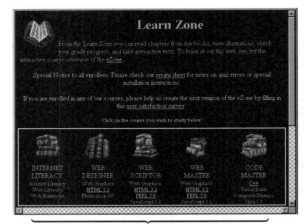

Figure 3
Use the Course
Matrix in the Learn
Zone to select
courses

Course Matrix

Passing Percentage

You can also set a minimum passing percentage for your course. This determines what percentage of test questions you need to answer correctly in order to pass the course. The percentage is preset at 70%, but you can select 50%, 60%, 70%, 80%, 90%, or 100%.

To set a minimum passing percentage, click the text box for this option to see a list of choices, then click the option you prefer. Once you've typed in the correct word and set the desired passing percentage, click the *Verify* button to enroll in the course. The Chapters Grid appears.

The Chapters Grid

The Chapters Grid, like the one featured in Figure 4, lets you select topics and quizzes for your course, while keeping track of your progress.

The Chapters column lists the chapters of the book; clicking a chapter lets you view and select its lessons. The middle column, Score, shows your current grade for the chapter (as a percentage). The Status column uses a colored indicator to let you know with a glance whether you've passed (green), failed (red), are still working through (yellow), or have not yet started (gray) a particular chapter.

Click a chapter, and the Lessons Grid appears for that chapter. (Remember, only Chapter 1 is enabled for Guests.)

Click here to go back to the
Course Matrix

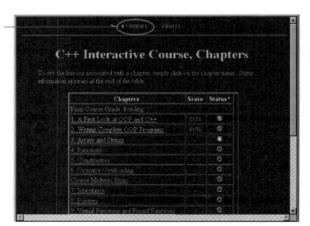

Figure 4
Work through the
course using the
Chapters Grid

The Lessons Grid

As you take the course, the Lessons Grid (Figure 5) tracks your performance within each chapter. You can use it to read a chapter lesson or take a lesson quiz.

To read a lesson, click the *Read* link in the Select column. To take a quiz, click the *Quiz* link in the Select column. The LEDs in the status column show whether you've passed (green), failed (red), or not yet started (gray) each quiz. A percentage grade appears for each completed quiz in the Score column.

Most likely, you'll achieve the best results if you read through the lessons, then take the quiz. If you prefer, however, you can jump directly to the corresponding quiz without reading through the lesson.

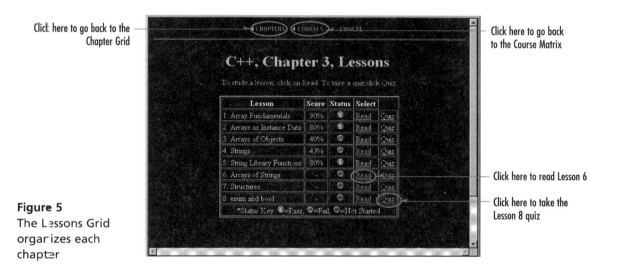

Click here to go back to the Chapter Grid

Click here to go back to the Course Matrix

Click here to read Lesson 6

Click here to take the Lesson 8 quiz

Figure 5
The Lessons Grid organizes each chapter

Testing

Each quiz is a multiple-choice questionnaire. In some courses, there is only one answer to each question, but other courses allow more than one answer. Read the instructions for your course so you know how the quizzes work.

Taking Quizzes

To answer a quiz question, click the check box next to the answer you want to choose. When you've answered all the questions, click the *Grade My Choices* button. Your quiz is corrected and your score shown. To record your score, click either the *Lessons* or *Chapters* link at the top of the main frame.

CAUTION

Do not use your browser's Back button after taking a quiz. If you use the Back button instead of the Lessons or Chapters link, your score will not be recorded.

Midterm and Final Exams

The Interactive Course includes midterm and final examinations. The midterm covers the first half of the book, while the final is comprehensive. These exams follow the same multiple-choice format as the quizzes. Because they cover more, however, they're somewhat longer. Once you have successfully passed all the quizzes, as well as the midterm and final exams, you'll be eligible to download a certificate of completion from Waite Group Press.

MENTOR ZONE

In the Mentor Zone, shown in Figure 6, you can review FAQs (Frequently Asked Questions) for each chapter. You can also ask a question of a live expert, called a mentor, who is standing by to assist you. The mentor is familiar with the book, an expert in the subject, and can provide you with a specific answer to your content-related question, usually within one business day. You can get to this area by clicking on the *Mentor* icon in the navigation frame.

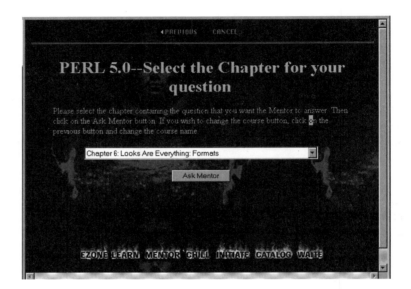

Figure 6
Get personalized help in the Mentor Zone

Just the FAQs

When you ask a mentor a question, you're first shown a set of FAQs. Be sure to read through the list. Since you have a limited number of questions you may ask, you'll want to use your questions carefully. Chances are that an answer to your question has already been posted, in which case you can get an answer without having to ask the question. In any event, you may learn about an issue you hadn't even considered.

If the FAQ list does not contain the answer you need, you'll want to submit your own question to the mentor.

Ask Your Mentor

eZone students may ask ten questions of their course mentor. This limit ensures that mentors will have the opportunity to answer all readers' questions. Questions must be directly related to chapter material. If you ask unrelated or inappropriate questions, you won't get an answer; however, the question will still be deducted from your allotment.

If the FAQ doesn't provide you with an answer to your question, click the button labeled *Ask Mentor*. Whenever you contact the mentor, the rules and conditions for the mentor questions are provided. After reading these, click the *Accept* button to continue. In a moment, a form like the one shown in Figure 7 appears.

This form specifies the course, the chapter, and other information pertinent to your question. The mentor emails the answer to your question directly to you, but keep in mind that Mentor Zone questions must be *directly* related to the chapter subject matter.

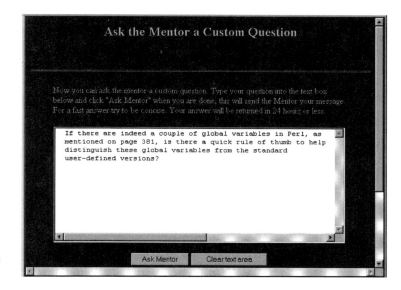

Figure 7
Use this form to
send your question
to your mentor

More Assistance

Keep in mind that there are other sources of assistance in the eZone, too. If you are experiencing technical problems with the book or CD, you'll want to contact the Webmaster; you'll find a link on the eZone's main page. If you want to discuss related issues, such as developments and applications, check out the newsgroups available in the Chill Zone. There are other ways to discuss issues with real people, as you'll discover, when you visit the eZone.

CHILL ZONE

Think of the Chill Zone as your student lounge, a place where students hang out and discuss their classes. But the Chill Zone does a student lounge one better—it's also a library chock full of information. It's a place where you can interact with others reading the same book and find expert resources to assist you as you develop and use your new skills. Perhaps the coolest thing about the Chill Zone is that its options are all included with the cost of your book.

To get into the Chill Zone, click the *Chill Zone* icon in the navigation frame. Once there, you can click three Chill Zone options:

Discussion List—You can subscribe (or unsubscribe) to a dedicated newsgroup centered on your book.

Newsletter—Select this option to subscribe (or unsubscribe) to the monthly eZone newsletter.

Resources—These are links to Web sites, tools, and other useful materials related to the course subject.

To select a Chill Zone option, click the link and follow the on-screen instructions.

THE EZONE AWAITS

As you have seen from this tour, this Interactive Course book is a lot more than the pages before you. It's a full-blown, personalized training system—including textbook, testing, guidance, certification, and support—that you can pick up and work through at your own pace and at your own convenience.

Don't settle for just a book when you can get a whole education. Thanks to this comprehensive package, you're ready to log on and learn in the eZone.

About the Authors

Noel Jerke manages Judd's, Inc.'s new OnLine Services department, assisting publishers of all types move to the Internet. Noel is an experienced programmer familiar with C, Basic, and Visual Basic; his current interests include client-server programming, Internet programming, and building Web sites. Noel co-authored Waite Group Press's *Visual Basic 4.0 Multimedia How-To* and *Visual Basic 4 API How-To*.

Michael D. Hatmaker is president of Smart Systems, Inc., a software development and consulting firm located in the Chicago area. Smart Systems has developed and marketed utilities for the Windows operating systems, and the company is currently developing a series of educational software for the Internet. Michael is a graduate of Purdue University in West Lafayette, Indiana, and is currently pursuing his executive M.B.A. degree from Loyola University of Chicago.

Jonny Anderson was born and raised in Scotland but now works as a freelance VB coder, living in London, England. His interests include formal systems, evolutionary biology, and artificial life. Jonny's only hobbies are playing Doom clones and his practice of unrelenting political cynicism.

Dedication

Noel Jerke: Once again, to my wonderful wife, who is more than any man could hope for. Thank you, Lord, for blessing me with her.

Michael D. Hatmaker: For my father, who taught me the value of hard work.

Jonny Anderson: To my Mum and Dad, Dave and Pippa, Ross (hi bro), Blair, and Billy-the-Dog. Especially to Lisa for making me happy and listening to me talk at nights. Finally, to Richard Dawkins, biologist, neo-Darwinist and visionary, for giving me the tools to think and the memes to evolve.

Acknowledgments

The authors would like to thank Waite Group Press and Mitch Waite for providing the opportunity to write this book. Project editor Kurt Stephan stayed on top of all the details and seemed to always have the right answers. Thanks for your patience and flexibility! Russ Jacobs and Steve Peschka did a great job of developmental and technical editing on the book.

Noel Jerke: Once again, I am very thankful for my wife, who has been very supportive and encouraging. Maria has been there through each hour with love and great patience. I also want to thank my coauthors for helping me endure the rapid rush of Internet technology and many beta releases (long awaited) of Internet Explorer. Last but certainly not least, I thank the Lord for providing me with the skills and capabilities to write this book—it's all for you.

Michael Hatmaker: My family, friends, and especially Laura deserve special thanks for their support during this lengthy project.

Jonny Anderson: My work on this book was made possible by the kindness of Lisa Sharpe, my confidante, and Zane Thomas, the wild-eyed Cyber Guru who got the whole thing started. Thank you both.

Contents

Part I Introduction

Part II Fundamentals

INTRODUCTION

VBScript Interactive Course is about building Internet applications using Microsoft's Visual Basic, Scripting Edition (VBScript) and a browser. VBScript provides many all-new possibilities for making your Web pages come alive. The ability to provide "intelligence" through VBScript and the browser on the client's machine where your Web pages run means that your Web pages no longer need be static. And, perhaps best of all, you will not have to master complicated CGI programming to add functionality to your Web site. There are bandwidth benefits as well; instead of traversing across the Internet to run a CGI application, your programming code can run right on the client's machine.

About *VBScript Interactive Course*

VBScript Interactive Course does not assume you are a programmer or an Internet expert. Instead, it gradually introduces and teaches VBScript in three distinct parts. Part I introduces you to the Web, HTML, and VBScript. From there, Part II takes you through the syntax and structure of the language, and shows you how to integrate it into your Web pages. Finally, Part III of the book teaches you to insert objects into your Web pages, explains how to interact with the browser from your scripts, and introduces you to many, many other advanced topics.

What's Different About This Book

This book is meant to be easy to understand, easy to follow, and most important of all, easy to learn from. It is a tutorial that aims to cover all aspects of Web page scripting and to teach you how to build great interactive pages. The tutorial will not just focus on scripting, but also on how the overall scripted Web page environment works.

Easy to Understand

VBScript Interactive Course starts off with very easy examples; we don't assume you're a rocket scientist. We try to explain everything with no assumptions about what you may or may not already know. We use plenty of figures and analogies to clarify the text. The program examples are well-documented to make everything as clear as possible. As you progress further through the book, the examples become more challenging, but the increasing difficulty level is gradual, so you're always ready for what comes next. Ultimately, we cover all the main features of VBScript.

eZone

Perhaps the most important way this book differs from other VBScript books is that it's a Waite Group Press Interactive Course book, which gives you access to the revolutionary new Web learning available through the eZone. This isn't just publisher's hype; by connecting you to Waite Group Press via the World Wide Web, the eZone plays a significant role in helping you learn VBScript.

About the CD-ROM

As a final plus, in addition to all the accompanying project code from the chapters, the CD-ROM contains Microsoft Internet Explorer 3.0, the Microsoft ActiveX Controls Gallery, and a number of other VBScript and ActiveX controls, bonus demos, and more. (Important note: Some or all of the third-party software—including ActiveX Controls Gallery—on the CD-ROM are intended for trial use only. Please refer to all read me files provided with these third-party items before using them.)

Organization and Installation of the CD-ROM

Source code that was developed for the book can be found in the SOURCE directory on the CD-ROM. Each chapter's and, where applicable, each session's source code is further broken out for your convenience: Chapter 1 has the corresponding directory CHAP01; Session 7 has the corresponding directory SESSION7. For example, if you want to find the code for Chapter 6, Session 8, you need to move to \SOURCE\ CHAP06\SESSION8.

The following instructions illustrate how to copy the source code from the CD-ROM drive to your hard drive. In this example, drive C: is assumed to be the hard drive you want to install the files to, and the D: is assumed to be the CD-ROM drive that you want to copy from. If your hard drive and CD-ROM drive are represented by different letters, substitute the drive letters in this example with ones that correspond to your system.

1. Exit to the DOS (or Command) Prompt.
2. Move to the root directory of your primary hard drive by typing

```
c:      <ENTER>
cd \      <ENTER>
```

3. Create a directory to store the source code, such as VBSCRIPT, by typing

```
md VBSCRIPT <ENTER>
```

4. Move into this directory by typing

```
cd VBSCRIPT   <ENTER>
```

5. Copy all of the source code from the CD-ROM by typing

```
xcopy d:\source\*.* /v /s
```

XCOPY allows you to copy all files and subdirectories (the /s switch turns on this feature), and as a by-product removes the Read-only attribute from the files copied to your hard drive. The /v switch tells XCOPY to verify the copy to ensure the copied files were copied correctly.

What Hardware and Software Do You Need?

To get started, you really only need two things to take advantage of the enclosed CD-ROM: Internet Explorer (version 3.0 is provided) and any text editor, such as Notepad.

You can also use tools such as Microsoft ActiveX Control Pad (included on the CD-ROM) or Microsoft Internet Studio. Visit Microsoft's Web site at **www.microsoft.com** to find out more about VBScript and the latest tools available for building scripts in your HTML documents.

Internet Explorer 3.0 is the first browser to fully support placing VBScript in your Web pages. For a full explanation of the features and use of Explorer 3.0, please refer to Appendix I, "Internet Explorer 3.0: A Field Guide."

Finally, we have provided many ActiveX controls from Microsoft to be used in sample pages on the CD as well as your own Web pages. The 3RDPARTY directory on the CD provides a read me file that provides instructions on how to install each set of software and gives last minute information on the CD-ROM contents.

Viewing the Sample CD Web Pages

Each chapter's corresponding sample Web pages and exercise answers are provided on the CD-ROM. Each chapter is labeled with the chapter number. Each session in the chapter has its own subdirectory within the chapter. Also provided in each chapter directory is an EXERCISES subdirectory. This is where sample solutions to the exercises in the book will be provided.

The Web pages provided on the CD can be easily opened by simply double-clicking on the Web page file indicated in the book text. If you wish to modify any of the sample Web pages, simply copy them to your hard drive and modify them as appropriate with your favorite text editing tool.

Connecting to the Internet

You do not need to be connected to the Internet to create VBScript Web pages. If you wish to find further resources on the Internet, to access Microsoft's VBScript Web pages, or to enter the eZone an Internet connection will be required.

INTRODUCTION

PART I

CHAPTER 1

WHAT IS THE WORLD WIDE WEB ANYWAY?

So you have heard a lot about the Web. You have used it; you may have even toyed around with building some Web pages. But how does it all fit together? What does it all mean? What about Netscape, HTML, HTTP, TCP/IP, forms, URLs, Navigator, Microsoft, Internet Explorer, Java, JavaScript, CGI, etc. Trying to keep it all straight is enough to make a person throw his or her hands up in the air and say, "Who cares!"

This chapter will introduce you to some of the basic concepts behind the Web, HTML, and getting started with Visual Basic Script. It is not meant to be an in-depth review of all the inner workings of every nook and cranny of Internet technology. But it does discuss some history, HTML, scripting, browsers, forms and, of course, a couple of Hello World examples to help get you up and going. There is no doubt that

it is a brave new Internet world, and together we will
tackle the basics so we can begin building truly activated Internet pages.

In this chapter, we will learn about:

- The World Wide Web and Why It's Important

- HTML and Its Place as the Fundamental Web Scripting Language

- How VBScript Applies to the Web

- Browsing and Browsers

- Building HTML Forms

- Creating "Hello World" Scripts in Both HTML and VBScript

THE WORLD WIDE WEB AND WHERE IT FITS

Probably the first thing to remember when getting started is that the World Wide Web
is a subset of the Internet. The Internet first appeared in the 1970s as an experiment
of the United States government's Advanced Research Projects Agency (ARPA). By the
late '70s it had grown into a global communication network. In the late '80s and early
'90s, commercial interest in the Internet began to blossom. You have to admit, those
government programs just seem to grow and grow! This one is infiltrating the whole
world!

The key technology foundation for the Internet is the TCP/IP transfer protocol. This
is the *glue* that connects computers around the world together.

TCP/IP

The Transmission Control Protocol is the method of data sharing between computers for all
Internet-connected computers. This data is broken down into packets using the Internet
Protocol. These packets are sent across the Internet independently. The TCP protocol provides error resolution to ensure that all the data has been sent correctly and that the individual IP packets are recombined appropriately on the client end.

The Internet is a huge, worldwide interconnection of computers via this TCP/IP protocol. The connections are made via phone lines and direct leased connections.
Typically, an individual will connect through an Internet service provider (ISP). An ISP
will work with a national service provider to provide high speed connections to the Internet
backbone. Figure 1-1 gives a top level view of the Internet.

As you can guess, the Internet is a huge, uncontrolled, mind-boggling phenome-
non that allows us to connect in a fashion not strictly controlled or planned out by anybody.

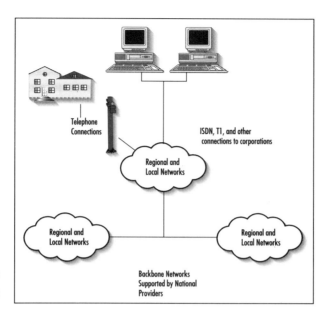

Figure 1-1
A top level view of
the Internet

When we share data across the Internet, it is not predetermined exactly how any one part of our data goes from point A to point B. But, the TCP/IP protocol always ensures that it does.

The Internet was becoming popular before the development of the World Wide Web, but nobody predicted the breathtaking growth of the Web, seemingly overnight. As with any big paradigm shift in the computer industry, this one caught many companies flat-footed, including Microsoft, and catapulted bright young stars such as Netscape's founders (not to mention millionaires) onto the scene.

The World Wide Web was originally developed as a government research project at the CERN laboratories in Switzerland. The World Wide Web is based on the Hyper-Text Transport Protocol (HTTP). This is the key to transferring hypertext documents and data across the Internet.

Hypertext Transport Protocol (HTTP)—Technical Note

With this protocol, a client machine will send a request to a server for a specified document. The server then sends the document back to the client. HTTP also supports sending data generated from server-based programs to the client. And, the server can take data generated from the client and pass it on to other programs on the server for processing. This server-based processing is carried out through the Common Gateway Interface (CGI). For example, this is how client-to-server database processing takes place for checking Web page passwords, credit card transactions, and so on.

One other key to understanding how to access World Wide Web documents is the use of Uniform Resource Locators (URLs). URLs are a naming convention for finding the location of any file on the Web. Every Web page has a unique Web address, usually a cryptic and unfriendly number such as 75.152.207.123, but it can be represented by a URL such as www.microsoft.com. URLs do not just point to a Web site; they also point to HTML documents on the Web. For example, www.microsoft.com/int-dev pulls up Microsoft's Internet developers' default HTML Web page. Note that you can also specify an address for a specific HTML document (**.HTM**).

SUMMARY

This is a very quick whirlwind overview of the basics, and there are plenty of references available about FTP, GOPHER, ARCHIE, and many other Internet-related topics beyond the scope of this book. Fortunately, for your purposes, you can assume all of the above is in place and begin to get down to what you need to build great Intranet or Internet Web pages: a browser, a good HTML editor, a server for Intranet/Internet pages and databases, and of course, Visual Basic Script. Not to mention a brilliant tome such as this one to help get you going! To find other books on these topics, try www.mcp.com.

1. TCP/IP is
    a. a really weird acronym.
    b. the primary protocol for sending data across the Internet.
    c. the World Wide Web HTML protocol interface.
    d. none of the above.

2. HTTP is
    a. a client/server protocol for transferring text documents and data on the Internet.
    b. a client/server protocol for transferring text documents and data on an Intranet.
    c. a tool used with the Common Gateway Interface (CGI) to transfer data.
    d. all of the above.

3. The Internet started
    a. as a garage experiment by two hackers in the '60s.
    b. as a research project at a leading corporation.
    c. as a government research project.
    d. with spontaneous generation between computers.

4. The World Wide Web
    a. consists of the HTTP protocol for transferring HTML documents and associated data (video, sound, and so on).
    b. is just one of many protocols on the Internet.
    c. was developed in a research laboratory in Switzerland.
    d. is all of the above.

5. Data is transferred across the Internet
   a. in one packet.
   b. in two packets taking any route.
   c. in multiple packets with error resolution and checking.
   d. in one packet with error resolution and checking.

WHAT IS HTML?

When getting started with HTML, the first thing to remember is not to confuse the acronym with its other popular representations such as **H**ow **T**o **M**ake **L**iverwurst, **H**oney **T**ake **M**e **L**ogging, and **H**old **T**he **M**ayo and **L**ettuce (remember the last time you told the waiter HTML). The **H**yper**T**ext**M**arkup **L**anguage (HTML) is the foundation for transferring data on the World Wide Web. And, as discussed in the last session, HTTP was developed as the transfer protocol for sending and retrieving HTML documents and data between Internet clients and servers.

The "Markup" part of HTML means that specific parts of the document are marked up to indicate how they should be presented by the viewing application (the browser). Look at the following example:

```
This is a <B><I>Visual Basic</I> Script</B> book.
```

In this example we have the string "This is a Visual Basic Script book." With the two markup tags for bold and italic, the string will be "This is a ***Visual Basic* Script** book." The `<B></B>` tags indicate when the text should become bold and end being bold. The `<I></I>` tags indicate when the text should become italic and end being italic.

This is not all that different from any word processor. Microsoft Word, for example, saves document formatting in a type of markup language which is certainly much more complex than HTML (at least for now). The HTML format is interpreted by Web browsers and the document displayed. The key to making the World Wide Web accessible from many different operating system platforms is the fact that the HTML document is simple ASCII text that can be read on nearly any operating system, including UNIX, DOS, Macintosh, or Windows.

Appendix G, "HTML 3.2 Quick Reference," contains many of the different HTML tags you can have in your document. These include input forms, tables, text formatting, and so on, which allow you to develop richly formatted documents. The current HTML standard is version 3.2, which is supported by the browser we will be working with, the Microsoft Internet Explorer. As HTML and Web pages begin to get more complex, I am sure that some day we will look back fondly on the days of version 3.2 and think how simple things were back then!

Typically an HTML document is formatted into logical document sections. Figure 1-2 displays these sections.

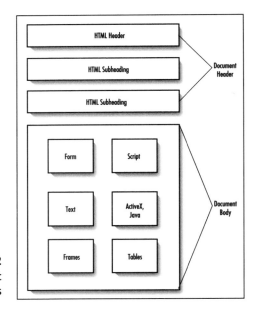

Figure 1-2
HTML document
sections

The document header, subheadings, body, script, and footer make up the formal structure of the document. None are required, but can be useful and important in building
the right look for your documents. Let's take a look at a very simple HTML document
to get us up and going.

```
<!-- Beginning HTML tag  -->
<HTML>

<!-- Head of the document  -->
<Head>
<Title> This is the Title of the Document</Title>
</Head>

<!-- Second heading  -->
<H1>This is the second heading body.<br><br><br><br></H1>

<!--  Start of the body  -->
<Body>

<!-- An input form  -->
<Form>
The form items would go here.
</Form>

<!-- Line Breaks  -->
<br><br>

<!-- Bold, Italic and regular text  -->
<B>This is some bold body text.</B><br>
<I>This is some italic body text.</I><br>
```

```
This is some regular text

<!--  Starts the script section  -->
<SCRIPT LANGUAGE="VBS">

'  This is where the Visual Basic script would go.

</Script>

<!--  End of the body  -->
</Body>

<!--  End of the HTML document  -->
</HTML>
```

Figure 1-3 shows the document in the Internet Explorer browser. Note the title bar text: This is the Title of the Document - Microsoft Internet Explorer.

This simple document builds the foundation for a basic HTML document. The overall document is defined by beginning **<HTML>** and ending **</HTML>** tags. The initial **HTML** tag is following by the first heading **<HEAD>**. This heading contains the title **<TITLE></TITLE>** of the document, which in the case of Microsoft's Internet Explorer shows up in the title bar of the browser window. That is followed by the secondary heading **<H1></H1>**. We then include a form structure **<FORM></FORM>**, which does not include any input elements. Next is some simple, formatted body text using **<B></B>** and **<I></I>** for bold and italic, respectively. Then we have our Visual Basic Script section of the document **<SCRIPT></SCRIPT>**, where the programming code will be placed. Finally, we show the body and HTML ending tags.

A quick note on placing code comments in your documents: If you want to place comments in the HTML sections or in your Visual Basic Script code, you can do so by using special syntax. For HTML, surround the comments with the **<!-- comments -->** tags. For Visual Basic Script, simply use the **['J** mark in front of the comments so the browser will not interpret the code. We will learn more about each as we move forward.

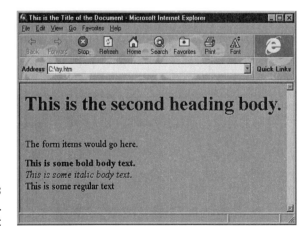

Figure 1-3
Sample HTML document

SUMMARY

If you are not already an HTML guru, you will soon find that these documents contain myriad tags that will build all kinds of documents, from games to references to serious business applications. But, as we will see in this book, it will be Visual Basic Script that will be just what the Microsoft doctor ordered to make these otherwise fairly static documents come alive.

1. Which of the following is not a basic HTML document structure?
   a. Title
   b. Body
   c. Heading
   d. Footer

2. How will the the following HTML text will be displayed?

```
An <B> easy </B> Quiz <I> Question </I>.
```

   a. **An easy Quiz *Question***
   b. **An easy *Quiz* Quiz** Question
   c. An **easy** Quiz *Question*
   d. **An easy Quiz *Question***

3. The `<BODY>` and `</BODY>` tags
   a. indicate the beginning and end of the body of an HTML document.
   b. indicate the beginning and end of the body of a paragraph.
   c. indicate the beginning and end of any section of an HTML document.
   d. do none of the above.

4. How will the following text be formatted?

```
<B>Working <I>with</B> the <B> Internet </B> is</I>
<I>Exciting</I>
```

   a. **Working *with* the *Internet*** is *Exciting*
   b. **Working** *with the* **Internet** is *Exciting*
   c. **Working with** *the **Internet*** is *Exciting*
   d. **Working** *with* the **Internet** is **Exciting**

5. Which of the following are valid HTML comments?
   a. `<!-- Comments -->`
   b. `<!-- Comments ->`
   c. `<-- Comments -->`
   d. `<!- Comments ->`

WHERE DOES SCRIPTING FIT IN?

In this whirlwind tour we have reviewed a little bit about the history and technology behind the Web as well as provided a quick introduction to HTML. We have yet to mention why we really need Visual Basic Script.

Think back to Session 1 when we discussed HTTP and the Common Gateway Interface (CGI) and how they allow for server-side processing of data to send to the client side (browser) as well as for processing of data sent from the client. If you think about this, every time we want to do any client-side activities to respond to the user, we must send the user's data to the server for the processing to take place and then send back the results. In other words, the client is really just a terminal (through a browser), with little actual processing taking place on the client side. With the likes of Visual Basic Script and JavaScript that *live* in the HTML document and can be executed by the host browser, we now have processing power on the client's side of the equation. For example, our Web page may require a user to enter his or her phone number to complete an order. We would rather check on the client side to make sure it is a valid phone number before sending the data to the server, which may be halfway around the world, and have to return an error. Figure 1-4 represents the difference between utilizing client-side and non-client-side processing.

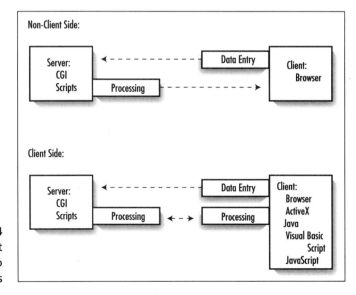

Figure 1-4
Where script languages fit into the Web process

The top part of the diagram shows the data flow and processing without a scripting engine in the browser. The bottom shows the addition of processing on the client side.

Imagine trying to do instant data validation of what the user is typing into a browser field if you had to send every keystroke to the server for validation. This would be monotonous indeed and, if you had a very slow server or extensive traffic, most likely the application would become unusable. But with Visual Basic Script, you can check every keystroke on the client side, without any server interaction. This will help reduce bandwidth requirements for your Web pages and reduce the amount of traffic across the net for your Web site.

Scripting, when combined with Microsoft's ActiveX technology and Sun's Java technology, provides a whole new set of possibilities for building interactive Web documents. For you Visual Basic programmers, imagine popping into your Web page any one of your favorite user interface ActiveX controls! Then, you could manipulate the control just like you do in Visual Basic by using Visual Basic Script. Or, you Java drinkers (programmers) could build your Java applets, include them in your HTML document and control their use through Visual Basic Script. Those of you who have been working in HTML for a while will now have all kinds of new opportunities to build truly interactive Web pages.

The Microsoft Internet Explorer is able to host ActiveX controls and Java applets right in the Web browser. When the HTML document is sent to the client from the server, these controls and applets are sent along with the document. For example, these controls might be a timer or charting tool. And, as mentioned, the key to utilizing and controlling these controls/applets in the browser will be Visual Basic Script. As you will learn in later chapters, you are going to be able to build powerful Web-based applications which will go far beyond traditional HTML. Figure 1-5 shows how adding the scripting capabilities coupled with ActiveX and Java to your Web pages will work.

If you are thinking about tracking any data with your applications, you may also be wondering how you can work with a server-based database to store and retrieve data and how scripting fits into this scenario. Visual Basic Script itself does not directly support working with the server database. The language was developed to ensure that it would be safe both for the client side and server side. If the language had the ability to work directly with server data, this could make the server data vulnerable to hackers. But, Visual Basic Script ensures that the data sent to be stored on the server is accurate by doing data validation before the data is sent. Also, it can be used as a powerful tool for presenting data entry options to the user. Combine this with ActiveX, and you will be able to build powerful Web applications. Figure 1-6 overviews the working process of a data entry Web application.

SUMMARY

This book will cover all aspects of using Visual Basic Script to get you up and going. The language will be reviewed, as will its interaction with HTML, with ActiveX, and with the server.

A whole new set of opportunities for building Web-based applications is opened up by being able to do client-side processing with Visual Basic Script.

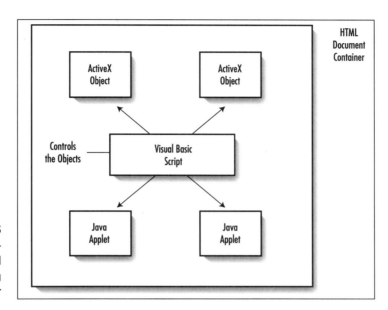

Figure 1-5
Visual Basic script-
ing, ActiveX and
Java working
together

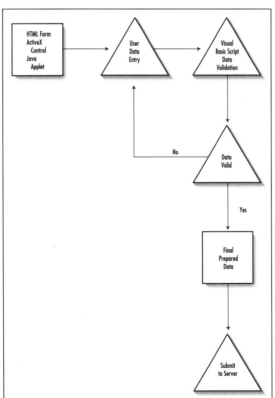

Figure 1-6
Visual Basic Script
and Web-based
data entry
applications

1. Visual Basic Script code is run
    a. on the server side.
    b. on the server side and client side.
    c. on the client side.
    d. by the operating system.

2. ActiveX technology allows you to
    a. run custom controls on the server.
    b. include custom controls in your HTML documents.
    c. build custom controls in Visual Basic Script.
    d. do none of the above.

3. An important use for Visual Basic Script is
    a. data validation on the client side.
    b. presenting data entry options to the user.
    c. controlling ActiveX custom controls and Java applets.
    d. all of the above.

4. Visual Basic Script helps to reduce
    a. server-side processing.
    b. client-side processing.
    c. the work load on the browser.
    d. database processing.

5. ActiveX controls and Java applets
    a. run on the server and are called by the Web browser.
    b. run on the server and temporarily are run on the local machine by the browser.
    c. are downloaded to the local machine and are run locally by the browser.
    d. are downloaded to the local machine and are run locally by the server.

SESSION 4

BROWSERS AND BROWSING

The browser, of course, is the fundamental tool for interacting with the Internet. There are many, many browsers available on the market for all different kinds of platforms. In fact, the '90s may well be remembered (for now) as the decade of the browser wars, primarily between Netscape's Navigator and Microsoft's Internet Explorer. Navigator has seen explosive growth along with the growth of the Web. Microsoft has been playing catch-up and is coming on strong with the version 3.0 incarnation of the Internet Explorer. This is the browser we will be using for this book, since it was the first to introduce Visual Basic Script support. With version 3.0, Microsoft has implemented both the Visual Basic Scripting language and the support for ActiveX and Java. Initially version 3.0 will be released for Windows 95 and Windows NT. But, at the time of publication of this book, Microsoft has promised both a Macintosh and Windows 3.1 version of the browser and is even promising a version for UNIX.

Microsoft is offering Visual Basic Script licenses free to any developers who wish to implement Visual Basic Script support in their browsers. Its goal is to ensure solid cross-platform support for the language. Fortunately, the Internet Explorer is provided free by Microsoft, so if you are planning on developing Intranet applications for your company, you can ensure support for your script code throughout your organization.

If you are a Visual Basic programmer, you may be wondering why you would want to use what would seem to be a limited browser interface for deploying applications. The key to making great applications is combining Visual Basic Script, ActiveX controls, Java applets, frames, tables, and HTML forms for building your user interfaces. Using tools such as these, you are not limited to just forward and back buttons, hypertext links, and static input interfaces. New possibilities will arise for building cross-platform applications and data entry programs, information reporting, games, a tribute to your dear spouse for his or her patience while you work on a new book, great references, and so on.

For those of you who may not be browser savvy, let's review the basics of negotiating through Web pages using the Internet Explorer. Figure 1-7 shows the Internet Explorer.

Double-click on the Internet Explorer to start the browser. In the address bar, type in the location of the CD-ROM provided with the CD. Now, go to the Chapter1 folder. Note the browser works just like the Windows Explorer for viewing your hard drive. In the Chapter1 folder, select the Session5 folder. In the Session5 folder, you will see the 1-5.HTM file. Double-click on that to bring the document up in the browser. From there, the following buttons allow you to browse through your HTML travels:

1. The Internet Explorer features a Home button (the house) that will take you back to your *home* or default page when the browser is started up.

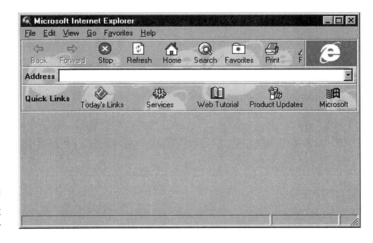

Figure 1-7
The Internet
Explorer

2. To go from the current page to the page just viewed, use the left arrow button or Back button.

3. To go to forward in the Web page history you have viewed, use the right arrow button or Forward button.

4. You can reload the Web page by clicking on the double green arrow button. This will ensure that you have a completely refreshed and up-to-date version of the Web page.

5. If you find that a Web page is taking a while to load and you don't wish to continue, select the Stop button (with a red X) to end the load.

6. Once you begin to surf the Web, you will find favorite Web pages you will wish to return to later. The Internet Explorer allows you to save favorite Web page locations under Favorites. Select the Favorites menu or the yellow folder icon and select the Add to Favorites item to include the current page in your list.

7. To view the source of any HTML document you are reviewing, select the View menu and then the Source option. Notepad will launch with the HTML document loaded. You will find this is the simplest way to modify the HTML documents provided on the CD-ROM.

SUMMARY

If you are unfamiliar with using a browser, a few minutes of surfing the Web will soon get you familiar with the basic fundamentals.

QUIZ 4

1. The Microsoft Internet Explorer supports
   a. Visual Basic Script.
   b. ActiveX.
   c. JavaScript/Java.
   d. all of the above.

2. Visual Basic Script will
   a. never be a cross-platform product.
   b. never work in another browser.
   c. only be supported in a limited way by the Internet Explorer.
   d. do none of the above.

3. Favorites are
    a. references stored by the Internet Explorer to your favorite Web sites.
    b. favorite Web sites Microsoft wants you to visit.
    c. tracked by the Internet Explorer to the Web sites you visit most often.
    d. none of the above.

4. Once a document has begun loading, the only way you can stop it is to
    a. shut down the browser.
    b. jump to another document.
    c. click on the red X Stop button.
    d. do none of the above.

5. To look at the HTML source of a Web page viewed in the browser you
    a. select the File menu and select View Source.
    b. select the View menu and select Source.
    c. select the Favorites menu and select Source.
    d. do none of the above.

BUILDING HTML FORMS

One of the more built-in ways to interact with your users directly from HTML is the use of forms and input elements. Forms allow HTML to be more than just data going out to the user. They also allow for data coming back to the server. We will not talk about working on the server side until later in the book, but we can review how to utilize and set up basic HTML forms that include text fields, check boxes, push buttons, radio buttons, and pop-up menus.

A Note for VB Gurus

HTML forms have no relation to Visual Basic forms. Their only link is conceptual. With HTML forms, you can add buttons, textboxes, and so on, and have that data sent to a server. But these are not the same as the ActiveX controls you are familiar with in Visual Basic.

Let's start out with the basic structure of a form in your HTML document. The tags for beginning and ending a form in your document are **<FORM>** and **</FORM>**. A couple attributes can be set for the form tag, as follows:

```
<FORM METHOD="Get or Post" ACTION="URL" ENCTYPE="type">
```

The method attribute indicates how the data should be sent to the server. The **"Get"** method sends the information in the form to the server indicated in the **Form** tag. The **"Post"** method sends the information in the form to the server, including all data in any HTML input elements. The default is **"Post"** for sending data to the server. The

ACTION attribute gives the address of the script that will process the form. In many cases this will be a PERL or C program or, as we will see later in the book, it can be a link to the Internet Database Connector (IDC) in Microsoft's Internet Information Server (IIS). The ENCTYPE attribute indicates how the data in the form will be encoded and applies only to the post method. The default and only answer is "application/w-vww-form-urlencoded". But, that is enough of the details for now; we will explore these further in later chapters. Let's review setting up a form with all the basic input elements.

Form Input Elements

The following outlines the basic tag formats for setting up a FORM, TEXTAREA, SELECT, and various input elements:

```
<FORM METHOD = "GET or POST" ACTION="URL" ENCTYPE="type">
<TEXTAREA NAME="NAME" ROWS="##" COLS="##"> </TEXTAREA>
<INPUT TYPE="TYPE" NAME="NAME" VALUE="######">
Types = CheckBox, TextBox, Submit, Reset, Radio, Button
<SELECT NAME="NAME"> <OPTION> Text </SELECT>
```

The CD-ROM in the Session5 subdirectory of Chapter1 contains a sample form complete with each input element. Figure 1-8 shows the Web page.

Let's look at the form section of the HTML code to see how each of the sections is utilized. The first input element of the form is a TextBox; we indicate that the size of the textbox will be 10 characters in length.

```
<!--  Start our form for display  -->

<FORM NAME="DataDisplay">
```

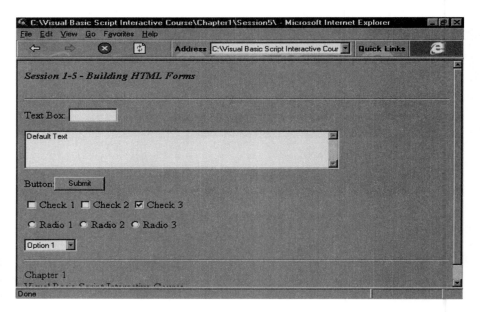

Figure 1-8
The form demo
Web page

```
<!--   Text Box   -->
```

```
Text Box: <INPUT NAME="TextBox" TYPE="TEXT" SIZE="10"><br><br>
```

Next in the form, we build a `TextArea` input box. We set up the textbox to have three rows and 90 columns. We also display the default text **"Default Text"** in the box when the form is shown.

```
<!--   TextArea Box   -->
```

```
<TEXTAREA NAME="TextArea" ROWS=3 COLS=90>Default
```

```
Text</TEXTAREA><br><br>
```

We build a **SUBMIT** button, which will submit the form to the server if we wish or, as we will see later in the book, we will be able to fire off Visual Basic Script events based on the button click.

```
<!--   Submit Button   -->
```

```
Button:<INPUT NAME="Button" TYPE="SUBMIT" VALUE="Submit"><br><br>
```

We also place a set of check boxes on the form. Note that there is a value set for each check box, but that this is different than the displayed text next to the check box. The last check box is set to be checked with the **CHECKED** keyword.

```
<!--   Check Box   -->
<INPUT TYPE="CHECKBOX" NAME="CHECK1" VALUE=1>Check 1
<INPUT TYPE="CHECKBOX" NAME="CHECK1" VALUE=2>Check 2
<INPUT TYPE="CHECKBOX" NAME="CHECK1" VALUE=3 CHECKED>Check 3
```

Forms also support radio buttons for selection of options. As with the check boxes, each radio button contains a value that is unique from the displayed text.

```
<!--   Radio Buttons   -->
<INPUT TYPE="RADIO" NAME="RADIO1" VALUE=1>Radio 1
<INPUT TYPE="RADIO" NAME="RADIO2" VALUE=1>Radio 2
<INPUT TYPE="RADIO" NAME="RADIO3" VALUE=1>Radio 3
```

Finally, we build a drop down menu box with three options for selection. The box can list as many options as you wish.

```
<!--   Select Box   -->
<SELECT NAME="SELECT">
<OPTION>Option 1
<OPTION>Option 2
<OPTION>Option 3
</SELECT>
```

```
</FORM>
```

SUMMARY

As we work with these input elements throughout the book, you will learn how to interact with each of these from your Visual Basic Script code to build powerful input capabilities for your users.

1. Forms can be used to
   a. retrieve input from the user.
   b. send user input to the server.
   c. interact with client input through Visual Basic Script.
   d. do all of the above.

2. Which of the following is not an HTML input type?
   a. `CheckBox`
   b. `Radio`
   c. `Button Bar`
   d. `TextBox`

3. Which of the following is a correct HTML input text element?
   a. `<INPUT NAME="TextBox" TYPE="TEXT" TEXTBOXSIZE="10">`
   b. `<INPUT NAME="TextBox" TYPE="TEXT" SIZE="10">`
   c. `<INPUT TEXTNAME="TextBox" TYPE="TEXT" SIZE="10">`
   d. `<INPUT NAME="TextBox" TEXTTYPE="TEXT" SIZE="10">`

4. The _____ method sends the information in the _____ to the _____ as a data body.
   a. `post`...form...server
   b. `get`...form...server
   c. `post`...document...server
   d. `get`...document...client

5. Which is the correct radio button element format?
   a. `<INPUT TYPE="RADIO" NAME="RADIO1" VALUE=1>`
   b. `<INPUT TYPE="RADIO" NAME="RADIO1">`
   c. `<INPUT TYPE="RADIO" NAME="RADIO1" VALUE=1>Radio1`
   d. all of the above

HELLO WORLD HTML

Well, what would we want to start with in our HTML introduction other than a good old Hello World example. We have had a review of basic HTML; let's utilize these tags to say "Hello World" in many new ways.

We can work with fonts, tables (an introduction), radio buttons, and check boxes to display our text in a number of ways. Let's review the sample HTML document provided on the CD-ROM in the Session6 subdirectory of Chapter1. To view the HTML source, select the View menu on the browser and select Source. Or, you can use your favorite HTML editing tool. Figure 1-9 shows the sample Web page.

You are beginning to get a little taste of what makes basic HTML easy to use. A few tags and you have colorful fonts, tables, and, of course, our input forms. You can review the last section on building HTML forms to see how the form section is built. But, let's review the first section on utilizing the colored fonts and the table. Select the View menu and the Source option to review the HTML document source.

HTML has several default color names supported for setting font colors. Our first section of Hello World! text is created by utilizing the font tags, **<Font>** and **</Font>**. When the font is defined, we set color.

```
<!-- Show the Text in Different Colors -->
<Font Color=BLUE> Hello World!</FONT>
<Font Color=GREEN> Hello World!</FONT>
<Font Color=RED> Hello World!</FONT><br>
```

Building an HTML table is also fairly straightforward. The basic tags include **<TABLE>** and **</TABLE>**. We can set the type of border for the table by using the BORDER attribute. Once the table is started, we define a row in the table by using the **<TR>** and **</TR>** tags.

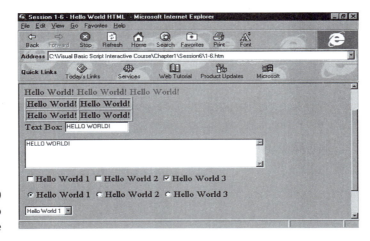

Figure 1-9
Hello World Web
sample

Within a table row, we use the **<TD>** and **</TD>** tags to define a column. In our table, we have two rows with two columns each.

```
<!-- Start the Table -->
<TABLE BORDER=1>

<!-- Start the Table Columns-->
<TR><TD>Hello World!</TD><TD>Hello World!</TD></TR>
<TR><TD>Hello World!</TD><TD>Hello World!</TD></TR>

</TABLE>
```

SUMMARY

As you become more familiar with the variety of formatting tags for your HTML documents, you will begin to find new and interesting ways to design your Web page that go beyond the simple formatting defined here.

What is ironic about an Internet Hello World example is that in some sense, with your Web pages, you have the ability to say "Hello" to the world. Once your pages are published on the Web, anyone anywhere in the world who is connected has the opportunity to see them!

1. The following table has how many columns?

```
<!-- Start the Table -->
<TABLE BORDER=1>

<!-- Start the Table Columns-->
<TR><TD>Data</TD><TD>Data</TD><TD>Data</TD></TR>
<TR><TD>Data</TD><TD>Data</TD><TD>Data</TD></TR>

</TABLE>
```

    a. 1
    b. 2
    c. 3
    d. 4

2. For radio buttons and check boxes, what attribute or keyword do you use to indicate if one of the items is selected?

    a. `Selected`
    b. `Check`

c. `Checked`
d. `Marked`

3. What is the text color of the second row, second table column?

```
<!-- Start the Table -->
<TABLE BORDER=1>

<!-- Start the Table Columns -->
<TR>
     <TD><Font Color=BLUE> Hello World!</FONT></TD>
     <TD><Font Color=GREEN> Hello World!</FONT></TD>
</TR>

<TR>
     <TD><Font Color=RED> Hello World!</FONT></TD>
     <TD><Font Color=YELLOW > Hello World!</FONT></TD>
</TR>

</TABLE>
```

a. Blue
b. Green
c. Red
d. Yellow

4. What kind of form input element does the second column of the table contain?

```
<TABLE BORDER=1>

<TR>
     <TD><Font Color=BLUE> Hello World!</FONT></TD>
     <TD><INPUT NAME="TextBox" TYPE="TEXT" SIZE="10"></TD>
     <TD><TEXTAREA NAME="TextArea" ROWS=3 COLS=30></TEXTAREA></TD>
</TR>

<TR>
     <TD><Font Color=RED> Hello World!</FONT></TD>
     <TD><INPUT NAME="TextBox" TYPE="TEXT" SIZE="10"></TD>
     <TD><TEXTAREA NAME="TextArea" ROWS=3 COLS=30></TEXTAREA></TD>
</TR>

</TABLE>
```

a. `TextBox`
b. `TextArea`
c. `Text`
d. `Area`

5. If the following table is supposed to have four rows and two columns, what is wrong?

```
<TABLE>

<TR>
    <TD>A</TD>  <TD>B</TD>  <TD>C</TD>  <TD>D</TD>
</TR>

<TR>
    <TD>AA</TD>  <TD>BB</TD>  <TD>CC</TD>
</TR>

<TR>
    <TD>AAA</TD>  <TD>BBB</TD>  <TD>CCC</TD>
</TR>
<TR>
    <TD>AAAA</TD>  <TD>BBBB</TD>  <TD>CCCC</TD>
</TR>

</TABLE>
```

    a. There are three columns.
    b. There are only three rows.
    c. There is no border for the table.
    d. The table is fine.

Difficulty: Easy

1. Modify the sample document to have the following changes:

    ● Change the table to have three columns with blue text.

    ● Change the Hello World 1 check box to be checked by default.

    ● Add additional line breaks around the table.

Difficulty: Intermediate

2. Write an HTML document that has a five-row table with the text in each column appearing as a different color.

'HELLO WORLD' VISUAL BASIC SCRIPT

We have seen how to say hello to the world in many different ways using HTML. Now let's dig into a programming example to get us up and going with Visual Basic Script. In this simple example, when the Web page is loaded, the script will run and pop up a dialog box telling us hello. You will notice a big difference between this example and the last. HTML is primarily utilized for text output, whereas Visual Basic Script is utilized for programming behind the scenes.

Figure 1-10 shows the sample Web page as it is being loaded. The Web page is found in the Session7 subdirectory of Chapter1 on the CD-ROM.

Note the dialog box that is showing 'Hello World!'. This is generated by a Visual Basic script embedded in the HTML document. The following is the standard HTML header for our example Web pages:

```
<HTML>

<!--   Show the title   -->
<TITLE> Session 1-7 - Hello World Visual Basic Script </TITLE>

<!--   Set the font size and color   -->
```

continued on next page

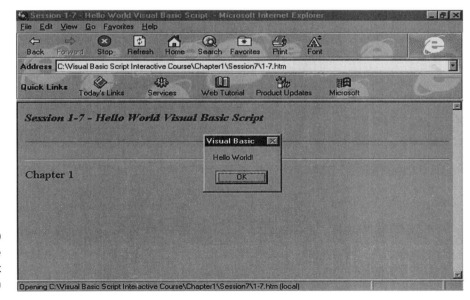

Figure 1-10
The sample
Visual Basic
Script program

continued from previous page

```
<H1><FONT SIZE=3 COLOR=MAROON>
<!--   Set this text to bold italic   -->
<B><I>Session 1-7 - Hello World Visual Basic Script</I></B>
</FONT></H1>

<!-- Show a graphic line and one line breaks -->
<HR>
```

When we start the body of the HTML document, we indicate that the scripting language will be Visual Basic Script (VBScript). We also indicate that the startup subroutine (segment of code) will be **StartSub**. Thus, when the page is loaded, the first segment of Visual Basic Script run is in the **StartSub** section.

```
<!--   Set the start up sub routine to StartSub   -->
<BODY LANGUAGE="VBScript" onLoad=StartSub>

<!--   Show a horizontal line   -->
<HR>
```

Now we indicate that the script in our document is starting. The tag is **<SCRIPT>** with the language indicated. Currently both Visual Basic Script and JavaScript are supported.

```
<!--   Start the Script   -->
<SCRIPT LANGUAGE="VBScript">
```

This is the subroutine, **StartSub**, mentioned earlier. You will learn more about subroutines in Chapter 5, "Danger—Program Construction." But for now, think of it as a way of breaking down or *segmenting* code into logical chunks. Within this subroutine, we call the MsgBox function which will display a common dialog box with the specified Hello World text. Note that comments are placed in the code using the ['] character.

MsgBox Definition
MsgBox(prompt[, buttons][, title][, helpfile, context]) See Appendix A, "Functions," for details on the different arguments. Note that arguments follow the function and are separated by commas.

```
' StartSub is our sub routine that is first loaded
Sub StartSub

    '  The MsgBox function with the first
    '  argument as "Hello World!" to define the message
    MsgBox "Hello World!"
End Sub

</SCRIPT>
```

Finally, we end our HTML document.

```
<!--   Change the font size and color   -->
<FONT SIZE=3 COLOR=MAROON>
Chapter 1 <br>
```

```
Visual Basic Script Interactive Course <br>
</FONT>

</BODY>
</HTML>
```

SUMMARY

Hopefully, at this point you are not too overwhelmed, especially if you are not a programmer. It is really as simple as that to place some Visual Basic Script code in your HTML document. Simply place starting **<SCRIPT>** and ending **</SCRIPT>** tags, add a little code, and, *voila*, you have an Active Internet page! So, you non-Visual Basic propellerheads will soon find there is no need to be intimidated by learning a little programming. But you Visual Basic veterans, don't worry. There will be plenty of challenge when you consider all the possibilities available by using the robust architecture of the Internet Explorer, ActiveX, Java, and Visual Basic Script.

1. In the following code example, what is the first subroutine that will be run when the script is executed?

```
<BODY LANGUAGE="VBScript" onLoad=AnotherSub>

<SCRIPT LANGUAGE="VBScript">

Sub StartSub

    MsgBox "Hello World!"

End Sub

Sub AnotherSub

    MsgBox "Hello World 2!"

End Sub

Sub EndSub

    MsgBox "Hello World 3!"
```

continued on next page

continued from previous page

```
End Sub

</SCRIPT>
```

       a. `StartSub`
       b. `EndSub`
       c. `AnotherSub`
       d. `onLoad`

2. What are the programming languages currently supported by Internet Explorer?
       a. Visual Basic and Cobol
       b. Visual Basic and Java
       c. Visual Basic Script and Java
       d. Visual Basic Script and JavaScript

3. With the MsgBox function, which of the following would show Yes and No buttons on the common dialog box?
       a. MsgBox Hello World!, 5
       b. MsgBox Hello World!, 3
       c. MsgBox Hello World!, 6
       d. MsgBox Hello World!, 4

4. With the MsgBox function, which of the following would show a "Hello" title?
       a. MsgBox Hello World!, Hello
       b. MsgBox Hello World!, Hello, 3
       c. MsgBox Hello World!, 0, Hello
       d. MsgBox Hello World!, 4, , Hello

5. What is wrong with the following code?

```
<SCRIPT LANGUAGE="VBScript">
Sub FirstSub
    ...
    ...
End Sub
Sub SecondSub
End
Sub ThirdSub
    ...
    ...
End Sub
</SCRIPT>
```

       a. There is no specified start up subroutine.
       b. There is no `End Sub` for the `SecondSub` subroutine.
       c. There is no language specified in the `<BODY>` tag.
       d. None of the above.

Difficulty: Easy

1. Modify the sample program so that the common dialog box shows Yes, No, and Cancel buttons. Also, add a title indicating that the code is for Chapter 1, Session 7.

HELLO WORLD: HTML AND VISUAL BASIC SCRIPT UNITED

In the last two sessions, we have seen how to tell the world hello both through HTML and Visual Basic Script. But, working independently does us little good. The power comes when we can combine the two to work together.

Let's take a look at the sample Web page provided in the Session8 subdirectory of Chapter1 on the CD-ROM. Figure 1-11 shows the Web page.

Now click the "Click Here!" button to show a Hello World! common dialog box. Figure 1-12 shows the common dialog box.

We have seen from the last session how to show a common dialog box using Visual Basic Script and the MsgBox function. And from the earlier chapter sessions, we learned how to build HTML input items such as buttons.

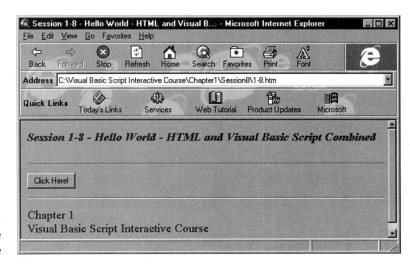

Figure 1-11
The sample
Web page

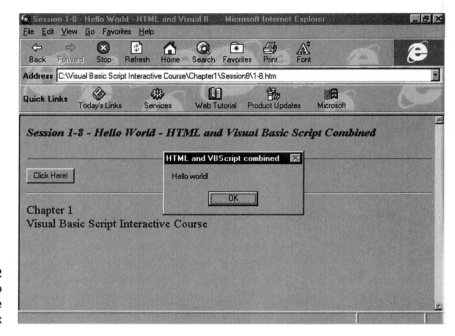

Figure 1-12
The sample Web page with the common dialog box

Now, let's look at the HTML and Visual Basic Script code. Select the View menu and the Source option to view the HTML source. First, the following HTML code builds the input button:

```
<INPUT TYPE=BUTTON VALUE="Click Here!" NAME="Hello">
```

This button is created to show the `"Click Here!"` text and has a name of `"Hello"`. Now, let's review the script code:

```
<SCRIPT LANGUAGE="VBScript">

    '   This subroutine is run when the
    '   button is selected
Sub Hello_OnClick

    '   Msgbox function with three parameters. The

    '   first is the message, the second indicates what

    '   buttons to show and the last is the title

    '   of the msgbox

    MsgBox "Hello world!", 0, "HTML and VBScript combined"
```

```
      End Sub

</SCRIPT>
```

The HTML section begins with the usual **<SCRIPT></SCRIPT>** tags. The key is defining a way for our code to run whenever the button is clicked. As you will learn in later chapters, the button has an **OnClick** event so that if we define the event in our script, the specified code will run. In this example, the **Hello_OnClick** subroutine in the script will be run whenever the button is clicked. And, in this case, we have a message box for our "Hello World!" message. An event is run whenever an *event* takes place in the browser. Thus, in our example, the click of a button fires off the **OnClick** event.

The tie between the HTML button click and script code means that you can interact in many ways to control the input and output options of your HTML documents.

SUMMARY

As we will see throughout the chapters, this link between HTML and your Visual Basic Script code will become integral to building Web pages.

 QUIZ 8

1. With _____ you can interact with _____ elements.
   a. Visual Basic Script…HTML input
   b. HTML…Visual Basic Script
   c. HTML…ActiveX
   d. None of the above

2. What is wrong with the following script?

```
<INPUT TYPE=BUTTON VALUE="Click Here!" NAME="Button">

<SCRIPT LANGUAGE="VBScript">

    Sub Button_Click

    MsgBox "Test"

    End Sub

</SCRIPT>
```

   a. The name of the HTML button cannot be **Button**.
   b. You cannot have a subroutine with **"Button"** in the name.
   c. The click event for the button is **OnClick**, not **Click**.
   d. The MsgBox button has no title.

3. What is wrong with the following script?

```
<INPUT TYPE=BUTTON NAME="Button">

<SCRIPT>

    Sub Button_OnClick

    End Sub

</SCRIPT>
```

    a. There is no language identifier in the **<SCRIPT>** tag.
    b. There is no value for the button HTML element.
    c. There is no code in the **Button_OnClick** subroutine.
    d. None of the above.

4. What is wrong with the following script?

```
<INPUT TYPE=BUTTON NAME="Button">

<SCRIPT>

Sub Button_Click

        Show a stuff message box to
        tell the user stuff
        MsgBox "Stuff", 0, "Stuff"

End Sub

</SCRIPT>
```

    a. There is no language identifier in the **<SCRIPT>** tag.
    b. The event is **OnClick**, not **Click**.
    c. There are no **'** characters in front of the code comments.
    d. All the above.

5. Events are
    a. segments of code that run whenever an action happens in the browser.
    b. segments of code that run only when you initiate them through code.
    c. code that makes an action happen in the browser.
    d. none of the above.

Difficulty: Intermediate

1. Modify the sample program to have two input buttons and two click event subroutines. In each, have a msgbox indicating the subroutine that has been fired off by the click of the buttons.

CHAPTER SUMMARY

This chapter has served as an introduction to basic concepts that make the Internet work. While we did not go into great depth, this should serve to get you up and going with a little Web technology, HTML tags, browsers, and a tad bit of scripting. In the next chapter, we will further explore building Web documents with HTML. Fully understanding how to build HTML documents is critical to understanding how we can enhance our Web pages using Visual Basic Script.

FUNDAMENTALS: BUILDING HTML DOCUMENTS

The HyperText Markup Language has taken corporate America and programmers by storm. It is not really a programming language in the sense of COBOL or Visual Basic, but it does provide powerful capabilities for text formatting and output display. The original purpose of HTML was primarily as a tool for making text documents readily available on the Internet. Basic graphic support was added, and then things started to take off. Now we have sound, live radio, video, live video, retail catalogs, and much, much more available to us.

CHAPTER 2

The HTML document is still the foundation for all basic Web pages. It is the interface presented when you visit a Web site. This basic language provides the necessary nuts and bolts for building Web pages. In this chapter we review some of the fundamentals of using HTML so that you will have a good foundation when we dive into Visual Basic Script. So, without further ado, let's get hyper!

In this chapter we will cover the following topics:

- Implementing HTML Basics

- How to Utilize Fancy Graphics in Your Web Pages

- Creating Terrific Text in Your Web Pages

- Building HTML Tables

- Implementing HTML Frames

- Adding Input Elements to Your Web Documents

- Creating Lists in Your HTML Documents

- Putting It All Together

HTML BASICS

In the last chapter, we had a brief introduction to HTML to get you started. Now we want to formally review the basics of what makes up HTML. The key word—*tag*—should be easy to remember; just think of that favorite childhood game. In HTML a section of the document is *tagged* in a certain way so that the browser knows how to display that portion of the document. Tags are surrounded by the **<** and **>** signs. And in many cases, there is a beginning tag and an ending tag. The following example will make text italic:

```
<I>Example</I> Text
```

The beginning tag for indicating text should be italic is **<I>**. The ending tag for when the text should return to normal is **</I>**. Most ending tags have a / character for the ending tag. But tags do not just perform formatting on a block of text, as we learned in Chapter 1, "What is the World Wide Web Anyway?" They can also divide an HTML document into sections. These sections can include document headings, title, and body and are also designated with tags. For example, the starting tag for the HTML body is **<BODY>** and the ending tag is **</BODY>**.

These tags, though, do not just have to have one set format or action. In fact, tags can have attributes that help to determine how the tag will be implemented. For example the **<SCRIPT>** and **</SCRIPT>** tags start and end the script section of an HTML document. But, since Internet Explorer supports both Visual Basic Script and JavaScript, we should indicate the type of script language we will be using. We can do this in the script tag by setting the **LANGUAGE** attribute as follows:

```
<SCRIPT LANGUAGE="VBScript">
```

This will indicate to the browser that the code that follows is Visual Basic Script. Appendix G, "HTML 3.2 Quick Reference," will give you a good overview of the different HTML tags available for formatting your documents. Figure 2-1 shows a sample document demonstrating several formatting tags.

Review the different tags used in the document. For example, the **<P>** and **</P>** tags are utilized for defining text paragraphs. And, in our example, we set an attribute for the paragraph, **ALIGN**, to **CENTER** so that the paragraph's text will be centered. There are many formatting tags for designing your HTML documents. This is just a start; the next several sessions will introduce you to many other types of document format options.

1. HTML tags
   a. indicate to the browser how to display the specified data.
   b. usually are surrounded by **< >** brackets.
   c. can have attributes that determine how the tag is applied.
   d. do all of the above.

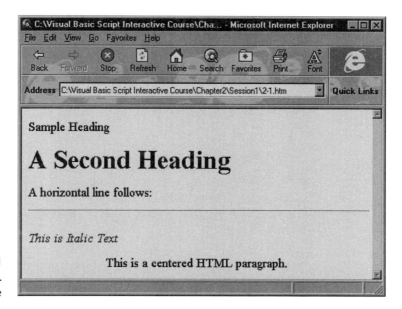

Figure 2-1
The sample HTML
Web page

2. The script tag contains what attribute?
   a. **LANGUAGE**
   b. Visual Basic Script
   c. **VBS**
   d. **TYPE**

3. Which HTML code creates the following output?
   This Is Displayed Text
   And this is **another line.**
   a. `<I>`This`</I>` Is Displayed Text,
      and this is another line.`</B>`
   b. `<I>`This`</I>` Is Displayed Text`<BR>`,
      and this is `<B>`another line.`</B>`
   c. `<I>`This`</I>` Is Displayed Text`<BR>`,
      and this is another line.
   d. This Is Displayed Text`<BR>`,
      and this is `<B>`another line.`</B>`

4. The following HTML code will

```
<P ALIGN=CENTER>
     Some Text
</P>
```

   a. align the **Some Text** text vertically in the browser window.
   b. align the **Some Text** text horizontally in the browser window.
   c. display text normally because the tags are incorrectly formatted.
   d. do all of the above.

5. What is wrong with the following code?

```
HTML
<H1>Heading</H1>
<HR><HR>
<BODY BGCLR=WHITE>
<I>Italic</I>
<BODY>
/HTML
```

   a. The ending body tag needs a **/** in the tag.
   b. **BGCLR** should be **BGCOLOR**.
   c. The beginning and ending HTML tags need beginning **<** and ending **>** characters.
   d. All of the above.

Difficulty: Easy

1. Change the sample so that the paragraph text is right-aligned. Also change the italic text to be bold.

SESSION 2

FANCY GRAPHICS?

Part of the appeal of the Web is not just nifty formatted text; the Web also has appealing graphics that make the eyes light up. And, we have quite a few options for how we integrate graphics into our documents.

Let's start with the simple **IMG** tag that adds an image to your document. The following code sample loads one of the Windows standard bitmaps, **Forest.bmp**, into the Web document:

```
<IMG SRC="FOREST.BMP">
```

The **IMG** tag indicates that an image is to be loaded. The **SRC** attribute sets the reference to the bitmap image. We have a few options available for us to set when aligning an image in the browser. The **ALIGN** attribute will align the text next to the graphic according to the setting of the attribute. The following figure outlines the text alignment attribute.

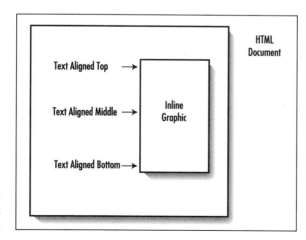

Figure 2-2
Text alignment
around graphics

Basic IMG Tag Options

```
<IMG>

ALIGN="TOP, CENTER, MIDDLE, BOTTOM, LEFT, or RIGHT"
ALT="Alternative text if the image is not shown"
SRC=GRAPHIC FILE NAME
```

One thing to keep in mind when building Web pages is that some browsers are not capable of displaying graphics, or certain types of graphics. Use the **ALT** attribute to display text where the image is displayed. This text is also visible if the image is slow to load. Of course, no Web designer has ever overloaded a page with graphics!

You might also be wondering how those psychedelic backgrounds that so many Web pages have are added to an HTML document. This is done with the **BACKGROUND** attribute of the **<BODY>** tag as follows:

```
<BODY BACKGROUND="FOREST.BMP">
```

That is all there is to it. Also, many Web pages have graphics and links to other HTML documents. Building a link to another HTML page is fairly simple as long as you know the location of the page by its URL (see Chapter 1).

HTML Links

HTML links are *hot spots* on a Web page that take you from the current page to another specified HTML Web page.

Basic Link Syntax:

<A>...</A>	Defines an anchor for a link with the display text.
HREF = URL	Specifies the destination of the link using its URL.

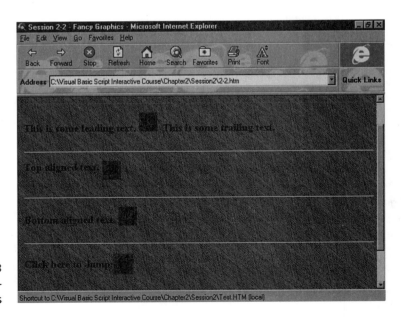

Figure 2-3
Sample HTML document with graphics

The following example builds a link to a document in the same directory as the currently loaded document. The clickable area to make the jump between the **<A>** and **</A>** tags is a graphic instead of text:

```
<A HREF="OtherDoc.HTM"><IMG SRC="forest.bmp"></A>
```

Thus, when the user clicks on the forest bitmap, he or she will jump to the **OtherDoc.HTM** HTML file. Let's take a quick look at an example of some of the techniques we have discussed. The sample document can be found in the Session2 subdirectory of Chapter2 on the CD-ROM.

The background graphic is set to the Windows standard sandstone bitmap. Even though the graphic does not fit the whole page, the browser tiles the image to fill the background. Following is the HTML code:

```
<!-- Start the Body and set the background image   -->
<BODY BACKGROUND="sandstone.bmp">
```

The first section of the document shows text surrounding the graphic. There are no line breaks between the text and graphic, and the text has no alignment attribute. The HTML is as follows:

```
This is some leading text.
<IMG SRC="CIRCLES.BMP">
This is some trailing text.
```

The next two sections align the text to the top and bottom of the image. This is done by simply setting the **ALIGN** attribute. The HTML code is as follows:

```
<!-- Show the Image with text aligned at the top-->
Top aligned text.
<IMG ALIGN=TOP SRC="CIRCLES.BMP">

... ...
... ...

<!-- Show the Image with text aligned at the bottom-->
Bottom aligned text.
<IMG ALIGN=BOTTOM SRC="CIRCLES.BMP">
```

Finally, we build a link to the **test.htm** HTML document using the graphic. We simply set up a link using the **<A>** and **</A>** tags and place a graphic between the two tags. The text before the image is placed in front of the **<A>** tag. Note in the **IMG** tag we set the alignment to **MIDDLE** so that the text will be centered with the graphic. Following is the HTML code:

```
<!-- Show text before the link   -->
Click here to Jump:

<!-- Build the link to test.htm with a graphic as the link
     Align the text in the middle of the graphic              -->
<A HREF="Test.HTM"><IMG ALIGN=MIDDLE SRC="CIRCLES.BMP"></A>
```

Adding images to your HTML pages is not difficult. You have many, many options available as to the size, color, and general characteristics of the images. Remember, there may be some poor souls out there who do not have T1 high bandwidth connections to the Internet and unlimited hard disk space who will not want to download the 20 megs worth of graphics you have placed on your page. To help make your pages successful, try to minimize size and general clutter.

1. You should use the ALT attribute when defining your images because
   a. some browsers do not support downloading and display of graphics.
   b. if the page is loading slowly, a description of the graphic is provided until the page is loaded.
   c. if a user interrupts the loading of a page, a description of the graphic is provided.
   d. of all of the above.

2. If a graphic you want to use as a background for your Web pages does not fill the entire Web page, which of the following will happen?
   a. The remainder of the document background will be white.
   b. The graphic will be tiled across the background.
   c. The rest of the background will be filled with a color of your choice.
   d. The graphic will be stretched across the background.

3. What is wrong with the following link?

`Jump to here:    <A><IMG ALIGN=MIDDLE SRC="CIRCLES.BMP"></A>`

   a. The `Jump to here:` text needs to be inside the `<A>` tag.
   b. There is no `HREF` attribute in the `<A>` tag indicating the document to jump to.
   c. There is no `HREF` attribute in the `</A>` tag indicating the document to jump to.
   d. There is no `HREF` attribute in the `<IMG>` tag indicating the document to jump to.

4. The following text will be

`<IMG ALIGN=TOP SRC="CIRCLES.BMP">`
`Some Text.`

   a. top-aligned to the right of the graphic.
   b. on top of the graphic.
   c. displayed on the graphic.
   d. top-aligned to the left of the graphic.

5. Which is not an `IMG` attribute?
   a. `ALIGN`
   b. `ALT`
   c. `SRC`
   d. `COLOR`

Difficulty: Intermediate

1. Change the sample so that the top- and bottom-aligned text appear to the right of the graphics, instead of the left.

SESSION 3

TERRIFIC TEXT

Throughout Chapter 1, and the first two sessions of this chapter, we have hinted at and used some HTML tags for formatting text. You will no longer have to wait to get a formal look at using these tags.

Many different tags can add character effects to your text. Of course, you are already familiar with the `<B></B>` and `<I></I>` tags for bold and italic. The following table overviews these two as well as the other tags you have available:

Tag	Description
`<B></B>`	Makes the text bold
`<I></I>`	Makes the text italic
`<U></U>`	Underlines the text
`<TT></TT>`	Uses a fixed width font for display
`<S></S>`	Places a strike through the text
`<SUP></SUP>`	Superscript
`<SUB></SUB>`	Subscript
`<EM></EM>`	Emphasizes the text
`<STRONG></STRONG>`	Strongly emphasizes the text
`<FONT SIZE=n></FONT>`	Sets the font size
`<FONT COLOR=color></FONT>`	Sets the font color

Table 2-1 *Text style tags*

This is only a subset of the tags available for formatting your text. These will provide the basics for most traditional text formatting. Note that it is up to the browser to determine how the actual text is displayed; the document author can only indicate how he or she would like the text to be shown. The sample document provided for this session gives examples of a formatted paragraph using these tags. The sample can be found on the CD-ROM in the Session3 subdirectory of Chapter2.

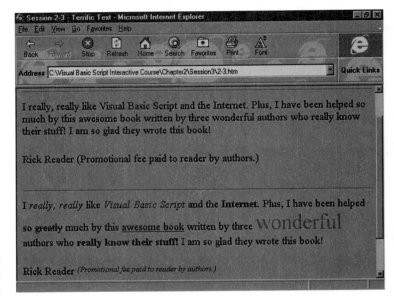

Figure 2-4
Sample Terrific
Text page

This example shows a sample quote by an obviously brilliant reader regarding this book. The first part of the document shows the text without any formatting. The second half shows the same basic paragraph with many text enhancements created through the use of the above tags. Note that you can have overlapping tags. This is the case with the authors' note that a small promotional fee was paid to the reader:

```
<!-- Italic superscript with a font size of 1   -->
<FONT SIZE=1 COLOR=BLUE>
    <I><SUP>(Promotional fee paid to reader by authors.)</SUP></I>
</FONT>
```

First, we set the font size and color. Next, the italic tag is set, followed by the superscript tag. The following text is then displayed with all three attributes. Finally, following the text, the ending tags indicate that each format option is to end.

1. What would be a simpler implementation of the following?

```
<FONT COLOR=BLUE>
<FONT SIZE=6>
    <I><B>Sample</B>  <B>Text</B></I>
</FONT>
</FONT>
```

```
a. <FONT COLOR=BLUE SIZE=6>
   <I><B>Sample Text</B></I>
   </FONT>
b. <FONT COLOR=BLUE> <FONT SIZE=6>
   <I><B>Sample Text</B></I>
   </FONT></FONT>
c. <FONT COLOR=BLUE>
   <FONT SIZE=6>
     <I><B>Sample</B>
     <B>Text</B></I>
   </FONT>
   </FONT>
d. <FONT SIZE=6>
   <FONT COLOR=BLUE>
   <I><B>Sample</B> <B>Text</B></I>
   </FONT>
   </FONT>
```

2. The Web page author
   a. has full control over how the text will be displayed in the browser.
   b. can utilize text tags to indicate how text should be displayed in the browser.
   c. can control complete Web page layout including pixel-level placement of text and graphics.
   d. does none of the above.

3. How will the following text be formatted?

```
<I><S>S</S>ample <B>T<U>ext</U></I></B>
```

   a. *Sample Text*
   b. *Sample **Text***
   c. S̶ample *Text*
   d. *Sample **Text***

4. What is wrong with the following HTML code?

```
<FONT COLOR=BLUE>
   <I></SUP>Sample</SUP> Text</I>
</FONT>
```

   a. The **</SUP>** tag should come after the **</I>** tag.
   b. The first **</SUP>** tag should be **<SUP>**.
   c. The **<FONT COLOR=BLUE>** tag should have **SIZE=n** in it.
   d. None of the above.

5. Which tag provides for a fixed width font?
   a. **<TT></TT>**
   b. **<T></T>**
   c. **<EM></EM>**
   d. **<U></U>**

Difficulty: Easy

1. Build a text paragraph that uses a fixed-width font versus the regular browser font. Try adding in some text effects to see how the text is displayed differently.

BUILDING TABLES

Don't let the title scare you; you won't need any power tools or varnish to work on this section. HTML tables are one of the more powerful formatting features you can utilize in your documents. The ability to organize your data into columns and rows will be invaluable in making a good presentation on your Web page. Figure 2-5 shows the basic format of HTML tables.

Fortunately, working with the fundamentals of building tables is not that difficult. The tag format is simple and straightforward. The most difficult (or annoying) aspect is that when your tables go beyond a few rows and columns, the HTML code can be lengthy!

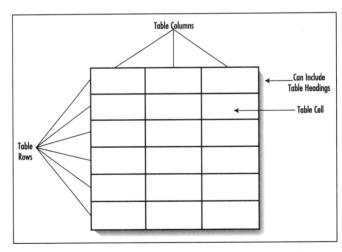

Figure 2-5
HTML tables

HTML Table Tags	
`<TABLE BORDER=n ></TABLE>`	Starts and ends the table.
`<TR></TR>`	Starts and ends a row in the table.
`<TD></TD>`	Starts and ends a column in a table.

Let's review a simple table with two rows and two columns:

```
<TABLE BORDER=2>

<TR>
      <TD>Row 1 Col 1</TD> <TD>Row 1 Col 2</TD>
</TR>

<TR>
      <TD>Row 2 Col 1</TD> <TD>Row 2 Col 2</TD>
</TR>

</TABLE>
```

This simple table illustrates the fundamentals of constructing a table. The table is initially built with the `<TABLE></TABLE>` tags. Then, each row is defined using the `<TR></TR>` tags. Finally we have two columns for each row indicated by the `<TD></TD>` tags. Don't let this simple example fool you, though; you can have very complicated tables complete with text formatting, input textboxes, buttons, and so on. The table is really just a formatting tool for your documents, and it is not limited to plain text.

Figure 2-6 shows a table using multiple column heading formats which are very useful in building reports. We use the `COLSPAN` attribute to indicate that a column should span more than one column in the table.

Figure 2-7 shows a more complicated table utilizing several of the formatting tags available and different formats for the column data.

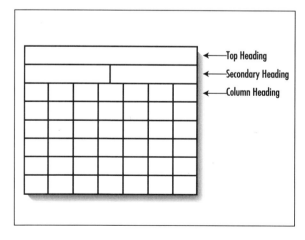

Figure 2-6
Table headings

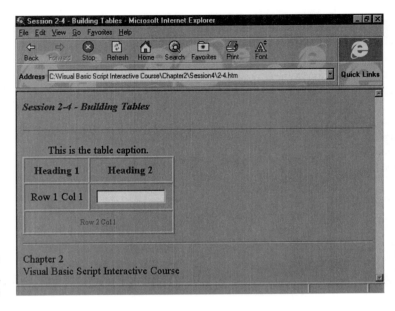

Figure 2-7
Sample HTML
table page

There are a couple of key points to discuss in the HTML document. First, note that when we set up the table, we set the border to 1 and the cell padding to 10. Cell padding places spaces around the contents of the cell.

```
<!-- Start the table with a border of 1   -->
<!-- and CELLPADDING of 10                -->
<TABLE BORDER=1 CELLPADDING=10>
```

Also included is a table caption which can be used to identify the table.

```
<!-- Show A table caption  -->
<CAPTION>This is the table caption.</CAPTION>
```

In the example, there are two table headings. Each has a different font color to display the heading. Note the **<TH></TH>** tags produce headings that are bold and stand out.

```
<!-- Show two table headings, each with a  -->
<!-- different color                       -->
<TH><FONT COLOR=MAROON>Heading 1</TH>
<TH><FONT COLOR=BLUE>Heading 2</TH>
```

Finally, our two rows are constructed. The first has two columns, and the second has one. The second column on the first row contains an input text box. Note that any of the standard HTML input elements can be placed in the table.

```
<!-- Start our first row  -->
  <TR>
     <!-- This row has two columns, one with  -->
     <!-- an input text box  -->
```

```
        <TD >Row 1 Col 1</TD>
        <TD ><INPUT TYPE=TEXT NAME=TEST></TD>
    </TR>

<!--  Start the second row  -->
    <TR>
        <!--  This column spans two columns and         -->
        <!--  the text is centered with a smaller font size  -->
        <TD ALIGN="CENTER" COLSPAN=2><FONT SIZE=1 COLOR=RED>Row 2 ⇐
            Col 1</TD>
    </TR>

</TABLE>
```

Tables can be fun and invaluable in formatting and displaying HTML documents for your user. We have just touched on what is possible with them in this example. Review Appendix G for more information on the various attribute tags that can be used with tables.

Use the following HTML code to answer these questions:

```
<TABLE BORDER=2>

<CAPTION>This is the table caption.</CAPTION>

<TH><FONT COLOR=MAROON>A Heading</TH>

<TR>
    <TD >Row 1 Col 1</TD>
    <TD ><INPUT TYPE=TEXT NAME=TEST></TD>
    <TD ><INPUT TYPE=BUTTON NAME=Button></TD>
</TR>

<TR>
    <TD COLSPAN=2><FONT SIZE=1 COLOR=RED>Row 2 Col 1</TD>
    <TD ALIGN="CENTER"><FONT SIZE=1 COLOR=GREEN>Row 2 Col 2</TD>
</TR>

</TABLE>
```

1. What is the cell padding for the above table?
   a. 18
   b. 25
   c. 20
   d. Default value

2. Row 2, column 3 contains
   a. an input button.
   b. an input text box.
   c. Row 2 Col 2.
   d. Row 2 Col 1.

3. The last row contains how many column boxes?
   a. 1
   b. 2
   c. 3
   d. 4

4. Row 2, column 1 has what color font?
   a. Red
   b. Maroon
   c. Green
   d. Blue

5. What table column attribute allows for a cell to cross more than one column?
   a. COLSPAN
   b. CSPAN
   c COLSPN
   d. COLUMNSPAN

Difficulty: Easy

1. Build a table which has two rows and four columns. Add one heading for the first two columns and one heading for the second two. Also include a table caption.

BUILDING FRAMES

Once again, don't worry, there will not be any heavy-duty construction going on here. We will not be installing any windows in our houses here, but we will be dividing HTML documents into multiple windows for viewing of several HTML documents at once. Frame technology allows us to add new dimensions to our documents. Figure 2-8 shows an HTML page broken down into different frames.

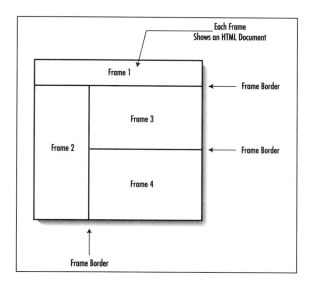

Figure 2-8
HTML frames

Frame Contructs
FRAMESET   This is a container which hosts the **FRAME**, **FRAMESET**, and **NOFRAMES** tags.
FRAME   Defines a single frame in a frameset. Note there is no matching end tag.
NOFRAMES   Content viewable by browsers that do not support frames.
TARGET   Allows you to specify which frame you would like to load a document into.

Frames allow you to provide multiple views within one browser window. Each view can contain its own unique HTML document. The many different attributes for formatting frames allow you to set features like scroll bars, frame border widths, and so on. Let's look at a simple frame example:

```
<FRAMESET COLS="*, *" FRAMESPACING="3">

    <FRAME SCROLLING="NO" NAME="FRAME1" SRC="Sample1.htm">

    <FRAME SCROLLING="YES" NAME="FRAME2" SRC="Sample2.htm">

</FRAMESET>
```

In this example, an HTML window will contain two frames in two columns. We need a **FRAMESET** container to hold our two frames. In the **FRAMESET** tag, we indicate there will be two columns in the browser window. The ***** value for the **COLS** attribute indicates the columns should be relative in size, which in this case means they will be evenly split across the screen.

We have two frames in the **FRAMESET**. The first frame will not have a scroll bar and the second will. Each shows an HTML document in the frame. The **SCROLLING** tag indicates whether or not to show scroll bars. And, the **SRC** tag indicates the source HTML document to show in the frame.

The sample Web page provided for this section sets up what is becoming a popular document style of having a top frame as the header of the document used for navigation, and so on. The left frame of the screen provides a menu of options for moving to different HTML documents, and the primary information frame is the body frame on the right. Figure 2-9 shows the sample document described above.

As you can see, we have three colorful HTML frames in our Web document—a header, menu bar, and body—each a different frame. This format will be effective for providing content in your main frame document, allowing browsing of menu options in the left frame and providing an overall application header. Let's look at how these frames were created:

```
<FRAMESET ROWS="72,*" FRAMESPACING="3">

    <FRAME SRC="Header.htm" NAME="HEADER" SCROLLING="NO" NORESIZE
           MARGINHEIGHT=6 MARGINWIDTH=8>


<FRAMESET COLS="150,*" FRAMESPACING=0>

    <FRAME SRC="Menu.htm" NAME="MENUS" SCROLLING="AUTO" NORESIZE
           MARGINHEIGHT=0 MARGINWIDTH=8>

    <FRAME SRC="Body.htm" NAME="BODY" NORESIZE MARGINHEIGHT=8
           MARGINWIDTH=8>


</FRAMESET>

</FRAMESET>
```

We have two framesets in our document. The first sets up the two rows of frames. We have arbitrarily set the height of the first row to 72, and the second will fill the remaining window space as indicated by the *. The first row shows the **header.htm** file. No scroll bars will be shown, and we won't allow a resize of the frame.

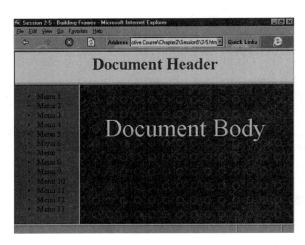

Figure 2-9
Frame HTML page

The second frameset sets up our two frame columns for the second row. The first shows our menu HTML file. Scrolling on this frame is set to automatic, and we will not allow resizing of this frame. The next frame shows the body document of our Web page.

Frames provide a wealth of opportunities for you to provide interactive documents to your user. The limit to the formatting and use of frames is just your imagination. In Chapter 12, "I Was Framed!," we will show you how to take control of these frames from Visual Basic Script so that you will have full control over the look and feel of your Web pages.

1. How will the following frame windows be displayed?

```
<FRAMESET ROWS="*,*">
```

    a. The document windows divided vertically into two equally sized frames.
    b. The document windows divided horizontally into two equally sized frames.
    c. The document window with two arbitrarily sized vertical frames.
    d. The document window with two arbitrarily sized horizontal frames.

2. The _____ tag defines a _____ in a frameset.
    a. frame…single document
    b. target…single frame
    c. frameset…single frame
    d. frame…single frame

3. Which of the following is a valid frame tag?
    a. SRC
    b. SCROLL
    c. HOME
    d. LENGTH

4. How many different frames will be displayed in the following Web page?

```
<FRAMESET ROWS="*,*">
  <FRAME SRC="doc1.htm" NAME="DOC1">
  <FRAMESET COLS="*,*,*">
     <FRAME SRC="doc2.htm" NAME="DOC2">
     <FRAME SRC="doc3.htm" NAME="DOC3">
     <FRAME SRC="doc4.htm" NAME="DOC4">
  </FRAMESET>
</FRAMESET>
```

    a. 1
    b. 4
    c. 3
    d. 2

5. Which frame tag indicates that the frame size cannot be adjusted?
   a. SCROLLING
   b. NORESIZE
   c. RESIZE
   d. LOCKED

Difficulty: Intermediate

1. Modify the sample HTML file for this session so the frames are resizable and have scroll bars.

ELEMENTAL DOCUMENTS

HTML is not all about text. There are many options for placing interactive input elements on your Web pages. The ones we are going to discuss here are just the elements directly supported by HTML. Chapter 10, "Objectifying Your Scripts," will discuss placing other objects into your HTML documents, including ActiveX controls and Java applets.

HTML Input Types	Description
CHECKBOX	Check box input
RADIO	Radio button input
IMAGE	Returns information where a user clicked on an image
TEXT	Single line text input
HIDDEN	A nonvisible input
RANGE	Number field with inputs limited to a specific range
SCRIBBLE	Lets user write on top of an image
SUBMIT	A button to submit form input
RESET	A button to reset the form
BUTTON	A general input button
SELECT	Menu of selections
TEXTAREA	Multiple line input

Table 2-2 *HTML input elements*

All these elements, except for **SELECT** and **TEXTAREA**, use the **INPUT** tag construct. There are several attributes that can be set for the **INPUT** as outlined below:

Attribute	Description
TYPE	Specifies the input type (such as CHECKBOX, RADIO, and so on)
NAME	The name of the input element
SIZE	Sets the size of the text display for a TEXT element
MAXLENGTH	The maximum length of a TEXT element
VALUE	Value used for initial value of HIDDEN, RANGE, and TEXT elements
DISABLED	Disables the input element from input
CHECKED	Initializes a field in a CHECKBOX or RADIO input element
SRC	Specifies the image file for IMAGE, SCRIBBLE, SUBMIT, or RESET

Table 2-3 *INPUT attributes*

The **TEXTAREA** and **SELECT** input elements have their own set of attributes that can be referenced in Appendix G. Figure 2-10 shows a sample HTML document with several input elements.

Let's review several of the input elements for this HTML document. The first is the textbox.

```
<INPUT NAME="TextBox" TYPE="TEXT" SIZE="10" MAXLENGTH=5>
```

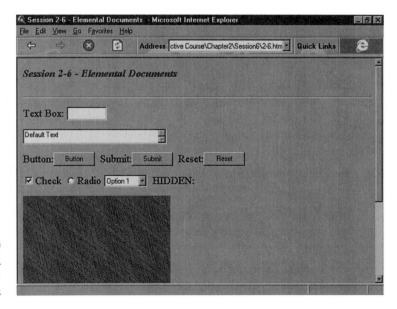

Figure 2-10
Sample HTML document wth input elements

The type is **TEXT** for a textbox. We have set the display size to 10 characters, but the maximum length is also set to 5 so that no more than 5 characters can be entered by the user. The following builds the HTML **TEXTAREA** input element:

```
<TEXTAREA NAME="TEXTAREA" ROWS=0 COLS=50>Default Text</TEXTAREA>
```

The type is **TEXTAREA**. The rows attribute is set to 0 to indicate that only one row is to be shown, and the columns are 50. Next we have three buttons:

```
<INPUT NAME="Button" TYPE=BUTTON VALUE="Button">
<INPUT NAME="Submit" TYPE=SUBMIT VALUE="Submit">
<INPUT NAME="Reset" TYPE=RESET VALUE="Reset">
```

There are three types of buttons: **BUTTON**, **SUBMIT**, and **RESET**. The **BUTTON** type is a standard input button. The **SUBMIT** button will execute an HTML form to send or retrieve data from the server. The **RESET** type will reset an HTML form.

The **HIDDEN** element provides a way for placing a hidden element on your form that can store data but not be visible.

```
HIDDEN:<INPUT TYPE="HIDDEN" NAME="HIDDEN" VALUE=10>
```

HTML elements provide many methods for providing input into your HTML documents. As we will see in later chapters, we can interact with these HTML elements from our scripts to build powerful data entry applications.

1. The _____ element allows the user to enter _____ of text.
    a. **TEXT**...multiple lines
    b. **HIDDEN**...hidden lines
    c. **TEXTAREA**...multiple lines
    d. none of the above

2. Which input element initiates a form action?
    a. **SELECT**
    b. **RANGE**
    c. **SUBMIT**
    d. **RESET**

3. How do you limit the input of the textbox?
    a. Set an initial value for the textbox.
    b. Use the **DISABLED** attribute.
    c. Set the **SIZE** attribute to the number of characters to be input.
    d. Set the **MAXLENGTH** attribute to the number of characters to be input.

4. How do you initialize a check box or radio button to be selected?
   a. Include the **CHECKED** attribute in the tag
   b. Set its initial value
   c. Set the **CHECKED** attribute to TRUE
   d. Set the **SELECTED** attribute to TRUE

5. Which **TEXT** input element attribute sets the display length of the element?
   a. **SIZE**
   b. **LENGTH**
   c. **CHARS**
   d. **WIDTH**

Difficulty: Intermediate

1. Build a table which has a drop-down select box for each column.

SESSION 7

CHECK THE LISTING

Often when presenting data to your users, you will need to use lists to display your information. HTML provides several methods of building formatted lists in your documents. You have already seen a list example earlier in the chapter.

HTML List Formats	
<DL>	A definition list is an automatically formatted two-column list with terms on the left and their definitions on the right.
<DIR>	A directory list consists of individual items, none containing more than 20 characters, which should be displayed in columns.
<MENU>	A general list of items.
<OL>	An ordered list consists of individual items which are numbered.
<UL>	A bulleted list consists of individual items which are bulleted.

Adding lists to your HTML documents is really as easy as adding a few tags to your document and typing in the list topic. As you can see from the above reference, you have a wide variety of lists you can add to your documents. Let's look at the code sample provided for this session on the CD. Open the HTML document in the Session7 subdirectory of the Chapter2 directory on the CD-ROM. Figure 2-11 shows the document.

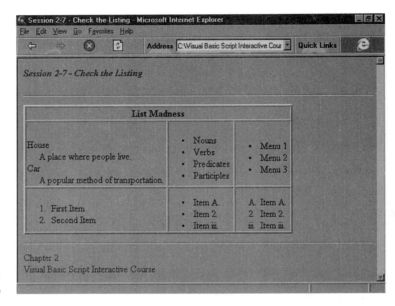

Figure 2-11
HTML list demo

The first table cell shows a definition list. This list shows the definition title and then the definition itself. The **<DL></DL>** tags start the list. The definition title is started by the **<DT>** tag, and the definition is defined by the **<DD>** tag.

```
<DL>
 <DT>House
 <DD>A place where people live.

 <DT>Car
 <DD>A popular method of transportation.
</DL>
```

Our next list, in row 1 column 2, shows a directory listing. The **<DIR></DIR>** tags start the listing and the **<LI>** tag indicates each list item.

```
<DIR>
 <LI>Nouns
 <LI>Verbs
 <LI>Predicates
 <LI>Participles
</DIR>
```

Next, we have a menu list. This list is started with the **<MENU></MENU>** tags and the list items are defined by the **<LI>** tag.

```
<MENU>
 <LI>Menu 1
 <LI>Menu 2
 <LI>Menu 3
</MENU>
```

Our next list in row 2 column 1, shows an ordered list. Note that the list items are numbered.

The **</OL>** tag starts the list, with the **<LI>** tag indicating each list item.

```
<OL>
  <LI>First Item
  <LI>Second Item
</OL>
```

The second column of row 2 shows a standard bulleted list. As with the other lists, the **<UL></UL>** tags define the list and each list item is designated by the **<LI>** tag. Note that we have included some attributes in the **<LI>** tag. These formats will be used in the order list but are shown here for contrast. Notice that they are ignored for this bulleted list, but in the last list example they change the listing numbers' style.

```
<UL>
  <LI TYPE=A>Item A.
  <LI TYPE=1>Item 2.
  <LI TYPE=i>Item iii.
</UL>
```

As mentioned above, with the ordered list, we can designate the appearance of the list item in the **<LI>** tag. The counter of the list can either be by alpha (A), numeric (1), or Roman numeral (i.).

```
<OL>
  <LI TYPE=A>Item A.
  <LI TYPE=1>Item 2.
  <LI TYPE=i>Item iii.
</OL>
```

As you build your HTML documents, you will find lists invaluable for presenting your data in an orderly way. Review Appendix E, "Properties," to find out more about your options for formatting HTML lists.

1. In the code below, Item 1 is a list element of what type of list?

```
<DIR>
<LI>Item 1
<LI>Item 2
<LI>Item 3
<MENU>
<LI>Item 4
<LI>Item 5
<LI>Item 6
</MENU>
<LI>Item 7
</DIR>
```

a. Directory
b. Menu
c. Bullet
d. None of the above

2. Using the listing below, the _____ list item will be counted using
_____.

```
<OL>
   <LI TYPE=A>Item
   <LI TYPE=1>Item
   <LI TYPE=I>Item
</OL>
```

a. first...Roman numerals
b. second...Roman numerals
c. third...Roman numerals
d. fourth...Alphabetical

3. In the listing below, the definition for W is:

```
<DL>
<DT>Q
<DD>H
<DT>N
<DD>A
<DT>P
<DD>W
<DT>K
<DD>G
<DT>V
<DD>E
<DT>M
<DD>Z
</DL>
```

a. K
b. P
c. V
d. None of the above

4. Which statement about the below list is NOT true?

```
<UL>
 <LI TYPE=I>Item
 <LI>Item
 <LI >Item
</UL>
```

a. Each list item will have a bullet in front of it.
b. There are three items in the list.
c. Every list item will show the text Item.
d. Each list item will have a Roman numeral in front of it.

5. What is the definition character limit for the DIR list?
   a. 10
   b. 20
   c. 30
   d. 40

Difficulty: Easy

1. Build a listing that will provide several categories of definitions, with each category counted with Roman numerals.

Difficulty: Easy

2. Add formatting to the above list to make each section stand out.

PUTTING IT ALL TOGETHER

We have been reviewing a lot of different aspects of HTML documents in this chapter. So, how do we put it all together to make exciting HTML documents? Well, we can throw in some tables, menus, frames, graphics, and so on, and we can build an eye-pleasing and intuitive Web page. And, when we begin adding some Visual Basic Script, we will be rolling.

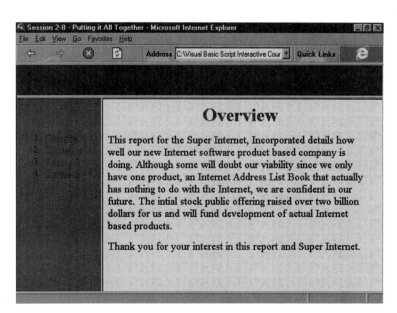

Figure 2-12
Sample annual
sales report

We will build a sample corporate annual sales report. Figure 2-12 shows the sample HTML Web page we will build.

Our document is broken down into three sections. The title shows that this is a company's annual sales report. The left frame shows a menu of options to review the sections of the sales report. Finally, the body, which shows the sales report, is in the right frame block.

The following HTML code shows the basic HTML document that displays the frames:

```
<!--  Begin our first frameset container  -->
<FRAMESET ROWS="54,*" FRAMESPACING="3">

   <!--  The first frame row shows the header  -->
   <FRAME SRC="Header.htm" NAME="HEADER" SCROLLING="NO"          NORESIZE ⇐
   MARGINHEIGHT=6 MARGINWIDTH=8>

   <!--  The second frame set will show our   -->
   <!--  next two frame columns               -->
   <FRAMESET COLS="150,*" FRAMESPACING=0>

      <!--  Show the menu frame  -->
      <FRAME SRC="Menu.htm" NAME="MENUS" SCROLLING="AUTO" NORESIZE ⇐
      MARGINHEIGHT=0 MARGINWIDTH=8>

      <!--  Show the body frame  -->
      <FRAME SRC="Body1.htm" NAME="BODY" NORESIZE MARGINHEIGHT=8 ⇐
      MARGINWIDTH=8>

   </FRAMESET>

</FRAMESET>
```

This HTML code builds our three frames. We are not allowing the frames to be resized, and we are ensuring that none of this *foundation* document is actually visible behind the frames. The header HTML frame document is fairly straight forward. Our menu is comprised of a list of links. As the following HTML code shows, each listing is an anchor to another document. When the list item is clicked on, the body frame is loaded with the specified HTML document. The target attribute in the link indicates which frame the document should be loaded in.

```
<OL>

<!--  Show our list items which are links -->
<!--  These links load the HTML documents -->
<!--  in the body frame                   -->
<LI><A href="BODY1.htm" TARGET="BODY">Overview</A>
<LI><A href="BODY2.htm" TARGET="BODY">Executives</A>
<LI><A href="BODY3.htm" TARGET="BODY">Sales</A>
<LI><A href="BODY4.htm" TARGET="BODY">Summary</A>

<!--  End Our List -->
</OL>
```

Last, the body frame shows the appropriate HTML document. In these documents, we have used various font formatting techniques, tables, and a neat background image for our document. By the way, this document was built using standard Windows Paint to give the SUPER background watermark effect.

Review and play around with the HTML sample provided. You have a wide arsenal of tools available to make your documents come alive. And, as we move into the next chapter, you will learn how to start adding scripts to your HTML Web pages to make them have depth through programming.

1. The _____ tag will indicate in which _____ an _____ will be loaded.
   a. `href`...table...HTML document
   b. `<A></A...`frame...HTML document
   c. `href`...frame...HTML document
   d. `TARGET`...frame...HTML document

2. How do we add Roman numerals to the sections of the annual sales section menu?
   a. `<LI TYPE=I>`
   b. `I <LI><A href="BODY1.htm" TARGET="BODY">Overview</A>`
   c. `<LI TYPE=ROMAN>`
   d. `<LI><A href="BODY1.htm" TARGET="BODY">I Overview</A>`

3. In the _____ document, the background image is set by the _____ statement.
   a. `BODY1` HTML...`BACKGROUND="SUPER.BMP"`
   b. `BODY1` HTML...`<BODY BACKGROUND="SUPER.BMP">`
   c. `MENU` HTML...`<BODY BACKGROUND="SUPER.BMP">`
   d. `HEADER` HTML...`<BODY BACKGROUND="SUPER.BMP">`

4. Which statement is true about frames?
   a. You are limited to just three frames in your documents.
   b. You can have resizable frames.
   c. You cannot display scroll bars on your frames.
   d. You cannot set the HTML document for one frame from another.

5. Which link attribute indicates which frame a document should be shown in?
   a. `TARGET`
   b. `JUMP`
   c. `LINK`
   d. `HREF`

Difficulty: Easy

1. Modify the sample HTML document to have the following changes:

- The background image on the title frame.

- Roman numerals on the menu items for the menu frame.

- Provide text formatting on the menu list.

CHAPTER SUMMARY

In this chapter we have reviewed the basics of building HTML documents. These include many of the most popular constructs such as tables and frames. As we will find in later chapters, with Visual Basic Script you can interact with many of these HTML elements to control the look, feel, and use of your Web pages.

CHAPTER 3

GREAT RUNNING SCRIPTS

n the first two chapters you heard a lot about what the World Wide Web is and how to get up and going with Web browsers and HTML documents. In this chapter we will take our first look at Visual Basic Script and its integration into your HTML documents.

We will look at some basics to get you familiar with how to embed a Visual Basic Script document into Web pages and run the script. And, an introduction will be provided to using ActiveX and interacting with the Internet Explorer scripting object model.

This chapter will not cover any one topic in depth, but will give you a good introduction to what it means to have Visual Basic Script available as a tool in your Web pages. Several concepts introduced in this chapter will be discussed in greater depth in subsequent chapters, but enough explanation will be provided here to get you up and going. So, without further discussion, let's get started!

In this chapter, we will cover the following topics:

- Differences Between Visual Basic Script and Visual Basic
- Adding a Script to your Web Page
- Building Our First Script
- Inserting ActiveX Controls in Your Web Pages
- Working with Objects in Your Browser
- Utilizing ActiveX Controls in Your Web Pages
- Utilizing the Visual Basic Script InputBox Function
- Building a Small Sample Application

 *SESSION 1*

DIFFERENCES BETWEEN VISUAL BASIC SCRIPT AND VISUAL BASIC

Microsoft Visual Basic, Scripting Edition, is the newest member of the Visual Basic line-up of programming tools. If you already know Visual Basic or Visual Basic for Applications, Visual Basic Script will be very familiar. And, if you don't know Visual Basic, once you learn the basics, you will find that it is not that complicated!

ActiveX Scripting

For you technical types out there: Visual Basic Script talks to the Internet Explorer using Microsoft's ActiveX Scripting. ActiveX Scripting acts like a general language interface to the Internet Explorer for other scripting languages. With ActiveX Scripting, language vendors can create standard language runtimes for their scripting implementations by having them interface to the browser with ActiveX scripts.

Microsoft has designed Visual Basic as a scalable development tool for a range of applications, including desktop, Internet, and client/server. The Visual Basic language can be used to create activated HTML documents with Visual Basic Script, to customize desktop applications using Microsoft Office and Visual Basic for Applications, and to build full scale client/server applications with Visual Basic. Figure 3-1 shows the relationship between these three flavors of Visual Basic.

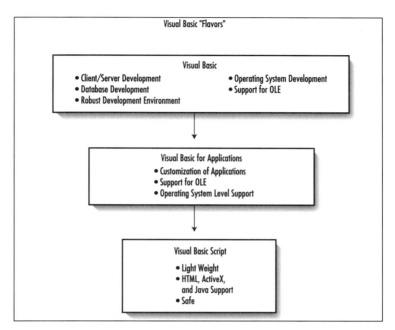

Figure 3-1
Visual Basic flavors

Visual Basic Script is a lightweight subset of the Microsoft Visual Basic programming language. Microsoft's goal is to provide Visual Basic Script on Windows and Macintosh platforms, and to work with third parties to provide UNIX versions for multiple platforms including Sun, HP, Digital, and IBM.

Visual Basic for Applications (VBA) is Microsoft's *all purpose* scripting language for incorporation into a wide range of desktop applications. Currently Microsoft Excel, Microsoft Project, and Microsoft Access have VBA support. Microsoft has committed to implementing VBA in the next version of Microsoft Word. Also, Microsoft has opened up VBA licensing to third parties so that they can include VBA in their products.

Visual Basic is the granddaddy of the Visual Basic tool set. Visual Basic version 4.0 provides a superset of the language and tool functionality found in Visual Basic for Applications. Key product features include client/server data access, multitier support, and team project development.

Visual Basic Script has been implemented to ensure that the product is completely secure and will have no negative effect on the system the script is running on. For example, there is no method for executing Windows Application Programming Interface (API) functions. Also there are no file I/O functions for reading and writing data from the user's hard drive. Think of Visual Basic Script as a tool for you to control the way your Web page users interact with your Web pages. It is not a tool for building complete client/server database applications. But, as we will see in later chapters, it will be invaluable in building great Web/Internet applications!

1. Which of the following provides the most robust functionality?
   a. Visual Basic
   b. Visual Basic for Applications
   c. Visual Basic Script
   d. None of the above

2. Which statement is true about programming with Visual Basic Script?
   a. You have to be careful not to make any *system* calls that might adversely affect the user's system.
   b. You have to be careful not to change any files stored on the hard drive.
   c. Visual Basic Script is safe and has been designed to not adversely affect the system that the code runs on.
   d. None of the above.

3. Visual Basic Script supports
   a. ActiveX scripting.
   b. ActiveY scripting.
   c. CGI programming.
   d. Java scripting.

4. Which of the following *can* you do in Visual Basic Script?
   a. Call Windows API functions.
   b. Read and write files from the end user's hard drive.
   c. Build complete client/server applications.
   d. Interact with an HTML document.

5. Visual Basic for Applications
   a. is designed for code scripting in desktop applications.
   b. is designed as a more robust version of Visual Basic Script for power Web programmers.
   c. is designed to compete directly with Java on the Internet.
   d. is currently not in use by any applications.

SESSION 2

ADDING A SCRIPT TO YOUR DOCUMENTS

You have seen small examples tags. The first tag will indicate the script language and the end tag will end the scripting section. Following is an example:

```
<SCRIPT LANGUAGE="VBScript">
<!--
...
...
...
-->
</SCRIPT>
```

You need to specify the language, since Microsoft Internet Explorer version 3.0 can support other scripting languages such as JavaScript. If you are deploying your HTML pages on the Internet for anyone to see, there is a good chance that someone who is using a browser that does not support Visual Basic Script may venture across your Web page. The HTML comment tags, **<!--** and **-->**, placed as shown, will prevent these browsers from displaying the script code.

Where you place script code in a page can be at your discretion. You can even break the script code up into different sections of the document. Most likely though, it will be easier to keep all your code together in one section of your HTML document.

You can attach Visual Basic Script code to your document in other ways, though keeping your code together in one section is generally recommended. One way to add short sections of code (inline) is in the tag defining an HTML element. For example, the following HTML input button has an **OnClick** event that shows a message box:

```
<INPUT NAME="AButton" TYPE=BUTTON
        VALUE="A Button" OnClick='MsgBox "I was Clicked!"'>
```

You can place the Visual Basic Script code right in the declaration of the input element. The event name, in this case **OnClick**, is followed by the Visual Basic Script code in single quotes. In our example, we will call the MsgBox function. Multiple Visual Basic Script statements can be included as long as they are separated with colons (**:**).

Events—What are they?

When you click on an HTML button, an *event* is fired that allows you to take some action based on the fact that the button was clicked. In our example, the HTML button input element has an **OnClick** event. We then attach code to this event which in this case will show a MsgBox dialog to the user. You will see, as we move forward, that you can use many different events to react to your user's input. These events are provided as part of the Internet Explorer Scripting Object Model which will be discussed in later sessions.

You can also write a **<SCRIPT>** tag so that it applies only to a particular event for a specific HTML input element. In the following example, we have the same code for the **Abutton** HTML button defined.

```
<INPUT NAME="AButton" TYPE=BUTTON VALUE="A Button">

<SCRIPT LANGUAGE="VBScript" EVENT="OnClick" FOR="AButton">
<!--
    MsgBox "I was clicked!"
-->
</SCRIPT>
```

continued on next page

continued from previous page

In this case, the sample script will just be run whenever the **Abutton** is clicked on by the user. Notice that in the script definition we have defined which event we want the script to run **FOR**, in this case the **OnClick** event for the button. In the next session, we will get started with *officially* writing our first script.

1. What is wrong with the following script?

```
<INPUT NAME="Button" TYPE=BUTTON VALUE="Button">

<SCRIPT LANGUAGE="VBScript" EVENT="OnClick" FOR="Button">
<!--
    MsgBox "Hello"

</SCRIPT>
-->
```

    a. The HTML input element should come after the script.
    b. The ending HTML comment tag should be before the **</SCRIPT>** tag.
    c. The event for the button is **Click**, not **OnClick**.
    d. None of the above.

2. What is wrong with the following script?

```
<SCRIPT>
<!--
    Sub StartSub()
      MsgBox "I was clicked!"
    End Sub
-->
</SCRIPT>
```

    a. There is no HTML input element defined for the script.
    b. There is no event defined for the script.
    c. There is no **Language** attribute for the script tag.
    d. The HTML comments tags should be inside the **Sub StartSub** and **End Sub** code lines.

3. Which statement is false?
    a. You can place multiple sets of script code in your document.
    b. You can define your own custom events for HTML input elements.
    c. You cannot directly place code in an HTML input element declaration.
    d. You can control the effects of an HTML input element event.

4. Which statement is true?
    a. You can only add Visual Basic Script to your documents.
    b. You can add other script code to your documents beside Visual Basic Script.
    c. You cannot have Java and Visual Basic Script in the same document.
    d. Microsoft Internet Explorer only supports Visual Basic Script.

5. Which of the following is not a method for adding Visual Basic Script code to your Web document?

    a. `<SCRIPT LANGUAGE="VBScript"> </SCRIPT>`

    b. `<INPUT NAME="Name" TYPE=BUTTON VALUE="Value" OnClick='MsgBox "Some Code!"'>`

    c. `<SCRIPT LANGUAGE="VBScript" EVENT="OnClick" FOR="AButton"></SCRIPT>`

    d. All of the above

SESSION 3

UNDER CONSTRUCTION—OUR FIRST SCRIPT

Put on the hard hat, take out the gloves—it is time to begin building great scripts. To get us up and running, the first thing we are going to do is learn how to do something familiar: write HTML code. But, this time, we are going to do it using Visual Basic Script!

We will do this by using some of the tools the Internet Explorer provides us. As you will learn throughout the book, the power of Visual Basic Script is in large part in what it can control. The *things* it can control include ActiveX controls, Java applets, and the Internet Explorer itself. So, let's learn how we can control the browser to write HTML code from our scripts.

As we will learn in Session 5, the Internet Explorer provides what is called an Object Model, which exposes different properties, methods, and events that allow us to control the browser from our scripts. One of these objects is the document object. You can think of this object as encompassing all aspects of your HTML document. Properties include settings like the background color, the location of the document, and so on. Methods would include things like `open`, `close`, and `write`.

The `write` method is the one we will use in our example. This method allows us to write HTML code directly from Visual Basic Script. The following code example shows how you would invoke this method to write a line of HTML code:

```
document.write "<BODY BGCOLOR=BLUE>"
```

In order to call the `write` method of the document object, we have to reference the fact that we want to use this particular method of the document object. We do this by using the '`.`' construct as the example shows. We then need to tell the `write` method what we want it to write. In this case it is a line of HTML code. Note that the code needs to be enclosed in double quotes since it will be a data type of `String`. We will learn much more about strings and data types in the next chapter.

Now, let's look at a more in-depth example to get us up and running. Our first script example will build a simple HTML table. This example can be found on the CD-ROM in the Session3 subdirectory of Chapter3. The following figure shows the Web page.

Let's look at how this script is created. First, we have the basic HTML **<SCRIPT>** tag indicating the start of our script. Also, we have a call to a subroutine called **StartSub**. We will learn more about subroutines in subsequent chapters, but for now simply think of it as a special container for Visual Basic Script code within the script. A subroutine organizes code into chunks that can be *run* independently of other code in your script. We can run this set of code by calling the name of the subroutine, which in this case is **StartSub**. Note that we have comments in our script. Script comments always follow an apostrophe character.

```
SCRIPT LANGUAGE="VBScript">

'  call start sub
StartSub
```

Now we will start our subroutine by using the **Sub** code construct followed by the name of the subroutine, in this case **StartSub**.

```
'  StartSub is our subroutine that is first loaded
Sub StartSub
```

Next, we will add our code to build the HTML table. First, we have several comments in our code. Then, we are going to call the **write** method of the document object several times. In all, we have six lines of code to make our table. Each line of code is represented by a new line in the script. You can only make one *statement* on each line in Visual Basic Script unless you separate two statements by using a ':'. We have an

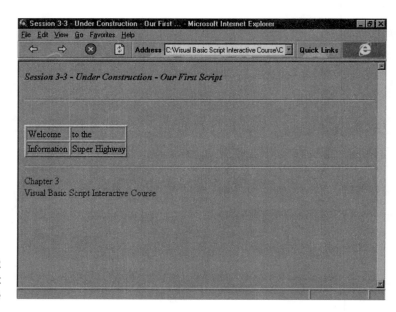

Figure 3-2
First script
Web page

example of this on line three of this code. If we were to take out that ':' character, when we went to run the script, an error would be returned.

```
'  The following document write statements
'  build an HTML table welcoming the
'  viewer to the information super
'  highway.
Document.write "<BR><BR><TABLE BORDER=2><TR>"
Document.write "<TD>Welcome</TD>"
Document.write "<TD>to the</TD>" : Document.write "</TR><TR>"
Document.write "<TD>Information</TD>"
Document.write "<TD>Super Highway</TD>"
Document.write "</TR></TABLE>"
```

With each call to the document **write** method, we are simply building an HTML table. The code statements are the same as if we were just writing HTML code, only here it is happening on the fly. Finally, the subroutine is ended by placing the **End Sub** statement and then ending our script by placing the closing script tag **</SCRIPT>**.

```
End Sub

</SCRIPT>
```

As you can see from the results in the browser, we have built a simple HTML table by using Visual Basic Script and the Internet Explorer document object. The next section will provide an exploration of how to add ActiveX controls to your documents. As we will see in later sessions, combining Visual Basic Script and ActiveX will provide the ability to build powerful Web pages.

1. Which statement is false about the **write** method of the document object?
   a. It can be called from Visual Basic Script.
   b. It is part of the Internet Explorer Object Model.
   c. It writes the specified text to the current HTML document.
   d. It can only be called once from Visual Basic Script.

2. The following Visual Basic Script code will

```
Document.write "<BODY BGCOLOR=GREEN>"
Document.write "<INPUT TYPE=TEXT NAME=TEXT1>"
Document.write "<BR>" Document.write "<INPUT TYPE=TEXT NAME=TEXT2>"
Document.write "<BR>"
Document.write "<INPUT TYPE=TEXT NAME=TEXT3>"
```

   a. create an HTML document with a green background.
   b. cause an error when the script is run.
   c. create an HTML document with three textboxes.
   d. display nothing because the HTML code is not correct.

3. Which of the following can Visual Basic Script not interact with?
   a. The Windows 95 desktop
   b. Java applets
   c. ActiveX controls
   d. Internet Explorer

4. What is wrong with the following script?

```
Document:write <BR><BR><TABLE BORDER=2>
Document:write <TR><TD>Welcome</TD>
Document:write <TD>to the</TD><TR>
Document:write <TR><TD>Information</TD>
Document:write <TD>Super Highway</TD>
Document:write </TR></TABLE>"
```

   a. There are ':' characters instead of '.' characters referencing the **write** method of the document object.
   b. There are no double quote characters surrounding the HTML code being passed into the **write** method.
   c. The HTML table is not built correctly.
   d. Both a. and b.

5. Which of the following is exposed by the Explorer object model?
   a. Events
   b. Methods
   c. Properties
   d. All of the above

Difficulty: Intermediate

1. Add another row onto the HTML table created in the example. The first column should say "Visit" and the second should say "Again". Also, center the text in the columns and add some cell padding to the table.

Difficulty: Intermediate

2. Add an HTML <BODY> tag and set the background to magenta for our example. Also, add some formatting to the columns of the table such as setting the font size and color.

GETTING ACTIVATED WITH ACTIVEX

ActiveX controls are software components that can be inserted into your Web pages and reused over and over. They are typically created by a variety of software vendors, but, if you are a Visual C++, Java, or Visual Basic programmer, you can create them yourself (see the ActiveX Software Developer's Kit from Microsoft). These controls can be used to quickly add specialized functionality to your Web pages, desktop applications, and development tools such as Visual Basic. For example, a chart control could be used to add charting capabilities to your Web page, or a label control could be used to display cool text.

> **Note to Programming Propeller Heads**
>
> ActiveX controls are simply a new name for OLE controls, which were also sometimes know as OCXs. But ActiveX controls can also be designed to be lightweight and small, which is more suitable for sending across the Internet.

The Internet Explorer 3.0 browser is the first Web browser to support ActiveX controls in Web pages. ActiveX controls can also be viewed in the Netscape Navigator using the ActiveX Plug-in for Netscape (see **http://www.ncompass.com**).

When Internet Explorer 3.0 encounters a Web page with an ActiveX control (or multiple controls), it first checks the user's local system registry to find out if that component is available on the user's machine. If it is, Internet Explorer will display the Web page by activating the control within the Web page. If the control is not already installed on the user's computer, Internet Explorer 3.0 will automatically find and install the component over the Web, based on where you want the control to be be on your Web site.

You insert an object into your document using the **<OBJECT>** tags and set its initial property values using **<PARAM>** tags. If you're a Visual Basic programmer, you'll recognize that the **<PARAM>** tags are just like setting properties for a control on a form. For example, the following set of **<OBJECT>** and **<PARAM>** tags adds the ActiveX Label control to a page:

```
<OBJECT ID="IELABEL1" WIDTH=100 HEIGHT=51
  CLASSID="CLSID:99B42120-6EC7-11CF-A6C7-00AA00A47DD2">
    <PARAM NAME="_ExtentX" VALUE="2646">
    <PARAM NAME="_ExtentY" VALUE="1323">
    <PARAM NAME="Caption" VALUE="Default">
    <PARAM NAME="Angle" VALUE="0">
    <PARAM NAME="Alignment" VALUE="4">
    <PARAM NAME="Mode" VALUE="1">
    <PARAM NAME="FillStyle" VALUE="0">
```

continued on next page

continued from previous page

```
        <PARAM NAME="FillStyle" VALUE="0">
        <PARAM NAME="ForeColor" VALUE="#000000">
        <PARAM NAME="BackColor" VALUE="#COCOCO">
        <PARAM NAME="FontName" VALUE="Arial">
        <PARAM NAME="FontSize" VALUE="12">
        <PARAM NAME="FontItalic" VALUE="0">
        <PARAM NAME="FontBold" VALUE="0">
        <PARAM NAME="FontUnderline" VALUE="0">
        <PARAM NAME="FontStrikeout" VALUE="0">
        <PARAM NAME="TopPoints" VALUE="0">
        <PARAM NAME="BotPoints" VALUE="0">
    </OBJECT>
```

In the **OBJECT** tag, you will first encounter the ID for the label. This defines the name of the label control, which can be customized by the programmer. Next, we set the width and the height of the control. Then we have the class ID; it is so obvious where this identifier comes from we will not bother to discuss it. Actually, Microsoft has a rather complex scheme for providing these unique class IDs (UUID) to identify an OLE object (i.e., ActiveX control). Fortunately, for our purposes, we can assume they are already assigned for us. Microsoft's ActiveX Control Pad or Internet Studio will automatically provide you with a listing of all ActiveX controls registered on your system. These tools scan the system registry and search for the control's UUIDs and provide you with a simple and easy way to insert the control into your HTML Web page.

An ActiveX control provides several properties, methods, and events for working with the control. This should sound similar to our discussion of the Internet Explorer Object Model in the last session. These properties, methods, and events help define the programmable functionality of the control. For example, a property might be used to set the color of the label text. Or the control might provide a **move** method for moving its location. Or an event might be triggered when the user clicks on the control. Figure 3-3 shows a conceptual model of an ActiveX control.

All the coding it took to make a control work is represented by the center of the model. This is not exposed to us in our Visual Basic scripts. This is good because frankly, we would much rather just use a chart than worry about all the complicated algorithms and code that make them work! The control exposes properties, methods, and events to the programmer that we will be able to manipulate from Visual Basic Script. The HTML object **PARAM** tags are used for setting the properties of the label control in the above code example. For example, one of the **PARAM** tags sets the font size to 12 point

Let's go ahead and look at a specific example of inserting three label controls into a Web page. Chapter 10, "Objectifying Your Scripts," has an in-depth discussion on adding and working with ActiveX controls to your Web pages. Figure 3-4 shows the sample Web page. The sample can be found in the Session4 subdirectory of Chapter3 on the CD-ROM.

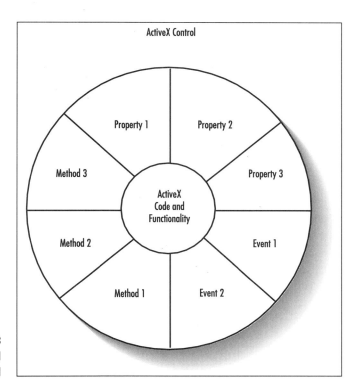

Figure 3-3
ActiveX control
model

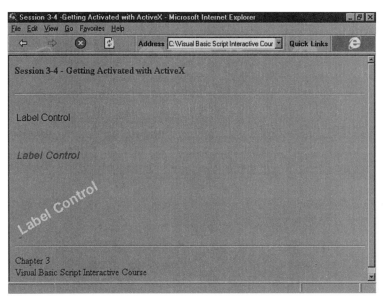

Figure 3-4
Sample ActiveX
control Web page

As you can see, this example is pretty straightforward. We have simply inserted three label controls into our document and set up the properties differently so that each label is unique in appearance. If you review the HTML code, you will find three label objects in the document with each of their **PARAM** properties defined differently. In Session 6 we will take a close look at how we can control an ActiveX control from our Visual Basic Script code.

1. Which statement is false about ActiveX controls?
   a. They are downloaded from your Web site to the user's system.
   b. These controls must be developed in C++ using the ActiveX SDK.
   c. You can have multiple ActiveX controls in your Web documents.
   d. With Visual Basic Script, you can work with the properties, methods, and events of an ActiveX control.

2. How many properties does the following control have?

```
<OBJECT ID="ACONTROL" WIDTH=10 HEIGHT=5
 CLASSID="CLSID:999 GOBLE D GOOK – 9023423 – STUFF">
    <PARAM NAME="XProperty" VALUE="AA">
    <PARAM NAME="YProperty" VALUE="BB">
    <PARAM NAME="ZProperty" VALUE="CC">
</OBJECT>
```

   a. 1
   b. 2
   c. 3
   d. 4

3. When Internet Explorer encounters a Web page with ActiveX controls, it first checks the _____ to find out if that component is available on the user's machine; otherwise it _____.
   a. local hard drive…aborts the HTML document
   b. local system registry…downloads the control
   c. local system registry…aborts the HTML document
   d. local hard drive…downloads the control

4. The _____ identifies a/an _____ for the browser.
   a. UUID…ActiveX control
   b. UUID…Java applet
   c. UUID…OLE object
   d. all of the above

5. The _____ indicates an _____ has been
   _____ into the browser.
   a. ActiveX tag...object...inserted
   b. object UUID...object...inserted
   c. UUID Object...ActiveX control...inserted
   d. object tag...object...inserted

EXERCISE 4

Difficulty: Easy

1. Modify the properties of the three label controls in our example to change each one's appearance.

Difficulty: Easy

2. Insert the chart ActiveX control into the document and manipulate its properties.

SESSION 5

INTRODUCING BROWSER OBJECTS

In Session 3 we touched on the fact that the Internet Explorer provides a scripting object model we can use to manipulate the browser and HTML document from our scripts. This object model exposes methods and properties to our HTML scripts so we can interact with the browser as well as various aspects of our HTML documents.

Several hierarchical levels to the object model allow us to work with various aspects of our Web pages and browser. The following diagram shows a graphical overview of this model.

You see many recognizable names in this model, including `Frame`, `Location`, `Link`, `Anchor`, `Form`, and `Element`. These are direct references to any such items you may have in your HTML document. For example, you might have an input element of type button that is on a form in your document that is part of the overall browser window. Or, you may have several frames in your browser window. This diagram provides a way for you to see how these *objects* are organized and related so you can reference their properties and methods.

For example, when we were calling `document.write` in Session 3, we were referencing the current document in Explorer Window and writing out a statement to that document.

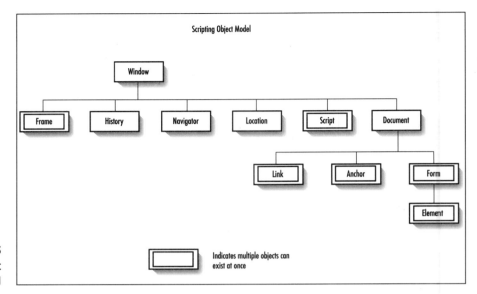

Figure 3-5
Scripting object
model

Object Model Definitions

Window—The top level object is a window. Every window contains a set of **Frame** objects, **History** objects, **Navigator** objects, **Location** objects, **Script** objects, and **Document** objects.

Frame—Set of contained frame windows in this window. Each frame is a window that has its own properties, including a document.

History—This object is used to access the list of documents previously explored during the current session of the browser.

Navigator—The **Navigator** object contains information about the browser application.

Location—Provides information about the location of the window's URL.

Script—Any scripting function defined using the **SCRIPT** element in the window scope.

Document—The document in the current window.

With Visual Basic Script we will be able to work with each one of these objects to have control over how our Web pages are presented and utilized. Figure 3-6 shows Visual Basic Script's relationship to the object model.

In Chapter 8, "Exploring Objects, Events, Methods, and Properties," we will explore the Scripting Object Model in depth and learn how we can control it from our script code. For now, with a few simple examples, we can give you a feel for how we can work with these different objects. Figure 3-7 shows the sample application provided in the Session5 subdirectory of Chapter3 on the CD-ROM.

As you can see, we have displayed many different properties, including the title of the document, the document background color value, the navigator appname and version, and the path of the document. These are all referenced by using the '**.**' reference method. Always starting with the **Window** object, we then reference the next object such as `window.document`. We then reference an appropriate property of the object such as `window.document.title`. This will provide us with the title for the current document.

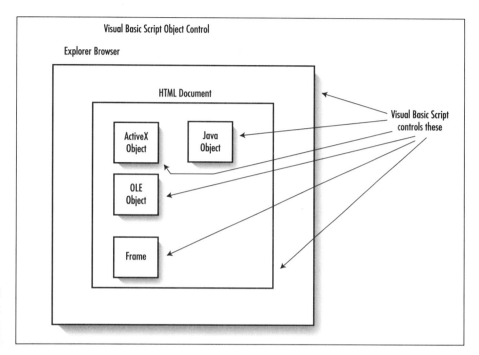

Figure 3-6
Visual Basic Script
and the scripting
object model

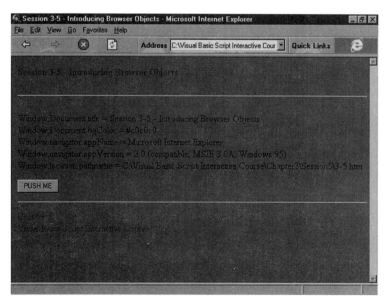

Figure 3-7
Sample object
model Web page

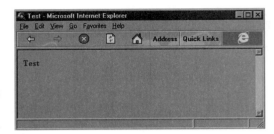

Figure 3-8
Document jumped
to on button click

When you click the HTML button, a small script is fired off that will change the currently referenced document to a simple test document also provided on the CD-ROM. This is done by setting the **Href** property of the **Location** object to a new HTML document. This document is then loaded. Figure 3-8 shows the document displayed after the button click.

Thus, we have manipulated the **Location** object **Href** property to change the currently displayed document. This will give you a taste of what is possible by using Visual Basic Script. As we will see in later chapters, having access to these objects from our Visual Basic Script code will be invaluable in creating interactive Web pages.

1. Which is not an object contained in the document object?
   a. **Link**
   b. **Anchor**
   c. **Location**
   d. **Form**

2. What is wrong with the following script statement?

```
MsgBox window.appname
```

   a. There is no such property as **appname** anywhere in the object model.
   b. It should be **window.document.appname**.
   c. It should be **window.location.appname**.
   d. It should be **window.navigator.appname**.

3. _____ provides information about the location of the _____.
   a. **Navigator**...Internet Explorer
   b. **Location**...window's URL
   c. **Location**...Internet Explorer
   d. **Navigator**...window's URL

4. Which is true about Visual Basic Script and the Scripting Object Model?
   a. You can add and delete properties from the object model.
   b. You can interact with all the methods and properties of the objects in the model.
   c. Only some of the exposed methods and properties are available to be referenced in Visual Basic Script.
   d. None of the above.

5. The _____ object contains the set of _____ in the main browser window.
   a. `Frame`...frame windows
   b. `Window`...frame windows
   c. `Frame`...window objects
   d. `Location`...frame windows

Difficulty: Advanced

1. Modify the test page to have two buttons on it. The first will not jump anywhere. The second will jump back to the original page by simply referencing the HTML document.

SESSION 6

WORKING WITH ACTIVEX CONTROLS

In this session, we are going to build an example of how we can utilize Visual Basic Script and ActiveX controls together. Let's see if we can spin up something interesting.

First, we will use two controls in our Web pages, a label control and a timer. We have already used the label control in Session 4. The timer control will allow us to execute a set of Visual Basic Script code on a timed interval. By combining these two controls and a little Visual Basic Script code, we will be able to spin our label control around and make it appear animated. The following figure shows our sample application with the label control in midspin. The code can be found in the Session6 subdirectory of Chapter3 on the CD-ROM.

First, we will need to insert a reference to our two ActiveX controls. The HTML code is not shown here, but you can reference it in the example provided on the CD-ROM. Note that for the timer control, the interval is set at 200 milliseconds. This indicates how often the timer will be *activated*.

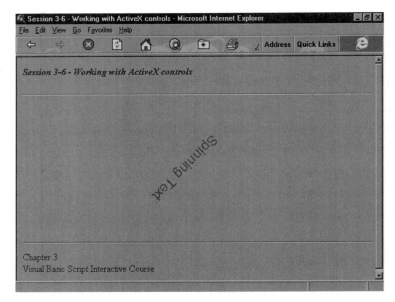

Figure 3-9
Spinning label
control Web page

Next in our document we will start the script. We will not be discussing variables until the next chapter, but we will have to use one for this demonstration, **NewAngle**. This variable will hold the value of the current angle of the label control and is declared using the DIM statement. We declare this variable right up front in our script.

```
<!-- Start the Script -->
<SCRIPT LANGUAGE="VBScript">

Option Explicit

Dim NewAngle
```

We then have a subroutine that is added to our script. This subroutine will be run every time the timer control counts off the 200 milliseconds value that we set the timer interval to. Note that the subroutine has the name of the timer, **IeTimer1**, and is then followed by an underscore and the name of the timer event. This is a standard naming convention for referring to events that will be run in our scripts. So, when the timer counts down 200 milliseconds, the **IeTimer1_Timer** event code is run.

```
Sub IeTimer1_Timer()
```

Each time this event is run, we will increase the value of the **NewAngle** variable by 5. We will also check the value and make it negative when we have reached 180 degrees so that it will continue to rotate. To do this we use an **If...Then...Else** statement. The **If...Then...Else** logic allows you to run different sets of code based on checking the value of the **NewAngle** variable. Finally, we set the **angle** property of the label control. We reference the **angle** property of the control using the same '.' notation that we used with Explorer objects (i.e., **document.write**). Thus, we use the ActiveX control's name, **IeLabel1**, and then reference the property. We then set the property equal to the new angle which is stored in **NewAngle**.

```
.....'  Increase the angle variable that will track the
.....'  angle of the label control
.....NewAngle = NewAngle + 5

.....'  Check to see if we have rotated half way, then
.....'  spin the other half
.....If NewAngle = 180 then NewAngle = -1 * NewAngle

.....'  Set the angle property on the label control
.....IeLabel1.angle = NewAngle


end sub


</SCRIPT>
```

The final result is that every 200 milliseconds the label control rotates. Run the sample document that came with the CD-ROM and you will see a spinning label control. This is just a small taste of what can be done with ActiveX controls and Visual Basic Script. As you can see, this goes far beyond what is possible with static HTML.

1. Which **PARAM** property of the label control sets the label text?
   a. **Caption**
   b. **Text**
   c. **Title**
   d. **Label**

2. The _____ of the timer control is run based upon the _____ property setting.
   a. timer event...interval
   b. interval event...interval
   c. timer event...time
   d. interval event...time

3. What **PARAM** property of the label control controls the text color?
   a. **BackColor**
   b. **ForeColor**
   c. **FontColor**
   d. **TextColor**

4. What will be the value of X the third time the timer event is run? Note that X starts with a value of 0.

```
<SCRIPT LANGUAGE="VBScript">

Dim X

Sub IeTimer1_Timer()

.....X = X + 2

End Sub

</SCRIPT>
```

    a. 2
    b. 4
    c. 6
    d. 8

5. Which label control **PARAM** property underlines the label text?
    a. `FontUnder`
    b. `Underline`
    c. `UnderlineFont`
    d. None of the above

EXERCISE 6

Difficulty: Intermediate

1. Add another spinning label control to the sample Web page. But, make this control spin in the opposite direction.

Difficulty: Easy

2. Change the color and font size of the second label control.

SESSION 7

WE NEED INPUT—INPUTBOX

Receiving input from the user will be a critical part of developing your Web applications. Certainly you can get input from HTML input elements such as a textbox or text area. But, what if you just want to get input quickly without adding these items to your Web pages? Well, coincidentally, there is a function provided by Visual Basic Script called InputBox that we can use. Figure 3-10 illustrates the InputBox function.

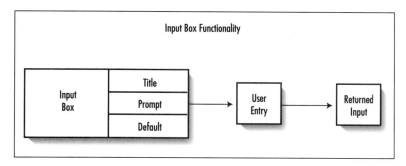

Figure 3-10
InputBox
functionality

InputBox functions similarly to the MsgBox function reviewed in Chapter 1, "What Is the World Wide Web Anyway?" But, with an InputBox we can have the user type in the response and then use it for later purposes. We have several options for controlling how the input box will be displayed, including setting the title, prompt, and a default value. Note that a function, when executed, will return a value to the section of code that called the function. That value can range from simple numbers to complete text strings.

InputBox

InputBox returns the data typed in by the user. The following are the arguments (we will learn more about these later) for the function. Note that these arguments will be located in parentheses after the InputBox function name.

prompt—This is the question or message you want to give to the user.

title—This is the text that will show on the top of the dialog box.

Default—Default value so the user does not have to do data entry.

Xpos—The x position on the screen where the box will be located.

Ypos—The y position on the screen where the box will be located.

The best way to review how this function works is to see it in action. Load the 3-7.htm Web page located in the Session7 subdirectory of Chapter3 on the CD-ROM. You will be prompted with three input boxes that are formatted differently based on the arguments passed into the function. Note that, whatever you type into each prompt, it will be written to the document using `document.write`. Figures 3-11, 3-12, and 3-13 show the sample InputBox calls.

The first input box will be located at position 10, 20 on the screen and will have a prompt of **InputBox Prompt**, a title of **InputBox Title**, and a default value of **InputBox Default**.

```
document.write InputBox("InputBox Prompt", _
                        "InputBox Title", _
                        "InputBox Default", _
                        10, _
                        20)
```

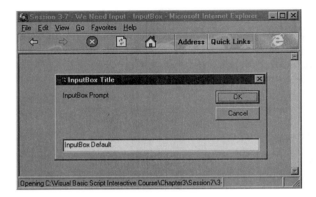

Figure 3-11
InputBox function-
ality—First Input
Box

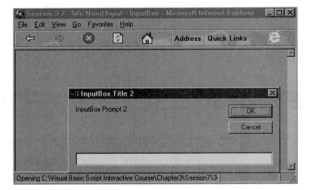

Figure 3-12
InputBox func-
tionality—Second
Input Box

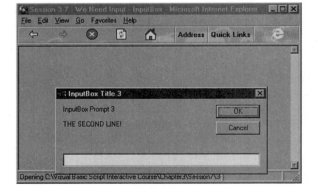

Figure 3-13
InputBox func-
tionality—Third
Input Box

The next input box simply changes the title and prompt. It also changes the location of the input box on the screen. Note that there is no default value.

```
document.write InputBox("InputBox Prompt 2", _
                    "InputBox Title 2", _
                    "", _
```

```
1940, _
2760)
```

The third input box will also change the location of the dialog box. But, we have added a twist to the prompt. Chapter 4, "Store That Data," will discuss this more in depth, but we are basically dividing the prompt into multiple lines. We do this by inserting a carriage return into the prompt using the CHR function and passing in a value of 10, which represents the value the computer recognizes as the Enter key on your keyboard. We use the '&' function to add the carriage return into the prompt. As you can see from the output, we have multiple lines in the prompt.

```
document.write InputBox("InputBox Prompt 3" & CHR(10) & CHR(10) &
                "THE SECOND LINE!", _
                "InputBox Title 3", _
                "", _
                2340, _
                3260)
```

The InputBox function will become an invaluable part of your programming toolbox. And as you can see, it is relatively easy to use. In the next session, we will build a simple game using the InputBox to provide you with an idea of how this functionality will be used.

1. What will be the title on the following input box?

```
InputBox("Some Text 1", "Some Text 2", "Some Text 3", 200, 500)
```

    a. Some Text 1
    b. Some Text 2
    c. Some Text 3
    d. 200

2. What is wrong with the following input box call?

```
InputBox "X", "Y"
```

    a. There is no X and Y position indicated.
    b. There is no default value specified for the user.
    c. There are no parentheses around the arguments.
    d. None of the above.

3. What will be the third line of the following input box prompt?

```
InputBox("ABCD" & CHR(10) & "ABC" & CHR(10) & "AB" & CHR(10) & "A")
```

    a. ABCD
    b. ABC
    c. AB
    d. A

4. Assuming that the user makes no entry into the input box, what will be written to the document?

```
document.write InputBox("Text1", "Text2", "Text3")
```

    a. Text1
    b. Text2
    c. Text3
    d. None of the above

5. What is the screen X coordinate position of the following InputBox call?

```
InputBox("Some Text 1", "Some Text 2", "Some Text 3", 200, 500)
```

    a. 200
    b. 500
    c. 700
    d. None of the above

Difficulty: Intermediate

1. Modify the last InputBox call to have four lines of input.

A SMALL SAMPLE APPLICATION

Enough learning; let's play games! Actually, this game is just a simple quiz, but we can build it to further demonstrate the InputBox function. Okay, we will have to use a few *advanced* tools like a variable and some If...Then...Else logic. But, you will find these are easy to work with.

Let's take the quiz first. Open the session document found in the Session8 subdirectory of Chapter3 on the CD-ROM. Click on the Take a Quiz button to take the quiz. Figures 3-14 and 3-15 show two of the quiz questions.

As you can guess, the quiz questions are built using the InputBox function. The button is a standard HTML button, but we have added the quiz code to the click event of the button. Let's look at the first section of code in the click event:

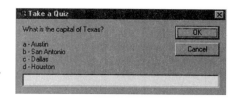

Figure 3-14
Quiz Question 1

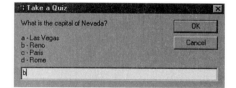

Figure 3-15
Quiz Question 2

```
Dim Answer1
Dim Answer2
Dim Answer3

Answer1 = InputBox("What is the capital of Texas?" & chr(10) _
                        & chr(10) & "a - Austin" _
                        & chr(10) & "b - San Antonio" _
                        & chr(10) & "c - Dallas" _
                        & chr(10) & "d - Houston" _
                        , "Take a Quiz", "", 10, 20)
```

Here we first have three variables declared that will hold the answer to each quiz question. Next, we have our first quiz question. You will recognize the CHR() function from the last session. This is how we build the multiple quiz questions line. The answer the user types in will be returned and stored in the **Answer1** variable. The following code will check to see if the user has answered correctly.

```
'  Next we will use the 'IF ... THEN ... ELSE' syntax
'  to check what the user entered.
If Answer1 <> "A" and Answer1 <> "a" then

'  Tell the user the answer was wrong
    MsgBox "Wrong Answer, try again!"

'  End the subroutine so the rest of the
'    code is not executed.
    Exit Sub


End If
```

This code uses the `If...Then...Else` construct to check the answer. We check to see if Answer1 is not equal (`<>`) to `"A"` or not equal to `"a"`. If so, we then will tell the user he or she entered the wrong answer using the `MsgBox` function. And, we use the `Exit Sub` syntax to exit the subroutine without executing the rest of the code in the subroutine. So, you cannot continue on to the next question until you have answered this one correctly. The next two questions each function in the same fashion as the first.

In the next two chapters you will learn more about using variables and things like `If...Then...Else`. This chapter will serve to get you thinking in the mode of adding scripts to your HTML documents. Combining all of these powerful tools will provide you with the ability to create trulyinteractive and activated Web applications.

1. What is wrong with the following code?

```
If Variable1 = Denver and Variable2 denver then

End
```

a. There are no double quotes around the **Denver** and **denver** answers.
b. There is no = sign between **Variable2** and **denver**.
c. There is no **If** in the **End** statement.
d. All of the above.

2. Which of the following would add a default answer to the following question?

```
Answer1 = InputBox("What is the capital of Texas?" & chr(10) _
               & chr(10) & "a - Austin" _
               & chr(10) & "b - San Antonio" _
               & chr(10) & "c - Dallas" _
               & chr(10) & "d - Houston" _
               , "Take a Quiz", "", 10, 20)
```

a. ..., "Take a Quiz", "A", 10, 20)
b. ..., InputBox("A", "What is...
c. ..., "Take a Quiz", "", 10, 20, "A")
d. ..., "A", "Take a Quiz", "", 10, 20)

3. Which symbol indicates the **not equal** relationship?
a. ( )
b. [ ]
c. < >
d. { }

4. Which syntax allows us to end a subroutine at any point during execution?
a. **End Subroutine**
b. **End Sub**
c. **End**
d. **End Function**

5. Which of the following is the correct way to declare a variable assuming X is the variable?

a. `Dim X`

b. `Variable X`

c. `Declare X`

d. `Var X`

Difficulty: Easy

1. Add the following question to the quiz with the specified answers:

Question: What is the capital of the United States?

Answers: a. Washington, DC

            b. Paris

            c. London

            d. None of the above

CHAPTER SUMMARY

Well, we have taken off with some Visual Basic Script coding. While we had to utilize a few items we have not discussed yet (i.e., `If...Then...Else`), you should have a good feel for how Visual Basic Script code is inserted into a Web page and a taste of how the two interact. In the next chapter we will take a formal look at how we work with variables and data in our scripts.

FUNDAMENTALS

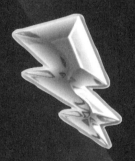

PART II

CHAPTER 4

STORE THAT DATA

Working with data is a key to being able to utilize Visual Basic Script in your HTML pages. If you are an experienced programmer, you will be surprised to find that the language only works with a variant data type and does not allow explicit declaration of data types. For you, this chapter will provide a solid overview of how to work with data in Visual Basic Script. If you are not a programmer, this chapter will give you a good overview of how to store and manipulate information in variables so that you can work with all the different types of data you need in your Web applications.

Data is stored in variables in your code. Think of variables as storage containers which remember one value or set of values when asked. For example, you might have a variable that will store someone's first name and another variable that will store his or her last name. Variables will do this until asked to remember a new value. Consider the following code snippet:

```
Dim X
Dim Y

X = 5

Y = X * 2
```

In this example, X and Y are our variables. First, we declare the variables by using the dimension statement, DIM. This directs Visual Basic Script to allocate memory for storing data in the variables. Initially we are asking X to store a value of 5. Then, we simply multiply the value of X times 2 and store that new value in the Y variable. Now, Y has been asked to store a value of 10 and X still has a value of 5.

"A Data Storage Container" is a good general definition for a variable, but to better define and use our data, variables can be defined in subgroups based on the type of data they store. For example, a variable that holds both alpha and numeric characters would be of subtype *string*. Variables that hold only whole number values between 0 and 255 are considered a *byte*. In this chapter, we will be reviewing all of these subtypes to determine how they will be used in our scripts. But, keep in mind that Visual Basic Script does not force a variable to always contain only one subtype during its life.

Each session in this chapter will explore a different aspect of working with data in Visual Basic Script. Once you work through these sessions, you should have a good understanding of how to work with data and variables in your program. So, without further discussion, let's jump into our exploration of utilizing data in our programs.

In this chapter we will cover the following topics:

- Utilizing Global and Local Variables
- Working with Strings
- Working with Numbers
- Working with Dates and Time
- Working with Arrays
- Utilizing Random Numbers
- Working with Upper- and Lowercase Characters
- Determining Variable Types

GOING GLOBAL OR STAYING LOCAL

One of the first things to understand about using variables in Visual Basic Script is how long the life of a variable is. Just because you may be working with variable Foozle in one section of your code does not mean the value of Foozle is available in another area of your code. You can think of this like a corporation. A global corporation will be accessed all over the world, whereas a local corporation will be accessed only in its home country, state, or city.

There are really three types of data to consider when working in a program. The first is called a Local variable, the second is a Global variable, and the third is Persistent Data. Generally we refer to a variable's *scope* to determine whether it is global or local. A variable can either be in scope, which means it is accessible, or out of scope, which means it is not.

A Note on Subroutines and Functions

As you will see, Global versus Local variables are in part defined by subroutines and functions. These will be discussed in depth in the next chapters. But for now, think of them as code segments that you can execute depending on your program logic. They take in values for the code to look at, called parameters. And, in the case of a function, they will return a value for whatever code invoked the function.

Let's take a look at this from a pictorial point of view. Figure 4-1 shows one big box that represents your overall script. The three smaller boxes represent procedures (functions or subroutines) in the script.

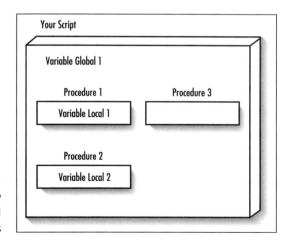

Figure 4-1
Graphic overview
of Global and Local
variables

In our picture, there is one Global variable declared, called **Global1**. In Procedure1, there is a Local variable, **Local1**, and in Procedure2 there is a Local variable, **Local2**. Procedure3 does not have any Local variables declared. Each procedure, 1 through 3, has the ability to see and modify **Global1**, which means its scope is global. So, if Procedure1 sets **Global1** to 5, then when Procedure2 reads the variable, it will have a value of 5. Conversely, if Procedure1 sets its locally scoped variable, **Local1**, to the value of 20, the other two procedures cannot access its value. The same goes for **Local2** and Procedure2. In this case, we consider **Global1** to have a Global or Script level scope. **Local1** and **Local2** have a Local or procedure level scope.

Definitions

Local Variable: A Local variable is available only within the subroutine or function that the variable is declared in.

Global Variable: A Global or Script level variable is one that is accessible anywhere inside your script, regardless of what subroutine or function your code resides in.

Persistent Data: Data that is stored in a file or database for later retrieval is considered persistent. In other words, this data will continue to be in existence even after the program and, for that matter, even when your HTML page is no longer running. This data is usually read into variables in your program for use.

There is one other key concept to consider and that is what happens when a variable goes out of scope. For a Global variable, this happens whenever the script stops running. For Local variables, the scope is only the lifetime of the procedure. So, **Local1** is only in existence from the beginning of Procedure1 until the time when Procedure1 is finished. The next time we enter Procedure1 again, **Local1** will be recreated and reinitialized.

Global Variables

Now that we have discussed the basic concepts of Global and Local variables, let's take a look at some code examples. Let's start with building a simple Global variable example.

```
<!-- Start the Script -->
<SCRIPT LANGUAGE="VBScript">
Dim OurGlobal
StartSub
Sub StartSub
.....OurGlobal = 5
.....CheckGlobal
.....MsgBox OurGlobal
End Sub
Sub CheckGlobal
```

```
.....MsgBox OurGlobal
.....OurGlobal = 10
End Sub
</Script>
```

This example simply embodies our `Global1` idea from Figure 4-1. In this case, the Global variable is named `OurGlobal`. `StartSub` is first run and `OurGlobal` is set to a value of 5. Then, the `CheckGlobal` routine is run to display the value of `OurGlobal`, which will still be 5. `CheckGlobal` also changes the value to 10 before it returns. Finally, we display the value of `OurGlobal` again in `StartSub` and the value is now 10. Try this code in the browser and play around with it to become more familiar with using Global variables.

Local Variables

Now let's take a look at utilizing Local variables in our script code.

```
<!-- Start the Script -->
<SCRIPT LANGUAGE="VBScript">
StartSub
Sub StartSub
.....Dim StartLocal
.....StartLocal = 10
.....DemoSub
.....MsgBox StartLocal
.....MsgBox DemoLocal
.....DemoSub
End Sub
Sub DemoSub
.....Dim DemoLocal
.....MsgBox "Demo Local = " & DemoLocal
.....DemoLocal = 30
.....MsgBox "StartLocal = " & StartLocal
End Sub
</Script>
```

In this example, our startup routine is `StartSub`, the set of code that will be run first when the browser starts the script. It initializes the `StartLocal` variable to 10. We then run `DemoSub`. In `DemoSub`, we have another Local variable, `DemoLocal`. To ensure that `DemoLocal` is empty, we display the value. We then set its value to 30. We also display the value of `StartLocal`. Since `DemoSub` has no reference to `StartLocal`, the value is empty. We then return to `StartSub` and this displays both the value of `StartLocal` and `DemoLocal`. Since `StartSub` has not yet finished executing, `StartLocal` is still 10 and of course `DemoLocal` is empty because `StartSub` has no access to its value. Finally, we run `DemoSub` again. Now, you might think the value of `DemoLocal` is still 30. But, our first running of `DemoSub` has finished; that means that the instance of `DemoLocal` we had then is no longer around. Thus, we are starting with a newly initialized value of `DemoLocal`, and it will be empty initially. Again, try this code in the browser and play around with it.

Local Variable Note

In two different procedures you can have two Local variables of the same name. In our diagram, Procedure1 and Procedure2 could both have had a Local variable named `FOO` (or any name). Since they are local, they have no relation to each other. Or, in our Local variable code example, `DemoSub` could have a variable called `StartLocal` that would be completely independent of the `StartLocal` variable in `StartSub`.

An Example

Finally, to tie all this together, a sample HTML document is provided in the Session1 subdirectory of Chapter4 on the CD-ROM. Run this example to demonstrate the code developed above. Figure 4-2 shows the example program.

Variable Naming Conventions

This code uses a three-letter prefix for some of the Global variables, such as `intGlobalVar`. The *int* moniker in this case indicates that this variable will only contain data of subtype integer. This is useful for referencing what kind of data a variable should contain. If you know that a variable is going to always contain a certain subtype, then using a three-letter prefix is good programming practice to help document the purpose of a variable in your program. For your reference, this naming convention is called Hungarian Notation.

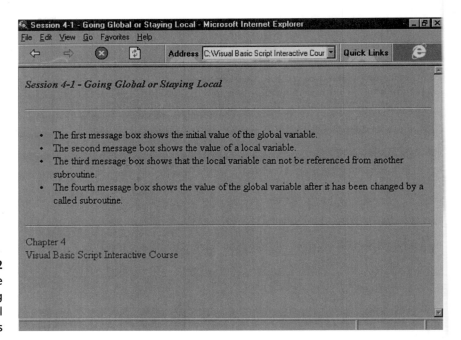

Figure 4-2
HTML example demonstrating Global and Local variables

We encourage you to play around with declaring variables at different points in your programs and see how you can affect the values.

Use the following code for the first three questions:

```
<!--  Start the Script  -->
<SCRIPT LANGUAGE="VBScript">
Dim A
StartSub
Sub StartSub
.....Dim B
.....B = 20
.....Work
.....A = A * 10
.....Work
End Sub
Sub Work
.....A = A + 5
End Sub
</Script>
```

1. Variable **A** has what kind of variable scope?
   a. Global
   b. Local
   c. Persistent
   d. Null

2. Variable **B** has what kind of variable scope?
   a. Global
   b. Local
   c. Persistent
   d. Byte

3. In **StartSub**, the first time **Work** is called, **A** has what value?
   a. 25
   b. 0
   c. 5
   d. 10

4. Which statement is true about local variables in two different procedures?
   a. They cannot have the same name.
   b. They must have the same name.
   c. They can have the same name.
   d. They must be of the same subtype.

5. For a variable, `Foo`, that will hold integer data, what would be an appropriate name using Hungarian Notation?
   a. `FooInt`
   b. `IFoo`
   c. `IntFoo`
   d. `FooI`

Difficulty: Easy

1. Write a program that has the following setup:

   ● Three Global variables.

   ● One startup subroutine that sets the Global variables and calls another subroutine to multiply them together and show the result.

   ● One calculating subroutine that multiplies the three Global variables together and displays the result to the user.

Difficulty: Intermediate

2. Write a program that declares two variables of the same name, but one is Global and one Local to a subroutine. In the subroutine, set the value of the Local variable to 5. Now in a StartUp subroutine, call the second subroutine with the Local variable set to 5. Then check the value of the Global variable. What is its value?

WORKING WITH STRINGS

In the first session, we talked generally about variables and mentioned that each variable can contain any type of data. We also discussed the fact that data in each variable can be classified into a *subtype* category (see Appendix E, Properties). In this session, we want to specifically look at the subtype *string*. In fact, you will quickly find out that Visual Basic Script is really *strung out* on strings. One of the long-time strengths of the BASIC language has been its string manipulation capabilities.

As mentioned earlier, all variables contain variant data. Variants in their basic form contain either numeric data or strings (alpha, numeric, and special characters). Strings are very important in working with data. For example, if you want someone to enter his or her name and address information, the data will be stored in a string. But, if you want the user to enter his or her weight, then that will be stored in a numeric subtype.

The first thing to point out about working with strings in Visual Basic Script is that they are always surrounded by double quotes (for example, **"Hello"**). The following is an example of how to set a variable to a string:

```
Dim strTest
strTest = "This is a String in Quotes!"
```

In this example, the variable **strTest** is set to contain the string: **This is a String in Quotes!**. You will always need to ensure that you utilize the double quotes or Visual Basic Script will politely inform you that you have an error.

Visual Basic Script provides a wide range of functions for working with strings. These include, but are not limited to, **Left**, **Right**, **Mid**, and **Trim**. Let's take a look at a few quick and simple examples of working with strings to help get some basic string manipulation ideas down. Let's first look at basic string concatenation (or addition) using the **&** operator. To get started, let's review a visual example.

Now, let's look at a Visual Basic Script example that builds on our above graphical example. The following code will build the string **"HelloWorld"**:

```
Dim strTest1
Dim strTest2
Dim strTest3
strTest1 = "Hello"
strTest2= "World"
strTest3 = strTest1 & strTest2
```

You can think of the **&** symbol as acting like addition, and in reality it concatenates (combines) two strings. Note that the new value is "HelloWorld" with no space between Hello and World. Taking from our visual example, the following example will build the string with a space:

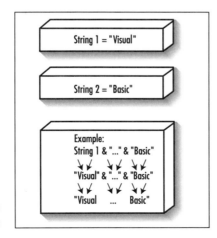

Figure 4-3
Building strings

```
Dim strTest1
Dim strTest2
Dim strTest3

strTest1 = "Hello"
strTest2= "World"

strTest3 = strTest1 & " " & strTest2
```

In this case, we don't have a variable that defines the space; we simply place a literal string of " " into our string concatenation equation. The result is that **strTest3** has **"Hello World"** with a space dividing the two words.

Simply adding strings together is not all we can do. We have access to powerful string manipulation functions including **Left**, **Right**, and **Instr** for parsing strings. Let's set up an example of splitting off the extension of a filename. In our example, the filename will be **"very wonderful.htm"**. In order to strip off the two parts surrounding the **"."**, we will have to find the location of the **"."** in this string. Knowing where this character is located will help us determine where the filename ends and the extension begins. Fortunately, we have many built-in utilities to help us tear this string apart.

Function Definitions

Instr: Returns the position of the first occurrence of one string within another.
Left: Returns a specified number of characters from the left side of a string.
Right: Returns a specified number of characters from the right side of a string.

To start out, let's use **Instr** to find the **"."**:

```
Dim intPos
Dim strFileName
Dim strLeft
Dim strRight

strFileName = "very wonderful.htm"

intpos = InStr(1, strFileName, ".")
```

Instr first wants to know where in the string we would like to start searching. In this case we will start in position 1. It then wants to know what string we are going to look in, which, in this case, is the filename stored in **strFileName**. Last we have to tell it what string to search for, which is **"."**.

In this case **intPos** will have a value of 15, which is the location of the **"."**. Now, let's get all of the characters to the left of the period using the **Left** function:

```
strLeft = Left(strFileName, intPos - 1)
```

This will return the string **"very wonderful"**. We know the **"."** is at position 15, so if we get the left 14 characters of the string, we will have **"very wonderful"**. Now, let's get the extension of the filename:

```
strRight = Right(strFileName, Len(StrFileName) - intPos)
```

In order to do this, we have to utilize one more string function, **Len**. This will return the length of the filename, which is 18. So, if we get the right set of characters of the string for a length of 3, we will have **"htm"**. Since the **"."** is at 15, and the length is 18, we can subtract the **"."** position from the length to get the extension (18–15).

Visual Basic Script is rich in string manipulation tools; this has always been one of the strengths of the Visual Basic language. In order to further explore the many functions we have available for string manipulation, let's take a look at the code sample provided on the CD-ROM for this session. Open the 4-2.HTM file in Chapter4, Session2 on the CD-ROM. Figure 4-4 shows the HTML document.

Let's first take a look at the use of the **ASC** and **Char** functions in the **ConvertAsc_ChrDemo** subroutine of the code. Every character in a string has a corresponding ASCII code value. For example, capital A has a corresponding value of 65. The **ASC** function will return the ASCII value of a character and the **CHR** function will convert an ASCII value into a character (string) representation. The first set of code in the subroutine converts integer 65 into a string, A.

```
.....'  Get the character representation
.....'   for ASCII 65
.....strWork = chr(65)
```

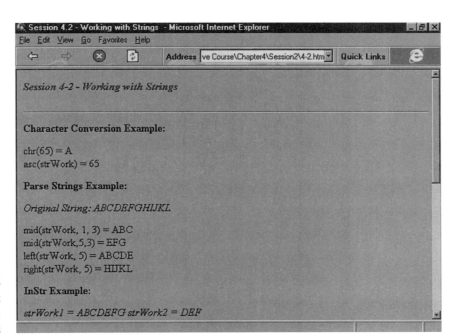

Figure 4-4
Sample Visual Basic Script string functions

The next set of code then converts that capital A back into a value of 65.

```
.....'  Retrieve the ASCII value for the
.....'  the character
.....intWork = asc(strWork)
```

The second subroutine, **ParseStringDemo**, demonstrates parsing, or taking apart, a string using a wide variety of functions. Let's review how a couple of these work. First, the **Mid** function is utilized as follows:

```
.....'  Set out working string
.....strWork = "ABCDEFGHIJKL"

.....'  Get the Mid
.....StrTemp = Mid(strWork,1, 3)
```

Definition
Mid returns a specified number of characters from a string from a starting position. Syntax: **Mid(string, start[, length])**

The **Mid** function is a powerful string parser. It allows you to select which part of a string you would like to work with. In the above code example, we will get the section of the **"ABCDEFGHIJKL"** starting with position 1 and ending with position 3, which in this case is **"ABC"**. To help you visualize some of the **Mid**, **Left**, **Right**, and **Instr** functions, Figure 4-5 shows several examples.

The rest of the function examples, combined with the definitions in Appendix A, "Functions," will help you get up and running with each. Just remember, if you need to twist, contort, tear apart, or do whatever to a string, there are plenty of functions to help you out.

1. Which of the following can be contained in a string?
   a. "ABCD"
   b. 1234
   c. Pounds"
   d. All of the above

2. What does the following evaluate to?

```
"A" & "CDE" & " " & "GH"
```

Note: The " " includes a space between the quotes.
   a. **"A CDEGH"**
   b. **"ACDE GH"**
   c. **"A CDE GH"**
   d. Invalid expression

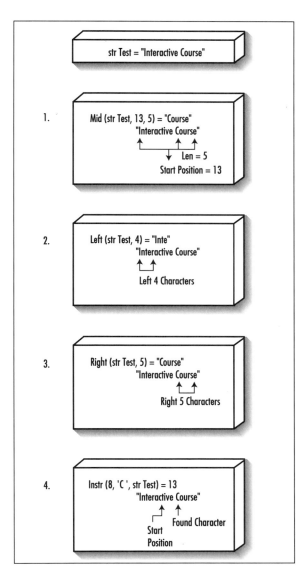

Figure 4-5
The Mid, Left, Right,
and Instr functions

3. What does the following evaluate to?

```
Left(Mid("VBSCRIPT", 2, 3), 2)
```

    a. "SC"
    b. "VB"
    c. "PT"
    d. "BS"

4. Which statement is true about variables?
   a. During the life of a variable, it can only contain one subtype.
   b. Basic variables contain either numeric or string values.
   c. String variables cannot be added together.
   d. There is no way to break apart a string variable.

5. Which function coverts a character into a corresponding integer value?
   a. `Chr`
   b. `Asc`
   c. `ChrInt`
   d. `Int`

Difficulty: Easy

1. Write a program fragment that will set a variable equal to "BOOK" from the string "AWESOME BOOK".

Difficulty: Intermediate

2. Write a program fragment that will find the position of the second 'c' in the string "Visual Basic Script is Easy!"

WORKING WITH NUMBERS

Now that we have taken a look at strings, let's move on to working with numbers. As mentioned in the last session, all variables are of a variant data type, which means they can contain any subtype whether it be a string, number, or date. Often, you will want to work with just variables that are numeric. So, if you are building a Web page to help millionaires track their money, you would want a long data type. If you are a science wizard calculating the nth root of the pie in the sky of the earth, you would want to use the double data type.

Of course when working with numeric data, there is not just one numeric subtype. In fact there are several, including Boolean, Byte, Integer, Long, Single, and Double.

Numeric Data Types
Boolean: Contains either True or False.
Byte: Contains an integer in the range 0 to 255.
Integer: Contains an integer in the range –32,768 to 32,767.
Long: Contains an integer in the range –2,147,483,648 to 2,147,483,647.

Single: Contains a single-precision, floating-point number in the range –3.402823E38 to –1.401298E-45 for negative values; 1.401298E-45 to 3.402823E38 for positive values. *Double:* Contains a double-precision, floating-point number in the range –1.79769313486232E308 to –4.94065645841247E-324 for negative values; 4.94065645841247E-324 to 1.79769313486232E308 for positive values.

Using these numeric data types comes down to how precisely you need to define your number. If it is a simple yes or no, then using a Double would be a little bit of an overkill. Likewise, if you are doing scientific work, an Integer or even a Long will most likely not cut it. But, fortunately, Visual Basic Script will handle adjusting the data subtype for you.

Visual Basic Script also provides a wide range of functions for working with numbers. These functions loosely fall into three categories: Standard Operators, Logical Operators, and Math Functions. Let's look at a couple of examples using Standard Operators.

Standard Operators consist of those familiar math operations such as +, –, *, /, and =. But this also includes some operators that may not be as familiar and obvious. For example, the integer division operator, \, is similar to the division operator, /, but performs a little different function. Let's look at the following example.

```
Dim intVar1
Dim intVar2

intVar1 = 17

intVar2 = intVar1 / 3
intVar3 = intVar1 \ 3
```

With normal division, **intVar2** will have a value of 5.66667 (17/3). With integer division, **intVar3** will have a value of 5. If you only need an integer after a division operation and want the remainder to be discarded, the \ integer division operator is a valuable tool.

Another function to utilize when working with division remainders is the **Mod** function. **Mod** performs modulus arithmetic on two numbers which return the remainder after the division of the two numbers. Let's look at another example.

```
Dim intVar1
Dim intVar2

intVar1 = 17

intVar2 = intVar1 mod 3
```

In this case, **sngVar2** will have a value of 2 (3 goes into 17 5 times with 2 left over) which is the remainder of the division.

Logical operators perform logical math operations on two variables. Let's look at a simple example of performing a logical AND operation.

```
Dim intVar1

intVar1 = 1 & 0
intVar1 = 1 & 1
intVar1 = 0 & 0
```

In the first case, `intVar1` is going to return 0. In the second, the return value is 1. In the last case, the return value is 0. The logical AND of two values will only be true if both values are 1 or TRUE. The OR operator combines the values differently, as outlined as follows:

```
Dim intVar1

intVar1 = 1 or 0
intVar1 = 1 or 1
intVar1 = 0 or 0
```

In the first and second cases, 1 will be returned; in the last, 0 will be returned. Appendix E, "Properties," will define all the logical operators and their results.

Provided on the CD-ROM in the Session3 subdirectory of Chapter4, is an example of using many of the different numeric operators and functions. Figure 4-6 shows the Web page.

There are four sections to the script: Standard Operators, then Logical Operators, followed by Math Functions, and the last section showing several miscellaneous functions. Let's take a look at two of these miscellaneous functions: `Int` and `Fix`. The code for working with these is as follows:

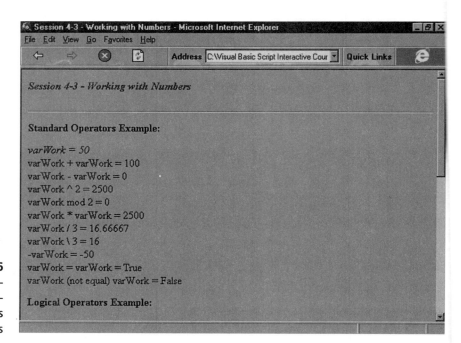

Figure 4-6
Web page demonstrating the numeric operators and functions

```
.....Dim varWork

.....'  Set the initial value
.....varWork = -57.98

.....'  Show the integer of the value
.....document.write "Int(varWork) = " & Int(varWork) & "<br>"

.....'  Show the 'fix' of the value which
.....'  will round down
.....document.write "Fix(varWork) = " & Fix(varWork) & "<br>"
```

The **Int** and **Fix** functions return the Integer portion of a number. But, if a number is negative, **Int** returns the first negative integer less than or equal to the number. **Fix** returns the first negative integer greater than or equal to the number. Review the other code examples to see the effect of the different operators and functions. Most of these will be as familiar as your high school math. Some will only be useful if you are a heavy-duty math person.

Working with numbers in Visual Basic is fairly straightforward and intuitive. The last session of this chapter will explore determining what kind of number you have and how to make conversions between the different number types.

1. Which of the following is not an integer?
   a. 1234
   b. 4.3
   c. 9
   d. −12

2. Which statement is true about the **Fix** function?
   a. It returns the first negative integer greater than or equal to the number.
   b. It returns the first negative integer less than or equal to the number.
   c. It rounds the number to the closest negative integer.
   d. None of the above.

3. What does the following evaluate to?

```
O OR (1 AND O)
```

   a. **2**
   b. **1**
   c. **NULL**
   d. **O**

4. The **Mod** function is used to _____ and return only the _____.
   a. multiply two numbers…remainder
   b. divide two numbers…integer
   c. multiply two numbers…integer
   d. divide two numbers…remainder

5. The Integer data type is
   a. an integer in the range of −32,768 to 32,767.
   b. an integer in the range of 0 to 65, 535.
   c. an integer between −256 and 256.
   d. an integer between 0 and 255.

Difficulty: Intermediate

1. Using only numeric expressions, write a code fragment that will divide the integer portion and the decimal remainder of the following equation into two variables:

```
5.25 = 21 / 4      (i.e. Var1 = 5 and Var2 = .25)
```

WORKING WITH DATES AND TIME

This session is good for single people to review since we will use Visual Basic Script to show you how to get a date and make time to be with that date. Aren't those computers just amazing! Of course, that is if you don't mind going out with something the likes of "1/1/96" or "10:30:20". But seriously, Visual Basic Script provides a variable subtype of Date that can be utilized for working with both dates and time. If you need to work with dates or time in your Visual Basic Script pages, you will be glad this data type is built into the language. There are many powerful built-in functions for manipulating both.

Date and Time Data Type
Represents a date between January 1, 100, to December 31, 9999.

Let's first look at how we can retrieve the current date and time using the **Date**, **Time**, and **Now** function:

```
Dim dtVar1
Dim dtVar2
Dim dtVar3

dtVar1 = Date
dtVar2 = Time
dtVar3 = Now
```

The **dtVar1** variable will contain the current system date in the format of "1/1/96". The **dtVar2** variable will contain the current system time in the format of "10:37:30 PM". Finally, the **dtVar3** variable will contain both the current system date and time in the format of "5/10/96 10:37:30 PM".

Table 4-1 briefly overviews the **Date** functions provided in Visual Basic Script.

Function	Description
Date	Returns the current system date.
Time	Returns a Variant of subtype Date indicating the current system time.
DateSerial	Returns a Variant of subtype Date for a specified year, month, and day.
DateValue	Returns a Variant of subtype Date.
Day	Returns a whole number between 1 and 31, inclusive, representing the day of the month.
Month	Returns a whole number between 1 and 12, inclusive, representing the month of the year.
Weekday	Returns a whole number representing the day of the week.
Year	Returns a whole number representing the year.
Hour	Returns a whole number between 0 and 23, inclusive, representing the hour of the day.
Minute	Returns a whole number between 0 and 59, inclusive, representing the minute of the hour.
Second	Returns a whole number between 0 and 59, inclusive, representing the second of the minute.
Now	Returns the current date and time according to the setting of your computer's system date and time.
TimeSerial	Returns a Variant of subtype Date containing the time for a specific hour, minute, and second.
TimeValue	Returns a Variant of subtype Date containing the time.

Table 4-1 Date *and* Time *functions.*

The sample program provided on the CD-ROM demonstrates most of these functions. Let's take a look at the output of the program:

In Figure 4-7, the first section demonstrates the **Date**, **Time**, and **Now** functions. The second section demonstrates working with dates. First, the **DateSerial** and **DateValue** functions are demonstrated for creating dates. **DateSerial** takes individual values for year, month, and day. **DateValue** will take a string subtype and create a date type subtype. Then, the **Day**, **Month**, **Year**, and **WeekDay** functions are demonstrated for breaking down the various components of a date.

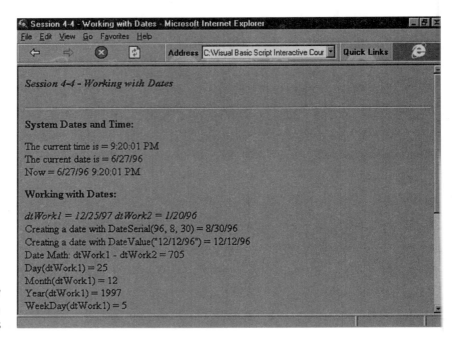

Figure 4-7
Demonstrating Date
functions

Figure 4-8 shows the **Time** functions in action. First, the **TimeSerial** and **TimeValue** functions are demonstrated. **TimeSerial** builds a time value based on hour, minute, and second. **TimeValue** returns the time represented in a string passed into the function. Finally, the hour, minute, and second components of the current time are broken down using the **Hour**, **Minute**, and **Second** functions.

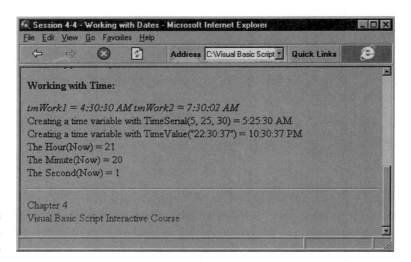

Figure 4-8
Demonstrating the
Time functions

Note that we can perform date math on two dates using the standard **+** and **−** operators. This will calculate the number of days between two dates, including leap years. This can be a powerful tool if you are building Web pages that have time-sensitive features.

Fortunately, Visual Basic Script provides solid, built-in functionality for working with dates and times. These functions are easy and straightforward to use.

1. Which of the following gives `intVar1` a value of 20?
   a. `dtWork1 = DateValue("02/05/93")`
      `intVar1 = Day(dtWork1) * 4`
   b. `dtWork1 = Mid("02/05/93"), 4, 1)`
      `intVar1 = Day(dtWork1) * 4`
   c. `intVar1 = Day(02/05/93) * 4`
   d. None of the above

2. `WeekDay` returns a(n) _____ representing the day of the week.
   a. string
   b. decimal
   c. integer number
   d. date

3. What does the following evaluate to?

`DateValue("12/12/96") - DateValue("12/02/96")`

   a. `2`
   b. `11`
   c. `4`
   d. `10`

4. What does the following evaluate to?

`DateValue("12/12/96") - DateValue("12/12/97")`

   a. `365`
   b. `-365`
   c. `1`
   d. `-1`

5. The _____ function returns the _____ and _____.
   a. `Today`...current date...time
   b. `Now`...hour, minute...second
   c. `Now`...current date...time
   d. `Now`...day, year...month

Difficulty: Easy

1. Find out the day of the week you were born.

Difficulty: Intermediate

2. Write a subroutine that will calculate the difference in years between two dates.

SESSION 5

WORKING WITH ARRAYS

So far we have been working with variables known as *scalars*. Scalar variables only allow you to assign a single value to the variable. Many times, however, you will want to easily track many values at one time. Let's say you have a Web page that, depending on a class number, shows all of the students in the class. And, this Web page will allow you to enter the grade for each student. There are several challenges to making this happen. First, each class might have a different number of students. Second, it would be very unwieldy to try to declare and work with enough variables to define each student and grade. Just imagine having variables `intStudent1` through `intStudent50` to try to do this.

Fortunately, there is a special type of variable in Visual Basic Script called an Array that allows us to easily work with large amounts of data in a convenient fashion. Dimensioning an Array variable is very easy, as follows:

```
Dim arrVar(5)
```

The array `arrVar` has a single dimension (we will discuss multidimensional arrays later) with six elements. Note that there are six elements and not five because the first element of the array starts at zero, not one. Let's look at an example defining an array of students from our class example.

```
<SCRIPT LANGUAGE="VBScript">

Dim arrStudents(50)

arrStudents(0) = "Noel Jerke"
arrStudents(1) = "Jonny Anderson"
arrStudents(2) = "Michael Hatmaker"
arrStudents(3) = "Mitch Waite"
```

```
arrStudents(4) = "Jill Pisoni"
arrStudents(5) = "Kurt Stephan"

</SCRIPT>
```

In this example, we have an array of students, **arrStudents(50)**, that has 51 elements. We have defined the first six elements to have the students' names by using a numerical index into the array. Note that the remaining elements remain empty. To access the value of an element in the array, simply use the index as follows:

```
strTestVar = arrStudents(1)
```

In this case **strTestVar** will be equal to Jonny Anderson. Arrays can also have two dimensions. Let's implement the ability to also store the students' grades along with their names as follows:

```
    dim arrStudents(50,1)

.....arrStudents(0,0) = "Noel Jerke"
.....arrStudents(0,1) = 5

.....arrStudents(1,0) = "Jonny Anderson"
.....arrStudents(1,1) = 15

.....arrStudents(2,0) = "Mitch Waite"
.....arrStudents(2,1) = 25
```

In this example, our **arrStudents** variable has two dimensions. To help visualize this, review Figure 4-9 to see how this array is set up.

The best way to think of two-dimensional arrays is as a table with columns and rows. You can have multidimensional arrays for working with all kinds of data relationships.

You may have noticed that in our examples with **arrStudent**, we have dimensioned 51 elements but are only using a few of these. Let's look at another way to dimension and work with array size.

```
<SCRIPT LANGUAGE="VBScript">

Dim arrStudents()
Dim intNumStudents

intNumStudents = GetNumberStudents

ReDim arrStudents(intNumStudents)

 .  .  .
 .  .  .
 .  .  .

intNumStudents = GetNumberStudents

ReDim Preserve arrStudents(intNumStudents)

</SCRIPT>
```

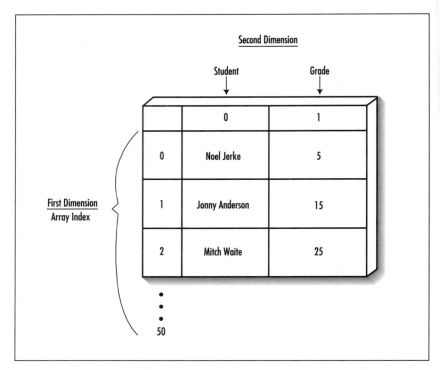

Figure 4-9
Two-dimensional
array

You can also declare an array whose size changes at any time your script is running. This is called a dynamic array. The array is initially declared locally within a procedure or globally using the **Dim** statement as with any other array. The difference is that no size or number of dimensions is placed inside the parentheses. To use a dynamic array, you must subsequently use **ReDim** to determine the number of dimensions and the size of each. In the above example, **ReDim** sets the initial size of the dynamic array to the value returned from a function called **GetNumberStudents**. Now let's say that later we need to check again how many students there are in a class, in case some have been added or deleted. A subsequent **ReDim** statement resizes the array to the new number of students, but uses the **Preserve** keyword to preserve the contents of the array. Without the **Preserve** keyword, all data in the array would have been erased.

The topic of our code example for this session is working with several of the array functions provided in Visual Basic Script. Utilizing these functions will help you in your endeavors with arrays. Figure 4-10 shows the program in action.

This sample introduces the **UBound**, **LBound**, and **IsArray** functions. The **Array** function handles building an array based on a set of initial parameter values. **IsArray** will determine whether a variable is an array or not. Finally, **UBound** and **LBound** will determine the upper and lower bounds of an array. Note that the second parameter of both functions indicates which dimension of the array to check.

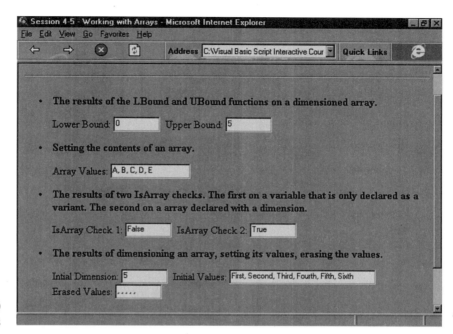

Figure 4-10
Array functions

Arrays are powerful tools for dealing with large amounts of data. Remember that an array's elements can be of any data subtype and allow you to mix and match what type of data you will be working with, as in our student name and grade example.

1. How many second-dimension elements are in the following array?

```
Dim arrWork( 2, 4)
```

    a. 4
    b. 3
    c. 5
    d. None of the above

2. At the end of the following code, what is the value in first element of **arrWork**?

```
Dim arrWork()
ReDim arrWork(5)
arrWork(0) = "I Love Quizzes"
ReDim Preserve arrWork(6)
arrWork(1) = "I Really Love Quizzes!"
```

     a. NULL
     b. EMPTY
     c. I Love Quizzes
     d. I Really Love Quizzes!

3. Which of the following is a true statement?
     a. An array can contain only one data subtype.
     b. An array can have only two dimensions.
     c. Once an array has been dimensioned, it can be resized.
     d. None of the above.

4. What does the following evaluate to?

```
Dim arrWork(3,4)
UBound(arrWork,1)
```
     a. 4
     b. 3
     c. 5
     d. Error

5. What does the following evaluate to?

```
Dim arrWork(3,4)
LBound(arrWork,1)
```
     a. 0
     b. 1
     c. 2
     d. 3

EXERCISE 5

Difficulty: Intermediate

1. Set up an array for a real estate broker that will store a list of 10 prospective home buyers and the names of up to five houses they are interested in.

Difficulty: Intermediate

2. Take the code fragment from the above exercise and resize the array to accept 20 prospective home buyers and 10 houses they are interested n. Be sure not to delete any of the current data in the array.

RANDOM OCCURRENCES

Working with random numbers can be fun! Visual Basic Script has a random number generation engine that, with a little programming, can generate a random number between any two values. The ability to utilize random numbers can be critical to any kind of game programming.

The random number generator in effect *simulates* the production of random numbers. It does this by starting with a *seed* value that will be needed by the random number generator to produce random values. In order to initialize the random number generator with this seed value, we will use the **Randomize** function. This will seed the number generator with an initial value that it will use to return the next random value. Typically, the best method for using **Randomize** is without any argument, because it then takes the initial seed value from the system time. You can seed it with your own pre-determined value if you wish

Definition
Randomize uses a number to initialize the **Rnd** function's random number generator, giving it a new seed value. If you omit the number, the value returned by the system timer is used as the new seed value.

Once we have initialized the random number generator, we can use the **Rnd** function to generate a random number between 0 and 1 if we provide no argument to the function. There are also several other options for utilizing **Rnd** as outlined in the following table.

Rnd **Parameter**	**Returned Value**
Less than zero	The same number every time, using number as the seed.
Greater than zero	The next random number in the sequence.
Equal to zero	The most recently generated number.
Not supplied	The next random number in the sequence.

Table 4-2   Rnd *argument options.*

Typically, the parameter is not supplied to retrieve the next random number in the sequence which is based on the seed value. Let's look at a simple code sample:

```
Dim sngRndVal
Randomize
sngRndVal = Rnd
```

In this case, **sngRndVal** will have a random value between 0 and 1. But what if we want a number between 0 and 100? There is a simple formula for using **Rnd** that will produce numbers between any range:

```
Int((UpperBound - LowerBound + 1) * Rnd + LowerBound)
```

Let's step through this code. If we assume that **Rnd** returns .25 and our **UpperBound** is 100 and our **LowerBound** is 0:

1. Rnd + LowerBound = .25

2. UpperBound - LowerBound + 1 = 101

3. 25 * 101 = 25.5

4. int(25.5) = 25

Based on these two functions, let's build a simple game that queries the user for the upper and lower bound of the random number range. We will then require the user to enter a guess. When he or she clicks on the Submit button, a random number will be generated and checked against the user's guess. The program is provided on the CD-ROM in the Session6 subdirectory of Chapter4. Figure 4-11 is a screen shot of the program.

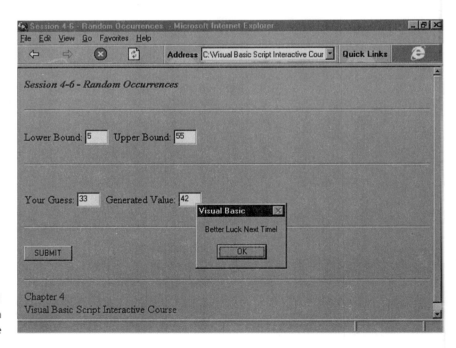

Figure 4-11
Random
number game

The first subroutine in the code handles seeding the random number generator:

```
Sub StartSub()

'   Seed the random number generator
Randomize

End Sub
```

A function, `GenerateRandomNumber`, is also provided to generate a random number between an upper and lower bound. The upper and lower bounds are passed into the function.

```
Function GenerateRandomNumber(UpperBound, LowerBound)

.....'   Upperbound is the highest number in the range
.....'   Lowerbound is the lowest number in the range
.....'   Rnd returns a decimal number
.....'   The difference between the bounds + 1 is multiplied
.....'   by the decimal. This plus the lower bound gives
.....'   us a number in the specified range.
.....'   Finally, the number is converted into an integer
.....GenerateRandomNumber = _
.......int((upperbound - lowerbound + 1) * Rnd + lowerbound)

End Function
```

The `CheckGuess` subroutine handles checking the value of the random number against the value entered by the user. Appropriate feedback is given by the `MsgBox` function.

```
Sub CheckGuess

Dim frmWork

'   Set frmWork to the form
set frmWork = Document.DataDisplay

'   Check the two values
if frmWork.txtUserGuess.value = frmWork.txtRandomNumber.value then
.....'   Tell the user they are correct
.....msgbox "Correct!"
else
.....'   Indicate they were not correct
.....msgbox "Better Luck Next Time!"
end if

End Sub
```

The `On_Click` method of the `cmdSubmit` button does all the necessary checking to ensure that the user has entered a lower and upper bound as well as a guess. This simple game is a good introduction to how the `Rnd` function can be utilized. If you need any unpredictability in your Web pages for games, security, and so on, this will be an invaluable tool for you.

1. If **Randomize** has _____ parameter, the value returned by the _____ is used as the new _____ value.
   a. no…system timer…seed
   b. one…system timer…initial
   c. a…system date…random
   d. None of the above

2. The following code will return a value between

```
INT((10 - 1 + 1) * Rnd + 10) + 5
```

   a. 0 and 10.
   b. 5 and 15.
   c. −5 and 5.
   d. 1 and 10.

3. What is the relationship of **intVar1** to **intVar2**?

```
Dim intVar1
Dim intVar2

intVar1 = INT((10 - 1 + 1) * Rnd + 10)

intVar2 = INT((10 - 1 + 1) * Rnd(0) + 10)
```

   a. Unknown; it is random
   b. Same value
   c. **intVar2** is greater than **intVar1**
   d. **intVar2** is less than **intVar1**

4. The **Rnd** function returns a value _____ but _____.
   a. less than 1…greater than 0
   b. less than 1…greater than or equal to 0
   c. less than or equal to 1…greater than or equal to 0
   d. less than or equal to 1…greater than to 0

5. If a parameter is not supplied to the **Rnd** function, then
   a. the previous random number in the sequence is returned.
   b. no random number is returned.
   c. the next random number in the sequence is returned.
   d. a random number larger than the previous number is returned.

Difficulty: Intermediate

1. Modify the sample program to track the number of guesses made and the number correct.

Difficulty: Intermediate

2. Modify the sample program to allow the user to enter the initial seed value for the Randomize function.

SESSION 7

WORKING ON THE CASE

Let's focus on a specific example of working with strings and the character case. Now that we have reviewed the fundamentals of using different data types, let's put an example into action.

Our task will be to take a string and convert the case of each character. An example would be converting "Visual Basic Script" to "vISUAL bASIC sCRIPT" (in case you are wondering, that would be an odd thing to do). To do this, we will need to examine each character in the string and determine whether or not it is an uppercase or lowercase character. This determination can be made by the character's ASCII value. Figure 4-12 overviews the process for converting "DOG-CAT" to "dog-cat".

As you can see, we will take each character, examine its value, and then either convert it or not convert it. Note that we do not want to convert non-alpha characters (such as, the '-' in our example) at all, but simply include them in the final string.

Our sample program provided on the CD-ROM performs this conversion. Let's examine the code to see how it is done. Figure 4-13 shows the Web page in action.

ASCII Character Code Set
American Standard Code for Information Interchange is used to represent letters and symbols found on a standard U.S. keyboard. Each letter and symbol is represented by an integer value between 0 and 255.

When the **cmdSubmit** button is clicked, we first check to see whether there has been a valid string entered to be converted. If not, we notify the user. Next, we make sure the output textbox is cleared of any current values. Once everything is set up, we will loop through each character in the string and call the **ConvertCharacter** function to convert the case of the character, if necessary. Note that we use the **Mid** function to get the current character we want to convert. We will use a loop, **For...Next**, to look at each character in the string.

	" D	O ↓	G	- ↓	C	A ↓	T "
Asc =	68	79	71	45	67	65	84
#1 7=65 or L=90	Y	Y	Y	N	Y	Y	Y
#2 7= 97 or L =122	N	N	N	N	N	N	N
If # 2 = Yes, then Asc val +32	100	111	103	45	99	97	116
If # 3 = Yes, then Asc val -32	--	--	--	--	--	--	--
Final Asc values	100	111	103	45	99	97	116
Chr of values	d	o	g	-	c	a	t

Figure 4-12 Converting "DOG-CAT" to "dog-cat"

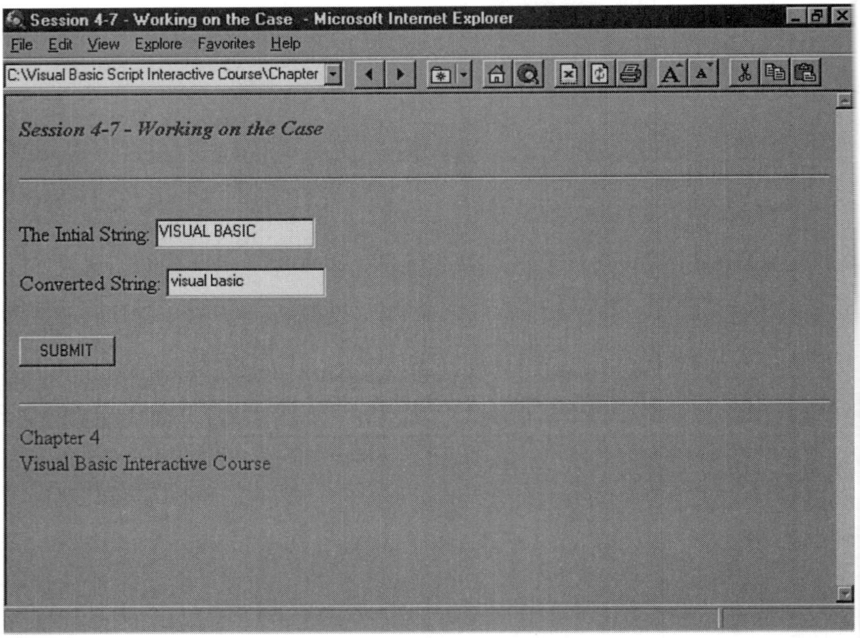

Figure 4-13 Converting string character case

The **For...Next** variable, **intForCnt**, will determine which character to start at in the **Mid** function, and we only get one character. So, essentially, we are looping through each character and will determine whether or not to convert it. The code in the loop is iterated through until the condition check in the **For** statement is true. Once it is true, we move on to the code after the loop.

We are also building a new string as we loop by storing the string in the **txtConvertedString** HTML text input element. We simply concatenate the latest converted character by using the **&** operator.

```
Sub cmdSubmit_OnClick()

Dim intForCnt
Dim intConvLen
Dim strConvStr
Dim frmWork

'  Set the display form
Set frmWork = Document.DataDisplay

'  Get the string to convert
strConvStr = frmWork.txtInitialString.Value

'  Get the length of the string
intConvLen = Len(strConvStr)

'  Check to ensure a string to
'  be converted was entered
if frmWork.txtInitialString.value = "" then

.....'  Tell the user no string was entered
.....msgbox "You have not entered in a string to be converted."

.....'  Exit the sub  routine
.....Exit Sub
end if

'  Clear the converted string field
frmWork.txtConvertedString.value = ""

'  Loop through each character
For intForCnt = 1 to intConvLen

.....'  Convert each character and tack it
.....'   on the currently build string
    frmWork.txtConvertedString.value = _
      frmWork.txtConvertedString.value & _
      ConvertCharacter(mid(strConvStr, intForCnt, 1))

Next

End Sub
```

Next, let's look at the **ConvertCharacter** function. This function takes in a single character string parameter, **strConvChar**, and returns a character string with the converted character by setting the function name, **ConvertCharacter**, to the new character.

First, the code retrieves the ASCII value of the character by using ASC. We then check to see whether the character is in the ASCII uppercase character range of 65 to 90. If so, we then add 32 to the value to move the ASCII value to the lowercase range (97 to

122). If it is not in the uppercase range, we then check to see whether it is in the lowercase range of 97 to 122. If so, then we subtract 32 to move it into the uppercase ASCII range (65 to 90). Finally, if it is in neither range, then we simply return the character unchanged. Note that the ASCII value is converted back to a character using the `Chr` function. The new character is returned by setting the function name equal to the character.

```
Function ConvertCharacter(strConvChar)

.....Dim IntAscChar

.....'  Get the ASCII value of the
.....'  sent in character
.....intAscChar = asc(strConvChar)

.....'  Check to see if the character is
.....'  in the Upper Case range
.....If intAscChar >= 65 and intAscChar <= 90 then

......'  If so then add 32 onto the ASCII
......'  value to convert is to Lower
......'  case
......ConvertCharacter = chr(intAscChar + 32)

.....Else

.......'  Check to see if the character is in the
...... '  lower case range
.......If intAscChar >= 97 and intAscChar <= 122 then

........'  If so then  subtract 32 from the
........'  ASCII value to convert it to
........'  Upper Case
........ConvertCharacter = chr(intAscChar - 32)

.......Else

........'  If it is not an alpha character
........'  then we simply pass back the character
........'   that was send in
........ConvertCharacter = strConvChar

.....End If

... End If

End Function
```

Converting a string in this fashion may be a little bit unusual, but it serves to demonstrate the power of string manipulation with Visual Basic Script. A real world example would be to ensure that the first name and last name entered by a user always begin with an uppercase character.

QUIZ 7

1. The _____ function returns the _____ associated with the specified _____.
   a. **Chr**...integer value...ASCII Code
   b. **ASC**...integer value...ASCII Code
   c. **Chr**...character...ASCII Code
   d. None of the above

2. The _____ function returns the _____ of a _____.
   a. **ASC**...ASCII code...character
   b. **ASC**...character string...character
   c. **Chr**...ASCII code...character
   d. **Chr**...Character string...character

3. What character is represented by (97–32)?
   a. a
   b. A
   c. z
   d. Z

4. What will be the result of the following?

```
UCASE(Mid("HelloWorld", 7, 3))
```

   a. **WOR**
   b. **WORL**
   c. **OWO**
   d. **OWOR**

5. What will be the result of the following?

```
LCASE(Left("HelloWorld", 7, 3))
```

   a. **wor**
   b. **Error**
   c. **orl**
   d. **owo**

EXERCISE 7

Difficulty: Intermediate

Modify the program to strip out all non-alpha characters.

WHAT TYPE OF VARIABLE AM I?

Since all variables in Visual Basic Script are of type **variant**, it will be important to be able to determine what subtype a variable is at any given time. For example, what if you need to know whether or not a user entered a number, or whether a variable contains a valid date, and so on.

Visual Basic Script provides a number of functions for determining the data type of a variable. One of the most powerful functions for making this determination is **VarType**. Table 4-3 outlines the different meanings of the return values from **VarType**.

Return Value	Data Type
0	Empty
1	Null
2	Integer
3	Long integer
4	Single-precision, floating-point number
5	Double-precision, floating-point number
6	Currency
7	Date
8	String
9	OLE Automation Object
10	Error
11	Boolean
12	Variant Array
13	Non–OLE Automation Object
17	Byte
8192	Array

Table 4-3   VarType *return values.*

As you can see, with **VarType** you can easily determine what type of variable is being utilized based on the return value. But, that is not the only set of functions provided for determining what data type a variable is. There is another set of **'IS'** functions that will check to see whether a function is a certain type or not. Table 4-4 illustrates these.

Function	Description
IsDate	Determines if a variable contains a valid date
IsArray	Determines if a variable contains a valid array
IsNumeric	Determines if a variable contains a valid number
IsEmpty	Determines if a variable is empty
IsNull	Determines if a variable contains NULL

Table 4-4 'IS' *Functions.*

These functions provide similar functionality to **VarType**, but explicitly work on only one data subtype. Each returns either True or False based on the check. The best way to review these functions is to review their use in code. Open the HTML document located in the Session8 subdirectory of the Chapter4 folder on the CD-ROM. Figure 4-14 shows the **'IS'** function demos.

The **'IS'** functions are demonstrated to show both True and False returns from testing of variables. The **varTest** variable is purposely left blank to show a false return from the functions. Figure 4-15 shows the **VarType** function. Also, included in an HTML table are the return values from the function.

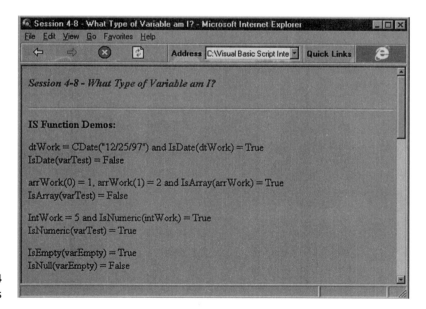

Figure 4-14
'IS' functions

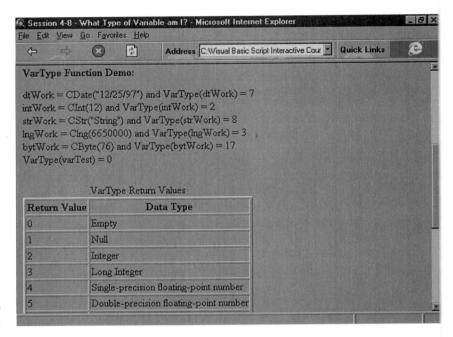

Figure 4-15
VarType function

Note that we also have a non-initialized variable, **varTest**, in this section of code. **VarType** returns 0 to indicate the variable is empty. In order to ensure that we are testing the right type of variable, we are using several data conversion functions, including **CDate**, **CInt**, **CStr**, **CLng**, and **CByte**. Each of these converts the data from another subtype to the specified subtype. By using these functions we ensure that the data subtype being passed into the **VarType** and **'IS'** functions is set appropriately for the check. Note that **IsNumeric("1234")** returns true, whereas **VarType("1234")** will return 8, which indicates it is a string. That is because **IsNumeric** is checking the variable to see whether the data in it can be used as a numeric, regardless of data subtype.

Utilizing all these tools will be the key to performing data validation in Chapter 10, "Objectifying Your Scripts". If we need to ensure that only numbers have been entered into a textbox, using **IsNumeric** will be invaluable. This will be true of any type of data we want to the user to enter.

1. When does the following return a value of 1 based on the following code?

```
Dim X
```

    a. **VarType(NULL)**
    b. **VarType(X)**
    c. **VarType(Y)**
    d. None of the above

2. What value will **Y** have based on the following code?

```
Dim Y

Y = 65
Y = Chr(Y)
Y = VarType(Y)
```

      a. 8
      b. 2
      c. 3
      d. 10

3. What will be returned from the following **IsNumeric** function?

```
Dim X

X = "IT IS 2 BASIC"
IsNumeric(MID(X, 7, 1))
```

      a. True
      b. False
      c. 5
      d. 8

4. What will be returned from the following?

```
IsDate(Str(Cdate("12/12/96")))
```

      a. True
      b. False
      c. −1
      d. 9

5. If a variable contains a value of '−24.56', what **'IS'** function will return true?
      a. IsReal
      b. IsLong
      c. IsInteger
      d. IsNumeric

Space holder for red flagged .eps. New .eps should fit in this spot perfectly

Difficulty: Easy

    1. Write a program subroutine that will check to see whether a variable is empty when it is passed in. If so, then set the value to 50.

Difficulty: Intermediate

    2. Write a program subroutine that will check to see whether a string passed in is a valid date. If not, then initialize the date to today's date.

CHAPTER SUMMARY

In this chapter we have taken our first formal look at how we work with data in our scripts. As you have seen, we can define the type of data we use in many different ways. We have many different functions provided in Visual Basic Script that will help us to manipulate that data. In the next chapter we will delve into utilizing those `If...Then ...Else` and `For...Next` constructs, as well as many others.

CHAPTER 5

DANGER—PROGRAM CONSTRUCTION

n this chapter we will discuss, first generally and then in more detail, how to construct and manipulate discrete blocks of code. This will allow you to apply structure to your Visual Basic Script programs. But before we get started, it will be useful to understand why programmers get so excited when they discuss the *structure* of their chosen language. Just why is the structure of a language so important?

Most traditional languages have a simple fundamental structure in common; they are *procedural*. This means the computer simply executes a program's code lines one after the other, in sequence, starting from the first line and ending at the last. This step-by-step approach is called the *procedural paradigm*, and it has the benefit of being quick and intuitive.

Unfortunately, by the time your programs become big enough to start impressing other people, this approach becomes severely limiting. It soon becomes clear that some sort of structure needs to be applied if programs of a useful size are to be manageable and efficient.

Definition: Code Structure

The manner in which a program's code is modularized into discrete, named blocks.

The theory used to apply structure to your Visual Basic Script code is not complex. If the code block is too big, chop it up into little pieces. Give each code block its own name and then work out some way to patch them all together so that all the blocks run in the intended order.

Within a code block, the processor will still run the code lines one after the other, but now the processor is free to jump from block to block. Just where and when to jump is dictated by code held within the blocks themselves. It is like trying to cross a river using many different stepping stones. You jump from stone to stone, occasionally testing a stone with your foot and sometimes doubling back. Different routes can be taken, but all will eventually lead from one bank to the other. Structure gives the processor stepping stones, allowing it to hop from the start block to the end block, hopefully doing some useful things along the way.

To add structure to your code, it must be split into blocks. These blocks are called *procedures*. In Visual Basic Script, as in most languages, the generic term *procedures* is divided up into *subroutines* and *functions*. Both are procedures as both consist of lines of code, but the detailed differences in how they operate justify giving them separate labels.

In this chapter, we will learn to:

- Create and Call Subroutines

- Structure Code with Functions

- Make Decisions Using the If...Then...Else Construct

- Repeat Lines of Code with the For...Next Loop

- Increase Flexibility with the Do Loop Construct

- Use the Select Case Statement to Run Different Code Blocks

- Link VBScript Code to the User Interface and Events

- Use Error Trapping to Create Code that Users Can't Easily Trip Up

CREATING AND CALLING SUBROUTINES

In Visual Basic Script, the most common procedure type is the Subroutine, or Sub for short. A Sub is a number of functionally related lines of code bundled together and given a name. The name is important because this is the identifier that will be used to call the Sub into action when it is needed. Precisely where the Sub starts and where it ends is determined by the Sub...End Sub delimiters.

Syntax

```
Sub name (parameter list)
        statements
                Exit Sub
        statements
End Sub
```

The subroutine is defined by the two delimiting statements Sub SubName...End Sub. The code between the subroutine delimiters will be run whenever this subroutine is called from elsewhere in the code.

This is how a Visual Basic Script Sub called Square might look.

```
Sub Square
        Dim X
        X = X * X
End Sub
```

If you look carefully at the code above (not the delimiters), you can see that this procedure is flawed. The variable X has been created, dimensioned, inside the Sub and is therefore a local variable (see Chapter 4, "Store That Data," Session 1). In this example, the variable X can only exist while the code inside Sub Square is actually being processed. The scope of the variable extends only as far as the delimiters of the Sub, so the variable is created, then destroyed, every time the Sub Square is run. As you know, when Visual Basic Script variables are first dimensioned, they are assigned a default value. For X, since it is being used to hold number values, the value will be zero. Since X is zeroed every time the Sub is run, the result of X = X * X will always be zero, which is not much use to anybody. What is needed is the ability to pass a value for X from outside the world of Sub Square and then give it to X after it has been dimensioned. The programmer needs to decide when they want Sub Square to run and what data Sub Square might need. A call is born.

In the example below, the subroutine called Square shows how the value of X can passed into the subroutine from elsewhere.

```
Sub Square(X)
        X = X * X
End Sub
```

Definition: Subroutine

A collection of code lines delimited by the `Sub...End Sub` markers. A fundamental structural component of Visual Basic Script, the subroutine allows code to be divided into manageable chunks and caters to the passing of data into the sub's code block. Although subroutines can receive data, they cannot return any values to the calling code.

In order to call a subroutine, you just write the sub's name and possibly some values or variables. When the name is read by the Visual Basic Script interpreter, it will not be confused; it keeps a record of all the procedures in a program. It uses the sub's name as a label to indicate where it should jump to find the sub's code. To call `Sub Square` and pass it a value, you would type the sub's name and beside it the value, or variable holding the value, you wish to pass. In our case it is `Sub Square` and the variable `X`, which has been given a value of **10**.

```
Sub Math
    Dim X
    X = 10
    Square X
End Sub
```

To be able to receive a value, `Sub Square` must be told to expect a variable from the calling procedure. In this case the value of `X` passed from `Sub Math` is popped into the `Sub Square` variable called `SqX`. Note the use of the keyword `ByVal` placed directly before each parameter the `Sub Square` is expecting to receive. This is required only when the value of the parameter is to be altered, as in this case. If the value is for reference only, then there is no need to use any prefix keyword.

`ByRef` is always assumed if `ByRef` is not used; it is the default mode of passing variables.

Definition: ByVal

If a parameter is passed to a procedure `ByVal`, then the value of the variable can be altered by the procedure it has been passed to. Visual Basic Script insists that this keyword be used if the procedure intends to alter the value of the parameter during the course of its processing.

The example below illustrates the `ByVal` method of passing variables to a procedure.

```
Sub Square (ByVal X)
    X = X * X
    MsgBox X
End Sub
```

Only use the `ByVal` keyword when the variable being sent is to have its value altered within the called procedure. In the case of `Sub Square`, the value of `X` is altered by the processing, and so the `ByVal` statement is used.

Also, this example shows the first use of a new command, **MsgBox**. This simple command causes a message box to appear displaying whatever message you like. In this case the value of **X** will be displayed. For simple message boxes, the syntax for the **MsgBox** command is just **MsgBox message**. The message can be a string or variable holding a string or a number.

Definition: ByRef

If a parameter is sent **ByRef**, then no changes can be made to the value of the variable within the body of the procedure. Visual Basic Script passes all variables **ByRef** as default, so this keyword is normally omitted.

With subroutines such as these you might create a whole library of mathematical functions to be called at your whim. Code organized and structured into subroutines is easy to read and maintain, but, most importantly, the same subroutine can be called from anywhere in your code as many times as needed. Since the code is reused time and again, it makes for enormous savings in time and cost. Subroutines also allow the programmer to concentrate on perfecting one piece of code at a time, which reduces the overall time spent debugging the code.

Summary

In this session we examined the first type of procedure, the subroutine. The code that comprises a subroutine was found sandwiched between two delimiters, the **Sub** and the **End Sub**. The syntax used to call a sub demonstrated that subroutines can be called from anywhere within the code. Simply declaring all variables for a sub inside the sub would result in local variables with default values. We solved this problem by passing values from calling code to the subroutine. The main limitation of subroutines is their inability to pass data values back to the calling code. The type of procedure that *can* manage this trick is called a *function*, which will be the subject for Session 2.

1. Applying structure to your code means
   a. filtering out bad data *before* it is processed.
   b. splitting the code into procedures.
   c. converting all the code into subroutines.
   d. ordering the code lines in ascending numerical order.

2. A subroutine is best defined as
   a. a group of lines that all do the same thing.
   b. structure applied by splitting the code into procedures.
   c. a type of procedure that can receive but cannot return values.
   d. a procedure that allows data to be sent to it.

3. Which is not an advantage of structured code?
   a. It saves on debugging time.
   b. It allows other programmers to understand your code.
   c. It always results in faster running code.
   d. It allows common procedures to be reused.

4. If a variable is passed to a procedure **ByVal**, then
   a. the procedure is allowed to change the value of the variable.
   b. the procedure can only change the value if it changes it back before ending.
   c. this has no effect because **ByVal** is the default.
   d. the procedure is not allowed to change the value of the variable.

5. If a variable is passed to a procedure **ByRef**, then
   a. the procedure cannot use the variable at all.
   b. a copy of the variable must be made.
   c. this has no effect because **ByRef** is the default.
   d. the procedure is not allowed to change the value of the variable.

Difficulty: Easy

1. Modify the subroutine Square to take more than one parameter, and use the parameters you pass to perform some simple arithmetic procedures. Use a message box to display your results.

Difficulty: Easy

2. Call a subroutine from within another subroutine. It is a good idea to place message boxes throughout your code to allow you to follow the code's progress.

Session 2

FUNCTIONS

In this session we will further extend your ability to structure your code into useful functional units. The main topics will be the definition, calling, and exiting of *functions*. If a subroutine is just code with structure applied, then a *function* is just a subroutine with a little more structure applied. The functional difference between the two lies in the function's ability to pass a data value back to the calling code. This value can be anything you like. It may be the result of successful calculation or perhaps an error code indicating why a function went wrong. Whatever they are used for, functions provide enhanced communication between the procedures that comprise a program. Figure 5-1 shows how a function call is processed.

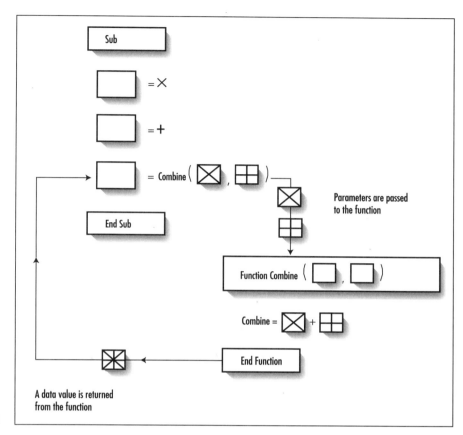

Figure 5-1
A function call

Defining a Function

Defining a function is no different from defining a sub, except you use the word *Function* instead of *Sub* in the procedure's declaration.

Syntax

```
Function name (parameter list)
        statements
             name = return_value
             Exit Function
        statements
        name = return_value
End Function
```

Function fSquare below returns the value it calculates back to the call by making the name of the function equal to the value or variable that needs returning. Here is function fSquare returning the value of the variable X.

```
Function fSquare(X)
         X = (X * X)
         fSquare = X
End Function
```

It is important to note that setting the return value of a function does not terminate the function. This statement is processed like any other and left behind. Although you can set the function's return value as often as you want, the value won't actually be returned until the function terminates at the **End Function** delimiter or the **Exit Function** command. It is good coding practice to set the return value of the function only when there is no possibility of further relevant processing—in other words, processing that could alter the value being returned. In simple functions such as **fSquareI**, the equation that sets the return variable is commonly the last line to be processed.

Calling a Function

Like a subroutine, a function can receive values passed by the call, but unlike a sub, a function can also return a value to the call. In order to be capable of receiving a value, the call must be in the form of an equation, which always takes the form:

Empty Variable = Function Name.

Just as with subroutines, if the function requires data to work with, you can send some winging its way by placing it (value or variable) to the right of the function name. There is a minor technicality at this point, and that is remembering to enclose the value to be sent to a function in brackets; subs do not need brackets, but functions do. In Visual Basic Script, the call to function **fSquare**, passing the value of **X**, looks like this.

```
X = fSquare(X)
```

Sub Math below shows the result returned from **fSquare** being displayed via a message box.

```
Sub Math
         Dim X
         X = 10
         X = fSquare(X)
         MsgBox X
End Sub
```

In the example above you can see that the procedure **Math** is using the function **fSquare** to perform the arithmetic for it. This helps keep **Sub Math** nice and simple. If any other procedures need to have a number squared, then they can call the same **fSquare** function which helps to prevent unnecessary duplication of code.

Forcing an Exit from a Sub or Function

A **Sub** or **Function** comes to an end when the **End Sub** or **End Function** delimiter is encountered. Here the processor returns to the point where the call was made and continues with the next line in the calling procedure. Occasionally it becomes imperative to stop processing mid-procedure; for example, if incorrect data is sent to a procedure and this is detected, then there is little point in carrying on with the rest of the processing.

In other cases it may simply be more efficient to leave the procedure before the **End** delimiter is reached. For example, a text search procedure might scan onscreen text for the first instance of a particular word. If successful, it would probably want to stop and return something meaningful (like the position of the word) as soon as it found the first instance of the word. Continuing to process all the remaining text after the procedure has been successful is just a waste of time. Being able to exit a procedure at just the right moment can be as important as knowing just when to call a procedure. How it's done is simplicity itself. The command is **Exit Sub** or **Exit Function**, depending on the procedure type you wish to exit from.

Summary

Session 2 has expanded your knowledge of procedures. Now that you have met the function, you have the ability to pass data both to and from code blocks. By using the calling syntax shown, functions may be chained together, each progressing the code in their own way until the processing goal is reached. Greater control over when a sub or function should stop running is achieved using the **Exit** command, either **Exit Sub** or **Exit Function**.

So far you have seen how to chop the code into procedures and how to call the procedures from the code. The next great leap forward will occur when you add decision-making power to your code. The mechanics of the command involved are covered in Session 3.

1. Which of the following statements is false?
    a. Functions are a type of procedure.
    b. Functions can return a value.
    c. Functions help prevent unnecessary code duplication.
    d. Functions should always be used in preference to subroutines.

2. A function can best be defined as
    a. a subroutine that does not change any data.
    b. a procedure that can return a value to the calling code.
    c. a faster version of a subroutine.
    d. a procedure that can call itself.

3. Which of the following lines of code sends the `TotalRads` variable to the function called `X_Ray`, returning a value into the `OncoActive` variable?
   a. `OncoActive  X_Ray TotalRads`
   b. `TotalRads  X_Ray OncoActive`
   c. `OncoActive = X_Ray (TotalRads)`
   d. `OncoActive TotalRads = X_Ray()`

4. An `Exit Function` statement is used
   a. when the program has finished running.
   b. when the user clicks the Quit button.
   c. to leave a function before the `End Function` statement.
   d. to prevent the `End function` statement from being run.

5. How many variables should be passed to a function?
   a. As many as the function requires
   b. No more than five
   c. No more than one
   d. From one to as many as the function requires

Difficulty: Easy

1. Write a function that allows more than one value to be passed to it. Perform some simple arithmetic with the values and send the result back to the calling code. After calling the function, display the value returned in a message box.

Difficulty: Easy

2. Write at least three arithmetic functions and create a controlling subroutine that calls the three functions in turn. Make sure to pass the return values from the previous function on to the next function. Display the final result of this compound calculation in a message box.

SESSION 3

If...Then...Else

This session deals with making decisions in Visual Basic Script. Programs can be seen as a series of actions, some of which will be carried out, some of which won't. It all depends on the data being processed.

The `If...Then...Else` construct allows the programmer to test data values and respond by running either one piece of code or another. A program with many `If` statements can react to a wide range of data and is not rigidly fixed into one particular processing pathway. Precisely which subset of the program's code actually runs depends on the data.

> **Definition:** If
>
> The primary decision-making component of Visual Basic Script. This command allows for the conditional branching of the code's logic. Which branch is pursued depends on whether the expressions being tested resolves to true or false.

Syntax

When only one line of code is dependent on the **If** condition being true, then it is fine to use the shorthand syntax shown below.

If *condition* Then statements

For more complex statements it is better to use the full syntax:

If *condition1* Then
          statements
ElseIf *condition2* Then
          statements
Else
          statements
End If

> **Definition: Condition**
>
> An equation whose value can be resolved to either true or false. The equation **X=10** is, at any given moment, either true or false. An equation becomes a condition when code decisions are taken depending on its value.

Decision Time

In procedures, decisions need to be made all the time. It is how the logic flows that determines the code's functionality. Such decisions can be defined by asking questions and then supplying instructions depending on the answers. Since computers are binary beasts, there is no such thing as a "well maybe" answer.

Consider the dilemma a traveller might face when confronted by a fork in the road:

"If left fork is way home then go left fork else if right fork is way home then go right fork else go backwards."

The example below uses the **If** construct to translate the traveller's dilemma into Visual Basic Script.

```
Sub TakeMeHome

    If  RightFork = Home Then
         GoRightFork
    Else
         GoLeftFork
    End If
End Sub
```

Before going anywhere, the traveller must examine his decision-making data or map as shown in Figure 5-2.

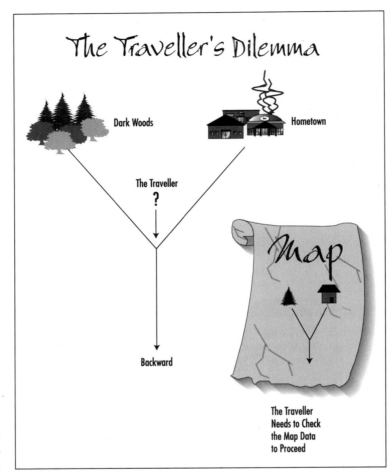

Figure 5-2
The traveller's
dilemma

While this answers the traveller's dilemma in part, it is not a complete solution, since it makes no mention of going backwards. Programmers must consider all possible alternatives, even highly unlikely alternatives. In this instance the original question was:

"If left fork is way home then go left fork else if right fork is way home then go right fork else go backwards."

The code below shows that translating the full question into Visual Basic Script does not present any problems.

```
Sub TakeMeHome

    If  RightFork = Home Then
            GoRightFork
    ElseIf LeftFork = Home Then
            GoLeftFork
    Else
```

```
              GoBackwards
         End If
   End Sub
```

Here are some sample **If** structures from Visual Basic Script. The first is the simplest.

```
If X<10 Then X=X+1
```

X will only be incremented if its value is less then **10**. When only one statement is dependent on the condition, in this case **X<10**, then it is acceptable to use this shorthand version of the **If** syntax. With the single-line syntax, it is possible to have multiple statements executed, but they must all be on the same line and separated by colons, as in the following example.

```
If X>10 Then X=X+1: Y=Y+1: Z=Z+1
```

It is usual practice not to format an **If** statement with multiple dependent lines in the manner shown above, even though it is perfectly legal. The recognized way of formatting exactly the same statement is as follows.

```
If X>10 Then
         X=X+1
         Y=Y+1
         Z=Z+1
End If
```

In both these examples, the dependent lines that increment **X**, **Y**, and **Z** will only be run if the value of **X** is greater than **10** when **X** is tested by the **If** statement. What would run if **X** was less than **10**? For these examples, the answer is nothing at all, but it raises an interesting point. If you are testing a condition to see if it is true, you are in fact making two tests: the first to see if it is true and also an implicit second test, to see if it is false, the logical opposite of true.

We use the statement **Else** to delimit lines that are dependent on the condition being tested not resolving to true.

Definition: Else

All conditions other than the conditions specified in the **If**. The **Else** statement represents the logical opposite of all the preceding **If** conditions combined.

In the following sample you can see the **Else** statement being used to take care of all logical possibilities other than the condition being tested in the **If** statement above it.

```
If X<10 Then
         X=X+1
Else
         X=X-1
End if
```

X will be incremented if its value is less than **10**; however, if **X** is not less than **10**, then the value of **X** is decremented. The **Else** statement acts as the logical opposite to whatever tests are being applied. What it really says is, "If none of the above conditions are true..."

The **Else** statement is not a specific test, since it represents the logical opposite of the tests being applied. There is a way to specify an **Else** statement to ensure that, in the event of the the first condition failing, there are secondary conditions to apply. The **ElseIf** statement allows a second and third (as many as you want) condition to be built into the **If...Then...Else** construct.

Definition: ElseIf

Used to define any further conditions required by the **If** block. Each **ElseIf** condition is dependent on all the conditions above it being false. If the **ElseIf** condition evaluates to true, then its dependent code is run.

In the following example you can see an **ElseIf** statement being used to specify a second condition. It is important to remember that although **ElseIf**s look like they are only testing one condition, in logical terms they represent a retest of all the conditions that went before, in addition to the condition the **ElseIf** specifies. In order to even test the **ElseIf** condition, we know the first **If** condition *must* have failed.

```
If X<10 Then
          X=X+1
ElseIf X>20 Then
          X=X-1
Else
          MsgBox "X > 10 and X < 20"
End if
```

X will be incremented if its value is less than **10**. **X** will be decremented if its value exceeds **20**. However, if neither of the conditions are true, then the code dependent on the **Else** statement is run and a message box displays an appropriate string. This shows how the logic of each failed condition is assumed for the next tested condition. The equivalent logic without using **ElseIf** or **Else** could be achieved like this:

```
If X<10 Then X=X+1
If Not (X<10) And X>20 Then X=X-1
If Not (X<10 And X>20) Then MsgBox "X is greater than 10 but less than 20"
```

This form of logic may appear to be the same at first glance, but it would potentially give very different results. Using the **If...Then...Else** construct, only one of the conditional branches can be run; using the three line logic shown above means this effect is not guaranteed.

The **Else** and **ElseIf** are both *optional*. You can have as many **ElseIf** clauses as you want, but none can appear after an **Else** statement.

Formatting an If Statement

In the example, certain lines are tabbed in and others are not. This is a near universal coding convention that implies the dependency of the tabbed code on the **If** statement. If code is tabbed in, then it is dependent on the decisions being taken above and one tab to the left.

Complex logical structures can be built easily using the `If...End If` control blocks. This lends the code a great deal of flexibility. All situations and all circumstances can be catered to. The `ElseIf` component allows each `ElseIf` branch to be a specific Yes–No question in its own right; you can have more than one `ElseIf` if required, so all valid possibilities can be checked for. In reasonably complex `If` structures, this `Else` code is often used "In Case of Emergency"; this is where error processing code is commonly found. If you have checked for all valid contingencies and none of them have resolved to true, then what is left over must be invalid. In the following example all valid conditions are checked and appropriate action taken if the value being tested turns out to be invalid.

```
If   X=42 Then
          MsgBox "This is the Magic Number"
ElseIf X>0 And X<1000
          MsgBox "X is Valid but not magic"
Else
          MsgBox "ERROR: X is an Invalid number"
End If
```

You can see that **X** has three logical states: **magic**, **valid**, or **invalid**. The first **If** condition tests to see if **X** is the magic number 42. If it is not the magic number, then the second test is performed to make sure that **X** is at least valid; that is, it lies between 0 and 1000. Failing both of these then, it is an iron-clad certainty that **X** lies outside the valid range and is certainly not the magic number. In this instance, the **Else** instance, appropriate error trapping takes place.

Nesting Ifs

Nesting means placing one thing inside another, like a Russian doll. Any code can be made dependent on an **If** statement, even another **If**. The example below shows two **If**s, one nested inside the other.

```
If X< 10 then
          If Y< 10 Then MsgBox "X and Y are both less than 10"
End if
```

The limit for nested **If** statements is so high it will never concern you. Here is an example of a triple-nested **If** statement.

```
If X< 10 then
          If Y< 10 Then
              If z< 10 Then
                                    MsgBox "X,Y,Z are all less than 10"
              End If
          End If
End if
```

The only line of code that actually does anything is the line that displays the message box, but, by nesting the **If** statements together, another form or compound test is being created. Nesting **If**s produces results very similar to those created by using **ElseIf**.

It is common to see a new nested If being created when a new test is being applied and ElseIfs being used when the test is a variation on the If condition. This is not a syntax rule, but it does make sense. In this final complex example, you see all the If components and formatting in action.

```
If X=10 Then
          MsgBox "X=10"
Else
          If Y<10 Then
                   MsgBox "X not=10 and Y<10"
          ElseIf Y=10
                   If Z=5 Then
                                      MsgBox "X not=10 and Y=10 and Z=5"
                   End If
          End If
End If
```

Don't worry if the example above looks a little daunting; just start at the top with the first If condition and work your way down and to the right. If you imagine some simple values for X, Y, and Z, then you can follow the logic-making decisions about which dependent code should run whenever a condition is being tested. The message boxes show the code's current logical position.

Summary

Decision-making lies at the heart of controlling a program's flow. In this session you were introduced to the If...Then...Else construct, Visual Basic Script's primary decision-making tool. In the syntax shown, you saw variables being tested to determine what, if any, code should be run in response. In real Visual Basic Script examples, you saw variables being repeatedly tested and error reporting code being initiated. The formatting conventions universally applied to If statements were demonstrated, as was the common practice of nesting the statements one within the other.

This session has shown you how to decide what to run. In the next session you will see how to make the same piece of code run again and again, stopping and starting under precise control.

1. Which of the following statements about the If construct is true?
    a. It cannot be used to initiate error reporting.
    b. It can only test one condition per If, ElseIf branch.
    c. It will run every dependent code block whose condition resolves to true.
    d. It will only run the *first* dependent code block whose condition resolves to true.

2. The **ElseIf** statement is used to
   a. add another specific condition to an **If** construct.
   b. create the logical opposite to all the following conditions.
   c. speed up the **If** construct.
   d. add error trapping.

3. The **Else** statement is used to
   a. terminate an **End If**.
   b. specify a new condition to be tested.
   c. represent all other non-tested conditions.
   d. promote world peace.

4. Programmers use **If** statements to
   a. make their code run faster.
   b. reduce the amount of time spent debugging.
   c. decrease the amount of code used overall.
   d. run specific code *only* when it is appropriate to do so.

5. Which of these is not a condition?
   a. `If X=10 Then`
   b. `If Z=5 And X=10 And MyName = "Jonny" Then`
   c. `X=X+1`
   d. `ElseIf X=Y+1 Then`

Difficulty: Easy

1. Create an arithmetic function that will act on even numbers only. If an odd number is sent to be processed, then the user should see a warning message box.

Difficulty: Easy

2. Create a program that can return a small range of messages based on the user's text input. For example, the program should establish the user's name and then greet them individually and personally.

Hint: Text input from the user is usually achieved using textbox controls.

THE For...Next LOOP

In this session, the techniques involved in repeating certain lines of code over and over again will be discussed. Such behavior is called *looping*; the same lines of code are run repeatedly, in a loop, until a condition is met and the loop stops looping. The

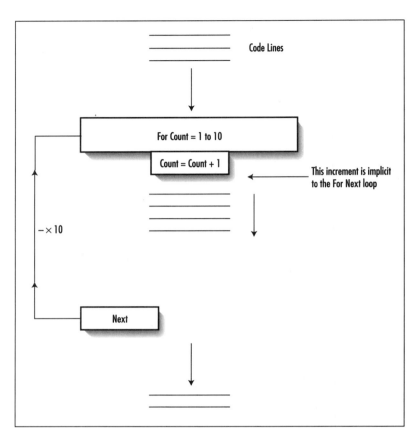

Code Lines

For Count = 1 to 10

Count = Count + 1

This increment is implicit
to the For Next loop

− × 10

Next

Figure 5.3
A loop being
processed

For...Next construct is used to show which lines are to be repeated and, very importantly, supplies a condition that can stop the loop when it is supposed to. Figure 5.3 shows how a loop is processed.

Definition: Loop

A group of lines within a body of code that can be selectively repeated a specified number of times.

Syntax

```
For counter = start To end [Step step]
          statements
          [Exit For]
          statements
Next
```

The For delimiter is made up of a number of a components that help to define the specific nature of the loop. The For Counter component sets up a predeclared variable to be used as a counter for the loop. The start and end components store the number at which to start looping and the number at which to end looping. A loop of this type works by setting the counter variable to the start number and then running the code in the body of the loop before jumping back to the top line again. After each run of the loop code, the counter variable is automatically incremented.

This process carries on until the counter variable has the same value as the **End** variable. The additional and *optional* component **Step** holds the increment value used by the loop. If **Step** is omitted from the statement, then an increment value of +1 is assumed. If there is no **Step** component, then the number of times a loop will repeat itself is equal to the **Start** variable minus the **End** variable.

The **Next** delimiter shows where the block of code to be repeated ends. All the lines of code contained between the **For** and the **Next** delimiters are part of the body of the loop and will therefore be repeated. When the processor reaches the **Next** delimiter, it jumps back up to the **For** statement and checks to see if it is okay to do another loop. Here is an example of a simple loop in Visual Basic Script.

```
For Counter = 1 to 10
        MsgBox Counter
Next
```

This code will display 10 message boxes, each displaying a number one larger than the previous message box. The number will start at 1, and the loop will end after the tenth message box is displayed.

The **Step** statement allows the counter to increment in values other than one. If the value of the **Step** variable is two, then the counter will increase it by two for each iteration of the loop. If the **Step** value is negative, then the counter will count down instead of up. In many circumstances, counting down can be just as useful as counting up.

```
For CountDown = 10 to 1 Step -1
        MsgXox CountDown
Next
```

In Formula One racing it is a common sight to see men with headphones leaning out over the railings at the edge of the track, holding aloft a large board with various numbers on it. Each time the driver comes around, he recognizes the stretch of track and, for an instant, glances up at the board. Now he knows his position, how many laps there are until the finish line, and other useful things. For the rest of the lap the driver need pay no attention to such details, concentrating all his energies into going as fast as possible. Only when he comes around again need the driver give up any of his resources to refresh his lap information. Such a system works well for racing drivers because it is a very efficient use of their resources.

The Visual Basic Script **For...Next** loop is like that Formula One driver. When the processor encounters a loop, it climbs into its car and speeds around and around the delimited code until the exit condition resolves to true.

This is what a **For...Next** car driving loop might look like in Visual Basic Script.

```
Sub GrandPrix
        Dim Lap
        Dim EndRace
        EndRace = 10
```

```
For Lap = 1 to EndRace
      MsgBox "This is Lap Number " & Lap
Next
MsgBox "The Race is Over"
End Sub
```

In this final example you can see the variable **EndRace** being set before the loop is started. This value could be set anywhere in the program and show how loops can be dynamically set to run as many or as few times as required, even if the value of the **EndRace** variable has been established elsewhere in the code.

Warning: Loops and Zero

Starting or ending a loop on zero will add an extra iteration to your loop since zero is counted as a valid number. If a loop starts on one and ends on five, then the loop will repeat the expected five times. If a loop starts at zero and ends at five, then the loop will run six times.

Summary

This session has tried to increase your coding power by introducing the concept of looping. The **For...Next** loop provides the programmer with the ability to rerun a delimited block of code a specified number of times. The code block is delimited using the **For** and the **Next** commands. The **For** command is accompanied by at least two and sometimes three separate values: the **Start** variable, the **Stop** variable, and the **Step** amount. The default **Step** value is +1. All three of the values are used to determine the number of times the loop will be rerun.

The **For...Next** loop is constrained to run a specific number of times. In the next session we will examine the **Do** loop. This is a more flexible loop construct that allows the programmer to run a loop while or until a *condition* is met.

1. A **For...Next** loop can be defined as a code block that is
   a. repeated a specified number of times.
   b. only run if a condition is true.
   c. only run if a condition is false.
   d. repeated until the user triggers an event.

2. The **Next** statement is used to
   a. start the loop repeating.
   b. create the end condition.
   c. delimit the lower boundary of the repeating code block.
   d. run the next line of code.

3. The **Step** command is used to
   a. set the value to be added to the counter variable.
   b. specify a new condition to be tested.
   c. skip the specified number of lines.
   d. force the loop to operate in reverse.

4. How many times will the message "Still looping" be displayed?

```
For X = 1 to 9
        MsgBox "Still looping"
Next
```

   a. 8 times
   b. 10 times
   c. 9 times
   d. None of the above

5. How many times will the message "Still looping" be displayed?

```
For X = 25 to -5 Step - 5
        MsgBox "Still looping"
Next
```

   a. 6 times
   b. 30 times
   c. -6 times
   d. 7 times

Difficulty: Easy

1. Write a For...Next loop that displays the counter value with each iteration. Try adding different Step values and various Start and End values to see how this affects the counter variable.

Difficulty: Moderate

2. Create an array and fill its elements with data. Starting with the first element (zero), display each data item in turn. The loop must finish on the last element, not before and not after.

Hint: The number of elements in any array can be found using Ubound(MyArray).

THE Do **LOOP CONSTRUCT**

In Session 4 the `For...Next` loop was introduced as a convenient way of repeating a block of code for a predetermined number of iterations. In this session, the looping concept will be taken one stage further. A new loop construct, the **Do** loop, will show how to create loops that will repeat *until* or *while* a condition, any condition chosen by the programmer, is found to be true. This adds enormous flexibility to the looping concept.

> **Definition: Do loop**
>
> Code found inside the **Do** loop delimiters will be repeated *while* a condition is true or *until* a condition becomes true.

Syntax (Top Check)

```
Do While | Until condition
          statements
                  Exit Do
          statements
Loop
```

> **Definition: Top Check**
>
> A **Do** loop that checks its condition before entering the loop. The conditional statement is found to the right of the **Do** keyword. If the condition resolves to true on this first check, then the loop code will not be run.

Do While **or** Do Until**?**

Do loops are used when you need to repeat a block of code, not for a set number of times but for as many times as it takes to complete a task. Remember, a condition is simply an equation that can be resolved to either true or false. Conditions are tested and used to decide whether or not to stop the loop. The form of **Do** loop that will continue *until* a condition is true is called a **Do Until** loop: Do until condition = true. The logical opposite of that statement is **Do While**. Visual Basic Script allows both logical types to be used so that the conditional tests are kept simple. Here are some **Do** loop examples.

```
X=0
Do While Not(X=10)
          X=X+1
Loop

X=0
Do Until X = 10
          X=X+1
Loop
```

Both these examples will loop for 10 iterations. You can see that the simplest code will be achieved by using the **Do Until**. The **Do While** is more complex because it uses the extra **Not**. Although the logic is the same, the clarity of the code is not.

Do Until isn't always the simpler method. Here are two more examples.

```
X=0
Do While X<10
          X=X+1
Loop

X=0
Do Until Not(X<10)
          X=X+1
Loop
```

As in the first set of **Do** loops, this pair is logically identical, and both will loop 10 times. From a computer's point of view, there is nothing to choose between them. From a Visual Basic Scripter's point of view, the **Do While** is much simpler to understand.

Syntax (Bottom Check)

```
Do
          statements
                    Exit Do
          statements
Loop While | Until condition
```

> **Definition: Bottom Check**
>
> A **Do** loop that checks its condition only after running through the loop code once. The conditional statement is found to the right of the **Loop** keyword. Even though the conditional statement might be true before the loop begins, the loop code will run once before this is checked.

Top/Bottom Checking

Another flexible feature of the **Do** loop is its ability to be either a top-checking loop or a bottom-checking loop. The top-checking loop checks its condition beside the **Do** keyword whereas the bottom-checking loop checks its condition beside the **Loop** keyword, at the bottom. If you remember how a computer reads one line at a time from the top of the code to the bottom, then you can see that a bottom-checking loop will have all of its code run at least once before the condition has a chance of being checked. Compare this to the top-checking loop, which always tests its condition *before* any loop-dependent code is run. For a top-checking loop, the exit condition must be false to start with before the loop is run at all. In contrast, a bottom-checking loop will always run the loop code at least once.

Each of the two types is used depending on the logic you want to express. Here are two examples of apparently equivalent loop logic.

```
X=10
Do While X<10
            X=X+1
Loop


X=10
Do
            X=X+1
Loop While X<10
```

The actions of the loops will not be the same though. In the first example **X** will not be incremented since the exit condition has been met. In the second loop **X** will be incremented by one because, although the exit condition has been met before the loop starts running, this is not tested until the loop has run once. It is more likely that correct loop structure for this case would be a top-checking loop, but as these next two examples show, that is not always the case.

```
X=10
Do While X>10 and X<20
            X=X+1
Loop

X=10
Do
            X=X+1
Loop While X>10 and X<20
```

In the first example the loop simply will never run. In the second example the loop is allowed to run once before testing the value of its condition. **X** has been incremented, and the loop continues for another nine iterations.

Loops Can Be Dangerous

The main asset of **Do** loops, their conditional testing, is also the source of their greatest danger. When you are running a loop that will stop *only* when its exit condition is met, what happens if its exit condition cannot be met? Consider the following example.

```
Do Until True = False
            X= X+1
Loop,
```

This is perfectly valid Visual Basic Script. You can type it in now if you want to, but it would not be advisable. If such a loop were to appear, the processor would treat it like any other. **X** would be incremented until **True = False**, which is just a logical way of saying the loop would never stop. Writing a loop like this is not as hard as it might seem. Here is an example of an innocuous-looking loop that would stop your code in its tracks.

```
X=10
Do
            X=X+1
Loop Until X=10
```

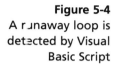

Figure 5-4
A runaway loop is
detected by Visual
Basic Script

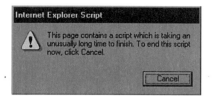

In this case the loop will stop only when **X** is equal to **10**. **X** is equal to **10** at the outset, but the loop is a bottom checker. This means the loop code will be run before the value of **X** is tested. Unfortunately, the loop code increases the value of **X** to 11, and so the loop condition, when it is finally tested, is found to be false. The loop will keep on looping, adding one to **X** and hopelessly rechecking the condition, but now things are out of control. **X** will never be equal to 10, and the loop will never exit.

If you do manage to get caught in an endlessly repeating loop, don't worry. It is such a common thing that Visual Basic Script has been programmed to detect when it happens. After entering a loop of this sort and spending about 15 seconds whirring away, Visual Basic Script will warn you that something is amiss and prompt you to stop running the code. Figure 5.4 shows the error reported when a runaway loop is detected. If this happens, be sure to check all your loops to find out which one cannot meet its specified exit condition.

Summary

Do loops add a great deal more flexibility to the looping concept. Through the use of **Do While** loops and **Do Until** loops, conditions can be expressed in their simplest form. Top-checking and bottom-checking loops were shown to extend the programmer's control even further to include most of the looping scenarios imaginable. We highlighted the danger of endlessly repeating loops, reinforcing the care that should be taken when deciding upon a loop's exit condition.

The next session returns to the decision-making theme left back in Session 3 with the **If** statement. The ability to direct the flow of processing will be extended allowing many more combinations of decisions to be made.

1. A **Do** loop can be defined as a code block that
   a. is repeated a specified number of times.
   b. will be run only while a condition is true.
   c. will only be run until a condition is false.
   d. will repeat while *or* until a specified condition is true.

2. An endless loop will occur when
   a. the start of the loop is not specified.
   b. the exit condition is met *while* not true.
   c. the exit condition cannot be met.
   d. a bottom-checking loop increments a value.

3. A top-checking loop checks the condition
   a. after the loop code has run.
   b. before the loop code is run.
   c. once at the beginning.
   d. once at the top.

4. A `Do While` loop will repeat
   a. while a condition is false.
   b. until a condition is true.
   c. while a condition is true.
   d. until a condition is false.

5. How many times will the message "Still looping" be displayed?

```
Do While Counter < 10
        MsgBox "Still looping"
        Counter = Counter + 1
Next
```

   a. 10 times.
   b. 9 times.
   c. 11 times.
   d. You cannot say without knowing the starting value of `Counter`.

EXERCISE 5

Difficulty: Moderate

1. Write a double nested `Do` loop that cycles through all the elements in a two-dimensional array.

Difficulty: Difficult

2. Create a two-dimensional array and fill its elements with names and descriptions of your friends. Add a search capability to the loop by checking each name in the array against a specified name. Stop the loop when the specified name is matched. Make the specified name user-enterable and display the description text of the match when found. Should no match be found, display an appropriate message. You have just written a database.

SESSION 6

THE Select Case **CONSTRUCT**

In Session 3 we saw that the `If...Then...Else` construct could be used to decide which code blocks should run. In this session, the running of different code blocks based on the value of a condition will be extended through the use of the `Select Case` statement. As your experience grows and the programming tasks you tackle increase in logical complexity, it is common to find large and unwieldy blocks of code emerging. One of the main culprits for this effect is the multiple nesting of `If` statements. The `Select Case` construct is a much neater way of packaging a series of conditional tests that direct the program flow. In many cases, it is the construct of choice simply because the resulting code is so much clearer and not because it adds extra functionality over a complex `If` statement.

Definition: Select Case

The `Select Case` statement will execute one of several groups of statements. The statements to be run will depend on the value of the expression tested by `Select Case`. If the value of the expression tested matches any more than one `Case` branch, *only* the statements following the *first* match are executed.

Syntax

```
Select Case testexpression
        Case expressionlist-1
               statements
        Case expressionlist-n
               statements
        Case Else
               statements
End Select
```

Definition: Expression

Any statement or variable that evaluates to either a string or a number.

Testing Multiple Values

The power of a `Select Case` statement lies in its ability to test any number of values for a given expression and then run the appropriate, dependent code block. Each case branch can have more than one possible value which will trigger the case-dependent code. Each value is separated by a comma. To illustrate this, consider the simple `Select Case` statement below.

```
X=5
Select Case X
          Case 1
                 MsgBox "X is equal to 1"
          Case 2,3,4
                 MsgBox "X is either 2 or 3 or 4"
          Case 5
                 MsgBox "X is equal to 5"
End Select
```

If this example was run, then the message **"X is equal to 5"** would be displayed in a message box. The **Select Case** statement first evaluates the value of **X**. It then tests each **Case** statement in turn. If the case has multiple values separated by commas, each value is tested in turn. This process continues until one of the values on one of the **Case** branches matches the test expression value. The code that is dependent on this **Case** statement is then run. After a case is found to be true, the processor ignores all the other case branches and restarts processing on the first line after the **End Select** statement. In the example, only the **Case** statement **Case 5** resolves to true since **X**, the test expression, was made equal to five before the **Select Case** was run.

Select Case statements can evaluate any type of data, not just numbers. The example below shows a **Select Case** statement testing the variable **MyName** to determine the appropriate code to run.

```
MyName = "Jonny"
Select Case MyName
          Case "Jonny"
                 MsgBox "Hello Jonny"
          Case "Billy", "Mike"
                 MsgBox "Hello Mike or Billy?"
End Select
```

You can see that this example will display the message "**Hello Jonny**", but what would have happened if the variable **MyName** had been set to a name that was not mentioned in any of the **Case** branches? In this situation, the **Select Case** would have simply ignored all the dependent code, and nothing would have happened. Sometimes it is useful to have some default code to deal with just such an eventuality. This default ability is provided by the **Case Else** statement. Like the **Else** component of an **If...Then...Else** construct, the **Case Else** stands for: if none of the above are true… Here is the same example as before, but this time it has default code to deal with any names it does not recognize.

```
MyName = "Lisa"
Select Case MyName
          Case "Jonny"
                 MsgBox "Hello Jonny"
          Case "Billy", "Mike"
                 MsgBox "Hello Mike or Billy?"
          Case Else
                 MsgBox "Howdy Stranger"
End Select
```

Now running the example would result in a welcoming **"Howdy Stranger"** message should **MyName** contain *any* name, indeed any string, other than those specified in the preceding **Case** statements. The code dependent on the **Case Else** statement will only be run if none of the previous specified conditions have been met.

Summary

In this session you have increased your ability to control the program flow. The **Select Case** construct improves the control by allowing individual blocks of code to be dependent on multiple expression values. Using the **Case Else** statement allows even the simplest **Select Case** construct to deal with all possible expression values. This is useful for detecting invalid data values. We saw that any data type can be tested; if Visual Basic Script can hold it in a variable, then it can be tested using a **Select Case**.

In the next session we will look at the world of *event driven* programming.

1. The code block dependent on a **Case** statement will be run when
   a. the processor reaches the **End Select**.
   b. the test expression value matches the **Case** value.
   c. at least one of the **Case** values matches the test expression value.
   d. all of the **Case** values match the test expression value.

2. A **Select Case** would be used instead of an **If** statement when
   a. the **If** statement could not code for the logical state required.
   b. extra processing speed is required.
   c. the resulting code is simpler to understand.
   d. there are more than two conditions to be tested.

3. Code dependent on the **Case Else** statement will run
   a. after the first conditional code block has run.
   b. before the first conditional code block has run.
   c. once at the end of the statement.
   d. only if none of the **Case** branch expressions have matched the test expression.

4. Multiple expressions on a **Case** branch
   a. are *not* allowed because there can only be one expression per **Case**.
   b. are *not* allowed because there would be no way to tell the expressions apart.
   c. *are* allowed if they are separated by commas.
   d. are *not* allowed because Visual Basic Script is only a subset of Visual Basic.

5. After a match has been found and the dependent code run,
   a. processing moves directly to the first line after the **End Select**.
   b. the next **Case** expression in turn is tested.
   c. the procedure is exited.
   d. you cannot say without knowing the expression value.

Difficulty: Moderate

1. Create a `Select Case` to determine which button from a group of buttons has been pressed.

Hint: The `Select Case` should only be written once and put into a procedure.
Difficulty: Difficult

2. Write a procedure that will display error messages depending on the number sent to it; use a `Select Case` construct. Create a series of procedures that will all call the same error handler with mock errors. Investigate the use of `Case Else` for calling your error-handling procedure.

EVENT DRIVEN CODING

In this session *events* and *event handlers* will be examined. This will allow you to link up the Visual Basic Script code you write to the user interface created using ActiveX controls.

Definition: Event

A user action which triggers the processing of a specified procedure in Visual Basic Script. Most controls have events; those that do not cannot interact with a user.

Linking Code to Events

Not all user actions generate events; there is no `Withering_Glare` event or any `Gesticulate_Wildly` event, which is a pity. However, all objects that interact with the user through windows must have a predefined set of events. These events are then used by the programmer as triggers to control how the program responds to user action. When users of a Visual Basic Script program click their mouse, press a key, or interact with the program in a machine in a recognizable manner, a wake-up call is sent to any code which has been expressly linked to that event. The special subroutines that are linked to specific events are called *event handlers*. It is within the event handler that you place your *event procedure*. The event procedure is automatically invoked in response to an event initiated by the user.

Definition: Event Handler

The subroutine that is invoked when its user event is generated. The *event procedure* is contained within the event handler.

Syntax

```
Sub ObjectName_Event
        Event Procedure Code
        Event Procedure Code
End Sub
```

Event handlers are subroutines that have been predefined by the inclusion of the object in a Visual Basic Script program. The subroutines do not contain any code until the programmer puts an event procedure in place. The event procedure will then be run whenever a user event causes an event handler to run its event procedure. The syntax of the event handler allows the programmer to easily identify both the event and the control to which it belongs. Below is an example of event handler from a button control called cmdClickMe.

```
Sub cmdClickMe_Click
        MsgBox "Button Clicked"
End Sub
```

The event handler above is for the single Click event of the button control cmdClickMe. When this button is single-clicked, this event handler is invoked, and the code in the event procedure is run.

Each object will have a range of events that defines its interactive capabilities. Button controls are nearly always either clicked or double-clicked by the user, and so these are its most frequently used events. It does cater to a wider range of interaction than just clicking though. Below is a list of the events that a standard HTML layout button control can react to.

AfterUpdate: Occurs after data in a control is changed through the user interface.

BeforeDragOver: Occurs when a drag-and-drop operation is in progress.

BeforeDroporPaste: Occurs when the user is about to drop or paste data onto an object.

BeforeUpdate: Occurs before data in a control is changed.

Click: Occurs when the user clicks the button with a mouse.

DblClick: Occurs when the user clicks a mouse button twice.

Enter: Occurs before the button receives the focus from another control.

Exit: Occurs immediately before the button loses the focus to another control.

KeyDown: Occurs when the user presses a key while the button has focus.

KeyUp: Occurs when the user releases a key while the button has focus.

KeyPress: Occurs when the user presses a key.

MouseDown: Occurs when the user presses the mouse button over the control.

MouseUp: Occurs when the user releases the mouse button after the button has been clicked.

MouseMove: Occurs when the user moves the mouse over the button.

Definition: Focus

When a control has focus, it has the ability to receive mouse clicks or keyboard input from the user. Only one control at a time can have this ability. The control that *has focus* is usually indicated by a highlighted caption or title bar. The focus can be set by the user or by the application.

Having this many events makes the control more flexible, although most of these will only be of use in unusual situations. More common is the use of the **MouseOver** event. The code for the double-click event handler is shown below.

```
Sub Sub cmdClickMe_DblClick
        MsgBox "Button Double Clicked"
End Sub
```

Exactly the same thing happens in the second example. This time you can see from the event handler that it is the **Double Click** event of the button **cmdClickMe** that will trigger the event procedure to run.

All controls that have any form of user interface have events to deal with the expected user actions. The richer the range of events a control caters to, the more varied Visual Basic Script's response can be. The reliance on the user for the code triggers necessary to run the software makes Visual Basic Script an *event driven* language.

Definition: Event Driven

Programs that can do nothing without regular contact via their user interface are said to be event driven. Such a coding structure requires the generation of standard user events by the processing layer, Windows, and interception of such events by the application layer, your program, where they are used to determine which of the application's procedures should run next.

Event driven code can be seen in two ways. Either the program relies on the user to dictate its every action, or the program itself controls the actions of the user. In fact they are both correct; each describes one side of user/code relationship. An event driven program can do nothing without a user to generate events, but the user can only generate those events allowed by the program.

Once inside the event handler, calls to any subroutine or function can be made. This is called the **Event Cascade** and is illustrated in Figure 5.5.

Visual Basic Script depends on the user to initiate the separate components that comprise its functionality. As soon as an event handler has run its course, Visual Basic Script can do nothing except hang around waiting for the user to trigger another event. This has a large impact on the design considerations of Visual Basic Script pages. As well as code efficiency and functionality considerations, the Visual Basic Scripter will learn to balance the data input and output needs in terms of graphical controls and displays.

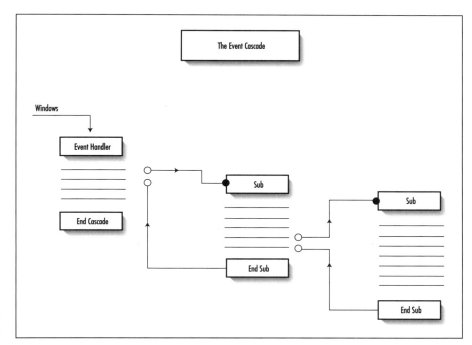

Figure 5-5
An Event Cascade

Summary

Session 7 has focused on events, the handlers that recognize them, and the code that can be generated as a result. We explored the close bond between the user and the code and the range of options available indicated by the flexibility of the events supported by the standard button control. Now the loop looks closed. In previous sessions you learned how to create procedures, but not much has been said about when they should run. This session should have changed that; now you know where to begin looking for the event handlers to get your code connecting to the user, and you can start the ball rolling.

In the next session we tackle the thorny issue of coding errors.

1. Which of the following best describes an event handler?
   a. The procedure that is invoked when its user event is generated
   b. The function that is invoked when its user event is generated
   c. The subroutine that is invoked when its user event is generated
   d. The event that is generated when its user interacts with a control

2. Which is correct syntax for `btnClickMe`'s `MouseUp` event?
    a. `Sub MyButton_MouseUp`
    b. `Function MyButton_Mouse Up`
    c. `Sub btnClickMe_MouseUp`
    d. `Sub btnClickMe Mouse_Up`

3. Which of the following events is *not* recognized by a standard button control?
    a. `KeyPress`
    b. `MouseMove`
    c. `DoubleClick`
    d. `Exit`

4. Event driven code is constrained by
    a. the actions of the user.
    b. the events supported by the controls.
    c. the size of the event procedures.
    d. answers a and b together.

5. If a code is initiated in the `Enter` event of a button control, it will terminate on the `End Sub` of which of the events shown?
    a. The `MouseUp` event
    b. The `Exit` event
    c. The `Enter` event
    d. The `KeyDown` event

Difficulty: Moderate

1. Place a button control and some check box controls in a page. Write the event procedures required to check the boxes if the event handler is triggered. Try interacting with the button to see how and when the events you choose are triggered.

Difficulty: Easy

2. Call a subroutine and a function from within an event handler. Place a `MsgBox` as a first and last line in each procedure. Note the order in which the procedures are called and terminated.

ERROR TRAPPING

Undeniably, humans are machines prone to error. Computers, on the other hand, are machines that simply cannot make mistakes. This realization leads to the rather depressing conclusion that, whenever something goes wrong with a program, it's fundamentally the fault of the programmer. It's no use beating around the bush; you created the code, so the buck stops dead at your feet. Some programmers are heard to berate the *user* as the source of all errors, but this is blatant blame avoidance. Your code should not *allow* the user to perform actions the program cannot deal with. The responsibility for making sure the code stays on its own two feet is entirely the programmers'; it is their job to anticipate the avenues that might lead to errors and choke them off.

Well-written code should have the ability to recognize potential error situations. This is perhaps most apparent when comparing all the user actions possible in Windows to the user actions actually required by the software. Errors often occur when the user performs an action or combination of actions that leads to a state for which there are no instructions. In cases like this, it should always be remembered that it is the *lack of instructions* that causes the error, not the user action.

> **Definition: Error**
>
> An error is a logical state that has no code to deal with it. It is any situation that causes a program to cease functioning or to function inappropriately. Errors can arise from the code syntax, from the application logic, from input data, or from unexpected user actions.

Error Trapping Components

Visual Basic Script supplies a set of options to help overcome the problem of error recognition: the **error** object, or more accurately the **Err** object and the **On Error** statements. The **Err** object and the **On Error** statements can be seen as a safe pair of hands to catch the code as it falls over. Working together, they will help you recognize an error as it happens, prevent the machine from falling over, fix the problem, and set the code off again from a safe point—all without rippling the surface of your user interface.

> **Definition: Error Trapping**
>
> A set of procedures whose only function is to recognize specific errors and deal with them appropriately.

The **Err** object will also allow access to handy bits of information so that you can tell what went wrong and where. Visual Basic Script really does do a lot of the work for you, but there is still much that can be done to make the user experience if not friendly, then at least less aggressive. But before the syntax and usage of the `On Error` statements and the `Err` object are explored, it will be useful to know what an *object* might be in the first place.

An Object Lesson

An object is a collection of related procedures. The procedures that make up an object define the functionality of the object. For example, a group of procedures, all of which are concerned with chart plotting, can be grouped together under a notional group and labeled `ChartDraw`. This is not quite an object though, because objects always *organize* their procedures in a certain way—in an *object-oriented* way, to be precise. The result of this object-oriented approach is a group of related procedures collected together, some of which are accessible and usable from within another program's code. The data or *properties* that the object's procedures use can be fed into the object; this is called *setting* its properties. The procedures or *methods* can be triggered by *invoking* the method.

Definition: Object

A procedure that has been structured in an object-oriented fashion. Such procedures are self-contained units with specific and defined functionality which require support from the program that hosts them. Objects present the programmer with an interface consisting of properties and methods.

When procedures have been grouped together as an object, the programmer gets to use their functionality by invoking the methods. To invoke a method, the object's name must first be stated, followed by the name of the method, as in these imaginary examples.

```
MyObject.Method
ChartDraw.ClearGraph
ChartDraw.PlotPieChart
```

The `ChartDraw` object in this example can plot a pie chart or blank the graph. Where is the data coming from to determine the slice size of the pie chart or which chart should be wiped? The answer lies, potentially, in two places. The first is sending data to the method when it is invoked, just like subroutines and functions. The second is setting an object's properties, storing the values required by the method, before the method is invoked. The first style is considered initially, and examples of the syntax are shown below.

```
MyObject.Method X, Y, n ..
ChartDraw.ClearChart "Pie Chart 1"
ChartDraw.PlotPieChart 25,14,13,2,65,3.14, "Pie Chart 2"
```

This time the `ChartDraw`'s methods are having data sent to them; this specifies precisely what the procedure is to do. The `ClearChart` method looks as if it should clear the chart called `"Pie Chart 1"`. The `PlotPieChart` method is having its pie slices sized by the values it is being sent. It also looks as if the `PlotPieChart` method is being sent the name `"Pie Chart 2"`; this could well be the new chart's title.

> ### Definition: Method
>
> The way in which a procedure within an object is invoked, thus triggering a component of the object's functionality. The procedures initiated in this manner will use any values sent to them as well as those values held in the object's properties.

Properties are just as important as methods. Properties hold values within the object. These values can be changed by the programmer or by the actions of the object's own methods. Properties are used to define the characteristics of the object.

Setting a property changes some characteristics of the object. The settings of all an object's properties, combined with the code contained within its methods, define any particular instance of an object. Although the code within the methods cannot be touched, the precise effect it has when run can be altered by presetting relevant property values. The imaginary `ChartDraw` object has had a new property added to it called `ChartType`. The old `PlotPieChart` method has been replaced with the simpler, more generic `PlotChart` method.

```
ChartDraw. ChartType = "Pie"
ChartDraw.PlotChart 6,1,9,34,6

ChartDraw. ChartType = "Bar"
ChartDraw.PlotChart 6,1,9,34,6
```

Now setting the value of the `ChartType` property will cause the `PlotChart` to plot the chart according to the setting. The exact shape of the chart, in this case the size of the pie slices, is mediated via the data values received by the `PlotChart` method. In the example, two charts are plotted: a pie chart and a bar chart. Both are plotted using the same method and the same data. The difference is in the setting of the `ChartType` property. Note how the property is set *before* the method is called.

> ### Definition: Property
>
> A property of an object is a unit of data which the object uses in the course of its function. Properties can be read/write—that is, programmer alterable—or read-only. For any particular function, an object's properties are set prior to invoking the appropriate method. The setting of some properties can automatically cause the object to internally invoke its own methods in order to process the new property value.

The `Err` **Object**

The `Err` object, in conjunction with the `On Error` statements (see below), is used primarily to manage runtime errors as they occur, although in more complex code it can also be used to create controlled errors defined by the programmer. `Err` has a number of properties which can be either read or set by the programmer and two methods which trigger its built-in functionality.

In practice this `Err` object is used to determine what went wrong and where. Using this information, the program can be written to ignore the error or act in a sensible manner to correct it. When an error occurs in a Visual Basic Script program, the `Err` object stores the details of the error as property values ready for the error trapping code written by the programmer to interrogate and take the appropriate action. Sometimes the appropriate action may be to invoke one of the **Err** object's methods.

Syntax

The syntax for the error object is the same as for all objects. You read (or set) its properties and invoke its methods.

```
Err.Property
```
or
```
Err.Method X,Y
```

Properties

The **Err** object has five read/write properties and no read-only properties. The properties are as follows:

Err.Number

This property is filled by the code where the error occurred or by Visual Basic Script if the error was not trapped by the programmer. The value returned or set is a numeric value uniquely specifying the error that has just occurred. **Number** is the **Err** object's default property.

Err.Description

The **Description** property comprises a short description of the error that has just occurred. Use this property to alert the user to an error that you cannot or do not want to handle. When generating a user-defined error, assign a short description of your error to this property.

Err.Source

The **Source** property specifies a string that identifies the procedure that caused the error. This property will also be set should an object that is being accessed by the Visual Basic Script code fail. Thus **Err.Source** can be used to provide your users with information when your code is unable to handle an error generated in an accessed object. For example, if you access Microsoft Excel and it generates a Division by zero error, Microsoft Excel sets **Err.Number** to its error code for that error and sets **Source** to **Excel.Application**.

Err.HelpFile

If a Help file and its full path are specified in the **Err.HelpFile** property, the **HelpContext** property automatically displays the Help topic that **HelpContext** identifies. If both **HelpFile** and **HelpContext** are empty, the value of **Err.Number** is checked, and if it corresponds to a Visual Basic Script runtime error value, the Visual Basic Script Help context ID for the error is used. If the **Number** value doesn't correspond to a Visual Basic Script error, the contents screen for the Visual Basic Script Help file is displayed.

Err.HelpContext

If a Help file is specified in the **Err.HelpFile** property, the **HelpContext** property automatically displays the Help topic that **HelpContext** identifies. If both **HelpFile** and

`HelpContext` are empty, the value of `Err.Number` is checked, and, if it corresponds to a Visual Basic Script runtime error value, the Visual Basic Script Help context ID for the error is used. If the `Number` value doesn't correspond to a Visual Basic Script error, the contents screen for the Visual Basic Script Help file is displayed.

Definition: Help

Help files are generated by programmers using readily available help file compilers. These convert textual documents into the standard Help file format. During the process of Help file creation, the author can assign numeric identifiers to individual topics within the Help file. These are called `HelpContextIDs` and allow the programmer to precisely define the Help text to be displayed.

Methods

When an error occurs, the `Err` object's primary function is to store the information placed there by Visual Basic Script to be examined and acted upon. This means that the methods are not as varied as might be expected; in fact there are only two of them.

Err.Clear

Use `Err.Clear` to explicitly clear the `Err` object after an error has been handled.

Err.Raise

It is hard to test any error handling code you may write unless there is a way of artificially inducing the error required. `Err.Raise` will cause Visual Basic Script to act just as if the error had happened. Precisely what error is raised must be preset in the properties described previously.

To summarize the functionality of the `Err` object:

- It contains information about runtime errors.

- It accepts the `Raise` and `Clear` methods for generating and clearing runtime errors.

- The properties of the `Err` object are set by the generator of an error, the Visual Basic Script programmer.

- The default property of the `Err` object is `Number`. It contains an integer which is the unique code for the error that has just occurred.

- When a runtime error occurs, Visual Basic Script automatically fills the properties of the `Err` object with information that uniquely identifies the error and information that can be used to handle it.

- To generate a runtime error in your code, set the properties to reflect the error you wish to generate and use the `Raise` method.

- The `Clear` method can be used to explicitly reset `Err`.

- The `Err` object is an intrinsic object with global scope, so it can be used anywhere without prior declaration.

The On Error **Statements**

How can the program tell if an error has occurred in the first place? When an error does occur, how can the now stricken machine know to what error code to run? Not to worry; assistance is at hand by using the On Error statements; they are On Error Goto, On Error Resume, and On Error Resume Next.

On Error Goto LabelName

In the example syntax shown below, the LabelName included in the On Error Goto statement is ErrLabel. This label is then repeated further down the page, but this time with a colon at its end. The On Error Goto statement is telling the processor where to go in the event of any recognizable error. The LabelName with the colon marks the spot where the error code is situated.

```
Sub MySubroutine
On Error Goto ErrLabel
          Processing..
          More Processing..
          Exit Sub
ErrLabel:
          Error Processing
End Sub
```

It is important to note the use of an Exit Sub before the actual label (the lower label with the colon) is encountered. This is to prevent the error code being run when there have been no errors. Unfortunately, Visual Basic Script does not automatically ignore any error trapping code it finds when things are running normally. Without the Exit Sub (or Exit function), the error code would be run as if it were just another part of the subroutine. Also, the label must be in the same procedure as the On Error statement; otherwise a compile-time error occurs.

After trapping the error, it is essential to find out precisely what error has occurred. This is where the Err's properties start to come in handy. Examining the Err.Number property allows the unique error number held there to be acted upon. If the number is an error that the code recognizes, then something can be done about it. In the example below, the error handling code has been placed under the label MyErrHandler:.

```
Sub AllMyProcessing
          On Error Goto MyErrHandler
          X=X+1
          MySubroutine X
          Exit Sub

          MyErrHandler:
          If Err.Number = MY_ERROR then
                    Dont_Panick
          Endif

End Sub
```

The error code is prevented from running during normal execution by the `Exit Sub` that precedes the `MyErrorHandler:` label. In the event of an error, the `On Error Goto`, `MyErrorHandler` ensures that `Exit Sub` is bypassed and processing goes straight to the error handling code. Each `On Error Goto Label` encountered resets the place that Visual Basic Script will go to in the event of an error. Visual Basic Script will only forget about an `On Error` statement when it has finished processing the procedure in which it appeared; that is, encountered its `End Sub`. This means that an error occurring in a nested procedure without error handling of its own may (in the example `MySubroutine X`) be handled in the parent procedure that called it. It is possible to create multiple layers of error trapping code in this way or to allow a number of functions to share the error trapping code held in the procedure that called them.

Resume

In order to deal with the error that has just occurred, the error handling code can make use of another Visual Basic Script command designed to aid error trapping, the `Resume` command. This command comes in three flavors:

- `Resume`
- `Resume Next`
- `Resume ErrLabel`

Here is an example of all three being used in an error handler.

```
MyErrHandler:
If Err.Number = MY_ERROR1 then
            Resume
ElseIf Err.Number = My_ERROR2
            Resume Next
Else
            Resume MyOtherErrorHandler
End If
```

All these commands cause the error to be ignored and processing to continue. The difference between them lies in just where the processing is to be restarted. `Resume` will restart on the same line that caused the error, whereas `Resume Next` will restart on the line following the line in error. Finally `Resume MyOtherErrorHandler` will restart the code at the first line following the `MyOtherErrorHandler:` label definition which must exist elsewhere in the same procedure.

On Error Resume Next

This specifies that when a runtime error occurs, control goes to the statement immediately following the statement where the error occurred. This is the same as using an `On Error Goto` statement and then issuing a `Resume` command in the error handling code. Doing it this way automatically resumes processing on the line after the line in error without the need to check the error number. This provides another way of structuring your error handling routines.

```
Sub Divide(ByVal X, ByVal Y)
        On Error Resume Next

        X=X/Y

        If Err.Number = DIV_BY_ZERO Then
                ProcessError DIV_BY_ZERO
                Err.Clear
        End If

        More Processing
End Sub
```

This example shows how to trap a division by zero error should the value of the variable Y ever be set to zero by the calling procedure. The **On Error Resume Next** ensures that the line that is run as soon as the **X=X/Y** line fails is the start of the error trapping code. Using this method allows specific errors to be trapped directly underneath the code that caused the error.

On Error Goto 0

Using this form of the **On Error** statement switches off all error trapping and prevents the **Err** object from being filled with the appropriate error information. Note that this statement does not specify line 0 as the start of the error-handling code, even if the procedure contains a line numbered 0. Without an **On Error Goto 0** statement, an error handler is automatically disabled when a procedure is exited.

After the Error

The **Err** object's properties are reset to zero or zero-length strings ("") after an **On Error Resume Next** statement and after an **Exit Sub** or **Exit Function** statement within an error-handling routine, and processing continues smoothly from that point on.

Summary

In the final session of this chapter you have had an introduction to objects, specifically to the **Err** object. You have seen how the properties and methods of the **Err** object can be used to gather all the information you need to trap the errors you might expect. The **On Error** statements showed how to guide the program flow to error handlers, switching the error handling on and off as necessary. The **Resume** statements showed how to restart the program after an error has been processed. Within the error handling routines, the **Err** object was used to determine the type of error that had just occurred and, therefore, the most appropriate action to take before restarting.

1. Whose fault is it when software crashes?
   a. The computer's
   b. The user's
   c. The programmer's
   d. The software's

2. An object is
   a. a collection of procedures.
   b. functionally related procedures.
   c. procedures accessed via properties and methods.
   d. answers b. and c. together.

3. The `Err` object *cannot* supply information about
   a. the reason for the error.
   b. the error number.
   c. Help files.
   d. the next line of code to process.

4. The `Err.Raise` method can be used to
   a. generate mock errors in order to debug error handling code.
   b. force the `Err` object to ignore the previous error.
   c. collate and display all of the error information.
   d. reboot a machine that has crashed.

5. `On Error Goto 0` will
   a. force a code restart after a fatal error.
   b. prevent errors from being reported.
   c. switch off the effects of any previous `On Error` statements.
   d. restart on the line following line zero.

Difficulty: Difficult

1. Write a procedure that can decode numbers sent to it and display a message relevant to the number. Using the `On Error Goto` statement, detect and trap a VBScript error of your choice. From the procedure's error handling code, make a call to the decoder. The call should include a number that results in the display of a message appropriate to the error trapped.

Test your error handling using the `Err.Raise` method to artificially trigger the error that you have chosen to trap. After the display of an appropriate message, restart the code at a suitable place using a form of the `Resume` command.

Difficulty: Moderate

2. Using `On Error Resume Next` statements, create an error handling routine that traps an error of your choice. The code must restart cleanly. Raise the error to test your error handling code.

CHAPTER SUMMARY

In this chapter, we learned the fundamentals of solid program construction by using a variety of techniques, including subroutines, functions, the **If...Then...Else** construct, the **For...Next** Loop, the **Do** loop construct, the **Select Case** statement, looping, and more. Finally, we explored linking VBScript code to the user interface and events, and discovered how to create robust code by using error trapping to anticipate the full range of possible user actions. In the next chapter, we will further explore interaction with the end user.

CHAPTER 6

TALK TO THE USER!

The first five chapters introduced you to the fundamentals of using HTML, Visual Basic Script, Internet Explorer, and ActiveX. Now, how do we begin to put this all together to build Web pages that allow us to interact with users in a new way?

In this chapter we will explore a variety of ways you can build Web pages that will provide a new experience for your Web page users. We will build things like spinning text, hypertext graphics, pop-up menus, and much, much more. These are the kinds of things that Web authors only dreamed about doing but that now will be fairly easy to implement. So without further ado, let's get started!

In this chapter we will cover the following topics:

- Utilizing the Visual Basic Script MsgBox Function
- Confirming User Input
- Using an Image Map for Navigation
- Building Dynamic Feedback Panels
- Building a Simple Image Browser
- Playing Sounds from Your Web Pages
- Utilizing the Pop-Up Menu ActiveX Control
- Building an Introduction Screen for Your Web Site

GETTING THE MESSAGE ACROSS

Do you ever feel as if you are really never understood? Well, this session is for you! With new tools provided in Visual Basic Script, a whole new set of opportunities is available for communicating directly with your users.

Now that we have the ability to manipulate ActiveX labels, HTML buttons, the windows status bar, and so on, the information displayed in these items can be dynamically controlled. For example, from Visual Basic Script we can change the caption of an HTML button with a simple statement, as follows:

```
button.value = "new value"
```

Simply by setting a new value for the button control, we have new options for making our controls *state* dependent. An example would be playing a game. While the game is stopped, the button value could be Play. While the game is in play, the button value could be Stop. Thus, this one HTML button can now be used for different purposes.

Another example of available options is the ability to set the status bar text of the Internet Explorer browser by referencing the **status** property of the **Window** object. We can set this status based on user actions in our Web document.

To dig deeper, a sample Web page of some of these examples in action is provided in the Session1 subdirectory of Chapter 6 on the CD-ROM. Figure 6-1 shows the Web page as it starts up.

Try clicking on all the buttons to see the resulting effects. The label in the first row and column will be updated by the button next to it, the next row of buttons will have its values updated, and the last three will set the window's status bar. Figure 6-2 shows a sample of the changes.

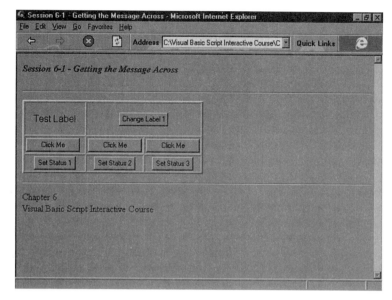

Figure 6-1
Sample message
Web page

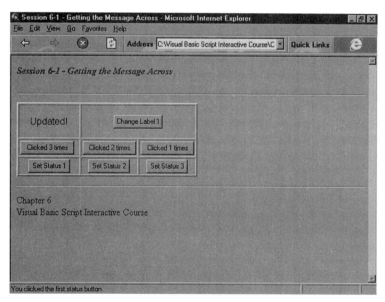

Figure 6-2
Updated message
Web page

Let's review how each update is accomplished. The following is the HTML code for updating the label control.

```
Sub LBLBtn_OnClick()
.....IeLabel1.caption = "Updated!"
End Sub
```

When the button is clicked on, the code references the caption value of the label control, and its caption is updated to display the new text, **"Updated!"**. The following code demonstrates the changes in the button values using Visual Basic Script:

```
Sub Button1_OnClick()

.....Click1Count = Click1Count + 1

.....Button1.value = "Clicked " & Click1Count & " times"

End Sub
```

In this example, there is a global counter that is incremented each time the button is clicked. We then display the new button value by concatenating the **"Clicked "** text with the counter value and then the **"times"** text. Each button will reflect the number of times each was clicked.

Finally, the browser status bar is set by clicking on the other three buttons using the following code:

```
Sub Status1_OnClick()

.....SetStatus "You clicked the first status button"

End Sub

Sub SetStatus(Status)

.....window.status = status

End Sub
```

A general subroutine, **SetStatus**, is provided to set the window status value based on the **Status** argument. Each click event for the buttons calls this subroutine and passes in the text to be displayed. Remember that the browser also uses the status bar based on various events the user may initiate on the Web page.

This example provides a few ideas of new ways in which you will be able to move beyond static HTML using Visual Basic Script. In the next session, we will get a taste of how a confirmation can be performed to ensure the user's actions were intended.

1. What will be the caption of the label control in the following code sample once the timer has fired twice? Assume the timer interval is 100 and it is enabled.

```
<SCRIPT LANGUAGE="VBScript">

Sub IeTimer1_Timer()

.....Counter = Counter + 1
```

```
.....IeLabel1.Caption = Counter

.....If Counter = 2 then Counter = 7

End Sub

</SCRIPT>
```

        a. 0
        b. 1
        c. 7
        d. 2

2. Which statement is true about setting the Window Status text?
    a. It can be set only from a click event of a button control.
    b. The status is also set by the browser and not just from Visual Basic Script code.
    c. The status bar can show several status messages at once based on multiple events.
    d. The status will be displayed only for a few brief seconds based on the user's preference settings for the browser.

3. What is wrong with the following code example?

```
<INPUT TYPE=BUTTON NAME=BUTTON VALUE="BUTTON">

<SCRIPT LANGUAGE="VBScript">

Dim Counter

Sub Button_OnClick()

.....Counter = Counter + 5

.....Button.caption = Counter

End Sub

</SCRIPT>
```

    a. The counter increment should be by 1, not 5.
    b. The input element should be after the script.
    c. You cannot set the button caption to just the value in `Counter`.
    d. `Caption` is not a property of the HTML button element.

4. What statement would have to be added to the `LBLBtn_OnClick` subroutine in our sample document to change the font size of the label to 20 point?
    a. `window.ielabel1.fontsize = 20`
    b. `ielabel1.fontsize=20`
    c. `ielabel1.fontsize=20`
    d. All of the above

5. Which variable in the sample document is a global variable?
   a. Click1Count
   b. Click1Count+1
   c. Click1Count&
   d. All of the above

Difficulty: Intermediate

1. Update the sample program provided on the CD-ROM so that when the Change Label 1 button is selected, the label caption will be updated and the text will be a larger point size and will have a random color.

Difficulty: Intermediate

2. Add a reset button to the table that, when clicked, will reset the label control, clear the status bar, and return the three Click Me buttons to their original state.

CONFIRMING A USER'S ACTION

In previous chapters, the **MsgBox** function has been used to display various values in our code examples, and we have purposely glossed over some of the available features of the function. In this session we will take a closer look at how the **MsgBox** function can be utilized to query the user to have the user provide feedback confirmation and then take appropriate action from our code.

There are many argument options available for configuring the display of the dialog box to the user. Specifically, the second **MsgBox** argument allows the developer to configure what icons and buttons are displayed. The following table overviews these argument settings:

Value	Description
0	OK button only
1	OK and Cancel buttons
2	Abort, Retry, and Ignore buttons
3	Yes, No, and Cancel buttons
4	Yes and No buttons
5	Retry and Cancel buttons
16	Critical Message icon
32	Warning Query icon

Value	Description
48	Warning Message icon
64	Information Message icon
0	First button is the default
256	Second button is the default
512	Third button is the default
768	Fourth button is the default
0	The message box is modal and the user must respond to the message box before continuing work in the current application.
4096	The message box is system-modal and no other system interaction can take place until the user responds to the message box.

Table 6-1 *Button Argument Options*

As you can see, there are many different configuration options. Keep in mind that you can combine these settings by adding up the values when setting the second argument. For example, the following code will show a message box with Yes and No buttons, and the second button will be the default:

```
ReturnValue = msgbox("Prompt", 4 + 256)
```

Also note that one does not have to have each argument of **MsgBox** defined to call the function. And a value does not have to be returned as shown in earlier sessions in the book. If a value is returned from the function, then that value indicates which button was selected. The following table describes what each return value means:

Value	Button
1	OK
2	Cancel
3	Abort
4	Retry
5	Ignore
6	Yes
7	No

Table 6-2 *MsgBox return values*

Now that these options have been reviewed, let's put them into action through some samples. Open the Web page provided in the Session2 subdirectory of Chapter6 on the CD-ROM. The Web page has three buttons and a text input element for data entry. Type some text into the input element and click on each button. Each resulting dialog box is configured differently. In Figure 6-3, the first button shows the following **MsgBox**:

Following is the **MsgBox** function call:

```
RetVal = msgbox(
         "Are you sure you wanted to enter the following text:"
         & chr(10) & chr(10) & txtInput.value, 3+64, "Verify1")
```

For the **Button** argument, the value has been set to 3 and 64 (67 total), which indicates that the Yes, No, and Cancel buttons will be shown as well as the information icon. If you select the No button, a value of 7, the text in the input text element is cleared. For the second message box, one more button argument value has been added, 256, to indicate that the No button should be the default. The third message box is shown in Figure 6-4.

The code for this message box is as follows:

```
RetVal = msgbox(
         "Are you sure you wanted to enter the following text:"
         & chr(10) & chr(10) & txtInput.value, 4+48, "Verify3")
```

In this example, the values of 4 and 48 are used to define the buttons and icon. The 4 value indicates that the Yes and No buttons should be shown, and the 48 shows the Warning Message icon.

The **MsgBox** dialog box can be customized to show different prompts, titles, buttons, icons, and so on, and based on the user response, appropriate action can be taken. As this example shows, the text box is cleared if the user indicates No to the query. The **MsgBox** function will become an important part of your Web page development tool set.

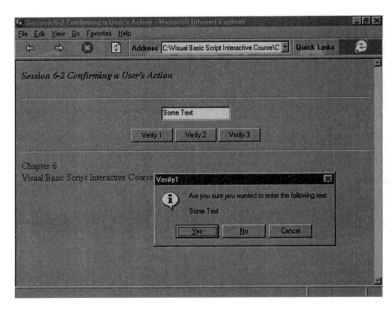

Figure 6-3
MsgBox Web page

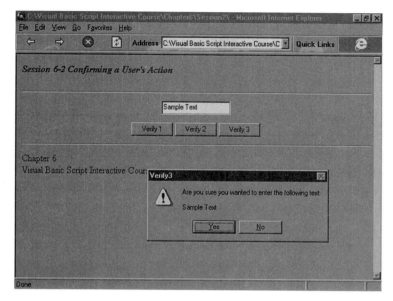

Figure 6-4
Final message box

1. What is wrong with the following **MsgBox** statement?

```
RetVal=MsgBox("Prompt", 3 & 44, "Title")
```

    a. Not all of the arguments are defined.
    b. The arguments are out of order.
    c. 3 and 44 are not valid values.
    d. None of the above.

2. What does the following code do?

```
RetVal = msgbox("Yes or No?", 4+48)

If RetVal = 5 then

.....RetVal=msgbox("Why?")

End If
```

    a. If the user answers "Yes", shows the second message box.
    b. If the user answers "No", shows the second message box.
    c. Only one message box is shown.
    d. An error will occur because no buttons are defined for the second message box.

3. What is the number of icons you can show in a single message box?
   a. 0
   b. 1
   c. 2
   d. 3

4. What is wrong with the following statement?

```
MsgBox("Line 1" chr(10) "Line 2", 4 + 48, "Title")
```

   a. There is no variable defined to retrieve the return value.
   b. There need to be '&' characters in the prompt to make it display correctly.
   c. Both a. and b.
   d. None of the above.

5. What will be the second parameter value of the **MsgBox** function if we want to show the Abort, Retry, Ignore buttons, the Critical Message icon, and have the second button as the default?
   a. 275
   b. 174
   c. 274
   d. 298

EXERCISE 2

Difficulty: Intermediate

1. Write a code fragment that will provide the user with three buttons: Abort, Retry, and Ignore. Use a `Select...Case` statement to effect an action based upon the response.

SESSION 3

USING AN IMAGE MAP FOR NAVIGATION

Well, now that we have played around with changing captions, values, and popping up message dialog boxes all over the place, we are now ready to move on to to some more *graphical* examples.

Image maps are useful for providing graphical hot links to other Web documents and other parts of your Web pages. But, we can use our Visual Basic Script toolbox to provide more capabilities to work with an image map.

In this session, an example will be built by providing feedback based on the mouse location over an image. Figure 6-5 shows the sample Web page which can be found in the Session3 subdirectory of Chapter6 on the CD-ROM.

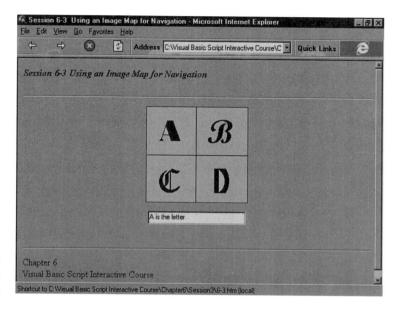

Figure 6-5
Image map
Web page

The following HTML code sets up the image map:

```
<!-- Build a link with no actual jump document -->
<A id="ImageLink" href="">

<!-- Show the bitmap image -->
<IMG SRC="6-3.bmp" WIDTH=176 HEIGHT=163 BORDER=1 NAME=Letters>

</A>
```

First, there is a link setup named "ImageLink". In this case, there is no reference document to jump to when the image is clicked on. Next, the image is shown using the **<IMG>** tag. The bitmap is also provided on the CD-ROM.

Next, an HTML input text box element is placed on the Web page. This is where feedback will be provided based on the mouse pointer location over the image. Then, the script starts as follows:

```
<!-- Start the script. -->
<SCRIPT language="VBScript">

'  The MouseMove event of the ImageLink
Sub ImageLink_MouseMove(Shift, Button, X, Y)
```

The first subroutine in the script is the **MouseMove** event of the link we set up in the document. This event will be fired off every time the mouse moves over the image. The four parameters are the status of the shift key, mouse button, X location, and Y location. In this session, we will be working with the X and Y location of the mouse over the image.

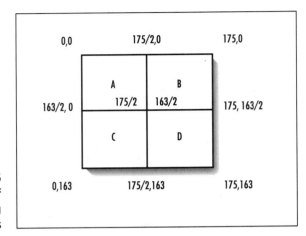

Figure 6-6
The coordinates of
the bounding
boxes

In the following code, a check is done to see which quadrant of the graphic the mouse is in. The width of the image is 175 pixels and the height is 163 pixels. Figure 6-6 shows the coordinates of the bounding boxes that surround each image.

Next in the code is the **InRect** subroutine which is being called to check if the X and Y location of the mouse is in the specified bounding box for each character. If the mouse is in the bounding box, then an appropriate message is displayed in the HTML input text box element.

```
'  We check to see if the mouse is over the 'A'
If (InRect(X, Y,  0, 0, 175/2, 163/2)=true) then

.....'  Indicate we are over the A
.....HelpText.value = "A is the letter"

Else

.....'  Check to see if we are over the 'C'
.....If (InRect(X, Y,  0, 163/2, 175/2, 163)=true) then

.......'  Indicate we are over the C
.......HelpText.value = "C is the letter"

.....Else

.......'  Check to see if we are over the 'B'
.......If (InRect(X, Y,  175/2, 0, 175, 163/2)=true) then

........'  Indicate we are over the B
........HelpText.value = "B is the letter"

...    ..Else

........'  Check to see if we are over the 'D'
........If (InRect(X, Y,  175/2, 163/2, 175, 163)=true) then
```

```
..........'  Indicate we are over the D
..........HelpText.value = "D is the letter"

........End If
......End If
....End If
End If

End Sub
```

The **InRect** function takes in the X and Y mouse location and the coordinates to check the location. A set of AND logic is done to check each coordinate. If all are true, then **InRect** will return true; otherwise, it will return false.

```
Function InRect(X, Y, X1, Y1, X2, Y2)

.....'  We check to see if the X coordinate
.....'  is between the two X boundaries. We also
     '  check to see if the Y coordinate is between
     '  the two boundaries. InRect will either return
     '  true or false.
     InRect =  X >= X1 AND X <= X2 AND Y >= Y1 AND Y <= Y2

End Function

</script>
```

The final result is that with each mouse move over the image, an appropriate message about that section of the image is displayed. Having this type of capability opens up many options for providing interactive graphics in your documents.

1. The Image Map **MouseMove** event
   a. is fired off whenever the mouse moves.
   b. is fired off whenever the mouse moves over the image map.
   c. controls the movement of the mouse.
   d. is fired off whenever the mouse moves onto the image map.

2. Which statement would correctly add a link document to our sample Web page link?
   a. `<A id="ImageLink" href="Link.htm">`
   b. `<IMG SRC="6-3.bmp" . .. href="Link.htm">`
   c. `<input type="text"  .. href="Link.htm">`
   d. None of the above.

3. What will the `InRect` subroutine return for the following values?
Function InRect(34, 90, 80, 10, 120, 100)
   a. True
   b. False
   c. 34
   d. 66

4. What is wrong with the following subroutine?

```
Sub Link_MouseMove(A, B)

.....IF A > 200 then

......MsgBox "You are over it now!"

.....Else

......MsgBox "You are not over it now!"

.....End if

End Sub
```

   a. Y is not checked and thus the location test will not be valid.
   b. There is no shift key and mouse button arguments for the `MouseMove` sub-routine declaration.
   c. The X and Y coordinates should be named X and Y, not A and B.
   d. `Link_MouseMove` is not a valid name for the script event.

5. What is wrong with the following Image Map?

```
<IMG SRC="XXX.bmp" HEIGHT=195 BORDER=2 NAME="Name">
```

   a. There is no width value.
   b. The border value should be 0 or 1.
   c. The height value cannot be greater than 100.
   d. None of the above.

Difficulty: Difficult

1. Update the sample Web page so that when one of the four quadrants is clicked on, a jump to a different Web page is performed.

BUILDING INFORMATION PANELS

In this session we are going to discuss paneling—not the dark, smoking room type, but help panels that provide information and feedback to your users. A good example of a panel built right into the browser is the status bar at the bottom. Our documents can go beyond that using the new tools we have at hand. Figure 6-7 shows an example of how a help panel might be implemented on a Web page.

The diagram depicts a Web browser with HTML input elements and a help panel below them. The idea is to have feedback on each input element as the user is interacting with each element. The CD-ROM provides a similar sample Web page located in the Session4 subdirectory of the Chapter6 directory. Figure 6-8 shows the Web page.

There are several input elements on the Web page in a table format. The last row on the Web page is the help panel for the input text elements. Figure 6-9 shows the help panel in action.

The help panel shows the text "Enter in Your First and Last Name". This was placed in the panel when the Name text element was selected. So you are wondering, how did this happen? Well, the code is fairly complicated, but let's see if it can be muddled through. The following is the code to place the Name help text in the panel:

```
'  The OnFocus event of the name text element
Sub NAME_OnFocus()
.....'  Set the caption
.....IeLabel1.Caption = "Enter in your First and Last Name"
End Sub
```

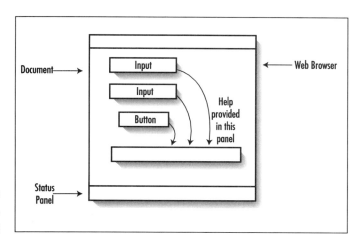

Figure 6-7
Web page help
panels

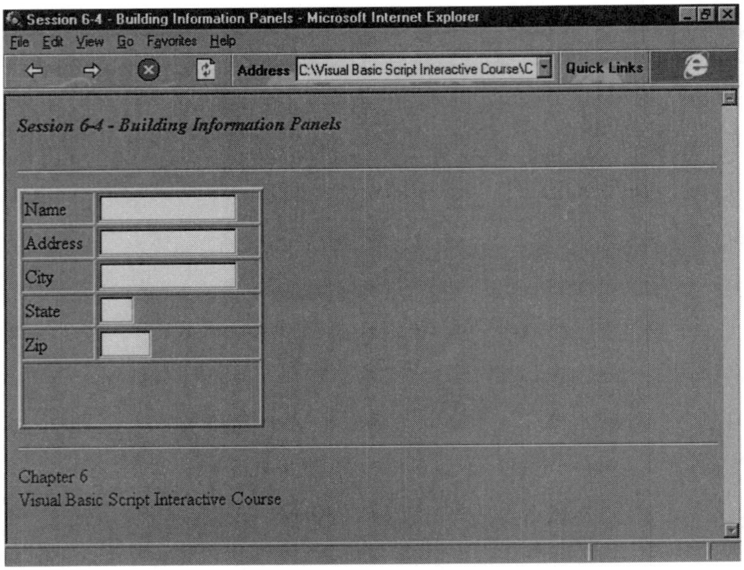

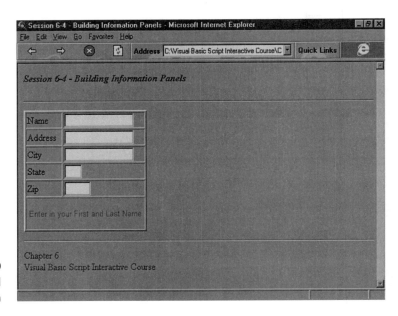

Figure 6-8
Sample help
panel Web page

Overwhelmed? As you can see, it is very simple! The **OnFocus** event of the Name HTML input element is used. An element gets *the focus* when it is selected for input. So, when the Name textbox is clicked on for input, the caption of an ActiveX label control that was placed in the last table row is updated. This same action is repeated for each textbox on the Web page.

Figure 6-9
Help panel
in action

There is also an opposite function of OnFocus, OnBlur, which is fired off when the user leaves the text element. This functionality can be used to test the data entered by the user and can take appropriate action.

Help panels can provide effective and easy feedback to your Web page users. You can, of course, modify all of the properties of the label control to change its point size, fore color, and so on, to make its appearance *fit* the situation.

1. Which of the following would be an appropriate implementation of the OnBlur event for the name label?
   a. `Dim Name_Blur() End Sub`
   b. `Dim Name_OnBlur() End Sub`
   c. `Dim NameOnBlur() End Sub`
   d. `Dim OnBlur_Name() End Sub`

2. Which statement is true?
   a. The HTML specification requires that help panels be provided for your input elements.
   b. The browser status bar can be moved around the Web page to act as a help panel.
   c. Help panels can only be manipulated through the OnFocus event.
   d. Help panels are built at the discretion of the Web page designer and can be a helpful tool.

3. With the _____ you can _____ any of its _____ to change the way the _____.
   a. label control…change…methods …label appears
   b. label control… change… properties…help message comes across
   c. text input element… change… properties…help message comes across
   d. label control… combine… properties…help message comes across

4. The help panel must appear _____ _____ all input elements that help will be provided on.
   a. directly before
   b. directly after
   c. beside
   d. none of the above

5. What event is fired when a text input element is exited?
   a. `Blur`
   b. `Exit`
   c. `OnBlur`
   d. `OnExit`

Difficulty: Intermediate

1. Add a feature to the sample help panel so that when the text in another help panel is clicked on, a link to a help page provides additional help on the current input item.

BUILDING A SIMPLE IMAGE BROWSER

We could not go any further in this chapter without playing around some more with displaying images in our Web pages. In this session, a simple image browser is going to be built that will allow the user to flip through a series of images. To do this, we will have to put together the use of frames and Visual Basic Script. In fact, this session will really give you an idea of how powerful it is to be able to build HTML on the fly from your scripts.

The image browser will utilize a frame that will essentially be the *browsing* window for viewing each image. This HTML code to display an image in this frame will be dynamically created from our script code. Figure 6-10 gives an overview of how this process will work.

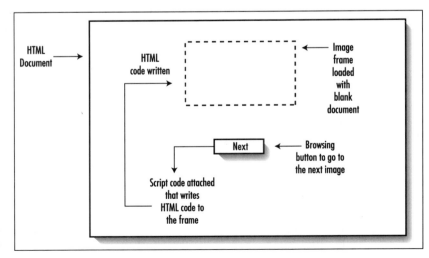

Figure 6-10
Image browser
overview

As you can see from this diagram, a frame has HTML code written to it based on the click of an HTML button element. To do this, a reference has to be made to the frame's document from the script in the parent document. The following statement is an example of doing this:

```
window.frames(0).document.write HTMLCODE
```

The window that the parent document resides in contains a collection that has all the frames for the document in it. Since we only have one frame in the document, the first indexed frame is the one we wish to write the HTML code to which is contained in the HTML code variable. Also, the frame can be referenced directly using the frame name or it can use the parent object to references the frames since the parent document is where our script is located. Once the code has been written to the frame document, it is a good idea to close the document as follows:

```
window.frames(0).document.close
```

Let's look at the sample document provided in the Session5 subdirectory of Chapter6 on the CD-ROM. Figure 6-11 shows the Web page.

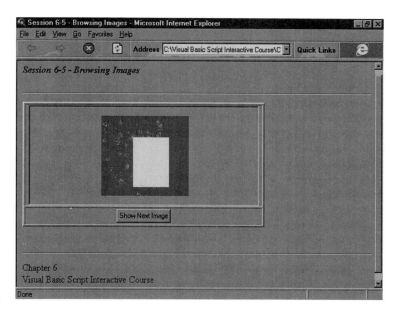

Figure 6-11
Image browser
Web page

First, let's review how the table is set up to display the frame and the button. The HTML code is as follows:

```
<!-- Start the table -->
<TABLE WIDTH=70% Border=2>

<!-- First row with the frame -->
<TR>
  <TD ALIGN=CENTER HEIGHT=100>
    <FRAME SCROLLING="NO" HEIGHT=170 WIDTH=400 SRC="empty.htm"
           NAME="Frame1">
  </TD>
</TR>

<!-- Second row with the browse button -->
<TR>
  <TD HEIGHT=30 WIDTH=100% ALIGN="CENTER">
  <INPUT TYPE="BUTTON" VALUE="Show Next Image"
         NAME="ImageBrowse" OnClick="ShowNext">
  </TD>
</TR>

</TABLE>
```

The first row builds a frame in the column that is named **Frame1**. An empty HTML text file is provided as the document to be initially loaded into the frame, and the frame is set up not to scroll. The second column will contain the HTML button element and we have defined the subroutine for the **OnClick** event to be **"ShowNext"**. The **ShowNext** subroutine is as follows:

```
' This subroutine will show the next image
Sub ShowNext()

    Dim NextImage

    ' Increase the image count
    ImageCount = ImageCount + 1

    ' Build the HTML line that will show the
    ' next image. Note that we need to
    ' use double quotes in our HTML code.
    ' So, in Visual Basic Script, we place
    ' two double quotes together - ""
    NextImage = "<CENTER><IMG SRC=""img" & CStr(ImageCount) &
                ".gif""></CENTER></BODY>"

    ' Write that HTML code to the frame to show
    ' the image.
    window.frames(0).document.write NextImage

    ' Close the document
    window.frames(0).document.close

end sub
```

The images are provided on the CD, and their filenames are `IMG#.gif` where the # sign indicates the image number. The `ShowNext` subroutine increments a global variable, `ImageCount`, that will indicate the image we are working with. Next, the `NextImage` variable is built to contain the necessary HTML code to display the image in the frame. This is done by building a simple `<IMG>` tag pointing to the GIF file to be displayed. The only tricky thing about building this HTML code is that we must include the last image number in the GIF filename. This is done by converting the `ImageCount` value into a string and concatenating this number between the `"img"` text and the `".gif"` text. Also note that where we need a double quote in the HTML code, we have to place two double quotes (`""`) together in the string.

Finally, the HTML code contained in NextImage is written to the frame using the frame reference techniques discussed earlier. The final result is that the image is displayed in the frame in the first row of our table, and each subsequent click of the button will move to the next image.

This technique of utilizing dynamic frames through Visual Basic Script code holds a wealth of opportunities for building dynamic Web pages. You can even write scripts to the frame from your parent document Visual Basic Script code as well as references to ActiveX controls and other objects.

1. Consider the following code. Which statement is true?

```
<FRAME HEIGHT=170 WIDTH=400 SRC="empty.htm" NAME="FOO">
<FRAME HEIGHT=170 WIDTH=400 SRC="empty.htm" NAME="FUM">
<FRAME HEIGHT=170 WIDTH=400 SRC="empty.htm" NAME="FI">

<SCRIPT>

window.frame(2).document.write "<BODY BGCOLOR=GREEN>"

</SCRIPT>
```

    a. The third frame will have a background color of green.
    b. The second frame will have a background color of green.
    c. The browser will have an error because there are three frames in the document.
    d. The "Foo" frame will have a background color of green.

2. Which of the following is another valid method for referencing the frame in the sample Web page?
    a. `Frame1.document.write "Stuff"`
    b. `Frames(0).document.write "Stuff"`
    c. `Parent.Frames(0).document.write "Stuff"`
    d. All of the above

3. Which statement does not correctly describe the following code?

```
Sub FOO()

    Dim HTMLCODE

    parent.frames(0).document.write NOW

    parent.frames(0).document.close

end sub
```

    a. The `FOO` subroutine when run will write to the first frame in the frames collection of the parent document.
    b. The frame will have the current date and time written to it.
    c. The frames will continuously have the date and time updated.
    d. Assuming the code works, there is at least one frame in the document.

4. Which statement, if placed immediately after the `ImageCount` variable is increased, will ensure that we do not move beyond the last image and will return us to the first image when the last is reached?
    a. `If ImageCount = 8 then ImageCount = 0`
    b. `If ImageCount = 8 then ImageCount = 1`
    c. `If ImageCount = 7 then ImageCount = 1`
    d. `If ImageCount = 7 then ImageCount = 0`

5. Once HTML code is written to a frame document, what should be done?
    a. The document should be refreshed.
    b. The document should be closed using the `Close` method.
    c. The document should be loaded in the frame.
    d. The browser window should be refreshed.

EXERCISE 5

Difficulty: Intermediate

1. Modify the sample Web page to have a back button as well. Make sure that both buttons will not move beyond the first or last image.

Difficulty: Easy

2. Add a caption to the image in the frame so the user will know the name of the file for the image.

PLAY A SOUND

What Web page would be complete without a beep or melody here and there? Fortunately, playing sounds from your HTML documents is not hard. By simply referencing a Wave or MIDI file on your system, you can have the file played. For example, the following script code will play the chimes wave file that comes standard with Windows 95:

```
location.href="/windows/media/chimes.wav"
```

Note that the forward slash (/) character is used to make the directory references. This is because the UNIX operating system directory system structure uses the '/' character instead of the backslash (\) used in Windows/DOS. Originally, most Internet servers were UNIX-based, and this convention has stuck. If no directory location is provided, the browser will look for the media file where the Web page document is located.

The key to using these media files effectively is how you apply them in your HTML documents. The Web page document provided for this session provides just a couple of ways in which you can use sound in your documents. Figure 6-12 shows the sample Web page.

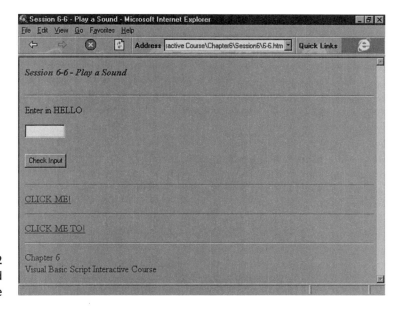

Figure 6-12
Play a sound
Web page

The first part of the document prompts you to enter the HELLO text in the text element. Try entering it correctly and then enter something else and click on the button each time. As you will hear, two different wave files are played. The traditional Chord wave file is played if the answer is incorrect and, if it is correct, the Ding wave file is played. If you review the HTML code, you will see that a simple check is being done on the contents of the HTML text element. But, this simple set of code provides for effective feedback for your Web page user.

The next two sections of the Web page provide hyper links that will actually play a wave file in the first case and play a MIDI file in the second. The **href** attribute of each link is set to the specified media file. But using Visual Basic Script, it is still possible to make a jump to another HTML document. This is done by adding **'location.href= document'** code in the **OnClick** event for each link. Thus, we have effectively played a sound when the link is clicked on, as well as jumped to a new page.

Adding sounds to your documents can be easy and provide effective feedback to your Web page user. Take advantage of the different events exposed to you by the scripting object model and ActiveX control events to effectively add sounds to your documents.

1. What is wrong with the following code?

```
Sub Button_OnClick

.....Location.href="\wavefiles\cool\windy.wav"

End Sub
```

    a. There is no window object referenced before the **Location.href** reference.
    b. The media files are always located in the \windows\media directory.
    c. Nothing; the statement is fine.
    d. The location of the file should be **"/wavefile/cool/windy.wav"**.

2. How can we add a sound playing when the browser window loads?
    a. Play the sound from a script in the **OnLoad** event of the window.
    b. Add **the <BGSOUND SRC="/windows/media/canyon.mid">** tag to the document.
    c. Play the sound from a subroutine in a script that is run when the script is loaded.
    d. All of the above.

3. If no directory location for the media file is specified, where will the browser look for the file?
    a. In the Windows Media directory
    b. On the root of the hard drive
    c. An error will be provided
    d. In the directory location of the Web page

4. What is wrong with the following?

```
<A "/windows/media/CANYON.MID" NAME="MIDLINK">CLICK ME TO!</A>
```

    a. No **HREF** for the document
    b. The beginning **<A** tag should be **<A>**
    c. Nothing is wrong.
    d. The name tag should come before the file location.

5. What operating system is responsible for HTML using '/' references instead of '\' references?
    a. Windows
    b. Windows 95
    c. UNIX
    d. DOS

Difficulty: Easy

1. Build a Web page that will allow the user to sample the Chord, Ding, and Chimes wave files based on a button click provided for each. Use an HTML table to provide a nice interface.

POPPING UP ALL OVER— POP-UP MENUS

We have available to us an ActiveX control that provides the ability to place customized pop-up menus on our HTML forms. This kind of tool provides many different opportunities for adding functionality to our Web pages. The pop-up menu can be invoked as the result of any user action or triggered event. Figure 6-13 shows some examples of how this could be used.

As the diagram shows, one of the most intuitive events to attach a pop-up menu to is the **click** event of an HTML input element or an ActiveX control. For example, we might provide a whole list of documents to jump to on a menu based on the click of a HTML hyper link. Or, when a label control is clicked on, we might provide formatting options for the text.

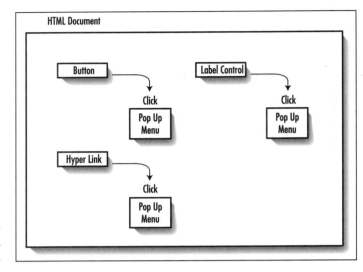

Figure 6-13
Pop-up menus
placed in HTML
documents

The pop-up menu control provides for dynamic menus to be created; reviewing this functionality will be the subject of the sample Web page provided for this session. Figure 6-14 shows the Web page.

If you click on the first button, a pop-up menu will be displayed. You can add and remove items from this menu using the second set of buttons. Figure 6-15 shows the pop-up menu after several menu items have been added.

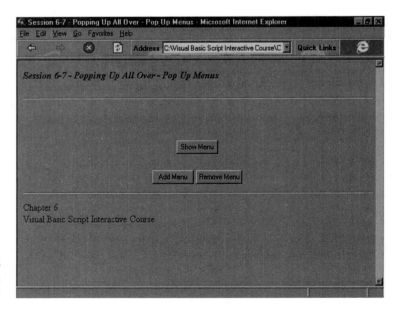

Figure 6-14
Pop-up menu
Web page

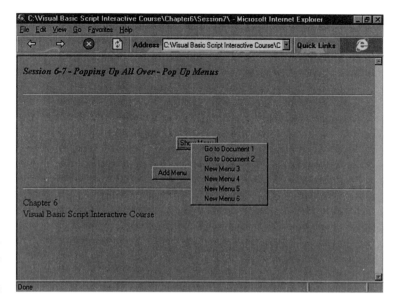

Figure 6-15
Pop-up menu Web
page with added
menu items

Select either of the first two menu items and the browser will jump to a sample document. This is accomplished by using the **Click** event of the menu. This event returns the index of the menu item selected.

Pop-Up Menu Methods and Events

Click—Fired off when one of the menu items is selected. The argument indicates which menu item was selected.
PopUp—Displays the pop-up menu.
AddItem—Adds another menu item to the menu with the text specified.
RemoveItem—Removes the menu item indicated by the passed in index.

The following is the click event code for the menu provided in the sample Web page:

```
'  Click event of the menu control
Sub Iepop1_Click(ByVal x)

.....'  Check the menu item clicked
.....select case x

.......'  First item
.......case 1

........'  Jump to document 1
........Location.href = "doc1.htm"

.......'  Second item
.......case 2
```

```
........'  Jump to document 2
........location.href = "doc2.htm"

........'  Any other menu items
........case Else

........'  Tell the user they clicked on a menu item
........MsgBox "You clicked on a new menu item!"

.....End Select

end sub
```

The **Select Case** construct is used to determine which menu item was selected. For the first two, a jump is made to another document. For the rest, a message box is shown.

For the **Click** events of the Add Menu and Remove Menu buttons, the **AddItem** and **RemoveItem** methods of the control are called. You can add and delete items to the menu as you wish. Keep in mind that it is good practice to not let your menus get overly large and overwhelm the user with selection options.

Adding pop-up menus to your documents is fairly easy. And, as you can see, it will be easy for you to begin using them immediately!

1. Assuming that the pop-up menu has two menu items to begin with, what will be the result of the following code fragment?

```
Iepop1.additem("Menu")
Iepop1.additem("Menu")
Iepop1.additem("Menu")

For N = 1 to 2
.....IePop1.RemoveItem(N)
Next N
```

    a. The menu will have no items left on it.
    b. The menu will have one item left on it.
    c. The menu will have two items left on it.
    d. The menu will have three items left on it.

2. The_____ method _____ the menu item _____.
    a. **RemoveItem**...removes...indicated by the passed in index.
    b. **AddItem**...adds...indicated by alphabetical value of the text.
    c. **PopUp**...displays...indicated by the passed in index.
    d. **Click**...displays...indicated by the passed in index.

3. What will be the caption of the fourth menu item, assuming there are no menu items to start with?

```
Iepop1.additem("Menu 1")
IePop1.RemoveItem(1)
Iepop1.additem("Menu 2")
Iepop1.additem("Menu 2")
Iepop1.additem("Menu 3")
Iepop1.additem("Menu 4")
Iepop1.additem("Menu 5")
IePop1.RemoveItem(1)
```

     a. Menu 2
     b. Menu 3
     c. Menu 1
     d. Menu 5

4. The click event of the pop-up menu control can only be activated by
     a. calling it from a button click event.
     b. calling it from a mouse move event.
     c. calling it from a link click event.
     d. all of the above.

5. The _____ _____ displays the _____ for the Pop-Up menu control.
     a. **PopUp** event…menu
     b. **Add Item**… item
     c. **Remove Item**… item
     d. **PopUp** event… list

EXERCISE 7

Difficulty: Intermediate

   1. Display a pop-up menu based on the click of a hyper link.

Difficulty: Intermediate

   2. Display a pop-up menu based on the click of an ActiveX label control.

BUILD AN INTRODUCTION SCREEN

In this last session, a little more razzle-dazzle will be built using the ActiveX timer control and label control. As we have seen in earlier sessions, we can combine these two to provide some interesting text effects.

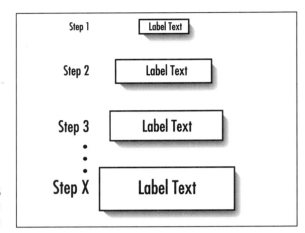

Figure 6-16
Expanding label
control

These two can be combined again to build an introduction screen to your HTML Web pages. Figure 6-16 shows the effect of changing the font size of a label control centered on our Web page over time.

With each step of the timer, we can increase the size of the font and have the text literally explode onto the Web page. The demonstration Web page provided with this session on the CD-ROM shows an example of building an introduction screen to our Web pages. Figures 6-17 and 6-18 show the different steps in the animation sequence.

So, how is this little bit of magic performed? First insert the ActiveX label control into the document. Set the initial point size to something relatively small, like 7. The key to ensure that larger font sizes will be visible is to make sure the width and height of the label control will allow the larger point size font to be visible. Decide on the point size you would like to expand to, set the label font size to that size, and then size the label accordingly for your caption text. Once sized properly, return the font size to the smaller size.

Figure 6-17
Initial step in the
welcome screen

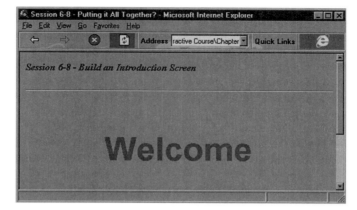

Figure 6-18
Near completion step in the welcome screen

Next, insert the timer control and set the interval at the speed at which you want the animation to take place. You can play around with different speeds to test the animation. In the sample Web page, the interval is set to a random value between 100 and 200.

The **Timer** event of the timer control is where the code will need to go to change the font size of the label control. The key will be to limit the number of size steps so the animation will come to an end. In the Web page example, this is done by allowing a global counter variable **SizeCount** to increment up to 25. Once the value is 25, the timer is disabled and the label control caption is cleared so that the text is not visible.

Providing these text effects is fairly simple and yet can be very effective in grabbing the Web page user's attention. Experiment with setting different properties of the label control to build all kind of welcome screens. And, remember, you can also dynamically change the caption of the label so you can have all kinds of words popping up in your introduction screen.

1. Assuming the same setup as provided in the sample Web page, what will be the effect of the following?

```
Sub IeTimer1_Timer()

.....If SizeCount = 25 then
.......ielabel1.caption = "DONE"
.....End If

.....SizeCount = SizeCount + 1

.....ieLabel1.fontsize = ielabel1.fontsize + 3

End Sub
```

a. The code will continue to increment the font size of the label by 3.

b. The timer will never stop ticking.

c. "DONE" will be displayed when the **SizeCount** reaches 25.

d. All of the above.

2. Assuming the same setup as provided in the sample Web page, what will be the effect of the following?

```
Sub IeTimer1_Timer()

.....SizeCount = SizeCount + 1

.....If SizeCount = 1 then
.......ielabel1.fontsize = 50
.......ieTimer1.enabled = False
.....   Exit Sub
.....End If

.....ieLabel1.fontsize = ielabel1.fontsize - 1

End Sub
```

a. The timer will only tick one time because **SizeCount** is initialized to 0 and the resulting Font Size will be 50 for the label.

b. This is in effect reversing the process of the original example. The label caption will start out large and continue to shrink.

c. This is in effect reversing the process of the original example. The label caption will start out large and continue to shrink until **SizeCount** is 1.

d. The label caption will start out small and continue to grow as the original example did.

3. Assuming the same setup as provided in the sample Web page, what will be the effect of the following?

```
Sub IeTimer1_Timer()

.....If SizeCount = 25 then
.......ieTimer1.enabled = False
.......ielabel1.caption = ""
.......Exit Sub
.....End If

.....SizeCount = SizeCount + 1

.....ieLabel1.angle = ielabel1.angle + 3

End Sub
```

a. The same as the original example.

b. Assuming a starting angle value of 0, the label will be rotated by 75 degrees.

c. Assuming a starting angle of 0, the label will be rotated by 72 degrees.

d. Assuming a starting angle of 0, the label will be rotated by 78 degrees.

4. Assuming the same setup as provided in the sample Web page, what will be the effect of the following?

```
Sub IeTimer1_Timer()

.....If SizeCount = 25 then
.......ieTimer1.enabled = False
.......ielabel1.caption = ""
.......Exit Sub
.....End If

.....ieLabel1.fontsize = ielabel1.fontsize + 2

End Sub
```

    a. Assuming an initial angle of 10, the label font size will be 60.
    b. Assuming an initial angle of 10, the label font size will be 50.
    c. Assuming an initial angle of 10, the label font size will be 70.
    d. The label font size will continue to be incremented.

5. How could the effect be reversed?

```
Sub IeTimer1_Timer()

.....If SizeCount = 25 then
.......ieTimer1.enabled = False
.......ielabel1.caption = ""
.......Exit Sub
.....End If

.....ieLabel1.fontsize = ielabel1.fontsize + 2

End Sub
```

    a. Start the font size out at a large point size and decrement the font size to 0.
    b. Decrement the font size to 0.
    c. Start the font size out at a large point size.
    d. Can't be done.

Difficulty: Easy

1. Add rotating and random color effects to the Introduction screen.

Difficulty: Easy

2. Build a Web page that, with each timer tick, will add one more letter onto an initial blank label control caption to build WELCOME.

CHAPTER SUMMARY

In this chapter, we have begun to see how we can apply Visual Basic Script to our Web pages to make them more interactive and responsive. And, we have begun to see how integrating objects such as ActiveX controls into our Web pages can really make them come alive. In the next several chapters, we will begin to take a look at how we can interact further with browser objects to control the Web page.

INPUT AND
OUTPUT

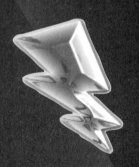

PART III

DOING DOCUMENTS AND WINDOWS

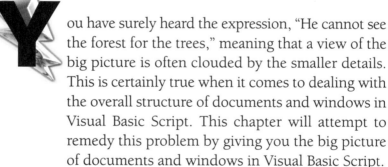

ou have surely heard the expression, "He cannot see the forest for the trees," meaning that a view of the big picture is often clouded by the smaller details. This is certainly true when it comes to dealing with the overall structure of documents and windows in Visual Basic Script. This chapter will attempt to remedy this problem by giving you the big picture of documents and windows in Visual Basic Script.

Let's start by looking at a diagram of the overall structure of documents and windows in Visual Basic Script. Figure 7-1 shows such a diagram. Notice that windows are the top level of objects within Visual Basic Script. Windows can contain a variety of other objects, including documents. In turn, documents can contain links, anchors, and forms.

217

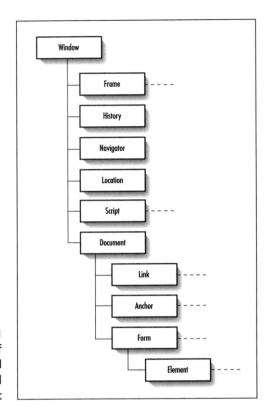

Figure 7-1
Overall structure of
documents and
windows in Visual
Basic Script

The **Frame** object simply references the frames contained in a specific window. Each of these frames is, in turn, a window with its own properties, including a document. Frames are covered briefly in Session 1, "Working with Windows and Frames," and they are covered in detail in Chapter 12, "I Was Framed!"

The **History** object allows you to access the URLs located in the history folder. These are the URLs previously loaded by the browser. This object is covered in detail in Session 2, "A Little History."

You can use the **Navigator** object to find out information about the particular browser software being used. You can obtain the application name and version, for instance, by using properties of the **Navigator** object. This object is covered in detail in Session 3, "Working with the Browser Program."

Location objects contain information about the location of a URL. The host, protocol, and full URL title are some of the items that can be obtained from the **Location** object. **Link** objects are similar to **Location** objects (they support many of the same properties and methods). However, **Link** objects refer to any **<A HREF=...>** links in a specified HTML document. Both of these objects are covered in detail in Session 4, "Working with Locations and Links."

The **Script** object represents the scripting code defined with the **SCRIPT** tag. Each window has an associated **Script** object. This object is covered in detail in Session 5, titled "Working with Scripts."

The **Document** object makes available a variety of information about the currently displayed document. This information includes the date and time when the document was last modified, various link colors for the document, and the title and location of the document. This object is covered in detail in Session 6, "Working with Documents."

You can use the **Anchor** object to retrieve information about anchor tags contained in an HTML document. This object is covered in detail in Session 7, "Anchors Away!"

Forms and elements are the display components of an HTML document. The **Form** object and **Element** object are used to access these forms and elements. These objects are covered in detail in Session 8, "Working with Forms and Elements."

 **1**

WORKING WITH WINDOWS AND FRAMES

Probably the most important object in the Visual Basic Script object hierarchy is the **Window** object. As shown in Figure 7-1, it contains all the other objects. To access frames, you start with a **Window** object; to access forms, you start with a **Window** object, and so on. The **Window** object that you will likely use most often is the top-level **Window** object because all other objects are descended from the top-level window. You can access the top-level **Window** object using the name *top*. This is not a window which you need to define. Rather, **top** will automatically refer to the top-level window in your object hierarchy. To refer to the main HTML document for a particular page, for example, you could use the top window as shown in Listing 7-1. Figure 7-2 shows the results.

Listing 7-1 Referring to the top-level window

```
<HTML>
<HEAD>
<TITLE>Top-Level Window Test</TITLE>
</HEAD>
<BODY>
<SCRIPT LANGUAGE="VBScript">
document.write "Document title is '" & top.document.title & "'."
</SCRIPT>
</BODY>
</HTML>
```

Using **top** to refer to the top-level window is particularly useful when you are dealing with a page that is divided into several frames. Next we will take a closer look at frames and the technique of using **top** to access the various frames on a page.

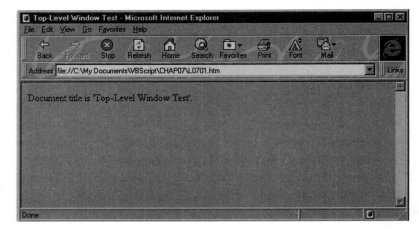

Figure 7-2
Displaying the main
document title

As shown in the object hierarchy of Figure 7-1, each **Window** object can contain multiple frame objects. If you have ever seen a Web page that is separated into several separate areas, each of which seems somewhat independent of the others, then you have seen frames in action. Figure 7-3 shows a simple Web page divided into three frames. Listing 7-2 contains the code to create this page. (The files **top.htm**, **left.htm**, and **main.htm** are not shown because they each simply contain a level-1 heading and some text.)

Listing 7-2 A simple frame example

```
<HTML>
<HEAD>
<TITLE>Frame Example</TITLE>
</HEAD>
<BODY>
<FRAMESET ROWS="70,*">
<FRAME NAME="frmAbove" SRC="above.htm" SCROLLING=NO>
<FRAMESET COLS="100,*">
<FRAME NAME="frmLeft" SRC="left.htm" SCROLLING=NO>
<FRAME NAME="frmMain" SRC="main.htm">
</BODY>
</HTML>
```

An entire chapter, Chapter 12, has been devoted to frames, so you do not need to under-stand how to create them at this time. The important thing to notice about Listing 7-2 is that each frame is given an arbitrary name which we will be able to use to identify that frame from our Visual Basic Script code. You specify the name of each frame using the **NAME="framename"** parameter of the **FRAME** tag. Although you are not required to give each frame a name, it is a good practice to always supply one.

There are at least two different ways to reference a frame within a window: by name and by number. In either case, you use a window's **frames** property to reference a specific frame.

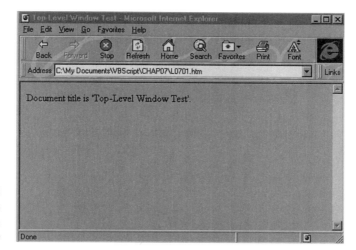

Figure 7-3
A simple example
of frames within a
window

To reference a frame by name, use the following syntax:

```
window.frames("framename")
```

To reference a frame by number, use the following syntax:

```
window.frames(framenumber)
```

In each of the above examples, you would replace **window** with a specific **Window** object. Using this syntax along with **top** to refer to the top-level window, we can reference each of the frames in Listing 7-2 by name as follows:

```
top.frames("frmAbove") ' the frame that is above the others

top.frames("frmLeft")  ' the left frame (bottom-left)

top.frames("frmMain")  ' the main frame (bottom-right)
```

As we learned earlier, the window referenced by **top** means something special to the browser: It means the top-level window. In our example, the top-level window is the window which contains the other three frames. Now let's see how we can reference each of the frames in our example by number:

```
top.frames(0)    ' the top frame

top.frames(1)    ' the left frame (bottom-left)

top.frames(2)    ' the main frame (bottom-right)
```

Notice that we reference our first frame with the number 0 rather than 1. Notice also that the frames are referenced by a number based on the order in which they were created. Since the top frame was the first frame we specified in Listing 7-2, we reference the top frame as number 0. Since the left frame was the second frame we specified in

Listing 7-2, we reference the left frame as number 1, and so on. Using numbers to reference your frames is inherently error-prone, and you can avoid a great deal of confusion just by naming your frames.

The topmost object is a `Window` object which, as we stated above, you can reference as top. This `top` window can contain a variety of frames. Each frame is, in turn, also a `Window` object. Therefore, any properties, events, or methods that exist for the `Window` object will also exist for a specific frame. Let's look at some of these properties, events, and methods now.

Accessing the Current Window

To refer to the current `Window` object, you can use the `self` property. If you do not explicitly specify a `Window` object, the current `Window` object will be assumed, so the `self` property may be unnecessary except to make it explicitly clear to which `Window` object you are referring. The `parent` property returns the `Window` object that is the parent of the specified window (or the current window if you do not explicitly specify the window). The `name` property returns the name of the specified `Window` object. Listings 7-3, 7-4, and 7-5 use these properties to demonstrate the various ways you can refer to the current window. The output is shown in Figure 7-4.

Listing 7-3 Set up two frames: a left frame and a right frame

```
<HTML>
<HEAD>
<TITLE>Current Window Test</TITLE>
</HEAD>
<BODY>
<FRAMESET COLS="50%,50%">
<FRAME SRC="L0704.htm" NAME="frmLeft">
<FRAME SRC="L0705.htm" NAME="frmRight">
</FRAMESET>
</BODY>
</HTML>
```

Listing 7-4 HTML for the left frame

```
<HTML>
<HEAD>
<TITLE>Left Frame</TITLE>
</HEAD>
<BODY>
<INPUT TYPE="Button" NAME="cmdDisplay" VALUE="Display">

<SCRIPT LANGUAGE="VBScript">
sub cmdDisplay_OnClick
     ' Refer to current window implicitly.
     st = "Current Window: " & name & Chr(13)

     ' Refer to current window with self property.
     st = st & "Current Window: " &  self.name & Chr(13)
```

```
        ' Refer to frame by name (using parent).
        st = st & "Current Window: " & parent.frames("frmLeft").name & Chr(13)

        ' Refer to frame by number (using parent).
        st = st & "Current Window: " & parent.frames(0).name & Chr(13)

        ' Refer to frame by name (using top).
        st = st & "Current Window: " & top.frames("frmLeft").name & Chr(13)

        ' Refer to frame by number (using top).
        st = st & "Current Window: " & top.frames(0).name & Chr(13)

        msgbox st
end sub
</SCRIPT>
</BODY>
</HTML>
```

Listing 7-5 HTML for the right frame

```
<HTML>
<HEAD>
<TITLE>Right Frame</TITLE>
</HEAD>
<BODY>
<INPUT TYPE="Button" NAME="cmdDisplay" VALUE="Display">

<SCRIPT LANGUAGE="VBScript">
sub cmdDisplay_OnClick
        ' Refer to current window implicitly.
        st = "Current Window: " & name & Chr(13)

        ' Refer to current window with self property.
        st = st & "Current Window: " &  self.name & Chr(13)

        ' Refer to frame by name (using parent).
        st = st & "Current Window: " & parent.frames("frmRight").name & Chr(13)

        ' Refer to frame by number (using parent)
        st = st & "Current Window: " & parent.frames(1).name & Chr(13)

        ' Refer to frame by name (using top).
        st = st & "Current Window: " & top.frames("frmRight").name & Chr(13)

        ' Refer to frame by number (using top).
        st = st & "Current Window: " & top.frames(1).name & Chr(13)

        msgbox st
end sub
</SCRIPT>
</BODY>
</HTML>
```

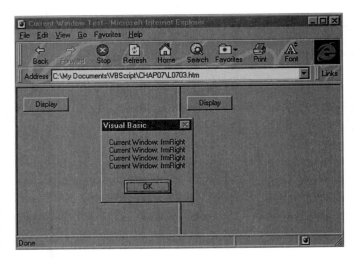

Figure 7-4
Referring to the current window

Notice in the output in Figure 7-4 that the same window name is returned even though we have specified this window in six different ways:

- Implicitly as the current window

- Explicitly as the current window using the self property

- As a frame of the parent window (by name)

- As a frame of the parent window (by number)

- As a frame of the top window (by name)

- As a frame of the top window (by number)

You can use each of these ways to refer to the current window. Which method you choose is largely personal preference.

Location, History, Navigator, and Document Objects

Like the frames property which lets you access the individual Frame objects of your window, the location, history, navigator, and document properties each allow you to access various other objects contained by a window. The full properties, events, and methods for the Location, History, Navigator, and Document objects are covered in separate sessions later in this chapter.

Navigating to Another URL

Several of the methods associated with the **Window** object allow you to navigate to a new URL and display the new page's contents in a window. To display a new page within an existing window, use the **Navigate** method. The **Navigate** method requires a single argument that is the URL of the page to display as follows:

```
[window.]navigate url
```

If you do not explicitly specify a **Window** object, the current window is assumed. Listing 7-6 demonstrates the **Navigate** method of the **Window** object. Figure 7-5 shows the output of this code.

Listing 7-6 Using the `Navigate` method of the `Window` object

```
<HTML>
<HEAD>
<TITLE>Navigate Test</TITLE>
</HEAD>
<BODY>
<INPUT TYPE="Button" NAME="cmdNavigate" VALUE="Visit Microsoft">
<SCRIPT LANGUAGE="VBScript">
sub cmdNavigate_OnClick
      navigate "http://www.microsoft.com"
end sub
</SCRIPT>
</BODY>
</HTML>
```

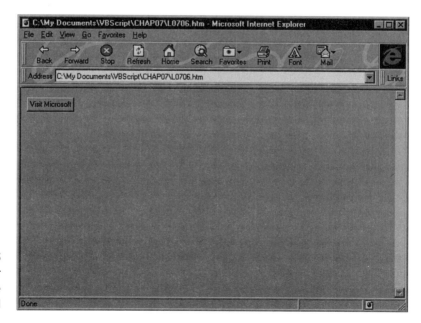

Figure 7-5
Displaying another page with the `Navigate` method

If you would prefer to display a new page's contents in an entirely new window, you can use the **Open** method of the **Window** object. This method will bring up an entirely new browser window in which you can display a Web page. The general syntax of the **Open** method is as follows:

```
[set newwindow =][window.]open url, target [,options]
```

where **options** is the following:

```
["[toolbar=bool] [,location=bool] [,directories=bool] [,status=bool] [,menubar=bool]
[,scrollbars=bool] [,resizeable=bool] [,width=pixels] [,height=pixels] [,top=pixels]
[,left=pixels]"]
```

Wow! That is a lot of options for one method, but they will be straightforward when we look at them individually. The first thing to notice is that you can (optionally) set a **Window** object equal to the return value of the **Open** method. This is because the **Open** method returns a **Window** object. Notice that you must use the keyword **set** when setting a variable equal to an object. Once again, you can specify a **Window** object explicitly or, if none is specified, the current window will be assumed.

The two arguments required are **url**, which is the URL of the new page, and **target**, which is the name of the target window in which to load this page. If a window with this name does not already exist, a new window is created with this name.

The **options** argument is a string that generally has the form **"optionname=bool, optionname=bool,..."** to determine whether or not the window is to display a toolbar, a location box, a status bar, and so on. Set the **bool** value to either 0 (false) or 1 (true). The final four arguments—width, height, left, and top—do not require 0 or 1 (Boolean) values, but rather they require an integer representing a number of pixels. For example, if you want a new window that is 300 pixels wide and 200 pixels high located at the top-left corner of the screen (0,0) and you want this window to display a toolbar, a location box, and a directories area, but no status bar, menu bar, or scroll bars and you want the window to be resizeable, you would use the following string for options:

```
"toolbar=1,location=1,directories=1,status=0,menubar=0,scrollbars=0,resizeable=1,⇐
width=300,height=200,left=0,top=0"
```

Listing 7-7 demonstrates the use of the **Open** method, and Figure 7-6 shows the results.

Listing 7-7 Opening a new window with the **Open** method

```
<HTML>
<HEAD>
<TITLE>Open Window Test</TITLE>
</HEAD>
<BODY>
<INPUT TYPE="Button" NAME="cmdNewWindow" VALUE="New Window">
<SCRIPT LANGUAGE="VBScript">
sub cmdNewWindow_OnClick
     top.open
"http://www.yahoo.com","frmYahoo","toolbar=0,location=0,directories=0,status=1,⇐
menubar=0,scrollbars=1,resizeable=1,width=400,height=300,top=100,left=100"
```

```
end sub
</SCRIPT>
</BODY>
</HTML>
```

When a window is opened using the **Open** method, you can use the **opener** property to find out which **Window** object was used to open this window. When you are finished with a newly created window, use the **Close** method to close it. Listing 7-8 demonstrates both of these. The resulting output windows are shown in Figures 7-7, 7-8, and 7-9.

Listing 7-8 Using the **Close** method and the **opener** property

```
<HTML>
<HEAD>
<TITLE>Open Window Test</TITLE>
</HEAD>
<BODY>
<INPUT TYPE="Button" NAME="cmdNewWindow" VALUE="New Window">
<INPUT TYPE="Button" NAME="cmdClose" VALUE="Close Window">
<INPUT TYPE="Button" NAME="cmdInfo" VALUE="Display Info">
<SCRIPT LANGUAGE="VBScript">
dim yahooWindow, smallYahooWindow
sub cmdNewWindow_OnClick
     set yahooWindow = top.open ("http://www.yahoo.com","frmYahoo","toolbar=0,⇐
location=0,directories=0,status=1,menubar=0,scrollbars=1,resizeable=1,width=400,⇐
height=300,top=100,left=100")
     set smallYahooWindow = yahooWindow.open
("http://www.yahoo.com","frmYahoo2","width=200,height=150")
end sub
sub cmdClose_OnClick
     yahooWindow.close
end sub
sub cmdInfo_OnClick
     msgbox "The small Yahoo window was opened by " & smallYahooWindow.opener.name &⇐
"."
end sub
</SCRIPT>
</BODY>
</HTML>
```

Interacting with the User

There are three methods of the **Window** which you can use to either display information to the user or request information from the user or both. These three methods are **Alert**, **Confirm**, and **Prompt**. In addition, you can display information in the status bar of a window using the window's **status** and **defaultStatus** properties.

The **Alert** method will display an alert dialog box in a specified window. The general syntax of the **Alert** method is as follows:

```
[window.]alert (string)
```

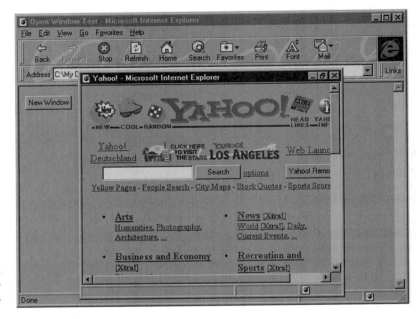

Figure 7-6
Displaying a new
browser window

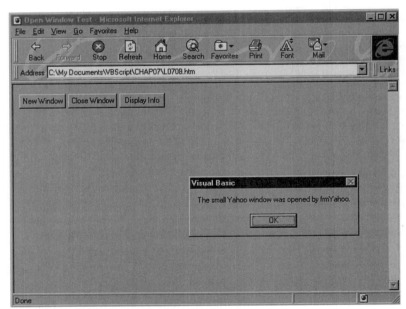

Figure 7-7
The main window
and information
dialog

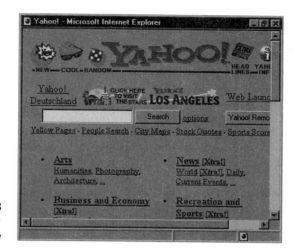

Figure 7-8
The larger Yahoo!
window

Figure 7-9
The smaller Yahoo!
window

The `Confirm` method will display a dialog box that allows the user to select either the OK or Cancel button. The general syntax of the `Confirm` method is as follows:

```
[bool=][window.]confirm (string)
```

The Boolean `return` value of the `Confirm` method will be true if the user clicked OK and false if not.

The `Prompt` method allows you to get some input from the user. The general syntax of the `Prompt` method is as follows:

```
[string=][window.]prompt [prompt][,default]
```

The `prompt` argument is the string you would like displayed in the dialog box. The `default` argument is the text you would like displayed in the input field initially. The value returned as `string` is the text entered by the user. If the user clicks the Cancel button rather than OK, the returned text will be null string (""). Listing 7-9 demonstrates the `Alert`, `Confirm`, and `Prompt` methods of the `Window` object. Figure 7-10 shows the resulting output.

Listing 7-9 Using the Alert, Confirm, and Prompt methods

```
<HTML>
<HEAD>
<TITLE>Dialog Box Test</TITLE>
</HEAD>
<BODY>
<INPUT TYPE="Button" NAME="cmdAlert" VALUE="Alert">
<INPUT TYPE="Button" NAME="cmdConfirm" VALUE="Confirm">
<INPUT TYPE="Button" NAME="cmdPrompt" VALUE="Prompt">
<SCRIPT LANGUAGE="VBScript">
sub cmdAlert_OnClick
     alert("This is an alert box.")
end sub
sub cmdConfirm_OnClick
     value=confirm("Do you want to click OK?")
     if value=TRUE then
       alert("You clicked OK.")
     else
       alert("You did not click OK.")
     end if
end sub
sub cmdPrompt_OnClick
     yourName=prompt("Please type your name:","John Doe")
     if yourName<>"" then
       alert("Your name is " & yourName)
     end if
end sub
</SCRIPT>
</BODY>
</HTML>
```

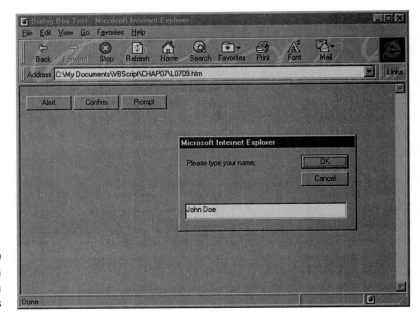

Figure 7-10
Interacting with
the user via
dialog boxes

If the information you need to display to the user is a simple string, you may consider using the status bar to display this information. The status bar is the single text line at the bottom of the browser window that often displays text messages regarding the current state of the browser (for example, "Connecting to site..."). You can set the default text to display in the status bar with the **defaultStatus** property. You can also use the **status** property to set the text to display in the status bar. In the current version of Internet Explorer, there seems to be little difference between these properties. Both **status** and **defaultStatus** change the text displayed in the status bar. Listing 7-10 demonstrates the **status** and **defaultStatus** properties. The resulting output is shown in Figure 7-11.

Listing 7-10 Using the **status** and **defaultStatus** properties

```
<HTML>
<HEAD>
<TITLE>Status Bar Test</TITLE>
</HEAD>
<BODY>
<INPUT TYPE="Button" NAME="cmdDefault" VALUE="Default">
<INPUT TYPE="Button" NAME="cmdStatus" VALUE="Status">
<P>
<A HREF="http://www.infoseek.com">Infoseek</A>
<SCRIPT LANGUAGE="VBScript">
sub cmdDefault_OnClick
     defaultStatus = "This is the default display text."
end sub
sub cmdStatus_OnClick
     status = "This is the status text."
end sub
</SCRIPT>
</BODY>
</HTML>
```

Calling Functions Automatically

Two methods associated with the **Window** object allow you to automatically call a function after a specific time delay. These methods are **setTimeout** and **clearTimeout**.

To automatically call a function after a specified time delay, use the **setTimeout** method. The general syntax of **setTimeout** is as follows:

```
id = [window.]setTimeout expression, msec, language
```

The **setTimeout** method returns a timer ID which you will use with the **clearTimeout** method to clear a timer when you no longer need it. The **expression** argument should evaluate to a particular function in your Visual Basic Script code, **msec** is the number of milliseconds to wait before attempting to make the function call, and **language** is either Visual Basic Script or Javascript, depending on the language in which the routine specified by **expression** is written.

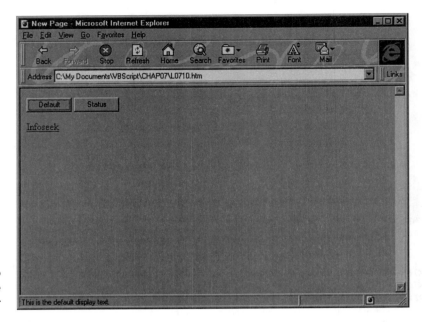

Figure 7-11
Setting the text to
display in the
status bar

When you no longer want a function to be called, you can use the `clearTimeout` method to clear a timer you have created with `setTimeout`. The general syntax of `clearTimeout` is as follows:

```
[window.]clearTimeout id
```

OnLoad **and** OnUnload **Events**

As a final exercise with the `Window` object, we will examine the two events associated with this object: `OnLoad` and `OnUnload`. As you might guess, the `OnLoad` event is triggered when the window loads (actually, *after* the window has finished processing the HTML code for its display) and the `OnUnload` event is triggered when the contents of the window are unloaded (as is the case when you jump to another Web page). To specify an `OnLoad` or `OnUnload` event, you need to add either `OnLoad="functionname"` or `OnUnload="functionname"` to the `BODY` tag of your HTML document. In addition, you must specify the scripting language in which the function is written by adding `Language="Visual Basic Script"` or `Language="JavaScript"` to the `BODY` tag. Listing 7-11 demonstrates the use of the `OnLoad` and `OnUnload` events. Figure 7-12 shows the results.

Listing 7-11 Using the OnLoad and OnUnload events

```
<HTML>
<HEAD>
<TITLE>Window Event Test</TITLE>
</HEAD>
<BODY LANGUAGE="VBScript" OnLoad="LoadProc" OnUnload="UnloadProc">
<A HREF="http://www.altavista.digital.com">Alta Vista Search</A>
<SCRIPT LANGUAGE="VBScript">
sub LoadProc
     alert ("This window's contents have finished loading.")
end sub
sub UnloadProc
     alert ("About to unload this window...")
end sub
</SCRIPT>
</BODY>
</HTML>
```

Table 7-1 contains a description of all the properties, methods, and events of the **Window** object.

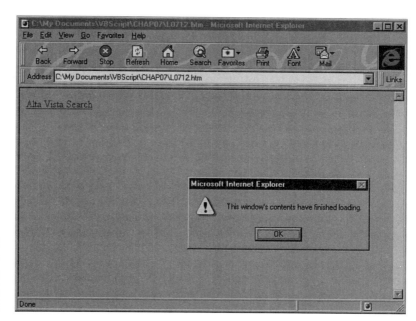

Figure 7-12
Executing code when a window's contents are loaded or unloaded

Name	Property, Event, or Method	Description
alert	method	Displays a message box
confirm	method	Displays a message box allowing the user to choose OK or Cancel
prompt	method	Brings up an input box to get input from the user
open	method	Creates a new window
close	method	Closes the window
setTimeout	method	Sets a timer to call a function after a specified delay
clearTimeout	method	Clears a timer created with setTimeout
navigate	method	Navigates the current window to a specified URL
navigator	property	Returns the Navigator object for the window
onLoad	event	Fires after all HTML has been processed
onUnload	event	Fires when the window contents are unloaded
name	property	Returns the name of the current window
parent	property	Returns the Window object of the window's parent
opener	property	Returns the Window object of the window that opened the current window

Name	Property, Event, or Method	Description
self	property	Returns the Window object of the current window
top	property	Returns the Window object of the topmost window
location	property	Returns the Location object of the window
defaultStatus	property	Sets the default text to be displayed in the browser's status bar
status	property	Sets the text to be displayed in the browser's status bar
frames	property	Returns the array of frames for the window
history	property	Returns the Navigator object for the window
document	property	Returns the Document object for the window

Table 7-1 *Properties, events, and methods of the Window object*

Summary

You can divide your Web page into frames that can each contain and display independent HTML commands. When creating frames, remember to give each frame a descriptive name (using the **NAME** parameter of the **FRAME** tag) which you can use to refer to that frame in your Visual Basic Script code. You can refer to frames either by the name that you specify or by a number which is based on the order in which the frames on a page are defined (with zero being the first frame defined). Finally, remember that a frame is also a window and, therefore, it has the same properties, methods, and events that a **Window** object has.

1. Which of the following is a somewhat independent unit into which you can divide your Web page?
   a. Frame
   b. Tile
   c. Webrect
   d. None of the above

2. Which of the following parameters of the `FRAME` tag is used to provide a frame name?
   a. `FRAMENAME`
   b. `ID`
   c. `NAME`
   d. None of the above

3. Which of the following is an example of referring to a frame by name?
   a. `top.frame("frmMain")`
   b. `top.frames("frmMain")`
   c. `top.frames(frmMain)`
   d. None of the above

4. Which of the following would refer to the first frame defined on a page?
   a. `top.frame(1)`
   b. `top.frames(1)`
   c. `top.frames("one")`
   d. None of the above

5. With which of the following does a `Frame` object share properties, events, and methods?
   a. `Script` object
   b. `Navigator` object
   c. `Window` object
   d. None of the above

Difficulty: Easy

1. Create a Web page containing several frames. Be sure to give each frame a descriptive name. How would you refer to these frames by name? By number?

Difficulty: Intermediate

2. Create a Web page containing multiple frames which bring up a message box when each frame is clicked. This message box will display the document title contained in that frame.

A LITTLE HISTORY

As a user surfs the World Wide Web in search of information, information is stored by the browser program which saves the various URLs that are visited. These recently visited URLs are typically accessible to the user through a browser menu (the Go menu in Internet Explorer 3.0, for instance). Figure 7-13 shows an open History folder in Internet Explorer 3.0. The History folder maintains a long list of recently visited URLs.

You can also access this history list from your Visual Basic Script code using the **History** object. The **History** object is contained by the **Window** object. You need not specify the **Window** object explicitly if you want to access the **History** object of the current window. For example, **history.length** would return the number of items in the history list for the current window.

You can retrieve the number of URLs that are saved in the history list by using the **Length** property of the **History** object. This property returns an integer value indicating how many URLs are saved in the **History** object. The code in Listing 7-12 demonstrates how to use the **Length** property.

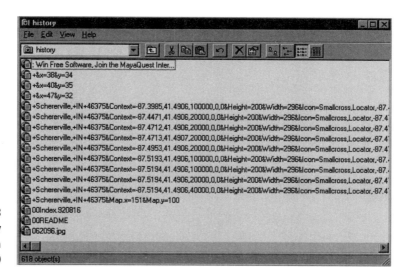

Figure 7-13
The History folder in Internet Explorer 3.0

Listing 7-12 Using the `Length` property of the `History` object

```
<SCRIPT language="VBScript>
...
    histCount = history.length
    alert "There are " & Str(histCount) & " entries in the _history list."
...
</SCRIPT>
```

You can also use the **History** object to access various URLs in the history list. To go forward in the history list (equivalent to clicking the forward button in your browser), use the **Forward** method. To go back in the history list (equivalent to clicking the back button in your browser), use the **Back** method. To go to a specific position in the history list, use the **Go** method. Listing 7-13 demonstrates these methods of the **History** object.

Listing 7-13 Using the methods of the `History` object

```
<SCRIPT language="VBScript>
sub btnForward_onClick
    history.back
end sub

sub btnBack_onClick
    history.forward
end sub

sub btnGo_onClick
    URLnum = val(txtGo.value)
    if URLnum > history.length then
      alert "That URL does not exist in the history!"
      exit sub
    end if
    history.go URLnum
end sub
</SCRIPT>
```

In this session we have covered the **History** object and seen how it can be used to access a list of URLs that have been visited recently. Table 7-2 contains a description of all the properties and methods of the **History** object.

Name	Property or Method	Description
back	method	Equivalent to pressing the browser back button
forward	method	Equivalent to pressing the browser forward button
go	method	Jumps to a specific position in the history list

TABLE 7-2

Name	Property or Method	Description
Length	property	Retrieves the number of entries in the history list

Table 7-2 *Properties and methods of the* History *object*

Summary

The History object can be used to access the URLs that have been visited. Use the Length property of the History object to determine the number of URLs that are currently being saved. To go to a specific URL in this history list, use the Go method, or use the Back and Forward methods to go backward and forward in the history list, respectively.

1. Which of the following is not a method of the History object?
   a. Forward
   b. Backward
   c. Go
   d. All the above are methods of the History object.

2. Which of the following methods of the History object can be used to jump to a URL at a specific position in the history list?
   a. Go
   b. Jump
   c. Position
   d. Location

3. Which of the following properties of the History object returns the number of URLs in the history list?
   a. elements
   b. itemcount
   c. length
   d. URLcount

4. To what is the Forward method of the History object similar?
   a. Clicking a specific entry in the browser's History folder
   b. Clicking the browser's forward button
   c. Clicking a specific entry in the browser's Go menu history list
   d. None of the above

5. Each **History** object is contained by which of the following?
    a. **Window** object
    b. **Navigator** object
    c. **Frame**
    d. Both a. and c.

Difficulty: Easy

1. Create a script which displays the number of items in the history list in an alert dialog.

Difficulty: Advanced

2. Use Visual Basic Script to create a mini-browser that brings up other URLs in a window, and implement custom forward and back buttons for your mini-browser.

WORKING WITH THE BROWSER PROGRAM

The browser can be considered the window on the Internet for the typical Web user. This is the application program that allows the user to jump from site to site on the vast expanse of the Internet. Unfortunately, not all browsers are created equal; you may need to take specific actions depending on the particular browser upon which your scripts are running. This is where the **Navigator** object fits in.

The **Navigator** object is contained by the **Window** object, and you need not specify the window explicitly if you want to use the current window. So **navigator.appName**, for instance, can be used to retrieve the name of the browser application program currently in use.

Each of the properties available for the **Navigator** object returns information about the specified browser. In general, the **Navigator** object gives the Microsoft Internet Explorer a degree of compatibility with Netscape's Navigator browser. Therefore, many of the properties will contain values relating to Netscape's browser for compatibility purposes (thus, the many references to "Mozilla").

You can find the application name and application code name using the **appName** and **appCodeName** properties, respectively. The application code name is generally an overall description of the browser compatibility (Internet Explorer returns **Mozilla**, for example), while the application name is the specific name of the browser application (such as **Microsoft Internet Explorer**).

The `appVersion` returns information about the version of the browser in use. Internet Explorer 3.0 returns `2.0 (compatible; MSIE 3.0A; Windows 95)`. The `userAgent` property is mainly supplied for compatibility with Netscape Navigator. It returns `Mozilla 2.0` for Internet Explorer 3.0. Listing 7-14 demonstrates the properties of the `Navigator` object.

Listing 7-14 Properties of the `Navigator` object

```
<SCRIPT language="VBScript">
sub Button1_OnClick
     alert "Code Name: " & navigator.appCodeName & chr(13) & "Name: " &⇐
navigator.appName & chr(13) & "Version: " & navigator.appVersion & chr(13) & "User⇐
Agent: " & navigator.userAgent
end sub
</SCRIPT>
```

In this session we have covered the properties of the **Navigator** object which allow you to determine information such as the type and version of the current browser. Table 7-3 contains a description of all the properties of the **Navigator** object.

Name	Property	Description
appCodeName	property	Gets the code name of the browser application
appName	property	Gets the name of the browser application
appVersion	property	Gets the version of the browser application
userAgent	property	Gets the user agent of the browser application

Table 7-3 *Properties of the* Navigator *object*

Summary

The **Navigator** object contains some properties that identify the current browser application. For example, the **appCodeName**, **appName**, and **appVersion** properties of the **Navigator** object can be used to identify the exact type and version of the browser that is currently in use.

QUIZ 3

1. Which of the following properties of the **Navigator** object returns the actual name of the browser application program?
   a. **appProgram**
   b. **appName**
   c. **appCodeName**
   d. None of the above

2. What is the most likely reason that **appVersion** returns "2.0…" rather than "3.0…" for Internet Explorer 3.0?
   a. A beta version of Internet Explorer is being used.
   b. The **appVersion** property returns the operating system version rather than the application version.
   c. To demonstrate that the capabilities of the browser are on par with those of Netscape Navigator 2.0.
   d. None of the above.

3. Which of the following properties will return **Mozilla...** under Microsoft Internet Explorer?
   a. **appCodeName**
   b. **userAgent**
   c. **appName**
   d. Both a. and b.

4. Which of the following identifies Microsoft Internet Explorer 3.0 within the string returned by the **appName** property?
   a. Internet Explorer
   b. MSIE
   c. INETEXP
   d. None of the above

5. Which of the following properties of the **Window** object refers to that window's **Navigator** object?
   a. **Navigator**
   b. **Nav**
   c. **Application**
   d. None of the above

EXERCISE 3

Difficulty: Intermediate

1. Modify the code in Listing 7-14 so that the results are written to the document itself rather than to an alert dialog.

Difficulty: Advanced

2. Modify the code in the first exercise so that the results are written to the document as links to other HTML documents which explain the results.

SESSION 4

WORKING WITH LOCATIONS AND LINKS

Links are what give the World Wide Web the ability to jump from location to location. This session will cover both the links themselves and the locations that appear at the end of each of these links.

The **Location** object returns information about the current location in cyberspace. The URL, host, port, pathname, and other information is available to you by using the **Location** object. The **Location** object is contained by the **Window** object, and you need not specify the window explicitly if you wish to use the current window. For example, **location.href** returns the complete URL of the current location. Listing 7-15 demonstrates the **Location** object.

Listing 7-15 The **Location** object in action

```
<SCRIPT language="VBScript">
sub btnClickMe_OnClick
     alert "Location is " & location.href
end sub
</SCRIPT>
```

The majority of the properties available for the **Location** object deal with obtaining the various parts of the whole URL. The best way to learn what these properties do is to look at an example. Listings 7-16 and 7-17 contain the Visual Basic Script code we will use to test the various properties of the **Location** object. A sample output dialog is displayed in Figure 7-14.

Listing 7-16 The frame layout used to test the `Location` object

```
<HTML>
<HEAD>
<TITLE>New Page</TITLE>
</HEAD>
<BODY>
<FRAMESET ROWS="20%,80%">
<FRAME NAME="top" SRC="L0717.htm">
<FRAME NAME="bottom" SRC="http://www.altavista.digital.com/">
</FRAMESET>
</BODY>
</HTML>
```

Listing 7-17 Using the various properties of the `Location` object

```
<HTML>
<HEAD>
<TITLE>Page2</TITLE>
</HEAD>
<BODY>
Hello Demo<P>
<INPUT TYPE=BUTTON NAME="Button1" VALUE="Click Me">
<P>
<SCRIPT language="VBScript">
sub Button1_OnClick
dim st
    st = "href: " & parent.frames(1).location.href & chr(13)
    st = st & "pathname: " & parent.frames(1).location.pathname & chr(13)
    st = st & "host: " & parent.frames(1).location.host & chr(13)
    st = st & "hostname: " & parent.frames(1).location.hostname & chr(13)
    st = st & "port: " & parent.frames(1).location.port & chr(13)
    st = st & "protocol: " & parent.frames(1).location.protocol & chr(13)
    st = st & "hash: " & parent.frames(1).location.hash & chr(13)
    st = st & "search: " & parent.frames(1).location.search & chr(13)

    alert st
end sub
</SCRIPT>
</BODY>
</HTML>
```

Notice that `location.href` returns the complete URL as you would expect to see it. The other properties (`hash`, `host`, `hostname`, `href`, `pathname`, `port`, `protocol`, and `search`) return smaller portions of this complete URL. Let's look at each of these properties in turn to see what they can tell us about a specific URL.

Let's begin with the following URL:

```
http://www.altavista.digital.com/cgi-bin/query?pg=q&what=web&fmt=.&q=apple
```

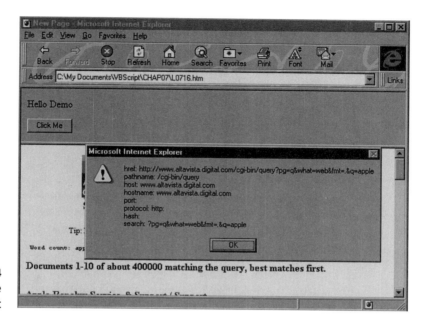

Figure 7-14
Properties of the
Location object

Table 7-4 shows what the various properties of the Location object return for this URL.

Property	Value Returned
location.hash	(no value)
location.host	www.altavista.digital.com
location.hostname	www.altavista.digital.com
location.href	http://www.altavista.digital.com/cgi-bin/query?pg=q&what=web&fmt=.&q=apple
location.pathname	/cgi-bin/query
location.port	(no value)
location.protocol	http:
location.search	?pg=q&what=web&fmt=.&q=apple

Table 7-4 *An example of the* Location *object's properties*

The Link object is very similar to a Location object, but a Link object represents one of the hyperlinks that exist in an HTML document. The Link object has one additional property that the Location object does not have: target. Use the target property to retrieve the target value of a specified link (if one is specified). The target value for a specific link determines the URL to which the user will be taken when he or she clicks on that link. You may need to know this information in order to do some processing before the user sees a specific Web page. For example, if a certain page is accessible only to a select group of users, you could check the target property of any link that is clicked and, if the target is the protected page, check the current user to see if he or she has permission to view the page.

You can access the various links in a document by using the Links object array. This array is zero based, so the first link in the document would be referenced as Links(0). You can find out how many links exist in a document by using the Length property of the Links array. The code in Listing 7-18, for example, displays the URL of every link in the current document.

Listing 7-18 Displaying the URL of every link in the current document

```
<SCRIPT language="VBScript">
sub Button1_OnClick
dim i, st
    st = ""
    for i = 0 to document.links.length - 1
      st = st & "Target: " & document.links(i).href & chr(13)
    next
    alert st
end sub
</SCRIPT>
```

Finally, there are three events associated with the Link object: mouseMove, onMouseOver, and onClick. These events are fired (or activated) when the mouse cursor is moved, when the mouse cursor is over a link, and when a link is clicked, respectively. Listing 7-19 demonstrates the use of these Link object events.

Listing 7-19 Events associated with the `Link` object

```
<HTML>
<HEAD>
<TITLE>New Page</TITLE>
</HEAD>
<BODY>
<A HREF="" ID="msLink">Visit Microsoft</A>
<P>
<A HREF="" ID="nsLink">Visit Netscape</A>
<SCRIPT LANGUAGE="VBScript">
sub msLink_onClick
     top.location.href="http://www.microsoft.com"
end sub

sub msLink_MouseMove(shift,button,x,y)
     status="Shift:" & CStr(shift) & "  Button:" & CStr(button) & "  x:" & CStr(x) &
"  y:" & CStr(y)
end sub

sub nsLink_onMouseOver
     top.status="Go to Netscape..."
end sub
</SCRIPT>
</BODY>
</HTML>
```

In Listing 7-19, we display different strings in the status bar at the bottom of the browser window, depending on the link to which the mouse is pointing. Moving the mouse over the Netscape link will display a static message, while moving the mouse over the Microsoft link will constantly update the status bar text with the current mouse position. Notice that the **MouseMove** event handler is passed four arguments which specify the status of the shift key, whether any of the mouse buttons are pressed, and the horizontal and vertical position of the mouse cursor (in pixels).

Table 7-5 contains a description of all the properties of the `Link` object.

Name	Property or Event	Description
hash	property	Gets or sets the hash portion of the URL
host	property	Returns the host and port portions of the URL
hostname	property	Returns the host portion of the URL
href	property	Returns the complete URL

continued on next page

continued from previous page

Name	Property or Event	Description
pathname	property	Returns the pathname of the URL
port	property	Returns the port portion of the URL
protocol	property	Returns the protocol portion of the URL
search	property	Gets or sets the search portion of the URL
target	property	Gets or sets the target of a link
mouseMove	event	Fires when the mouse is moved
onMouseOver	event	Fires when the mouse cursor is over the link
onClick	event	Fires when the link is clicked

Table 7-5 *Properties and events of the* Link *object*

Summary

The Location object can be used to obtain information about the URL of the page currently being displayed. The **href** property returns the complete URL of the current page, and the various other properties of the Location object return portions of the complete URL (such as the path, any search parameters, and so on). Setting the **href** property equal to a URL string will cause the browser to navigate to that URL.

The Link object is associated with hypertext links in your document. In addition to the same properties possessed by the Location object to return a link's URL information, the Link object has a **target** property which returns the target of the link and three events that deal with the mouse: **mouseMove**, **onClick**, and **onMouseOver**.

1. Which of the properties is valid for the Link object but not valid for the Location object?
   a. search
   b. target
   c. protocol
   d. hash

2. Which of the following events can be used to determine when the mouse cursor is over a specific link?
   a. `onClick`
   b. `mouseMove`
   c. `onMouse`
   d. None of the above

3. Which of the following properties returns both the host and port of a specified URL?
   a. `host`
   b. `hostname`
   c. `port`
   d. None of the above

4. Which of the following represents the number of links in the current document?
   a. `document.linkCount`
   b. `document.links.Count`
   c. `document.count`
   d. `document.links.length`

5. Which of the following properties returns the complete URL of a `Link` or `Location` object?
   a. `URLname`
   b. `href`
   c. `name`
   d. Either a. or c.

Difficulty: Easy

1. Modify Listing 7-19 to display other information about each link in a document.

Difficulty: Advanced

2. Create a script that displays a link's URL whenever the mouse cursor passes over a specific URL.

WORKING WITH SCRIPTS

Each window has an associated `Script` object that represents the code defined using the `SCRIPT` tag within that window's HTML document. Listing 7-20 demonstrates the use of the `SCRIPT` tag to create some simple Visual Basic Script code.

Listing 7-20 Sample use of the SCRIPT tag

```
<HTML>
<HEAD>
<TITLE>Script Test</TITLE>
</HEAD>
<BODY>
<SCRIPT LANGUAGE="VBScript">
randomize

if rnd > .5 then
     document.write "Hello"
else
     document.write "Hi"
end if
</SCRIPT>
</BODY>
</HTML>
```

Currently, there are two values you can specify for the **LANGUAGE** parameter: Visual Basic Script or JavaScript. You can, in fact, have scripts for each type of language in a single HTML file.

Calling a Script in a Different Window

You can call a script function in a different window by prefacing the script function with the name of the window that contains the script. Listings 7-21 and 7-22 demonstrate calling a function within another window.

Listing 7-21 The window that defines the scripting function

```
<HTML>
<HEAD>
<TITLE>Main Page</TITLE>
</HEAD>
<BODY>
<FRAMESET ROWS="50%,50%">
<FRAME SRC="LO722.htm" NAME="frmTop">
<FRAME SRC="LO722.htm" NAME="frmBottom">
<SCRIPT LANGUAGE="VBScript">
sub mySub(st)
     frmBottom.document.open
     frmBottom.document.write st
     frmBottom.document.close
end sub
</BODY>
</HTML>
```

Listing 7-22 The window that calls the scripting function

```
<HTML>
<HEAD>
<TITLE>Script Test</TITLE>
</HEAD>
<BODY>
<SCRIPT LANGUAGE="VBScript">
      top.mySub("Hello")
</SCRIPT>
</BODY>
</HTML>
```

Summary

The **Script** object associated with each window represents the code defined with the **SCRIPT** tag for that window. There currently are no properties, events, or methods associated with the **Script** object. You can call a script in another window by prefacing the script function with the name of the window in which the script resides.

1. Which of the following is a property of the **Script** object?
   a. **forms**
   b. **elements**
   c. **window**
   d. None of the above

2. How can you call a script function in another window?
   a. By prefacing the window name to the function
   b. By placing the window name in parentheses after the function
   c. By just using the function name by itself
   d. None of the above

3. A different **Script** object is associated with each of which of the following objects?
   a. **Form**
   b. **Window**
   c. **Element**
   d. None of the above

4. Which of the following is a possible value of the **LANGUAGE** parameter of the **SCRIPT** tag?
   a. **VBScript**
   b. **JScript**
   c. **JavaScript**
   d. Both a. and c.

5. Which of the following tags is used to end a script?
   a. `</END>`
   b. `</SCRIPT>`
   c. `<NOSCRIPT>`
   d. None of the above

Difficulty: Intermediate

1. Create some Visual Basic Script functions in a main window and call these functions from other windows.

Difficulty: Advanced

2. Modify the first exercise of this session so that one of the functions in the main window modifies the document of the window that is calling the function. How do you reference this document object from the main window?

WORKING WITH DOCUMENTS

The `Document` object is one of the most important objects available in Visual Basic Script. `Link`, `Anchor`, and `Form` objects are all contained by a `Document` object. Additionally, you can add information to Web pages on the fly by using the `write` and `writeln` methods of the `Document` object. Since `Link` objects, `Anchor` objects, and `Form` objects are all covered in different sessions of this chapter, we will concentrate on the properties and methods which are unique to the `Document` object. However, it is worth mentioning that the links, anchors, and forms contained within a document are all accessed through the zero-based arrays we have seen earlier in this chapter. Use the `anchors`, `forms`, and `links` properties of the `Document` object to access these zero-based arrays. As before, you can use the `length` property of anchors, forms, or links to determine the number of these objects contained in a document.

Changing Document Colors

You can change the color scheme for a document in a variety of ways. The colors of the various links can be set with the `linkColor`, `aLinkColor`, and `vLinkColor` properties (`aLinkColor` specifies the color for active links and `vLinkColor` specifies the color for visited links). The foreground and background color of a document can also be set using the `bgColor` and `fgColor` properties. Note that all these color properties must be set before the document is actually displayed (place your script code in the `<HEAD>` section of the HTML document). You cannot change these colors after the document has

been displayed. Listing 7-23 demonstrates the use of these color properties. The resulting page is shown in Figure 7-15.

Listing 7-23 Using the various color properties of the Document object

```
<HTML>
<HEAD>
<TITLE>Color Test</TITLE>
<SCRIPT LANGUAGE="VBScript">
' Red foreground text.
document.fgColor="#0000FF"
' White background.
document.bgColor="#FFFFFF"
' Black links.
document.linkColor="#000000"
' Red active links.
document.aLinkColor="#FF0000"
' Gray visited links.
document.vLinkColor="#888888"
</SCRIPT>
</HEAD>
<BODY>
<H1>Color Test</H1>
<A HREF="http://www.microsoft.com">Microsoft</A>
<P><A HREF="http://www.netscape.com">Netscape</A>
</BODY>
</HTML>
```

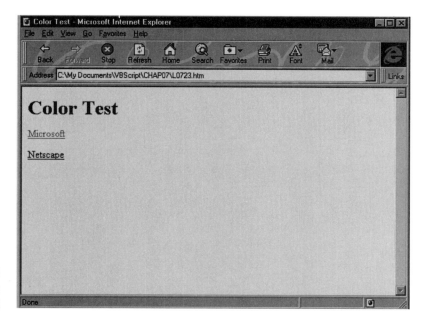

Figure 7-15
Properties of the
Location object

Document Information

You can obtain specific information about a document using the `lastModified`, `title`, and `referrer` properties. The `lastModified` property returns the date that the document was last changed. The `title` property simply returns the document title, and the `referrer` property tells you which document the user was viewing when he jumped to your document (assuming the user did jump to your document from a previous one). These properties are demonstrated in Listing 7-24. The resulting output is shown in Figure 7-16.

Listing 7-24 Using the `lastModified`, `title`, and `referrer` properties of the `Document` object

```
<HTML>
<HEAD>
<TITLE>Document Info Test</TITLE>
</HEAD>
<BODY>
<INPUT TYPE="Button" NAME="cmdInfo" VALUE="Document Info">
<SCRIPT LANGUAGE="VBScript">
sub cmdInfo_OnClick
     st = "Title: " & document.title & chr(13)
     st = st & "Last Modified: " & document.lastModified & chr(13)
     st = st & "Referrer: " & document.referrer & chr(13)

     msgbox st
end sub
</SCRIPT>
</BODY>
</HTML>
```

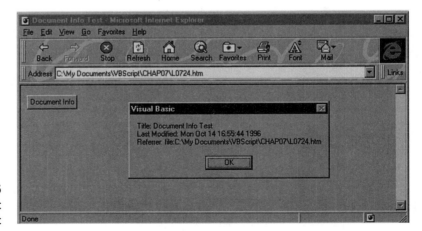

Figure 7-16
Information about
the `Document` object

Location, Anchor, Link, **and** Form Objects

You can use the **location**, **anchors**, **links**, and **forms** properties to access these various objects related to a specific document. See Session 4 of this chapter for a complete discussion of the **Location** object and the **Link** object, Session 7 of this chapter for a complete discussion of the **Anchor** object, and Session 8 of this chapter for a complete discussion of the **Form** object.

Creating Documents Dynamically

The real fun begins when you can dynamically create HTML documents using Visual Basic Script code, and this is exactly what the various methods of the **Document** object allow you to do. First, you must open a document using the **Open** method. Then, use the **write** and **writeln** methods to add content to the document. Finally, close the document using the **Close** method. If you need to clear the contents of a document, you can use the **Clear** method to do so. The resulting Web page is shown in Figure 7-17.

Have a Cookie

A cookie is an odd name for what is a very useful concept in Visual Basic Script programming: A cookie is a small packet of information stored on a user's machine. For security purposes, very little input and output is tolerated by Visual Basic Script and its supporting browsers, but the Visual Basic Script designers did realize the need to occasionally save information for individual users (such as their preferences for your particular Web site). Cookies provide just such an ability.

To place a cookie on the user's machine, you need to set the **cookie** property of the **Document** object. Likewise, you can read the value of a previously set cookie by reading the **cookie** property. Listing 7-25 is a simple example of setting and reading the **cookie** property.

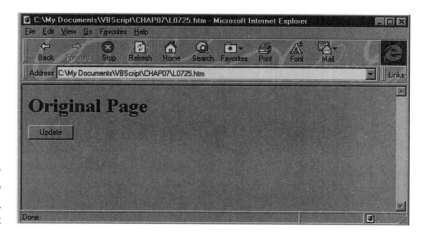

Figure 7-17
A dynamically created HTML document

Listing 7-25 Using the `cookie` property of the `Document` object

```
<HTML>
<HEAD>
<TITLE>Cookie Test</TITLE>
</HEAD>
<BODY>
<INPUT TYPE="Button" NAME="cmdSet" VALUE="Set Cookie">
<INPUT TYPE="Button" NAME="cmdRead" VALUE="Read Cookie">
<SCRIPT LANGUAGE="VBScript">
sub cmdSet_OnClick
     st = prompt("Enter a cookie string to save:","")
     if st<>"" then
       document.cookie = st
     end if
end sub
sub cmdRead_OnClick
     alert("The cookie string you entered is '" & document.cookie & "'.")
end sub
</SCRIPT>
</BODY>
</HTML>
```

Problems Using a Cookie with a Local Page

There is a problem when using a cookie on a Web page loaded from one of your computer's local drives (as is the case with the examples on the accompanying CD-ROM for this book). Cookies will simply not work when a page is loaded from a local drive. This problem exists with Internet Explorer 3.0, but it will hopefully be corrected in a future version. Nevertheless, these same pages will correctly function with cookies when they are loaded from a remote site (i.e., via the Internet).

Unfortunately, a cookie that you set in the manner shown in Listing 7-25 will expire at the end of the user's session. To create a cookie that lasts longer, you need to specify an expiration date for the cookie. You set expiration date by appending a date string of the following format to the end of your cookie:

```
";expires=10-Aug-97 GMT"
```

Listing 7-26 demonstrates the use of a cookie with an expiration date.

Listing 7-26 A cookie with an expiration date

```
<HTML>
<HEAD>
<TITLE>Cookie Test</TITLE>
</HEAD>
<BODY>
<INPUT TYPE="Button" NAME="cmdSet" VALUE="Set Cookie">
<INPUT TYPE="Button" NAME="cmdRead" VALUE="Read Cookie">
<SCRIPT LANGUAGE="VBScript">
sub cmdSet_OnClick
     st = prompt("Enter a cookie string to save:","")
```

```
        if st<>"" then
          document.cookie = st & ";expires=10-Aug-97 GMT"
        end if
end sub
sub cmdRead_OnClick
        alert("The cookie string you entered is '" & document.cookie & "'.")
end sub
</SCRIPT>
</BODY>
</HTML>
```

The **Document** object has many powerful properties and methods that allow you to customize the look of your displayed pages. This session has demonstrated these various properties and methods. Table 7-6 contains a description of all the properties and methods of the **Document** object.

7-6

Name	Property or Method	Description
linkColor	property	Gets or sets the color of links in the document
aLinkColor	property	Gets or sets the color of active links in the document
vLinkColor	property	Gets or sets the color of visited links in the document
bgColor	property	Gets or sets the document background color
fgColor	property	Gets or sets the document foreground color
anchors	property	Accesses all anchors in a document
links	property	Accesses all links in a document
forms	property	Accesses all forms in a document
location	property	The Location object associated with the document

continued on next page

continued from previous page

Name	Property or Method	Description
lastModified	property	When the document was last modified
title	property	Title of the document
cookie	property	Used to transfer saved information across documents
referrer	property	From which Web document did the user jump to the current one
write	method	Outputs to a document
writeln	method	Outputs to a document with a carriage return
open	method	Opens a document for output
close	method	Closes a document
clear	method	Clears the contents of a document

Table 7-6 *Properties of the* Document *object*

Summary

The Document object is the object that represents the actual HTML code that makes up a document along with various display properties of the document (such as foreground color, background color, link color, and so on). You can get information about the document using the Document object properties. In addition, you can dynamically construct documents using the various methods of the document object such as Open, Write, and Close. Finally, the Document object provides the cookie property which allows you to store small packets of data on the user's machine. These cookies can be used to save individual user preferences for your Web pages.

1. Which of the following properties can be used to set the color of links that have already been visited?
   a. `aLinkColor`
   b. `linkColor`
   c. `vLinkColor`
   d. None of the above

2. Which of the following methods is used to send output to a document?
   a. `write`
   b. `writeln`
   c. `output`
   d. Both a. and b.

3. Which of the following properties of the `Document` object return zero-based arrays of other objects?
   a. `forms`
   b. `anchors`
   c. `links`
   d. All of the above

4. Which of the following properties can be used to transfer information from one page to another?
   a. `transValue`
   b. `open`
   c. `referrer`
   d. `cookie`

5. Which of the following is the correct way of accessing the URL of the current document?
   a. `document.location.href`
   b. `document.href`
   c. `document.url`
   d. None of the above

Difficulty: Intermediate

1. Create a script which allows you to set the various color properties of a document by typing values into textboxes.

Difficulty: Advanced

2. Create a pseudo-browser which lets you open up documents by typing a URL into a textbox. Display information about the document displayed including its title, last modification date, referring document, and so on.

SESSION 7
ANCHORS AWAY!

An anchor is a bookmark which you establish in your document in order to mark a specific location in your HTML document to which you can hyperlink from elsewhere within the document or from other documents entirely. You create an anchor within your document by setting the **NAME** parameter of the anchor tag as follows (don't forget the ending anchor tag, **</A>**):

```
<A NAME="anchorname"></A>
```

Subsequently, you can link to this particular location within your document by setting the **HREF** parameter of the anchor tag equal to **"#anchorname"** as in the following example:

```
<A HREF="#anchorname">Jump to anchor</A>
```

Listing 7-27 demonstrates an example of specifying anchors in an HTML document. Figure 7-18 shows the resulting Web page.

Listing 7-27 Specifying anchors in a document

```
<HTML>
<HEAD>
<TITLE>Anchors Example</TITLE>
</HEAD>
<BODY>
<H2>Select:</H2>
<A HREF="#first">Read first paragraph</A>
<BR>
<A HREF="#second">Read second paragraph</A>
<HR>
<A NAME="first"></A><H1>First Paragraph</H1>
This is the text in the first paragraph.
<HR>
<A NAME="second"></A><H1>Second Paragraph</H1>
This is the text in the second paragraph.
</BODY>
</HTML>
```

As we touched upon earlier in this chapter, each document has an **anchors** property which can be used to access the anchors on a particular page. You can find the number of anchors within a document by checking **anchors.length**, and you can access each individual anchor as an array with the first anchor represented as element zero.

Listing 7-28 demonstrates these concepts by adding to the code in Listing 7-27. The output is shown in Figure 7-19.

Listing 7-28 Using the `anchors` property of a document

```
<HTML>
<HEAD>
<TITLE>Anchors Example</TITLE>
</HEAD>
<BODY>
<INPUT TYPE="Button" NAME="cmdAnchors" VALUE="Anchors">
<HR>
<H2>Select:</H2>
<A HREF="#first">Read first paragraph</A>
<BR>
<A HREF="#second">Read second paragraph</A>
<HR>
<A NAME="first"></A><H1>First Paragraph</H1>
This is the text in the first paragraph.
<HR>
<A NAME="second"></A><H1>Second Paragraph</H1>
This is the text in the second paragraph.
<SCRIPT LANGUAGE="VBScript">
sub cmdAnchors_OnClick
     st = "Number of anchors: " & document.anchors.length & chr(13)

     st = st & "First anchor is named: " & document.anchors(0).name

     msgbox st
end sub
</SCRIPT>
</BODY>
</HTML>
```

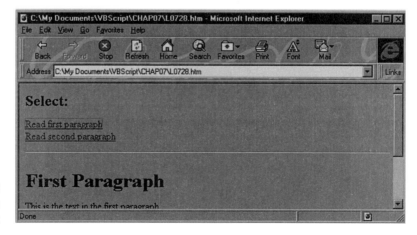

Figure 7-18
Anchors within a
document

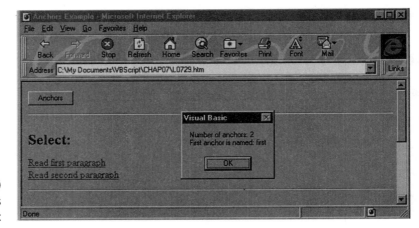

Figure 7-19
More anchors
within a document

The **Anchor** object itself has only one property, **name**, which returns the name of a specific anchor.

Summary

You can set an anchor within your HTML document using the anchor tag (**<A>**) along with a **NAME="anchorname"** parameter. To reference this anchor from elsewhere in your document, use the anchor tag along with an **HREF="#anchorname"** parameter. The **Document** object has an **anchors** property which returns an array containing the anchors in a document. The **length** property of the **anchors** array reveals the number of anchors in a document, and you can access the names of each of these anchors individually using the following syntax: **document.anchors(anchornumber).name**.

Remember that the **anchors** array is zero-based, so the first anchor in a document is actually **document.anchors(0)**.

1. Which of the following is a property of the **Anchor** object?
    a. **target**
    b. **href**
    c. **name**
    d. both a. and c.

2. Which of the following will return the number of anchors in a specific document?
   a. `document.anchorCount`
   b. `document.anchors.length`
   c. `document.anchors.Count`
   d. None of the above

3. Which of the following is a method of the `Anchor` object?
   a. `close`
   b. `go`
   c. `back`
   d. There are no methods associated with the `Anchor` object.

4. Which of the following is a correct way to establish an anchor within your document?
   a. `<A HREF="anchorname">`
   b. `<A HREF="#anchorname">`
   c. `<A NAME="#anchorname">`
   d. None of the above

5. Which of the following is a correct way to jump to a previously established anchor within your document?
   a. `<A HREF="anchorname">`
   b. `<A HREF="#anchorname">`
   c. `<A NAME="#anchorname">`
   d. None of the above

EXERCISE 7

Difficulty: Intermediate

1. Create a Web page which contains four anchors. Be sure to name each anchor with an arbitrary name. Then write the Visual Basic Script code to display the name of each anchor on the page.

Difficulty: Intermediate

2. Create a script that displays the name of each anchor in the current document. (Hint: Use the `status` property of the `Window` object to display a text string in the status bar at the bottom of the browser window).

WORKING WITH FORMS AND ELEMENTS

Forms and elements are the visual components that allow the user to interact with your HTML documents. This session looks briefly at how you can access the **Form** and **Element** objects of a document and then refers you to Chapter 9, "Data Validation," and Chapter 10, "Objectifying Your Scripts," for more information.

Establishing a Form

To create a form on a Web page, use the **<FORM>** and **</FORM>** tags. You add any elements (textboxes, check boxes, buttons, and so on) to the form by using the **<INPUT>** tag along with the appropriate parameters to specify the type of element along with its name, value, and other options. Listing 7-29 shows a simple example of a form containing three different elements. Figure 7-20 shows the resulting page.

Listing 7-29 Creating a simple form

```
<HTML>
<HEAD>
<TITLE>Form Test</TITLE>
</HEAD>
<BODY>
<FORM ACTION="http://www.someserver.com/bin/search.cgi" METHOD=GET>
<INPUT NAME="cmdButton" TYPE="Button" VALUE="Press Me">
<P><INPUT NAME="txtInput" TYPE="Text" VALUE="Text goes here...">
<P><INPUT NAME="chkBox" TYPE="CheckBox" CHECKED>
</FORM>
</BODY>
</HTML>
```

The **ACTION** and **METHOD** parameters of the **FORM** tag are used to determine the appropriate server-side code to execute when the form is submitted. You will need to contact your Internet Service Provider to find out if you are able to create and/or use such server-side code.

Elements on a Form

As we learned in the previous example, each element of a form is defined with the **INPUT** tag. The **INPUT** tag has the following general syntax:

```
<INPUT NAME="elementname" TYPE="elementtype" VALUE="value">
```

Certain elements also have additional properties that can be set (for example, the **CheckBox** element has a **CHECKED** parameter). The type of element is determined by the

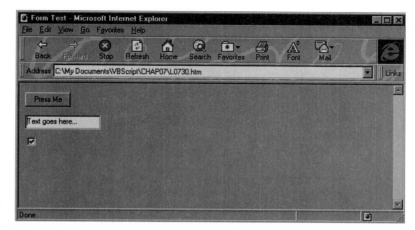

Figure 7-20
A simple form

value you specify for TYPE="elementtype." Some acceptable element types are Button, Text,CheckBox, TextArea, Radio, Password, and Submit.

Referencing Forms and Elements

Each **Document** object has an associated **forms** array which you can use to get at the various forms within a document and subsequent elements contained by these forms. Use the **forms** property of a document to retrieve the **Forms** array for that document. Each **Form** object has an associated **elements** property. Use the **elements** property of the **Form** object to access the elements contained by that form. Listing 7-30 demonstrates the use of the **Forms** array and the **Elements** array. The output is shown in Figure 7-21.

Listing 7-30 Using the Forms array and Elements array

```
<HTML>
<HEAD>
<TITLE>Form Test</TITLE>
</HEAD>
<BODY>
<INPUT NAME="cmdDisplay" TYPE="Button" VALUE="Display Info">
<HR>
<FORM ACTION="http://www.someserver.com/bin/search.cgi" METHOD=GET>
<INPUT NAME="cmdButton" TYPE="Button" VALUE="Press Me">
<P><INPUT NAME="txtInput" TYPE="Text" VALUE="Text goes here...">
<P><INPUT NAME="chkBox" TYPE="CheckBox" CHECKED>
</FORM>
<SCRIPT LANGUAGE="VBScript">
sub cmdDisplay_OnClick
    st = "Number of forms: " & document.forms.length & chr(13)
    st = st & "Number of elements on form(0): " & document.forms(0).elements.⇐
length & chr(13)
    st = st & "Name of 2nd element on form(0): " & ocument.forms(0).elements(1).name
```

continued on next page

continued from previous page

```
        msgbox st
end sub
</SCRIPT>
</BODY>
</HTML>
```

In the same manner as many of the object arrays we have seen in this chapter, both the `Forms` array and the `Elements` array are zero-based. In addition, each has a `length` property that you can use to retrieve the number of forms or elements, respectively.

Handling Events

Each of the various form elements can respond to a variety of events (such as when the user clicks the element or when the element receives focus), and you can specify that a specific Visual Basic Script subroutine be executed when an event occurs. There are two basic ways in which you can assign subroutines to handle these events:

1. Define the subroutine for an event within the INPUT tag

2. Define the subroutine for an event within the SCRIPT tag

Let's see how we would add an event-handling subroutine using each of these methods.

First, to define an event-handling subroutine within the INPUT tag, simply use the format `event="subroutinename"` as shown in Listing 7-31.

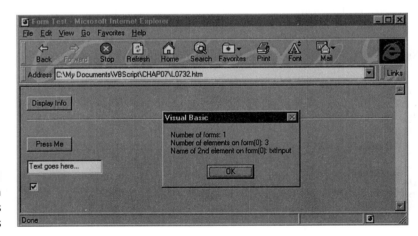

Figure 7-21
Display information
about various
forms and elements

Listing 7-31 One method of defining an event-handling subroutine

```
<FORM NAME="frmMain">
<INPUT NAME="cmdButton" TYPE="Button" VALUE="Press Me" OnClick="PressSub">
</FORM>
<SCRIPT LANGUAGE="VBScript">
sub PressSub
     alert("You have pressed the button!")
end sub
</SCRIPT>
```

The second method of specifying an event-handling subroutine is to define the subroutine within the **SCRIPT** tag as shown in Listing 7-32.

Listing 7-32 A second method of defining an event-handling subroutine

```
<FORM NAME="frmMain">
<INPUT NAME="cmdButton" TYPE="Button" VALUE="Press Me">
<SCRIPT FOR="cmdButton" EVENT="OnClick" LANGUAGE="VBScript">
     alert("You have pressed the button!")
</SCRIPT>
</FORM>
```

Table 7-7 contains a description of all the properties, events, and methods of the **Form** object. Table 7-8 contains a description of all the properties, events, and methods of the **Element** object. Forms and elements are discussed again in Chapter 9.

Name	Property, Event, or Method	Description
action	property	Gets or sets the submit action of the form
encoding	property	Gets or sets the encoding for a form
method	property	Indicates how the form should be sent to the server
target	property	Specifies the target window in which to display the form results
elements	property	Returns the array of elements contained in a form
submit	method	Submits the form
OnSubmit	event	Triggers when the form is submitted

Table 7-7 *Properties, events, and methods of the* Form *object*

TABLE 7-8

Name	Property, Event, or Method	Description
form	property	Gets the form object that contains the element
name	property	Gets or sets the name of the element
value	property	Gets or sets the value of the element
defaultValue	property	Gets or sets the default value of the element
checked	property	Gets or sets the checked state of a check box element
defaultChecked	property	Gets or sets the default checked property of a check box element
length	property	Gets the number of options in an element
options	property	Gets the <OPTIONS> tags for an element
selectedIndex	property	Gets the index for the selected option
click	method	Clicks the element
focus	method	Sets the focus to a specific element
blur	method	Clears the focus from a specific element
select	method	Selects the contents of an element
onClick	event	Triggers when the element is clicked
onFocus	event	Triggers when the element receives focus
onBlur	event	Triggers when the element loses focus

Name	Property, Event, or Method	Description
onChange	event	Triggers when the element has changed
onSelect	event	Triggers when the contents of an element are selected

Table 7-8 *Properties, events, and methods of the* Element *object*

Summary

To create a form on your page, use the FORM tag. Elements within the <FORM> and </FORM> tags are contained by that particular form. Each document has an associated Forms array which you can access with the Forms property of the document. The Length property of the Forms array tells you how many forms are contained by the document. The Forms array is zero-based so the first form is referenced as document.forms(0).

1. Which of the following is a correct way of finding the number of elements on the first form in a document?
   a. `document.forms(0).elements.length`
   b. `document.forms(1).elements.length`
   c. `document.elements.length`
   d. `document.elements(0).length`

2. Which of the following is the correct way of finding the number of forms on a document?
   a. `document.forms.elements`
   b. `document.forms.length`
   c. `document.forms.count`
   d. None of the above

3. Which of the following is not a correct statement?
   a. Elements are contained by forms.
   b. Forms are contained by documents.
   c. Documents are contained by windows.
   d. All of the above are correct.

4. Which of the following is a correct statement?
   a. Scripts are contained by forms.
   b. Elements can contain several forms.
   c. Locations are contained by windows.
   d. None of the above are correct.

5. Which is the correct way to specify an event handler for a form element?
   a. `<INPUT TYPE="Button" NAME="cmdPressMe" VALUE="Press Me" OnClick="Pressed">`
   b. `<SCRIPT FOR="cmdPressMe" EVENT="OnClick" LANGUAGE="VBScript">`
   c. Both a. and b. are correct.
   d. None of the above.

Difficulty: Intermediate

1. Create a script that displays the name of each element in a form when that form is clicked.

Difficulty: Advanced

2. Modify the previous exercise so that the output is written to a new HTML document.

CHAPTER SUMMARY

The scripting object model is an integral part of Visual Basic Script programming. By learning the various properties, methods, and events associated with the various scripting objects, you will be able to add considerable power to your Visual Basic Script applications.

CHAPTER 8

EXPLORING OBJECTS, EVENTS, METHODS, AND PROPERTIES

Throughout the previous chapters you have been working with objects. You may not have realized it, but you have been subjected to things like events, methods, and properties. Before you begin to worry about ill effects, the only known long-term ones are a few words added to your vocabulary and an easy and intuitive way of doing script programming.

In fact, in the last chapter you reviewed how to work with the Document and Window objects of the Internet Explorer. You also worked with ActiveX controls, which are types of objects, and beginning in Chapter 3, "Great Running Scripts," with the label and timer control. And each time we used the button or text HTML input elements, you were working with objects.

This chapter will serve to formalize your introduction to using the Internet Explorer Scripting Object

Model. You can think of the Internet Explorer as one big object whose role in life is to connect to the Internet/Intranet to display Web pages, play sounds, and so on. Within your scripts, you have the ability to control this big object to make it work for you to build your Web pages. The first four sessions in this chapter will go over some basics of how you can manipulate different aspects of the Internet Explorer input elements, frames, and forms to work for you. Then, in the last four sessions, we will take a closer look at how all the different objects of the Internet Explorer are exposed and how we can further use them. So, hold on to your hats—think objects.

In this chapter we will cover the following topics:

● **Building HTML Forms on the Fly**

● **Interacting with HTML Text Elements**

● **Interacting with HTML Check Box Elements**

● **Interacting with HTML Button Elements**

● **Exploring Microsoft Internet Explorer Browser Objects**

● **Working with Form Objects**

● **Working with Multiple Forms on Your Web Pages**

● **Combining All of These Techniques to Build Great Web Pages**

BUILDING A FORM ON THE FLY

To get started with learning how the power of working with objects can help us, let's explore how we can use the Internet Explorer object model to build forms on the fly. As you remember from Chapter 6, "Talk to the User!," we built a simple image browser that flips through a series of images. This was done by controlling the document displayed in a frame on the Web page.

To build a form on the fly, we can utilize the same technique. The key to making this successful is knowing how to manipulate the object structure of the Internet Explorer. In the sample provided in the Session1 subdirectory of Chapter8 on the CD-ROM, a simple button click builds a form in a frame. The click event fires the **ShowForm** script subroutine to build the form. Following is one of the lines of code from the subroutine that builds a set of HTML code in the frame.

```
Window.Frames(0).Document.Write "<CENTER><FORM>"
```

In this code fragment, we are maneuvering through the object model to be able to write the **CENTER** and **FORM** tags to the frame document. Figure 8-1 overviews the object hierarchy that pulls this code together:

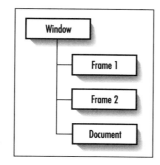

Figure 8-1
Frame object
hierarchy

Each window has a set of frames. The current window can, in fact, be a frame that is part of a set of frames in another window. There can be multiple levels with each frame having a corresponding **Document** object. In our example, we want to write from the topmost document to a child frame on our new form. In the above code fragment we reference an array, sometimes called a collection, that holds a reference to each frame in the current window. In our example, we have only one frame, so we would reference the first element of the array. Thus **window.frames(0)** will directly reference the frame that we want to build the form in.

If the document has five frames, then you will be able to reference five elements in the **frames(x)** collection. Also note that you do not have to directly reference *window* in the statement since it is a *top* level object and will be assumed by Visual Basic Script.

What Is an Object?

An object can be thought of as any entity that has attributes and plays a role in life. For example, an airplane is an object. It may have all kinds of attributes, such as the number of passengers it will carry, its length, year made, and so on. But it also has all kinds of methods we can *do* to it. For example, the landing gear can be lowered or raised, it can be flown, landed, and so on. It can fire off events such as a low fuel warning and other types of indicators that give feedback. The objects that will be worked with in Visual Basic Script will also have attributes, methods, and events.

To write the document to the frame, we simply reference the **Document** object of that frame. To do the writing, we use the **write** method of the **Document** object. The **Document** object knows how to create HTML on the fly using its **write** method.

To end the writing of the document to the frame, we use another method of the **Document** object, **close**. This will end the document. Figure 8-2 shows the sample document provided on the CD-ROM in the Session1 subdirectory of Chapter8. Note the form is not shown.

Figure 8-3 shows the form built by clicking on the HTML element Build Form button.

Review the code provided on the CD-ROM to see how the form is built. Once you have the appropriate referencing down on how to reach the **Frame** object in order to write HTML code to it, building forms on the fly will be easy.

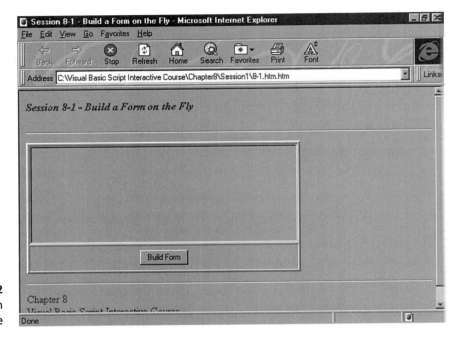

Figure 8-2
Sample form on
the fly Web page

Figure 8-3
Sample form build

1. Which statement is false about an Internet Explorer scripting object?
   a. It can contain events, properties, and methods.
   b. **write** is a subobject of documents.
   c. **frames(x)** is a subobject of the **Window** object.
   d. **close** is a method of the **Document** object.

2. What is wrong with the following statement? Assume there is at least one frame in the parent window.

```
frame.document.write "HTML CODE"
```

   a. The **WINDOW** tag is missing to reference the frame.
   b. The name of the frame needs to be referenced.
   c. The **frame** object is not referenced appropriately.
   d. Both b. and c.

3. Which statement best characterizes an **Object** method?
   a. Provides factual information about the object such as its name, status, and so on.
   b. Is triggered by the object itself, such as the **OnClick** event of an HTML button.
   c. Can be invoked from a script to perform some function the object is capable of performing such as writing HTML code to a document.
   d. None of the above.

4. Which is a true statement?
   a. The **frames** collection is limited only to the number of frames on the current HTML document.
   b. The **frames** collection is limited to three frames.
   c. The **frames** collection is limited to three frames for each HTML document.
   d. The **frames** collection is limited to 3 times the number of HTML documents for the current frame window.

5. Which statement best characterizes an **object** property?
   a. Defines a specific action that will take place when the user interacts with the object.
   b. Defines a specific action you can have the control perform.
   c. Defines a specific attribute or characteristic of the object.
   d. None of the above.

Difficulty: Easy

1. Add an additional button to the form that will build a form with several radio buttons on it in the same frame. The idea is to provide different form functionality based on user selection.

INTERACTING WITH AN HTML TEXT ELEMENT

The HTML Text input element that we have been working with throughout the book is an object that we can manipulate through its properties, methods, and events. For example, one of the properties of the textbox is its value, which we can set and manipulate from our scripts to control the text in the textbox.

Table 8-1 overviews the different properties, events, and methods available for the HTML Text input element as well as the TextArea input element:

Name	Description
Properties	
form	Gets the form object containing the element
name	Gets or sets the name of the element
value	Gets or sets the value of the element
defaultValue	Gets or sets the default value of the element
enabled	Gets or sets whether the control is enabled
Methods	
Focus	Sets the focus to the element
Blur	Clears the focus from the element
Select	Selects the contents of the element
Events	
OnFocus	Fired when the element gets the focus
OnBlur	Fired when the element loses the focus
OnChange	Fired when the element has changed
OnSelect	Fired when the contents of the element are selected

Table 8-1 Text *and* TextArea *properties, events, and methods*

As you can see, we have a wide range of options for controlling how the `text` and `textarea` input elements behave in our Web pages. To see some of these in action, let's review the sample provided in the Session2 subdirectory of Chapter8 on the CD-ROM. Figure 8-4 shows the Web page.

There are two sections on the Web page; the first is a sample demonstration for the `Text` element, and the second half is a sample demonstration for the `TextArea` element. Try clicking on the first element in each section, typing text, and exiting each. You will notice that the following text gives feedback elements as to what events were fired off for each text input. If you review the code, you will see that the `OnFocus`, `OnBlur`, and `OnChange` event subroutines are defined for each. Within these, we are using the `value` property of the other textboxes to display the event that was fired. Figure 8-5 shows the events fired for the `Text` element.

A button is also provided that will demonstrate using the `Focus` method of both elements. This will change the input focus from the current section of the document to the textbox. This is useful for not allowing a user to exit a text element until all appropriate data has been entered.

This session serves to provide a good example of how utilizing the properties, methods, and events of objects such as the `Text` and `TextArea` elements can be powerful in customizing how your Web page is utilized. In the next session, we will work with the `CheckBox` element.

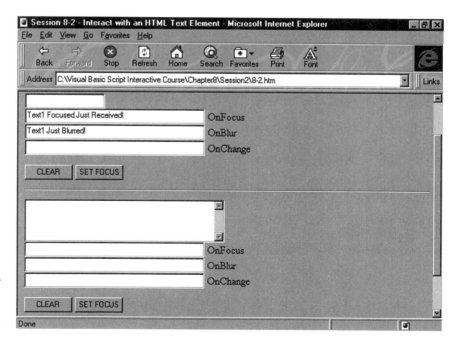

Figure 8-4
Sample `Text` element interaction Web page

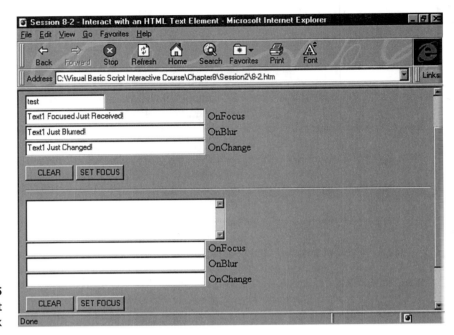

Figure 8-5
Text element event
feedback

1. This event can be used to check any changes that the Web page user may have entered.
   a. OnSelect
   b. OnChange
   c. OnBlur
   d. OnFocus

2. Which property controls the ability of the user to place text in the Text or TextArea input elements?
   a. defaultvalue
   b. value
   c. enabled
   d. name

3. What Visual Basic Script subroutine event is fired when a user exits a Text input element?
   a. Blur
   b. OnBlur
   c. OnSelect
   d. OnFocus

4. With the **Focus** method you can set the input focus to a **Text** or **TextArea** element. Which method do you use to take the focus away?
   a. **Blur**
   b. **Form**
   c. **Select**
   d. **Enabled**

5. Which property value will be used if no other value has been entered?
   a. **value**
   b. **defaultValue**
   c. **enabled**
   d. **focus**

Difficulty: Easy

1. Build a Web page that will ensure the user made some type of input into a textbox before exiting.

Difficulty: Intermediate

2. Build a Web page that will convert the text entered by the user into a **Text** element to be all uppercase.

INTERACTING WITH HTML
CheckBox **ELEMENTS**

Just like the **Text** and **TextArea** input elements, the **CheckBox** input element also has a set of events, methods, and properties. These can be used for controlling and working with how the user interacts with the Web page and specifically makes input selections.

Table 8-2 overviews the **CheckBox** properties, methods, and events:

Name	Description
Properties	
form	Gets the form object containing the element
name	Gets or sets the name of the element
value	Gets or sets the value of the element
checked	Gets or sets the checked state of the check box—True or False

continued on next page

continued from previous page

Name	Description
Properties	
defaultChecked	Gets or sets the default checked property of the check box
enabled	Gets or sets whether the control is enabled
Methods	
Click	Invokes the button click event
Focus	Sets the input focus to the element
Events	
OnClick	Fires when the element is clicked
OnFocus	Fires when the element gets the focus

Table 8-2 CheckBox *properties, methods, and events*

As you can see, many of these are very similar to the same properties, events, and meth-ods of the textbox control. Let's review the sample provided on the CD-ROM to see some of the CheckBox properties in action. The example can be found in the Session3 sub-directory of Chapter8. Figure 8-6 shows the Web page.

There are three check boxes, three buttons, and three status textboxes. Click on each button in succession. When you click on the button, the value, name, and checked properties of the check box above the button are shown. Note that the CheckBox value is set in the HTML <INPUT> tag code. Also, when the button is clicked, the next check box is either checked or unchecked based on its current state. Figure 8-7 shows an example of the first and second buttons being clicked.

Below is the code for the first button click. The value property of the textbox is set to display the check box value property, name property, and checked property. The CheckBox value is set up in the HTML <INPUT> tag code, the name is also set, and the checked property indicates whether or not the check box is currently checked. In the follow-ing line of code, the next corresponding check box is either checked or unchecked, based on its current status. To do this, the NOT operator is used to take the current checked true or false value and reverse it.

```
'   First button click
Sub SHOWBTN1_OnClick()

    '   Show the status of the first check box
    SHOWTEXT.Value = "Value = " & Check1.value & "    Name = " & _
                     Check1.name & "   Checked = " & check1.checked

    '   Set the value for the next check box to the
    '   opposite of the current value
    Check2.checked = Not Check2.Checked

End Sub
```

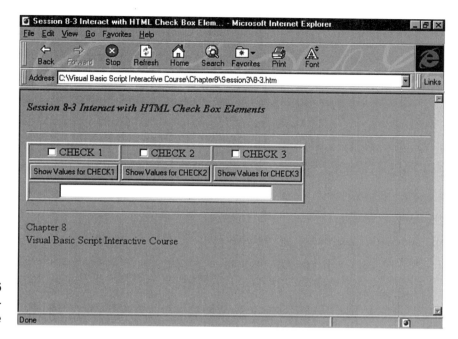

Figure 8-6
CheckBox demonstration Web page

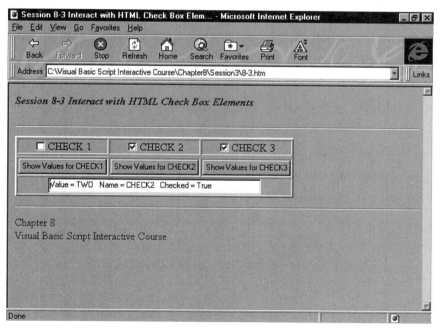

Figure 8-7
Results of the first two button clicks

The other two buttons work similarly. This example demonstrates how the current properties and status of a check box can be utilized to control the behavior of each check box. As we will see in the next chapter, having access to these will enable us to perform data validation on the user's input.

The code below is used for questions 1 and 2:

```
<INPUT TYPE=CHECKBOX NAME="CHECK1" VALUE=1 CHECKED>CHECK 1
<INPUT TYPE=CHECKBOX NAME="CHECK2" VALUE=2>CHECK 2
<INPUT TYPE=CHECKBOX NAME="CHECK3" VALUE=3>CHECK 3

<SCRIPT LANGUAGE="VBScript">

Sub Check1_OnClick()

     Check1.value = Check1.value * 3

End Sub

Sub Check2_OnClick()

     If check2.checked = "False" then
       Check2.value = Check2.value * 2
     End If

End Sub

Sub Check3_OnClick()

     If check3.checked = "True" then
       Check3.value = Check3.value * 4
     End If

End Sub

</SCRIPT>
```

1. Using the above code, what is the value of the third check box after three clicks?
   a. 58
   b. 48
   c. 12
   d. 36

2. Using the above code, what will be the value of the first check box after one click?
   a. 1
   b. 9
   c. 3
   d. 6

3. Which of the following cannot be controlled, called, or set for the check box?
   a. `value`
   b. `focus`
   c. `position`
   d. `enabled`

4. Which of the following statements would be a correct declaration of the `focus` event subroutine for the `Check1` check box in the code sample above?
   a. `Sub Check1_Focus()`
   b. `Sub Check1_OnFocus()`
   c. `Check1_Focus`
   d. `Check1_OnFocus`

5. Which is not a valid property, event, or method of the `CheckBox` input element?
   a. `form`
   b. `Click`
   c. `OnBlur`
   d. `OnFocus`

Difficulty: Intermediate

1. Build a series of three check boxes so that when one is checked, the other two will be unchecked. The functionality should be the same as three radio buttons.

SESSION 4

INTERACTING WITH AN HTML BUTTON ELEMENT

The last input element we will take a close look at is the button. We have been using the button throughout these past chapters to help build the demonstration Web pages. Let's take a formal look at the properties, events, and methods of the button control and how we can use these to build functionality into our applications.

Table 8-3 overviews the properties, methods, and events of the `Button` input element. Note that these events also apply to the Submit and Reset button types.

Name	Description
Properties	
form	Gets the form object containing the element
name	Gets or sets the name of the element
value	Gets or sets the value of the element
enabled	Gets or sets whether the control is enabled
Methods	
Click	Clicks the element
Focus	Sets the focus to the element
Events	
OnClick	Fires when the element is clicked
OnFocus	Fires when the element gets the focus

Table 8-3 `Button`, `Submit`, *and* `Reset` *properties, methods, and events*

By now I am sure these events, properties, and methods are becoming fairly familiar, so let's go ahead and dive into the sample provided on the CD-ROM. Figure 8-8 shows the sample Web page.

We revisit the spinning label control utilized in earlier chapters. This is done using the ActiveX label and timer controls. In fact, we are utilizing the **angle** property of the label to make it spin and the **interval** property of the timer to control the spin speed. The **timer** event of the Timer control is used to perform our manipulation on the label control.

For the button control, we have three buttons which will control the spinning of the label. The first starts and stops the spinning; the next two speed up and slow down the spinning of the label.

For the StartStop button, the key is setting the timer interval to either **0** to stop it or to the original interval value. This is done by checking the value, or caption, of the button. Based on that, our **If** logic in the **OnClick** event of the button will manipulate the timer appropriately. In the following code from the **OnClick** event, you can see that the **If** statements check the value of the button. Based on the value, the timer is manipulated, and the value of the button is changed.

```
If StartStop.Value = "STOP" then

   StartStop.Value="START"

   IeTimer1.Interval = 0

Else
```

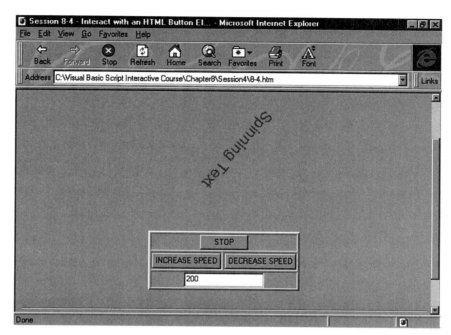

Figure 8-8
HTML Button
element
demonstration

```
StartStop.Value="STOP"

IeTimer1.Interval = Interval

End If
```

For the other two buttons, we simply increment or decrement the time period for the timer when the button is clicked on. This is done with the familiar OnClick event of the button. In the OnClick event, the timer interval property is updated.

In these four sessions, we have reviewed several examples of how to utilize properties, events, and methods and manipulate different objects in the Explorer object model. In the last half of this chapter, we will explore the Internet Explorer Scripting Object Model in greater detail. In addition, we will take a close look at the whole model, forms, and frames.

1. The _____ will set the _____ of an _____.
    a. focus event...focus...element
    b. click event...focus...element
    c. blur event...text...element
    d. OnFocus event...focus...element

2. What will be the result of the following code?

```
<INPUT TYPE=BUTTON NAME=BTN1 VALUE="Some Value 1">
<INPUT TYPE=BUTTON NAME=BTN2 VALUE="Some Value 2">

<SCRIPT LANGUAGE="VBScript">

Sub Btn1_OnClick()
     Btn2.Click
End Sub

Sub Btn2_OnClick()
     Btn1.Click
End Sub

</SCRIPT>
```

    a. When the first button is clicked, the second one is clicked.
    b. When the second button is clicked, the first one is clicked.
    c. This will cause an endless loop of button clicks.
    d. All of the above.

3. What does the following code accomplish?

```
<INPUT TYPE=TEXT NAME=TEXT1>
<INPUT TYPE=BUTTON NAME=BTN VALUE="">

<SCRIPT LANGUAGE="VBScript">

Sub Btn_OnClick()
     Btn.value = Text1.value
End Sub

</SCRIPT>
```

    a. An error; the **Btn** and the **Text1** values are not compatible.
    b. The **Btn** value will be set to the name of the textbox.
    c. The **Btn** name will be set to the value of the textbox.
    d. Whatever text is in the textbox will be the value or caption of the button when it is clicked.

4. Which statement best describes the uses of the StartStop button in the example Web page?
    a. The effect of the button changes based on the value of the button.
    b. It controls the starting and stopping of the label control.
    c. The **OnClick** event is utilized to provide the button functionality.
    d. All of the above.

5. Which is not a property of the button input element?
   a. `form`
   b. `name`
   c. `disabled`
   d. `value`

Difficulty: Easy

1. Add a button to the sample Web page that will flip the label's text color between blue and red.

EXPLORING EXPLORER OBJECTS

In the last chapter we were introduced to the `Window` and `Document` objects; also, we have taken a look at input elements in the first sessions of this chapter. But there is more to the Internet Explorer scripting object model. Figure 8-9 provides an overview of the object model.

As you can see, our familiar `Window` and `Document` objects are represented as well as the `Element` object. But there are also several other objects available to us for working with from our scripts. Table 8-4 outlines each.

Name	Description
Window	The `Window` object represents the Internet Explorer window and its methods and properties.
Frame	Array of frame windows contained by a parent window. Each frame is a window that has its own properties, including a document.
History	The `History` object exposes methods for navigating through the current history of Web pages.
Navigator	This object represents `stub` variables for the Netscape Navigator browser. The `Navigator` object makes your code compatible with the Navigator browser.
Location	Setting any portion of the `Location` object causes the browser to navigate to the newly constructed URL.

continued on next page

continued from previous page

Name	Description
Script	Any scripting function defined using the SCRIPT element in the window scope.
Document	The Document object reflects the HTML document currently in the browser and objects on the page, such as links, forms, buttons, and ActiveX objects.
Link	The Link object is referenced as a read-only property array. A Link object is constructed for every link that appears in the HTML document. All properties of the Link object are read-only and are the same as the Location object's properties. It is only accessible through the indexed array.
Anchor	The Anchor object is referenced as a read-only property array. It is only accessible through the indexed array.
Form	Forms are kept in the Document object both as an array and by name. Script forms are accessible either by index (the documents forms array) or by name (given in the NAME="somename" attribute of the HTML <FORM> tag).
Element	Elements are intrinsic HTML controls (placed on a page through the input tag <INPUT>) or objects that are insertable in HTML via the object tag <OBJECT>. These include ActiveX Controls. They can be referenced either by array or name, but this reference must follow the form identifier.

Table 8-4 *Internet Explorer object descriptions*

All of these objects have their appropriate properties, methods, and events to query, control, and interact with. As the object hierarchy diagram above shows, the **Document** object has three objects that help to define it, and the **Form** object has the **Element** object to help define it. Note that one of the best references for each and every property, method, and event is Microsoft's ActiveX Software Developer's Kit (SDK).

When working with objects in your scripts, the object reference can become rather complicated. For example, referencing an **Element** object on a form can have a rather long '.' reference. The following code fragment gives an example:

```
window.document.form.text.value
```

In this case, we are referencing the value of a **Text** input element on the form. But this nomenclature would get cumbersome if we needed to reference that object over and over. With Visual Basic Script, we have options for shortening this reference. The following sample demonstrates this technique:

```
<FORM NAME=FORM1>

    <INPUT TYPE=TEXT NAME=TEXT1 VALUE="Some Text"><BR>
    <INPUT TYPE=BUTTON NAME=BUTTON1>
```

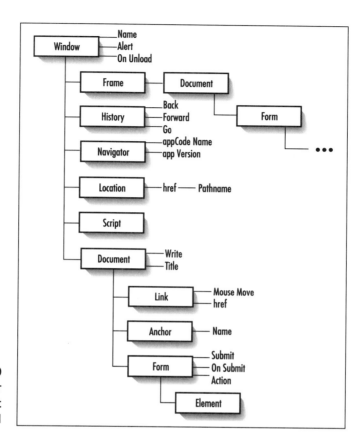

Figure 8-9
Internet Explorer
scripting object
model

```
</FORM>

<BR><BR>

<SCRIPT LANGUAGE="VBScript">

Sub Button1_OnClick()

    Dim FORMREF

    Set FORMREF = window.document.Form1

    msgbox FORMREF.Text1.value

End Sub

</SCRIPT>
```

In this sample, we have a form, **Form1**, with two input elements, **Button1** and **Text1**. When the button is clicked, the value of the textbox will be displayed. But, as you can see in the **OnClick** code, we have referenced the **Form** object and placed that reference into the variable `FORMREF`. Then in the next line of code, the `FORMREF` variable is used to then reference the `text1` element and its value.

In the next two sessions we will further explore the `Form` object to understand how we can reference multiple forms on a document as well as the input elements contained on each form.

1. The _____ exposes methods for _____ through the current _____ of Web pages.
   a. `History` object…navigating…history
   b. `Link` object…navigating…history
   c. `Link` object…viewing…history
   d. `Anchor` object…navigating…`Link` objects

2. Which is a correct reference for the button element object below?

```
<FORM NAME=FORM1>

    <INPUT TYPE=BUTTON NAME=BUTTON1 VALUE="BUTTON 1">

</FORM>
```

   a. `Window.Document.Form.Button.Value`
   b. `Window.Document.Form1.Button.Value`
   c. `Window.Document.Form.Button1.Value`
   d. `Window.Document.Form1.Button1.Value`

3. Which is a correct reference for the text element object below?

```
<FORM NAME=FORM>

    <INPUT TYPE=BUTTON NAME=TEXT1 VALUE="TEXT 1">

</FORM>
```

   a. `Var = Window.Document.Form`
      `Text1.Value`
   b. `Var = Window.Document`
      `Var.Text1.Value`
   c. `Var = Window.Document.Form`
      `Var.Text1.Value`
   d. `Var = Window.Document.Form`

4. Which two objects are referenced through arrays?
   a. `Window` and `Document`
   b. `Anchor` and `Document`
   c. `Anchor` and `Form`
   d. `Link` and `Frame`

5. The _____ object allows you to _____ the _____ for the browser.
   a. **Location**…change…URL
   b. **History**…delete…URL
   c. **Location**…change…location
   d. **Anchor**…update…history

Session 6

Form **OBJECTS**

The **Form** object provides the ability to work with the data that will be sent to the server and processed by your forms. There are many properties, events, and methods that define a form; how we can interact with it is from our script code. Table 8-5 overviews each.

Name	Description
Properties	
action	Gets or sets the address to be used to carry out the action of the form
encoding	Gets or sets the encoding for the form
method	Indicates how the form data should be sent to the server
target	Specifies the name of the target window in which to display the form results
elements	Returns the array of elements contained in the form
Methods	
Submit	Submits the form
Events	
OnSubmit	Fired when the form is submitted

Table 8-5 Form *properties, events, and methods*

The key to using these is to control the actions of the form. With these properties, you have control over how the form is to be handled by setting the method, encoding, and so on. Let's take a look at the sample Web page found in the Session6 subdirectory of Chapter8 on the CD-ROM. Figure 8-10 shows the document.

Click on both buttons to see the results of the Visual Basic Script included in the document. As you can see, the message box shown indicates the method used by the form as well as the name of the two elements on the form. The second button calls the **Submit** method to fire off the form, even though that element is not a Submit button of the form.

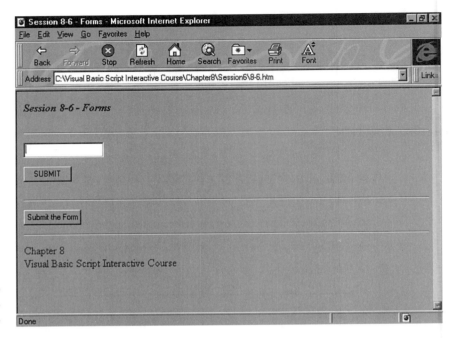

Figure 8-10
Sample interactive
form Web page

Review the script code for this sample, and you will see the straightforward ways in which you can interact with the form submission. In the next chapter, we will review many different options for performing data validation, which will be an invaluable tool in ensuring that the data sent to the server is valid.

1. The **Submit** method of the form
   a. allows the form action to be submitted to the server.
   b. initiates the submit from outside the form.
   c. performs data validation before the submit is initiated.
   d. does all of the above.

2. What is the value of the variable **Var**?

```
<FORM NAME=FORM>
  <INPUT TYPE=TEXT NAME=TEXT1>
  <INPUT TYPE=BUTTON NAME=BUTTON1>
  <INPUT TYPE=TEXT NAME=TEXT2>
</FORM>

<SCRIPT LANGUAGE="VBScript">
StartSub
```

```
Sub StartSub()
      Var = Form.Elements(1).Name
End Sub
</SCRIPT>
```

       a. Text1
       b. Button1
       c. Text2
       d. Form

3. The _____ property specifies the name of the _____ to display the _____ results in.
       a. target...target window...form
       b. action...HTML document...query
       c. submit...HTML element...query
       d. encoding...target window...form

4. The Form object is a child object of which object?
       a. Window
       b. Element
       c. Navigator
       d. Document

5. This event is fired when a forms data is sent to the server.
       a. Submit
       b. Form
       c. OnSubmit
       d. Post

Difficulty: Intermediate

    1. Build a Web page that will require the Web page user to enter 'hello' in a textbox before the form can be submitted.

WORKING WITH MULTIPLE FORMS

In the last session, we reviewed an example with a single form, but a document can have multiple forms on it. The **Document** object has an array of forms that can be referenced for all forms on the document. Figure 8-11 shows this relationship.

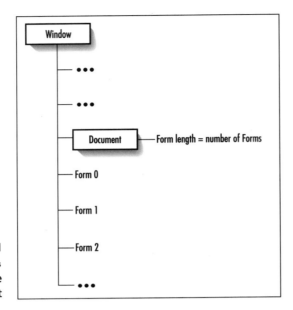

Figure 8-11
Multiple Forms
objects for one
Document object

The **Forms** object has a **Length** property that will indicate the number of forms on the document. This will indicate the number of forms that can be referenced in the array. The following code fragment shows this:

```
document.forms.length
```

And, the **forms** array is referenced as follows:

```
document.forms(##)
```

The **##** indicates the index into the array, which cannot be greater than **forms length** minus 1. This is because the array index begins counting at 0 and not 1. Thus for a document with 4 forms, the **##** array index would be 0 through 3. The **forms** events, methods, and properties are referenced in the same way as using the specific form name shown in the last session.

A sample Web page is provided in the Session7 subdirectory of Chapter8 on the CD-ROM. Figure 8-12 demonstrates referencing the elements on several forms of the document.

In this document, the three textboxes are each placed on a separate form. The button submits all forms by calling the **Submit** method of the form. The next section

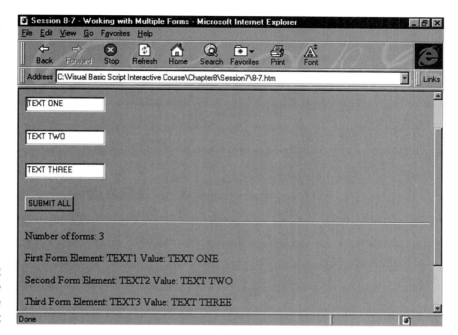

Figure 8-12
Sample multiple
form Web page
document

is the output of a startup subroutine that references the number of forms on the document and the first element on each form. The following code shows how the first form is referenced:

```
Document.write "Number of forms:   " &
          document.forms.length & "<BR><BR>"

Document.write "First Form Element:   " & _
          document.forms(0).elements(0).name & "    "

Document.write "Value:   " & document.forms(0).elements(0).value _
          & "<BR><BR>"
```

As you can see, the number of forms on the document is referenced through the **length** property. Then, to retrieve the first form on the document, we reference the document **forms()** property and then the **elements** property of **forms**. If you have a large number of forms or elements on your document, consider using a **For...Next** loop if you need to reference each. You can easily reference each by looping through the array and performing similar functions such as clearing each element on a form.

In the last session, a sample Web page will be built that will pull together many of the concepts demonstrated in this chapter. It will demonstrate how dynamic Web pages can be built using forms, frames, and elements.

1. What is wrong with the following code, assuming there is one form on the document?

```
MsgBox Document.Forms.Method
```

    a. There is no **method** property for the **Forms** object.
    b. It should be: **Document.Forms(0).Method**.
    c. It should be: **Document.Forms(1).Method**.
    d. The method cannot be determined until the form has been submitted.

2. What is the upper bound value of the **Forms** array for a document if there are six forms?
    a. 7
    b. 6
    c. 5
    d. Unknown

3. What is wrong with the following code fragment?

```
<FORM NAME=Form1 Method="POST">
<INPUT TYPE=TEXT1 NAME=TEXT1 VALUE="Some Text">
</FORM

<FORM NAME=Form2 Method="POST">
<INUT TYPE=TEXT2 NAME=TEXT2 VALUE="Some More Text">
</FORM>

<SCRIPT LANGUAGE="VBScript">

StartSub

Sub StartSub()

    For N = 0 to Document.Forms.Length
      Msgbox Document.Forms.Method
    Next N

End Sub

</SCRIPT>
```

    a. The **MsgBox** forms reference is not correct.
    b. The script will crash because the loop will try to access an invalid index in the **Forms** array.
    c. **"POST"** is not a correct form method.
    d. Both a. and b.

4. Which property indicates the number of forms on the form?
   a. `Name`
   b. `Method`
   c. `Submit`
   d. `OnSubmit`

5. Which of the following is not a valid property, event, or method of the `Forms` object?
   a. `FormNum`
   b. `Length`
   c. `Number`
   d. `Numb`

EXERCISE 7

Difficulty: Advanced

1. Build a Web document with six text input elements on a single form. Use the `Elements` array of the `Forms` array to loop through each element on the form.

PUTTING IT ALL TOGETHER

So, you may be thinking that this stuff is cool, but how do I put it all together? To answer this question, let's take a look at a sample Web page that will be based on the first session on building forms on the fly.

In our example, we will build two forms on the fly based on button clicks. The key in this example will be interacting with the form created in the frame. To get started, let's look at how we reference the object hierarchy for forms in a frame from our Visual Basic Scripts. Figure 8-13 shows this hierarchy.

The `Frames` attribute of the `Window` object is an array that will reference each frame on the top-level document. Each frame contains a document which has all the same attributes of the `Document` object discussed in the last chapter. The `Document` object of the frame would be referenced as follows:

```
Window.Frames(##).Document
```

The `##` indicates an index into the set of frames on the `Window` object. Once you have the `Document` object for the frame referenced, you can then reference all subobjects of the document. Figure 8-14 shows this.

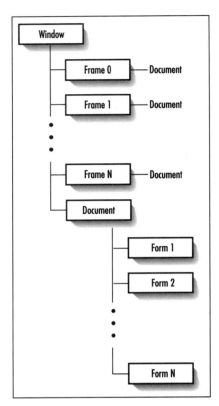

Figure 8-13
Frame object
hierarchy

As you can see, once you have the **Document** object of the frame referenced, you can use the same reference techniques we have used throughout the chapter. The following code fragment shows how to reference an element on a form contained in a frame document.

```
Window.Frames(##).Document.Forms(##).Elements(##)
```

The top-level object is referenced; then the **Frames** array will be referenced with an appropriate index to indicate which frame. Next, the document contained in the frame is referenced followed by the array of forms contained in the document. Finally, for the form indicated by the index, we can reference the array of elements on that form. Thus even though we have windows within windows created by using frames, through the object model we can reach down to these frames and manipulate their objects.

So, without further discussion, let's dive into our Web page example for this session. The document can be found in the Session8 subdirectory of Chapter8 on the CD-ROM. Figure 8-15 shows the Web page.

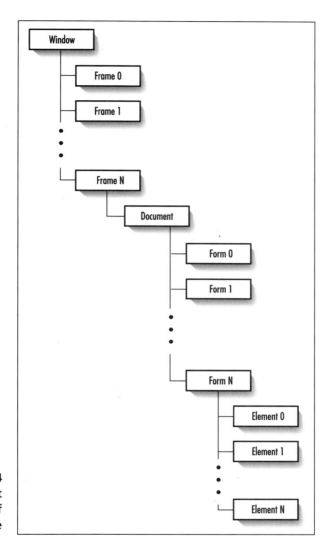

Figure 8-14
Document
reference of
a frame

Click on the Build Form A button to build the first form in the frame. Once the frame is built, the middle two buttons will allow you to either clear the form contained in the frame or submit it. Click on the Build Form B button, and a different form will be built. The middle two buttons will perform the same operations.

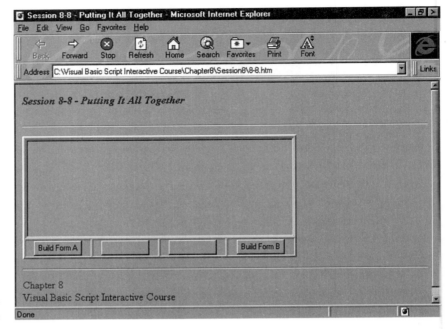

Figure 8-15
Putting It All
Together Web page
sample

The creation of the two forms in the frame follows the same basic steps shown in the first session. The Clear Form button references the complete object hierarchy shown in the code fragment above. The following is the loop which clears the values of all the form elements:

```
FrameDocForm = Window.Frames(0).Document.Forms(0)

For N = 0 to FrameDocForm.Elements.Length - 1
     FrameDocForm.Elements(N).Value = ""
Next
```

First, to make our code easier to read, we set the variable **FrameDocForm** to reference the **Form** object of the frame document. Then, in the **For...Next** loop, we reference the number of elements in the form just as we learned in earlier sessions. Finally, each element is then referenced to clear the array.

```
If ClearForm.Value = "Clear Form B" then

     FrameDocForm.Check1.Checked = False
     FrameDocForm.Check2.Checked = False
     FrameDocForm.Check3.Checked = False

End If
```

In the next section of the subroutine code shown above, we check to see what the status of the button value is. If we are working on Form B, then the check boxes are unchecked. Again, the same reference can be made to these elements through the **FrameDocForm** variable, but instead of using the **Elements** array, the check boxes are referenced by name.

For the Submit Form button, the **Submit** method of the form in the frame is called to submit the form. The window status bar is updated to indicate that the form was submitted.

With the object hierarchy at your disposal, you can build very complex Web pages and still have control over any part of the Web page in your script code. The key is navigating the different levels of the hierarchy to appropriately reference each object.

1. What is wrong with the following reference, considering that the **Window** document has two frames each with two forms containing six elements?

```
Window.Document.Frames(0).Form(1).Element(0).Value
```

    a. The element needs to be referenced by name.
    b. The form on the frame must be referenced by name.
    c. A check should be done to ensure that each object can be referenced.
    d. There is nothing wrong with the reference.

2. In the **ClearForm_OnClick** subroutine of the Web page sample, which of the following would work as a way to reference the **Checked** property of the first check box?

    a. `Window.Frames(0).Document.Forms(0).Elements(1).Checked`
    b. `Window.Frames(0).Document.Forms(0).Elements(2).Checked`
    c. `Window.Frames(0).Document.Forms(0).Elements(3).Checked`
    d. `Window.Frames(0).Document.Forms(0).Elements(4).Checked`

3. A frame can contain an HTML document that contains other _____, _____, and _____.
    a. frames…tables…elements
    b. forms…elements…scripts
    c. frames…elements…scripts
    d. All of the above

4. The top-level object in the Internet Explorer Scripting Object model is the
    a. **Window** object.
    b. **Document** object.
    c. **Length** object.
    d. **HTML** object.

5. Which is the correct way to set **Var1** to the second form on the first frame of the browser window document?

   a. `Var1 = Window.Frames(0).Document.Forms(0)`

   b. `Var1 = Window.Frames(0).Document.Forms(1)`

   c. `Var1 = Window.Frames(0).Document.Forms(2)`

   d. `Var1 = Window.Frames(1).Document.Forms(1)`

Difficulty: Advanced

1. Change the sample Web page so that the two forms are shown in different frames. Add a Build and Submit button for each frame.

Difficulty: Intermediate

2. Add to your solution for the first exercise a check on the form submit click to ensure that data has been entered in the various form input elements.

CHAPTER SUMMARY

Microsoft Internet Explorer objects can be powerful to utilize and manipulate from your scripts. Each object has events, methods, and properties that can be manipulated from your code. Whether you are building forms on the fly or interacting with textboxes or check boxes, the possibilities are wide open. In the next chapter we will explore how we can support the user by entering input and validating the data input.

DATA VALIDATION

One of the fundamental uses of Visual Basic Script is the client-side validation. For example, if we need dollar values to be entered into a textbox, we might not want to allow a number with three or more decimal places. Perhaps we need to ensure that a valid state was entered in a person's address. Even using ActiveX controls, we can build different ways of validating and supporting user input into Web pages. By doing validation on the client side, we don't need to send the data to the server, have it checked, and then have any errors returned all the way back across the Internet. With a little scripting on the client side, we can quickly check and give feedback.

You will find many different data validation needs as you begin to build Web pages and check for input. In this chapter, we will review handling and checking both numeric and alphanumeric text. We can validate a list of selections, add them to pop-up menus, provide tips, and validate an entire form. Through the techniques presented here, and many more demonstrated throughout the entire book, you will have many options for how you can work with the user-entered data to provide validation and feed-back.

In this chapter we will cover the following topics:

- ● Validating Text Entered into a Textbox

- ● Validate Numbers Entered into a Textbox

- ● Validate a Date Entered into a Textbox

- ● Validate Selections Made in a Listbox

- ● Validate Capitalization in a Text Paragraph

- ● Using the ActiveX Pop-Up Window Control to Provide Feedback to the User

- ● Validating User Selections with the ActiveX Menu Control

- ● Validating Data Entered into a Form

VALIDATE TEXT ENTERED INTO A TEXTBOX

One of the basic techniques used for data validation is checking text entered into a textbox. An example may be needing all text input to be in uppercase or lowercase, or perhaps checking to make sure that the answer fits within a range of possible answers.

As with most of the sessions in this chapter, we will work primarily with a Web page example to get a taste of how we can perform this type of validation. Figure 9-1 shows the sample Web page provided in the Session1 subdirectory of Chapter9 on the CD-ROM.

The Web page provides an input box for entering text. We have three check boxes that will set the type of check done when the Validate button is selected. The first check is to ensure that the data entered into the textbox is all uppercase. The second check is to ensure that the text is all lowercase. The last check will ensure that the text entered is a valid state abbreviation. There are also two buttons provided for performing the conversion of the text to either upper- or lowercase.

DATA VALIDATION

One of the fundamental uses of Visual Basic Script is the client-side validation. For example, if we need dollar values to be entered into a textbox, we might not want to allow a number with three or more decimal places. Perhaps we need to ensure that a valid state was entered in a person's address. Even using ActiveX controls, we can build different ways of validating and supporting user input into Web pages. By doing validation on the client side, we don't need to send the data to the server, have it checked, and then have any errors returned all the way back across the Internet. With a little scripting on the client side, we can quickly check and give feedback.

You will find many different data validation needs as you begin to build Web pages and check for input. In this chapter, we will review handling and checking both numeric and alphanumeric text. We can validate a list of selections, add them to pop-up menus, provide tips, and validate an entire form. Through the techniques presented here, and many more demonstrated throughout the entire book, you will have many options for how you can work with the user-entered data to provide validation and feedback.

In this chapter we will cover the following topics:

- Validating Text Entered into a Textbox

- Validate Numbers Entered into a Textbox

- Validate a Date Entered into a Textbox

- Validate Selections Made in a Listbox

- Validate Capitalization in a Text Paragraph

- Using the ActiveX Pop-Up Window Control to Provide Feedback to the User

- Validating User Selections with the ActiveX Menu Control

- Validating Data Entered into a Form

VALIDATE TEXT ENTERED INTO A TEXTBOX

One of the basic techniques used for data validation is checking text entered into a textbox. An example may be needing all text input to be in uppercase or lowercase, or perhaps checking to make sure that the answer fits within a range of possible answers.

As with most of the sessions in this chapter, we will work primarily with a Web page example to get a taste of how we can perform this type of validation. Figure 9-1 shows the sample Web page provided in the Session1 subdirectory of Chapter9 on the CD-ROM.

The Web page provides an input box for entering text. We have three check boxes that will set the type of check done when the Validate button is selected. The first check is to ensure that the data entered into the textbox is all uppercase. The second check is to ensure that the text is all lowercase. The last check will ensure that the text entered is a valid state abbreviation. There are also two buttons provided for performing the conversion of the text to either upper- or lowercase.

DATA VALIDATION

One of the fundamental uses of Visual Basic Script is the client-side validation. For example, if we need dollar values to be entered into a textbox, we might not want to allow a number with three or more decimal places. Perhaps we need to ensure that a valid state was entered in a person's address. Even using ActiveX controls, we can build different ways of validating and supporting user input into Web pages. By doing validation on the client side, we don't need to send the data to the server, have it checked, and then have any errors returned all the way back across the Internet. With a little scripting on the client side, we can quickly check and give feedback.

You will find many different data validation needs as you begin to build Web pages and check for input. In this chapter, we will review handling and checking both numeric and alphanumeric text. We can validate a list of selections, add them to pop-up menus, provide tips, and validate an entire form. Through the techniques presented here, and many more demonstrated throughout the entire book, you will have many options for how you can work with the user-entered data to provide validation and feedback.

In this chapter we will cover the following topics:

- Validating Text Entered into a Textbox
- Validate Numbers Entered into a Textbox
- Validate a Date Entered into a Textbox
- Validate Selections Made in a Listbox
- Validate Capitalization in a Text Paragraph
- Using the ActiveX Pop-Up Window Control to Provide Feedback to the User
- Validating User Selections with the ActiveX Menu Control
- Validating Data Entered into a Form

VALIDATE TEXT ENTERED INTO A TEXTBOX

One of the basic techniques used for data validation is checking text entered into a textbox. An example may be needing all text input to be in uppercase or lowercase, or perhaps checking to make sure that the answer fits within a range of possible answers.

As with most of the sessions in this chapter, we will work primarily with a Web page example to get a taste of how we can perform this type of validation. Figure 9-1 shows the sample Web page provided in the Session1 subdirectory of Chapter9 on the CD-ROM.

The Web page provides an input box for entering text. We have three check boxes that will set the type of check done when the Validate button is selected. The first check is to ensure that the data entered into the textbox is all uppercase. The second check is to ensure that the text is all lowercase. The last check will ensure that the text entered is a valid state abbreviation. There are also two buttons provided for performing the conversion of the text to either upper- or lowercase.

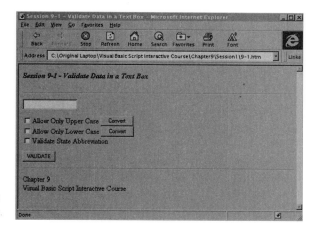

Figure 9-1
Textbox validation
Web page example

Try entering different values in the textbox and performing the different checks. Then click on the convert buttons to change the text appropriately. To get started, let's review the uppercase and lowercase checks. The following is the code for the uppercase check:

```
Sub UpperCase()

    If UCASE(Text1.Value) <> Text1.Value then

        MsgBox "You did not enter the text in Upper Case - Try Again!"

        Text1.Focus

    Else

        MsgBox "The Text is all Upper Case."

    End If

End Sub
```

First, the UCASE function is used to convert the string to uppercase, and then it is checked against the original string. If it was originally entered in uppercase, then the two will match. If they do not match, then the user is notified and the focus is set back to the textbox for input. The lowercase example works in the same fashion. To convert the strings to upper- and lowercase, the LCASE and UCASE functions are used.

The state abbreviation checking is fairly straightforward. A SELECT CASE construct is used to check the value entered in the text element. To make the check easy, the value in the textbox is converted to uppercase. Then each state is checked in the select. For purposes of this example, only a few states are checked. If there is no match, then a message box is provided to the user.

You can validate almost any type of data entered into a textbox based on whatever criteria you may have. As we will see in later sessions, we can tear apart, twist, and manipulate strings to our heart's content to validate and format data. In the next session, we will look specifically at how to validate numerical data.

1. In the sample Web page, if we are doing a check for uppercase data entry, what will be the result of entering "NIGHT 1" into the check box and why?
   a. The check would return true because the alpha characters are all uppercase.
   b. The check would return false because the '1' is not an alpha character.
   c. The check would return false because the space is not an alpha character.
   d. Both b. and c.

2. What will the following check do?

```
Flag = True

For N = 1 to Len(Text.Value)
        If Mid(Text.Value, N, 1) = "(space)" then Flag = False
Next
```

   a. Check for a space in the text entered in the textbox.
   b. Loop through each character in the text entered in the input element.
   c. Set the Flag to false if the text value is "Hello There".
   d. All of the above.

3. Assume that a user might enter a period after the state abbreviation. How can this period be ignored when validating the text?
   a. `Text.Value = Left(Text.Value, 2)`
   b. `Text.Value = Left(Text.Value, 2)`
   c. `Text.Value = Right(Text.Value, Len(Text.Value) - 2)`
   d. `Text.Value = Left(Text.Value, Len(Text.Value) - 2)`

4. If the Validate button were part of a form, and the check was successful, what method would be used to activate the form?
   a. `POST`
   b. `GET`
   c. `Submit`
   d. `OnSubmit`

5. What textbox event could be used to validate the entered data immediately when the textbox is exited?
   a. `OnLeave`
   b. `OnExit`
   c. `OnBlur`
   d. `Blur`

EXERCISE 1

Difficulty: Easy

1. Add a check to the sample Web page that will check for spaces in the entered text.

Difficulty: Intermediate

2. Write a sample code fragment that will check whether the first character of the input is upper- or lowercase.

SESSION 2

VALIDATE NUMBERS ENTERED INTO A TEXTBOX

Not only do we need to work with validating strings, we need to validate numbers. The precision of a number can depend on whether we are working with values ranging from precise scientific numbers to two-digit decimal place money. If we are asking a person for his age, we need to check to make sure a negative number was not entered. And, for that matter, there should be no decimals in the age number.

To get a feel for how to do this kind of validation, see the sample Web page found in the Session2 subdirectory of Chapter9 on the CD-ROM. Figure 9-2 shows the Web page.

As with the last session, this Web page demonstrates several different types of validation. The first button will round any number entered into the text input element to two decimal places. The next two options will check for integers and positive numbers. Two Convert buttons are provided to convert the numbers from a decimal to an integer and from a negative to a positive.

Let's first look at the following code, which rounds any decimal number entered into the textbox to two decimal places.

```
Sub ROUND_OnClick()

    Numbers.Value = Numbers.Value * 100

    Numbers.Value = CInt(Numbers.Value)

    Numbers.Value = Numbers.Value / 100

End Sub
```

Here, we move the two decimal digits we want to keep to the left of the decimal point by multiplying the value times 100. Then the CInt function is used to convert that number to an integer. CInt will round that number automatically. Finally, the number is divided

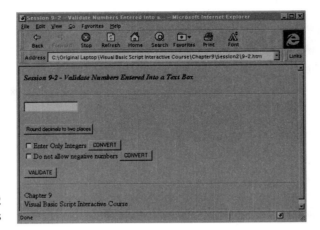

Figure 9-2
Validating numbers

by 100 to move the two decimal points to the right of the decimal point. Figure 9-3 shows the process of rounding the number.

Of course, this method can be used to round the number to any precision by changing the value we are multiplying and dividing by. A number of approaches can be taken to check for an integer. One of the simplest is to do two easy checks found in the IntCheck function of the sample. The first is to use the IsNumeric function to ensure that a number was entered into the text input element. Second, we can check the text entered for a decimal point using the InStr function. That will return the position of the decimal point in the number if there is one. The only other check needed is to ensure that just a decimal was entered, with no digits to the right. A check is done to see whether there are any numbers to the right of the decimal by checking the length versus the decimal position. To convert the number to an integer, the CInt function is used.

The final check is to ensure that a negative number is not entered into the input element. The simple check is to see whether a negative sign (-) was entered into the input element. A Trim function is performed to ensure that no leading or trailing spaces are on the input text. Then we simply use the Left function to see whether the left-most character is a negative sign. If so, then the negative sign is shaved off to convert it to a positive number.

Figure 9-3
Rounding numbers
to two decimal
points (HAND)

(1)	Multiply by 100	$xxxxx.1234$ $\times 100$
		$xxxxx12.34$
(2)	Use the CInt Function	CInt ($xxxxx12.34$) $\longrightarrow$ $xxxxx12$
(3)	Divide by 100	($xxxxx12$ $\div$ $100 = xxxxx.12$

These are just three types of validations that can be performed on numbers entered into an input element. In these examples we used some string manipulation and other techniques to manipulate and convert these numbers. With Visual Basic Script you have a wide range of options for working with numbers.

1. What multiplier and divisor would we need to use to round a number to four decimal places?
   a. 1100
   b. 10000
   c. 1000
   d. 11000

2. Which of the following checks will ensure that a number, **Val1**, falls between to values, **Val2** and **Val3**?
   a. If **Val1 >= Val2** and **Val1 <= Val3** then....
   b. If **Val1 > Val2** and **Val1 < Val3** then....
   c. If **Val1 >= Val2** or **Val1 <= Val3** then....
   d. If **Val1 > Val2** or **Val1 < Val3** then....

3. There is another Visual Basic Script function that can be used to convert a negative number to a positive. Which of the following will do this?
   a. ABS
   b. CINT
   c. CLNG
   d. CSNG

4. There are two more functions, Int and Fix, which can be used to convert a number into an integer. What is the difference between the two?
   a. Int only works on a current integer and turns it into a positive.
   b. Fix only works on a current integer and turns it into a positive.
   c. Int returns the first negative integer less or equal to the number, while Fix returns the first negative integer greater or equal to the number.
   d. None of the above.

5. Which function can be utilized to ensure that the data in the textbox is converted into a numerical format?
   a. CInt
   b. CLong
   c. CSng
   d. All of the above

Difficulty: Easy

1. Use the ABS function in the sample to convert the negative number to an integer.

SESSION 3

VALIDATE A DATE ENTERED INTO A TEXTBOX

Dates are another key type of data we need to validate. We can perform different types of validation such as ensuring that a valid date is entered or that a date falls within a range, and check time values as well.

So, without further discussion about what we can do, let's look at examples of how to perform these checks. Figure 9-4 shows the sample Web page provided in the Session3 subdirectory of Chapter9 on the CD-ROM.

There are four **Text** input elements provided for doing different types of checks. The first prompts you to enter a date that falls between two dates. The next prompts you to enter a date that falls in the current decade. We can also check to ensure that the day of the week entered falls on a specified day, in this case Monday. The final example checks to see whether a time entered by the user falls between two time frames.

The first key function we need to use to ensure a valid date entered is the IsDate function. This will ensure that a valid date, time, or date and time has been entered into the input elements.

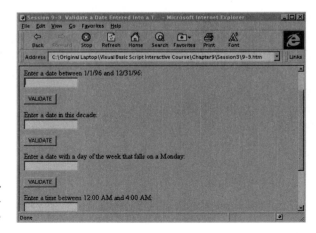

Figure 9-4
Date and time validation Web page

The second and third examples check a part of the date to ensure that it falls within a range. The Year function returns the value of the year in a valid date. This can be compared with the value Year returns from the Now function. In this case, we ensure that the year falls in the current decade. To check for a day entered that falls on Monday, the Day function is used. This returns a value that indicates which day of the week the date falls on. In this case, **2** is the value returned for Monday.

The first and last checks use simple date math checking to ensure that the date and time fall between two values. These checks can be done with the same mathematical operators you are used to using for regular math expressions.

Dates can be picked apart using the Day, Month, and Year functions as well as any string functions since the values are entered into text input elements. Also, don't forget the DateSerial and DateValue functions as well as CDate for building and converting strings and the corresponding time functions. As with strings and numbers, Visual Basic Script provides a wealth of opportunity for working with, validating, and manipulating dates.

1. What will the following code fragments return?

```
Year("01/05/1996")
Year("01/05/96")
```

      a. 1996, 96
      b. 96, 1996
      c. 96, 96
      d. 1996, 1996

2. What will be the result of the following code fragment assuming **Val1 = "21/01/1954"**?

```
If Val1 >= CDate(1/5/92) then
   msgbox "Date is in range)
End If
```

      a. An error will be returned by the CDate function call.
      b. An error will be returned by the MsgBox function call.
      c. False will be returned because **Val1** does not contain a valid date.
      d. All of the above.

3. Which function returns a Date subtype that contains a specific hour, minute, and second based on passed in values for each?
      a. TimeValue
      b. DateSerial
      c. DateValue
      d. TimeSerial

4. What functions can be used to separate the different sections of a time variable?
   a. Hour
   b. Minute
   c. Second
   d. All of the above

5. Which function can be used to ensure that a date is stored with a subtype of Date?
   a. CDate
   b. ConvDate
   c. IsDate
   d. All of the above

Difficulty: Intermediate

1. Write a code fragment that will return the three primary sections of a time variable.

VALIDATE LIST SELECTIONS

Lists of options for the user to select are a common way of presenting data for the Web page reader to choose from. But, like any other input from the user, it will be critical to validate it before it is sent to the server. The **SELECT** input element can be interacted with in your scripts to perform validation on the user selections. Table 9-1 reviews the properties, events, and methods:

Property, Method, or Event	Description
Properties	
Name	Gets or sets the name of the element
Length	Gets the number of options in a select element
Options	Gets the <OPTIONS> tags for a select element in an array
SelectedIndex	Gets the index for the first selected option

Property, Method, or Event	Description
Method	
Focus	Sets the focus to the element
Blur	Clears the focus from the element
Event	
OnFocus	Fired when the element gets the focus
OnBlur	Fired when the element loses the focus
OnChange	Fired when the element has changed

Table 9-1 *Select properties, methods, and events*

Each option in a select box can be reviewed to retrieve its text description as well as whether or not it is selected. The key to performing the validation will be using the Options array that provides an index into the option list in the Select input element. Each option has a Selected and Text property that allows you to check whether that option is selected and retrieve the text of the option. Thus, each array entry can be checked to review the selections of the user.

The example provided for this session can be found in the Session4 subdirectory of Chapter9 on the CD-ROM. This Web page provides a list of selections about three different luxury cars. Once the selections are made, click the Select button to perform whatever the next appropriate action would be.

When you click the Select button, the script code searches through each select list to ensure that the appropriate selections were made before continuing. Figure 9-5 shows the Web page in action.

There are four selection lists provided: one for picking a car manufacturer, one for the car color, another for the car style, and the last for selecting the features desired on the car. Make your selections and click the Select button. Try selecting and not selecting different options and clicking on the button. If all the selections are made appropriately, feedback is given on the selections, and the user can choose to proceed or not.

The Select button click event is where the primary logic for the validation takes place. First, in the code, we need to check that only one manufacturer, color, and body style were selected as well as ensure that any selection was made at all. The following code does this for the manufacturer list. The For...Next loop checks each option in the Options array to see whether it is selected. A count is made to track the number of selections.

```
For N = 0 to Cars.Length -1

    If Cars.Options(n).Selected = 1 then Cnt2 = Cnt2 + 1

Next
```

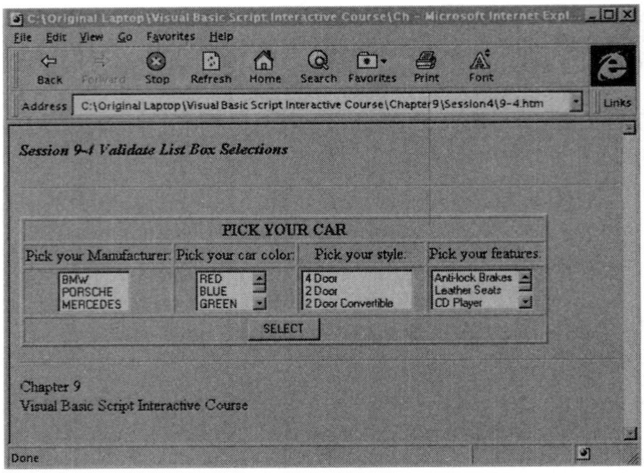

Figure 9-5
Select list
validation
Web page

Based on the count, we check to see whether more than one option was selected. If so, the user gets a notification and the subroutine is exited. If no selection was made, a similar notification is given and the subroutine exited.

```
If Cnt2 > 1 then

    MsgBox "You picked more than one manufacturer. Please try again."

    Exit Sub

End If

If Cnt2 = 0 then

    MsgBox "You did not pick a manufacturer. Please try again."

    Exit Sub

End If
```

Once all checks are done, the text for each selected item is added up in a string to be displayed in a message box that will give feedback to the user on the selections made and allow a decision by the user.

Review the code to see how each selected text item is retrieved and added to the display string. In the next session we will return to text validation and provide a sample for how to ensure that appropriate sentence capitalization has been provided.

1. Which property returns the list item chosen by the user?
   a. `SelectedIndex`
   b. `SelectedItem`
   c. `Selected`
   d. None of the above

2. What will be the results of the following code fragment assuming the SELECTLIST has five items and two selected?

```
Sub CheckList()

    Dim Cnt

    For N = 1 to SELECTLIST.Length

      If SELECTLIST.OPTIONS(N).SELECTED = 1 then CNT = CNT + 1

    Next

End Sub
```

   a. CNT will equal 2.
   b. CNT will equal 1.
   c. The `Options` array is not referenced properly.
   d. The `Options` array is referenced properly but the `For` loop should start at 0 and go to the Length minus 1.

3. Which code fragment will compare the text values of two select lists?
   a. `If Select1.Options(Selected) = Select2.Options(Selected) then...`
   b. `If Select1.Options(Select1.SelectedIndex) = Select2.Options(Selected1.SelectedIndex) then...`
   c. `If Select1.Options(Select1.SelectededIndex).Text = Select2.Options(Selected1.SelectedIndex).Text then...`
   d. `If Select1 = Select2 then...`

4. The _____ _____ references the _____ _____ in a/an _____ for the `Select` element.
   a. `list` property...`<OPTIONS>` tags...array
   b. `options` property... `<OPTIONS>` tags...list
   c. `list` property... `<OPTIONS>` tags ...list
   d. `options` property...`<OPTIONS>` tags...array

5. Which is not an event of the `Select` object?
   a. `Focus`
   b. `OnBlur`
   c. `OnChange`
   d. `OnUpdate`

Difficulty: Intermediate

1. Write a code fragment that will allow a user to select all the items in a listbox except for one.

Difficulty: Intermediate

2. Write a code fragment that will check to see whether the single selections of twolist boxes are the same.

VALIDATE THE CAPITALIZATION IN A TEXT PARAGRAPH

Verifying an entire paragraph of text can be a daunting task. This could range from basic checking to ensure that any text was entered all the way to a complete spelling and grammar check. As we saw in the first session, we can make some basic checks to ensure text entered into a textbox is correct.

In this session, we are going to check the capitalization of a paragraph entered into a `TextArea` input element. Normally, the first word of each sentence should be capitalized. What we want to demonstrate in this session is how to search for the first letter of each sentence and capitalize it. Figure 9-6 shows the sample Web page that can be found in the Session5 subdirectory of Chapter9 on the CD-ROM.

As the Web page shows, there is just one `TextArea` input element and one Input button. The default text provided has several sentences with no capitalization. Click on the button to check capitalization of the paragraph. You can also type in your own paragraph with different punctuation and capitalization and test the algorithm.

Speaking of algorithms, let's take a look at how this validation technique is done. The key is to look for the end of one sentence for a punctuation identifier which would be either a '?', '!', or '.'. Once we find one of these punctuation marks, we can check two positions to the right for the first letter of the next sentence. Note that the two spaces separating two sentences is done by convention; you could easily check for one space as well. Figure 9-7 shows a graphical representation of how this check is done.

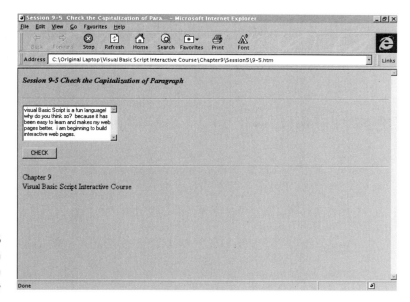

Figure 9-6
Paragraph
capitalization
sample Web page

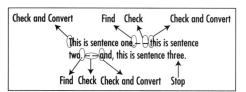

Figure 9-7
Checking for
capitalization of
sentences (HAND)

As the diagram shows, we check the first character of the paragraph, then we look for the next punctuation mark for the end of the sentence. Then a check is done for two spaces, then for the beginning of the next sentence and finally, we capitalize the first character.

Of course we will need to check the first character of the paragraph to ensure that it is capitalized. The first section of the code in the click event of the button makes this check as follows:

```
TextStr = Trim(TextInput.Value)

If Asc(Mid(TextStr,1,1)) >=97  or Asc(Mid(TextStr,1,1)) <=122 then

    RightStr = Right(TextStr, Len(TextStr) - 1)

    TextStr = UCASE(Mid(TextStr, 1, 1)) & RightStr

End If
```

First, the text is retrieved from the paragraph into the `TextStr` variable. The next line of text checks the ASCII value of the first character to ensure that it falls within the range of uppercase characters. If it does not, we take all the characters to the right of the first character and tack on the first character converted to uppercase using UCASE.

In the next section of code, the rest of the text is checked. Each character is looped through, beginning at the second character of the string since we already checked the first. What we will be searching for in the string is one of the three sentence ending punctuation characters, '!', '?', and '.'. The following code accomplishes the check and conversion.

```
For N = 2 to Len(TextStr) - 1

    If Mid(TextStr, N, 1) = "." or Mid(TextStr, N, 1) = "!" or ->
       Mid(TextStr, N, 1) = "?" then

      If Mid(TextStr, N + 1, 1) = " " and Mid(TextStr, N + 2, 1) ->
         = " " then

      If Mid(TextStr, N + 3, 1) <> " " then

        LeftStr = Left(TextStr, N + 2)

        RightStr = Right(TextStr, Len(TextStr) - N - 3)

        TextStr = LeftStr & UCase(Mid(TextStr, N + 3, 1)) & ->
        RightStr

        N = N + 3

      End If
    End If
  End If
Next
```

The first `If...Then` statement checks for the punctuation mark. The next `If...Then` statement checks the next two characters beyond the current loop position to ensure these are spaces. The next check ensures that the third character is not a space, so that the next character can be converted to an uppercase character. Once we are sure we have the first character of a sentence, the text is broken into two segments—the text to the left of the first character and the text to the right. These two sections are melded together with the original character converted to uppercase. Figure 9-8 shows this process.

When you click on the Check button on the Web page, the check is quick and simple and provides for easy formatting of the text. This type of validation can be simple and effective; many similar types of checks can be performed.

Figure 9-8
Converting
beginning of
sentence characters
to uppercase (AND)

```
String = " This is sentence one. _ _ this is
             sentence two."

A = Left (String, 23) = " This is sentence one. _ _ "
B = Ucase (Mid (String, 24,1)) = " T "
C = Right (String, Len (String) – 21) = " his is sentence two."

A & B & C = " This is sentence one. _ _ This is
               sentence two."
```

QUIZ 5

1. What will be the value of the following string?

```
Var1 = "String1 String2 String3"

Var1 = Left( Mid(Var1, 9, 7) , 3)
```

    a. "Str"
    b. "Stri"
    c. Error
    d. "ng2"

2. What will be the result of the following string manipulation?

```
Var1 = "This is a CAPITAL sentence."

For N = 1 to Len(Var1)

    If UCASE( MID(Var1, N, 1) ) = MID(Var1, N, 1) then

      Var2 = Mid(Var1, N, 1)

    End If

Next N
```

    a. `Var2` will equal `"T"`.
    b. `Var2` will equal `"L"`.
    c. `Var2` will equal `"TCAPITAL"`.
    d. `Var2` will equal `"CAPITAL"`.

3. Which string manipulation function will check for one string in another?
    a. Mid
    b. CheckIn
    c. Instr
    d. MidIn

4. Which set of code will retrieve the first character of a string?
   a. Left(Var1, 1)
   b. Mid(Var1, 1, 1)
   c. Left(Mid(Var1,1,5) , 1)
   d. All of the above

5. If we wish to ensure that there are no spaces surrounding a string, what functions would we use?
   a. LTrim, RTrim, Trim
   b. LSpace, RSpace, Space
   c. LSpc, RSpc, Spc
   d. None of the above

EXERCISE 5

Difficulty: Intermediate

1. Convert the sample provided on the Web page so that paragraphs that have single spaces between sentences will be checked appropriately.

SESSION 6

USE AN ACTIVEX POP-UP WINDOW TO SUPPORT USER INPUT

Data validation can be supported in many different ways. The check after the data has been entered is key, but support can be given up front. This session will use the ActiveX Pop-Up Window control. We can use this control to provide pop-up help in many different ways.

ActiveX Pop-Up Control
This control, when activated, pops up a window that shows another HTML Web page. The key method to be called is **PopUp**. It takes two parameters, with the first indicating the Web page to show and the second whether the window should be expanded or not.

The sample provided for this session builds a simple quiz that asks for the capitals of two states and the name of a Star Trek character. For each quiz question a button is provided that will show some hints on answering. When the Hint button is clicked, a pop-up window shows an HTML page that has hints regarding how to answer the question. Figure 9-9 shows the sample Web page that can be found on the CD-ROM in the Session6 subdirectory of Chapter 9.

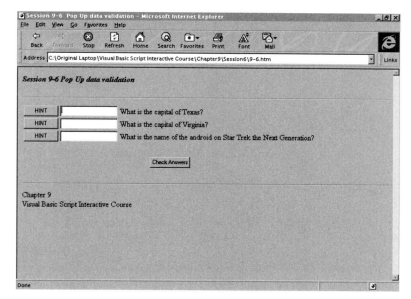

Figure 9-9
ActiveX pop-up
sample Web page

First, answer the three questions. Click on each button to show a hint. This click activates the ActiveX control and shows an appropriate HTML document. These documents can also be found on the CD-ROM.

The pop-up window is called using the **PopUp** method of the ActiveX control. The following code calls one of the hint HTML pages:

```
PopObj.Popup "d:\Chapter9\Session6\DataTip.htm", False
```

The first parameter indicates the Web page that should be shown and the second indicates whether or not the window should expand to fit the Web page. Using this pop-up control provides a technique to help the user make his data entry selections. These pop-up windows could be used to provide helpful hints if a user is stuck or unsure of how to respond. They could provide quick help for guiding new users through your new interactive Web page.

Of course, the check on the answers to the quiz is a straightforward text validation. More could be provided as feedback, such as setting the focus to the wrong answer to provide additional feedback, showing the appropriate hint, and so on. In the next session we will utilize another ActiveX control to provide feedback selections based on user-selected input.

1. What is wrong with the following code for showing the hint when an incorrect answer is given?

```
If UCASE(Answer.Value) <> ANSVAR1 then

  MsgBox "Try again!"

  Exit Sub

  PopObj.Popup "hint.htm", False


End If
```

    a. A full UNC must be provided to find the HTM hint file.
    b. The 'Pop Up' object should come right after the MsgBox function.
    c. ANSVAR1 should be converted to uppercase.
    d. None of the above.

2. Which button method could be called to show one of the Hint windows?
    a. `OnClick`
    b. `Click`
    c. `Focus`
    d. `OnFocus`

3. What is wrong with the following click event subroutine?

```
Sub Button_Click()

    PopObj.Popup

Exit Sub
```

    a. There is no document specified to be shown in the pop-up window.
    b. The event should be `Button_Onclick`.
    c. The end of the subroutine should be `End Sub`.
    d. All of the above.

4. What is missing from the following pop-up menu declaration?

```
<OBJECT ID="PopObj" WIDTH=31 HEIGHT=17
    <PARAM NAME="_ExtentX" VALUE="8281">
    <PARAM NAME="_ExtentY" VALUE="4498">
</OBJECT>
```

    a. No parameters are specified for the document to show.
    b. The `'OBJECT ID'` should be `'OBJECT CLASSID'`.
    c. There is no class ID for the object.
    d. There is no directory location for where the object is located on the local hard drive.

5. The pop-up menu can accept how many parameters?
    a. 1
    b. 2
    c. 3
    d. 4

EXERCISE 6

Difficulty: Intermediate

1. Update the sample so that the appropriate hint will be given for the first incorrect answer encountered.

SESSION 7

ACTIVEX MENU CONTROL VALIDATION

To continue providing additional information to help users make the right selections, this session will utilize another type of ActiveX control, the Menu control. We reviewed this control in earlier chapters, but here we will apply it to our car selection Web page developed in Session 4. With the Menu control, we can provide a list of the selections for the user to jump to an information Web page.

We know from our techniques developed in Session 4 that we can determine what selections the user has made. We can add these selections to the ActiveX Menu control. Figure 9-10 shows the Web page with the ActiveX control.

The Menu control shows the list of selections made by the user. Try selecting any combination of options. When you click on one of the menu options, a Web page appears that can provide more information regarding the car selection made.

We have modified the last section of the **ShowMenu** click event to add the selected items to the menu. The **AddItem** method of the ActiveX control is used to add the list item to the menu. The list item is referenced through the **Text** property of the **Option** array. The pop-up menu is cleared with each click of the button using the **Clear** method

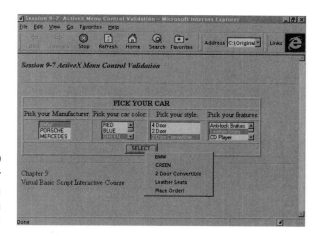

Figure 9-10 Validating user selections with the ActiveX Menu control

of the ActiveX control. Note that only one HTML file is jumped to for each of the card add-on options.

```
IePop1.Clear

IePop1.additem(Cars.Options(Cars.SelectedIndex).Text)

IePop1.additem(Colors.Options(Colors.SelectedIndex).Text)

IePop1.additem(Style.Options(Style.SelectedIndex).Text)

For N = 0 to Features.Length - 1

     If Features.Options(n).Selected = 1 then

        IePop1.additem(Features.Options(n).Text)

     End If

Next

IePop1.additem("Place Order!")

call Iepop1.PopUp()
```

The very last item added to the listbox is an option to "Place the order". This could be any option to move the user to the next logical step in the process. This method is an example of how you can provide quick feedback on what the user selected and provide options for him or her to validate the selections he or she made by retrieving additional help. The final session will put together a larger example of validating an entire HTML input form using Visual Basic Script.

1. Which of the following is not an event or method you can use with the pop-up menu ActiveX control?
   a. OnClick
   b. PopUp
   c. RemoveItem
   d. AddItem

2. Which of the following general descriptions would produce a method for providing an information HTML link for each car feature?
   a. Case 3 in the IePop_Click event of the sample would need to reference the exact menu item feature selected by the user and then jump to the appropriate page.
   b. The For...Next loop in the ShowMenu click event needs to be modified to store the ID for the feature selected in the listbox.

c. When the menu is clicked on, all items should be removed except for the menu item selected.

d. Both a. and c.

3. ActiveX pop-up menu buttons could be added
   a. to allow the user to easily jump to description Web pages for each select option.
   b. to provide for a selection of a set of default configurations.
   c. All of the above.
   d. None of the above.

4. This ActiveX pop-up menu method allows the menu to be refreshed.
   a. `Refresh`
   b. `Clear`
   c. `RemoveItem`
   d. `Empty`

5. What is wrong with the following declaration of the pop-up menu ActiveX control?

```
<OBJECT
     id=Iepop1
     classid="clsid:7823A620-9DD9-11CF-A662-00AA00C066D2"
     width=1
     height=1
>
</OBJECT>
```

a. There is no name attribute defined for the object.
b. There are no parameters defined for the object.
c. Both the above.
d. None of the above.

Difficulty: Advanced

1. Modify the program to provide a help Web page for each feature that can be selected.

VALIDATE A FORM'S CONTENTS

The final session for this chapter will take a look at a standard data entry form validation example. Any commercial Web site is most likely going to have some need for a standard order form Web page. This is the typical page that will ask for name, address, rank, phone number, and so on. There are some key data validation techniques that will prove the power of having client-side validation and Visual Basic Script.

Our form will not be submitted until all the data appears to be valid in format. This validation will include checking dates, phone numbers, zip codes, state abbreviations, and general data entry. The sample Web page is provided on the CD-ROM in the Session8 subdirectory of Chapter9 on the CD. Figure 9-11 shows the sample Web page.

Attempt to fill out each element on the form. Try answering different sections of the form incorrectly and see how the form validation takes place. When you click on the Submit button, the form will not be submitted to the server until the data has been completely validated.

The first step in helping the user to fill out the form correctly is to provide the current date in the Order Date fields on the form in the **OnLoad** event of the window. Next, the **Submit 'OnClick'** event checks all the basic text elements to ensure that they are not blank. These include the name, address, and city. We cannot strictly validate these fields other than to ensure that they are not blank.

The rest of the fields can be validated in particular ways. And, in the **Submit OnClick** event, a subroutine is called for each check including **ValidateState**, **ValidateDeliveryDate**, **ValidateZipCode**, and **ValidatePhoneNumber**. We have seen the basics from early in this chapter on how to do text validation, numeric validation, and date validation as well as how to do simple state validation.

We have provided the date in three input elements to make the date entry as well as the validation easier. In the **ValidateDeliveryDate** subroutine, we first check to see whether any of the entries are blank. If they are not blank, then the three elements are combined into a text string and validated to be a correct date.

The section of the phone number and zip code can be validated by simple numeric validation using IsNumeric. We can also ensure that the correct number of digits have been entered for each using the Len function.

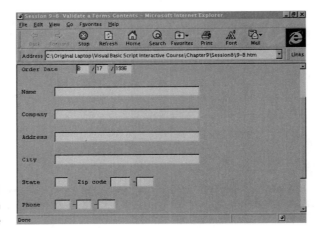

Figure 9-11
Form validation
Web page

For the state validation, we simply use the Select Case construct to validate that a correct state abbreviation has been entered. For this example, only a few states are validated.

It is hard to gauge all the ways in which Web page builders might need to validate data entry, whether it is to validate standard form elements, check a user's input into a game, and so on. As has been demonstrated throughout this chapter, by using Visual Basic Script functions, ActiveX controls, a little programming logic, and creativity, we can provide ways for our Web pages to be easy to use, quick to respond, and intuitive to navigate.

1. For which of the following will IsNumeric return False?
   a. " 1233"
   b. " –2323.23"
   c. " 8"
   d. None of the above

2. What is wrong with the following validation of a Social Security number such as "522-25-0675"?

```
Sub Validate

If Len(SN) <> 11 then MsgBox "Invalid Number" : Exit Sub
If Mid(SN, 4, 1) <> "-" then MsgBox "Invalid Number" : Exit Sub
If Mid(SN, 7, 1) <> "-" then MsgBox "Invalid Number" : Exit Sub

If IsNumeric(Mid(SN, 1, 3)) <> True then

    MsgBox "Invalid Number" : Exit Sub

Exit Sub

If IsNumeric(Mid(SN, 5, 2)) <> True then

    MsgBox "Invalid Number" : Exit Sub

Exit Sub

If IsNumeric(Mid(SN, 7, 3)) <> True then

    MsgBox "Invalid Number" : Exit Sub

Exit Sub

End Sub
```

a. The length check should be for 12, not 11 characters.
b. The last IsNumeric should start at position 8, not position 7.
c. The second IsNumeric should start at position 6, not 5.
d. The check for the first dash should start at position 3, not 4.

3. Which function cannot be used to help us convert and validate numbers?
   a. ABS
   b. INT
   c. DOLLAR
   d. FIX

4. Which Visual Basic construct could be used to easily validate whether an area code falls within a set range of values?
   a. `Select...Case`
   b. `If...Then...Else`
   c. `For...Next`
   d. All of the above

5. When the form is submitted to the server, which happens (assume the `Post` method is used)?
   a. The data in the input elements of the form is sent to the server.
   b. The `OnSubmit` event is fired off.
   c. Both of the above.
   d. None of the above.

Difficulty: Intermediate

1. Write a code fragment that will validate month abbreviations.

CHAPTER SUMMARY

Data validation is one of the key uses for Visual Basic Script. As you have seen in this chapter, we can assist the user both with making valid selections as well as validating those selections after the data has been entered. Also, knowing how to interact with the Internet Explorer object model and ActiveX controls is critical to being able to validate the data and interact with the Web page user. In the next chapter, we will learn how to utilize many different ActiveX controls and other types of objects from our scripts.

CHAPTER 10

OBJECTIFYING YOUR SCRIPTS

The main plank of Microsoft's new Internet philosophy is the ActiveX object architecture. It promises to unleash hitherto undreamed of power to Net programmers, especially those who use Microsoft's Internet Explorer.

ActiveX controls are compact objects which provide the VBScripter with a gallery of bolt-in, high-powered functionality to mix with standard windows components. The approach allows the programmer to glue together Windows and Net functions using Visual Basic Script.

With ActiveX controls you will soon be able to start adding customizable labels, dynamic charts, real-time timers, and much more onto your Web pages. Soon you will be producing pages that offer a genuine and instantaneous response to the user's demands. To achieve this in only one short chapter, you will learn about the following:

- Using and Manipulating Objects within Visual Basic Script

- The VBScript Wizard

- The HTML Layout Control

- Inserting ActiveX Controls into a Web Page

- Various ActiveX Controls, Including Many Familiar from the Windows Environment

- The IEChart Control

- The IELabel Control

- The IETimer Control

- An Overview of the Object Architecture, Properties, and Methods

- An Overview of the Java and JavaScript Languages

SESSION 1

GETTING ACTIVE WITH ACTIVEX

The default coding environment for Visual Basic Script is the HTML file displayed in Notepad. This is fine if you want to change or add a coding detail, but Notepad is really just text display software. Coding the control references used by IE entails looking up the *ClassID* for the control you want (ClassID: a hieroglyphic stream of numbers used to identify each control type) and then typing it in correctly. This results in HTML code blocks which are hard to decipher.

Fortunately, adding controls to the HTML page can be simple if the Microsoft ActiveXpad is used (see Figure 10.1). This application is designed to work a three-way split between HTML, Visual Basic Script, and ActiveX objects. This is no ordinary HTML editor. Xpad comes fully equipped with its own drag-and-drop interface for adding the ActiveX control components to the page. Xpad supplies the Visual Basic Script shown in Figure 10-1. This tool far outstrips the title of Wizard being, in effect, the Visual Basic Script programming environment. Xpad also offers the HTML Layout Control which Session 2 shows to be invaluable.

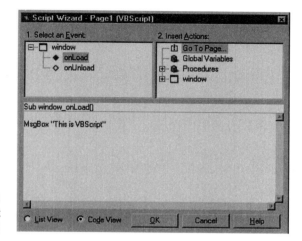

Figure 10-1
The VBScript
Wizard

The VBScript Wizard

This session assumes you have already tried running ActiveXPad (Xpad) to see what it looks like and have experimented with some of the features. Below is a list of suggested actions you should try before going much further with this text.

- Write some HTML tags in the HTML environment

- Save an .HTM file to disk

- Load an .HTM into the Internet Explorer to check your HTML

- Click Tools from the menu, then ScriptWizard

Before we take a look at adding your Visual Basic Script code via the Wizard, it is best to understand where the Visual Basic Script fits in. Although the Xpad makes things easier for you, it is always possible to type the Visual Basic Script directly onto the HTML page using the appropriate tags. The default page produced by Xpad contains the following HTML.

```
<HTML>
<HEAD>
<TITLE>New Page</TITLE>

VBScript Can go Here

</HEAD>
<BODY>

VBScript Can go Here

</BODY>
</HTML>
```

To start inserting Visual Basic Script code into this document, just begin typing. If you want to write the OnLoad event handler for the **Window** object, you could simply write the following straight into the textpad that displays the HTML and save the file.

```
<SCRIPT LANGUAGE="VBScript">
<!--
Sub Window_OnLoad
      MsgBox "This is VBScript"
End Sub
-->
</SCRIPT>
```

This works fine, but writing event-handler declarations (**Sub Object_OnEvent...
End Sub**) over and over is an error-prone business.

On top of this, having all the events strung out in a linear fashion on a flat page makes it hard to correlate the event handlers with the controls to which they are attached. In a straightforward text display, it is harder to get the whole, *event-driven* picture. The very same **Window_OnLoad** event handler can be coded from within the Wizard and displayed on its own or collected together with other handlers. Unless you are experienced, it is almost impossible to write event-driven code in a linear fashion. Take a look at Figure 10-1 again, and you will see the code in its code window.

On the left of the **Wizard** window sits the list of all the objects currently on the form. In this case, there is only the main IE object called **Window**. The right-hand frame contains a list of all the objects on the form plus a heading for **Procedures** and one for **Global Variables**. Below all this there is an empty script window with the Option button set to **Code View** (or at least it should be for the moment).

The left-hand list of objects shows all the Events for the chosen object. Clicking on the **Window** entry in the left-hand list reveals the two events exposed by the IE **Window** object:

 OnLoad

 OnUnload

Definition: Exposed

If an object exposes a property, then that property becomes available to the programmer. An object's designer decides which properties and methods to keep internal to the object and which to expose to the programmer. If the VBScripter exposes an object's properties or methods to the user, those properties or methods can be deliberately set or invoked by the user.

Clicking on the **OnLoad** event brings the definition for the **Window_OnLoad** event handler into the script window as shown in Figure 10-1. If the event handler does not appear in the script window, make sure the Code View option button is selected.

Xpad has kindly placed the correct event handler definition on the top line for you. Clicking on the right mouse button in the **Script** window allows you to edit the event-handler name; however, since **Window** is an object native to IE, you cannot change its name. Since changing the spelling of **OnLoad** bears no relation to sane behavior, there is no need to change the definition provided. Underneath the event definition sits a blank space; this is the coding window, the place where all the Visual Basic Script you write actually goes.

Xpad does not include the **End Sub** delimiter in the code window and you don't need to type this. Xpad treats the subroutine's definition lines, both top and bottom, as its own. The **End Sub** will be written into the HTML automatically, but since this line should never change, there is no need to display it in the Wizard.

Now it is time to actually write a line of Visual Basic Script into the Wizard's code window. Make sure the event handler is still the **Window_OnLoad** event and enter the message box line shown below.

```
MsgBox "This is VBScript"
```

Click on the OK button. Tell the Wizard you are happy with your work and you want to see how it looks in the HTML document. Figure 10-2 illustrates how the parent HTML file should look.

You can see the Wizard has placed the event handler inside a set of **<SCRIPT>** tags and inside a pair of comments. It has generated both the **Sub** and the **End Sub** delimiters required to create a valid subroutine. To the left of the **<SCRIPT>** tag sits a little button with a scroll on it. This calls up the **Script Wizard** window with the associated subroutine displayed in the code window. Last, but not least, comes the code that actually does the work—your code.

Certainly it would seem that for the native components of the IE, such as the **Windows** object, it is easy to add code, but what about user-defined procedures? Go back to the Wizard and have a look at the top right-hand section. There is *another* list of all the objects currently referenced in the HTML file. There is still only one object, the default **Window** object. The entry marked **Procedures**, when clicked, will show a list of all the

Figure 10-2
The generated
HTML code

Visual Basic Script procedures present in the HTML document. An entry for the `Window_OnLoad` event should be present here. Right clicking on the procedure and selecting `Edit Procedure` brings it up into the code window if you want to check whether your message box line is still looking good. To create a new procedure, just right-click over the word Procedure and then select New Procedure; Xpad then provides a brand new `Script` window. The event handler should look like the one below.

```
Sub Procedure1()
```

Now change the subroutine's name to `Display` and allow it to receive one parameter called `Message`. Inside the code window, display the variable in a message box. The code should look like the sample shown (also see Figure 10-3). Remember there is no need to use the `End Sub` delimiter at the bottom of each subroutine.

```
Sub Display(Message)
     MsgBox Message
```

Finally, change the code attached to the `Window_OnLoad` event so that it calls `Display` and passes it to `Message` to put in the message box. Click the Wizard's OK to confirm all the changes and have a look at the code generated back in the parent HTML. There you can see the two lines of hand-crafted Visual Basic Script, each in the separate subroutines yet connected via the variable `Message`. The HTML code should now look like the sample below.

```
<HTML>
<HEAD>
<SCRIPT LANGUAGE="VBScript">
<!--
Sub window_onLoad()
        Display "This is VBScript"
end sub
-->
</SCRIPT>
<SCRIPT LANGUAGE="VBScript">
<!--
Sub Display(Message)
        MsgBox Message
end sub
-->
</SCRIPT>
<TITLE>New Page</TITLE>
</HEAD>
<BODY>

</BODY>
</HTML>
```

That's enough checking back to the parent HTML for now. Use the Wizard's visual structures to show where the code is and what events a control has.

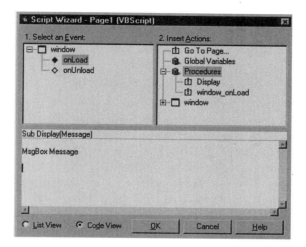

Figure 10-3
A new subroutine
in the Wizard's
window

Although the **Message** variable, in the example above, was local to the **Display** subroutine, many cases require Global variables to be available to all the procedures.

To allow for the addition of globals, there is a **New Global Variable** option on the same list as the **New Procedure** (right mouse button over **Procedures**). Selecting this option displays an input box for the new variable's name. To try this out, just type in the name of the variable you want to be global. If it is an array, add the number of elements you require in brackets. If you want to check the globals already dimensioned, then click on the **Global Variables** list entry to see a list of those created so far. You can now use this variable name anywhere in the Wizard. Like **End Sub**, the **dimension** (**Dim**) statements for the Global variables are hidden unless you look at the parent HTML file. Look closely (one last time) and there they are. To check how these Global variables work, replace the variable being passed to the **Display** subroutine with a Global variable with the same name (**Message**). Now the HTML listing should look like the listing shown below.

```
<HTML>
<HEAD>
<SCRIPT LANGUAGE="VBScript">
<!--
dim Message

Sub Display()
      MsgBox Message
end sub

Sub Window_onLoad()
      Message =  "This is VBScript"
      Display Message
end sub
-->
</SCRIPT>
```

continued on next page

continued from previous page

```
<TITLE>New Page</TITLE>
</HEAD>

<BODY>
</BODY>
</HTML>
```

The VBScript Wizard has many useful functions. For example, the code can be viewed in List View, which attempts to show the code more clearly in terms of actions on objects rather than commands. This may benefit those unfamiliar with any form of coding. Also, the list of objects on the left-hand side will expand to show all the properties, methods, and child objects related to them and is a very handy reference guide for the objects used. There are lots of useful shortcuts and reminders and they can be learned by writing code, using the Wizard, and developing your own style.

Note: Parent and Child Objects

If an object contains another object, then it is a **Parent** to the contained object. When an object is contained within another object, then it is a child of the container object. Objects can be both parents and children.

Summary

This session has given an introduction to the software used to create Web pages with active content. Although it is certainly possible to code all your Visual Basic Script directly into a text editor, the increases in performance gained by using supportive environments such as ActiveXpad outweigh the small loss in coding flexibility. We saw that the Xpad provided the coder with an object-based view of IE compatible Web pages, and exposed the properties and methods of all the objects held on the page. The VBScript Wizard component showed how it could position your VBScript code between correctly generated HTML tags as well as handle global variables, procedure declarations, and event declarations.

As the complexity of a Web page grows, it becomes increasingly useful for programmers to be able to package up their HTML+VBScript+ActiveX into reusable chunks or objects. This means that once the functionality of the object has been finalized, tested, and saved by the VBscripter, all subsequent usage of that functionality will require only the inclusion of the desired object. The ability to package all the code into an object, called the *HTML layout file,* is also found in ActiveXpad, which we discuss in Session 2.

Quiz 1

1. The **End Sub** delimiter is not required with the VBScript Wizard because
   a. the Wizard cannot produce the correct syntax.
   b. **End Sub** is no longer required by VBScript.
   c. the Wizard automatically inserts **End Sub** into the parent HTML.
   d. you cannot create subroutines with the Wizard.

2. The default coding environment for VBScript is
   a. a text editor like Windows Notepad.
   b. the VBScript Wizard.
   c. the Internet Explorer.
   d. HTML editor packages.

3. The VBScript Wizard does not provide
   a. an onscreen list of all the objects within an HTML file.
   b. a list of all the properties and methods for each object.
   c. a list of all the available events for each object.
   d. a list of all the available error codes.

4. To add a new global variable you must
   a. click on **New Procedure** and dimension a variable.
   b. click on **New Procedure** and add a parameter to the subdeclaration.
   c. click on **New Global Variable** and type in the variable name.
   d. dimension a variable in the **Window_OnLoad** event.

5. The Xpad application does not allow
   a. the manipulation of ActiveX controls.
   b. HTML authoring.
   c. VBScript authoring.
   d. changes to the **Window** object's event handlers.

Exercise 1

Difficulty: Easy

1. Using only the VBScript Wizard, create a Web page that welcomes the user with a message box when the page is loaded and displays a second message when the page is left.

Difficulty: Easy

2. Create an HTML file that contains a number of VBScript procedures, a global variable, and a global array of ten elements. Examine the HTML generated by the Wizard and identify the End Sub delimiters of the procedures as well as the lines responsible for dimensioning the globals.

USING THE HTML LAYOUT CONTROL

Xpad's ability to store and retrieve composite blocks of Web functionality that include mixtures of HTML, VBScript, and ActiveX controls allows the Web author to create sophisticated Web pages with the minimum of fuss. In Session 1 you saw how to add VBScript code to the HTML file via the VBScript Wizard. In this session you will see how to add ActiveX controls to your pages via the HTML layout control. Figure 10-4 shows how the HTML layout control should look.

The layout control is an ActiveX control in its own right but, rather paradoxically, it is designed to contain groups of ActiveX controls and the VBScript used to manipulate them. Once all the controls have been added, the layout control is saved as a layout file with the extension `.alx`. After saving, it is now ready for inclusion into the main body of the parent HTML document by hand coding `<OBJECT>` tags or, more simply, via the Xpad menu.

Definition: Layout File

This file type has the extension `.alx` and is generated by the HTML layout control. It consists of ActiveX control references and VBScript code. A reference to the layout file is included within the main body of the parent HTML file.

Figure 10-4
The HTML layout control

In its heart, the layout control is really just another kind of HTML code generator, although it also functions as a container for storing ActiveX controls. When a layout file is created, it is really a set of HTML tags (including the **<OBJECT>** tags that refer to the ActiveX controls added to the layout) and imbedded VBScript. The whole lot is then wrapped up and saved as a reusable object in its own right. Whenever an **<OBJECT>** reference to the layout control appears in a parent HTML file, the visual components of the layout control, the buttons, listboxes, etc., all appear on the page as they did when the layout file was created. To a user, it seems as if all the HTML code itself was present within the body of the parent file instead of just an **<OBJECT>** reference to a layout file.

One of the advantages of using the layout control is that, once completed and debugged, the same code can be used repeatedly. Considering the layout control's ability to hold multiple ActiveX objects and as much VBScript code as is required, the programmer can create a library of layout files to be included as composite elements of any HTML parent file.

To create an HTML Layout control, start by clicking the New HTML Layout on the File menu. The new HTML Layout control is displayed in the HTML Layout editor. It allows the user to select controls from a toolbar and drag them onto a form.

The default controls that make up the Toolkit are:

- CheckBox
- ComboBox
- CommandButton
- HotSpot
- Image
- Label
- ListBox
- OptionBar
- ScrollBar
- SpinButton
- TabStrip
- TextBox
- ToggleButton

This toolset is enough to build most ActiveX HTML documents, although any new ActiveX controls that are registered will also be available to be added to the toolbar. Figure 10-5 shows what a typical Layout control looks like during construction in ActiveXpad.

Figure 10-5
Working with the
Layout control

Once you have dragged and dropped some objects to the layout page, you should start up the VBScript Wizard by clicking the top left button with the yellow scroll icon. This time, in addition to the IE **Window** object, the list of objects also contains the controls you have added to the layout. Each control will display a list of its events and will allow VBScript to be placed in the event handlers. New procedures and global variables can be added to the layout file, allowing entire VBScript applications to be written inside a single, reusable, layout file.

Note: Adding Layout Files to the Parent HTML File

Place the cursor in the parent HTML file as displayed in the main Xpad screen. Select the menu option Edit. Select the submenu option Insert HTML Layout. You will be presented with an open file dialog box. Select the `.alx` file you wish to add and press Open. The selected layout file will automatically be added to the parent file complete with `<OBJECT>` tags and setup information.

The VBScript interacts with the objects held in the layout control by accessing the properties and methods from the code. The control must be present on the layout page before the Wizard will recognize it. Below is an example of a textbox control having the text it displays set to a new string.

```
Sub ChangeText()
    Textbox1.Text = "My New String"
```

The example above shows that objects added to a layout file are manipulated in the same way as any other object. The syntax is the object's name followed by the property name followed by the new value, as shown below.

```
ObjectName.Property = NewValue
```

If you would like to review the current property settings for an object, leave the VBScript Wizard and return to the layout file interface. Double-click on the object you are interested in, and a large property list should appear. Figure 10-6 shows the property list for a textbox control.

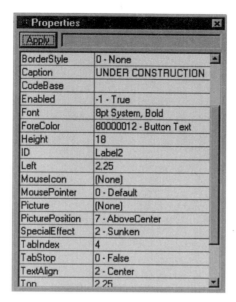

Figure 10-6
The property list of a textbox control

ActiveX methods are invoked in much the same way— the object name, then the method, followed by any parameters required.

```
ObjectName.Method parameterlist
```

For example, to add a new item into a listbox object, the **AddItem** method should be invoked. Included with the statement is the string value or variable to be added to the list. The example below shows a loop adding string elements from an array of strings into a listbox control.

```
For X = 1 to 10
      ListBox1.AddItem MyStringArray(X)
Next
```

Summary

Session 2 has dealt with another of Xpad's main components, the HTML Layout controls. These controls can be added to any HTML file using object references, with Xpad stepping in to generate the appropriate HTML to include them correctly. The layout files were seen to allow ActiveX objects, the code necessary for their action, and user interaction to be blended together. The resulting object can then be added to any HTML file, instantly conferring the layout file's functionality to the page. We saw that the layout control's toolbar contains many of the fundamental controls to be found in the windows environment. Also, any ActiveX control registered with your system can be added to the toolbar and used in your own pages. Once added to a layout file, the ActiveX objects were manipulated via their properties and methods using VBScript to control the logic and flow of data.

To make a start on your library of useful layout files, the next session will show you how to create a layout file that adds some Web navigator functionality to any page.

1. A layout control is referenced in the parent HTML file using
    a. globally dimensioned arrays.
    b. the `<OBJECT> </OBJECT>` tags.
    c. `Sub...End Sub` delimiters.
    d. none of the above.

2. The layout control does not provide as standard
    a. a textbox control.
    b. a listbox control.
    c. a voice activation control.
    d. an option button control.

3. Controls added to a layout file are manipulated in VBScript via their
    a. subroutines and properties.
    b. functions and methods.
    c. subroutines and functions.
    d. properties and methods.

4. To add a new textbox control with an ID property of `"MyTextBox"`
    a. drag a textbox object onto the layout page.
    b. dimension in global variables an object called `MyTextBox`.
    c. drag a textbox object onto the layout page and set its ID property to "MyTextBox".
    d. drag a textbox object onto the layout page and alter its `OnLoad` event-handler name.

5. The methods of an ActiveX control are invoked using which syntax?
    a. `ObjectName.Method.Parameter`
    b. `ObjectName.Method Parameterlist`
    c. `Method.Object Parameterlist`
    d. `ObjectName.Method(parameterlist)`

Difficulty: Easy

1. Create a layout file that contains several controls of your choice and save it to disk giving it the name "MyTest". Now insert the new layout file into a parent HTML file. The filename will be `"MyTest.alx"`.

Difficulty: Moderate

2. Create a layout file that contains a listbox. When the layout file first loads, add some data items to the listbox so they are seen when the page is first displayed.

USING THE DEFAULT ACTIVEX CONTROLS

Whenever you begin an HTML layout session, a square toolbox appears. This contains a default set of controls that come supplied with the Xpad software. Using only these objects, you can build almost any windows-style interface. This session concentrates on building your first HTML layout file and then including it into a working Web page. Figure 10-7 shows the navigator included into its HTML page and loaded in IE.

The navigator layout file allows the user to select a URL category and then see all the available URLs for that category. Alongside the cryptic URLs, there appears a short description of the actual site. When the user clicks on the Launch button, the currently selected URL is used to open the requested Web page.

Figure 10-7 shows what the page looks like when it has been created from a standard HTML file. In fact, it has been created using a *single* HTML layout control. There is no HTML present in the parent HTML file which codes for the listbox or combobox. The parent HTML file which proves the point is shown below.

```
<BODY>
<BR>
<CENTER>
<OBJECT
      CLASSID="CLSID:812AE312-8B8E-11CF-93C8-00AA00C08FDF"
      ID="NavBar"
      STYLE="LEFT:0;TOP:0">
      <PARAM NAME="ALXPATH" REF VALUE="file:C:\Visual Basic Interactive
      Course\Chapter 10\Navigate.alx">
</OBJECT>
</CENTER>
</BODY>
```

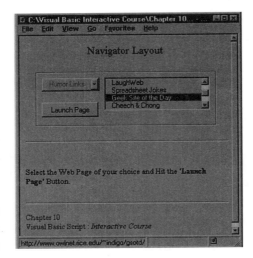

Figure 10-7
The navigator
layout in action

The little HTML that comes before and after the layout file reference is there to set up the look and feel. The bulk code is found in the **Navigate.alx** file. This includes all the **<OBJECT>** tags for the listbox, button, combobox, and frame controls plus all the VBScript code used to manipulate the object. All the VBscripter need really care about are the events triggered by the user and the event procedures that will be triggered by them. To recreate the **navigate.alx** object yourself, go back to your Xpad session. If you have not already created a new HTML layout file, do so now. From the toolbar, add the following objects to the layout control. All the properties of the objects can be left at their default values except those indicated below. The precise size and positioning of each object is up to you.

● **Listbox**

  Special Effect = 2 - Sunken

  BackColor = Gray

● **Combobox**

  ForeColor = Red

  Special Effect = 1 - Raised

  BackColor = Gray

● **Command Button**

ID = cmdLaunch

Caption = "Launch Page"

● **Image**

Special Effect = 3 - Etched

The following VBScript has been spooled together to form a listing. You will be taken through the VBScript step by step to enable you to create a useful layout file without too much suffering on the way. This example contains a number of URL links but, since these may well be out of date, you might like to replace those mentioned with your own favorite links.

The best place to begin is with the Global variables. This is because they do not sit inside any subroutine or function (see Session 1).

```
Public variables
Dim CategoryList (3)
Dim URLList (3,15,2)
Dim CurrentList
```

In the code shown above you see three Global variables being dimensioned. Two of them are arrays and are therefore capable of holding multiple values. The **CategoryList** array will hold the three categories of links available: Humor, Music, and Internet. The **URLList** array will hold the URLs and their descriptions by category. Finally the **CurrentList** variable will hold the currently selected category.

When the layout file is first loaded, its **OnLoad** event is triggered. The code below shows the event declaration and the event procedure.

```
Sub Navigate_OnLoad()
        Call Init()
End Sub
```

The **onLoad** event is generated when the object in question is first loaded by the IE, as the parent HTML file is parsed and processed at download. In this case, as soon as the Layout file **Navigate.alx** is loaded into memory, the subroutine **Init** is called. The code below shows the subroutine **Init**.

```
Sub Init()
        CategoryList(1)="Humor Links"
        CategoryList(2)="Music Links"
        CategoryList(3)="Internet Links"

'       Fill the category list combobox
        For i= 1 to 3
                ComboBox1.AddItem (CategoryList(i))
        Next
```

```
'HUMOR
        URLList(1,1,1)="Howard Stern"
        URLList(1,1,2)="http://haven.ios.com/~koam/"
        URLList(1,2,1)="Humor archives"
        URLList(1,2,2)="http://www.cs.cornell.edu/Info/People/ckline/
                        humor.html"

'MUSIC
        URLList(2,1,1)="Tori Amos"
        URLList(2,1,2)="http://www.iac.net/~cdwagner/torimain.htm"
        URLList(2,2,1)="Edie Brickell"
        URLList(2,2,2)="http://www.crl.com/~phantom/edie/edie.html"


        URLList(3,1,1)="Search using Alta Vista"
        URLList(3,1,2)="http://www.altavista.digital.com"
        URLList(3,2,1)="Bandwidth Conversation Society"
        URLList(3,2,2)="http://www.infohiway.com/way/faster/"


        ComboBox1.ListIndex=0
        CurrentList=1
End Sub
```

This initialization section sets up the array **CategoryList** with the three main catagories of URL. The combobox showing the catagories is filled with the new values from the **CategoryList** array. The **URLList** array is filled with all the site descriptions and site URLs. Remember that the **URLList** variable has been dimensioned to hold 15 URLs, so you can add more of your favorite links to the category lists if you wish.

Now that the combobox has been filled, the user can click on it and change the selected item. The code below shows the change event handler and its code.

```
Sub ComboBox1_Change()
on error resume next
        CurrentList=ComboBox1.ListIndex+1
    Call FillList()
End Sub
```

The **ComboBox1_Change** event is generated by **ComboBox1** whenever the user selects a different Category from the box's list. When a new Category is selected, the **CurrentList** variable is updated to reflect the user's new section selection. The **CurrentList** variable specifies the currently selected Category and is used in the subroutine **FillList** shown below.

```
Sub FillList()
Dim i
'       Clear the list

ListBox1.Clear

'       Fill the list

For i = 1 to Ubound(URLList,2)
        If URLList(CurrentList,i,1)<> "" then ListBox1.AddItem
```

```
⇐(URLList(CurrentList,i,1))
        Next
        ListBox1.ListIndex=0
End Sub
```

The **FillList** subroutine is called whenever a new selection is made from the combobox. Changing the value selected from the combobox alters the value of the **CurrentList** variable and so the list is filled from a different portion of the **URLList(CurrentList,x,x)** array. Before the listbox is filled with the URLs for the **CurrentList** Category, the listbox is cleared. If this was not done, the new items would just be appended to the end of the old list.

After the user has selected a category and the listbox has been filled with URLs, the user will probably try to click on the listbox. This will trigger the change event, and the interesting line shown below is run.

```
Sub ListBox1_Change()
    Parent.defaultStatus=URLList(CurrentList,ListBox1.ListIndex+1,2)
end sub
```

The single line event procedure above shows the object-oriented nature of the IE 3.0 (not to worry, the object hierarchy will be covered in later sessions). For now, note that the **DefaultStatus** property of the **Parent** window will be set to the string value of the URL held in the **URLList** array. The **DefaultStatus** property holds the string that is displayed in the status bar at the foot of the browser. The Parent tag refers to the **Parent** object, i.e., one object higher in the hierarchy. In this case the **Parent** object is the IE Window itself . Setting the **DefaultStatus** property of the **Window** object makes the URL string appear at the foot of the IE browser.

The user has selected the category, then selected the URL within that category. The URL has been displayed at the foot of the browser, so all that remains is for the user to press the Launch button. When he does, a click event is generated and the **cmdLaunch_Click** event handler code shown below is run.

```
Sub cmdLaunch_Click()
    URLIndex=ListBox1.ListIndex + 1
    TheURL=URLList(CurrentList,URLIndex,2)
    Parent.Location.Href=TheURL
end sub
```

The single URL element required to launch a page is being specified using the number held in the **CurrentList** variable and then further by the selection made from the listbox. The current listbox selection is found by adding one to the listindex property of the listbox. Each item in a listbox has a **ListIndex** value. The values start at zero; the first item has a **ListIndex** = 0, but the array index for URLList starts at one. The **ListIndex** has one added to it for each item to bring it in line with the array index.

The two values combined will specify a pair of elements: the URL description, used in the Listbox, and the URL itself. It is the URL value which is assigned to the **TheURL** variable. It is then used to set the **Location.Href** property of the **Window** object which forces IE to load the page it points to. Note again the use of the *Parent* identifier to access the properties and methods of the parent (**Window**) object.

Now that you have a working copy of the navigator layout file saved, add it into any HTML page using Xpad. When you load the page into IE, you will see your navigator. Any page can now contain the **Navigator.alx** file, so any page can have the navigator without additional coding.

Summary

We saw that the HTML layout file will provide the programmer reusable composite elements which can be used to build or augment Web pages. This session put Sessions 1 and 2 into practice, showing how the HTML layout control is used in close partnership with the VBScript Wizard. A reusable layout file was created that had the look and feel of a normal windows application showing that mastering the skills of VBScript really can start to produce useful results.

In the next session, this hands-on experience is broadened when you meet a pair of ActiveX objects no VBScript programmer can do without— the **IELabel** control and the **IETimer** control.

1. The **End Sub** delimiter is not required with the VBScript Wizard because
   a. the Wizard cannot produce the correct syntax.
   b. **End Sub** is no longer required by VBScript.
   c. the Wizard automatically inserts **End Sub** into the parent HTML.
   d. you cannot create subroutines with the Wizard.

2. The default coding environment for VBScript is
   a. a text editor like Windows Notepad.
   b. the VBScript Wizard.
   c. the Internet Explorer.
   d. HTML editor packages.

3. The VBScript Wizard does not provide
   a. an on-screen list of all the objects within an HTML file.
   b. a list of all the properties and methods for each object.
   c. a list of all the available events for each object.
   d. a list of all the available error codes.

4. To add a new global variable you must
   a. click on New Procedure and dimension a variable.
   b. click on New Procedure and add a parameter to the subdeclaration.
   c. click on New Global Variable and type in the variable name.
   d. dimension a variable in the **Window_Onload** event.

5. The Xpad application does not allow
   a. the manipulation of ActiveX controls.
   b. HTML authoring.
   c. VBScript authoring.
   d. changes to the **Window** object's event handlers.

EXERCISE 3

Difficulty: Easy

1. Using only the VBScript Wizard, create a Web page that welcomes the user with a message box when the page is loaded and displays a second message when the page is left.

Difficulty: Easy

2. Create an HTML file that contains a number of VBScript procedures, a global variable, and a global array of 10 elements. Examine the HTML generated by the Wizard and identify the End Sub delimiters of the procedures as well as the lines responsible for dimensioning the globals.

SESSION 4

USING THE ACTIVEX LABEL AND TIMER CONTROLS

In the previous session you saw how to drag and drop ActiveX controls onto a Web page and add functionality through VBScript. Those skills will be expanded over the course of this session with the introduction of ActiveX controls that are not part of the layout's default toolbox.

> **Hint: Adding Controls to the HTML Layout Toolbox**
>
> Position the mouse over any part of the toolbox square and right click. Select Additional Controls from the pop-up menu. An Additional Controls dialog box should appear that presents the user with a list of available, i.e., registered controls. Check the controls you wish to appear on the toolbox and click OK.

The ActiveX IELabel and Timer Controls

Two controls that do not appear as default controls, but are found on many Web pages, are the IETimer control and the IELabel control. They are *safely scriptable,* which means they pass the Microsoft internal tests for ActiveX legitimacy. This is good, since Microsoft was responsible for the release of these controls.

The IELabel Control

Unlike the label control found in the standard HTML layout toolbox, this label control allows the text to be positioned at any angle. The angle can also be set at runtime, allowing for a rotating-text style of animation. It is also possible to manipulate the forecolor, backcolor, and font properties, which combine to produce eye-catching effects. The example application detailed in this session will show some of the label's animation features and how they can be further enhanced when used in combination with the IETimer control.

The IETimer Control

Code operating within an event-driven structure can ultimately trace the functionality of the program back to an originating user action (event). If there is something that the programmer specifically wants to do *in between* the user-triggered event procedures, then a problem occurs, as there will be no event to attach the event procedure to. The timer control neatly fills this gap by offering an event handler that is triggered at specified intervals set by the programmer. The timer can be switched on, in which case the event procedure will run every specified interval, or off, in which case it does nothing. An example of the `Timer` event is shown below.

```
Sub IETimer1_Timer
    MessageBox "Hello Again"
```

The interval between each firing of the `Timer` event is specified by setting the `IETimer.Interval` property. The interval time is measured in milliseconds (1000 milliseconds per second), and any number between 1 (0.001 seconds) and 65534 (65.5 seconds) can be entered. This property is commonly set at design time and not usually changed from within the code, although this can be done if the situation demands it. The `IETimer.Enabled` property is used to toggle the timer control on and off. When the enabled property is set to True, the timer will start triggering its `Timer` event at every `Interval` value. When the `Enabled` property is set to False, it resets its countdown and shuts down. This means every time a timer is enabled, the counter will always be starting from the beginning again.

A Little Label Magic

This session's code sample is intended to highlight a number of controls besides the Timer and Label controls. Below is a list of controls that have been used. All the controls, other than Label and Timer, are present on the default toolbox.

- The Checkbox Control
- The OptionButton Control
- The SpinButton Control
- The Image Control as a frame

- The CommandButton Control
- The default Label Control
- The TextBox Control
- The ListBox Control
- The IELabel Control
- The Timer Control

In essence, all this page succeeds in doing is exposing selected properties of the Label control to the user. This application exposes only those properties of the label that are relevant to the user. It only allows the user to input data within a specified range by restricting them through the interface. This is called *Front Ending,* i.e., building a visual component that sits between the user and the control. To achieve the desired functionality, this demo exposes the following IELabel properties:

- `IELabel1.Caption`—Determines the text to be displayed.
- `IELabel1.Angle`—Determines the display angle of the label's caption.
- `IELabel1.ForeColor`—Determines the color of the caption text.
- `IELabel1.FontName`—Determines the font used to display the caption text.
- `IELabel1.FontSize`—Determines the point size used to display the caption text.

When it is up and running, your copy of IE should look like Figure 10-8.

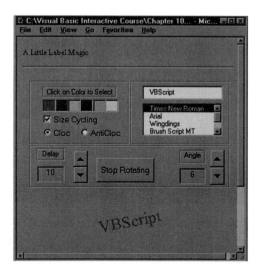

Figure 10-8
A little Label magic
spinning away

The vast majority of the VBScript and all the controls that make the page will be stored in a layout file. This layout file needs to be added to a parent HTML file as described in Session 2. Below is the relevant HTML from the parent file showing the layout file reference.

```
<CENTER>
<OBJECT ID="Label"
        CLASSID="CLSID:812AE312-8B8E-11CF-93C8-00AA00C08FDF">
                            <PARAM NAME="ALXPATH" REF VALUE="file:C:⇐
\Visual Basic Interactive
        Course\Chapter 12\.alx">
</OBJECT>
</CENTER>
```

The VBScript

Please remember that with VBScript listings, the order in which each event and its associated code is presented is not of great importance, since all the procedures except the **Timer** event are run when they are triggered by the user. Let's start the listing with something you saw in Session 2, adding items to a listbox. The event that triggers this code is the layout file **OnLoad** event; the code is shown below.

```
Sub LayoutLabel_OnLoad
        lstFonts.AddItem "Times New Roman"
        lstFonts.AddItem "Arial"
        lstFonts.AddItem "Wingdings"
        lstFonts.AddItem "Brush Script MT"
        lstFonts.AddItem "Lucida Handwriting"
        lstFonts.AddItem "Symbol"
End Sub
```

The code shown above will be triggered when the layout file is first loaded. This always happens when the page is first loaded and is a good place to put any initialization code for objects contained within the layout. If your system does not support any of the fonts mentioned above, then just change the names shown to fonts of your own.

The application requires three variables that are global to the entire layout file. They must be dimensioned outside of any subroutine declaration to achieve this, but Xpad's New Global Variable option will help you here. The variables are shown below.

```
dim Toggle
dim Inc
dim FontSize
```

Remember, these variables are not typed directly into the parent HTML file, but added via the Global Variable option in the VBScript Wizard (see Session 1). They are shown in a listing format for the sake of clarity.

If you take another look at the page as it runs, you will see two spinbutton controls. The first is called **spnDelay** and the second **spnAngle**. Below is the **change** event handler for **spnDelay**. This event is triggered whenever the user changes the **Value** property of the spinbutton by clicking one of its arrows.

```
Sub spnDelay_Change()
      lblDelay.Caption = spnDelay.Value
      tmrRotate.Interval = spnDelay.Value
end sub
```

Spinbuttons are useful if there is a defined range of contiguous values the user can select from. Depending on which arrow button was pressed, the spinbutton's value is automatically increased or decreased (the amount is specified by the spinbutton's **SmallChange** property) before the **Change** event is triggered. The **Change** event procedure takes the new spinbutton value and passes it on to the label **lblDelay**'s caption property for display. The primary purpose of this spinbutton is to speed up or slow down the rate at which the timer control fires its event. The Timer property **tmrRotate.Interval** is also set to the new spinbutton value. It is unusual for applications to speed up and slow down timers in this way simply because few situations demand it.

The higher the spin value, the higher the Interval value and the less frequently the timer will trigger a timer event and vice versa. It is the **Timer** event procedure that will determine what happens when the **Timer** event is fired, and that will appear a little later. For now let us consider the change event of the second spinbutton **spnAngle**.

```
Sub spnAngle_Change()
      lblAngle.Caption = spnAngle.Value
end sub
```

This event handler is used to display the current number held in **spnAngle**'s **Value** property. The label **lblAngle** is not an IELabel but is a default label control from the HTML layout toolbox. It is only used to display the current **Value** property of the spinbutton. This same **spnAngle.Value** will be used to increase or decrease the rotation angle of the label, but that too belongs to the **Timer** event coming soon.

The **txtCaption** textbox allows the user to alter the text being displayed. You may have noticed that changing the text in the textbox dynamically changes the spinning label's text display. The code below shows how this is achieved.

```
Sub txtCaption_Change()
      lblMain.Caption = txtCaption.Text
end sub
```

The **Change** event of the textbox is used so that any changes in the **txtCaption.Text** property trigger the change event procedure. The newly typed string held in **txtCaption.Text** is passed on to the IELabel control, called **lblMain**, for display via its **Caption** property. Any changes in the text of the textbox **txtCaption** will instantly appear as the text is being displayed by the label.

Next, we'll examine the setting of a new display color. The interface for this was just a line of colored labels which, when clicked, caused the display text to match the color of the clicked label. The click event handlers for all the colored labels are shown below.

```
Sub lblBlue_Click()
     ChangeColor lblBlue.BackColor
end sub

Sub lblCyan_Click()
     ChangeColor lblCyan.BackColor
end sub

Sub lblYellow_Click()
     ChangeColor lblYellow.BackColor
end sub

Sub lblRed_Click()
     ChangeColor lblRed.BackColor
end sub

Sub lblMaroon_Click()
     ChangeColor lblMaroon.BackColor
end sub

Sub lblGreen_Click()
     ChangeColor lblGreen.BackColor
end sub
```

The colored labels were colored by setting their **BackColor** properties to differing values. When the label is clicked, the **Click** event procedure sends the value of their **Backcolor** property to a subroutine called **ChangeColor**. **Sub Changecolor** is shown below.

```
Sub ChangeColor(color)
     lblMain.ForeColor = Color
end sub
```

This is a stand-alone subroutine and is only called when a colored label is clicked. The IELabel control, **lblMain**, has its **ForeColor** property set to the value of the **color** parameter. The **ForeColor** property is used by **lblMain** to set the color of the text it displays.

The controls that make up the interface will also allow the user to select a new font to be used for the rotating label text. The effect is triggered when the user clicks on a font in the listbox control. It is logical therefore that the event handler should be the listbox **Click** event. This event handler is shown below.

```
Sub lstFonts_Click()
     lblMain.FontName = lstFonts.Text
end sub
```

The listbox control is called **lstFonts**, as can be seen from its click event handler above. When the event procedure is triggered, the selected font is passed to the **FontName** property of **lblMain** (the IELabel object). As soon as **FontName** property is set, the text held in **lblMain's Caption** property is automatically reformatted to reflect the new value specified by the **FontName** property.

The **cmdRotate** command button is used to stop and start the rotation of the label caption. This is achieved by toggling the value of the Global variable **Toggle** from True to False and back again, one toggle per button push. This allows the button to become bivalent; it is either in its "Push to Start Rotating" mode or its "Push to Stop Rotating" mode. The code that controls this toggling is held in the **Click** event of **cmdRotate**, as shown below.

```
Sub cmdRotate_Click()
     Toggle = Not(Toggle)

     If Toggle then
          tmrRotate.Enabled = True
          cmdRotate.Caption = "Stop Rotating"
     Else
          tmrRotate.Enabled = False
          cmdRotate.Caption = "Start Rotating"
     End If
end sub
```

The first line of the event procedure above shows the simple trick used to toggle True/False values. If you make the new value of **Toggle** the logical opposite of the old value, you will always be setting it from True to False or back again. The actual control over the rotation is achieved by enabling and disabling the **tmrRotate** timer control based on an If test of **Toggle**'s current value. The **Caption** property of **cmdRotate** is also updated each time to reflect the current state of the button.

You may have noticed a number of references to the code contained in the **tmrRotate** Timer event handler. It is now time to have a look at that event procedure to see just how the values set by the user are processed. The **tmrRotate** Timer event is shown below.

```
Sub tmrRotate_Timer()

     If optClock.Value = True Then
          lblMain.Angle = lblMain.Angle + spnAngle.Value
Else
          lblMain.Angle = lblMain.Angle - spnAngle.Value
End If

If chkSize.Value = True Then
          If FontSize + Inc > 64 Then Inc = -1
          If FontSize + Inc < 8 Then Inc = 1

          FontSize= FontSize+ Inc
          lblMain.FontSize = FontSize
     End If
end sub
```

If the **cmdRotate** Click event procedure has enabled the timer, and if its interval has elapsed, then the Timer event is triggered. The event procedure first checks the current direction of spin chosen by the user as indicated by the **optClock** OptionButton. If its **Value** property is true, then the angle of the displayed text is increased and it spins clockwise. If this is reversed and the value is subtracted, the `optClock.Value` is set to false, and the text spins counterclockwise.

The user is allowed to determine the direction of rotation, either clockwise or anti-clockwise, by clicking the option button `optClock`. If the option button is checked, then its `Value` property is set to True. If it is unchecked, its `Value` property is set to False. There is no need for any VBScript code. Once set, the value will remain until it is reset. It can therefore be used to make code flow decisions like the one shown above.

Perhaps the most attention grabbing feature of this sample application is the way the rotating text appears to go off into the distance then come forward again. This effect is created by smoothly varying the size of the text being displayed. The user can switch the option on or off via a checkbox control. If a check box is checked, then its `Value` property is set to True; otherwise its `Value` is False. Whatever the current `Value` setting, the property can be tested in any procedure to help decide which code should be run.

In the final `If` statement of this session, the checkbox control `chkSize` has its `Value` property tested. The text will only be affected if the `chkSize` has a `Value` property set to True, i.e., the box has been checked. The `lblMain.Fontsize` is varied up and down the font's point size scale. If the font size has risen to 64, then it is set to decrease. Conversely, if the font size has shrunk to 8, then it is set to increase again. Fortunately, if the font does not support the font size, then the attempt is ignored.

Summary

This session has continued to expand the available toolset by including in a sample application two ActiveX controls which, although commonly used, are not found on the HTML layout control's default Toolbox. The Label control had a number of its properties exposed to user manipulation, and dynamic results were obtained. The animation effect was created by the first use of Timer control, an essential tool in any event-driven environment. The Timer control demonstrated its ability to trigger code without the aid of a user event, the code run being entirely at the programmer's discretion. Finally, a number of common events and properties were manipulated to achieve some familiarity with these everyday coding techniques.

In the next session, one final ActiveX control, the IEChart control, will be examined. This is a more complex control requiring a little more code preparation and support. The session will also be used to continue the theme of object manipulation within VBScript.

1. Which of the following best describes a `Timer` object's function?
   a. Creates an autofiring eventhandler for the programmer's use
   b. Allows animation effects to be created
   c. Fires off a predetermined sequence of events
   d. None of the above

2. Which statement about the **IELabel** object is True?
   a. The **Forecolor** property sets the label's border color.
   b. The **FontName** property sets the color of the display text.
   c. The **Angle** property specifies the text's display angle.
   d. The **FontSize** property automatically cycles from largest to smallest.

3. Which line of code will toggle the value of **MyVar** from True to False?
   a. `Toggle (MyVar)`
   b. `Not(MyVar)`
   c. `Not (MyVar) = MyVar`
   d. `MyVar = Not (MyVar)`

4. When a check box is checked its caption property is
   a. set to True.
   b. set to False.
   c. unaffected.
   d. set to empty string.

5. CheckBox controls and optionButton controls are often used to
   a. provide event handlers to process user actions.
   b. provide the user with onscreen verification of a selected option.
   c. make logic flow decisions within the code.
   d. answers a., b., and c. together.

Difficulty: Easy

1. Create an onscreen clock accurate to the second. The time display format is not important.

Difficulty: Moderate

2. Now create an onscreen clock that can be positioned both horizontally and vertically. Clicking on the button should toggle between horizontal and vertical modes.

SESSION 5

USING THE ACTIVEX CHART CONTROL

The Microsoft-written IEChart control does not boast 3D graphs nor ray-traced shading, but it does neatly package all the basic charting functionality normally required. For the VBscripter who wants a simple path to simple charts, it is just a matter of setting a few properties and entering some data, and the IEChart control will dynamically convert your data into a variety of common chart types.

This session seeks to extend your knowledge of ActiveX types, as well as give more hands-on experience manipulating ActiveX objects. It also seeks to explain the workings of the IEChart control by exposing a subset of its properties, primarily those responsible for its more useful or interesting features. The properties are exposed to the user so that the control can be dynamically altered onscreen, showing a range of the control's functionality.

The Chart Attack Application

The Chart Attack application uses the following components:

- Textbox Control

- Standard Label Control

- CheckBox Control

- ComboBox Control

- SpinButton Control

- IE Chart Control

The Chart properties manipulated in the code are

- IEChart.*RowName*

- IEChart.*Rows*

- IEChart.*Columns*

- IEChart.*ColumnIndex*

- IEChart.*DataItem*

- IEChart.*ChartType*

- IEChart.*ColorScheme*

- IEChart.*vgridStyle*

- IEChart.*hgridStyle*

When you have the Chart Attack running, your copy of IE should be similar to Figure 10-9.

The data used in this session is meaningless. Clicking on the Refresh button generates single data values (random within specified bounds) for each of the five columns generating a random graph. The row of spinbuttons will alter that single data value up and down. The altered value is fed into the graph object, and the display reacts accordingly. The sample has been designed this way to avoid the tedium of typing in test data.

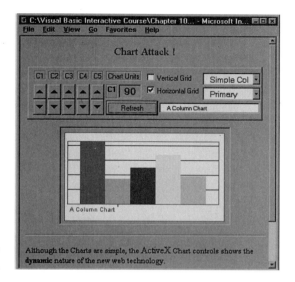

Figure 10-9
Chart Attack

The VBScript Code

The code shown below is the **Onload** event generated when the **Chart.alx** file is first loaded into the parent HTML file.

```
Sub Graph_Onload()


        cmbStyle.additem "Simple Pie"
        cmbStyle.additem "Special Pie"
        cmbStyle.additem "Simple Col"
        cmbStyle.additem "Simple Bar"
        cmbStyle.listindex = 2

        cmbColor.additem "Primary"
        cmbColor.additem "Mute"
        cmbColor.additem "Color Blind"
        cmbColor.additem "Poor Taste"
        cmbColor.additem "New Age"
        cmbColor.listindex = 0

        txtLegend = "Chart Legend"
        chkHGrid.Value = True
         Chart.Rows = 1
        Chart.Columns = 5
        ChartRefresh
end sub
```

The **Onload** event sets the interface components to their startup values and calls the **ChartRefresh** subroutine, which provides the first set of initialization data to draw the first graph. The chart refresh subroutine and the commandbutton **cmdRefresh**'s **Click** event are shown below.

```
Sub ChartRefresh()

        Randomize

        SpinButton2.value = (Rnd*50)+50
        SpinButton3.value = (Rnd*50)+50
        SpinButton4.value = (Rnd*50)+50
        SpinButton5.value = (Rnd*50)+50
        SpinButton1.value = (Rnd*50)+50
end sub

Sub cmdRefresh_Click()
        ChartRefresh
end sub
```

The **ChartRefresh** subroutine is called as an initialization procedure from the **Chart_Unload** event and then subsequently whenever the Refresh commandbutton is clicked. It simply sets each spinbutton value (and hence data column value seen later) to a random number that lies between 50 and 100.

X = Rnd*50 choses values for **X** from **0** to **50** at **Rand**om.

X = (Rnd*50)+50 means **X = (0 to 50) + 50** therefore **X = (50 to 100)**.

Note the use of the command **Randomize**; this reseeds the internal random number generator to prevent the same sequence of random numbers being thrown out. The **RefreshChart** subroutine is used to set up the initial chart data and, when called from the **cmdRefresh** Click event, to restore the chart to a reasonable data position.

> **Definition: Reseed**
>
> **Randomize** initializes the **Rnd** function's random-number generator, giving it a new seed value. The value returned by the system timer is used as the new seed value.
>
> If **Randomize** is not used, the **Rnd** function uses the same number as a seed the first time it is called, and thereafter uses the last generated number as a seed value. This results in the same sequence of random numbers every time the random number generating application is run.

The random values generated are used to set the value of the spinbutton, but how does that affect the graph? The spinbutton **Change** event procedures make calls to a common procedure called **SpinClick**. The individual calls are shown below.

```
Sub SpinButton1_Change()
        SpinClick 0,SpinButton1.Value
end sub

Sub SpinButton2_Change()
        SpinClick 1,SpinButton2.Value
end sub

Sub SpinButton3_Change()
        SpinClick 2,SpinButton3.Value
end sub
```

```
Sub SpinButton4_Change()
      SpinClick 3,SpinButton4.Value
end sub

Sub SpinButton5_Change()
      SpinClick 4,SpinButton5.Value
end sub
```

Each event handler does essentially the same thing. It passes an index number and the current value of its own **Value** property as parameters to the **SpinClick** subroutine. The index number will be used to determine which column (or pie slice) on the chart should be updated. The value is used to determine the new column's value. Since the buttons are named from 1 to 5, but the column index values for an IEChart object run from 0 to 4, the index sent is always one less than the **SpinButtonX** sending it. The **SpinClick** subroutine is shown below.

```
Sub SpinClick(Index,Value)
      Chart.ColumnIndex = Index
      Chart.DataItem = Value
      lblChartValue.Caption = Value
      lblColumn.Caption = "C" & Index+1
end sub
```

The **SpinClick** subroutine receives data from the spinbuttons. It receives an index number for the column to be updated and the new value the user has set for the spinbutton. These values are then used to manipulate the chart object.

Setting the **Chart.ColumnIndex** property tells the object which column is about to be updated. Setting the **Chart.DataItem** property sets the column's value. The **Caption** properties of the two display labels **lblChartValue** and **lblColumn** are also updated with the two parameter values. The labels are used to show the user which column is currently selected and what its current value is.

One of the features of Chart Attack is the ability to dynamically alter the chart style without losing the data. In order to achieve this, a select case construct was used in the combobox **cmbStyle**'s Change event handler. The code for this is shown below.

```
Sub cmbStyle_Change()
    Select Case cmbStyle.value
          Case "Simple Pie"
                Chart.ChartType=0

          Case "Special Pie"
                Chart.ChartType=1

          Case "Simple Col"
                Chart.ChartType=11

          Case "Simple Bar"
                Chart.ChartType=14
    End Select
end sub
```

In order to dynamically alter the style of graph used, the code that switches from style to style is called whenever the item selected in **cmbStyles** is changed. The combobox **cmbStyles** was preloaded with values back in the Layout **OnLoad** event procedure. The **Value** property of **cmbStyle** holds the text string of the currently selected item.

The **Select Case** statement shown above tests the string held in the **Value** property and compares it to those shown on the Case branches. The **Select Case** ensures that only the code relevant to the selected chart style is actually run. Setting the **ChartType** property to a numerical value instantly affects the graph, converting all the data from the old chart style into the newly selected style. The numbers that correspond to the various chart styles were copied from the property listbox in the HTML layout environment.

Another IEChart property exposed to the user is the **RowName** property. This takes a string and displays it as a chart legend. The user dynamically changes the chart legend by changing the text held in the textbox **txtLegend**. The Change event handler for **txtLegend** is shown below.

```
Sub txtLegend_Change()
      Chart.RowName = txtLegend.Text
end sub
```

When the user changes the **Text** property value of **txtLegend**, the event procedure above is triggered. This causes the new value of the **Text** property to be passed to the **RowName** property of the **Chart** object, and the Chart display is automatically updated to reflect this.

The **ColorScheme** property acts like the IEChart's **Style** property. Setting the **ColorScheme** to a numeric value will select one of the built-in color schemes. When a new color scheme is selected from the combobox **cmbColor**, the **Change** event handler is triggered. The **Change** event handler for **cmbColor** is shown below.

```
Sub cmbColor_Change()
      Chart.ColorScheme = cmbColor.Listindex
end sub
```

The **listindex** property of comboboxes such as **cmbColor** holds the numerical Index value of the currently selected list item. The index value always starts from zero for the first item in the list. This index value can be passed directly to the **ColorScheme** property of the **Chart** object, where it is used to represent a particular, built-in color scheme.

Finally, the user can select whether or not to have either horizontal or vertical grid lines shown on the display. The **Chart** object has two properties to toggle the grid lines on and off. The user determines the grid line's state by toggling a pair of check boxes called **chkVGrid** and **chkHGrid**. When the values of these check boxes change, the properties of the **Chart** object need to be updated. The change event handlers for both the check boxes are shown below.

```
Sub chkVGrid_Change()
      Chart.vgridStyle = chkVGrid.Value
end sub
```

```
Sub chkHGrid_Change()
      Chart.hgridStyle = chkHGrid.Value
end sub
```

The code to toggle both horizontal and vertical grid lines works by linking the **Value** property of the check boxes to the **hgridStyle** or **vgridStyle** properties of the **Chart** object. Should the user change the check box value (this can only be True or False), then the chart's grid properties are updated and the grid lines toggle on and off.

Summary

In this session you saw how setting just a few of the IEChart's properties can cause the object to change its display without losing any of the data already entered. Random numbers were generated within specified bounds to provide some raw data to initialize or reset the graph. The **Randomize** statement was employed to prevent the duplication of any series of random numbers. The IEChart was dynamically linked to the user interface via spinbuttons, an example of user control through interface design. A number of the IEChart's properties were exposed to the user and manipulated in the code giving an overview of the object's somewhat limited potential. It should be noted that this is the simplest **Chart** object found. There are many more third party controls with far greater functionality, although you can be sure that they will integrate with VBScript in much the same way as the **IEChart** object.

The next session will show you around the objects inherent to the Internet Explorer. Understanding the nature of these objects will provide you with an even greater repertoire of properties and methods you can manipulate when creating your Web pages.

1. The command **Randomize**
   a. produces a random number between 1 and 50.
   b. reseeds the random number generator.
   c. creates a random number of random numbers.
   d. None of the above.

2. The IEchart object's **ChartType** property *always* takes a
   a. text string value indicating the chart type.
   b. a numeric value indicating the chart type.
   c. value from a Click event handler.
   d. value from a Change event handler.

3. Which line of code will toggle the value of **MyVar** from True to False?
   a. **Toggle (MyVar)**
   b. **Not(MyVar)**
   c. **Not (MyVar) = MyVar**
   d. **MyVar = Not (MyVar)**

4. A Select Case construct is *always* used to
   a. determine the logic flow based on the value of a single test expression.
   b. determine the logic flow based on the value of many test expressions.
   c. set the value of a test expression to the value show in the *Case* branch.
   d. set the `ChartType` property to a numeric value.

5. Which statement most accurately describes the `ListIndex` property of both comboboxes and listboxes?
   a. A string value indicating the currently selected list item starting from zero
   b. An index value starting from one
   c. A numeric value indicating the currently selected list item starting from one
   d. A numeric value indicating the currently selected list item starting from zero

Difficulty: Moderate

1. Create a layout file that allows the user to select a chart column and alter its value. Make sure the graph reflects any alterations in the chart data.

Difficulty: Difficult

2. Create a multidimensional array to hold numeric chart data. Use the array to create a graph. Write a subroutine that will allow the user to alter one or more columns by a percentage amount. Allow the user to select the chart type, color scheme, and grid lines.

SESSION 6

EXPLORING THE EXPLORER

The Internet Explorer is itself little more than a collection of objects, albeit a large and complex collection. Many of the IE's component objects are exposed to programmers, presenting a range of properties and methods for their use. The IE Object model shown in Figure 10-10 shows the major object-based components.

When you load an HTML page into IE, it creates a number of objects. These objects correspond to that page, its contents, and other pertinent information. Below are four of the more important objects created whenever an HTML file is loaded in IE.

- *Window*: the top-level object; contains properties that apply to the main HTML page.

- *Location*: contains properties on the current URL

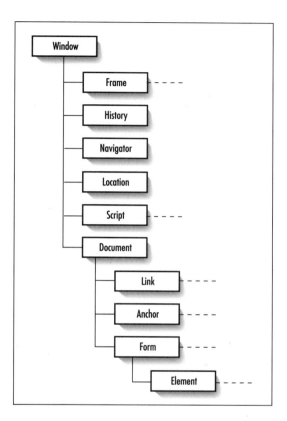

Figure 10-10
The Internet
Explorer object
model

- *History*: contains properties representing URLs the user has previously visited

- *Document*: contains properties for content in the current document, such as title, background color, and forms

These objects all have properties and methods which can be useful to the programmer. Many of the objects will also contain objects themselves.

The properties of the **Document** object are created based on the HTML of the document the object refers to. For example, the **Document** object has a property for each Form (**<FORM>**) and each Anchor (**<A>**) in the document.

The power of the Object Model comes from the ability to ascertain information about the current environment and then use that information in VBScript. For example, you may wish to discover the URL of the currently displayed HTML file. The **Window** object contains the child object **Location**. This object has a property called **Href**, and this property contains the URL string of the currently displayed page. The VBScript code to copy the current URL to a variable **MyURL** is shown below.

```
MyURL = Window.Location.Href
```

Some properties can be set as well as just read. The URL property of the **Location** object is one of them. Setting the URL causes IE to search out and load the document. The VBScript code to set the **Href** property is shown below.

```
Window.Location.Href = "http://Dummy.Com/Myfile.htm"
```

The objects that make up the IE object model also supply useful methods. A good example is the **Document.Write** method. This method allows HTML to be sent to a currently loaded document, allowing dynamic alteration of any displayed page. If the document is contained within a frame, then it can be accessed and HTML sent to it. The code below shows the **Document.Write** method being invoked.

```
Document.Write "<B>The IE Object Model</B>"
```

The example above shows a few words flanked by the HTML tags for bold text. The HTML must be sent *before* any HTML can be written to a document; it must first be opened using the **Document.Open** method. The **Document.Write** method is then used with its string of HTML sent as a parameter (strings can be up to 255 characters long but no more). Each string sent is added to the newly opened document. The **Document.Write** method can be used as often as is required to complete the HTML page. In order to allow IE to process and display the document, the **Document.Close** method needs to be invoked. The complete process is shown below.

```
Document.Open
Document.Write "<CENTER><B>The IE Object Model</B></CENTER>"
Document.Close
```

The sample above uses **Document** as the object name. If this code were run, then the HTML would be sent to the main document object, i.e., the parent HTML file. The code to specify a document object within a **Frame** object is shown below.

```
Document.Open
MyFrame.Document.Write "<B>This appears in the Frame Document</B>"
Document.Close
```

Frame objects are created when the page is first loaded, but only if there are **<FRAME>** tags in the document. The most important thing to remember about frames is that an HTML page with frame tags consists of more than one HTML file. If you have a page with two frames in it (a frameset), three HTML files are needed. One file is required for each of the frames, and one to describe how the the frames will be laid out; this is the parent HTML file. An example of the HTML **<FRAMESET>** tag is shown below.

```
<FRAMESET ROWS="20%, *">
        <FRAME NAME = "Frame1" SRC="Frame1.htm">
        <FRAME NAME = "Viewer" SRC="Viewer.htm">
</FRAMESET>
```

Part of this HTML statement is the NAME component. The name specified here will be used by IE as the frame's object name; in the case above the objects would be called

Frame1 and Viewer. To send the document held in the viewer frame some HTML, the Document.Write method should be invoked. The code below shows this happening for the Viewer frame object.

```
Viewer.Open
Viewer.Document.Write "<B>This appears in the Viewer frame Document</B>"
Viewer.Close
```

The Window object has other useful methods. Three more are shown below.

```
Window.Prompt(Message, Default Text)
Window.Alert (Message)
Window.Confirm(Message)
```

The Prompt method displays an input dialog box. It prompts the user for some input text and returns it to the code like a function. Alert works in just the same way as the MsgBox command you have already met. The Confirm method simply displays a message box with Yes and No buttons and returns True or False. In the code shown below, they are used in combination.

```
Sub GetInput()
    Dim UserMsg

    Do
            UserMsg = Prompt ("Please Enter Message","Some Text")
            If UserMsg = "" Then
                    If Confirm "Do you want to Quit?" Then Exit Do
            Else
                    Alert "You entered : " & UserMsg
            End If
    Loop Until Not (UserMsg="")

    Alert "GoodBye"
End Sub
```

The code sample above will present the user with an input box that returns inputted text into the UserMsg variable. The user is now caught in a Do loop, which will repeat the input box and alert box for as long as the user types a message into the input box. To quit, he must force the UserMsg to be an empty string. UserMsg will be an empty string if the user presses OK without first typing anything into the input box. The Confirm box gives the user a Yes and a No option. The return value, True or False, can be directly tested in an If statement. If the user says Yes, true is returned and the Do loop is exited. A final alert box gives an exit message.

Summary

The Internet Explorer is not simply a passive HTML viewer. This session has shown that it dynamically creates objects that contain information relating to the page. Altering this information by setting the properties of the IE objects effectively rewrites portions of the page *in situ*. We also examined some of the primary objects, such as the Window object and the Document object. The window's Href property showed how easy Web navigation is with IE. The Document object was manipulated through its Write method, opening up the possibility of creating dynamic HTML pages on screen. A cursory glance was made in the direction of floating frames to illustrate how the HTML is converted into objects within IE. Finally, the window object's **Prompt**, **Alert**, and **Confirm** methods were used to illustrate some of the IE features useful to the VBScript programmer.

In the next session, we will examine another Net-related language called Java and its sister JavaScript in overview.

1. The Window object is
   a. the **Parent** object to all the objects created for a Web page.
   b. the HTML that controls the window formatting.
   c. the way Xpad displays object information.
   d. the lowest level Object model component.

2. From the statement below, which is the *child* object and which is the *parent* object?

   ```
   Window.Document.Href
   ```
   a. **Window** is the child object and **Href** is the parent object.
   b. **Document** is the child object and **Href** is the parent object.
   c. **Href** is the parent object and **Window** is the child object.
   d. **Window** is the parent object and **Document** is the child object.

3. A *frame* object is created when
   a. the user clicks on a frame.
   b. a page is loaded that contains HTML frame tags.
   c. the user opens a link within a frame.
   d. a page is loaded that contains HTML link tags.

4. After sending HTML using the **Document.Write** method, the page is processed and displayed by invoking which method?
   a. **Document.Open**
   b. **Document.Input**
   c. **Document.Close**
   d. **Window.Document.Write**

5. The Confirm returns
   a. Yes or No, depending on which button is pressed.
   b. True or False, depending on which button is pressed.
   c. a value indicating whether the user wishes to quit the application.
   d. a numeric value indicating the currently selected list item.

Difficulty: Difficult

1. Create a layout file that displays the URL of the current page on the Web page. You can choose to display the URL in a textbox or by writing it directly to the Web page using the `write` method. Allow the user to input a URL and make IE load up the file specified.

Difficulty: Moderate

2. Choose an object from the Object model. Display all the property values for that object in a framed document.

SESSION 7

A LITTLE JAVA, PLEASE!

Java is intended to be a universal standard for the transfer of functionality embedded in HTML. Although this would seem to be at loggerheads with the ActiveX technology, this is not necessarily the case. Catching on to the growing need for a universal solution to the problems of hardware and software diversity on the Net, Microsoft has ensured that the IE comes fully equipped with Java capabilities. Both ActiveX controls and their Java equivalents called applets (which means small application) will be able to live side-by-side in the same HTML. Not only that, they will be able to talk to one another via the common language of objects, properties, and methods. This is where VBScript comes in. VBScript can be seen as the glue that holds together all the objects on a page. A Java object is treated in much the same way as an ActiveX object, so both can be present on any one Web page.

This duality allows the IE to display a very wide range of functionality indeed. C programmers can write ActiveX controls, and Java programmers can write applets. IE Explorer can utilize the functionality of both via its Object model. IE also provides support for JavaScript, a language similar in function to VBScript but different in syntax and style.

Here is a quick technical resumé of Java's capabilities.

- **Object-Oriented.** The language is, to its very core, object-oriented, allowing inheritance and the reuse of code in both a static and dynamic fashion.

- **High Performance.** Being a C++ derivative with "Just-in-time" compilation and the ability to link in native C methods makes Java fairly sing along. It also implements an efficient multithreading capability to make better use of the available processor resource.

● **Portable.** Any machine, regardless of its architecture, will download and run Java code as long as it has a (machine-specific) Java interpreter written for it. This is an important feature for a language that is intended primarily for Internet use with its infinitely variable hardware base.

● **Robust.** The pressures of being portable and the fear of bringing down business systems forced the architects of Java to turn out a remarkably well-behaved programming environment.

Java is an interpreted language. This means that every computer user who wants to run some Java must have installed a program to convert the Java code statements into the native machine code for that computer. This program is called the *interpreter*. Unlike other interpreted languages such as Visual Basic and VBScript, Java is totally committed to being an object-oriented language. This allows any part of the language to be augmented as the library of Java component objects grows over time.

Java functionality is normally packaged into applets that work in much the same way as the ActiveX controls. References to the applets are embedded into the HTML file; when it is *parsed,* the host browser requests a copy of the applet and stores it in the memory of the host machine ready for use. Because Java is fast and compact, it can be used to create complex functionality, which can then be incorporated as a black box object into a standard HTML 3.0 document by any Web author.

Definition: Parse

The splitting of a sentence into recognizable words. This is normally done as a first stage in extricating the meaning of the sentence. In order to be parsed, a string must contain delimiting characters. You are currently using spaces as your primary delimiter as you read this. All computer languages are parsed before being processed.

The JavaScript Language

JavaScript is a compact, object-based scripting language for developing client/server applications. The IE browser interprets JavaScript statements embedded directly in an HTML page in much the same way it interprets VBScript. An example of some JavaScript is shown below.

```
<SCRIPT LANGUAGE="JavaScript">
      function compute(form) {
            if (confirm("Are you sure?"))
                  form.result.value = eval(form.expr.value)
            else
                  alert("Thats All Folks.")
      }
</SCRIPT>
```

JavaScript occupies the same niche in the IE browser as VBScript. When we examine the JavaScript sample above, some familiar objects and methods become apparent. The IE Window object is having its **Confirm** and **Alert** methods triggered which will produce dialog boxes for the user. The **<SCRIPT>** tag tells the browser what language to expect with the **LANGUAGE="JavaScript"** element. When running, JavaScript is indistinguishable from VBScript.

JavaScript and Java

The JavaScript language resembles Java, but without Java's static typing and strong type checking. JavaScript stands to Java as VBScript stands to C. JavaScript supports most of Java's expression syntax and code flow control constructs. In contrast to VBScript's single *variant* data type, JavaScript supports a runtime system based on data types representing numeric, Boolean, and string values, making the programmer's life a little more flexible.

JavaScript complements Java by exposing useful properties of Java applets to script authors. JavaScript statements can get and set exposed properties to query the state or alter the performance of an applet or plug-in. This methodology is precisely equivalent to the VBScript/ActiveX approach.

Java programs consist exclusively of classes and their methods. Java's requirements for declaring classes, writing methods, and ensuring type safety make programming more complex than JavaScript authoring. Java's inheritance and strong typing also tend to require tightly coupled object hierarchies.

In contrast to Java, JavaScript descends in spirit from a line of smaller, dynamically typed languages like HyperTalk and dBASE. These scripting languages offer programming tools to a much wider audience because of their easier syntax, specialized built-in functionality, and minimal requirements for object creation.

Summary

This session has tried to flesh out your understanding of the Net environment by introducing you to Java and JavaScript. These are two languages you will probably hear a lot about, and for some very good reasons. Java promises to be a universal solution to the problem of hardware diversity on the Net. It achieves this as an interpreted language, but it still manages to be fully object-oriented, robust, and high performance. Applets written in Java are compatible with ActiveX controls since both will reside in the IE. Being IE objects makes them available to either VBScript or JavaScript. Both scripting languages share the same niche and therefore exhibit many similar characteristics. Both languages are parsed by IE when they are first loaded, and both are imbedded into HTML via **<SCRIPT>** tags.

1. Java is *not*
   a. high performance.
   b. object-oriented.
   c. hardware-specific.
   d. interpreted.

2. Which of the following is not a JavaScript data type?
   a. Boolean
   b. Variant
   c. Numeric
   d. String

3. JavaScript can invoke which of the following IE methods?
   a. Alert
   b. Prompt and Alert
   c. Confirm
   d. Any method exposed by the IE object model

4. Which of the following describes a statement that has been *parsed*?
   a. Chopped into words and rearranged to make machine code
   b. Chopped into component words based on delimiting characters
   c. Converted from VBScript into JavaScript
   d. Invoked by an IE object method

5. The HTML `<SCRIPT>` tags are used to embed which of the following languages?
   a. VBScript
   b VBScript and Java
   c. Java and JavaScript
   d. VBScript and JavaScript

Difficulty: Easy

1. Surf the Net and check out some Java and JavaScript pages. See if the Internet Explorer really can use Java applets like it says. View the HTML source from these pages and see if you can spot where the applet is being referenced.

Difficulty: Difficult

2. Create an HTML file that includes a Java applet. Apply your knowledge of objects, especially ActiveX controls, to work out how this should be done. You will need to establish the technique yourself; it is not available from the session's text.

AN OLE OVERVIEW

OLE is not nearly as confusing as many sources make out. The acronym stands for *Object Linking and Embedding*, a name that used to describe the entire functionality of OLE, but nowadays describes only a small part of it. This session aims to provide an overview of Microsoft's OLE architecture and a little of its history. By gaining a general insight into the construction of this exciting new technology, you will come to understand its potential for the applications you write.

A Brief History

When Microsoft released the original OLE 1.0, its only purpose was to allow the user to imbed OLE compatiable components within one another. For example, a user could place a Word document *inside* an Excel spreadsheet and then, without leaving the Excel spreadsheet, use Word to edit the text by double-clicking on the image of the Word document object. Documents that contain one or more objects from other OLE compatiable applications are called *compound documents*.

There are two ways that the object components of a compound document can be organized. From the example given, if the Word document was stored as a separate file from the Excel spreadsheet, then the two are said to be linked. If the Word document is stored as an intrinsic part of the Excel spreadsheet, then the Word document is said to be embedded. Hence the original usage of the term *object linking and embedding*.

After OLE 1.0 came OLE 2.0. Its release changed the face of windows programming forever. Up until this point, the programming community was pulling its collective beard out trying to resolve problems created by the frightening growth in software complexity. As user demand soared, programs such as Word or Excel grew into monolithic applications. The problem with this incremental growth approach is that any change to the application, no matter how small, required a full rewrite and rerelease of the entire application. This and many other profit-squeezing reasons led to the formulation of OLE 2.0 which, at a stroke, solved most of the problems by throwing windows wide open to the world of objects.

After version 2, Microsoft stopped releasing versions of OLE. The company did not give up on the subject—quite the opposite—it was just that version numbers had become irrelevant. Understanding why OLE is now just called OLE and not OLE 3.0 or 4.0 is the key to understanding why OLE affects everybody who intends to program within the windows environment. So why did Microsoft get rid of the numbers?

What Happened to the Numbers?

OLE relies on its ability to coordinate software components to form a coherent application with functionality exposed internally to the member components and externally to the user. OLE is a server; it provides a communications service to its clients. Users are clients of OLE, as are the software components that make up an OLE application. A client-server relationship exists when a centralized body acts as a distribution hub for the services required by its client attachments.

Definition: Software Component

A reusable piece of code and data that can be plugged into any other software component that presents a set of funtions to the user or another software component. Software components are commonly compounded to form aggregate applications.

An analogy for the role of OLE, although Microsoft may not agree, is the United Nations. In principle, the UN supplies all its UN-compatible countries with a series of common interfaces that allows every member country to speak to one another. A message directed to one country from another will be routed by the UN from the sender to the recipient and probably translated on the way. This allows different countries using different languages to cooperate without ever having to consider the complexities of translation or location.

OLE provides the same function, allowing software components to make use of its translating and locating abilities. Although Word and Excel and VBScript might all be written in different languages at different times by different people, under the auspices of OLE they can all be mixed and matched together within single, aggregate application.

But it need not stop there. Huge applications like Word can be broken down into functional components and each one made into an OLE-compatible object in its own right. This will not affect how Word actually operates, since all the same functionality is still present, only now it is chopped up and coordinated through OLE. The difference OLE makes becomes apparent when it is realized that now any programmer can interact with the software components of Word itself. To give an example, if you want to add a spell-checking function to your application, you could include the software component of Word that has this function. Every function of Word is made available to any program that can speak to the OLE interface. So why did all this objectification of Windows make Microsoft forget about OLE's version number?

Imagine you had created a program that had 10 functions in its original form, release 1.0. Adding a further function would require the release of version 2.0. Now imagine that each function was a software component that existed independently within the OLE architecture. Adding the 11th function would mean delivering a single extra software component with instructions on how to add this to the other 10 existing software components, usually a simple installation program. What would you call this extra function, since it is not a full release but really a sophisticated add-on? Microsoft solved the naming dilemma created by the new programming approach by forgetting about releases all together and delivering the additions to OLE as OLE components themselves.

That is why OLE is now called OLE and not OLE 3.0; it has become an approach to programming rather than an application in its own right.

> **Definition: OLE Components**
>
> A unified environment for object-based software components with the capability of altering and expanding the architecture through the addition of further OLE components. The concepts that form the idea of an OLE object are collectively called the *component object model*, or COM.

OLE and VBScript

The Internet Explorer consists of many objects, some of which relate to the data represented by an HTML page. If the HTML page contains VBScript, then this is directed to the VBScript component of the Internet explorer for compilation and execution. As you have seen earlier in this chapter, a convenient way to program VBScript is within the Xpad environment; this is because Xpad provides a single point of access to VBScript HTML and the ActiveX software component library.

This means you have already been using OLE like a seasoned veteran, although you may not have fully realized the fact. Xpad is a visualization of OLE in action—it allows the user to create an aggregate application consisting of ActiveX objects plus data (some of which act as instructions in the form of VBScript and HTML) to be used by components of IE when the page is loaded.

OLE is the reason that ActiveX programmers can write their new controls in the language of their choice (normally it would be C++, but Java might change this) providing whatever functionality they want to provide, and yet you can access all of this by simply including the control in your HTML layout.

This helps to clarify the role of the HTML layout control itself. It acts as a container object for all the other ActiveX controls and VBScript data you want to collect together in a Web page.

> **Definition: Container**
>
> A container object holds information describing the objects which are grouped into that container.

Xpad will automatically provide all the technical backup required to allow the controls to coexist under OLE despite their disparate backgrounds. It does this by integrating all the objects you include and the VBScript you write using the common OLE interface. The Web page itself is therefore OLE-compatiable, and so it can be recognized and used by any other OLE component or aggregate application such as IE.

The Dangers of OLE

The greatest strength of OLE—its ability to expose component functionality to any other OLE application—is also its greatest security compromise. OLE holds out the potential to create applications that can access any part of the client's component architecture and manipulate it to the author's own ends. This has been the case since OLE 2.0 was released, but since getting full-blown OLE applications surreptitiously into a client's machine is not easy, people tend to know where their software has come from. With the advent of the anonymous Web, this has changed.

Any Web page that contains controls not currently installed on the client machine will have to install those controls before it can be loaded and displayed correctly. Allowing a page to install any control it likes is not very clever, especially since those controls can access every part of the OLE architecture resident on the client machine.

This problem has been partially resolved by Microsoft through its use of security levels, certificates, and electronic signatures. This allows users to have greater confidence in the providence of the controls they allow to be installed onto their machines. but it certainly does not rule out the possibility of downloading rogue OLE components with dubious intentions.

Summary

In this session you have seen how OLE transformed and continues to transform the way Windows applications are produced. VBScript via IE and ActiveX has been fully committed to the OLE architecture and object-based programming approach. Although the mechanics of OLE are not relevant at this stage, chasing the answer to the missing OLE version numbers has shown how profound OLE impact can be. You have seen that you already use OLE whenever you create a Web page that includes ActiveX or VBScript components although as a client the use of its services should have been transparent to you.

Finally, we pointed out the potential danger arising from the misuse of OLE technology over the hugely expanded and anonymous Web.

1. Which of the following best defines a `Container` object?
   a. It holds information describing the objects that are grouped into that container.
   b. It acts as a repository for OLE data.
   c. It is a software component.
   d. It provides IE with its VBScript capabilities.

2. Which of the following is not a compound document?
   a. A Word document within an Excel spreadsheet
   b. An Excel spreadsheet within a Word document
   c. A bitmap within a Word document
   d. A bitmap in Word document which is linked to an Excel spreadsheet

3. Which of the following does not show a client-server relationship?
   a. OLE and software components
   b. Web site and Net surfer
   c. Democracy
   d. A mouse and its mouse mat

4. The HTML layout control is
   a. an object.
   b. an OLE software component.
   c. a container object.
   d. all of the above.

5. Why might OLE on the Web have security implications?
   a. The Web is anonymous.
   b. Missing controls must be downloaded onto the client machine before pages can display.
   c. Not everybody in the world is honest, not even programmers.
   d. All of the above.

Difficulty: Easy

1. Visit Web sites whose pages contain ActiveX controls. Observe closely what happens when you access a page with ActiveX objects your machine does not recognize. You should see the automatic download occur before the Web page is displayed.

Difficulty: Easy

2. Experiment with security settings for the Internet Explorer. These are found in the View menu under Options. Visit sites with novel ActiveX controls and watch them download to see the effect your changes have made. Decide the security level that best suits your needs.

CHAPTER SUMMARY

In this chapter, you've learned to use and manipulate objects within VBScript, and have become acquainted with the VBScript Wizard and the HTML layout control. In addition, you've discovered ActiveX controls, and learned how to insert them into a Web page. Finally, you've pulled it all together with an overview of object architecture, properties, and methods.

ADVANCED TECHNIQUES

PART IV

MULTIMEDIA

sers have come to expect more than static text HTML pages. They expect sound, graphics, and animation. In this chapter, we will look at each of these elements and discuss how they can be used and modified with Visual Basic Script.

In this chapter, you will learn to:

- Display a Graphic
- Create a Clickable Image Using VBScript
- Load Background Graphics
- Show a Marquee in Internet Explorer
- Add Sound to Your Web Pages
- Apply Animation Techniques
- Add Videos to Your Web Pages
- Combine All the Previous Techniques to Create a VBScript Game

DISPLAYING A GRAPHIC

In this session, you will learn how to display a graphic image within your HTML document. Although this session deals solely with HTML, later sections in this chapter will show you how to use Visual Basic Script to manipulate these images.

Creating a Graphic Image

Before you add a graphic image to your HTML document, you must create the image or find an existing image to use.

There are generally two types of images which can be displayed with standard Internet browsers: GIF images and JPEG images. GIF images will usually have the .GIF extension in the filename (for example, PICTURE.GIF), and JPEG images will usually have the .JPG extension in the filename (for example, PICTURE.JPG). Each of these types of images is compressed to take up less space and to transfer faster over the Internet. JPEG images provide better compression for photographic images, but they generally take longer to display. Possibly for this reason, GIF images seem to be used more frequently in HTML documents.

JPEG Image Files

JPEG compression is a *lossy* compression scheme. This means that the resulting compressed image is not *exactly* the same as the original. However, the compressed image is often so close to the original that the average observer will notice no difference. If you are creating your own JPEG files, your paint program may give you the option to set a compression ratio for the resulting graphic file. The more compression you use, the less the resulting file will look like the original, but the file size will be smaller. Experiment with different values for this compression ratio. Generally, compression of 25 to 50 percent can be achieved without significant loss of image quality.

To create your own images, you will need to use a drawing program that allows you to create either GIF or JPEG images. Such programs are often available free from the Internet or services such as CompuServe and America Online.

In addition, you may be able to use images from existing HTML pages on the Internet. If you do decide to use existing GIF or JPEG images, make sure they are not copyrighted.

Windows and Windows 95 Users

Starting with version 3.0 of Microsoft Internet Explorer, you can use the Paint program that is included with Windows and Windows 95 to create images for the Internet. This is because Internet Explorer 3.0 supports BMP image files which you can produce directly with the free Paint program included with your version of Windows.

Displaying a Graphic Image

Now that you know how to create or obtain a GIF or JPEG image, you are ready to display it within your HTML page. To display the image, we will use the **IMG** tag.

The basic form of the **IMG** tag is as follows:

```
<IMG SRC="URL">
```

where **"URL"** is the quoted string specifying the exact location of the image you wish to display. Here is a simple HTML document which displays an image named **"MOUNTAIN.GIF"** (examine Figure 11-1 to see the result of this code).

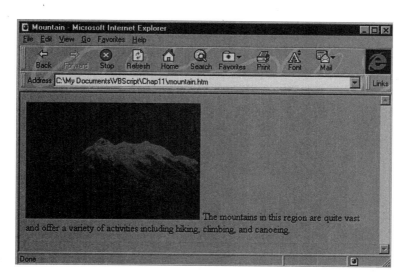

Figure 11-1
Displaying a
graphic image

```
<HTML>
<HEAD><TITLE>Sample Image</TITLE></HEAD>
<BODY>
<IMG SRC="MOUNTAIN.GIF">
The mountains in this region are quite vast and offer
a variety of activities including hiking, climbing, and
canoeing.
</BODY>
</HTML>
```

The above example specifies **"MOUNTAIN.GIF"** as the URL of the image to display. Because we did not precede **"MOUNTAIN.GIF"** with a specific URL location, it is assumed that the **"MOUNTAIN.GIF"** image is located in the current URL (the URL of the currently displayed HTML document). If the image you want to display does not exist in the same location as the currently displayed HTML document, you need to indicate the full URL location of the image as in the following code:

```
<HTML>
<HEAD><TITLE>Sample Image</TITLE></HEAD>
<BODY>
<IMG SRC="HTTP://WWW.ACME.COM/IMAGES/NATURE/OCEAN.GIF">
</BODY>

</HTML>
```

Advanced Options for Graphic Images

We have already seen how to display a graphic image within an HTML document. Now let's find out how to use more advanced options of the HTML **IMG** tag.

Aligning an Image with Text

The **ALIGN** option of the **IMG** HTML tag allows you to adjust the alignment of an image to the surrounding text. Here is the general format of the **ALIGN** option:

```
<IMG ALIGN=position SRC="PICTURE.GIF">
```

where position is either **TOP**, **BOTTOM**, or **MIDDLE**.

Here is a simple HTML document which displays an image with the top of the image aligned with the proceeding text:

```
<HTML>
<HEAD><TITLE>Sample Image</TITLE></HEAD>
<BODY>
<IMG ALIGN=TOP SRC="SMILEY.GIF">
</BODY>
</HTML>
```

Figures 11-2, 11-3, and 11-4 show the difference between the **TOP**, **BOTTOM**, and **MIDDLE** arguments of the **ALIGN** option. The following listing shows an example of using all three alignment options, and the output from this listing is shown in Figure 11-5.

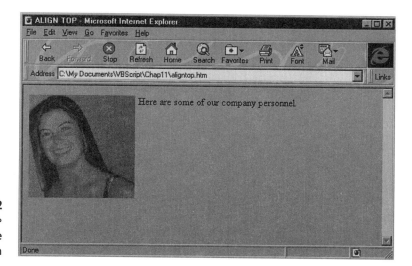

Figure 11-2
Using the TOP
argument of the
ALIGN option

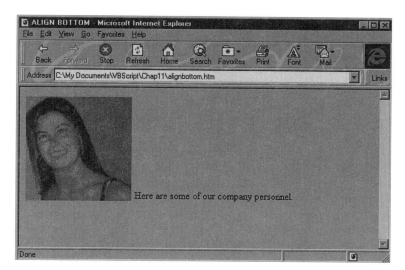

Figure 11-3
Using the BOTTOM
argument of the
ALIGN option

```
<HTML>
<HEAD><TITLE>Alignment Test</TITLE></HEAD>
<BODY>
<H1>Different Image Alignments</H1>
<IMG ALIGN=TOP SRC="SQUARE.GIF">This text is aligned with the top of the image.
<P>
<IMG ALIGN=MIDDLE SRC="SQUARE.GIF">This text is aligned with the middle of the image.
<P>
<IMG ALIGN=BOTTOM SRC="SQUARE.GIF">This text is aligned with the bottom of the image.
</BODY>
</HTML>
```

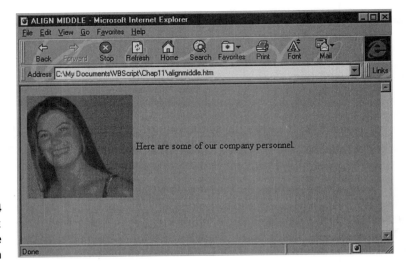

Figure 11-4
Using the MIDDLE
argument of the
ALIGN option

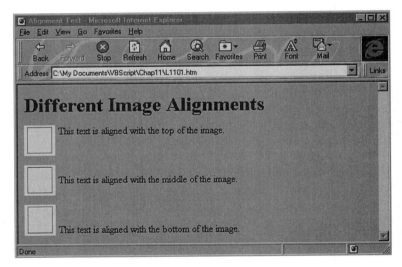

Figure 11-5
How TOP, MIDDLE,
and BOTTOM
alignment display

Allowing for Non-Graphical Browsers

As surprising as it may be, not all browsers have support for graphics. In particular, the visually-impaired computer users who browse the World Wide Web typically do so using a browser called Lynx, which does not support graphics. In addition, those with a slow modem connection (i.e., 2400 baud) generally use browsers that will not display graphics. To accommodate those who have non-graphical browsers, use the ALT parameter of the IMG tag to specify some alternate text to be displayed in place of the image. The following listing demonstrates the ALT parameter.

```
<HTML>
<HEAD>
<TITLE>Non-Graphical Browser Test</TITLE>
</HEAD>
<BODY>
<IMG SRC="smiley.gif" ALT="A Smiley Face">
</BODY>
</HTML>
```

Making the Image Background Transparent

Setting the background color attributes for your images can make a big difference in how your images are displayed on a Web page. Look at the difference between Figure 11-6 and Figure 11-7.

Notice how the image in Figure 11-6 has a square border around it while the image in Figure 11-7 does not. Although it may sometimes be preferable to have such a border, it is not so in this case. Unfortunately, you cannot make a change to your HTML or VBScript code to correct the problem with the background of the image. This is a property of the image itself, so you must use a separate drawing or painting program that supports the ability to specify a transparent background (such as Paint Shop Pro or GIF Contruction Set).

Summary

To create images to display within your HTML page, you must use a drawing or painting program which can create GIF or JPEG image files.

Use the **IMG** tag to display images on your HTML page. If the image you want to display is not at the same URL as the currently displayed HTML document, you must specify

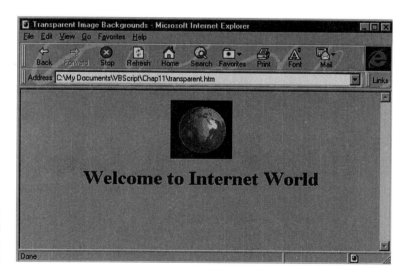

Figure 11-6
An image without a transparent background

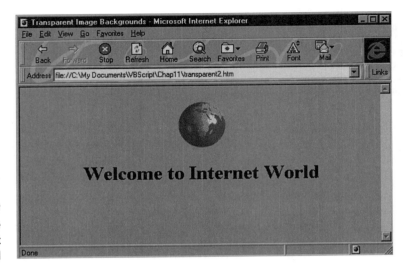

Figure 11-7
The same image
with a transparent
background

the full URL of the image. The **ALIGN** option and the **TOP**, **BOTTOM**, and **MIDDLE** arguments align the image with the surrounding text.

1. The two standard types of graphic images you can use in your HTML documents are
   a. JIF and MPEG.
   b. IMG and VRES.
   c. GIF and JPEG.
   d. TAR and ZIP.

2. Which of the following graphic images referenced within the **IMG** tag *must* exist at the same URL as the currently displayed HTML document?
   a. `<IMG SRC="PICTURE.GIF">`
   b. `<IMG SRC="FILE://IMAGES/PICTURE.GIF">`
   c. `<IMG SRC="HTTP://WWW.COMPANY.COM/PICTS/PICTURE.GIF">`
   d. `<IMG SRC="HTTP://PICTURE.GIF">`

3. What are the three arguments that can be used with the **ALIGN** option of the **IMG** tag?
   a. `LEFT, RIGHT, CENTER`
   b. `TOP, BOTTOM, MIDDLE`
   c. `FIRST, SECOND, THIRD`
   d. `UPPER, LOWER, CENTER`

4. Which of the following HTML parameters can be used to substitute text in place of graphic images for non-graphical browsers?
   a. `NOGRAPH`
   b. `SUBSTITUTE`
   c. `ALIGN`
   d. `ALT`

5. Which of the following demonstrates the correct method of using an image as a link?
   a. `<A HREF="PAGE2.HTML"><IMG SRC="GOPAGE2.GIF"></A>`
   b. `<SRC HREF="PAGE2.HTML"><IMG SRC="GOPAGE2.GIF"></SRC>`
   c. `<IMG HREF="PAGE2.HTML   SRC="GOPAGE2.GIF">`
   d. `<IMG SRC="GOPAGE2.GIF">`

Difficulty: Easy

1. Create your own graphic image and display it on an HTML page preceded by the words "Here is my image:" and aligned with its middle at the position of the text.

Difficulty: Intermediate

2. Create a Web page which has images that connect you to the various popular search sites such as Yahoo!, Excite, Lycos, and so on.

WHERE DID I CLICK?

Before VBScript, there were cryptic scripting tools such as CGI and Perl which allowed you to perform various activities on the server. Unfortunately, the server is usually kept pretty busy just satisfying requests for HTML documents, and when you add any additional processing (such as with these server-side scripts), you run the risk of slowing the server to a crawl.

Using server-side scripts may not seem like a big deal to you, but consider this: One of the most-used server-side scripting activities is creating a clickable image in an HTML document. That's right—before VBScript, you had to use the server just to tell where users clicked inside one of the images on your Web page! In this session, we will see how we can accomplish this same activity by using VBScript and leaving the server free to do more important tasks.

Tracking the Mouse with Events

By now, you are probably comfortable with the fact that many objects on your Web page can generate events which you can respond to with VBScript routines. It turns out that an image is no different—well, only slightly different. Because an image does not inherently generate mouse events, we must wrap the image with a dummy anchor tag. This dummy anchor tag will use a format similar to the following:

```
<A ID="name" HREF=""><IMG SRC="image_name"></A>
```

Notice that the **HREF** parameter of the anchor tag is set to null string (**""**). This prevents the users from jumping somewhere when they click anywhere in the image.

Using a Dummy Anchor Tag

You can use the technique of providing a dummy anchor tag to attach mouse events to items on your Web page which do not normally have these events attached to them (such as an inline image).

MouseMove **and** OnClick **Events**

For our purposes, there are two important events related to the mouse: **MouseMove** and **OnClick**. **OnClick** is certainly important, because we need to jump to a specific URL when the user clicks on a section of the image on our Web page. But why is **MouseMove** important, and how can it be used in the context of an image map?

The basic format of the **OnClick** event is as follows:

```
objectname_OnClick
```

An underscore and the event name are appended to the name of the object for which we want to track the event. Notice that the **OnClick** event has no parameters.

The **MouseMove** event has several important uses. First and foremost, no x- and y-coordinates are passed to the **OnClick** event, so we *need* the **MouseMove** event in order to determine the latest position of the mouse pointer (we will store this position in a global variable so we can access it in any of our subroutines or functions). Another important use of the **MouseMove** event is to provide the user with a *tip* regarding what the region he or she is currently positioned over represents. In our example below, we simply output to a text control some text stating either Red Box, Blue Box, or Green Box. You could use more meaningful text in your Web pages such as "Click here to see a map of Indonesia" or "Send an e-mail to customer support." You may also want to use the **MouseOver** event to generate these tips.

The basic format of the **MouseMove** event is as follows:

```
objectname_MouseMove(shift, button, x, y)
```

As we have seen before, an underscore and the event name are appended to the name of the object for which we want to track the event. The four parameters (**shift**, **button**, **x**, and **y**) represent the status of the shift key, an indicator for which button is pressed (if any), the x-coordinate of the mouse (relative to the object), and the y-coordinate of the mouse (relative to the object), respectively.

Let's look at an example: Suppose we have a button on a Web page that we have named cmdMenu. If we want to jump to another Web page when the button is clicked, we could use the following VBScript code:

```
<SCRIPT LANGUAGE="VBScript">
sub cmdMenu_OnClick
      top.location.href="menu.htm"
end sub
</SCRIPT>
```

When the cmdMenu button is clicked, the **cmdMenu_OnClick** event is generated, which means that the VBScript subroutine named **cmdMenu_OnClick** will be executed (if it exists, of course). In this case we have placed code in the subroutine to jump to a new page titled **"menu.htm"**.

Creating a Clickable Image Map

Now that we know how to use the **MouseMove** and **OnClick** events to track mouse movement within an image, it is a simple matter to implement the code to create a clickable image map.

Basically, the following example displays an image containing three differently colored boxes (as shown in Figure 11-8). When the user moves the mouse pointer over one of the colored boxes, the color of the box is displayed in the text control beneath the image. When the user clicks the mouse, a simple HTML file is displayed for each of the colored boxes. You should be able to expand this basic example to implement a variety of clickable image maps within your Web pages.

```
<HTML>
<HEAD>
<TITLE>Clickable Image Maps</TITLE>
</HEAD>
<BODY>

<A ID="image" HREF=""><IMG SRC="image map.gif"></A>

<BR>

<INPUT TYPE="text" NAME="txtDisplay" SIZE=50>

<SCRIPT Language="VBScript">
<!--
dim mX, mY

sub image_MouseMove(s,b,x,y)

    ' Save the mouse coordinates.
    mX = x
    mY = y

    ' Check to see if we are in a specified rectangular region.
    if InRect(x,y,10,10,50,30) then
```

continued on next page

continued from previous page

```
            DisplayInfo "Red Box"
        elseif InRect(x,y,10,40,50,60) then
            DisplayInfo "Blue Box"
        elseif InRect(x,y,60,10,100,30) then
            DisplayInfo "Green Box"
        else
            DisplayInfo ""
        end if
    end sub

    sub image_OnClick

        ' The OnClick event does not receive x and y coords, so
        ' use the mX and mY variables that we saved in MouseMove.
        if InRect(mX,mY,10,10,50,30) then
            location.href = "red.htm"
        elseif InRect(mX,mY,10,40,50,60) then
            location.href = "blue.htm"
        elseif InRect(mX,mY,60,10,100,30) then
            location.href = "green.htm"
        end if
    end sub

    function InRect(x,y,x1,y1,x2,y2)
        ' Check to see if x and y fall within the specified boundaries.
        if x >= x1 and x <= x2 and y >= y1 and y <= y2 then
            InRect = true
        else
            InRect = false
        end if
    end function

    sub DisplayInfo(outputString)
        txtDisplay.value = outputString
    end sub
-->
</SCRIPT>
</BODY>
</HTML>
```

In the previous listing, we began by placing an anchor on our Web page using the <A ID="image" HREF=""> tag. We used ID to set the name of the anchor (image) and HREF to set the URL of the page to display when the anchor is clicked. You must specify an HREF value even if you do not want to automatically display another page when the anchor is clicked. Therefore, we set **HREF=""**, which will do nothing.

After the anchor is established, we place a textbox on our page using the **<INPUT TYPE="text" NAME="txtDisplay" SIZE=50>** tag. This tag specifies that we want a textbox whose name is **"txtDisplay"** and whose size is 50 pixels wide.

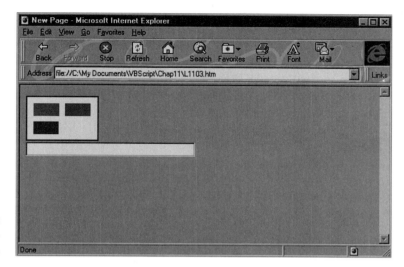

Figure 11-8
The clickable image
map in action

Next, we start our VBScript code to track the mouse while it is in the image area. This is accomplished using the **image_MouseMove** subroutine. (Remember: Because **Image** is the name of the object, **image_MouseMove** is the name of the event subroutine that will track the mouse movement). Within the **image_MouseMove** subroutine we use the **InRect** function (declared later in our VBScript code) to see if the mouse is currently in a specified rectangle. If the mouse is currently positioned within one of the specified regions, we display a message using the **DisplayInfo** subroutine (also declared later in our VBScript code). Notice that we save the mouse position in the **mX** and **mY** variables. Because these variables are dimensioned outside a specific subroutine, they are considered global and are accessible to all the VBScript subroutines and functions. These mouse position coordinates will be needed in the **image_OnClick** event subroutine because no mouse position information is passed to the **OnClick** subroutine.

The **image_OnClick** subroutine checks to see if we are in a specified region using code similar to that used in the **image_MouseMove** subroutine. The difference is in the action that we take in the **image_OnClick** subroutine. Rather than display a message, we actually jump to a new page entirely. The page to which we jump is determined by the region in which the mouse is positioned when the **OnClick** event occurred.

The InRect function is defined next. It is the function that was used in the **image_MouseMove** and **image_OnClick** subroutines. This function simply returns either True or False, depending on whether or not the mouse coordinates (which are passed to this function in the **x** and **y** parameters) are contained in the region specified by x1, y1, x2, and y2, which are also passed to the InRect function.

Finally, the **DisplayInfo** subroutine accepts one parameter (**outputString**) which it displays in the txtDisplay textbox that we defined earlier.

Summary

Wrap an object in a dummy anchor tag to attach mouse events to the object.

Use the **MouseMove** and **OnClick** events to track mouse movement and button presses. Since the **OnClick** event does not contain information about the current x- and y-coordinates of the mouse, constantly monitor this information in the **MouseMove** event (if you need it).

QUIZ 2

1. To create a clickable image map, why do we surround an image with a dummy anchor tag?
   a. Because we want the user to jump to the link specified in the anchor
   b. Because the image will not be displayed without the dummy anchor tag
   c. Because an image does not inherently have mouse events attached to it
   d. None of the above

2. From which event do we get the x- and y-coordinates of the mouse cursor?
   a. **MouseMove**
   b. **OnClick**
   c. **MousePos**
   d. **OnNewPos**

3. Which of the following is a use for the **shift** parameter of the **MouseMove** event?
   a. To see if the mouse position has changed
   b. To determine which mouse button is pressed (if any)
   c. To determine the status of the keyboard shift key
   d. None of the above

4. Which of the following events can be used to generate *tips* when the user passes the mouse cursor over specified areas?
   a. **MouseMove**
   b. **MouseOver**
   c. Both a and b
   d. None of the above

5. How do we obtain the mouse position within the **OnClick** event subroutine?
   a. The x- and y-coordinates are passed to the **OnClick** subroutine as arguments.
   b. We use the **MousePos()** function within the **OnClick** subroutine.
   c. We save the mouse position coordinates in global variables within the **MouseMove** subroutine.
   d. None of the above.

Difficulty: Easy

1. Modify the listing in the "Creating a Clickable Image Map" section to use your own image (you will need to update the listing with new coordinates for clickable regions).

Difficulty: Advanced

2. Create a clickable image map in which the clickable areas are not rectangles (circles perhaps?).

LOADING GRAPHICS IN THE BACKGROUND

Many current Web pages feature a background that contains a graphic image. Often, these graphic images are texture patterns that can be tiled throughout a Web page to produce the effect of a textured background (marble, gravel, paper, and so on). In this session, we will learn how to add background images to your Web pages and to specify whether the image is fixed (this is known as a watermark) or scrollable.

Background Images

You can add a background image to your Web page using the **BACKGROUND** parameter of the **BODY** tag. Simply set the **BACKGROUND** parameter equal to the URL of the image you want to display as the background (GIF, JPEG, and BMP format images can all be used). If this image is smaller than the display area of your document (which is usually the case), then the image will be tiled to fill the entire display. The following example illustrates using the **BACKGROUND** parameter of the **BODY** tag:

```
<BODY BACKGROUND="bgimage.gif">
```

This **BODY** tag will attempt to load a GIF image titled **"bgimage.gif"** as the background of the current Web page. Because we did not specify a complete URL, **bgimage.gif** must exist in the same directory as our Web page.

Adding Background Images to Tables

You can also add background images to an entire table, a table cell, or a table row by adding **BACKGROUND="image_url"** to any **TABLE**, **TD**, or **TR** tag, respectively. See Chapter 2, "Fundamentals: Building HTML Documents," for more information on creating tables.

Watermarks

Normally, a background image will scroll with the information on a Web page when a user uses the browser's vertical scroll bar to scroll through a Web page. However, you may want to keep your background image static and have the text and other information scroll over this static background image. In this case the static background image is referred to as a watermark and can be created by setting the **BGPROPERTIES** parameter of the **BODY** tag to **FIXED** as in the following example:

```
<BODY BACKGROUND="testbg.gif" BGPROPERTIES=FIXED>
```

This would load the **"testbg.gif"** image into the background and keep it fixed while the other contents of the Web page are scrolled over the background. To wrap up everything we have learned in this session, the following listing contains a complete example of displaying a background image for a Web page. Figure 11-9 shows the output from this code. Try this example on your own and experiment with modifying the properties of the **BODY** tag.

```
<HTML>
<HEAD>
<TITLE>Background Graphics</TITLE>
</HEAD>
<BODY BACKGROUND="testbg.jpg" BGPROPERTIES=FIXED>
<H1>
This is some large text.
<P>
We are going to put quite a bit of text on this page so we can scroll and see what
effect the BGPROPERTIES parameter of the BODY tag has on scrolling.
<P>
This is some more large text.
<P>
Are we scrolling yet?
<P>
If not, perhaps you can add some more text of your own to this HTML file.
<P>
How about now?
<P>
Do you like the clouds effect?
<P>
It almost makes you feel like you are flying, doesn't it?
<P>
OK, not really, but it's still pretty cool.
<P>
Try some other background images if you would like to.
<P>
```

```
I hope we are scrolling, because this is the last line of text.
<P>
</H1>
</BODY>
</HTML>
```

Summary

Use the **BACKGROUND** parameter of the **BODY** tag to specify a background image for your Web page. Set **BGPROPERTIES=FIXED** within the **BODY** tag in order to keep the background image static and scroll the other contents of the page over this static image (the default will scroll the background image also).

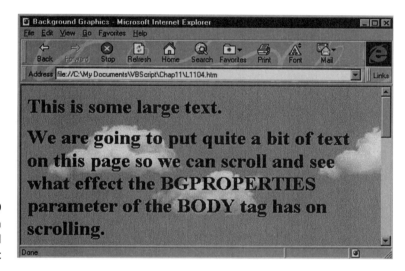

Figure 11-9
A Web page with a background graphic

QUIZ 3

1. Which of the following tags is used to display a background image in your Web pages?
   a. `PICTURE`
   b. `IMG`
   c. `HEAD`
   d. `BODY`

2. Which of the following parameters of the `BODY` tag specifies the URL of the image to use as a background for your Web pages?
   a. `BACKGROUND`
   b. `BGURL`
   c. `URL`
   d. `BGSRC`

3. What is a watermark?
   a. A background image that scrolls with other contents of its Web page
   b. A small mark at the bottom of your Web page to indicate that it contains a background
   c. A background image that is static and does not scroll with the other contents of its Web page
   d. None of the above

4. Which of the following is the appropriate parameter setting of the `BODY` tag to implement a watermark?
   a. `BACKGROUND=WATERMARK`
   b. `BACKGROUND=FIXED`
   c. `BGPROPERTIES=FIXED`
   d. `FIXED=TRUE`

5. Which of the following is a default characteristic of a background image for your Web pages?
   a. It is static and will not scroll with the other contents of its Web page.
   b. It is tiled to fill the entire display area.
   c. It is enlarged to fill the entire display area.
   d. None of the above.

EXERCISE 3

Difficulty: Easy

1. Modify the code in the "Watermarks" section so that the background image is *not* fixed (so that it will scroll with the other contents of the Web page).

Difficulty: Intermediate

2. Give the user a choice of displaying a Web page that has the background fixed and one that does not, and display the appropriate page when the user makes a selection.

SHOWING A MARQUEE

The latest version of Internet Explorer provides the ability to display a text string that scrolls across your HTML page in marquee style. In addition, this effect requires very little programming effort on your part. This session will explain how to use this marquee effect to liven up your HTML documents.

Displaying Marquee Text

To display marquee text within your HTML document, use the **MARQUEE** HTML tag. The basic form of this tag is as follows:

```
<MARQUEE>text to display</MARQUEE>
```

Using the **MARQUEE** tag with no parameters will cause the text to scroll from right to left indefinitely. You can modify the behavior of the **MARQUEE** tag by using the parameters shown in Table 11-1.

Parameter	Value	Description
BEHAVIOR	"alternate"	Bounce the text back and forth across the display
BEHAVIOR	"scroll"	Start the text off the screen and scroll the text so that it is off the screen before wrapping
BEHAVIOR	"slide"	Start the text off the screen and scroll the text until it touches the margin
DIRECTION	"right"	Scroll text to the right
DIRECTION	"left"	Scroll text to the left
SCROLLAMOUNT	(numeric)	Number of pixels to scroll with each movement of the text

continued on next page

continued from previous page

Parameter	Value	Description
SCROLLDELAY	(numeric)	Delay (in milliseconds) between each text movement
LOOP	(numeric) or "infinite"	Number of times to loop the text
BGCOLOR	"#xxxxxx" or (color name)	Set the background color to either the defined hex value (i.e., "#FF0000" for red) or the defined color name ("Red").
WIDTH	(numeric)	Width in pixels or percent
HEIGHT	(numeric)	Width in pixels or percent
ALIGN	"top", "middle", or "bottom"	Align nearby text with top, middle, or bottom of marquee
VSPACE	(numeric)	Adjust vertical margin of marquee
HSPACE	(numeric)	Adjust horizontal margin of marquee

Table 11-1 *Parameters and values of the* MARQUEE *tag*

The parameters of the **MARQUEE** tag that are most significant are the **BEHAVIOR**, **DIRECTION**, and **LOOP** parameters.

Set the **BEHAVIOR** parameter to either "alternate" (which bounces the text back and forth across the screen), "scroll" (which scrolls the text from off the screen on one side of the display to off the screen on the other side and then repeats) or "slide" (which scrolls the text only to the margin of the display and then repeats).

Use the **DIRECTION** parameter to specify whether you want the text to scroll to the "right" or to the "left" within the marquee.

Finally, the **LOOP** parameter can be set to a numeric value if you want the marquee to scroll only a set number of times (after that, nothing will be displayed). If you want the marquee to loop indefinitely, set the **LOOP** parameter to "infinite" (this should also be the default value).

The following listing demonstrates many of the techniques outlined in this session. Four different marquees are displayed on the same page, each with slightly different parameter settings. Figure 11-10 shows a snapshot of these marquees in action. Try it out, and examine the code to see how the different settings affect the **MARQUEE** display.

```
<HTML>
<HEAD>
<TITLE>Marquee Test</TITLE>
</HEAD>
<BODY>
<MARQUEE>This is a standard marquee.</MARQUEE>
<BR>
<MARQUEE BEHAVIOR="alternate" SCROLLAMOUNT=1 SCROLLDELAY=1>This is a marquee with a
few parameters set.</MARQUEE>
<BR>
<MARQUEE SCROLLAMOUNT=10 SCROLLDELAY=2 LOOP=2>This marquee will only loop
twice.</MARQUEE>
<BR>
<MARQUEE DIRECTION="right" BGCOLOR="#FF0000">This marquee will have a red background
color.</MARQUEE>
<BR>
</BODY>
</HTML>
```

Summary

Use the **MARQUEE** tag to display marquee-style text within your Web pages. The **BEHAVIOR**, **DIRECTION**, and **LOOP** parameters of the **MARQUEE** tag adjust the main settings of your marquee. The **SCROLLAMOUNT** and **SCROLLDELAY** parameters of the **MARQUEE** tag determine the speed that your text moves across the display.

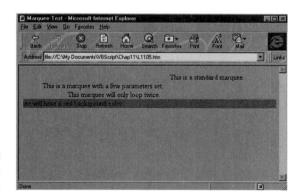

Figure 11-10
The marquee
examples in action

QUIZ 4

1. Which of the following tags is used to display marquee-style text?
   a. `<SCROLLTEXT>`
   b. `<MARQUEETEXT>`
   c. `<MARQUEE>`
   d. `<SCROLL>`

2. Which of the following parameters of the `MARQUEE` tag is used to determine if the text should scroll in a single direction or alternate back and forth?
   a. `BEHAVIOR`
   b. `ALT`
   c. `DIRECTION`
   d. `ALTERNATE`

3. Which of the following is a correct way to set the `BGCOLOR` parameter of the `MARQUEE` tag?
   a. `BGCOLOR="#FF0000"`
   b. `BGCOLOR="Red"`
   c. `BGCOLOR="#0000FF"`
   d. All are correct

4. When you set the parameter `SCROLLAMOUNT=5`, what are you setting?
   a. The marquee text will scroll once every five seconds.
   b. The marquee text will scroll five inches every minute.
   c. The marquee text will scroll five pixels each time it moves.
   d. None of the above is correct.

5. When you set the parameter `SCROLLDELAY=5`, what are you setting?
   a. The delay between each text movement to five seconds
   b. The delay between each text movement to five milliseconds
   c. The delay for movement across the entire marquee to five seconds
   d. None of the above is correct.

EXERCISE 4

Difficulty: Easy

1. Create your own Web page using several `MARQUEE` tags. Experiment with the different parameters of the `MARQUEE` tag to generate different effects.

Difficulty: Advanced

2. Experiment with VBScript code that could imitate the functionality of the `MARQUEE` tag.

WHAT ABOUT SOME SOUND?

The World Wide Web is no longer just a collection of static information pages. More and more, Web page designers are adding multimedia elements to their sites in order to capture Web surfers' attention and keep them coming back to their site. One feature that you can add to your sites to make them more interesting is sound. This session explains the type of sound you can add to your Web pages and the proper procedures for doing so.

Playing MIDI Music

MIDI is a standard format of music files which is easy to incorporate in your Web pages. Rather than attempt to save an exact sound (as is the case with the WAV and AU digitized audio formats discussed later in this session), MIDI files simply store the musical notes and instrument types for musical scores. It is then up to the synthesizer in your computer's sound card to reproduce the music. This results in much smaller files than digitized audio files.

To play a MIDI music file while your Web page is displayed, use the **BGSOUND** tag. This tag has a few parameters you can set. The **SRC** parameter specifies the URL of the MIDI file to play and the **LOOP** parameter specifies the number of times you want to play the MIDI song.

Using the **BGSOUND** tag, you can select background music for your Web site. Simply set the **SRC** parameter of the **BGSOUND** tag equal to the URL of the MIDI file which you want to play while your Web page is displayed. For example, you could use code similar to the following:

```
<BGSOUND SRC="sample.mid" LOOP=2>
```

This modified **BODY** tag will load the **"sample.mid"** file and play it two times while your Web page is displayed. It assumes, of course, that the **"sample.mid"** file is located in the current directory, since a complete URL was not included. If you want the specified MIDI file to loop continuously, specify **LOOP=INFINITE** within the **BGSOUND** tag.

Random Background Music

The whole idea of having a scripting language for your Web pages is to make them interesting and interactive, right? Assuming that's the case, let's try to add a little spice to the standard **BGSOUND** technique of playing MIDI files. Let's create a short VBScript subroutine that will play a random song each time your Web page is displayed.

The technique we will use to play a random MIDI file is the same as we have learned already: We will use the **BGSOUND** tag. But rather than explicitly place the **BGSOUND** tag in your HTML document, we will use the **document.write** method to place a slightly different **BGSOUND** tag in our document for each MIDI file. The complete code for this method is as follows.

```
<HTML>
<HEAD>
<TITLE>Random Background Music</TITLE>
</HEAD>
<BODY>

<SCRIPT Language="VBScript">
const MAX_SONG = 3

document.write "<BGSOUND SRC=" & Chr(34) & RandomMusic & Chr(34) & ">"

Function RandomMusic
    Dim iSong

    iSong = Int(Rnd(1)*MAX_SONG) + 1

    Select Case iSong
    Case 1
      RandomMusic = "night.mid"
    Case 2
      RandomMusic = "silence.mid"
    Case 3
      RandomMusic = "starry.mid"
    End Select
End Function
</SCRIPT>

You should be hearing a random MIDI song now. Refresh the page to hear another random
song.
</BODY>
</HTML>
```

Our code begins by setting a constant, **MAX_SONG**, equal to the number of random songs we will be choosing from. In our example we will be choosing from three different MIDI songs, so we set **MAX_SONG = 3**. Next, we use **document.write** to output the **BGSOUND** tag with the **SRC** parameter set to **Chr(34) & RandomMusic & Chr(34)**. **Chr(34)** is used to insert a quotation mark simply because quotation marks are required around the name of the sound file specified within the **BGSOUND** tag. **RandomMusic** is a function that we define next in VBScript. The **RandomMusic** function returns a string based on a random number from **1** to **MAX_SONG**. We use a **SELECT...CASE** structure to assign the actual function return value. In this case the **RandomMusic** function will return either **"night.mid"**, **"silence.mid"**, or **"starry.mid"**.

Using **document.write** works much like inserting HTML code directly. In our example from the previous listing, if the **RandomMusic** function returned **"silence.mid"**, our resulting HTML file would be equivalent to the code contained in the following listing.

```
<HTML>
<HEAD>
<TITLE>Random Background Music</TITLE>
</HEAD>
<BODY>

<BGSOUND SRC="silence.mid">

You should be hearing a random MIDI song now. Refresh the page to hear another random
song.
</BODY>
</HTML>
```

Notice that the placement of our VBScript code containing the `document.write` method is critical. We must place the VBScript code at the location in our HTML file where we would want the resulting `document.write` output to appear. In our example, because we would want the `BGSOUND` tag to appear immediately following the `BODY` tag, this is where we place our VBScript code containing the `document.write` method.

Playing Digitized Sounds

MIDI music is nice because the MIDI files are usually small and download to the user's computer fairly quickly, but they can only play *synthesized* music. What if you want to play your voice saying, "Welcome to my Web page," or play a few bars of your symphonic band playing the "Star Spangled Banner"? In this case, you need to use a *digitized* audio file.

A digitized audio file contains the information to reproduce a sound exactly (or close to exactly depending on how much information you save in the file). When creating your own digitized audio (using the Windows 95 Sound Recorder, for example), you generally have the option of specifying the frequency at which the sound is sampled. The higher the frequency you choose, the better the quality of the sound will be, but the file size will also be larger. Therefore, the size of a digitized audio file will depend on both the length of the audio segment which is digitized and the frequency at which it was digitized. Experiment with different frequencies to determine what produces sound files that are accurate but do not take too long to download.

Once a digitized audio sample is created, it is generally saved in one of two formats: WAV (pronounced "wave") files or AU (pronounced "Ay-Yoo") files.

Resampling Digitized Audio

If you want to decrease the size of a digitized audio file, you may be able to use a sound utility program (such as the shareware Goldwave program for Windows 95) to resample the audio file. Using resampling, you can adjust the sampling frequency of an existing audio file to sacrifice sound quality for file size.

WAV Audio

The WAV file format originated with the Windows platform and is used quite often today to store digitized audio. Generally, the compression will not be great with WAV files, and the file sizes can be quite large (so be careful that your users don't have to wait too long for your WAV files to download). To play a WAV audio file, use the **BGSOUND** tag as we did with MIDI files. So, for example, to play a file titled **"hello.wav"** use the following code:

```
<BGSOUND SRC="hello.wav">
```

Once again, if you do not specify a **LOOP** parameter, the sound will be played one time only.

AU Audio

The AU file format originated with Unix machines, and it is optomized for storing digitized audio. Generally, compression of AU files will be better than compression of WAV files. To play an AU audio file, we also use the **BGSOUND** tag. So, for example, to play a file titled **"boing.au"**, use the following code:

```
<BGSOUND SRC="boing.au" LOOP=5>
```

This would play the sound in the **"boing.au"** file five times.

Summary

MIDI music can be easily added to your Web pages using the **BGSOUND** tag. Set the **SRC** parameter of the **BGSOUND** tag to the filename of the MIDI music file. MIDI files typically have a **".mid"** filename extension.

Digitized sound files can also be included on your Web pages by using the **BGSOUND** tag. The two types of digitized audio files inherently supported by the Microsoft Internet Explorer are WAV audio and AU audio. The file size of digitized audio files in either of these formats is a function of both the length of the audio and the sampling frequency with which the file was created.

QUIZ 5

1. Which of the following tags can be used to add MIDI music to your Web pages?
   a. MUSIC
   b. BGMUSIC
   c. MIDISRC
   d. None of the above

2. Which of the following types of digitized audio files are inherently supported by Microsoft Internet Explorer?
   a. WAV
   b. AIFF

    c. AU

    d. Both a. and c.

3. Which of the following should be the smallest (relative to file size) version of the "Star Spangled Banner"?

    a. MIDI

    b. WAV

    c. AU

    d. Both a. and b.

4. Which of the following parameters of the `BGSOUND` tag is used to repeat a sound or MIDI song?

    a. `REPEAT`

    b. `AGAIN`

    c. `LOOP`

    d. None of the above

5. Within a `BGSOUND` tag, how do you specify that you want a song or sound to repeat indefinitely?

    a. `LOOP=INFINITE`

    b. `LOOP=INDEFINITE`

    c. `REPEAT=CONTINUOUS`

    d `INFINITE`

Difficulty: Easy

1. Add some background MIDI music to one of your existing Web pages.

Difficulty: Advanced

2. Create a Web page that plays different sounds when different links on the page are clicked. (Hint: See Chapter 12, "I Was Framed!", for information about hidden frames).

SESSION 6

ANIMATION

This session introduces you to some simple animation techniques that you can use in your own HTML pages. If you would like more information about the ActiveX controls discussed in this session, refer to Chapter 10, "Objectifying Your Scripts." Later in this chapter, we will examine some more advanced animation using Visual Basic Script.

Animation Using the LABEL Control

Although the label control was designed primarily to display text, it can also be used to animate text using the **ANGLE** option.

The LABEL control is an ActiveX control that allows you to display a string of text within your HTML document. Although you have already seen how to display strings of text on your HTML page, the LABEL control gives you many options to change the font, color, position, and angle of a string of text. The following listing is a simple example which uses the LABEL control to display Hello, world. on an HTML page. The output from this example is shown in Figure 11-11.

```
<HTML>
<HEAD>
<TITLE>New Page</TITLE>
</HEAD>
<BODY>
<OBJECT ID="lblHello" WIDTH=115 HEIGHT=27
 CLASSID="CLSID:99B42120-6EC7-11CF-A6C7-00AA00A47DD2">
    <PARAM NAME="_ExtentX" VALUE="3043">
    <PARAM NAME="_ExtentY" VALUE="714">
    <PARAM NAME="Caption" VALUE="Hello, world.">
    <PARAM NAME="Angle" VALUE="0">
    <PARAM NAME="Alignment" VALUE="4">
    <PARAM NAME="Mode" VALUE="1">
    <PARAM NAME="FillStyle" VALUE="0">
    <PARAM NAME="FillStyle" VALUE="0">
    <PARAM NAME="ForeColor" VALUE="#000000">
    <PARAM NAME="BackColor" VALUE="#C0C0C0">
    <PARAM NAME="FontName" VALUE="Arial">
    <PARAM NAME="FontSize" VALUE="12">
    <PARAM NAME="FontItalic" VALUE="0">
    <PARAM NAME="FontBold" VALUE="0">
    <PARAM NAME="FontUnderline" VALUE="0">
    <PARAM NAME="FontStrikeout" VALUE="0">
    <PARAM NAME="TopPoints" VALUE="0">
    <PARAM NAME="BotPoints" VALUE="0">
</OBJECT>
</BODY>
</HTML>
```

You can see that the LABEL control requires a variety of parameters: **ExtentX** and **ExtentY** to set the width and height; **FontName**, **FontSize**, **FontItalic**, **FontBold**, **FontUnderline**, **FontStrikeout**, **TopPoints**, and **BotPoints** to set the font characteristics; **ForeColor** and **BackColor** to set the foreground and background colors; and so on. Actually, the code for all of these parameters and values was created automatically using the ActiveX Control Pad, which is covered in detail in Chapter 14, "Make the Leap—Advanced Topics."

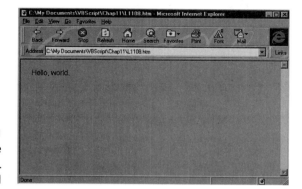

Figure 11-11
A simple example
of the LABEL
control

The parameter we are most interested in for this session is the **ANGLE** parameter. The **ANGLE** parameter of the LABEL control allows you to set the angle at which you would like the text displayed. We can perform some simple animation by repeatedly changing the **ANGLE** parameter. The following listing uses a TIMER control in conjunction with a LABEL control to repeatedly rotate the text Hello, world. Figure 11-12 shows this code in action.

```
<HTML>
<HEAD>
<TITLE>Simple Animation with the Label Control</TITLE>
</HEAD>
<BODY>
    <OBJECT ID="lblHello" WIDTH=115 HEIGHT=115
 CLASSID="CLSID:99B42120-6EC7-11CF-A6C7-00AA00A47DD2">
    <PARAM NAME="_ExtentX" VALUE="3043">
    <PARAM NAME="_ExtentY" VALUE="3043">
    <PARAM NAME="Caption" VALUE="Hello, World.">
    <PARAM NAME="Angle" VALUE="0">
    <PARAM NAME="Alignment" VALUE="4">
    <PARAM NAME="Mode" VALUE="1">
    <PARAM NAME="FillStyle" VALUE="0">
    <PARAM NAME="FillStyle" VALUE="0">
    <PARAM NAME="ForeColor" VALUE="#FFFF00">
    <PARAM NAME="BackColor" VALUE="#C0C0C0">
    <PARAM NAME="FontName" VALUE="Arial">
    <PARAM NAME="FontSize" VALUE="12">
    <PARAM NAME="FontItalic" VALUE="0">
    <PARAM NAME="FontBold" VALUE="1">
    <PARAM NAME="FontUnderline" VALUE="0">
    <PARAM NAME="FontStrikeout" VALUE="0">
    <PARAM NAME="TopPoints" VALUE="0">
    <PARAM NAME="BotPoints" VALUE="0">
</OBJECT>
    <OBJECT ID="timer1" WIDTH=39 HEIGHT=39
     CLASSID="CLSID:59CCB4A0-727D-11CF-AC36-00AA00A47DD2">
        <PARAM NAME="_ExtentX" VALUE="1005">
```

continued on next page

continued from previous page

```
            <PARAM NAME="_ExtentY" VALUE="1005">
            <PARAM NAME="Interval" VALUE="100">
    </OBJECT>

<SCRIPT Language="VBScript">
sub timer1_Timer
    dim temp

    ' Rotate the label text by 5 degrees.
    temp = lblHello.angle + 5

    ' Degrees of rotation are from 0 to 360.
    if temp > 360 then temp = temp - 360

    lblHello.Angle = temp
end sub
</SCRIPT>
</BODY>
</HTML>
```

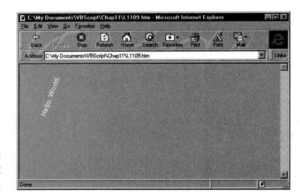

Figure 11-12
Rotating text
in action

Animation Using the MARQUEE Tag

In Session 4 of this chapter, we saw how the **MARQUEE** tag can be used to generate interesting marquee effects for text. Now let's see how we can use our knowledge of the **MARQUEE** tag to produce simple animation.

The **MARQUEE** tag is used to move or animate text characters within a marquee field. But what if we were able to get the **MARQUEE** tag to animate pictures instead of text characters? Actually, we can do just that with a little ingenuity.

The **MARQUEE** tag only works with text, but we are still in control of what font we want to use to display the text in the **MARQUEE** tag. Therefore, if we select a font that contains pictures rather than text characters (such as the WingDings font), we can perform simple animation. The following listing demonstrates this technique by showing a hand pointing to the left that scrolls in from the right of the text box using a **MARQUEE** tag. You can see the **MARQUEE** in action in Figure 11-13. This effect could be useful to draw attention to certain areas of your Web page.

```
<HTML>
<HEAD>
<TITLE>Simple MARQUEE Animation</TITLE>
</HEAD>
<BODY>
<FONT FACE="WingDings" SIZE=20>
<INPUT TYPE="text" NAME="txtInput" VALUE="Type your name here" WIDTH=50>
<MARQUEE BEHAVIOR="slide" WIDTH="30%">E</MARQUEE>
</FONT>
</BODY>
</HTML>
```

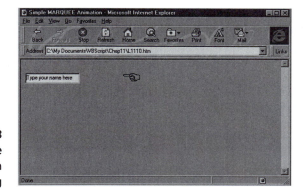

Figure 11-13
Simple
animation with
the MARQUEE tag

Animated GIF Files

Session 1 of this chapter introduced you to several types of graphic image formats, including the GIF format. We will now revisit GIF files to discuss a special type of GIF file—animated GIFs. Animated GIFs are essentially *flipbook-style* animation in which successive animation frames are overlaid on top of the current frame. Fortunately, animated GIFs need not save all the information from every frame. Instead, the parts of the image that change from frame to frame are saved. This results in much smaller files that won't put the user to sleep while the animated image downloads.

Online Sources for Animated GIF Files
Check out these Web sites that contain animated GIF files: http://www.yahoo.com/Computers_and_Internet/Graphics/Computer_Animation/Animated_GIFs/ http://www.usadvertiser.com/master/animated.htm http://www.vr-mall.com/bagg/bagg.html http://members.aol.com/royalef/galframe.htm http://rodent.lib.rochester.edu/webtools/whatsnew.htm http://www.starnet.com.au/~graphics/graphics/gifw001.htm

The advantage of animated GIF files is that you are not required to have any special client or server applications to use them. Simply insert the animated GIF file with the **IMG** tag as we did in Session 1. For example, look at the following code:

```
<IMG SRC="animtest.gif">
```

Assuming that **"animtest.gif"** is an animated GIF file, this code is all you would need to insert the animated GIF in your Web page.

To create animated GIF files, use a shareware or freeware GIF utility program. Many of these programs can be found on the Internet. A good one to try is GIF Construction Set by Alchemy Mindworks. These GIF utility programs will let you import GIF images one at a time and specify an animation order for the images. In addition, you can set options such as transparency, color, delay between frames, and image position.

Summary

For simple animation, you may be able to use either the LABEL ActiveX control or the **MARQUEE** tag. The LABEL ActiveX control has an **ANGLE** parameter which you can set to change the angle of displayed text. This effect is good for rotating text on your Web pages. The **MARQUEE** tag can be used in conjunction with a font such as WingDings (which contains a variety of small images) to perform simple animation.

More complex animation can be stored as an animated GIF file and displayed using the standard **IMG** tag. You will need a separate program to create animated GIF files, but once created, they can be inserted directly into your Web page like a standard image.

1. To perform some simple animation which rotates a text string, which of the following could you use?
   a. The **MARQUEE** tag
   b. The TEXT control
   c. The LABEL control
   d. None of the above

2. Which of the following could you use to perform some simple animation which scrolls a picture across the display?
   a. The **MARQUEE** tag
   b. The TEXT control
   c. The SCROLLBOX control
   d. None of the above

3. Which of the following tags might you use to setup the MARQUEE control to display small pictures?
   a. **FONT**
   b. **IMG**
   c. **A**
   d. **HR**

4. What is an advantage of using animated GIF files for animation?
   a. The server-side software is very fast.
   b. No additional client or server software is needed.
   c. Both a. and b.
   d. None of the above.

5. Which of the following fonts contains tiny pictures you can use in MARQUEE animation?
   a. Arial
   b. WingDings
   c. Courier
   d. None of the above

Difficulty: Intermediate

1. Create a Web page that contains several label controls of a variety of colors and sizes and animate each of them.

Difficulty: Advanced

2. Create a Web page that allows the user to select an image from the WingDings font that will scroll across the screen with the MARQUEE tag.

PLAYING WITH VIDEO

Music and still graphic images are great, but nothing captures a viewer's attention more than live video. Today, the World Wide Web still consists mostly of static images and text, but this will change as users continue to connect to the Internet at higher speeds. Even today, when a majority of Web surfers are using 14.4 and 28.8 modems, you can still achieve a variety of effects using video on your Web pages. This session will demonstrate some techniques for working with video on your Web pages.

Standard Video

There are two basic types of video available on the Internet today: standard video and streamed video. Standard video requires that (as with most images, sound, and music files) you download the entire video before viewing it. Streamed video (which we will discuss next) begins to play almost immediately and continues to download as the user views the video.

The AVI (pronounced Ay-Vee-Eye) format is a popular file format for use with video under Microsoft Windows and Windows 95. In fact, AVI is also referred to as the Video for Windows format. This file type is supported in Microsoft Internet Explorer without any additional helper applications. Filenames for files in AVI format will generally have an **".avi"** extension. Other video file types supported in Microsoft Internet Explorer include MPEG and Quicktime. Filenames for files in these formats will generally have a **".mpg"** or a **".mov"** extension, respectively.

To insert a video clip in your Web page, simply use the **IMG** tag which we discussed in Session 1 of this chapter along with the **DYNSRC** parameter. Set the **DYNSRC** parameter equal to the URL of the video file you want to display as in the following:

```
<IMG DYNSRC="testvid.avi">
```

This code will load the **"testvid.avi"** video file and display it. You can specify the **WIDTH** and **HEIGHT** of the video display area just as you can with a standard graphic image. If you do not specify a width and height, these values will default to the size of the video footage. The other parameters you can use when displaying video files in your Web page are **LOOP**, **START**, and **CONTROLS**.

Set the **LOOP** parameter equal to the number of times you want the video to be shown. If you set **LOOP=INFINITE**, then the video clip will repeat indefinitely. The **START** parameter can be used to specify when the video clip will begin to play. You can set the **START** parameter equal to one of two values: **FILEOPEN** (if you want the video clip to play as soon as it is loaded) or MOUSEOVER (if you want the video clip to play when the user moves the mouse over the video area. If you set START=MOUSEOVER, the first frame of the video will be displayed as the default static image until the user moves the mouse pointer over the video image. If you would rather have another image displayed until the video plays, insert an SRC="imagename" parameter in addition to the DYNSRC parameter. Here is some sample code that will wait until the user places the mouse pointer over the video area to start the video:

```
<IMG DYNSRC="sample.avi" START=MOUSEOVER>
```

If you want to display a set of controls beneath your video clip so the user can control playback, then include the CONTROLS parameter with your IMG tag. Here is an IMG tag that includes user playback controls:

```
<IMG DYNSRC="morevideo.avi" CONTROLS>
```

Table 11-2 contains a summary of the parameters you can use when displaying video on your Web pages. The following listing uses some of these parameters to display an AVI video on a Web page. Figure 11-14 shows the output of this Web page. Notice that we have chosen to display the controls beneath the video clip by specifying the CONTROLS parameter.

```
<HTML>
<HEAD>
<TITLE>Video on a Web Page</TITLE>
</HEAD>
<BODY>
<H1>Sample .AVI Video</H1>
This page contains an .AVI video clip.
<P>
Move your mouse over the video area to start the video.
<P>
<IMG DYNSRC="sample.avi" START=MOUSEOVER CONTROLS>
</BODY>
</HTML>
```

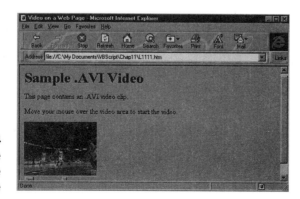

Figure 11-14
The look of the video clip on the Web page

Parameter	Value	Description
DYNSRC	(video filename)	Name of video to display
WIDTH	(numeric)	Width of video area in pixels
HEIGHT	(numeric)	Height of video area in pixels
LOOP	(numeric) or INFINITE	Number of times to show video
START	FILEOPEN	Plays video clip as soon as it is loaded
START	MOUSEOVER	Plays video clip when the mouse passes over the video area
CONTROLS		Displays video controls beneath your video clip

Table 11-2 *Parameters to adjust video display*

Streamed Video

The advantage that streamed video has over standard video is that the user can start viewing the video footage almost immediately. Video footage is displayed for the user while other, subsequent video footage is downloaded. The disadvantage of streamed video is that it sometimes requires special software on the server to provide the streamed video footage. Microsoft Internet Explorer has the built-in ability to stream MPEG, AVI, and Quicktime video files using ActiveMovie technology, but AVI and Quicktime files must be specially modified to take advantage of this streaming effect.

Summary

The two types of video that you may present in your Web pages are standard video and streamed video. Streamed video will begin to display almost immediately with subsequent video frames displayed as they are downloaded. The disadvantage to streamed video is that it generally requires separate helper software to be installed in addition to Microsoft Internet Explorer.

You can use the **IMG** tag to insert AVI video files into your Web page by specifying the **DYNSRC** parameter. There are also a host of other parameters you can include to determine when the video clip will play, the size of the display area, and whether or not video controls will be displayed for the user.

1. What are the two main types of video content?
   a. Standard and Active
   b. Standard and Streamed
   c. Live and Streamed
   d. None of the above

2. Which of the following is the main characteristic of streamed video?
   a. It always requires special server software.
   b. Video begins playing before the entire file is downloaded.
   c. The entire video must be downloaded to the user's machine before playing.
   d. None of the above.

3. Which of the following tags can be used to insert an AVI video in your Web page?
   a. AVI
   b. VIDEO
   c. IMG
   d. DYNIMG

4. Which of the following parameters of the IMG tag is used to indicate a video source?
   a. DYNSRC
   b. VIDEO
   c. SRC
   d. AVI

5. Which of the following parameters of the IMG tag is used to play a video when the mouse pointer moves over the video area?
   a. START=FILEOPEN
   b. START=MOUSEMOVE
   c. START=MOUSEOVER
   d. MOUSE=STARTVIDEO

Difficulty: Easy

   1. Create a Web page that contains an AVI video.

Difficulty: Intermediate

   2. Create a Web page that contains several *animated buttons* using the IMG tag and the START parameter as links to other sites.

ANYONE UP FOR A GAME?

This session pulls together many of the graphic, sound, and animation techniques presented in this chapter in order to create a simple Visual Basic Script game. The game we will create in this session is a memory game, similar to the classic Concentration game. We will create rows and columns of hidden images that the user must click on to view. Each time the user clicks on two images that are the same, those two pieces disappear. The object is to make all of the images disappear.

Laying Out the Playfield

The first step in creating the memory game is to create the playfield. In this case we need to display rows and columns of images. We will use the IMAGE ActiveX control to display our images. Also, we will need to store what the hidden image is at each row and column location. For the purposes of this game, let's use a grid that is four rows by three columns for a total of 12 images. 12 images will require six matching pairs of hidden images. We will store the index of the hidden image at each image location by using a simple array of numbers (1 to 12 for each of the 12 images). The `CreatePlayfield` subroutine does this work:

```
sub CreatePlayfield
    ' The cards() array will hold the number of the bitmap image at each card
location.
    ' There are 12 cards, so there will be six bitmaps (each must appear twice).
    for i = 0 to 12
      cards(i) = 0
    next

    for i = 1 to 6
      r = Int(rnd * 12) + 1
      while cards(r) <>0
        r = Int(rnd * 12) + 1
      wend
      cards(r) = i

      r = Int(rnd * 12) + 1
      while cards(r) <>0
        r = Int(rnd * 12) + 1
      wend
      cards(r) = i
    next
end sub
```

As we discussed earlier, the IMAGE control is used to display an image at each position. Because we are using 12 different IMAGE controls, it would be handy if we had these controls in an array that we could go through and process each image. It turns out we can create an array, but only indirectly. The `Initialize` routine fills the `imgCard()` array by using the SET command. You must use SET if you are assigning an object to a variable:

```
sub Initialize
    ' We want the display to be different each time.
    randomize

    ' Create an array of card objects from the image controls.
    set imgCard(1) = imgCard1
    set imgCard(2)= imgCard2
    set imgCard(3)= imgCard3
    set imgCard(4) = imgCard4
    set imgCard(5) = imgCard5
    set imgCard(6) = imgCard6
    set imgCard(7) = imgCard7
    set imgCard(8) = imgCard8
    set imgCard(9) = imgCard9
    set imgCard(10) = imgCard10
    set imgCard(11) = imgCard11
    set imgCard(12) = imgCard12

    ' No cards are turned over at this point, so turn1 and turn2 are zero.
    turn1=0
    turn2=0

    ' Initialize the number of matches to zero.
    match = 0
end sub
```

The `imgCard()` array is declared outside of any VBScript subroutine so that we can reference this object array from within any of the VBScript subroutines and functions.

Getting User Input

Once we have the playfield established, we need to allow for user input. For our memory game, we will use the `Click` event procedure for each image control we have on our page. For example, the `Click` procedure for the first image is as follows:

```
sub imgCard1_Click
    if cards(1) =0 or turn1=1 then exit sub

    imgCard1.SpecialEffect = 2
    call PlaySound(1)
    ShowPicture(1)
end sub
```

When the user clicks on a card, we check to see if the card has been turned over previously. If it has, we exit the subroutine and do nothing else. If it has not, we adjust the **SpecialEffect** property of the image (this gives the effect of pressing down on the image) and call the **PlaySound** subroutine. Finally, we display the appropriate hidden picture for image number 1.

Responding to the User

The **PlaySound** subroutine deserves a special look. When you look at the complete source code for the memory game (found on the accompanying CD-ROM), you will see that the game consists of three HTML files. The first (**"gamemain.htm"**) lays out two separate frames for the game. The top frame is actually not even visible. We will just use it along with the **document.write** method to execute HTML commands on the fly The **PlaySound** subroutine uses this hidden frame to output the **BGSOUND** tag in order to play sounds when the user clicks a button or when a match is uncovered.

```
sub PlaySound(soundNumber)
    parent.hidden.document.open
    select case soundNumber
    case 1
      parent.hidden.document.write "<BGSOUND SRC='moog14.wav'>"
    case 2
      parent.hidden.document.write "<BGSOUND SRC='moog20.wav'>"
    end select
    parent.hidden.document.close
end sub
```

> **Quotes within HTML Tags**
>
> VBScript will interpret a single quote (') as a double quote (") within an HTML tag. So, for example, the following would be a legal use of the **document.write** method:
>
> `document.write "<IMG SRC='testimg.jpg'>"`

The Completed Game

The final thing we need to cover is what to do when the user completes the game. In the case of the memory game, the game is completed when all the matched image pairs are uncovered. We know there are six pair of images, so we keep track of the number of matches with a global variable (**"match"**). When this global variable is equal to six, we bring up a message box stating that the user has won, and we reload the game with the following line of code:

`parent.navigate parent.location.href`

Because **parent.location.href** should contain the URL of the current location, we can use the **Navigate** method to this URL in order to achieve the effect of reloading the current page.

The following listing contains the complete source code for the VBScript section of the memory game. Figure 11-15 shows the game in action. The complete game (two HTML files along with various sounds and images) can be found on the accompanying CD-ROM.

```vbscript
<SCRIPT Language="VBScript">
dim cards(13)
dim imgCard(13)
dim turn1, turn2
dim match

call Initialize
call CreatePlayfield

sub PlaySound(soundNumber)
    parent.hidden.document.open
    select case soundNumber
    case 1
      parent.hidden.document.write "<BGSOUND SRC='moog14.wav'>"
    case 2
      parent.hidden.document.write "<BGSOUND SRC='moog20.wav'>"
    end select
    parent.hidden.document.close
end sub

sub imgCard1_Click
    if cards(1) =0 or turn1=1 then exit sub

    imgCard1.SpecialEffect = 2
    call PlaySound(1)
    ShowPicture(1)
end sub

sub imgCard2_Click
    if cards(2) =0 or turn1=2 then exit sub

    imgCard2.SpecialEffect = 2
    call PlaySound(1)
    ShowPicture(2)
end sub

sub imgCard3_Click
    if cards(3) =0 or turn1=3 then exit sub

    imgCard3.SpecialEffect = 2
    call PlaySound(1)
    ShowPicture(3)
end sub

sub imgCard4_Click
    if cards(4) =0 or turn1=4  then exit sub
```

continued on next page

continued from previous page

```
            imgCard4.SpecialEffect = 2
            call PlaySound(1)
            ShowPicture(4)
      end sub

      sub imgCard5_Click
            if cards(5) =0 or turn1=5   then exit sub

            imgCard5.SpecialEffect = 2
            call PlaySound(1)
            ShowPicture(5)
      end sub

      sub imgCard6_Click
            if cards(6) =0 or turn1=6 then exit sub

            imgCard6.SpecialEffect = 2
            call PlaySound(1)
            ShowPicture(6)
      end sub

      sub imgCard7_Click
            if cards(7) =0 or turn1=7 then exit sub

            imgCard7.SpecialEffect = 2
            call PlaySound(1)
            ShowPicture(7)
      end sub

      sub imgCard8_Click
            if cards(8) =0 or turn1=8 then exit sub

            imgCard8.SpecialEffect = 2
            call PlaySound(1)
            ShowPicture(8)
      end sub

      sub imgCard9_Click
            if cards(9) =0 or turn1=9 then exit sub

            imgCard9.SpecialEffect = 2
            call PlaySound(1)
            ShowPicture(9)
      end sub

      sub imgCard10_Click
            if cards(10) =0 or turn1=10 then exit sub

            imgCard10.SpecialEffect = 2
            call PlaySound(1)
            ShowPicture(10)
      end sub
```

```
sub imgCard11_Click
    if cards(11) =0 or turn1=11 then exit sub

    imgCard11.SpecialEffect = 2
    call PlaySound(1)
    ShowPicture(11)
end sub

sub imgCard12_Click
    if cards(12) =0 or turn1=12 then exit sub

    imgCard12.SpecialEffect = 2
    call PlaySound(1)
    ShowPicture(12)
end sub

sub tmrGraphic_Timer
    ' See if any of the card images need to be changed.
    for i = 1 to 12
      if cards(i)>12 then
        imgCard(i).PicturePath = "qmark.bmp"
        imgCard(i).SpecialEffect = 1
        cards(i) = cards(i) - 12
      end if

      if cards(i) = 0 then
        imgCard(i).PicturePath = "blank.bmp"
        imgCard(i).SpecialEffect = 1
      end if
    next
end sub

sub CreatePlayfield
    ' The cards() array will hold the number of the bitmap image at each card
location.
    ' There are 12 cards, so there will be six bitmaps (each must appear twice).
    for i = 0 to 12
      cards(i) = 0
    next

    for i = 1 to 6
      r = Int(rnd * 12) + 1
      while cards(r) <>0
        r = Int(rnd * 12) + 1
      wend
      cards(r) = i

      r = Int(rnd * 12) + 1
      while cards(r) <>0
        r = Int(rnd * 12) + 1
      wend
      cards(r) = i
    next
end sub
```

continued on next page

continued from previous page

```
sub ShowPicture(cardIndex)
    ' Create a string containing the appropriate bitmap file for a specified card
number.
    st = "card" & CStr(cards(cardIndex)) & + ".bmp"

    imgCard(cardIndex).PicturePath = st

    if turn1 = 0 then
      ' Save the number of the first card picked.
      turn1 = cardIndex
    elseif turn2 = 0 then
      turn2 = cardIndex

      ' If the cards match...
      if cards(turn1) = cards(turn2) then
       call PlaySound(2)
       cards(turn1) = 0
       cards(turn2) = 0
       match = match + 1

        ' After 6 matches, the user wins.
        if match >= 6 then
         msgbox "You win!"
         ' Reload the page.
         parent.navigate parent.location.href
       end if
      else
        ' Cards do not match...adding 12 will indicate image
        ' needs to be redrawn as question mark.
        cards(turn1) = cards(turn1) + 12
        cards(turn2) = cards(turn2) + 12
      end if
      turn1 = 0
      turn2 = 0
    end if

end sub

sub Initialize
    ' We want the display to be different each time.
    randomize

    ' Create an array of card objects from the image controls.
    set imgCard(1) = imgCard1
    set imgCard(2)= imgCard2
    set imgCard(3)= imgCard3
    set imgCard(4) = imgCard4
    set imgCard(5) = imgCard5
    set imgCard(6) = imgCard6
    set imgCard(7) = imgCard7
    set imgCard(8) = imgCard8
    set imgCard(9) = imgCard9
    set imgCard(10) = imgCard10
```

```
        set imgCard(11) = imgCard11
        set imgCard(12) = imgCard12

        ' No cards are turned over at this point, so turn1 and turn2 are zero.
        turn1=0
        turn2=0

        ' Initialize the number of matches to zero.
        match = 0
    end sub
</SCRIPT>
```

Summary

You cannot directly create a `control` array, but you can use the SET command to simulate such an array. A `control` array can be very helpful for containing a series of images to display. These images can be separate frames of an animation or entirely separate images (as was the case in the memory game).

One method of playing various sounds is to use a hidden frame along with `document.write`. The `document.write` method outputs HTML to a document, and using a hidden frame for output ensures that the user is not visually distracted when a frame is updated.

You will often need to use double quotes within a string when using the `document.write` method. In order to facilitate this, you can use single quotes in place of double quotes within an HTML tag.

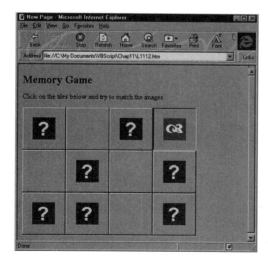

Figure 11-15
The VBScript
memory game

1. Which of the following is the method used with the memory game to play a sound?
   a. The **BGSOUND** tag
   b. A hidden frame
   c. Both a and b
   d. None of the above

2. Which of the following is the correct way to assign an ActiveX control to a variable?
   a. `varname = control`
   b. `SET control, varname`
   c. `SET varname = control`
   d. `control = varname`

3. What is the purpose of the **SpecialEffect** property of the image control?
   a. To give the image a 3-D look
   b. To dither the image
   c. To display an animation in place of an image
   d. None of the above

4. Which of the following is the proper way to play a sound using the `document.write` method?
   a. `document.write "<BGSOUND="chicken.wav">"`
   b. `document.write "<BGSOUND=""chicken.wav"">"`
   c. `document.write "<BGSOUND=\"chicken.wav\">"`
   d. None of the above

5. Which of the following is a correct example of assigning an image to an array of images?
   a. `set imgArray(1) = imgNumber1`
   b. `imgArray(1) = imgNumber1`
   c. `imgArray[1] = imgNumber1`
   d. `set imgArray[1] = imgNumber1`

Difficulty: Easy

1. Add more tiles to the memory game and modify the BMP images with any standard paint program (including Microsoft Paint).

Difficulty: Intermediate

2. Modify the memory game so that certain tiles contain a *wildcard* image that will match with any other image.

CHAPTER SUMMARY

In this chapter, you've learned how to jazz up your Web pages by employing such multimedia techniques as graphics, clickable images, backgrounds, marquees, and sound. In addition, you've added motion to your pages with animation and video, and tied all you've learned together to create a VBScript game. In the next chapter, you'll take your pages to a new level of sophistication with frames.

CHAPTER 12

I WAS FRAMED!

At this point in the book, you should have a good understanding of creating a basic Web page using HTML and VBScript. This chapter will show you how to split up your Web documents into multiple sections called *frames*.

A frame is a rectangular region of your Web page in which the contents of a separate HTML file are displayed. A *frameset* is the actual layout of the multiple frames. As you might guess, you must first design the layout, or frameset, before you attempt to specify the format of the individual frames. This chapter will lead you through the process of creating the frameset layouts and formatting the individual frames to display your page's data.

Here are the topics we will cover in this chapter:

- Creating Framesets and Filling Frames
- Using Hyperlinks with Frames
- Nesting Multiple Framesets
- Advanced Frame Formatting and Floating Frames
- Making Reference to Another Frame
- Making Reference to Another Document's Frame
- Dealing with Browsers That Do Not Support Frames
- Creating a Complete Frame Application

After completing this chapter, you will be able to use frames within your Web pages to present a variety of information in a format easier for your users to view.

GETTING FRAMED

If you have seen Web pages divided into multiple, rectangular sections, then you have seen frames in action. Frames give you the ability to view multiple HTML documents in one browser window.

Think of it this way: A standard HTML document has a single display area but, by using frames, you can create multiple display areas. Each of these areas is given a name that can be used to reference the frame in other parts of your document (or other documents). Figure 12-1 shows a sample Web page which uses frames to divide the display area into two columns.

Now let's take a look at Listings 12-1, 12-2, and 12-3, which show the HTML required to create these frames.

Input **Listing 12-1** A sample HTML document that uses frames

```
<HTML>
<HEAD><TITLE>Frames Example</TITLE></HEAD>
<BODY>
<FRAMESET COLS="50%,*">
<FRAME SRC="frame1.htm" NAME="Frame1">
<FRAME SRC="frame2.htm" NAME="Frame2">
</FRAMESET>
</BODY>
</HTML>
```

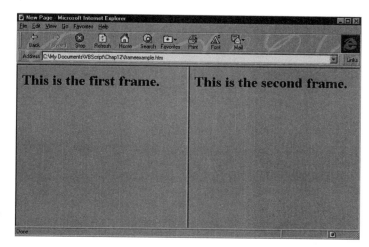

Figure 12-1
An example of
using frames

Input | **Listing 12-2** Code for FRAME1.HTM

```
<HTML>
<HEAD><TITLE>Frame One</TITLE></HEAD>
<BODY>
<H1>This is the first frame.</H1>
</BODY>
</HTML>
```

Input | **Listing 12-3** Code for FRAME2.HTM

```
<HTML>
<HEAD><TITLE>Frame Two</TITLE></HEAD>
<BODY>
<H1>This is the second frame.</H1>
</BODY>
</HTML>
```

In these listings, two frames are created and named, unimaginatively enough, "Frame1" and "Frame2". The "FRAME1.HTM" file is displayed in "Frame1", and the "FRAME2.HTM" file is displayed in "Frame2". Notice that Listings 12-2 and 12-3 are simple HTML files. It is Listing 12-1 that sets up the layout of the frames using two new HTML tags: FRAMESET and FRAME. The FRAMESET tag, which we will look at in detail next, determines the number of frames and their placement into either rows or columns. The FRAME tag specifies the HTML source which will be placed in each frame.

The First Step: Using FRAMESET

Before you can begin to format the individual frames, you must first use the FRAME-SET tag to tell your browser the general format of your document. Here are some of the questions you will answer using the FRAMESET tag:

- How many frames will you have?

- Will the frames separate your document into columns or rows?

- How big should each column or row be?

- Should there be extra space between the frames?

- Will these frames have a border or not?

Each of these questions can be answered using the four properties of the FRAME-SET tag: ROWS, COLS, FRAMEBORDER, and FRAMESPACING. Here is the general syntax of these four properties:

```
<FRAMESET ROWS="row_description" COLS="column_description" FRAMEBORDER=[YES/NO]
FRAMESPACING=number_of_pixels>
```

The row description and column description are strings which determine the number of rows or columns into which you want your page divided and the size of each row or column. These row and column description strings can take a variety of formats, but each will generally look like one of the following:

```
<FRAMESET ROWS="row1_size[,row2_size]...[,rown_size]">
```

```
<FRAMESET COLS="column1_size[,column2_size]...[,columnn_size]">
```

Notice that the number of rows or columns is determined by the number of sizes you specify. Also notice that only ROWS or COLS can be specified for each FRAMESET. You cannot specify both in the same FRAMESET. If you want a mixture of rows *and* columns, you need to use separate FRAMESET tags to embed one set of frames within another. We will look at this method in the Session 3.

For each row or column you specify in a FRAMESET tag, you must indicate the size of that row or column in one of three ways:

1. Indicating the row height or column width in pixels (see Listings 12-4 and 12-5 which are demonstrated in Figures 12-2 and 12-3).

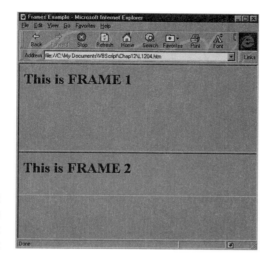

Figure 12-2
Creating frame rows of a specific height

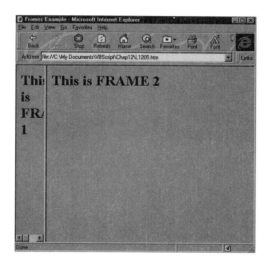

Figure 12-3
Creating frame columns of a specific width

Input   **Listing 12-4** Specifying a pixel height for frame rows

```
<HTML>
<HEAD><TITLE>Frames Example</TITLE></HEAD>
<BODY>
<!-- Create three rows which are 200 pixels in height, 100 pixels in height, and 100
pixels in height, respectively -->
<FRAMESET ROWS="200,100,100">
<FRAME SRC="frame1.htm" NAME="Frame1">
<FRAME SRC="frame2.htm" NAME="Frame2">
</FRAMESET>
</BODY>
</HTML>
```

Input   **Listing 12-5** Specifying a width in pixels for frame columns

```
<HTML>
<HEAD><TITLE>Frames Example</TITLE></HEAD>
<BODY>
<!-- Create two columns which are 80 pixels wide and 560 pixels wide, respectively -->
<FRAMESET COLS="80,560">
<FRAME SRC="frame1.htm" NAME="Frame1">
<FRAME SRC="frame2.htm" NAME="Frame2">
</FRAMESET>
</BODY>
</HTML>
```

2. Indicating the row height or column width as a percentage (see Listings 12-6 and 12-7 which are demonstrated in Figures 12-4 and 12-5).

Input   **Listing 12-6** Specifying frame row height as a percentage of the display area

```
<HTML>
<HEAD><TITLE>Frames Example</TITLE></HEAD>
<BODY>
<!-- Create two rows which are 30% and 70% of the display area height, respectively -->
<FRAMESET ROWS="30%,70%">
<FRAME SRC="frame1.htm" NAME="Frame1">
<FRAME SRC="frame2.htm" NAME="Frame2">
</FRAMESET>
</BODY>
</HTML>
```

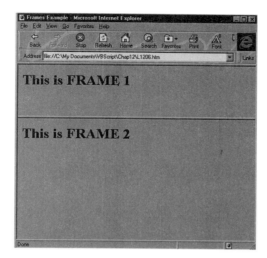

Figure 12-4
Creating frame
rows with a per-
centage height

Figure 12-5
Creating frame
columns with a per-
centage width

Input

Listing 12-7 Specifying a frame column width as a percentage of the display area

```
<HTML>
<HEAD><TITLE>Frames Example</TITLE></HEAD>
<BODY>
<!-- Create two columns which are each half of the display area width -->
<FRAMESET COLS="50%,50%">
<FRAME SRC="frame1.htm" NAME="Frame1">
<FRAME SRC="frame2.htm" NAME="Frame2">
</FRAMESET>
</BODY>
</HTML>
```

3. Using the "*" symbol with either of the above two methods denotes the remaining space in the display area (see Listings 12-8 and 12-9 which are demonstrated in Figures 12-6 and 12-7).

Input

Listing 12-8 Using "*" to specify the remainder of the display area height

```
<HTML>
<HEAD><TITLE>Frames Example</TITLE></HEAD>
<BODY>
<!-- Create one row that is 200 pixels in height and a second row that takes up the
remainder of the display area -->
<FRAMESET ROWS="200,*">
<FRAME SRC="frame1.htm" NAME="Frame1">
<FRAME SRC="frame2.htm" NAME="Frame2">
</FRAMESET>
</BODY>
</HTML>


<HTML>
<HEAD><TITLE>Frames Example</TITLE></HEAD>
<BODY>
<!-- Create a column which is 20% of the display area and a second column that takes
up the remainder of the display area -->
<FRAMESET COLS="20%,*">
<FRAME SRC="frame1.htm" NAME="Frame1">
<FRAME SRC="frame2.htm" NAME="Frame2">
</FRAMESET>
</BODY>
</HTML>
```

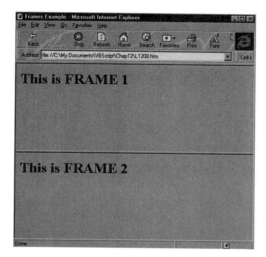

Figure 12-6
Creating frame
rows that use the
entire display area

Figure 12-7
Creating frame
columns that
use the entire
display area

Input
Listing 12-9 Using "*" to specify the remainder of the display area width

Separating Frames with a Color or a Background Image

You can separate frames by a solid color of your choosing or by a specified background graphic pattern. This is normally accomplished by setting FRAMEBORDER=0 and FRAMESPACING=*number_of_pixels* within the **FRAMESET** tag. This will create a space of *number_of_pixels* between each frame on the page. The areas between the frames will contain either the color specified by BGCOLOR=*color* or the background image specified by BACKGROUND="*image_url*" within the **BODY** tag of the parent document.

Here are some more examples of **FRAMESET** tags which make use of the three methods of specifying the size of rows and columns:

```
<!-- Two rows: top uses 30% of space, bottom uses 70% of space -->
<FRAMESET ROWS="30%,70%"> or <FRAMESET ROWS="30%,*">

<!-- Three columns: first is 100 pixels wide, last is 50 pixels wide, middle uses
remaining space -->
<FRAMESET COLS="100,*,50">

<!-- Two equally sized columns which, together, use all available space -->
<FRAMESET COLS="*,*"> or <FRAMESET COLS="50%,50%">

<!-- Two columns, the first of which uses 2/3 of the available space and the second
of which uses 1/3 -->
<FRAMESET COLS="2*,*"> or <FRAMESET COLS="66%,*">
```

As you can see, there are often several ways to specify the format of frames within your documents. Which of these formats you choose is entirely up to you, but sticking with one throughout will make it easier for others to understand your HTML code.

The **FRAMEBORDER** property can be set to either Yes or No. When set to No, the frames are displayed without borders. The default method is to display frames with borders, and this is how they will be displayed if you do not specify a **FRAMEBORDER** property or if you set **FRAMEBORDER=YES**. Listing 12-10 demonstrates borderless frames. The output from this listing is displayed in Figure 12-8.

Input
Listing 12-10 Borderless frames using the **FRAMEBORDER** property

```
<HTML>
<HEAD><TITLE>Borderless Frames Example</TITLE></HEAD>
<BODY>
<FRAMESET COLS="50%,*" FRAMEBORDER=NO>
<FRAME SRC="framet1.htm" NAME="Frame1">
<FRAME SRC="framet2.htm" NAME="Frame2">
</FRAMESET>
</BODY>
</HTML>
```

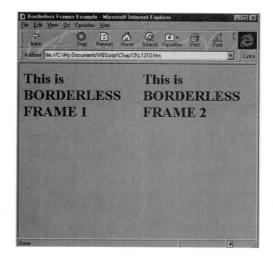

Figure 12-8
Frames with
FRAMEBORDER=NO
in their
FRAMESET tag

The **FRAMESPACING** property can be used to introduce extra space between the frames on your Web document. Set **FRAMESPACING** equal to the number of pixels you would like displayed between frames. Listing 12-11 sets FRAMESPACING=10 to create more space between each frame. Figure 12-9 shows the resulting page.

Figure 12-9
Increased space
between frames

Input

Listing 12-11 Increasing the space between frames with the
FRAMESPACING property

```
<HTML>
<HEAD><TITLE>Framespacing Example</TITLE></HEAD>
<BODY>
<FRAMESET COLS="50%,*" FRAMESPACING=10>
<FRAME SRC="frames1.htm" NAME="Frame1">
<FRAME SRC="frames2.htm" NAME="Frame2">
</FRAMESET>
</BODY>
</HTML>
```

> **Inheriting the FRAMEBORDER and FRAMESPACING Properties**
>
> The FRAMEBORDER and FRAMESPACING properties are inherited from any containing
> FRAMESET tags. This means that any attributes you set with the FRAMEBORDER and
> FRAMESPACING properties of a specific frameset will be inherited by frames and other
> framesets that the frameset contains. This will be important when you nest FRAMESET
> tags as described in Session 3 of this chapter.

Fill Those Frames

OK, we have the layout of frames on your Web page covered. Now let's fill 'em up with
lots of important information (that is the only kind of information you publish,
right?).

We will use the SRC property to tell our browser what information goes in each frame.
Set the SRC property equal to the URL of the HTML you wish to display in the frame.
It's that simple. So, for example, we could use some code like that in Listing 12-12 to
fill two frames with the contents of the "TEST1.HTM" and "TEST2.HTM" Web pages.

Input

Listing 12-12 A simple two-frame test

```
<HTML>
<HEAD><TITLE>Test</TITLE></HEAD>
<BODY>
<FRAMESET ROWS="*,*">
<FRAME SRC="TEST1.HTM" NAME="FirstPage">
<FRAME SRC="TEST2.HTM" NAME="SecondPage">
</FRAMESET>
</BODY>
</HTML>
```

This HTML code in Listing 12-12 will attempt to separate your display into two rows
using frames and display the **"TEST1.HTM"** page in the first row and the **"TEST2.HTM"**
page in the second row (see Figure 12-10). In this case, because we did not specify the
entire URL to the **"TEST1.HTM"** and **"TEST2.HTM"** pages, your browser will assume they
are located at the same place as this **"TEST.HTM"** file. If the HTML you want to display

is located elsewhere, you need to include the entire URL (such as SRC="http://www.somesite.com/index3.htm").

You may have noticed that in each of the examples in this chapter we have used the **NAME** property of the **FRAME** tag to set an arbitrary name for our frames. The **NAME** property allows you to select a name for each frame that you can subsequently use to reference that particular frame from elsewhere within the current HTML document or from within other documents. This name is case-sensitive, so you may want to stick with all lowercase or all uppercase for your frame names to avoid confusion when you attempt to reference a frame in your VBScript code.

We will learn some of the important uses of the **NAME** property in the upcoming sessions of this chapter. For now, it is enough that you remember to specify a name for each of the frames you create. Even though the **NAME** property is not required, it will make your work *much* easier when you need to refer to a specific frame from your VBScript code.

Summary

Use the **FRAMESET** tag to create a frame layout for your page. Use either the **COLS** property or the **ROWS** property to designate the number and size of columns or rows, respectively. When specifying the size of the columns or rows, you can either specify the size in pixels, the size as a percentage of the display area, or use the asterisk ("*") to signify the remainder of the display area. The **FRAMEBORDER** property can be set to either Yes or No to create frames with or without borders, and the **FRAMESPACING** property can be set to the number of pixels you want between frames.

Finally, use the **FRAME** tag to specify the contents of each frame within a frameset.

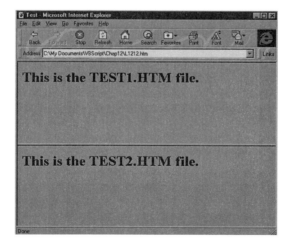

Figure 12-10
A simple
two-frame test

1. Which of the following properties is used to designate the layout of the frames on your page?
    a. FRAMESET
    b. FRAMELAYOUT
    c. FRAMERELAY
    d. FRAME

2. Which of the following is the correct way to create two equally sized columns using frames?
    a. `<FRAMESET COLS="*,*">`
    b. `<FRAMESET COLS="50%,50%">`
    c. `<FRAMESET COLS="*,50%">`
    d. All of the above are correct.

3. Which of the following tags might be used to specify the content of a particular frame?
    a. `<FRAME URL="http://www.mycompany.com/" NAME="Link">`
    b. `<FRAMESET SRC="http://www.mycompany.com/" NAME="Link">`
    c. `<FRAMECONTENT SRC="http://www.mycompany.com/" NAME="Link">`
    d. `<FRAME SRC="http://www.mycompany.com/" NAME="Link">`

4. The two allowable properties of the FRAMESET tag are
    a. ROWS and COLUMNS.
    b. ROWS and COLS.
    c. SRC and NAME.
    d. HROWS and VCOLS.

5. What is the purpose of the NAME property of the FRAME tag?
    a. To reference a frame from elsewhere in the same document
    b. To set the source document for a frame
    c. To reference a frame from within another document
    d. Both a. and c.

Difficulty: Easy

1. Create an HTML document which is divided into two equally sized rows. Create and display a ROW1.HTM document in the first row and a ROW2.HTM document in the second row. These documents can contain whatever you like.

Difficulty: Easy

2. Create an HTML document which is divided into three columns of varying sizes. Experiment with the FRAMEBORDER and FRAMESPACING properties to see what effect they have on the resulting Web page.

HYPERLINKING AND FRAMES

In a standard HTML document, it is straightforward to use the anchor tag (<A...>) to hyperlink to other documents. In this session we will see how frames affect this simple hyperlinking structure.

When a frame in your document contains hyperlinks, clicking on these hyperlinks will, by default, bring up the new URL *in the same frame*. Listings 12-13 and 12-14 demonstrate a simple example which brings up three separate pages in the top frame, depending on which link is clicked. The files **"first.htm"**, **"second.htm"**, and **"third.htm"** are not shown because they simply contain a level 1 heading stating, "This is the (*first/second/third*) page." The file **"bottom.htm"** (also not shown) is a blank page (it contains nothing in the BODY section). Figure 12-11 shows this example before a link is clicked, and Figure 12-12 shows this example after the "First Page" link is clicked.

Input	**Listing 12-13** The layout of two simple frames

```
<HTML>
<HEAD>
<TITLE>Frames and Hyperlinking</TITLE>
</HEAD>
<BODY>
<FRAMESET ROWS="30%,70%">
<FRAME SRC="top.htm" NAME="frmTop">
<FRAME SRC="bottom.htm" NAME="frmBottom">
</BODY>
</HTML>
```

Figure 12-11
Before clicking
on the "First
Page" link

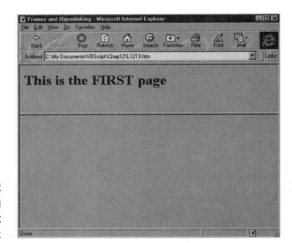

Figure 12-12
After clicking
on the "First
Page" link

Listing 12-14 The HTML for the top frame

```
<HTML>
<HEAD>
<TITLE>Frames and Hyperlinking</TITLE>
</HEAD>
<BODY>
<A HREF="first.htm">First Page</A>
<A HREF="second.htm">Second Page</A>
<A HREF="third.htm">Third Page</A>
</BODY>
</HTML>
```

As you can see, clicking on the "First Page" link brings up the first page in the top frame as we expected. Although this may be useful in some circumstances, it would also be helpful if we could click a link in the top frame, which would update the bottom frame. In other words, if we click on some hypertext in the *top* frame, we would like the *bottom* frame to display the contents of the new location and the top frame to remain the same.

We can accomplish this by using the **TARGET** parameter of the anchor tag. To load the destination of a link in a separate frame, set **TARGET="framename"** in the anchor tag of your link where **"framename"** is the name you specified using **NAME="framename"** in the **FRAME** tag. In our case we set **NAME="frmBottom"** for the bottom of our two frames (refer to Listing 12-13). Listing 12-15 demonstrates the updated HTML code for the top frame, and Figures 12-13 and 12-14 display the results of this new code before and after the "First Page" link is clicked.

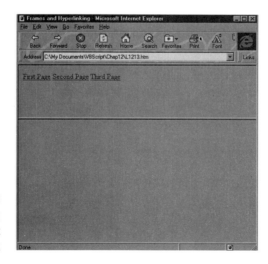

Figure 12-13
Before clicking
on the "First
Page" link

Figure 12-14
After clicking
on the "First
Page" link

Input   **Listing 12-15** The revised HTML for the top frame

```
<HTML>
<HEAD>
<TITLE>Frames and Hyperlinking</TITLE>
</HEAD>
<BODY>
<A HREF="first.htm" TARGET="frmBottom">First Page</A>
<A HREF="second.htm" TARGET="frmBottom">Second Page</A>
<A HREF="third.htm" TARGET="frmBottom">Third Page</A>
</BODY>
</HTML>
```

Using the BASE Tag

You can use the **BASE** tag to set a target for multiple links in your HTML code. For example, look at the following **BASE** tag:

```
<BASE TARGET="frmMain">
```

This tag would cause all subsequent links (up until a **</BASE>** tag is encountered) to use the frame titled **"frmMain"** as their target. Using the **BASE** tag can save you time if you have many links that use the same frame as their target.

Notice that the contents of the top frame remain unchanged while the new page is displayed in the bottom frame. You could use this method to create a menu for your site by placing the major areas of your site as links in a frame and setting the TARGET of these links to a separate frame.

Summary

Hyperlinks can be used within frames in much the same way they are used in standard documents. By default, clicking on a link within a frame will bring up the destination of that link in the same frame. If you want the destination of a link within a frame to display in a *different* frame, use the **TARGET** parameter of the anchor tag. Set the **TARGET** parameter equal to the name of the frame that you specified with **NAME="framename"** in the **FRAME** tag.

1. To which of the following locations will the destination of a hyperlink within a frame be displayed by default?
   a. The topmost window
   b. The frame that contains the link
   c. The next frame that was created
   d. None of the above

2. Which of the following parameters of the anchor tag is used to specify the frame in which you would like a link's contents displayed?
   a. **OUTPUT**
   b. **WRITEFRAME**
   c. **TARGET**
   d. None of the above

3. Which of the following is used to set the name of a frame that is later referenced by the **TARGET** parameter?
   a. The **FRAMESET** tag
   b. The **FRAME** tag
   c. The **NAME** tag
   d. None of the above

4. Which of the following anchor tags could display its contents in a different frame?
   a. `<A HREF="other.htm">`
   b. `<A HREF="other.htm" TARGET="frame2">`
   c. `<A HREF="other.htm" FRAME="frame2">`
   d. Both b. and c.

5. Which of the following is incorrect?
   a. `<A HREF="new.htm">`
   b. `<A HREF="new.htm" TARGET="frmNew">`
   c. `<A TARGET="frmNew">`
   d. They are all correct.

Difficulty: Easy

1. Create a page with two frames. Put links to some of your favorite sites in each frame and try clicking on the links. Notice how these sites come up within the frame where the link exists. Try using links to sites that themselves contain frames. What happens?

Difficulty: Intermediate

2. Create a Web site with three main areas. Design the site so that there are always two frames displayed: a small top frame that shows links to the various main areas of the site and a large bottom frame which displays the actual contents of these areas.

CREATING MULTIPLE FRAMES

In Session 1 of this chapter, we learned how to partition the display area into rows or columns using the **FRAMESET** tag. Now we will learn how to split the display area into rows *and* columns by nesting the **FRAMESET** tags.

Let's say, for example, that we want to create a series of frames which separate our display area into regions resembling those in Figure 12-15. We can use FRAMESET to split the display into rows or columns, but Figure 12-15 contains both rows and columns, so how can we accomplish this? The answer is by nesting the **FRAMESET** tags, as shown in Listing 12-16.

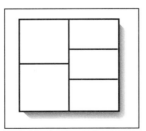

Figure 12-15
Frames which
create rows
and columns

Input **Listing 12-16** Nesting multiple FRAMESET tags

```
<FRAMESET COLS="50%,50%">
<FRAMESET ROWS="50%,50%">
<FRAME SRC="CELL1.HTM" NAME="Cell1">
<FRAME SRC="CELL2.HTM" NAME="Cell2">
</FRAMESET>
<FRAMESET ROWS="33%,33%,*">
<FRAME SRC="CELL3.HTM" NAME="Cell3">
<FRAME SRC="CELL4.HTM" NAME="Cell4">
<FRAME SRC="CELL5.HTM" NAME="Cell5">
</FRAMESET>
```

The code in Listing 12-16 will begin by dividing the display area into two columns, each 50 percent of the total size. Then, the first column is divided into two equally sized rows with the <FRAMESET ROWS="50%,50%"> tag. Finally, the <FRAMESET ROWS="33%,33%,*"> divides the second column into three rows, each with approximately 33 percent of the display height. Figure 12-16 shows some sample output from Listing 12-16.

The FRAMESET tag can be nested to more than two levels (the number of levels you can nest to is pretty much unlimited), but be aware that having too many frames on a page will cause each frame to be very small. Unless you are planning on distributing magnifying glasses with your HTML documents, it is best to limit the number of frames on your display!

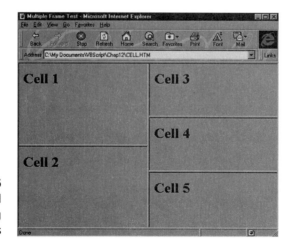

Figure 12-16
Multiple rows and columns using frames

Summary

You can use nested FRAMESET tags to create both rows and columns of frames. This is important because each FRAMESET tag can only specify either ROWS or COLS but not both.

1. Which tag is used to create multiple frames on a single page?
   a. MFRAME
   b. MULTI
   c. FRAMESET
   d. ROW

2. To how many levels can you nest the FRAMESET tag?
   a. 1
   b. 2
   c. 3
   d. Limited only by the size of your display area

3. Which of the following is a consideration when adding several frames on a single page?
   a. Adding more frames will make each frame smaller.
   b. Adding more frames will make your HTML too large to execute.
   c. Adding more frames will cause a "TOO MANY FRAMES" error.
   d. All of the above.

4. Which of the properties cannot be used within a nested FRAMESET?
   a. FRAMEBORDER
   b. FRAMESPACING
   c. NAME
   d. All FRAMESET properties can be used.

5. When dividing the display area into both rows and columns of frames, in which of the following ways should you proceed?
   a. Create the rows first, then nest the columns.
   b. Create the columns first, then nest the rows.
   c. Create them both at the same time with one FRAMESET tag.
   d. The order in which you create rows and columns of frames is unimportant.

Difficulty: Easy

1. Create the CELL1.HTM, CELL2.HTM, CELL3.HTM, CELL4.HTM, and CELL5.HTM files which contain whatever information you want. Then insert the code in Listing 12-16 into a complete HTML document and display the whole thing.

Difficulty: Intermediate

2. Create the HTML code to display frames in the formats shown in Figure 12-17.

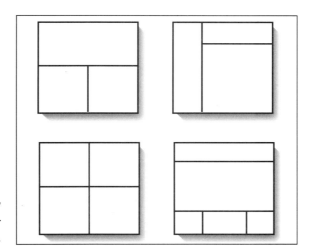

Figure 12-17
Frame formats for
Exercise 3, No. 2.

ADVANCED FRAME FORMATTING AND FLOATING FRAMES

We already know that frames are a cool way to separate the display area on your Web pages, and we have learned how to get a few frames up and running. For a quick review of the HTML frame tags we have looked at so far in this chapter and their respective properties, check out Table 12-1.

Tag or Property	Purpose
FRAMESET	Determines layout of frames
ROWS="*row_height_list*"	Sets number of rows and size of each
COLS="*column_width_list*"	Sets number of columns and size of each
FRAMEBORDER=YES|NO	Creates borderless frames
FRAMESPACING=*number_of_pixels*	Sets extra spacing between frames
FRAME	Determines specific frame properties
SRC="*url*"	Sets content of frame
NAME="*frame_name*"	Sets name used to reference frame

Table 12-1   *Some HTML tags and properties related to frames*

In this section, we will learn to use the remaining properties of frames. These properties are listed in Table 12-2.

Property	Purpose
MARGINWIDTH=*number_of_pixels*	Sets the width of the frame margin
MARGINHEIGHT= *number_of_pixels*	Sets the height of the frame margin
SCROLLING=YES|NO|AUTO	Shows or hides scrollbars
NORESIZE	Doesn't allow user to resize the frame
FRAMEBORDER=YES|NO	Creates borderless frames

Table 12-2   *Remaining properties of the* FRAME *tag*

The **MARGINWIDTH** and **MARGINHEIGHT** properties allow you to set the exact size of your frame margins. If you do not specifically set these properties, your browser will give your frames a default margin size. Both of these properties require that you specify an amount in pixels as the size of the respective margin. Listing 12-17 demonstrates the **MARGINWIDTH** and **MARGINHEIGHT** properties. Figure 12-18 shows the resulting Web page.

Input

Listing 12-17 Using the MARGINWIDTH and MARGINHEIGHT properties

```
<HTML>
<HEAD><TITLE>Frames Example</TITLE></HEAD>
<BODY>
<FRAMESET COLS="50%,*">
<FRAME SRC="frames1.htm" NAME="Frame1" MARGINWIDTH=20 MARGINHEIGHT=5>
<FRAME SRC="frames2.htm" NAME="Frame2" MARGINWIDTH=5 MARGINHEIGHT=20>
</FRAMESET>
</BODY>
</HTML>
```

Use the **SCROLLING** property to determine whether scroll bars will appear on the specified frame. Setting **SCROLLING** to YES ensures that a scroll bar will always be present on your frame (although it will not be active unless the output displayed in the frame is larger than the actual size of the frame). Setting **SCROLLING** to NO ensures that a scroll bar will never be visible, even if the output displayed in a frame does not fit within the frame borders. Finally, setting **SCROLLING** to AUTO will cause a scroll bar to appear only if it is needed (when the output to a frame is larger than the actual frame size). If you do not explicitly set the **SCROLLING** property, AUTO will be assumed. Listings 12-18, 12-19, and 12-20 demonstrate frames with the **SCROLLING** property set to YES, NO, and AUTO, respectively. The output of these listings is displayed in Figures 12-19, 12-20, and 12-21.

Figure 12-18
Changing the
MARGINWIDTH and
MARGINHEIGHT
properties of
frames

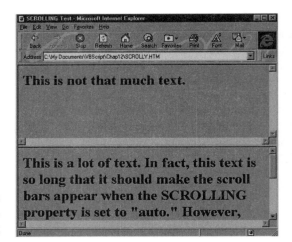

Figure 12-19
SCROLLING property
set to YES

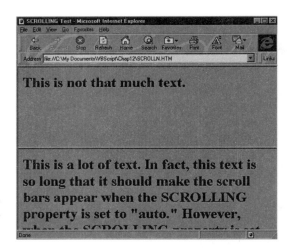

Figure 12-20
SCROLLING property
set to NO

Input   **Listing 12-18** Setting the SCROLLING property to YES

```
<HTML>
<HEAD><TITLE>Frame Scrolling Example</TITLE></HEAD>
<BODY>
<FRAMESET COLS="50%,*">
<FRAME SRC="scroll1.htm" NAME="Frame1" SCROLLING=YES>
<FRAME SRC="scroll2.htm" NAME="Frame2" SCROLLING=YES>
</FRAMESET>
</BODY>
</HTML>
```

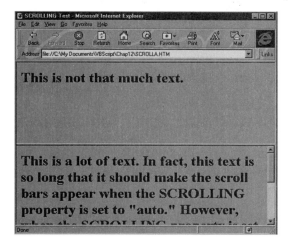

Figure 12-21
SCROLLING property
set to AUTO

 Listing 12-19 Setting the SCROLLING property to NO

```
<HTML>
<HEAD><TITLE>Frame Scrolling Example</TITLE></HEAD>
<BODY>
<FRAMESET COLS="50%,*">
<FRAME SRC="scroll1.htm" NAME="Frame1" SCROLLING=NO>
<FRAME SRC="scroll2.htm" NAME="Frame2" SCROLLING=NO>
</FRAMESET>
</BODY>
</HTML>
```

Listing 12-20 Setting the SCROLLING property to AUTO

```
<HTML>
<HEAD><TITLE>Frame Scrolling Example</TITLE></HEAD>
<BODY>
<FRAMESET COLS="50%,*">
<FRAME SRC="scroll1.htm" NAME="Frame1" SCROLLING=AUTO>
<FRAME SRC="scroll2.htm" NAME="Frame2" SCROLLING=AUTO>
</FRAMESET>
</BODY>
</HTML>
```

The **NORESIZE** property indicates that the frame is not able to be resized by the user. Frames can normally be resized if the **NORESIZE** property is not indicated. You do not assign a value to this particular property. Instead, it functions as a flag and merely placing it in your **FRAME** tag marks the frame as unable to be resized. Listing 12-21 demonstrates the **NORESIZE** property. Figure 12-22 displays the output.

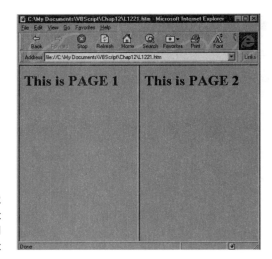

Figure 12-22
Some frames that
can be resized and
some that cannot

Input   **Listing 12-21** Using the NORESIZE property in a FRAME tag

```
<HTML>
<HEAD><TITLE>Frame Resizing Example</TITLE></HEAD>
<BODY>
<FRAMESET COLS="50%,*">
<FRAME SRC="page1.htm" NAME="Frame1">
<FRAME SRC="page2.htm" NAME="Frame2" NORESIZE>
</FRAMESET>
</BODY>
</HTML>
```

The final property of the FRAME tag that we will cover here is the FRAMEBORDER property. This property functions like the FRAMEBORDER property of the FRAMESET tag. It can be set to 1 if you would like your frame to display a border or 0 if you do not want a border on your frames. The default value for FRAMEBORDER is 1.

Any FRAMEBORDER property that you specify for a specific frame will override the FRAME-BORDER setting of the enclosing FRAMESET. Listing 12-22 demonstrates this (the output is displayed in Figure 12-23). Notice that the first frame does not specify a FRAMEBORDER property, so it inherits the FRAMEBORDER=0 setting from the FRAMESET tag. The second frame functions in the same way, but the third and final frame sets FRAMEBORDER=1. This setting overrides the FRAMESET tag's FRAMEBORDER setting so that a border is displayed on the final frame.

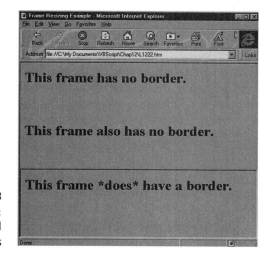

Figure 12-23
Using FRAMEBORDER
with individual
frames

    Listing 12-22 Overriding the FRAMEBORDER setting in a
FRAME tag

```
<HTML>
<HEAD><TITLE>Frame Resizing Example</TITLE></HEAD>
<BODY>
<FRAMESET ROWS="30%,30%,*" FRAMEBORDER=0>
<FRAME SRC="border1.htm" NAME="Frame1">
<FRAME SRC="border2.htm" NAME="Frame2">
<FRAME SRC="border3.htm" NAME="Frame3" FRAMEBORDER=1>
</FRAMESET>
</BODY>
</HTML>
```

Floating Frames

As we have seen in our previous coverage of frames, you must establish a frame lay-out using the **FRAMESET** tag before you can specify any frame content. This is not the case with *floating frames* which are defined with the **IFRAME** tag. A floating frame is a frame which can be placed directly in your HTML code in much the same way as an image is placed on your page with the IMG tag. Listing 12-23 demonstrates the **IFRAME** tag. As with the standard **FRAME** tag, you specify the content of a floating frame with the SRC parameter. The output from this listing is shown in Figure 12-24.

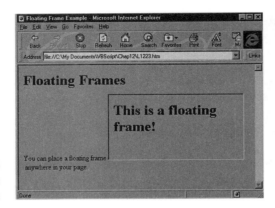

Figure 12-24
A floating frame
example

| Input | **Listing 12-23** Using a floating frame |

```
<HTML>
<HEAD><TITLE>Floating Frame Example</TITLE></HEAD>
<BODY>
<H1>Floating Frames</H1>
You can place a floating frame
<IFRAME SRC="float.htm">
<H1>***Your browser does not handle floating frames!***</H1>
</IFRAME>
anywhere in your page.
</BODY>
</HTML>
```

Notice that we have used the **</IFRAME>** tag in Listing 12-23 to denote the end of the floating frame. You can place HTML between the **<IFRAME>** and **</IFRAME>** tags specifically for browsers that do not support floating frames. Figure 12-25 shows the output of Listing 12-23 in a browser that does not support floating frames.

You can specify the width and height of your floating frame using the **WIDTH** and **HEIGHT** parameters which can be specified either in pixels or as a percentage of the display size. To specify **WIDTH** and **HEIGHT** as a percentage of the display size, simply use the % symbol. Listing 12-24 demonstrates setting the width and height of a floating frame. Figure 12-26 shows the resulting output.

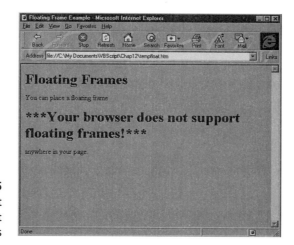

Figure 12-25
A browser that
does not support
floating frames

Figure 12-26
Floating frames
with a specified
width and height

Listing 12-24 Setting the width and height of a floating frame

```
<HTML>
<HEAD><TITLE>Floating Frame Example</TITLE></HEAD>
<BODY>
<H1>Floating Frames</H1>
Here is the Microsoft site:
<IFRAME WIDTH=50% HEIGHT=25% SRC="http://www.microsoft.com">
</IFRAME>
<P>Here is the Netscape site:
<IFRAME WIDTH=200 HEIGHT=150 SRC="http://home.netscape.com">
</IFRAME>
</BODY>
</HTML>
```

Specifying a Border for Floating Frame Content

Use the **TOPBORDER** and **LEFTBORDER** properties of the **BODY** tag to specify a border (in pixels) for your floating frame content. For example, to align the content of your floating frame flush with the top and left sides of the floating frame border, use the following **BODY** tag for the page that will be displayed in the floating frame:

```
<BODY TOPBORDER=0 LEFTBORDER=0>
```

The default style of a floating frame will have a 3-D recessed look. If you want a more seamless look, you can eliminate a floating frame's border by using the **FRAMEBORDER** parameter. To create a borderless floating frame, set **FRAMEBORDER=0** as shown in Listing 12-25. Notice the difference between the two frames in Figure 12-27.

Listing 12-25 Using the FRAMEBORDER property with a floating frame

```
<HTML>
<HEAD><TITLE>Floating Frame Example</TITLE></HEAD>
<BODY>
Here is a frame with standard borders:
<IFRAME WIDTH=300 HEIGHT=100 SRC="iborder.htm">
</IFRAME>
<P>Here is a frame with no borders:
<IFRAME WIDTH=300 HEIGHT=100 FRAMEBORDER=0 SRC="iborder.htm">
</IFRAME>
</BODY>
</HTML>
```

A floating frame will also default to having horizontal and/or vertical scroll bars as they are needed. This is the same as setting SCROLLING=AUTO within the **IFRAME** tag. If you do not want your user to be able to scroll within your floating frame, you can use the **SCROLLING** parameter as in the following example:

```
<IFRAME WIDTH=200 HEIGHT=200 SCROLLING=NO SRC="test.htm">
```

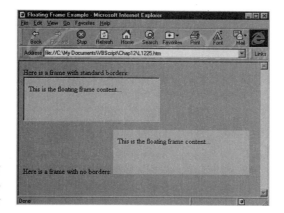

Figure 12-27
A floating frame
with no border

Advanced Notes on Floating Frames

Floating frames are added to the document object rather than the standard frames collection. This has important consequences for accessing the contents of floating frames.
To access a floating frame on the current page, use the following:

```
document.FloatingFrameName.whatever
```

To access a floating frame in a different frame, use the following:

```
top.frames(n).document.FloatingFrameName.whatever
```

or

```
top.frames("framename").document.FloatingFrameName.whatever
```

The possible values of the **SCROLLING** parameter are the same as those of the **SCROLLING** parameter used with standard frames (YES, NO, AUTO).

You can establish margins for your floating frame using the **HSPACE** and **VSPACE** parameters. Set the **HSPACE** and **VSPACE** parameters equal to the number of pixels you would like as a margin in your floating frame. Listing 12-26 shows two frames with different HSPACE and VSPACE settings. The resulting page is displayed in Figure 12-28.

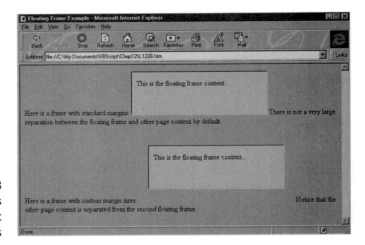

Figure 12-28
Floating frames
with different
margin sizes

Input

Listing 12-26 Using the HSPACE and VSPACE properties of a floating frame

```
<HTML>
<HEAD><TITLE>Floating Frame Example</TITLE></HEAD>
<BODY>
Here is a frame with standard margins:
<IFRAME WIDTH=300 HEIGHT=100 SRC="iborder.htm">
</IFRAME>
There is not a very large separation between the floating frame and other page con-
tent by default.
<P>Here is a frame with custom margin sizes:
<IFRAME WIDTH=300 HEIGHT=100 HSPACE=20 VSPACE=30 SRC="iborder.htm">
</IFRAME>
Notice that the other page content is separated from
the second floating frame.
</BODY>
</HTML>
```

Wrapping Text Around a Floating Frame

You can align a floating frame to either the left or right of the display using the ALIGN parameter just as you use the ALIGN parameter of the IMG tag. You can use the line break tag along with the CLEAR parameter (<BR CLEAR=RIGHT>, <BR CLEAR=LEFT>, or <BR CLEAR=ALL>) to wrap text around a floating frame as you would around an image.

Updating Floating Frame Content

Let's end this session with a little bit of trickery that can add some interesting effects to your Web pages. Often, there are cameras at various sites on the World Wide Web that provide continuously updated images. An example of one such camera is located at Netscape's headquarters. This particular camera features a view of the office fishtank that is updated every 30 seconds. Listing 12-27 takes advantage of this continuously updating image, by automatically updating itself every 30 seconds through a special use of the **META** tag. (Those familiar with the client-pull technique will recognize the third line as the one that makes the page refresh every 30 seconds.)

 Listing 12-27 A page that automatically updates itself every 30 seconds

```
<HTML>
<HEAD>
<META HTTP-EQUIV="REFRESH" CONTENT="30; URL="L1227.htm">
<TITLE>My Fish</TITLE>
</HEAD>
<BODY TOPMARGIN=0 LEFTMARGIN=0>
<IMG SRC="http://www1.netscape.com/fishcam/livefishcamsmall.cgi?livefishcamsmall.jpg">
</BODY>
</HTML>
```

Now that we have a page which automatically updates itself, we can place a floating frame with its **SRC** property set to this page we have created. This is an easy way to add some interesting effects to your Web pages. Listing 12-28 demonstrates the code to add the floating frame:

 Listing 12-28 Using a floating frame to display a continuously updating page

```
<HTML>
<HEAD>
<TITLE>My Fish</TITLE>
</HEAD>
<BODY>
Here is an updated view of the Netscape fishtank:
<IFRAME WIDTH=110 HEIGHT=110 FRAMEBORDER=0 SRC="L1227.htm">
</IFRAME>
</BODY>
</HTML>
```

For more information on the client-pull technique, see Chapter 14, "Make the Leap—Advanced Topics."

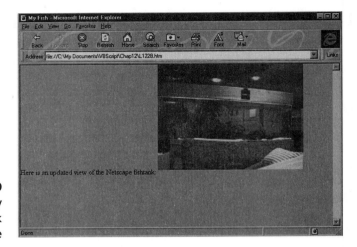

Figure 12-29
The automatically
updating fish tank
image

Summary

You can use advanced formatting properties of the **FRAME** tag to achieve a variety of effects with your frames. The **MARGINWIDTH** and **MARGINHEIGHT** properties control the margin size of your frame. The **SCROLLING** property can be set to YES, NO, or AUTO to determine whether or not scroll bars will be displayed in your frame. The **FRAMEBORDER** property can be set to 0 or 1 to determine if your frame will have a border. The **NORESIZE** property can be added to your **FRAME** tag to indicate that a frame cannot be resized by the user.

Additionally, many of these properties also apply to floating frames. A floating frame has many of the qualities of a standard frame, but it can be inserted directly into your HTML code with the IFRAME tag. You can place HTML between the **<IFRAME>** and **</IFRAME>** tags which will be displayed by browsers that do not support floating frames.

1. Which of the following properties can be used with both the **FRAMESET** and **FRAME** tags?
   a. **NORESIZE**
   b. **SCROLLING**
   c. **SRC**
   d. **FRAMEBORDER**

2. In what units are **MARGINWIDTH** and **MARGINHEIGHT** specified?
   a. pixels
   b. inches
   c. picas
   d. centimeters

3. What is the appropriate setting of the **SCROLLING** property if you want scroll bars to be displayed only when they are needed because the output to be displayed will not all fit in the designated frame?
   a. SCROLLING=YES
   b. SCROLLING=NO
   c. SCROLLING=SOMETIMES
   d. SCROLLING=AUTO

4. Which of the following properties are currently unsupported by browsers other than the Microsoft Internet Explorer?
   a. **NORESIZE**
   b. **FRAMEBORDER**
   c. **FRAMESPACING**
   d. Both b. and c.

5. Which of the following statements is true?
   a. Frames can be resized by default.
   b. You must set NORESIZE to YES to disallow resizing of frames.
   c. You must set NORESIZE to NO to disallow resizing of frames.
   d. Resizing frames is never allowed.

EXERCISE 4

Difficulty: Easy

1. Create a sample HTML document that makes use of borderless frames.

Difficulty: Advanced

2. Use Visual Basic Script to create a program which allows users to select various properties of the FRAMESET and FRAME tags and dynamically create HTML frame documents. (Hint: Use document.write to create a new HTML document.)

MAKING REFERENCE TO ANOTHER FRAME WITHIN A WINDOW

You have already seen how to create multiple frames for your Web documents, and you have also displayed simple output in these frames. In this session we will learn how to reference the various frames in the same window by name and by number.

Referencing Frames by Name

Every window has an associated **frames** array which you can use to reference all the frames contained by that window. If you need to read or set a property from a frame other than the current frame, you can use the **frames** array to reference a specific frame. Here is the general syntax for referencing another frame within your document using the name of the frame:

```
frames("framename").property
```

where **"framename"** is the name you assigned to the frame when it was created (using the **NAME** property of the **FRAME** tag), and **property** is the name of a property associated with a frame object. For a complete list and description of the properties associated with a frame object, see Chapter 7, "Doing Documents and Windows."

Why would you want or need to reference another frame? There are many reasons. Listings 12-29, 12-30, and 12-31 present an example to illustrate a potential use for referencing one frame from another.

Input   **Listing 12-29** An example of accessing a frame by name

```
<HTML>
<HEAD>
<TITLE>Frame Example</TITLE>
</HEAD>
<BODY>
<FRAMESET COLS="*,*">
<FRAME SRC="COLUMN1.HTM" NAME="InputFrame">
<FRAME SRC="COLUMN2.HTM" NAME="OutputFrame">
</FRAMESET>
</BODY>
</HTML>
```

Input **Listing 12-30** Sample COLUMN1.HTM file

```
<HTML>
<HEAD>
<TITLE>Frame Example</TITLE>
</HEAD>
<BODY>
<FORM>
<INPUT TYPE="TEXT" NAME="txtFirstName" VALUE="John">
</FORM>
</BODY>
</HTML>
```

Input **Listing 12-31** Sample COLUMN2.HTM file

```
<HTML>
<HEAD>
<SCRIPT LANG="VBSCRIPT">
Sub cmdSubmitClick()
     If InputFrame.txtFirstName = "John" Then
       MessageBox "Your name is John."
     Else
       MessageBox "I don't know your name."
     End If
End Sub
</SCRIPT>
</HEAD>
<BODY>
<FORM>
<INPUT TYPE="BUTTON" NAME="cmdSubmit" VALUE="Submit:" & InputFrame.txtFirstName>
</FORM>
</BODY>
</HTML>
```

This example initially sets up a command button in the output frame and gives it the same caption as the text in the input frame (initially this will be "John"). If the user clicks this submit button without changing the name, the script will bring up a dialog informing the user that his name is "John"; otherwise, the script will bring up a dialog informing the user that his name is not known. Figure 12-30 shows the sample output of this HTML code.

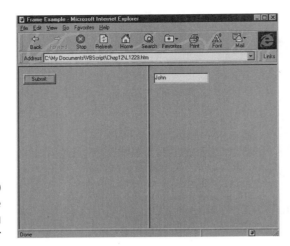

Figure 12-30
Sample of one
frame accessing
data in another

Referencing Frames by Number

The preferable way to reference a frame within your document is by name. Not only are names easier for you to remember, but frame numbering will change if you adjust the order in which the frames are created within your HTML code. Nevertheless, you can reference a frame by number using the **frames** array. Here is the general syntax for referencing a frame by number:

```
Frames(framenumber).property
```

The frames are numbered based on the order in which they are created within your HTML code.

That's about it for referencing a specific frame. Just use sensible and descriptive names for your frames, and you will have an easy time locating the data you need.

Summary

You can reference frames in your document by name or by number. It is preferable to reference your frames by name because the frame numbering may change if you add or remove frames from your page. The name with which you refer to a frame is the arbitrary name which you specify using the **NAME** property of the **FRAME** tag. If you do reference a frame by number, remember that numbering starts at zero, not one.

1. Which of the following is a correct way to reference a frame by name?
    a. frames("myframe").*property*
    b. frame(myframe).*property*
    c. frame("myframe").*property*
    d. frame!myframe.*property*

2. Which of the following is a correct way to reference a frame by number?
   a. frame("0").*property*
   b. frame(0).*property*
   c. frames(0).*property*
   d. none of the above

3. Where do you set the name of each frame?
   a. Within the **FRAME** tag
   b. Within the **FRAMESET** tag
   c. Within the **frames** array
   d. None of the above

4. Which of the following references the first frame of your page?
   a. frame(first).*property*
   b. frame(0).*property*
   c. frame(1).*property*
   d. none of the above

5. On which of the following is the numbering of the frames based?
   a. The alphabetical position of a frame's name
   b. The number specified with the **NUMBER** property
   c. The order in which the frames are created in the HTML code
   d. None of the above

Difficulty: Intermediate

1. Modify the HTML in Listings 12-29, 12-30, and 12-31 to include other controls, such as check boxes and radio buttons. Place these controls on the input form and access their values from the output form.

Difficulty: Advanced

2. Create a simple page with two frames. Have each frame display the title of the other frame's page. (Hint: Use the properties of the document object.)

MAKING REFERENCE TO A FRAME IN ANOTHER WINDOW

In the previous session, you learned to reference another frame within a window but what if you need to reference a frame that is in another window altogether? This session will show you how to get at the frames that exist in another window.

As mentioned in Session 5 of this chapter, each window has an associated **frames** array that can be used to reference all the frames contained by that window. To reference a frame in another window, simply preface the **frames** array with the name of the appropriate window as in the following example:

```
window.frames("framename").property
```

or

```
window.frames(framenumber).property
```

where **window** is a window object, **"framename"** is the name given to a frame with the **NAME** property of the **FRAME** tag, **framenumber** is an integer which represents an existing frame, and **property** is any property of a frame object. (Once again, see Chapter 7 for a description of all properties, events, and methods of the **Frame** object.)

Let's look at an example that should make this topic clearer. Listing 12-32 shows the HTML for our top level window. This window contains two frames, **"frmTop"** and **"frmBottom"**. Listing 12-33 shows the HTML code to be used to create the top frame's content while Listing 12-34 shows the HTML code to be used to create the bottom frame's content. Notice that the bottom frame also contains two frames called **"frmTop"** and **"frmBottom"**, respectively.

Input

Listing 12-32 The HTML code for the top-level window

```
<HTML>
<HEAD>
<TITLE>Frames Example</TITLE>
</HEAD>
<BODY>
<FRAMESET ROWS="50%,50%">
<FRAME NAME="frmTop" SRC="L1233.htm">
<FRAME NAME="frmBottom" SRC="L1234.htm">
</BODY>
</HTML>
```

Listing 12-33 The HTML code for top of the two frames

```
<HTML>
<HEAD>
<TITLE>Top Frame</TITLE>
</HEAD>
<BODY>
<H1>This is the top frame.</H1>
</BODY>
</HTML>
```

 Listing 12-34 The HTML code for bottom of the two frames

```
<HTML>
<HEAD>
<TITLE>Bottom Frame</TITLE>
</HEAD>
<BODY>
<FRAMESET ROWS="50%,50%">
<FRAME NAME="frmTop" SRC="L1235.htm">
<FRAME NAME="frmBottom" SRC="L1236.htm">
</BODY>
</HTML>
```

Finally, Listings 12-35 and 12-36 show the HTML code that will create the display for the two bottom subframes. Notice in Listing 12-35 that when the user clicks the **"Click Me"** button, two message dialogs are displayed that print the title of the document objects contained by the two different frames that have **"frmTop"** as their name. To reference the top-level window, we use the special **"top"** keyword.

 Listing 12-35 The HTML code for top of the two bottom frames

```
<HTML>
<HEAD>
<TITLE>Top-Bottom Frame</TITLE>
</HEAD>
<BODY>
<INPUT TYPE=BUTTON NAME="cmdClick" VALUE="Click Me">

<SCRIPT LANGUAGE="VBScript">
sub cmdClick_OnClick
     msgbox "The title of the top frame is " & top.frames("frmTop").document.title
     msgbox "The title of the top-bottom frame is " &
top.frames("frmBottom").frames("frmTop").document.title
end sub
</SCRIPT>
</BODY>
</HTML>
```

Listing 12-36 The HTML code for bottom of the two bottom frames

```
<HTML>
<HEAD>
<TITLE>Bottom-Bottom Frame</TITLE>
</HEAD>
<BODY>
<H1>This is the bottom of the bottom frames.</H1>
</BODY>
</HTML>
```

So referencing a frame in another window is not really any more difficult than referencing a frame in the same window (as long as you know the name of the appropriate window object). Using this technique, you can get at the properties, methods, and events of any frame, even those contained in a window other than the current window.

Summary

A separate **frames** array exists for each window object. To reference a frame within another window, preface the **frames** array with the name of the appropriate **Window** object. Once again, frames within each window can be referenced either by name or by number.

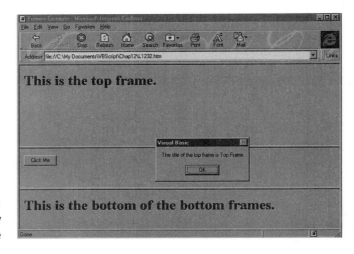

Figure 12-31
A multiple-window example

1. Which of the following is a correct way to reference a frame in a window other than the current window?
   a. frames("myframe").*property*
   b. frame("myframe").*property*
   c. mywindow.frames("myframe").*property*
   d. none of the above

2. Which of the following references a frame within the top-level window?
   a. frames("myframe"). *property*
   b. top.frames("myframe"). *property*
   c. mywindow.frames("myframe"). *property*
   d. It could be either a. or b., depending on where this code resides.

3. Which of following is syntactically correct?
   a. top.top.frames("myframe").*property*
   b. top.frames("myframe").frames("frame2").frames("frmBottom").*property*
   c. top.("myframe").*property*
   d. none of the above

4. What is the keyword that refers to the top-level window object?
   a. primary
   b. main
   c. wndTop
   d. none of the above

5. A separate `frames` array is associated with which of the following objects?
   a. window
   b. frame
   c. document
   d. Both a. and b.

EXERCISE 6

Difficulty: Intermediate

1. Create the HTML code to implement two separate documents. On the first document there should be two textboxes, and on the second document there should be two command buttons. Hyperlink the documents and change the caption of the command buttons on the second document to match the text in the textboxes on the first document.

Difficulty: Intermediate

2. Create a Web page which consists of multiple windows, each of which contains multiple frames. Place a command button on each frame that tells various information about the document contained in that frame including its title, URL, and so on.

SUPPORTING BROWSERS THAT DO NOT DISPLAY FRAMES

Frames are a powerful feature for formatting your documents, but what about those Netsurfers who use older browsers without frame support? A document that relies on frames for formatting can look pretty bad in a browser that does not support them. Fortunately, there is an HTML tag designed especially for those browsers that do not support frames: **<NOFRAMES>**.

Look at the example in Listing 12-37. It uses the **NOFRAMES** tag to display a different page layout in browsers that do not support frames.

Input

Listing 12-37 Allowing for browsers that do not support frames

```
<HTML>
<HEAD><TITLE>Supporting Browsers Without Frames</TITLE></HEAD>
<BODY>
<FRAMESET ROWS="70,*">
<FRAME SRC="LOGO.HTM" NAME="LOGO" SCROLLING="no">
<FRAME SRC="WELCOME.HTM" NAME="MAIN">
</FRAMESET>
<NOFRAMES>
<IMG SRC="LOGO.GIF">
<HR>
<H1>Welcome to this web site!</H1>
</NOFRAMES>
</BODY>
</HTML>
```

Figures 12-32 and 12-33 display the results of this code in a browser that supports frames and one that does not, respectively.

The **<NOFRAMES>** and corresponding **</NOFRAMES>** tags are used to enclose the HTML and text that should be displayed by any browser that does not support frames. As in the example above, you can often format the **<NOFRAMES>** section so that the result is similar to what will be displayed by a browser that does support frames. At the very least, you can use the **<NOFRAMES>** tag to display a message that your Web page requires a frame-enabled browser to be viewed correctly.

To display your page with a different layout in browsers that do not support frames, simply place the HTML code for those browsers between the **\<NOFRAMES\>** and **\</NOFRAMES\>** tags. Only browsers that do not support frames will execute the HTML code between these tags. Other browsers (such as Microsoft Internet Explorer 3.0) will ignore the HTML code between the **\<NOFRAMES\>** and **\</NOFRAMES\>** tags.

As browsers become increasingly advanced, it is becoming more and more difficult to find a browser that does not support frames. This brings up an interesting question: How do you know what your Web page will look like for those people who view it with browsers that do not support frames? The answer is actually quite simple: Just place the code between the **\<NOFRAMES\>** and **\</NOFRAMES\>** tags into a temporary, separate HTML document and display it using any browser. Make sure that you do not include the actual **\<NOFRAMES\>** and **\</NOFRAMES\>** tags in this temporary file.

Figure 12-32
A frame example in a browser that supports frames

Figure 12-33
A frame example in a browser that does not support frames

For example, to test the `<NOFRAMES>` section of the document in Listing 12-1, paste the code between the `<NOFRAMES>` and `</NOFRAMES>` tags into a generic HTML format as shown in Listing 12-38.

Input

Listing 12-38 Testing the output for browsers that do not support frames

```
<HTML>
<HEAD><TITLE>No Frames Test</TITLE></HEAD>
<BODY>
<IMG SRC="LOGO.GIF">
<HR>
<H1>Welcome to this web site!</H1>
</BODY>
</HTML>
```

One final note about frames: Not everybody likes them! Remember that partitioning your document into multiple frames reduces the display size for each of these frames. It is especially important to keep this in mind if you are using a high resolution monitor to do your development. Many people still use the World Wide Web at 640x400 resolution, so make sure to view your pages at this resolution to see if they are still easy to view. (Most operating systems give the option to adjust the screen resolution so that even if your video card and monitor support a 1024x768 or higher resolution, you can temporarily change to a lower resolution like 640x400 for testing purposes.) Some of the best Web sites even offer the option of using frames or not. This requires a good deal more work though because two separate versions of the framed pages must be maintained.

Summary

When developing Web sites which will be viewed by a large variety of browsers, keep in mind that some browsers still do not support frames. For compatibility with these browsers, you can maintain an alternate page layout between the `<NOFRAMES>` and `</NOFRAMES>` tags which will only be displayed by browsers that do not support frames.

Quiz 7

1. Which of the following tags can be used to display a section of HTML only in browsers that cannot correctly handle frames?
   a. `<ALT>`
   b. `<FRAME SECTION="NOFRAMES">`
   c. `<NOFRAMES>`
   d. `<NF>`

2. In order to make your Web page useful to the widest variety of browsers you should:
    a. use frames on every Web page.
    b. use frames when necessary, but supply alternate displays with the `<NOFRAMES>` tag.
    c. use the `<NOFRAMES>` tag to display a message that a frame-enabled browser is required.
    d. none of the above.

3. What happens to the HTML code placed between the `<NOFRAMES>` and `</NOFRAMES>` tags?
    a. It is displayed by all browsers.
    b. It is only displayed by Microsoft Internet Explorer.
    c. It is only displayed by browsers that support frames.
    d. None of the above.

4. If your browser does support frames, how can you test a layout designed for browsers that do not support frames?
    a. Locate another browser which does not support frames.
    b. Use your current browser and page as is.
    c. Place the code between the `<NOFRAMES>` and `</NOFRAMES>` tags into a temporary HTML file and view that file with your current browser.
    d. Either a. or c.

5. For what reason should you test your Web pages at low resolutions such as 640x400?
    a. 640x400 is the maximum size for a browser window.
    b. Quite a few people still view Web pages at low resolutions.
    c. Web pages often look better at lower resolutions than at higher ones.
    d. None of the above.

EXERCISE 7

Difficulty: Easy

1. Create a Web page that displays two frames or, for browsers that do not support frames, displays the message "This page is optimized for frame-enabled browsers."

Difficulty: Advanced

2. Create a Web page that consists of five frames (rows and columns), and include a `<NOFRAMES>` section which uses HTML tables to imitate this formatting.

SESSION 8
PUTTING IT ALL TOGETHER

Learning about a topic is fine and good, but if you cannot make practical use of your knowledge, it will not benefit you. Therefore, this session shows you a practical example program using frames.

The example we will use is that of a small image archive. Let's suppose that you have several images (tasteful ones, of course, so as not to stimulate more legislation like the Communications Decency Act) that you would like to display on a Web page. You would like the user to be able to select an image from a thumbnail version of the image itself, and then display information about the image (its author, when it was created, and so on). Well, have we got the code for you!

Listings 12-39, 12-40, and 12-41 show the code to create the bulk of this site. Listing 12-39 is the main page which establishes the framed layout and loads the contents of each frame. Listing 12-40 is the code for the left pane, which is where the thumbnail images are located. Listing 12-41 is the code for the first of the full-sized images. Subsequent IMAGEx.HTM files will follow the format of the Listing 12-41 with only slight differences for each image.

Input   **Listing 12-39** The main layout of the example program

```
<HTML>
<HEAD><TITLE>Frames Example Program</TITLE></HEAD>
<BODY>
<FRAMESET COLS="20%,80%">
<FRAME SRC="IMAGES.HTM" NAME="Images" SCROLLING="yes">
<FRAMESET ROWS="60,*">
<FRAME SRC="LOGO.HTM" NAME="Logo" SCROLLING="no" FRAMEBORDER="no">
<FRAME SRC="IMAGE1.HTM" NAME="Main">
</FRAMESET>
</FRAMESET>
</BODY>
</HTML>
```

Input   **Listing 12-40** Displaying the image thumbnails in the left-most pane

```
<HTML>
<HEAD><TITLE>Image Selection Code</TITLE></HEAD>
<BODY>
<BASE TARGET="Main">
Choose an image:
<A HREF="IMAGE1.HTM"><IMG SRC="IMAGE1.GIF"></A><P>
<A HREF="IMAGE2.HTM"><IMG SRC="IMAGE2.GIF"></A><P>
<A HREF="IMAGE3.HTM"><IMG SRC="IMAGE3.GIF"></A><P>
```

```
<A HREF="IMAGE4.HTM"><IMG SRC="IMAGE4.GIF"></A><P>
<A HREF="IMAGE5.HTM"><IMG SRC="IMAGE5.GIF"></A><P>
</BODY>
</HTML>
```

 Listing 12-41 A sample IMAGEx.HTM file which will be displayed in the "Main" frame

```
<HTML>
<HEAD><TITLE>Image 1</TITLE></HEAD>
<BODY>
<H1>You have selected Image 1</H1>
<HR>
Image 1 was created on July 4, 1996 by the famous
Italian numeral designer Richard Vermatelli.
</BODY>
</HTML>
```

HOW IT WORKS

We set up the leftmost frame to provide the access to the image thumbnails. Because we will have several images, we have set SCROLLING equal to YES to provide a scroll bar for the user. The top-right frame is set to SCROLLING+NO because we do not want the corporate logo to scroll in this frame. Finally, SCROLLING is not defined for the bottom-right frame so AUTO is assumed. This will work out fine because we would only need scroll bars displayed if the information we want to present to the user is too large to fit in the frame.

When the user clicks one of the images in the leftmost frame, an anchor is activated to one of the IMAGEx.HTM files. Because we set **<BASE TARGET="Main">** in Listing 12-40, the output from clicking any of these images is displayed in the frame named "Main." Figure 12-34 shows the example program in action.

Summary

Using what you have learned about frames in this chapter, you can create an image archive on the Web. Create small thumbnail images (using any popular paint program) in one frame which the user can click to display the full-size version of the image.

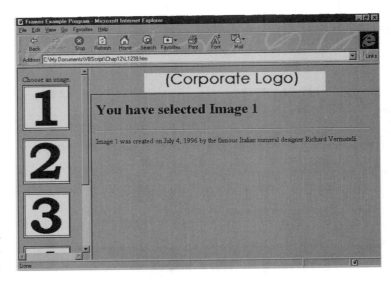

Figure 12-34
The example pro-
gram in action

1. What is a thumbnail image?
    a. A picture of a person's thumb
    b. A picture of a person's index finger
    c. A smaller representation of a large image
    d. None of the above

2. How do you ensure that scroll bars will *always* appear on a given frame?
    a. Set SCROLLBARS=TRUE in the **FRAME** tag.
    b. Set SCROLLING=TRUE in the **FRAME** tag.
    c. Set SCROLLBARS=YES in the **FRAME** tag.
    d. Set SCROLLING=YES in the **FRAME** tag.

3. What is the purpose of the **<BASE TARGET="framename">** tag?
    a. To immediately load the contents of the frame named "*framename*"
    b. To specify that subsequent links should use the frame named "*framename*" as
       their target
    c. To set the target of a frame named "BASE"
    d. None of the above

4. What does the asterisk ("*") represent in the ROWS="…" or COLS="…" properties?
    a. Create as many rows or columns as possible
    b. Do not give a size to a specified row or column
    c. Create a row or column which uses the remaining display space
    d. None of the above

5. Which tag is used to display another page when an image is clicked?
   a. The Anchor tag
   b. The OnClick tag
   c. The URL tag
   d. None of the above

Difficulty: Easy

1. Modify the sample program in this session to contain images from your own image library with information about each.

Difficulty: Intermediate

2. Modify the sample program in this session so that when one of the image buttons is clicked by the user, it appears to be in a depressed or highlighted state.

CHAPTER SUMMARY

Framesets specify the layout of various frames within your Web page, and each frame can display the contents of a separate HTML file. If you need to place a frame within your HTML document, you can do so using a floating frame (with the **IFRAME** tag) rather than the standard FRAMESET/FRAME duo. Regardless of how you create your frames, it is a good practice to give each one a name with the **NAME** property so you can refer to it later in the following way:

```
document.frames("framename").property
```

Finally, if you do not want to ignore those who have browsers which do not support frames, include the **NOFRAMES** tag with the appropriate information to display to those users. Fortunately, this is currently not that great a concern if you are using VBScript because the only browser that supports VBScript natively is Microsoft's Internet Explorer which also supports full frame functionality.

CHAPTER 13

PUTTING IT ALL TOGETHER

This chapter focuses primarily on the practice of writing VBScript code. It consists of sessions that actually get up and do something. Some of the code is quite complex and other bits are easy, but they all show VBScript techniques in action. There is a repetition of certain concepts across the sessions showing the techniques which are useful and repeatable across many problems. The look and feel has been guided by Windows 95 in order to distinguish these applications from the usual HTML look and feel. These applications show how VBScript is not just a language to liven up HTML; it actually puts real Windows programs on the Web.

In this chapter, we will explore:

- Grouping Controls and Sharing Procedures
- Multidimensional Arrays
- Interface-constrained Design
- Windows Style Menus
- Context-sensitive Help
- Client-side Data Validation

GROUPING CONTROLS

In the graphical environment of Windows, the user can be guided through an interface if the designer has given thought to the way the various controls are organized and grouped. This gives the program's interface an *intuitive* feel which pleases the user and makes the code easier to use.

The intuitive nature of grouped controls extends into VBScript code through the use of control arrays. Imagine a form with 10 option buttons. In order to work out the option selected, each control would have to be checked individually. The code below shows how such a subroutine might look in VBScript.

```
Sub CheckOption
If chkOption1.Value = True Then MsgBox "You have selected option 1"
If chkOption2.Value = True Then MsgBox "You have selected option 2"
. . . . VBScript to check options 3 - 9
If chkOption10.Value = True Then MsgBox "You have selected option 10"
End Sub
```

Each line does exactly the same thing but uses a different option button. All this repetition is very wasteful; it would be better to write one line and substitute the name of the control 10 times. With VBScript this can be done: Simply put the option buttons in an array. Remember, arrays are variables that can hold more than one value. Each separate value is given an index so it can be selectively retrieved when required. By way of a reminder, the code below shows an array being dimensioned and used in a message box.

```
Sub ShowName
Dim Names(2)
Names(0) = "Manny"
Name(1) = "Pam"
Name(2) =  "Ross"
MsgBox "Hi There " & Name(2)
End Sub
```

The example above would display a message box with the message "Hi There Ross" because the variable **Name**, value number (2), is equal to the string "Ross". If array variables can hold strings, then why not make them hold controls? Using the index, the user could reference each control individually; the array name plus the correct index would become the control name. The example below shows how to put some textbox controls into an array.

```
Sub SetText
Dim TextBoxes(2)
Set TextBoxes(0) = txtControl1
Set TextBoxes(1) = txtControl2
Set TextBoxes(2) = txtControl3

TextBoxes(1).Text = "Hello There Ross"
End Sub
```

The **Set** command tells VBScript that it should prepare the array element to receive an object instead of the normal variant data type. This command must be used to place an object, such as a control, into an array.

The last line of the sample shows why arrays of controls are so useful. Because using the name of the array plus the index is equivalent to using the control's real name, all its properties and methods can be accessed. This leads to much simpler code when applying the same operation to more than one control. Consider again the option button example given earlier and compare the original solution to the one given below.

```
Sub CheckOption
Dim Loopy

For Loopy = 0 to 9
        If Options(Loopy).Value = True Then
                MsgBox "You have selected option " & Loopy
                Exit For
        End If
Next

End Sub
```

The variable **Loopy** is incremented by one for each loop iteration. Because it is reused as the array's index value, each option button held in the array will be checked in turn. The partnership between the array and any of the loop constructs is very common in VBScript.

If the **Value** property of the current option button is True, the message box is displayed and, because only one option button will be True, the loop is exited. Add 10 more controls to the form. All that needs to be changed in the example above is the termination value of the **For...Next** loop from 9 to 19 (arrays always begin at zero). In its original form, 10 more **If** statements must be added to cater to the additional controls.

SHARING COMMON CODE

Another way of cutting down on written code is to allow controls to share the same code. This trick allows different objects to behave in a precisely coordinated way and makes debugging and rewriting much simpler.

In order to share a common subroutine, the controls must share a common event. Normally all the controls in an array are of the same type, so this is not a problem. If five buttons are to call the same code when clicked, then a call to the subroutine should be placed into each button's **Click** event procedure. The example below shows two such event handlers for **Button1** and **Button2**, both of which form part of a global array called **Buttons**.

```
Sub Button1_Click
      ButtonClick(1)
End Sub
Sub Button2_Click
      ButtonClick(2)
End Sub
```

No matter which button is pressed, the subroutine **ButtonClick** will be run. The difference lies in the argument each event procedure sends to the subroutine. For **Button1** the argument is one; for **Button2** the argument is two. The subroutine **ButtonClick** shown below indicates why this is necessary.

```
Sub ButtonClick(Index)
Buttons(Index).Caption = "Clicked"
MsgBox You clicked button " & Index
End Sub
```

The argument sent from the button's event procedure is passed to the variable called **Index** used to access the correct control from the global array **Buttons**. No matter which button is clicked, the same lines of code will be reused to perform the same actions. The effect will be applied only to the control indicated by the value of the **Index** variable. Logically, each control shares an abstracted event procedure. The subroutine **ButtonClick** is the event procedure for all the buttons. The only other way to achieve an equivalent functionality would be to repeat the code from **ButtonClick** in every event procedure. This makes debugging and code updating very laborious.

VBScript allows complex forms with multiple controls to be organized and manipulated. Combining arrays of controls with shared code makes it easier to achieve a higher level of code organization. For this reason, similar techniques can be found in most event-driven languages.

Summary

The first session briefly examined how to create functional groups of controls in code and then allow them to share code. Creating arrays containing objects may seem a little esoteric at the outset, but as virtually all the following sessions will show, they can be used across a wide range of problems.

Session 2 begins the process of real coding with an example of client-side data validation.

1. Which of the following best describes when an array of controls should be used?
   a. When the user requires an intuitive interface
   b. When the amount of code needs to be reduced
   c. When a number of controls share a similar function
   d. When more than five controls are found on a page

2. Which line correctly places a textbox control in the **Boxes** array?
   a. `Boxes(1) = TextBox1`
   b. `TextBox1= Boxes(1)`
   c. `Let Boxes(1) = TextBox1`
   d. `Set Boxes(1) = TextBox1`

3. Putting a control into an array allows access to
   a. none of its properties; all of its methods.
   b. all of its properties; some of its methods.
   c. all of its properties; all of its methods.
   d. none of its properties; none of its methods.

4. Which of the following is *not* an advantage of sharing code?
   a. Faster debugging
   b. Greater choice of events and event handlers
   c. Easier code updates
   d. Tighter code organization

5. Arrays of controls are commonly used in conjunction with
   a. `For...Next` loops.
   b. `Do...While` loops.
   c. event procedures.
   d. all of the above.

Difficulty: Moderate

1. Place five option buttons and one command button on an HTML layout page. In the `Onload` event of the page, place the five option buttons into a global array. Pressing the command button should makes a message appear indicating the currently selected option.

Difficulty: Difficult

2. Place five check boxes and a command button on an HTML layout page. Place them into a global array when the page first loads. Normally more than one check box can be selected at any one time. Write a single procedure that only allows the currently selected check box to remain selected. Pressing the command button should deselect all the check boxes at once.

CLIENT-SIDE DATA VALIDATION

When collecting data from any source, it is always a good idea to ensure that the data is acceptable before attempting to process it. Client-side data validation is an attempt to ensure, as far as possible, that the data being *sent* to the server for processing consists of only acceptable data types in the expected places. Gone are the days when client machines were treated as simple dumb terminals. VBScript's reason for existing is to free up some of that spare capacity and allow tasks to be performed on the client's machine.

It should, therefore, come as no surprise that one of the first genuine uses for VBScript touted by Microsoft was that of client-side validation. In fact, VBScript turns out to be very flexible when it comes to string manipulation, the technique at the heart of validating alphanumeric information.

The example in this session will demonstrate easy to intermediate string manipulation and show shared events in action. Figure 13-1 shows the application running in IE.

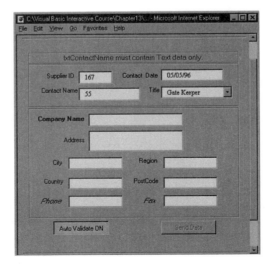

Figure 13-1
Client-side data
validation

VBScript has a number of useful commands for testing the contents of strings, a useful ability when checking data from the interface. The **IsNumeric** function will return True or False, indicating whether the string consists only of numbers. Unfortunately, VBScript lacks a simple **IsText** test. It does offer a test for a string to determine whether or not it is pure text.

In this example, the user can choose whether to validate data as it is typed in or to validate all the entries when the form is completed and the data is sent. An ActiveX timer is used as part of the simple error message display.

All in all, this example will provide all the fundamentals necessary to perform generic data validation on the client's machine while keeping the frills, and therefore the transmission time, to a minimum. Be sure to play with the example extensively before diving into the following code analysis. Understanding the functionality is prerequisite to understanding the code.

There are three global variables employed by the validation procedures. **Auto** is a flag determining whether or not the users want their data to be checked as they type it in; **Valid** is a flag which indicates the current state of the form and is set to False if an error is detected. **PreviousText** will be explained a little later. The code below shows the variables being dimensioned and the code that is run when the page first loads. Remember, using Xpad's Script Wizard eliminates the need to dimension global variables directly in the code.

```
Dim Auto
Dim Valid
Dim PreviousText

Sub LayoutValidate_OnLoad()
      cmbTitle.Additem "Director"
      cmbTitle.Additem "Gate Keeper"
      cmbTitle.Additem "Insect Doctor"
      cmbTitle.Additem "Ink Blender"
      cmbTitle.listindex = 1

      txtSupplierID.SetFocus
      Auto = False
End Sub
```

The **LayoutValidate_OnLoad** event initializes the combobox control **cmbTitle** so that the choices it displays are available from the outset. This is, incidentally, one of the easiest levels of data validation. Restricting the user to inputting only valid choices does the job. Setting the **ListIndex** property of the combobox to one sets the default selection to the first item (it goes blue). Using the **SetFocus** function of the textbox **txtSupplierID** gives that control focus. The **Auto** flag is set to False which, as demonstrated in the code below, disables the auto validation option.

```
Sub txtContactName_Change()
      If Auto Then Validate txtContactName, "Text"
End Sub
```

Every textbox that supports the auto validate feature shares the same **Validate** sub-routine. The code above will call **Validate** only when the **Auto** flag is set to True. That is why the **Auto** flag is global, so all the **change** events can see it and act accordingly. Note the parameters passed to the validate subroutine. The first is the control's name, and the second is the type of data valid for this textbox. In this session's example, the controls have not been placed in an array; the control's name, not an index value, is sent as a parameter. This still allows the **Validate** subroutine to access its properties, as can be seen below.

```
Sub Validate(TextBox,TypeOfCheck)
Valid = True
Valid = IsTextValid (TypeOfCheck, TextBox.Text)

If Not Valid Then
      ProcessInvalidForm TypeOfCheck, TextBox.Text, TextBox.ID
End If

TextBox.SetFocus
End Sub
```

The global variable **Valid** is set to True at the start of the procedure; it will be reset to False if any of the subsequent validation tests fail. All of the validation tests are held in the function **IsTextValid**. As shown, it performs tests on the text, and if any fail, it returns a value of False into the **Valid** variable.

The **Valid** variable is tested straightaway to see if the text has passed or failed its validation. If **Valid** is False, then the subroutine **ProcessInvalidForm** is called passing the type of test, the text that failed that test, and the name of the textbox that was holding the text. Finally, the focus is set to the current **TextBox** object.

So, the **Validate** procedure gets the text to be checked and sends it off for analysis. If the text is invalid, then it calls the procedure that deals with this eventuality, making sure it has all the information it needs. Nothing too tricky yet. What, though, is meant by *invalid text*? The function **IsTextValid**, shown below, will answer this question. Remember, the **Validate** subroutine calls this function and sends the text to be checked as well as the type of check to be performed.

```
Function IsTextValid(TypeOfCheck,Target)
IsTextValid= True

      Select Case TypeOfCheck
            Case "Numeric"
                  If Not IsNumeric(Text) Then
                        IsTextValid= False
                  End If
            Case "Date"
                  If Not IsDate(Text) Then
                        IsTextValid= False
                  End If
```

```
        Case "Text"
                If NotText(Text) Then
                        IsTextValid= False
                End If
    End Select

    If Not(Auto) and Text = "" Then  IsTextValid = False
End If
```

The first line of this function sets the function's return value to True. This will be reset to False if any of the subsequent checks fail.

The **Select Case** tests the value of the parameter **TypeOfCheck** and runs one of three checks depending on the string it contains. This string was originally sent to the **Validate** sub from the textbox's **Change** event procedure. This allows each individual textbox to determine the type of check applicable to the data it intends holding.

The three types of data checked are Numeric, Date, and Text. VBScript supplies two commands, **IsNumeric** and **IsDate**, that allow the characters in the string to be tested directly. **IsNumeric** returns True if the string contains only numbers. **IsDate** returns True if the string consists of a valid date format. Valid text is harder to describe, and really comes down to the individual program requirements. This is why VBScript has no **IsText** function, but this has been solved by writing a home-grown version of an **IsText** function. Should any of the checks fail, then the function's return value is set to False.

The final line is a generic check. If the **Auto** option is disabled (the **Auto** variable is set to False), then the user must press the Send button to ensure all the data is of the correct type. A blank entry is invalid if the users think they are finished and attempt to send the data. Blanks are valid while typing with the **Auto** option enabled.

The checks shown above are all fairly straightforward except, perhaps, for the **IsText** function. The code below shows how the **IsText** function decides whether the text is invalid.

```
Function IsText(Text)
Dim Loopy

IsText = True
Dim Nibble
        For Loopy = 1 to Len(Text)
                Nibble = Left(Text, Loopy)
                Nibble = Right(Nibble,1)

                If IsNumeric(Nibble) Then IsText = False
        Next
End function
```

Testing for textual validity is achieved via some moderately complex string manipulation. The **Left** function takes a string and a number and returns a substring. The number parameter determines the substring's length. In this example, the **Loopy** variable determines the length of the substring by and increases by one character per loop iteration. The loop will stop looping when its counter reaches the number of characters in the string. The length of a string, in characters, is found using the **Len** function.

The string returned using **Loopy** always contains one more character than the previous loop's, with the new character always appearing as the first one on the right. This new character is clipped off the right-hand side by using the **Right** function, which counts along a string from the right for the specified number of characters. In this case, it is always just the one new character that appears per loop.

The newly isolated character is then checked to make sure it is not a number; this process is repeated for the whole length of the string. If the text string contains any numeric characters at all, then **IsText** returns False and the validation fails. This test assumes that all non-numeric characters are text, which is fine for this example. Should other characters be deemed unacceptable as text, then they could be tested for individually.

Remember that the **IsText** function was called, previously, as part of the **IsTextValid** function. It, in turn, was called from the **Validate** subroutine. Back in the **Validate** procedure, a failure triggers the **ProcessInvalidForm** sub. This takes the type of check that failed, the text that failed, and the name of the textbox that is holding the invalid data. This is all shown below.

```
Sub ProcessInvalidForm (TypeOfCheck,Text,Name)

    If   Not(Text = "") Then
            Report Name & " must contain " & TypeOfCheck & " data only."

    ElseIf   Not(Auto) Then
            Report Name & " cannot be left blank."
    End If

End sub
```

When the user has presented invalid data, an error message is constructed and displayed. This makes for a more helpful user interface.

The first message appears when the **Text** variable is not an empty string. This message means one of the three tests—**IsNumeric**, **Isdate,** or **IsText**—has failed. The second message is constructed only if the **Text** is an empty string and the auto validate option is disabled (**Auto = False**). This is important because a string containing invalid text is a crime with no excuses, whereas an empty string is only invalid when the data is actually sent.

The error message is sent to the subroutine **Report** for display, as shown below.

```
Sub Report(Reason)
        lblBanner.Caption = Reason
        tmrBanner.Enabled = True
End Sub
```

Now the message is assembled, and it is passed here for display in the label control called **lblBanner**. In order to make the message return to the default text after a short display interval, a timer called **tmrBanner** was set up to trigger after two seconds. This was done by setting the **Interval** property to 2000 (milliseconds) at design time. It hasn't fired until this point because its **enabled** property has also been set to False at design time. Resetting the **enabled** property to True in this procedure sets the timer's clock ticking down, and two seconds later its event procedure runs. The **tmrBanner's** **Timer** event handler and procedure are shown below.

```
Sub tmrBanner_Timer()
        tmrBanner.Enabled = False
        lblBanner.Caption = "Data Validation"
End Sub
```

The first line disables the timer again. This prevents it from repeatedly running once every two seconds. The label control **LnlBanner** has its **Caption** property set to the default display **"Data Validation"**. This wipes out the error message placed there by the **ProcessInvalidForm** subroutine.

The validation can be run automatically, but the Send button is pressed and all the data is checked regardless of the auto option selected. The **Click** event for the **cmdSend** button is shown below.

```
Sub cmdSend_Click()

        Validate txtSupplierID, "Numeric"

If Valid Then Validate txtContactName, "Text"
If Valid Then Validate txtCompanyName, "Text"
If Valid Then Validate txtAddress, ""
If Valid Then Validate txtCity, "Text"
If Valid Then Validate txtRegion, "Text"
If Valid Then Validate txtCountry, "Text"
If Valid Then Validate txtPostCode, ""
If Valid Then Validate txtPhone, "Numeric"
If Valid Then Validate txtFax, "Numeric"

If Valid Then
            Report "All data checked successfully"
            'Send Data to Server
End Sub
```

Each control has a line of code to check its contents by sending the control and the type of check to the **Validate** subroutine. The interesting point to note is that all the tests, apart from the very first one, depend on the **Valid** variable still being True. If any of the tests fail, then no further testing will take place. This is efficient and also prevents the first error message from being instantly superimposed by any subsequent error messages.

The **Auto Validate** option is toggled on and off by pressing the toggle button control called **tglAutoValidate**. The button stays down when clicked and pops up again when reclicked. The **Click** event procedure for **tglAutoValidate** is shown below.

```
Sub tglAutoValidate_Click()
      If tglAutoValidate.Value = True Then
            tglAutoValidate.Caption = "Auto Validate ON"
      Else
            tglAutoValidate.Caption = "Auto Validate OFF"
      End If

      cmdSend.Enabled = Not(tglAutoValidate.Value)

      Auto = tglAutoValidate.Value

End Sub
```

A toggle button has a **Value** property equal to True when pressed and a **Value** property of False when clicked back up. Whenever it is clicked, the new **Value** is set before the event handler is triggered. This means that the **If** statement inside the event procedure checks the *current* state of the toggle button. It uses the True or False value to decide on the button's caption, either "ON" or "OFF".

Whenever the **auto** option is selected, the Send button **cmdSend** is disabled (you can run the example and check this out). This is achieved by setting its **Enabled** property to the logical opposite of the toggle button's **Value** property. When the auto validate is on (True) the **Enabled** property is **Not (True)**,which equals False, and vice versa.

Finally the value of the global variable **Auto** is set to **tglAutoValidate**'s True or False value. Thus, when the toggle button is pressed, the caption changes, the **Auto** variable is set, and the Send button is enabled or disabled.

Summary

This example showed data validation routines that could be adapted for a wide range of simple data input pages. The resulting functionality provides a level of service that might surprise many Web users accustomed to raw HTML. The textboxes all shared a common validation routine, although the text boxes were not themselves, held in an array. We examined the functions **IsNumeric** and **IsDate** and wrote the new check **IsText**, employing some effective string manipulation.

The error message was created by manipulating a combination of string data, including an explanation of the error and the preprocessed object name derived from the object's **ID** property. Using a timer to reset the error message after a short display period pepped up the interface a little.

QUIZ 2

1. Which of the following strings would cause the `IsNumeric` function to return True?
   a. "1,2,3"
   b. "23"
   c. "**##"
   d. "One Two Three Four"

2. If a Timer control has an Interval value of 1602, then it will fire every
   a. 16.02 seconds
   b. 0.1602 seconds
   c. 160.2 seconds
   d. 1.602 seconds

3. If a variable called `Toggle` is True, then `Not (Toggle)` is
   a. True
   b. Null
   c. False
   d. 1

4. The code statement shown below would result in which substring?

```
SubString = Right ("Able was I ere I saw Elba", 4)
```

   a. "Elba"
   b. "I ere I"
   c. "Able"
   d. The string would be blank.

5. How many iterations would a `For...Next` loop starting at zero and ending at `Len ("123456")` complete?
   a. 6
   b. 5
   c. 7
   d. You cannot tell from the information given.

EXERCISE 2

Difficulty: Moderate

1. Write an `IsText` function that defines valid text in the following manner: no numbers, no colons, no back slashes, and definitely no percentage symbols. Incorporate this into an HTML page and test it by sending text from a textbox whenever the user changes the value of its `Text` property. Use a message box to indicate failed text.

Difficulty: Difficult

2. Upgrade the `IsText` function so that now it returns a single value that not only indicates failure but also why the failure occurred. Decode any failure codes into an appropriate error message that indicates to the user what went wrong. The message should be wiped out after a 2.5 second display period.

QUIZ TIME

The multiple-choice format is an excellent way to gather data from users. It provides an interface that does not require data validation because the user must answer from the choices presented.

This session aims to provide a fully working model of a multiple-choice test, complete with a question navigator, score evaluation, and a current status. It also directly demonstrates how to synchronize separate arrays by forcing them to share a common index variable. This technique illustrates how to keep tabs on different information in different arrays with ease.

Once completed, the principles learned in this session can be applied wherever a user groups together more than one option button or whenever a user must choose from a defined set of responses.

Before starting this session, you should run the quiz page and make sure you achieve a reasonable score. All the questions have been selected from previous chapters, so you will have met them before. By the time you are satisfied with your score, the functionality of the Quiz Time application should be familiar. Needless to say, the answers are in the code, although not all are reproduced in this session. Figure 13-2 shows the quiz page.

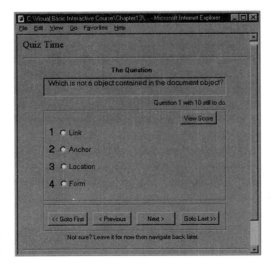

Figure 13-2
The Quiz page

To begin the code analysis, take a look at the global variables being dimensioned below. As in the previous session, the listing is being included for clarity, although the variables themselves were generated using Xpad's Script Wizard.

```
Dim QText()
Dim QChoices()
Dim Responses()
Dim Answers()
Dim optButton(4)

Dim QCurrent
Dim Qnum
```

Because these variables are global, they will be available throughout the code. A grand total of five arrays is dimensioned here. Note how `Qtext()`, `Qchoices()`, `Responses()`, and `Answers()` all are dimensioned as arrays without any members. This is so they can be redimensioned to their correct size prior to the array being filled with question-and-answer data. Adding or deleting questions becomes far simpler because the only code that needs adjusting is the value of the `QNum` variable. The initialization code to do this is found in the `OnLoad` event of the HTML layout control used for this example and is shown below.

```
Sub QuizLayout_OnLoad()
Dim Q
QNum=10

ReDim QText(Qnum)
ReDim Qchoices (Qnum,4)
ReDim Answers(Qnum)
ReDim Responses (Qnum)

Set optButton(1)=Option1
Set optButton(2)=Option2
Set optButton(3)=Option3
Set optButton(4)=Option4

Q = 1
QText(Q)="  Which is not an object contained in the document object?"
Qchoices(Q,1)="Link"
Qchoices(Q,2)="Anchor"
Qchoices(Q,3)="Location"
Qchoices(Q,4)="Form"
Answers(Q)=3

Q = Q + 1
QText(Q)="The menu control can only be activated by a click event."
Qchoices(Q,1)="True"
Qchoices(Q,2)="False"
Answers(Q)=2
```

continued on next page

continued from previous page

```
    . . . 8 more questions

cmdGotoFirst_Click
End Sub
```

For this quiz of 10 questions, the arrays are redimensioned to their correct sizes. Note that the `QChoices` array has two dimensions.

The `optButton(4)` array is being created to hold the four option buttons—with element zero being ignored. Holding the controls in an array like this makes it much easier to check the values or reset a property for each control by using a simple loop.

Each of the questions is set up using three separate arrays. The `QText` array holds the text of the question, the `QChoices` array holds all four of the answer options *per question* (hence its two dimensions), and `Answers` holds the number of the correct answer.

For each question (only the first two are shown above) the index value `Q` is incremented by one and used in all three arrays. This ensures that the answer and the options are correct for the question. The arrays are synchronized.

The final line calls the `cmdGotoFirst` event procedure. This shows that the event handler is just another subroutine that can be called from the code. The <<Goto First button sets the current question to question number one. This is using the navigator (see Figure 13-3) normally triggered by the user clicking on the <<Goto First button. It is perfectly acceptable to artificially trigger event procedures in this way. The `cmdGotoFirst` and the `cmdGotoLast` event procedures are shown below.

```
Sub cmdGotoFirst_Click()
QCurrent = 1
QDisplay
End Sub

Sub cmdGotoLast_Click()
QCurrent = QNum
QDisplay
End Sub
```

Figure 13-3
The navigator
toolbar

The navigator code is very simple but produces useful results. QCurrent is a global variable that represents the question currently displayed. Qcurrent is used as a common index value for the three question arrays QText, QChoices, and Answers. Using QCurrent as a common index variable ensures that the arrays will always be pointing to the correct information for the current question.

This makes it easy to navigate through the questions. If the user wants the *final* question to be displayed, then UQCurrent is simply set to the highest index value of the array. To jump to the first question, the global index variable should be set to the value one, the first index value to contain a question (zero has been ignored in this example).

The above code shows this happening to the QCurrent variable. The first question has an index value of one and the last an index value of QNum (see QuizLayout_OnLoad). After the index variable has been set, the subroutine QDisplay is called. This displays the new question and its options.

The navigator also allows the user to step through the questions both forward and backward. The code for this is shown below.

```
Sub cmdPrevious_Click()
If Not(Qcurrent - 1 < 1) Then
        Qcurrent   = Qcurrent - 1
        QDisplay
End if
End Sub

Sub cmdNext_Click()
If Not(Qcurrent + 1 > Qnum)   Then
        Qcurrent = Qcurrent + 1
        QDisplay
End if
End Sub
```

To go forward, just add one to the global index and all the arrays will point to the next question. To go backward, just subtract one from the global index. Note how the alteration will only occur if it is valid to do so. It is invalid for the Qcurrent variable to be less than one or greater than QNum because there are no questions stored outside this range.

All the navigator buttons do much the same thing; they alter the value of Qcurrent and call the subroutine QDisplay, the code for which is shown below.

```
Sub QDisplay(QCurrent)
Dim Loopy
lblQuestion.Caption = QText(QCurrent)
ResetOptions

For Loopy = 1 to 4
        optButton(Loopy).Caption = Qchoices(QCurrent,Loopy)
        optButton(Loopy).Enabled = Not(QChoices(QCurrent,Loopy) = "")
        If Loopy = Responses(QCurrent) Then optButton(Loopy).Value = True
Next

DisplayStatus
End Sub
```

A lot of functionality is packed into a tiny amount of code here. This is great news for a language intended to be transmitted across the Net where every second of extra download time may lose potential customers; however, it does present difficulties when trying to decipher what is going on. Everything should be fine if it is taken line by line.

After dimensioning the local variables **Msg** and **Loopy**, the first line simply displays the current question's text using the **Caption** property of **lblQuestion**. Note how the **QText** array (it holds the questions) is being accessed using the **QCurrent** variable as its index.

Next there is a call to **ResetOptions**. This sets all the option buttons to unselected.

The **For Next** loop that follows will run four times, one for each of the options for the question being displayed. For each iteration of the loop, the value **Loopy** goes up by one. Any arrays that are using **Loopy** as their index variable will point to their next member every time **Loopy** is incremented. Here again is the first line inside the loop:

```
optButton(Loopy).Caption = QChoices(QCurrent,Loopy)
```

This line will set the **Caption** property of each option button to one of the four options contained per question in the **QChoices** array. **Qcurrent** is being used to indicate the current question and **Loopy** is being used to indicate the current option. Remember that the **optButton** array is the array of option controls. As **Loopy** increases, so each option button has its caption property set to one of the four options.

The next line inside the loop does a similar thing.

```
optButton(Loopy).Enabled = Not(QChoices(QCurrent,Loopy) = "")
```

This time it is the **Enabled** property of each option button being affected. It is set to False (that is, disabled) when the current choice for the current question, **QChoices(QCurrent,Loopy)**, is equal to an empty string. It is set to True when the current choice for the current question is not equal to an empty string. This means that option buttons without corresponding options are disabled while option buttons with corresponding options are enabled.

The last line inside the loop again uses **Loopy** to index the option buttons and **Qcurrent** to index the questions.

```
If Loopy = Responses(QCurrent) Then optButton(Loopy).Value = True
```

During the course of the quiz, a user may answer some questions and then return to them later. The responses are saved in an array called **Responses**; one value is held per question, and the array is indexed using **Qcurrent**. This means the user's last answer is recalled when the question is displayed. If no option has yet been selected, then none of the option buttons is selected.

The final line of the subroutine calls the subroutine **DisplayStatus**, which is used to update the status line constantly displayed on the page. The code to do this is shown below.

```
Sub DisplayStatus()
Dim Msg
If QCurrent = QNum Then
                Msg = "This is the Last question"
Else
                Msg = "Question " & QCurrent
                If QMissed Then Msg  = Msg  &  " with " & QMissed  & " still to
  do."
End If

lblStatus.Caption = Msg
End Sub
```

The status line tells the users the current question number and how many questions they have completed so far. The **If** statement is used to see if the current question number held in **Qcurrent** is equal to the last question number, held in **QNum**. If it is not the last question, then the number of questions to go is calculated by the **QMissed** function, which returns the number of questions that remain unattempted or the value False if all have been attempted. Finally, the newly constructed message held in the **Msg** variable is displayed using **lblStatus.Caption**.

You may remember that near the start of the **Qdisplay** subroutine, the **ResetOptions** sub was called. This was done to reset all the option button values to False. The **ResetOptions** procedure is shown below.

```
Sub ResetOptions()
Dim Loopy

For Loopy = 1 to 4
      optButton(Loopy).Value = False
Next
End Sub
```

The code above demonstrates another reason for putting the option buttons in the array **OptButtons**. It makes it easy to apply the same action to each control in turn by using the **Loopy** variable to index the array of controls one member at a time. Each member has its **Value** property set to False, assuring all the option buttons are unselected.

You may have noticed that the **ResetOptions** procedure does not store the user's selected option if the user has chosen one. That is because it will have already been stored if the user has clicked an option button. The code to do this is found in the option button's **Click** event procedures. All four of the event procedures are shown below.

```
Sub Option1_Click()
Responses(QCurrent)=1
End Sub

Sub Option2_Click()
Responses(QCurrent)=2
End Sub
```

continued on next page

continued from previous page

```
Sub Option3_Click()
Responses(QCurrent)=3
End Sub

Sub Option4_Click()
Responses(QCurrent)=4
End Sub
```

The **QDisplay** procedure has a line that refers to an array called **Responses**. It uses a stored value to set the correct option button to selected if the user decides to revisit a question.

When the user clicks on an option button, a number corresponding to the response is stored in the **Response** array. The index of this stored number is the current question number, held in **Qcurrent**. When **QDisplay** is called upon to display the same question again, **Qcurrent** will be used to access the response value. The **Responses** array is therefore synchronized with all the other question-related data through the use of the common index **Qcurrent**.

At any point in the quiz, the user can check his or her running score as a percentage correct out of the total number of questions. The string also includes a note of the number of questions yet to be completed. If all the questions have been completed, then the message will alter slightly to replace the **X questions still to go** message with a final message appropriate to the score. The code that determines the message to be displayed is shown below.

```
Sub cmdScore_Click()
        Dim Msg1, Msg2, Msg3, Msg14
        Dim Score

Msg1="Not so good. A little more practice is required"
Msg2="A solid performance. Keep this up."
Msg3="So close it makes you weep."
Msg4="Good grief, we have a Guru on our hands!"

Msg="Your score so far is " & (QCorrect / QNum) * 100 & "%" & chr(13) &
chr(13)

If QMissed Then
        Msg = Msg  & "You still have " & QMissed & " questions to
complete."
Else
        Score = QCorrect
        If Score = 10 Then Msg=Msg & Msg4
If Score = 9 Then Msg=Msg & Msg3
        If Score >5 and <= 8 Then Msg=Msg & Msg2
        If Score <= 5 Then Msg=Msg & Msg1
End If

MsgBox Msg, 32, "...and the scores on the doors?"
End Sub
```

The message must always contain the number of questions answered and the percentage score. The **Msg** variable is set to hold this information. Note the use of two **chr(13)** added to the end of the **Msg** variable. **Chr(13)** codes for a new line character.

The second part of the message should be added only if all the questions have been answered. The function **QMissed** is used to determine how many questions there are still to go. This function will return False if all the questions have been attempted.

If **QMissed** is not False, then some questions remain unanswered. The **Msg** message text is augmented with number of questions still to go, again supplied by the **Qmissed** function.

If all the questions have been attempted, the **Msg** text is augmented with either **Msg1**, **Msg2**, **Msg3**, or **Msg4**; each one contains a message appropriate to a certain score range. The **QCorrect** function sets the **Score** variable, which calculates and returns the number of correct answers. Remember the **chr(13)** new line characters on the end of the **Msg** variable? They were put there to separate the two messages with a blank line.

The final line of code displays the completed message in a message box. The number 32 is used to make the **msgbox** a 'Warning query' type. In practice, this means a little graphic of a bubble with a question mark appears on the message box.

The **cmdScore Click** event procedure used two functions to gather information about the user's efforts so far. The first was **QMissed**, and the second was **QCorrect**. The code for **QMissed** is shown below.

```
Function QMissed()
Dim Loopy
QMissed = False

For Loopy = 1 to QNum
            If Responses(Loopy)= 0 Then QMissed = QMissed + 1
Next
End Function
```

If no questions remain to be answered, this function will return False; if questions do remain to be answered, **QMissed** returns the total number. If a question has not been attempted, then it will not have had the corresponding member in the **Response** array set to value. All this function does is count the number of Response members whose values are unset (equal to zero). Setting the **QMissed** return value to False at the outset makes this the default value which will be returned if none of the members of **Response** are set to zero.

The second function used by the **cmdScore** event procedure was **QCorrect**. This was called only if all the questions had been attempted and returns the number of correct responses. The code for **QCorrect** is shown below.

```
Function QCorrect()
Dim Loopy
For Loopy = 1 to QNum
            If Responses(Loopy) = Answers(Loopy) Then QCorrect = QCorrect + 1
Next
End function
```

QCorrect uses a direct comparison between the members in the **Responses** array, which holds the user's selection for each question, and the **Answers** array. The **Answers** array was set up way back in the initialization code and holds the correct answer for each question. Should there be a match, then the user response is the same as the value held in the answer array and the **QCorrect** return variable is incremented by one. Using the **Loopy** variable to index both arrays ensures that the user response for a question is compared to the correct answer.

Summary

Although the primary purpose of this session was to show how to use option buttons in a multiple-choice format, a number of programming issues were revealed. For instance, the synchronizing of multiple arrays by sharing a common index variable allowed complex navigator functionality to be created from a few simple lines. The use of functions returned either False or a meaningful value, which allowed them to serve in two capacities— as an absolute check and as a calculation with a return value. Overall, following the code through from start to finish allows a user to build up exposure to actual code and real coding techniques.

1. Which of the following best describes how to synchronize two arrays?
    a. Ensure that they share the same data.
    b. Ensure that they share the same name.
    c. Ensure that they share the same **Index** variable.
    d. Ensure that they are dimensioned together.

2. Event procedures can be triggered by which of the following?
    a. The user
    b. The code making a call
    c. A timer control
    d. All of the above

3. Using **Chr(13)** in a string variable causes the string
    a. to end.
    b. to start a new line.
    c. to reset to empty.
    d. none of the above.

4. How many members will **MyArray** shown below contain?

```
Dim MyArray(1,4)
```

    a. 8
    b. 10
    c. 9
    d. 12

5. When are loops commonly used with arrays of controls?
    a. When a different action needs to be applied to each control
    b. When an action needs to be applied to one control
    c. When the same actions need to be applied to each control in turn
    d. When resetting the controls to their default values

Difficulty: Moderate

1. Create a two-dimensional array with two blocks of five members and fill it with data. Create a single dimensioned array with two members. Now display the values held, ensuring that the index arrays are synchronized. The multidimensional array should be synchronized using its first dimension.

Difficulty: Difficult

2. Create a Web page with five option buttons and two command buttons. The command buttons will be used to move backward and forward through an array. The current position of the array should be held internally. When the current position of the array is altered, the option selected by the user should be stored in the array so that returning to the same position later will redisplay the option previously selected.

A SIMPLE GAME

This session demonstrates how to write a simple game for the Web. The game is not very exciting, but writing even a simple game can present the programmer with significant challenges. Games often require their interfaces to operate in unusual ways, and the game code will nearly always allow for interesting diversions and experimentation.

The example presented in this session is called Flip-Flop. The user is presented with 12 blank squares (see Figure 13-4). Hidden behind each square is a single letter from A to F. This results in six pairs of letters being created behind the squares. The user has to click on pairs of squares which will pop up if no match is found and stay down if the two letters are the same. Every pair of clicks is counted as an attempt, and the running total of attempts is displayed. When the user has matched all six pairs, the game is over and Flip-Flop resets itself for another go. To help out the frustrated player, there is a Reveal All option that toggles all the squares down to reveal the position of all the hidden letters.

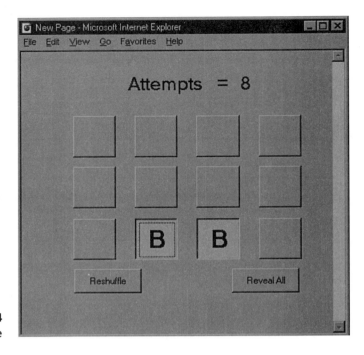

Figure 13-4
The Flip-Flop game

The code below shows the global variables used in this example being dimensioned. Remember, Xpad's Script Wizard allows a user to dimension these global variables using the **New Global Variable** option.

```
dim Toggle(12)
dim Store(12)
dim Reveal
dim Index
dim FirstIndex
```

The two variables of interest at this point are the arrays **Toggle(12)** and **Store(12)**. There are 12 toggle buttons on the page, and each one does the same thing. When clicked using the **Caption** property, each button shows a large capital letter. Because their functionality is so similar, they will all be placed in the **Toggle** array. The letters they display will be held in the **Store** array so that they can be kept hidden.

The code shown below is the **OnLoad** event procedure for the FlipFlop HTML layout file. This procedure will run as soon as the page loads.

```
Sub FlipFlop_OnLoad()
Set Toggle(1) = tgl1
Set Toggle(2) = tgl2
Set Toggle(3) = tgl3
Set Toggle(4) = tgl4
Set Toggle(5) = tgl5
      . . .
```

```
          Set Toggle(12) = tgl12

Shuffle
End Sub
```

The code above (not complete) places 12 toggle buttons into the **Toggle** array. It then calls a procedure called **Shuffle**.

The initialization code is held in the **Onload** event so it will be run when the page first loads. Here all 12 of the toggle buttons are put into the **Toggle** array using the **Set** statement. Putting all the toggle buttons in an array will help simplify the common processing they all share.

The **Shuffle** procedure is responsible for the random distribution of the letters to each toggle button. The code for **Shuffle** is shown below.

```
Sub Shuffle()
Dim Loopy
Dim Ascii
Randomize

For Index = 1 to 12
      Store(Index) = ""
Next

Ascii = Asc("A")
For Loopy = 1 to 2
      Do
              Index = CInt(RND*11) + 1
              If Store(Index) = "" Then
                    If Reveal Then Toggle(Index).Caption=Chr(Ascii)
                            Store(Index) = Chr(Ascii)
                      Ascii = Ascii + 1
              End If
      Loop Until Ascii > Asc("F")
      Ascii = Asc("A")
Next

lblCounter = "0"
FirstIndex = 0
End Sub
```

This procedure will be generating random numbers, so it starts with the **Randomize** statement. This prevents the same sequence of random numbers being thrown out every time the program is run. A **For...Next** loop is then used to quickly set all the members of the **Store** array to empty strings. This array will be used later to store the new batch of capital letters. The first time the code runs, the array will be blank anyway, but this does not matter.

In the next line the **Asc()** function converts the letter "A" into its ASCII equivalent (65) and this is put into a variable called Ascii. The number itself does not matter, what does is that 66 is "B", 67 is "C", and so on. This means a loop can be run from A to F if the characters are first converted to ASCII values (65 to 70).

Definition: ASCII

ASCII is the standard numerical representation of characters. The number range begins at 0 and ends at 255.

The **Do** loop shown above does just this. It will keep on looping until the **Ascii** variable has been incremented to a number greater than Asc("F"), which is 70.

Inside the loop, a random number between 1 and 12 is generated and stored in the variable called **Index**. This number is then used to access the **Store** array and test the value of the member held at that index number. If there is nothing stored there, then a copy of the current value of **Ascii** is placed at that position. The copy of **Ascii** is converted from a number to the equivalent character using the **Chr()** function.

After the converted **Ascii** value has been saved into the **Store** array (at a randomly selected index point, remember) the numeric variable **Ascii** is incremented by one.

This process continues; first A is placed in a randomly selected point in the **Store** array, then B, then C, and so on, with each increment of the **Ascii** variable. Note that the random number held in **Index** is used only if it has not been used before by checking to see if the slot is still blank before assigning the value.

After six empty slots are used up, the **Ascii** variable will have been incremented to a value greater than Asc("F") and so the loop stops looping. It may have taken more than six loops to select six empty slots in the **Store** array but that does not matter; the loop will keep on trying out random numbers until it finds the empty slots.

Twelve buttons require values, so the whole of the **Do** loop is repeated. Because the value of **Ascii** is reset to the value of Asc("A"), the next six empty slots will also contain the letters A to F. Six sets of pairs will be created, scattered randomly throughout the **Store** array.

The penultimate line of the **Shuffle** procedure initializes the attempts total to zero. The label **lblCounter** is used to display the value on the page.

The last line resets the global variable **FirstIndex** to zero. This is used later to indicate which toggle button, of a pair, was pressed first.

All the capital letters are held in the **Store** array to hide them from the user. They are revealed only singly when the user presses a button. Pressing a button will trigger that button's **Click** event. Three of the 12 toggle button **Click** event procedures are shown below.

```
Sub tgl1_Click()
Index = 1
ToggleClick
End Sub

Sub tgl2_Click()
Index = 2
ToggleClick
End Sub

Sub tgl3_Click()
Index = 3
ToggleClick
End Sub
```

All 12 of the toggle button event procedures do the same thing: They set a global variable called **Index** to the position they occupy in the **Toggle** array and then they all call the *same* subroutine called **ToggleClick**.

When the user presses the first button in a pair it must stay down. The second button in a pair must stay down as well. How long they both remain down depends on whether or not the capital letters displayed in their captions are the same. If they are the same, the buttons stay down; if they are not the same, the buttons pop back up again after 200 milliseconds. If the buttons do match and there are no more buttons left unmatched (they are all pressed down), then the game must be over.

The code to do all this is held in the **ToggleClick** procedure, called by clicking any of the 12 toggle buttons. **ToggleClick** is shown below.

```
Sub ToggleClick()
If Toggle(Index).Value = True And Not(Reveal) Then
        Toggle(Index).Caption = Store(Index)
        If FirstIndex = 0 Then
                FirstIndex = Index
        Else
                lblCounter = lblCounter + 1
                If Not (Store(Index) = Store(FirstIndex)) Then
                        tmrButtonsUp.Enabled = True
                Else
                        If Not(Finished) Then
                                FirstIndex = 0
                        Else
Alert "Well Done. Your Ordeal is Over"
                                NewGame
                        End If
                End If
        End If
End If
End Sub
```

In the toggle button **Click** event procedure, the global variable **Index** was set to the number of the button just pressed. This **Index** variable is used above to access the properties of the last pressed button from the **Toggle** array.

The **ToggleClick** procedure will be called regardless of whether the button is pressed down or popped up. To prevent the pop-up click events from running **ToggleClick**, the toggle button's **Value** property is tested to ensure it is True (pressed down) and not False (popped up). One last condition is applied before the **ToggleClick** procedure is allowed to carry on: The global variable **Reveal** must be False.

Reveal is set to True when the user presses the Reveal All button. This causes all the buttons to simultaneously toggle either up or down. Toggling the buttons from the code still triggers the **Click** event procedure, so revealing all 12 values by toggling the buttons down results in 12 unwanted calls to **ToggleClick**. The first **If** statement ensures that the rest of the procedure will be run only if the button being tested is clicked down and this is not as a result of the reveal option.

The `ToggleClick` code shown above deals with the following four scenarios:

- First button is pressed.

- Second button is pressed but no match.

- Second button is pressed; there is a match but the game is not yet finished.

- Second button is pressed; there is a match and the game is finished.

In all cases, the newly pressed button needs to display its letter. The letter is held in the `Store` array and displayed on the button by passing the letter into the button's `Caption` property.

The value of the global variable `FirstIndex` is tested. If this is the first button of a pair to be pressed, then `FirstIndex` will be at its default value of zero. All that needs to be done is store the `Index` value of the button in the `FirstIndex` variable. That is all `ToggleClick` will do for the first button in a pair.

When you call `ToggleClick` for a second button in a pair, `FirstIndex` will not be equal to zero. In this case, the Attempts counter is increased by one (note that VBScript permits the number to be added directly to the string value held in `lblCounter`'s `Caption` property). The next `If` statement checks to see if there has been a match between the letter used for the second button (using the `Index` value) and the letter used for the first button (using the `FirstIndex` value). If there is not a match, then only the line that enables the timer called `tmrButtonsUp` is run. This timer will pop the buttons up as soon as its *Interval* of 200 milliseconds has elapsed.

Should the two buttons match, then `tmrButtonsUp` is not enabled and so the buttons will stay down. It may be that this match represents the final pair required to finish the game. To check, use a function called `Finished`, which returns True if all the buttons are down and False if any remain popped up.

If `Finished` does not return True, then the game is not yet over. The global variable `FirstIndex` is set to zero. This ensures that the next time `ToggleClick` is run, the button will be treated as the first in a pair.

When `Finished` does return True, then the game ends. An appropriate message is displayed and a call is made to the subroutine called `NewGame`. This resets Flip-Flop for another go.

When two buttons have been pressed but the letters they display do not match, use The Timer control `tmrButtonsUp`. The timer `Interval` property was set to 200 (milliseconds) at design time. After 0.2 seconds the `tmrButtonsUp Timer` event procedure will run. The code for this procedure is shown below.

```
Sub tmrButtonsUp_Timer()

Toggle(Index).Value = False
Toggle(FirstIndex).Value = False

Toggle(Index).Caption = ""
Toggle(FirstIndex).Caption = ""
```

```
tmrButtonsUp.Enabled = False
FirstIndex = 0
End Sub
```

The **Timer** event procedure pops up the two mismatched buttons. It must also wipe the letters from the button face. The **Index** variable indicates the last button pressed (the second button) and the **FirstIndex** variable indicates the first button pressed. Using these indexes, both buttons are popped up by setting their **Value** properties to False and both their **Caption** properties are wiped by setting them to empty strings.

The timer then disables itself (sets its **Enabled** property to False) to prevent it rerunning in 200 milliseconds. The global variable **FirstIndex** is set to its default value of zero. This ensures that the next button that calls the **ToggleClick** procedure will be correctly recognized as the first button of a new pair.

As you saw in the **ToggleClick** code, when two buttons did match it was necessary to check if the game was finished. This was done by calling the function **Finished**, the code for which is shown below.

```
Function Finished()
Finished = True

For Index = 1 to 12
     If Toggle(Index).Value = False Then
              Finished = False
              Exit For
        End If
Next
End function
```

The function above will return True if all the buttons are down (**Value** property is True) and False if any buttons remain popped up (**Value** property is False).

The first line sets the return value of **Finished** to True. Following this, there is a **For...Next** loop that runs from 1 to 12 The loop's counter variable, called **Index**, indexes each toggle button in turn from the **Toggle** array. If any of the toggle buttons has a value of False, then the return value for **Finished** is set to False. The **Exit...For** that directly follows this line prevents the loop wastefully checking any more buttons. If one is still popped up, then the rest are irrelevant.

If **Finished** returns a value of True to the **ToggleClick** procedure, then the game is over. The interface is prepared for a new game by calling the procedure **NewGame**. The code for **NewGame** is shown below.

```
Sub NewGame()
Reveal = False
HideShow
Shuffle
End Sub
```

The global variable **Reveal** is set to False. This is relevant to the **HideShow** procedure that follows. The **HideShow** procedure ensures that all the buttons are popped up. Finally, a call is made to **Shuffle** to randomly rearrange the letters held in the **Store** array.

The `HideShow` procedure will click either all the buttons up or all the buttons down depending on the value of the `Reveal` variable. The code for this procedure is shown below.

```
Sub HideShow()
For Index = 1 to 12
            If Reveal Then
            Toggle(Index).Caption = Store(Index)
            Else
            Toggle(Index).Caption = ""
        End If
            Toggle(Index).Value = Reveal
Next
End Sub
```

This procedure uses a `For...Next` loop to cycle through all the toggle buttons held in the `Toggle` array. Each button has its `Value` property set to the current value (True or False) of the `Reveal` variable. This causes all the buttons to be set to the same state, either up or down.

The value of `Reveal` is set by clicking on the Reveal All button called `cmdReveal`. When `cmdReveal` is clicked, it changes its caption and causes all the buttons to click either up or down. The code for `cmdReveal`'s `Click` event procedure is shown below.

```
Sub cmdReveal_Click()
Reveal = Not(Reveal)

If Reveal Then
      cmdReveal.Caption = "Hide Again"
Else
      cmdReveal.Caption = "Reveal All"
End If

HideShow
End Sub
```

The first line toggles the value of the `Reveal` variable; if it was True, it is made Not True, which means False and if it was False, it is made Not False, which means True.

The new value of `Reveal` is then tested and `cmdReveal`'s `Caption` property is updated with its new caption text. Finally, the procedure `HideShow` is called to toggle the buttons as described previously. If the new value of `Reveal` is True, `HideShow` will press all the buttons; if it is False, `HideShow` will pop them all back up again.

Summary

This session demonstrated how to manipulate both the interface and text values in an unusual way. Using the numerical ASCII equivalents instead of real letters allowed a loop to be created that could produce genuinely unpredictable results by generating random index values. Two arrays were synchronized, and importantly, one of them was an array of controls.

The tedious task of manipulating 12 toggle buttons was greatly eased by creating loops to do all the work. The toggle buttons were enhanced by the use of a timer. We also demonstrated the possible dangers of generating unwanted effects by clicking the buttons from the code.

1. Which of the following best describes the actions of a Timer control?
    a. After the Interval has elapsed, the Timer's `Click` event is run.
    b. After the Timer has elapsed, the Timer's `Click` event is run.
    c. After the Interval has elapsed, the Timer is disabled.
    d. After the Interval has elapsed, the Timer's `Timer` event is run.

2. Which of the following best describes the `Asc()` function?
    a. It converts numbers to letters.
    b. It converts letters to numbers.
    c. It converts characters to their ASCII value.
    d. It converts letters to their ASCII value.

3. Using `Chr(13)` in a string variable causes the string
    a. to end.
    b. to start a new line.
    c. to reset to empty.
    d. none of the above.

4. How many times will a loop that runs from Asc("A") to Asc("H") loop?
    a. 8
    b. 5
    c. 26
    d. It is impossible to determine.

5. When are loops commonly used with arrays of controls?
    a. When a different action needs to be applied to each control
    b. When an action needs to be applied to one control
    c. When the same actions need to be applied to each control in turn
    d. When resetting the controls to their default values

Difficulty: Moderate

1. Place more than five toggle buttons on a page. Clicking the first toggle should cause the second toggle button to press down. The second pressing down should cause the first to pop up and the third to press down. The third should cause the second to pop up and the fourth to press down and so on. Remember the unwanted click events.

Difficulty: Difficult

2. Write a set of procedures that will generate an English word using randomly generated letters. The word must start with a consonant, followed by a vowel and then end in another consonant. The middle letters should be entirely random. The word length is up to you.

A WEB CALCULATOR

Calculator programs represent an interesting programming challenge. In a calculator program, the interface must look like a physical calculator to be instantly recognizable. It is not good enough to write code for addition, division—this code must work within the constraints of the interface.

The problem with transposing a real calculator to software lies not in the arithmetic but in the coordination of the interface components. The plastic buttons of a calculator spring back automatically after being pressed because they sit on a bed of rubber. Unless told to do so, buttons do not spring back in a VBScript interface.

In this session we use the ActiveX control IEPOP to create a pop-up menu and then reuse it to create a drop-down menu. This allows the calculator to support a Windows-style menubar. In addition, the menu items are also toggle switches that allow special options to be switched on or off, with the menu displaying the current state of the option.

This session is not meant to be easy. The code has been deliberately compressed to present a smaller ALX file (see note on next page) while still retaining its relatively advanced (at least for the Net) interface design.

Figure 13-5 shows the Web calculator sample in action.

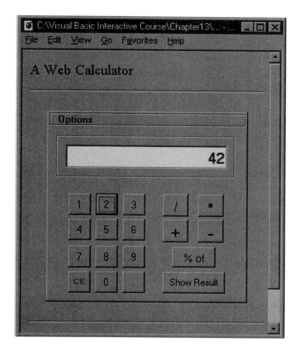

Figure 13-5
The Web Calculator
sample running

> **Note: Less Code = Faster Download**
>
> Unlike most languages, VBScript is distributed in its source-code form because it is part of an HTML text file. When the code is delivered to the client machine, the browser is responsible for converting (compiling) this text into a machine-readable form. The less VBScript and the fewer controls, the smaller the resulting HTML file and the faster the subsequent download.

The global variables used throughout the code are shown below. As in the previous sessions, the listing is being included for clarity, although the variables themselves were generated using Xpad's Script Wizard.

```
Dim Action
Dim ClearDisplay
Dim RoundUp
Dim Auto
Dim AllUp
Dim Number1
Dim Number2
```

These variables will be visible to the entire set of procedures contained within the HTML layout file. Their function will be explained as they arise in the following code analysis.

The calculator does not need much of an initialization procedure, as is shown in the `OnLoad` event procedure of the **Calculate** HTML layout file below. This event is triggered when the page first loads up and is therefore ideal for initialization code.

```
Sub Calculate_OnLoad()
popOptions.AddItem "RoundUp - OFF"
popOptions.AddItem "Auto - OFF"

ClearDisplay = True
End Sub
```

The IEPOP menu control is called **popOptions**. In the code above, **popOptions** is preloaded with its menu items. These will be displayed as windows menu when the **popOptions.Popup** method is invoked.

Each of the Number buttons shares the same code, a subroutine **NumberClick**. A sample of the **Click** event handlers is shown below.

```
Sub cmdZero_Click()
NumberClick "0"
End Sub

Sub cmdPoint_Click()
NumberClick "."
End Sub

Sub cmd9_Click()
NumberClick "9"
End Sub

Sub cmd8_Click()
NumberClick "8"
End Sub
```

The numbers are buttons calling the common procedure **NumberClick**. Each button passes its number to the **NumberClick** procedure. The point character is treated as if it were a number.

The **NumberClick** subroutine called by all the number buttons on the form is shown below.

```
Sub NumberClick(Number)
If ClearDisplay = True Then
        txtDisplay = ""
        ClearDisplay = False
End If

txtDisplay = txtDisplay & Number
End Sub
```

To keep the calculator's display showing the correct digits, it must be periodically wiped. For example, after pressing an action button (see code below), the display must be wiped so the second number can be seen correctly. This is mediated by the **ClearDisplay** global flag. This can be set to True anywhere in the code and the next time any number button is pressed, the display is cleared before another number is displayed. `ClearDisplay` is set back to False to prevent the display from being cleared every time a number is pressed.

The final line places the new number on the end of the display string held in `txtDisplay`.

The action buttons determine what arithmetic procedure to carry out on the numbers the user inputs. This example has the usual range: plus, minus, divide, and multiply, with one additional extended calculation which works out percentages. The `Click` event handlers for all the action buttons are shown below.

```
Sub tglPlus_Click()
If tglPlus.Value = True Then ActionClick "+"
End Sub

Sub tglPercent_Click()
If tglPercent.Value = True Then ActionClick "% of"
End Sub

Sub tglMultiply_Click()
If tglMultiply.Value = True Then ActionClick "*"
End Sub

Sub tglDivide_Click()
If tglDivide.Value = True Then ActionClick "/"
End Sub

Sub tglMinus_Click()
If tglMinus.Value = True Then ActionClick "-"
End Sub
```

The toggle button's `Click` event is generated for both the up and the down actions. The `ActionClick` procedure should be run only when the toggle button is being clicked down. When clicked down, a toggle button's `Value` property is True. Therefore, the `Value` property is checked before the `ActionClick` procedure is called.

You can see from the code above that each call to `ActionClick` is accompanied by the button's function, either + , - , /, and so on. The `ActionClick` code is shown below. The value sent to it is now is passed into `BtnPressed`.

```
Sub ActionClick(BtnPressed)
If Auto Then
        ToggleButtons BtnPressed
Else
        ToggleButtons AllUp
End If

Action = BtnPressed
Number1 = txtDisplay
ClearDisplay = True
End Sub
```

When the **Auto** option is True, the action button pressed last must stay depressed to indicate the action is to be reapplied. The procedure **ToggleButtons** is called and sent the **BtnPressed** variable to indicate which button should stay down. If the **Auto** option is set to False, then the procedure **ToggleButtons** is called with the constant **AllUp** whose value is always False. This forces all the action buttons to spring back up.

We store the action to be performed in the global variable **Action**. The number, taken from the display window **txtxDisplay**, is stored in the global variable **Number**. We will use both in the **Calculate** procedure later on.

Note that the **ClearDisplay** flag is also set to True. This means that the next time a number button is pressed, the display will be reset.

The code shown above indicates that **ToggleButtons can set** the state of the toggle buttons. The **ToggleButtons** procedure is shown below.

```
Sub ToggleButtons(btnPressed)
If tglDivide.Value = True And Not(tglDivide.Caption = btnPress) Then
      tglDivide.Value = False
End If

If tglMinus.Value = True And Not(tglMinus.Caption = btnPress) Then
      tglMinus.Value = False
End If

If tglMultiply.Value = True And Not(tglMultiply.Caption= btnPress) Then
      tglMultiply.Value = False
End If

If tglPercent.Value = True And Not(tglPercent.Caption = btnPress) Then
      tglPercent.Value = False
End If

If tglPlus.Value = True And Not(tglPlus.Caption = btnPress) Then
      tglPlus.Value = False
End If
End Sub
```

This procedure receives a parameter that will be False or a symbol denoting a button that should stay pressed down. Shown below is an excerpt from **ToggleButtons**; it shows how **tglDivide** determines whether it should spring back up or stay depressed.

```
If tglDivide.Value And Not(tglDivide.Caption = btnPress) Then
            tglDivide.Value = False
End If
```

Only one of the toggle buttons can be pressed at any one time. To see if **tglDivide** has been pressed, its **Value** property is checked. If False, the **If** statement fails and we test the next button. The next test compares the button's caption to the value of **btnPressed**; remember the button identifier passed to **btnPressed** from the Togglebuttons call was + or * and so on.

If the button is pressed and it is not the button indicated by the **btnPress** variable, then the button is popped back up. If a pressed button is the button indicated by the **btnPressed** variable, then it stays down. The **Value** property is always used to determine a toggle button's current state.

If **btnPressed** is a value that cannot match any of the action button's captions, then they will all be popped back up. The constant **AllUp**, sent by the calling code if all the buttons are to spring back, has a value of False which cannot match any of the captions, and so each of the checks will cause its buttons to spring back up.

The heart of the calculator's functionality lies in the **Calculate** procedure. This is called from the **cmdCalculate Click** event procedure (the Show Result button). Both the event handler and the **Calculate** procedure are shown below.

```
Sub cmdCalculate_Click()
Calculate
End Sub

Sub Calculate()
Dim Solution

If Number2 = "" Then Number2 = txtDisplay

Solution =  DoMath

If Auto Then
        Number1 = Solution
Else
        Number1 = ""
        Number2 = ""
End If

txtDisplay.Text = Solution
ClearDisplay = True
End Sub
```

The variable **Number2** holds the second number the user inputs. If **Auto** is True, then the second number needs to be preserved so it can be reused. **Number2** will be an empty string if **Auto** is False or the user has pressed the Clear All (CE) button (regardless of **Auto's** current setting). Only under these conditions will the number held in the display be passed to the **Number2** variable.

The **DoMath** procedure, the actual calculation code, passes the calculated value back into the variable **Solution**.

If the **Auto** option is set to True, then the solution to the last operation must be used as the basis for the next. To achieve this, place the newly calculated **Solution** into the **Number1** variable. If the **Auto** option is False, then the next operation must be treated as a separate entity and so both **Number** variables are reset to empty.

The **Text** property of **txtDisplay** now displays the newly calculated **Solution**.

The **ClearDisplay** flag is set to True. This will display the next time the user presses a number button.

The **DoMath** function does the number crunching and checks to see if the solution is to be rounded (an option from the menu). The code for **DoMath** is shown below.

```
Sub DoMath()
Select Case Action
        Case "+"
                DoMath = Number1 + Number2
        Case "-"
                DoMath = Number1 - Number2
        Case "*"
                DoMath = Number1 * Number2
        Case "/"
                DoMath = Number1 / Number2
        Case "% of"
                DoMath = (Number2/100) * Number1
End Select

If RoundON Then DoMath = CLng(DoMath)

End Sub
```

The global variable **Action** is tested to determine the type of calculation. **Action** was set way back in the **ActionClick** procedure. The calculation performed depends on which action button the user pressed.

If the **Rounding** option has been switched ON, then the **RoundON** variable is True. The rounding is done by forcing the newly calculated return value of **DoMath** into a Long datatype using the **CLng** function. Longs do not support decimal places, so VBScript will automatically round the number up or down to make it fit into the new data type.

We mentioned the menu options **Auto** and **Rounding** earlier. The ActiveX control uses IEPOP to give the page its menu functionality. In this application the IEPOP control has been called **PopOptions**. This control will cause a menu of preloaded items (see **Calculate_OnLoad**) to appear at the current mouse coordinates whenever its **PopUp** method is invoked. This method is called from the blue Options label **Click** event procedure. The code for the event procedure is shown below.

```
Sub lblOptions_MouseDown(Button, Shift, X, Y)
If Button = 1 Then PopOptions.Popup
End Sub
```

Clicking on the blue Options label will cause the menu to pop up at the current mouse coordinates. Although it is not perfect, this gives a good impression of a standard windows drop-down menu. Note how the **Button** parameter (automatically sent by VBScript to this event handler) is checked before the menu is popped up. A **Button** value of one means the left button was clicked; a value of two means the right. The drop-down menus will respond only to a left click.

After the menu has popped up, the user clicks on the option of his or her choice. This triggers the **popOptions** control's **Click** event. The event handler is sent the numeric value, starting from one, representing the menu option the user clicked. The **Click** event procedure for the menu control **popOptions** follows.

```
Sub popOptions_Click(item)
popOptions.RemoveItem Item

Select Case Item
          Case 1
          If RoundUp = False Then
                         popOptions.AddItem "Round Up - ON", 1
          Else
                         popOptions.AddItem "Round Up - OFF", 1
          End If
          RoundON = Not (RoundON)
          Case 2
          If Auto = False Then
                         popOptions.AddItem "Auto - ON", 2
          Else
                         popOptions.AddItem "Auto - OFF", 2
                         ToggleButtons AllUp
          End If
          Auto = Not (Auto)
End Select
End Sub
```

The clicked menu item is removed from the pop-up menu. The **Item** parameter holds the value of the selected option and so is used to remove it from the menu. The **Select Case** statement determines which option was selected and directs the processing accordingly. In both cases, the new menu text is added back into the pop up menu. This updates the menu to reflect the current setting of the options. The **Not** function toggles the flag for the selected option.

Switching the **Auto** option OFF also calls the **ToggleButtons** procedure with the **AllUp** parameter. This forces all the action buttons to pop back up again.

The only button not yet mentioned is the reset or CE button. The **Click** event procedure for **cmdCE** calls the procedure **Reset**. Both the event handler and the **Reset** procedure are shown below.

```
Sub cmdCE_Click()
Reset
End Sub

Sub Reset()
Number1 = ""
Number2 = ""

txtDisplay = "0"
ClearDisplay = True

ToggleButtons AllUp
End Sub
```

If the user wishes to cancel the operation, he or she presses the **cmdCE** button, which calls the **Reset** procedure. This resets the **Number1** and **Number2** variables and the display to the calculator default of "0". It sets the **ClearDisplay** flag to True, which ensures that the "0" will be wiped out when the next number button is clicked. This prevents the "0" from forming part of the calculation number. The last line makes sure all the action buttons are popped up.

Summary

This session has shown the value of sharing code between controls, especially between controls which can be grouped by virtue of their related functionality. In more general terms, this session has highlighted some of the complexity that starts to evolve whenever code is being constrained by an interface. It has shown how you can keep track of the interface by making sure that each interface component identifies itself to the procedures it calls. The state of the menu options was maintained through the use of global flags. That said, some pretty neat tricks were employed to pack the functionality in: the recasting of variables to a different data type to force the number rounding, the use of the pop-up menu as a pretend drop-down menu, the dynamic-toggling menu items, and the **Auto** option.

1. The code to process a user's menu selection is commonly found
   a. in the pop-up control's menu item.
   b. in the pop-up control's **PopUp** method.
   c. in the pop-up control's **Click** event procedure.
   d. in the pop-up control's **Change** event procedure.

2. If VBScript is held in an HTML layout file, then the initialization code is commonly found
   a. in the layout's **UpLoad** event procedure.
   b. in the layout's **OnLoad** event procedure.
   c. in the layout's **Initialize** event procedure.
   d. in the layout's **Init** event procedure.

3. Which best describes the state of a Toggle button **Value** property?
   a. True when up
   b. True when down
   c. True when down and False when up
   d. False when down and True when up

4. Why does recasting a number using the **CLng** round the number?
   a. Long variables are used only to perform simple calculations.
   b. Long variables can support only whole numbers.
   c. It is a quirk of VBScript.
   d. String variables can support only whole numbers.

5. Which method is used to add the menu items to an IEPOP menu control?
   a. `AddOption`
   b. `PopUp`
   c. `AddItem`
   d. `InsertItem`

EXERCISE 5

Difficulty: Easy

1. Create a page that has one small rectangular label on top of another large square label. Now make a pop-up menu appear when the right mouse button is clicked on the larger background label. Make the same menu appear when the left mouse button is clicked over the smaller label. The same menu is now being used as both a pop-up and a drop-down menu.

Difficulty: Moderate

2. Create a page with five toggle buttons and a check box control. When the check box is checked, only one button may remain down at any one time. When the check box is unchecked, all the buttons can be down at the same time.

BUSINESS ON THE WEB

This session demonstrates how to create a true business application. Business applications on the Web have, until now, been no more than electronic PR brochures; all that is about to change. With ActiveX controls and VBScript, if it can be done in Windows, it can be done on the Web. This allows real business processing to be directed at a huge customer base for a minimal outlay; no wonder managers around the world are pricking their ears up.

Although there are as many business applications as there are businesses, much of their core functionality tends to revolve around data retrieval or dissemination. This session demonstrates how to construct a front end that allows for data entry, search, and manipulation. In addition to this core functionality, the Supplier sample also features context-sensitive help, bookmarks, drop-down menus, an onscreen clock, a navigator bar, and Windows 95 styling.

It is a *front end* because, like all Web pages, it must rely on a server for permanent information storage. However, unlike standard Web pages, this front end has its own temporary storage (the client machine's memory) to hold chunks of data. The server can now deliver or receive its data in large blocks, which means the communication between the front end and its server is greatly reduced. Providing the server with client-side data buffers like this will enhance the performance of the system as a whole.

The Supplier page (see Figure 13-6) contains information relating to the fictional company Gromit Industries and its database of supplier information. In practice, the Supplier front end would communicate with a server to send and receive data. To keep things simple, however, the code for the data transfer is not presented in this session.

To begin the code analysis, take a look at the global variables being dimensioned below. All the variables were generated using Xpad's Script Wizard.

```
Dim ContactName(10)
Dim Title(10)
Dim CompanyName(10)
Dim Address(10)
Dim PostCode(10)
Dim City(10)
Dim Region(10)
Dim Country(10)
Dim Phone(10)
Dim Fax(10)

Dim BookMark
Dim HelpOn
Dim LastSupplierID
Dim SupplierID
```

The 10 arrays, each with 10 members, dimensioned above hold the data to be manipulated by the user. The arrays will be synchronized by using a common index variable to access them all. This allows all the various data items for a particular supplier to be presented and updated together. The final four global variables will be used later in the processing.

The **OnLoad** event contains the initialization code of the Supplier HTML layout file. This code will therefore be run as soon as the page loads into the Internet Explorer.

```
Sub Supplier_OnLoad()
SetUpDummyData
SetUpMenus

SupplierID = 1
LastSupplierID = 2
DisplayDetails

lblDate.Caption = Date
lblTime.Caption = Time

End Sub
```

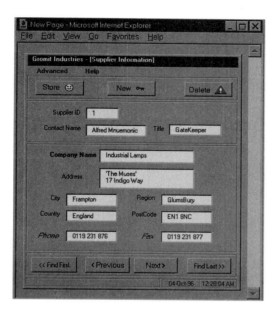

Figure 13-6
The Supplier
front end

The Supplier page starts with two full pages of supplier data to give an idea of how it might look in practice. This dummy data is fed into the various arrays by calling the **SetUpDummyData** procedure. Supplier also has two drop-down menus triggered from the blue **Advanced** and **Help** labels. The **SetUpMenus** procedure adds the menu options to the menus. The code for both procedures will follow shortly.

The next line makes the first mention of **SupplierID**, probably the most important variable in this example. It is used to index all the data arrays, thus synchronizing the data they hold. All the arrays in Supplier have 10 members; however, this need not be the case. The arrays could hold the information for 1000 suppliers if necessary. If the arrays are not filled (that is, they have not used all their available members), the variable **LastSupplierID** is used to mark the highest index value that references supplier data; if it were any higher, it would reference a series of blank members. The code above shows **LastSupplierID** initialized to two, the number of dummy suppliers already loaded. The lowest (first) **SupplierID** is always one.

Next, a function named **DisplayDetails** is called. This function displays the details of the selected supplier by using the **SupplierID** to index all the data arrays.

In the bottom right-hand corner of the page, the current date and time are displayed in two labels, **lblDate** and **lblTime**. The **Caption** property displays the system date and time returned from the VBScripts functions **Date** and **Time**.

The initialization code used the procedure **SetUpDummyData** to fill two members for each of the variables. A representative sample of the code for **SetUpDummyData** is shown below.

```
Sub SetUpDummyData()
ContactName(1) = "Alfred Mnemonic"
ContactName(2) = "Oprah Saxophone"
. . . deleted lines
Fax(1) = "0119 231 877"
Fax(2) = "02 876 174"
cmbTitle.Additem "Llama Trainer"
cmbTitle.Additem "Ice Melter"
cmbTitle.Additem "Director"
cmbTitle.Additem "Ink Blender"
cmbTitle.listindex = 1
End Sub
```

To prevent tedious repetition, we don't show all the arrays in the code sample above. Even so, we can see that members one and two from each array will be loaded with supplier data. The combobox called **cmbTitle** is also initialized to hold the Title options made available when the user creates a new supplier.

Setting the combobox's **ListIndex** property to one selects the first item in the list and makes it appear in the textbox portion of the combobox. This combobox is hidden from view when the page is first loaded (its **Visible** property set to False at design time). We will fully explain its use later.

The second initialization procedure was **SetUpMenus**, the code for which is shown below.

```
Sub SetUpMenus()
popAdvanced.AddItem "Search by ID"
popAdvanced.AddItem "BookMark - Create"
popAdvanced.AddItem "BookMark - GOTO"

popHelp.Additem "Help - OFF"
End Sub
```

Two IEPOP controls provide Supplier with its menu functionality: **popAdvanced** and **popHelp**. You can see in the code above that each menu control has its options added using the **AddItem** method. The **popHelp** control has only one option, which doubles up to give two in one because it can be set either ON or OFF. To start, the Help option is loaded with its OFF caption.

The initialization code running from the **OnLoad** procedure continues with a call to **DisplayDetails**. This occurs just after the value of **SupplierID** index variable is set to one. An abridged version of the code for **DisplayDetails** is shown below.

```
Sub DisplayDetails()
txtSupplierID = SupplierID
txtCity = City(SupplierID)
. . . . more display lines
txtPhone = Phone(SupplierID)
txtFax = Fax(SupplierID)
End Sub
```

Each line moves a data value held in one of the data arrays into a textbox used for display to the user. The exception is the **txtSupplierID** textbox that displays the current value of the **SupplierID** variable.

At the point of initialization, the **SupplierID** is one. This procedure will display all the details relating to the supplier who has an ID of one.

Thinking ahead for a moment, if the **SupplierID** value is incremented by one and the **DisplayDetails** procedure is called again, then the details relating to supplier two will be displayed. If the **SupplierID** is set to **LastSupplierID,** then the details of the last supplier available will be displayed. Finally, if the **SupplierID** is set to one and **DisplayDetails** called, the details of the first supplier will be redisplayed. This could provide a simple way to navigate through the data.

The code needed to navigate through the supplier information is found in the **Click** event procedure for **cmdFindFirst**, **cmdPrevious**, **cmdNext**, and **cmdFindLast**. This code is shown below.

```
Sub cmdFindFirst_Click()
SupplierID = 1
DisplayDetails
End Sub

Sub cmdPrevious_Click()
SupplierID = supplierID - 1
If SupplierID < 1 Then SupplierID = 1
DisplayDetails
End Sub

Sub cmdNext_Click()
SupplierID = supplierID + 1
If SupplierID > LastSupplierID Then SupplierID = LastSupplierID
DisplayDetails
End Sub

Sub cmdFindLast_Click()
SupplierID = LastSupplierID
DisplayDetails
End Sub
```

In each case, the **SupplierID** value is altered and the **DisplayDetails** procedure called to update the interface with the new information. Only the **cmdNext_Click** and **cmdPrevious_Click** procedures have to make an extra check to ensure the new value of **SupplierID** stays within the range allowable. For **Supplier** the range is one to the value of **LastSupplierID**. If the new value of **SupplierID** lies outside this range, it is reset to the range limits. This prevents the user from navigating beyond the available data.

Other than allowing the user to examine the data, the three main functions of **Supplier** are adding, deleting or modifying data. These functions are triggered via the **cmdNew**, **cmdDelete**, and **cmdStore** command buttons, respectively.

The code for the first of these functions is held in the **cmdNew Click** event procedure.

To save a new set of supplier data, the New button must first be clicked. The user should then type in the data and finally, to save the new data into the arrays, click on the Store button.

The command button **cmdNew** plays two roles. After it is first clicked, **cmdNew**'s **Caption** changes to Cancel. Clicking on the button in this mode will restore the interface to what it was before the New button was clicked. The code for **cmdNew**'s **Click** event procedure is shown below.

```
Sub cmdNew_Click()

If cmdNew.Caption = "New" Then
        cmdNew.Caption = "Cancel"
    LastSupplierID = LastSupplierID + 1

    If LastSupplierID > 10 then
        LastSupplierID = 10
        MsgBox "No more than 10 Records can be stored."
    End If

    SupplierID = LastSupplierID
    txtTitle.Visible = False
    cmbTitle.Visible = True
Else
    cmdNew.Caption       = "New"
    DeleteCurrent
End If

DisplayDetails
End Sub
```

The first line shows the **Caption** property of **cmdNew** being tested using an **If** statement. The **If** splits the button's functionality in two: When the caption reads New, one branch will run and when it reads Cancel, the alternative (Else) branch will run.

In the first case, the **Caption** will read New. This sets the **SupplierID** to the next available slot in the data arrays. The new data needs to be stored in the next set of empty array members. The index value for this will always be one greater than the **LastSupplierID** (assuming arrays are not full). The **Caption** property is updated to Cancel, which will force the button to perform its alternative function when it is next clicked. **LastSupplierID** is then incremented by one to allow for the new set of data about to be entered by the user.

After incrementing the **LastSupplierID**, its new value is checked to make sure it does not exceed the total number of members available per array. If the new value is greater than allowed (for this example the limit is ten members, although this need not be the case) then the **LastSupplierID** is reset to the available limit and a warning message is displayed to the user.

If the new value of **LastSupplierID** is valid, then the **SupplierID** is updated to match this new value. If this was not done, the **Next** and **Previous** functions would still be using the old value of **SupplierID** as their starting point, causing an unexpected jump in supplier position when they are next clicked.

Finally the combobox **cmbTitles** is used in a rather neat way. In normal display mode, the supplier's job title is displayed in a textbox control. When the user wishes to add a new supplier, this textbox is replaced by a combobox which contains all the valid job titles. This is achieved by setting the **Visible** property of the textbox control, **txtTitle**, to False and the **Visible** property of **cmbTitles** to True, as seen in the code shown above.

At any time during a New operation, the user can cancel out and return to where he or she stopped. As demonstrated earlier, this functionality is triggered only when the **cmdNew**'s caption reads Cancel. When this is the case, the code sets cmdNew button's **Caption** back to New and the **DeleteCurrent** procedure is called.

The **DeleteCurrent** procedure will remove all the information about a particular supplier. **DeleteCurrent** is called when the user clicks on the **cmdDelete** command button and, as was shown above, when users wish to discard the unwanted New supplier attempt. The code for **DeleteCurrent** and the **Click** event procedure for the **cmdDelete** command button are both shown below.

```
sub cmdDelete_Click()
DeleteCurrent
End Sub

sub DeleteCurrent()
Dim Loopy

For Loopy = SupplierID To LastSupplierID
        ContactName(LastSupplierID) = ""
. . . deleted lines
                Fax(Loopy) =Fax(Loopy+1)
Next

ContactName(LastSupplierID) = ""
. . . deleted lines
Fax(LastSupplierID) = ""

LastSupplierID = LastSupplierID - 1

If SupplierID > LastSupplierID Then
        SupplierID = LastSupplierID
End If

DisplayDetails
End Sub
```

If a supplier's information is to be deleted from any part of the array other than the last member, then a blank space will appear at deletion points across all the arrays. To fill in this gap, all the members that lie above the blank slot are shuffled down one. This leaves two copies of the next highest supplier's information held in each array. A **For...Next** loop is used to continue this process of shuffling each set of elements down one index value. When the loop ends, the last two members will hold the same information. The last slot is blanked to remove this duplication. This shuffling process succeeds in compressing the array each time a supplier is removed, filling in any gaps left in the array and ensuring that the value **LastSupplierID** plus one is always the first empty member in the array.

The **For...Next** loop starts at the **SupplierID** to be deleted and ends at the value for the **LastSupplierID** variable. The loop variable **Loopy** indexes each array within the loop. Copies of the member held at **Loopy** plus one are placed at the index value of **Loopy**. The first time this happens, the data to be deleted is overwritten by a copy of the data held at **SupplierID** plus one and lost (deleted). As the loop continues, no more data is lost; it is only shuffled down by one. When the loop is finished, the extra copy of the last supplier's information is blanked out and the **LastSupplierID** is reduced by one. The sum effect of this loop is to delete the data requested while preserving all the other data. The newly freed slot finally appears at **LastSupplierID** plus one, ready to be used again.

One final test is carried out on **SupplierID** to make sure that its value is not greater than the new value of **LastSupplierID**. This would happen if the current supplier being deleted was also the last supplier held in the arrays.

Now that the current supplier information has been deleted and different information has been shuffled into its old slot, the latter needs to be displayed. Displaying supplier information requires a call to the **DisplayDetails** procedure. The final line of **cmdNew's** **Click** procedure shows this call to the **DisplayDetails** procedure being made.

Supplier comes with two Windows-style drop-down menus. In fact they are really pop-up menus (IEPOP controls), but forcing them to appear only when the blue labels **Advanced** or **Help** are clicked makes them act like drop-down menus. The two IEPOP controls **popAdvanced** and **popHelp** were initialized in the Supplier **OnLoad** event procedure at the beginning of this session.

The code below shows the **Click** procedure for the **popHelp** control. Note the parameter **Item**, which carries the number of the option the user has clicked. The menu control **popHelp** has only one option, so this parameter can be ignored in the code below.

```
Sub popHelp_Click(Item)

popHelp.RemoveItem 1
HelpOn = Not(HelpOn)
If HelpOn then
        popHelp.Additem "Help - ON"
Else
        popHelp.Additem "Help - OFF"
End If

End Sub
```

The option in **popHelp** toggles the context-sensitive help on and off. It does this by setting the variable **HelpOn** to either True or False.

The first line removes the (only) option from the menu control using the **DeleteItem** method. The option to be deleted is specified by sending the **DeleteItem** method the option's Item number; in this case it will always be one because there is only one option.

The **Not** command on the next line logically inverts the value of the **HelpOn** variable, toggling it from True to False and back again.

The new value of **HelpOn** is then tested to determine which option text should be displayed. The menu option is then recreated using the **AddItem** method to indicate the new help setting.

The help menu will appear only if the user clicks the left mouse button while over the blue Help label called **mnuHelp**. The **MouseDown** event procedure for **mnuHelp** is shown below. The **MouseDown** event—not the **Click** event—is used because the **Click** event does not receive the **Button** parameter. This is needed to test which mouse button (right or left) the user clicked.

```
Sub mnuHelp_MouseDown(Button, Shift, X, Y)
If Button = 1 Then popHelp.PopUp
End Sub
```

The **MouseDown** event is sent the **Button** parameter and the code above shows it being tested. A right click sends a **Button** value of two and a left click a **Button** value of one. If the user has clicked with their left button, then the **popHelp** IEPOP control has its **PopUp** method invoked, causing the **Help** menu options to appear at the current mouse coordinates.

The same reasoning applies to the **MouseDown** event handler for the **mnuAdvanced** label control. The code is shown below.

```
Sub mnuAdvanced_MouseDown(Button, Shift, X, Y)
If Button = 1 then popAdvanced.PopUp
End Sub
```

Before considering the advanced options, the **Help** functionality needs further explanation.

After switching the **Help** option ON, the user will see short explanations of **Supplier's** functionality in the status bar at the foot of the layout. The relevant messages appear when the user places the mouse over a control and they disappear when moved off the control. This effect is achieved very simply, as the code below shows.

```
Sub cmdFindFirst_MouseMove(Button, Shift, X, Y)
If HelpOn Then lblHelp.Caption = "Go to the first record available"
End Sub
```

```
Sub cmdDelete_MouseMove(Button, Shift, X, Y)
If HelpOn Then lblHelp.Caption = "Warning - Deletes current record"
End Sub
```

Each control that has context-sensitive help available has a **MouseDown** event handler identical (apart from the help text) to the two shown above. The single line checks the value of the **HelpOn** variable. Only if the user has toggled the **Help** option on will **HelpOn** variable be True and the help text displayed. The label control called **lblHelp** is used to display the help text.

When the user moves off the control, the **Caption** property of **lblHelp** needs to be reset to a blank string. You achieve this by using the **MouseDown** event handlers from the controls that do not have context-sensitive help, for example, the label control **lblWindow**. The code for two of these **MouseDown** event procedures is shown below.

```
Sub lblWindow_MouseMove(Button, Shift, X, Y)
lblHelp.Caption = ""
End Sub
Sub lblTopBtnBar_MouseMove(Button, Shift, X, Y)
lblHelp.Caption = ""
End Sub
```

Whenever the user passes the mouse over these controls, the **Caption** property for the **lblHelp** control is set to an empty string. Normally, this goes unnoticed, but if the user has just displayed some context-sensitive help, it will be wiped out.

As soon as a user moves from one control to another, the help text will be replaced by another help message (if the control has help available) or will be wiped out (if the control has no help available).

The Advanced menu is controlled by another IEPOP control called **popAdvanced**. Below is the **Click** event procedure for **popAdvanced**. The Advanced options consist of a search by **SupplierID**, the bookmarking of a particular supplier, and, finally, a goto bookmarked supplier option. Consequently, the Advanced menu has three options and the **popAdvanced Click** procedure, shown below, must test the **Item** parameter to determine which option the user selected.

```
Sub popAdvanced_Click(item)
Select Case Item
      Case 1
            Do
                  SupplierID = parent.Prompt ("Please Enter Supplier ID","")
                  If  cInt(SupplierID) <= cInt(LastSupplierID) Then
Exit Do
                  End If
MsgBox "Record " & SupplierID & " does not exist.Please
try again."
            Loop
            DisplayDetails
      Case 2
            BookMark = SupplierID
      Case 3
            SupplierID = BookMark
            DisplayDetails
End Select
End Sub
```

A **Select Case** structure tests the value of the **Item** parameter it uses to determine which menu option the user selected.

Option number one is the search function. Going into this branch, the code enters what appears to be an eternal **Do** loop (there is no escape clause on either the **Do** or the **Loop** statements). The user is presented with an Input box asking for the value of the **SupplierID** he or she wants to see. The value entered is returned into the **SupplierID** variable, which is tested immediately. If the number is less than or equal to the **LastSupplierID**, it is valid (if it were greater then the members displayed would be blank), and the loop is exited. Here is the escape clause, right in the middle of the loop. Note that before a comparison can be made between the new value of **SupplierID** and the value of **LastSupplierID**, both are converted into integer data types. This is required for a *numerical* comparison, which will not work if either of the values is a string data type.

If the user has entered an invalid supplier ID, the exit **Do** is ignored and a warning message is displayed. The loop will then restart, which redisplays the Input box. This continues until the user enters a valid supplier ID.

After a valid supplier ID is entered, **DisplayDetails** is called to update the interface with the information specified by the new **SupplierID** value.

Option number two sets the bookmark to the current **SupplierID**. This saves the current value of **SupplierID** into the global variable **BookMark**. Now, no matter where the users navigate, they can quickly go back to the supplier they marked by selecting the third option.

Option number three goes to the bookmark created by option number two. It sets the **SupplierID** to the stored bookmark value held in the **BookMark** variable and then calls **DisplayDetails** to update the display.

Because it is so easy to achieve, **Supplier** comes with an onscreen clock. The first procedure in this example (the layout's **OnLoad** event procedure) showed the label **lblTime** having its caption set to the current system time returned by the **Time** function. The clock is created by updating **lblTime** with the latest system time every second. A Timer control with an **Interval** property set to 1000 triggers the update code.

```
Sub tmrUpdateTime_Timer
lblTime = Time
End Sub
```

The final procedure is the **Timer** event procedure for **tmrUpdateTime**. It shows the clock update code putting the latest system time into **lblTime**'s **Caption** property using the return value from the **Time** function.

Summary

This session demonstrated how to construct a front end that allows for data entry, search, and manipulation. It showed how the application of synchronized arrays can lead to additional features such as bookmarks and data navigators. This type of functionality is found throughout windows applications and is already appearing throughout the Internet. In addition to its core functionality, the Supplier sample also features context-sensitive help, drop-down menus, an onscreen clock, and Windows 95 styling, all of which can be applied anywhere users need to feel instantly at home with the interface.

From a technical point of view, Supplier was interesting for two reasons: First, it employed the concept of using the client machine's memory to hold data instead of making repeated requests to a server; second, it used automatic array compression to keep the arrays from filling up with blank spaces after supplier data had been deleted.

1. Which of the following best describes the **Button** parameter?
    a. 1 = Left : 2 = Right.
    b. 2 = Left : 1 = Right.
    c. 0 = Left : 1 = Right.
    d. 1 = Left : 0 = Right.

2. Select the most accurate description of the IEPOP control's **PopUp** method.
    a. Causes the menu options to be displayed
    b. Causes the **Click** procedure to be run
    c. Causes the menu options to be displayed at the current mouse coordinates
    d. Sends the **Click** procedure the selected option's **Item** parameter

3. Placing data in the client's memory is more efficient because
    a. the server is freed up to complete other tasks.
    b. there is less frequent communication between the client and the server.
    c. there is less data to transfer.
    d. answers a. and b.

4. Which of the following is *not* an advantage of arrays sharing a common index?
    a. The arrays cannot get out of step.
    b. It is easy to navigate through the data.
    c. Code can depend on the position of data within the arrays.
    d. You can loop through the array to simplify common processing.

5. Numerical comparisons (< or >) cannot be used with which data type?
    a. Integer
    b. String
    c. Long
    d. Double

Difficulty: Moderate

1. Create a page with at least three textboxes. Using synchronized arrays, allow the user to store and retrieve the data he or she types into the textboxes. Add a search facility that uses a text search string.

Difficulty: Difficult

2. The Supplier example is flawed. If a user deletes a record, every supplier above the deleted record has its supplier ID decreased by one. The supplier ID is part of the data and should not be changed in this way. This bug also prevents the bookmarks from operating properly. The solution is to create a separate index variable that is not part of the data. Modify Supplier by adding an index variable that will correctly synchronize the arrays while preserving intact the original supplier data.

CHAPTER SUMMARY

Congratulations! You've graduated to the world of advanced VBScript coding by mastering such high-level concepts as grouping controls and sharing procedures, creating multidimensional arrays, and designing Windows style menus. You've also gotten a handle on interface-constrained design and context-sensitive help. With these skills, you've taken VBScript beyond the realm of conventional Web page design—you're designing real Windows applications for the Web. In the final chapter, we will take things even further with more advanced VBScript topics.

CHAPTER 14

MAKE THE LEAP—ADVANCED TOPICS

The previous 13 chapters of this book have presented a solid overall view of the VBScript scripting language. Now, in Chapter 14, we will look at some advanced topics in VBScript. Here are a few of the topics we will cover in this chapter:

- ActiveX Control Pad
- HTML Layout Control
- Style Sheets
- Advanced ActiveX Controls
- Working with Java

Some of these concepts are difficult, but you should be able to implement all of them using the VBScript knowledge you have learned throughout this book.

ACTIVEX CONTROL PAD

After working your way through the chapters in this book, you should be fairly proficient in the use of VBScript. The difficult part is actually writing some useful VBScript programs! The ActiveX Control Pad is a free (at the time of this writing) program available from Microsoft which makes it easier to create Web pages which incorporate ActiveX controls. It is included on the CD-ROM for this book; please see the Introduction for more details.

Obtaining the ActiveX Control Pad

The ActiveX Control Pad can also be obtained with the HTML Layout Control (discussed in Session 2, "HTML Layout Control") from the Microsoft Web site at the following URL:

`http://www.microsoft.com/workshop/author/cpad/`

Adding an ActiveX Control

The ActiveX Control Pad is essentially a text editor with the ability to insert and manipulate ActiveX controls and VBScript subroutines. When you start the ActiveX Control Pad, a simple HTML file is displayed. This HTML file contains all the required tags (such as HTML, HEAD, BODY, and so on). You can open several different HTML files at once. To begin editing a new HTML file, select New HTML from the File menu. (Selecting New HTML Layout from the File menu will create an HTML Layout. HTML Layouts will be discussed in Session 2). Figure 14-1 shows the ActiveX Control Pad with a new HTML file open.

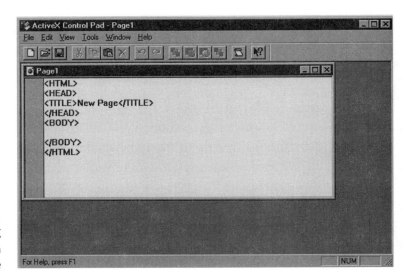

Figure 14-1
The ActiveX
Control Pad with a
new HTML file

To add content to your Web pages, type your HTML tags into the ActiveX Control Pad windows as you normally would. When you need to insert an ActiveX control in your HTML page, select Insert ActiveX Control from the Edit menu. The ActiveX Control Pad will bring up a list of the ActiveX controls installed on your system (as seen in Figure 14-2). Select an ActiveX control from this list, and the ActiveX Control Pad will add the necessary HTML code for the ActiveX control to your document.

Display and Properties Windows

After adding an ActiveX control to your document, the ActiveX Control Pad will automatically open a display window and a properties window for the control that you selected. Figure 14-3 shows the display window for the ActiveMovie control and Figure 14-4 shows the properties window for this control. The display window and the properties window will be different depending on which ActiveX control you have added. You will also notice that a small cube icon has been added to the left margin of your document window. This icon, shown in Figure 14-5, represents the newly added ActiveX control. You can click on this cube icon at any time to bring up the display window and properties window for a particular ActiveX control.

The display window shows you what the ActiveX control will look like when displayed on your HTML page. Using the display window, you can change the basic display properties of the ActiveX control such as width and height. To change the width or height of the control, click on one of the white squares along the border of the control and drag the control to the size that you want. The ActiveX Control Pad will automatically update the width and height values in the HTML code itself.

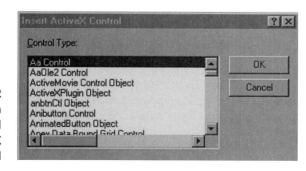

Figure 14-2
Choosing an
ActiveX control
from the ActiveX
Control Pad

Figure 14-3
The display window
for the ActiveMovie
control

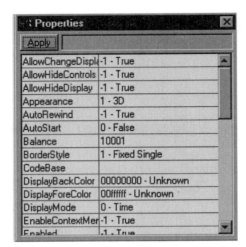

Figure 14-4
The properties
window for the
ActiveMovie
control

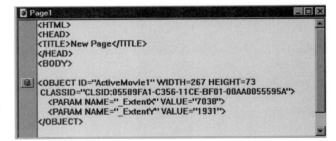

Figure 14-5
The icon in the left
margin represents
an ActiveX control

The properties window shows you the various properties and their values for a specific ActiveX control. You can edit these properties by double-clicking on the property you want to change and typing the new value. This is similar to editing control properties in Visual Basic, Delphi, and other popular programming environments. Once again, any changes you make in the properties window will be reflected in the actual HTML code for the ActiveX control you have selected. In addition, any changes you make in the properties window will be reflected in the display window so you can see how your changes affect the display of the control.

Adding Scripts

If all the ActiveX Control Pad allowed you to do is easily add ActiveX controls to your Web pages, it would still be pretty cool, but the ActiveX Control Pad also makes it easy to add scripting (both VBScript and JavaScript) to your HTML.

To insert a script, select Script Wizard from the Tools menu or click on the scroll icon at the top of the ActiveX Control Pad window. This will bring up the Script Wizard window as shown in Figure 14-6. In similar fashion to adding ActiveX controls, adding a script places a script icon in the left margin of the document window. Clicking on this script icon brings up the Script Wizard for that particular script.

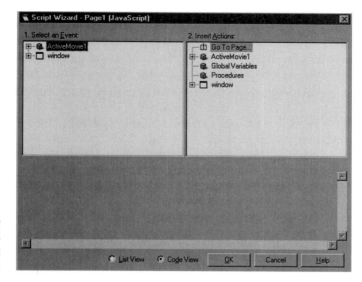

Figure 14-6
The ActiveX
Control Pad Script
Wizard

The Script Wizard window is divided into three panes: The top-left pane (the *event* pane) displays events to which you can add a script, the top-right pane (the *action* pane) displays actions which can be placed in the script, and the bottom pane (the *script* pane) displays the actual script code or script actions (depending on whether List View or Code View is selected at the bottom of the Script Wizard window).

To add a script, begin by selecting an event from the top-left pane. For each ActiveX object that you add to your document, events will be available in the event pane. Even if you have not added any ActiveX controls to your document, the Window object will have two events available by default: onLoad and onUnload. Let's use the onLoad event to automatically display a different Web page. This might be helpful if your Web site has moved and you want anyone who goes to the old site URL to automatically be taken to the new site URL.

Changing the Script Options

You can use the script options to change the way in which the script code is displayed within the Script Wizard. Select Script from the Options submenu of the Tools menu to change the script options.

First, click on the small plus sign next to the **Window** object in the event pane. This will display the various events available for the **Window** object (in this case, just onLoad and onUnload). Clicking on the onLoad event and the script pane (at the bottom of the Script Wizard window) should change and display "<SCRIPT FOR=Window EVENT=onLoad()>." Next, double-click on the Go To Page... action in the action pane. This will add the appropriate script code to go to a specified Web page. The following script code should be displayed at the bottom of the Script Wizard window in the script pane:

```
Window.location.href = ""
```

This code will go to a specified Web page. You need to specify the Web page to which you want to go by typing the complete URL inside the quotation marks as follows:

```
Window.location.href = "http://www.newsite.com/"
```

That's it! You have completed adding a simple script to your Web page which will automatically open a different Web page when the original page is opened. Figure 14-7 shows the Script Wizard window after the above actions have been completed.

The Script Wizard is a powerful tool for adding scripting to your Web pages. This session has just scratched the surface of what you can do with the Script Wizard, but hopefully you have a basic understanding of how to add ActiveX controls and scripting capabilities to your Web pages using the ActiveX Control Pad. The next session will look at a specific ActiveX control which is tightly integrated with the ActiveX Control Pad: the HTML Layout control.

Summary

Use the ActiveX Control Pad to create HTML documents which contain ActiveX controls. To insert an ActiveX control into your document, select Insert ActiveX Control from the Edit menu in the ActiveX Control Pad. Clicking on the cube icon in the left margin of a document brings up the display window and properties window for a particular control. Use the display window of a control to change basic display properties (such as height and width) and to see how the control will look at runtime. The properties window of a control allows you to change any of the control's available properties. Finally, use the Script Wizard to attach VBScript or JavaScript code to specific events.

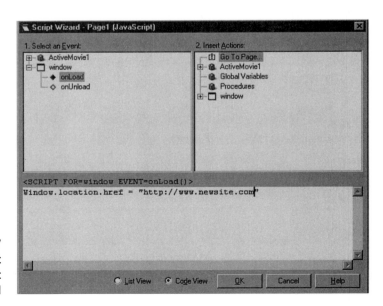

Figure 14-7
Adding a script with the Script Wizard

1. Which of the following best describes the ActiveX Control Pad?
   a. A simple HTML editor with the ability to insert ActiveX controls
   b. A complete, WYSIWYG HTML editor
   c. An ActiveX control editor without any HTML editing capabilities
   d. None of the above

2. What happens when you click on the cube icon in the left margin of the ActiveX Control Pad?
   a. The ActiveX control is removed from your Web page.
   b. The properties window for the ActiveX control is shown.
   c. The display window for the ActiveX control is shown.
   d. Both b. and c.

3. What is the purpose of the display window?
   a. To generally show how the ActiveX control will be displayed
   b. To allow you to change basic display properties such as width and height
   c. Both a. and b.
   d. None of the above

4. Which of the following occur when you make changes to the property window?
   a. The display window is updated.
   b. The actual HTML code for the ActiveX control is updated.
   c. The values in the property window are updated.
   d. All of the above.

5. The Script Wizard window is divided into which of the following:
   a. The script pane, the ActiveX pane, and the Java pane
   b. The JavaScript pane, the VBScript pane, and the ActiveX pane
   c. The property pane, the method pane, and the event pane
   d. The event pane, the action pane, and the script pane

Difficulty: Easy

1. Create a Web page with a several ActiveX controls. Adjust the various properties for the various controls and look at the revised page to see how each control is affected.

HTML LAYOUT

The HTML Layout control is an ActiveX control which gives you the ability to speci-fy a precise layout for ActiveX controls on your Web page. The HTML Layout control is tightly integrated with the ActiveX Control Pad which was discussed in the previ-ous session. We will be using the ActiveX Control Pad in this session to create HTML Layouts and to add these layouts to our HTML documents.

Creating an HTML Layout

To create an HTML Layout, select New HTML Layout from the File menu of the ActiveX Control Pad. This will display a blank HTML Layout form and a toolbox of form con-trols similar to those shown in Figure 14-8.

Adding Controls to an HTML Layout

Now that we have a blank HTML Layout, let's add some controls. To add controls to an HTML Layout, select a control from the control toolbox then click inside the lay-out form at the location you would like the control displayed. This will place the chosen control on the HTML Layout with standard size dimensions. You can hold down the button and drag the mouse when placing a control to add a control with custom size dimensions. You can also move and resize a control after you have placed it on an HTML

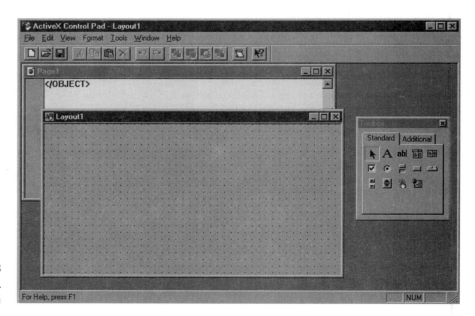

Figure 14-8
A blank HTML
Layout form

Layout form by selecting the standard mouse cursor in the control toolbox and clicking and dragging on the control or on the control borders. Figure 14-9 shows two Label controls: one that was added by simply clicking the mouse and one that was added by clicking and dragging to increase the size of the label.

Changing Properties of Individual Controls

You can set the properties for the individual controls on your HTML Layout by highlighting a control and selecting Properties from the View menu or by right-clicking on a control and selecting Properties from the pop-up menu. These properties can be adjusted in the same way as the properties for individual ActiveX controls by double-clicking on a specific property and typing a new value. Figure 14-10 shows the properties window for the Label controls. Notice that the BorderStyle has been changed from the default value of zero to display a border around the labels of Figure 14-9.

When you have finished setting up an HTML Layout control, you will be prompted to save the layout in a file with an ".ALX" extension. These .ALX files contain all the information needed to recreate the complete HTML Layout that you created. To actually display this HTML Layout on our Web page, we need to add the HTML Layout control to our document and specify the location of the appropriate .ALX file. Add the HTML Layout control selecting Insert HTML Layout from the Edit menu of the ActiveX Control Pad. Use the dialog box that appears (it will be similar to the dialog box in Figure 14-11) to specify the location of the .ALX file you want displayed.

Notice in Figure 14-12 that a single ActiveX control (the HTML Layout control) has been added to your HTML source file. If you want to modify the HTML Layout that you have inserted, just click the layout icon in the left margin next to the HTML Layout control in our document. This will bring up the HTML Layout editor for this particular layout.

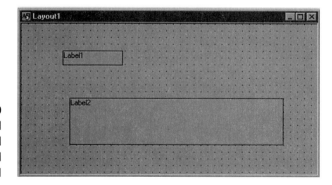

Figure 14-9
One standard-sized
Label control and
one custom-sized
Label control

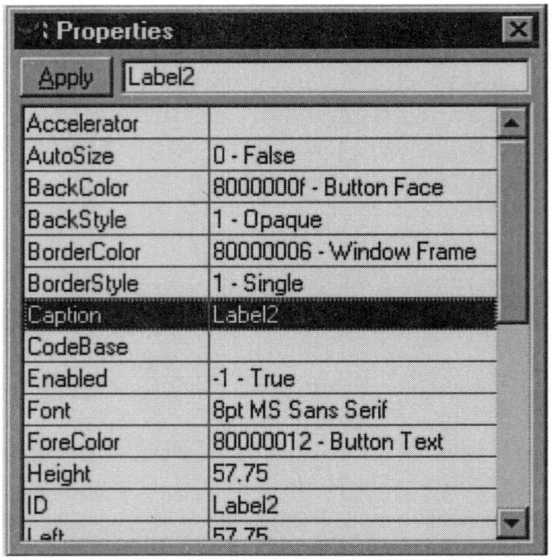

Figure 14-10
Properties of the
Label controls

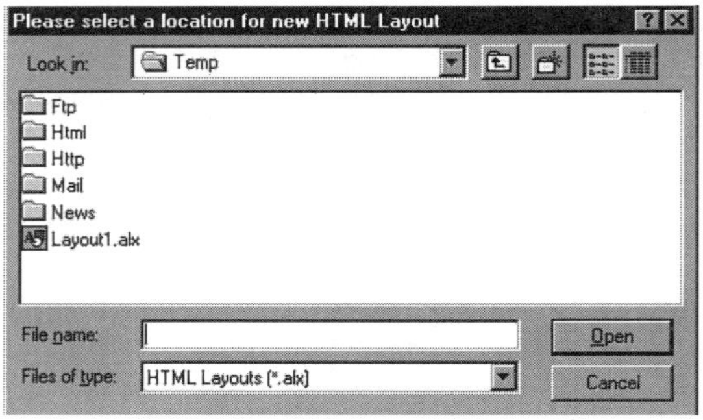

Figure 14-11
Adding the HTML
Layout control to
your document

Figure 14-12
A document with
an HTML Layout
control

When using HTML Layouts on your Web pages, remember that because an HTML Layout requires that a specific .ALX file be downloaded in addition to the standard HTML document, it may take longer for the user to view your Web pages. In fact, version 3.0 of Internet Explorer does not cache the .ALX files, so they must be reloaded each time the Web page containing an HTML Layout is displayed.

Referencing Controls within an HTML Layout

In order to change the properties of various controls that you have placed within an HTML Layout, you will need to reference those controls within the layout. To reference controls within an HTML Layout, use the following syntax:

```
layoutname.controlname.property
```

where **layoutname** is the name of your HTML Layout, **controlname** is the name of the control within the layout (also specified by the ID property), and **property** is the specific property you want to reference. For example, the code in Listing 14-1 changes the text property of a textbox control within an HTML Layout. The results are shown in Figure 14-13.

Listing 14-1 Referencing a control within an HTML Layout

```
<HTML>
<HEAD>
<TITLE>HTML Layout Test</TITLE>
</HEAD>
<BODY>

<INPUT TYPE="Button" NAME="cmdShow" VALUE="Show Text">

<SCRIPT LANGUAGE="VBScript">
sub cmdShow_OnClick
     Layout1_alx.txtDisplay.Text = "Hello"
end sub
</SCRIPT>

<OBJECT CLASSID="CLSID:812AE312-8B8E-11CF-93C8-00AA00C08FDF"
ID="Layout1_alx" STYLE="LEFT:0;TOP:0">
<PARAM NAME="ALXPATH" REF VALUE="file:C:\My Documents\VBScript\CHAP14\Layout1.alx">
 </OBJECT>

</BODY>
</HTML>
```

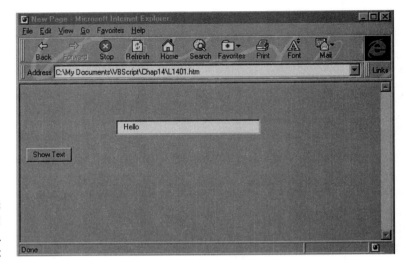

Figure 14-13
A textbox control
within an HTML
Layout

Summary

Use the ActiveX Control Pad to create HTML Layouts and to include these layouts in a Web page. To insert an HTML Layout into your document, select Insert HTML Layout from the Edit menu in the ActiveX Control Pad. Clicking on the layout icon in the left margin of a document in the ActiveX Control Pad will bring up the HTML Layout editor for that particular layout.

To add controls to an HTML Layout, select the controls from the control toolbox and click in the layout form at the location you want the control displayed. HTML Layouts are saved in files with an ".ALX" extension. These .ALX files contain all the information necessary to recreate the HTML Layout exactly.

1. Which of the following is a feature of the HTML Layout control?
   a. You do not need to add an ActiveX object to your page to display an HTML Layout.
   b. HTML Layouts decrease the load time of your Web pages.
   c. You can specify the exact placement and size of controls within the HTML Layout.
   d. None of the above.

2. Which of the following is an advantage of clicking and dragging the mouse when placing a control on an HTML Layout (rather than simply clicking)?
   a. You can specify the placement of the control.
   b. You can specify the size of the control.
   c. You can specify any of the control properties.
   d. None of the above.

3. The contents of an HTML Layout are saved in which of the following?
   a. A separate .ALX file
   b. The HTML source itself
   c. A separate .GIF image file
   d. Both a. and c.

4. To display an HTML Layout within your Web page, which of the following must you do?
   a. Create an HTML Layout.
   b. Save the Layout as an .ALX file.
   c. Add an HTML Layout ActiveX control to your document.
   d. All of the above.

5. Which of the following is the correct way to reference controls within an HTML Layout?
   a. `layoutname.controlname.property`
   b. `layoutname.controls("controlname").property`
   c. `layouts("layoutname").controlname.property`
   d. none of the above

Difficulty: Easy

1. **Create an HTML Layout with various controls on a form and display this layout on a Web page.**

Difficulty: Intermediate

2. **Create an HTML Layout which responds to the user clicking on a command button by displaying text within a text control.**

STYLE SHEETS

The HTML format has many advantages such as readability and portability, but its major weakness is that the same Web page displayed on one browser may look quite different on another browser. To help alleviate this problem, Microsoft has implemented styles and cascading style sheets in Internet Explorer version 3.0. This session will introduce you to styles and explain how they can be used to precisely format sections of your documents.

In-Line Style Information

The easiest way to quickly insert style information is in-line, meaning that the style information is intermingled with the actual document text. There are two ways to insert in-line style information: using the STYLE parameter of the standard paragraph tag (`<P>`) or using the new SPAN tag.

To set a style for a paragraph, add the STYLE parameter to the paragraph tag. Table 14-1 lists the various options that are available for text formatting by using styles. If you want to set more than one style, separate the styles with semicolons. Listing 14-1 demonstrates setting the style within the paragraph tag and setting multiple styles separated by semicolons. The resulting Web page is shown in Figure 14-14.

Listing 14-2 Using in-line styles

```
<HTML>
<HEAD><TITLE>Styles</TITLE></HEAD>
<BODY>
<P>This is the first paragraph.</P>
<P STYLE=font:bold;background:#FFFF00>This is the second paragraph, and it is bold
with a yellow background.</P>
</BODY>
</HTML>
```

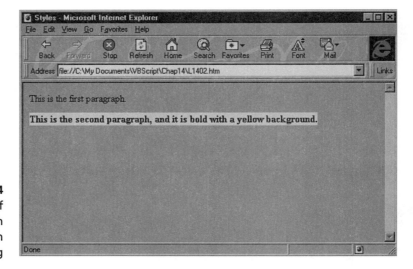

Figure 14-14
A demonstration of in-line styles with the paragraph (`<P>`) tag

Style	Description	Example
font: [bold] [italic] [[font size][/font leading]] [list of font names]	Sets font properties	font:12pt Arial font:bold 10pt/12pt "Times,Helv,.Arial"
font-family: [list of font names]	Sets font type	font-family:Courier New font-family: "Arial,Sans Serif"
font-size: size	Sets font size	font-size:10pt font-size:3cm
font-weight: bold or normal	Sets the font weight (currently normal or bold)	font-weight:bold
font-style: italic	Sets text styles (currently only italic)	font-style:italic
text-decoration: none, underline, italic, or line-through	Sets text decoration	text-decoration:none
line-height: [measurement]	Sets leading (height of each line of text)	line-height:20pt
background: #rrggbb, color name, or URL ([address of image])	Places a color or image behind text	background:#ffffff background:white background:URL (http://www.somesite. com/images/marble .gif)

Table 14-1 *Styles for text formatting*

You can also set an in-line style by using the new **SPAN** tag. Setting a style with the **SPAN** tag is almost identical to setting a style with the paragraph tag. Listing 14-3 shows how the **SPAN** tag can be used to set in-line styles. Figure 14-15 displays the results.

Listing 14-3 Setting in-line styles with the new SPAN tag

```
<HTML>
<HEAD><TITLE>Styles</TITLE></HEAD>
<BODY>
<P>This is the first paragraph.</P>
<P>Use the SPAN tag to <SPAN STYLE=background:#FFFF00>highlight</SPAN> words or⇐
phrases.</P>
</BODY>
</HTML>
```

Style Tips

When using the line-height style, be aware that the extra spacing is currently added before lines, not after. This may be changed later to match the standards set by desktop publishing applications.

Use the background style to "highlight" portions of text. Here is an example: You can use styles to `<SPAN STYLE=background:#FFFF00>` highlight `</SPAN>` some text in your document.

Using the Layout Options

In addition to using styles to format your text, you can also use styles to specify certain layout information for your document. Margins, indentation, and alignment can each be specified using styles. Table 14-2 lists the styles that deal with document layout. As with the formatting options above, all measurements can be set in inches, centimeters, or pixels.

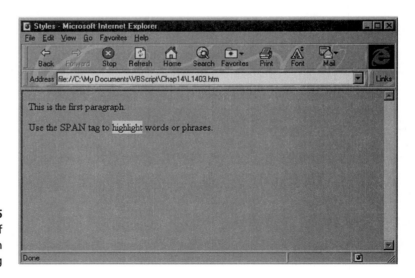

Figure 14-15
A demonstration of in-line styles with the SPAN tag

Style	Description	Example
margin-left: [measurement]	Sets the left margin	margin-left:1.2in
margin-right: [measurement]	Sets the right margin	margin-right:.7cm
text-indent: [measurement]	Sets the paragraph indentation	text-indent:0.35in
text-align: left, right, or center	Sets text alignment	text-align:center

Table 14-2 *Styles for text layout*

Designating Style Information for the Entire Page

Although in-line styles are convenient, they have a major disadvantage: If you want to reformat certain text throughout your document, you must change every occurrence of in-line styles within the document. Wouldn't it be nice if you could specify, say, all level one headings (**<H1>**) as 14 point Arial font? It turns out that you can do just that by placing style sheet information at the beginning of your document.

The **STYLE** tag is used to specify a style sheet for your document. It should appear before the **BODY** tag within your HTML. A style sheet indicates specific formatting for the general HTML tags. You can specify formatting and layout for paragraphs, headings, body text, and so on. Listing 14-4 demonstrates a style sheet for an entire document. The results are shown in Figure 14-16.

Listing 14-4 A style sheet within a single document

```
<HTML>
<STYLE>
BODY {background: URL(http://www.mysite.com/images/marble.jpg); color: blue}
H1 {font: italic 14pt/18pt Arial }
P {font: 12pt Arial; text-indent: 1.0in}
A {text-decoration: italic; color: red}
</STYLE>
<BODY>
<H1>Level one headlines are in 14-point Arial italics.</H1>
<P>Here is some paragraph text and a <A HREF="http://www.wgp.com"> link</A> that is
italicized because we set text-decoration for links to "italic."</P>
</BODY>
</HTML>
```

Notice that you first specify the general HTML tag which you want to format (H1, for example), then you specify the specific style attributes within curly braces ({}). Even if you specify a style sheet in this way, you can override these styles in specific sections of your document using in-line styles as mentioned above.

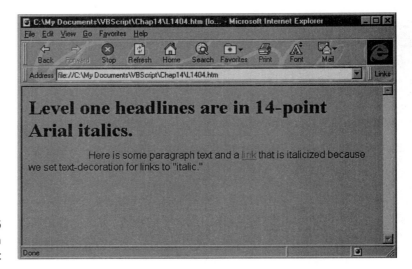

Figure 14-16
A style sheet for an
entire document

External Style Sheets

We have now seen how to specify in-line styles for specific areas of a document and how to specify styles for an entire document, but there is one very powerful aspect of style sheets that we have not yet covered: external style sheets.

An external style sheet is simply a text file containing the style formatting as it appears for style sheets within a document (minus the **<STYLE>** and **</STYLE>** tags). The advantage of an external style sheet is that you can use styles in more than one document, and change the styles throughout your site simply by changing the external style sheet. Listing 14-5 is the complete contents of a sample external style sheet file. These external style sheets are normally saved with a ".css" extension, which stands for Cascading Style Sheet.

Listing 14-5 An external style sheet file (sample.css)

```
BODY {background: white; color: black}
H2 {font: 14pt Arial bold}
P {font: 10pt Arial; text-indent: 0.5in}
A {text-decoration: none}
```

Notice that an external style sheet does not contain any HTML formatting. There are no <HTML>, <HEAD>, or <BODY> sections in an external style sheet. As you can see, the general HTML tags are listed along with specific formatting styles for each (as we saw with the **STYLE** tag above). To make use of an external style sheet, you must place a **LINK** tag in the HEAD section of each HTML document for which you want the formatting and layout used. Listing 14-6 demonstrates this technique.

Listing 14-6 Using an external style sheet in your HTML documents

```
<HTML>
<HEAD>
<TITLE>Style Sheet Sample</TITLE>
<LINK REL=STYLE TYPE="text/css" SRC="sample.css">
</HEAD>
<BODY>
Body text is black on a white background.
<H2>This should be 14-point Arial bold.</H2>
<P>Paragraph fonts are 10-point Arial, and <A HREF="http://www.somesite.com">links⇐
</A> are not underlined because we specified "none" as the text-decoration.
</BODY>
</HTML>
```

Summary

You can use style sheets to select specific colors, fonts, and text styles for various HTML formatting tags. To specify a style for a small section of text, you can use the **<SPAN>** tag. If you would like consistent formatting throughout your document, it is better to specify a style sheet in your document header with the **<STYLE>** tag. Finally, you can use external style sheets (using the **<LINK>** tag) to specify a consistent style sheet for multiple documents.

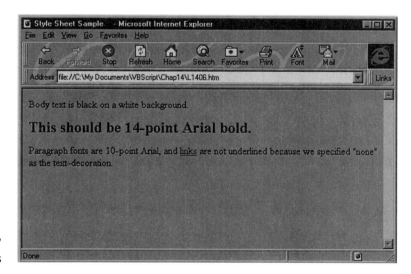

Figure 14-17
External file sheets

QUIZ 3

1. Which of the following is an advantage of in-line styles?
   a. They are easy to change throughout a document.
   b. They are easy to change in multiple documents.
   c. Both a. and b.
   d. None of the above.

2. Which tag can be used to specify in-line styles?
   a. P
   b. SPAN
   c. Both a. and b.
   d. None of the above

3. Which of the following is an advantage of styles placed at the top of your HTML document?
   a. They provide the quickest way to insert style information.
   b. They are easy to change throughout a document.
   c. They are easy to change in multiple documents.
   d. None of the above.

4. Which of the following tags is used to specify styles at the top of an HTML document?
   a. HEAD
   b. STYLE
   c. BODY
   d. LINK

5. Which of the following tags is used to specify an external style sheet for a document?
   a. HEAD
   b. STYLE
   c. BODY
   d. LINK

EXERCISE 3

Difficulty: Easy

1. Use both the paragraph (<P>) and <SPAN> tags to insert styles throughout an HTML document.

Difficulty: Intermediate

2. Create an external style sheet for two HTML documents. Change the style sheet styles and reload the Web pages to see that the changes are implemented in both.

ADVANCED ACTIVEX CONTROL USAGE

In previous chapters, you have been introduced to a variety of ActiveX controls which you can use to enhance the look and interactivity of your Web pages. This session takes a look at some of the more advanced aspects of ActiveX controls and their usage.

Using Control Properties and Methods at Runtime

There are times when you may want to use the properties and methods of various controls *after* the Web page on which they reside has completed loading. An example of this is adding items to an ActiveX button-menu control.

To add items to an ActiveX button-menu control, we must use the **AddItem** method. Unfortunately, if the button-menu control does not exist when we attempt to add items to it, an error will occur. To be safe, we will use a timer function in our VBScript code to test for the existence of the appropriate **button-menu** object. We do this with the IsObject function. The IsObject function will return true if the specified object exists and false if it does not. Once we are sure the object exists, we can disable the timer control (to avoid adding the items to the menu twice) and proceed to add the items safely. Listing 14-7 contains the code to add menu items to a button-menu control using the above technique.

Listing 14-7 Checking for the existence of an object before setting its properties

```
<HTML>
<HEAD>
<TITLE>Button-Menu Test</TITLE>
</HEAD>
<BODY>

<OBJECT ID="mnuFile" WIDTH=93 HEIGHT=27
  CLASSID="CLSID:52DFAE60-CEBF-11CF-A3A9-00A0C9034920">
    <PARAM NAME="_ExtentX" VALUE="2461">
    <PARAM NAME="_ExtentY" VALUE="714">
    <PARAM NAME="Caption" VALUE="&amp;File">
</OBJECT>
```

continued on next page

continued from previous page

```
<OBJECT ID="mnuEdit" WIDTH=127 HEIGHT=27
 CLASSID="CLSID:52DFAE60-CEBF-11CF-A3A9-00A0C9034920">
     <PARAM NAME="_ExtentX" VALUE="3334">
     <PARAM NAME="_ExtentY" VALUE="714">
     <PARAM NAME="Caption" VALUE="&amp;Edit">
</OBJECT>

<OBJECT ID="Timer1" WIDTH=39 HEIGHT=39
 CLASSID="CLSID:59CCB4A0-727D-11CF-AC36-00AA00A47DD2">
     <PARAM NAME="_ExtentX" VALUE="1005">
     <PARAM NAME="_ExtentY" VALUE="1005">
     <PARAM NAME="Interval" VALUE="100">
</OBJECT>

<SCRIPT LANGUAGE="VBScript">
sub Timer1_Timer
     if IsObject(mnuEdit) then
       Timer1.Enabled="0"
       mnuFile.AddItem "New", 1
       mnuFile.AddItem "Open", 2
       mnuFile.AddItem "Save", 3
       mnuFile.AddItem "Save As...", 4

       mnuEdit.AddItem "Cut", 1
       mnuEdit.AddItem "Copy", 2
       mnuEdit.AddItem "Paste", 3
       mnuEdit.AddItem "Delete", 4
     end if
end sub
</SCRIPT>
</BODY>
</HTML>
```

PreLoader Control

Have you noticed that during a session of using the World Wide Web, you will often visit a page with a large number of graphic images that may take a while to load the first time you view the page but show up almost instantaneously when you subsequently view the same page? On a similar note, if the same graphic image is used on multiple pages, it will show up almost instantaneously after the first time it is loaded. What causes this behavior?

Many popular World Wide Web browsers (including Microsoft's Internet Explorer) implement a *cache*. A cache is a storage area on your local computer (generally on your hard drive) where recently viewed Web pages and elements of Web pages (images, music, video, and so on) are stored so they can be retrieved quickly if they are needed again. This makes a lot of sense when you think about it, because you will often look at the same Web page many times due to using the back and forward buttons of your browser.

In effect, the PreLoader control allows you to selectively place in the cache the elements you will use on your Web pages so they can be retrieved instantly. For example, if your initial Web site screen has a good amount of text that may take the typical person viewing your site 30 seconds or so to read, why not take advantage of this time to "preload" images, music, and video that will be used on subsequent pages. This will make your Web pages appear faster, which will certainly make the person viewing the page happier.

To use the PreLoader control, simply set the URL property of the PreLoader control to the URL of the element you want to place in the cache and set the **Enable** property to 1. This will begin downloading the specified URL to the cache. When the process is finished, the Complete event will be generated for the PreLoader control, and the Error event will be generated if an error occurs during the download. Additionally, you can check the status of three read-only properties of the PreLoader control: CacheFile is the name of the local file after it is downloaded, Bytes returns the number of bytes that have been downloaded to the cache thus far, and Percentage returns the percentage amount of bytes for the current element that have been downloaded to the cache thus far. Table 14-3 summarizes these properties and events of the PreLoader control. Listing 14-8 demonstrates using the PreLoader control to load an image and subsequently view it.

Name	Property or event	Description
URL	property	URL of the file to load
Enable	property	Enables or disables the PreLoader control
CacheFile	property	Filename of cached copy
Bytes	property	Current number of bytes loaded
Percentage	property	Percentage of total bytes loaded
Complete	event	Fires when loading is complete
Error	event	Fires if an error occurs during loading

Table 14-3 *Properties and events of the PreLoader control*

Listing 14-8 Using the PreLoader control to retrieve a JPEG image

```
<HTML>
<HEAD>
<TITLE>Preloader Test</TITLE>
</HEAD>
<BODY>

URL: <INPUT TYPE="Text" NAME="txtURL" VALUE="" SIZE=90>
<P>
<INPUT TYPE="Button" NAME="cmdLoad" VALUE="Load">

<OBJECT ID="PreLoader1" WIDTH=0 HEIGHT=0
 CLASSID="CLSID:16E349E0-702C-11CF-A3A9-00A0C9034920">
    <PARAM NAME="_ExtentX" VALUE="0">
    <PARAM NAME="_ExtentY" VALUE="0">
    <PARAM NAME="enable" VALUE="0">
</OBJECT>

<OBJECT ID="Timer1" WIDTH=39 HEIGHT=39
 CLASSID="CLSID:59CCB4A0-727D-11CF-AC36-00AA00A47DD2">
    <PARAM NAME="_ExtentX" VALUE="1005">
    <PARAM NAME="_ExtentY" VALUE="1005">
    <PARAM NAME="Interval" VALUE="100">
</OBJECT>

<SCRIPT LANGUAGE="VBScript">
sub cmdLoad_OnClick
    PreLoader1.URL = txtURL.Value
    PreLoader1.Enable="1"
    Timer1.Enabled="1"
end sub
sub PreLoader1_Complete
    PreLoader1.Enable="0"
    alert ("Image has completed loading.")
    Timer1.Enabled="0"

    document.open
    document.write "<IMG SRC='" & txtURL.Value & "'>"
    document.close
end sub
sub PreLoader1_Error
    alert("An error has occurred.")
    Timer1.Enabled="0"
    status = "Preloader Error!"
end sub
sub Timer1_Timer
    status = "Bytes: " & PreLoader1.Bytes & "  Percentage: " & PreLoader1.⇐
Percentage & "%"
end sub
</SCRIPT>
</BODY>
</HTML>
```

Listing 14-8 begins by setting up a textbox and a command button on the Web page. The user is expected to type the URL of an image in the textbox and click on the Load button. Clicking on the Load button causes the code in the cmdLoad_OnClick subroutine to be executed. This code sets the URL value of the PreLoader control, enables the PreLoader control, and enables the Timer control. The Timer control displays the current status of the load in the status bar (bytes and percentage). The code for the Timer control is located in the Timer1_Timer subroutine. Finally, when the load has finished, the PreLoader1_Complete event subroutine is executed. This code brings up an alert box to inform you that the download has finished and then displays the image by replacing the current HTML document with an **IMG** tag that references the image we have just preloaded. You should see that the image is displayed instantaneously.

Summary

You can use control properties and methods at runtime by placing the appropriate code in a timer procedure and checking for the existence of the object before setting its properties or calling its methods. This ensures that you do not cause an error by attempting to use the properties and methods of an object that does not yet exist.

The PreLoader control is a special ActiveX control that allows you to load specific files into the cache to be displayed instantaneously at a later time. You can use this method to load large graphics, sounds, and videos while displaying other information to the user. This will decrease the perceived loading time of your site for the user.

1. Which of the following is a reason to use a timer function to set object properties?
   a. To set an object's properties before the page loads
   b. To ensure the existence of an object before setting its properties
   c. Both a. and b.
   d. None of the above

2. Which of the following functions checks for the existence of an object in VBScript?
   a. Exists
   b. IsObject
   c. ObjectExists
   d. None of the above

3. When we add items to a menu control from the timer function, why do we immediately disable the timer function after we add the items?
   a. To ensure that the object exists
   b. To ensure that the object does not exist
   c. To ensure that we do not add the menu items more than once
   d. None of the above

4. What is the function of the URL property of the PreLoader control?
   a. To set the file to load
   b. To set the filename within the local cache
   c. To retrieve the current number of bytes that have been loaded
   d. None of the above

5. Which property of the PreLoader control can be used to inform the user about how much of a particular file has been loaded?
   a. Bytes
   b. Percentage
   c. Both a. and b.
   d. None of the above

Difficulty: Intermediate

1. Use the PreLoader control to load a graphic image to the local cache, then display it when it has completed loading.

Difficulty: Intermediate

2. Use a timer function to add items to a menu from VBScript. Be sure to check for the menu object's existence with IsObject before adding items to the menu.

INTRODUCTION TO JAVA

When it comes to programming for the World Wide Web, no other technology has generated as much interest and excitement as the Java programming language developed by Sun Microsystems. Fortunately, VBScript can serve as an excellent complement to Java. In fact, you can use VBScript to control the various properties of Java applets on your Web pages.

Simple Java

It is beyond the scope of this book to try and teach the Java language to you. There are many volumes of books devoted to the subject. What we will do is show you a simple Java program and explain its major parts.

The Java programming language has its roots in C++, so if you have seen any C++ code you will recognize the similarities to Java. To produce Java code, you will need a Java compiler for your system. There are a variety of Java compilers available including those from Symantec, Microsoft, and Sun Microsystems (the inventors of the Java language). The code in this book was produced with the Symantec Café development environment.

Obtaining a Free Java Compiler

Sun Microsystems has free Java compilers available for Windows, Macintosh, and Unix systems at the following URL:

`http://java.sun.com`

Look for the Java Developer's Kit which contains several utilities relating to the Java programming language.

A Java compiler does not function in exactly the same way as a typical compiler on your system. Typically, a compiler will take programming code (source code) and convert it to native machine language instructions for your system. A Java compiler takes Java source code (typically a file that ends with a ".java" extension) and converts it to Java bytecodes which are symbolic Java instructions. These Java bytecodes will normally reside in a file which ends with a ".class" extension. So for example, you might create a simple Java program called "simple.java" with any text editor, then pass this source code through a Java compiler to create a "simple.class" file containing the resulting Java bytecodes.

To actually execute your Java code, you will need to use a Java interpreter. Alternatively, the newest versions of both Netscape Navigator and Microsoft Internet Explorer include the built-in ability to execute Java code. Although you can create free-standing applications in Java, its popularity to this point has been largely centered around creating smaller applications called *applets*. A Java applet is a small Java program that is created specifically to be embedded in an HTML document.

As mentioned above, either Netscape Navigator or Microsoft Internet Explorer can execute a Java applet. To instruct the browser program to execute a Java applet, you use the **APPLET** tag as shown in Listing 14-9.

Listing 14-9 The HTML to include a simple Java applet

```
<HTML>
<HEAD>
<TITLE> A simple program </TITLE>
</HEAD>
<BODY>

<APPLET CODE="simple.class" WIDTH=283 HEIGHT=190></APPLET>

</BODY>
</HTML>
```

In Listing 14-9 we specify the name of the Java code to execute using the **CODE** parameter of the **APPLET** tag. **WIDTH** and **HEIGHT** are two other parameters which we can use to specify the size of the applet display area in pixels. In the example above, we have designated the Java applet display to be 283 pixels wide and 190 pixels high.

Now that we know how to insert an applet in a Web document, let's look at an example Java applet. Listing 14-10 contains the code for a simple Java applet. This program simply displays the string "Hello, world!" in a textbox. We will use the previous HTML code (Listing 14-9) to display our simple applet. See the output in Figure 14-18.

Listing 14-10 A simple Java program

```java
import java.awt.*;
import java.applet.*;

public class simple extends Applet {

    public void init() {

        super.init();

        //{{INIT_CONTROLS
        setLayout(null);
        resize(283,103);
        label1=new Label("simple Applet", Label.CENTER);
        add(label1);
        label1.reshape(63,15,147,15);
        edit1=new TextField(26);
        add(edit1);
        edit1.reshape(28,52,217,23);
        edit1.setText("Hello, world!");
        //}}
    }

    public boolean handleEvent(Event event) {
        return super.handleEvent(event);
    }

    //{{DECLARE_CONTROLS
    Label label1;
    TextField edit1;
    //}}
}
```

The import keyword is used to indicate that we will be using Java functions from a specific library of functions. In the example of Listing 14-10, we indicated that functions from all libraries that are of type java.applet (applet functions) or java.awt (graphics and windowing functions) will be used. We indicated the use of all functions from these two general library classes by using an asterisk ("*") in place of an actual library name. Alternatively, you can specify an exact library name such as "java.awt.Graphics."

The next line after our import lines creates a new Java class called "simple" and indicates that it is extending the existing Java class of type Applet. This is the correct way to indicate that our Java code is indeed an applet rather than a full-blown application.

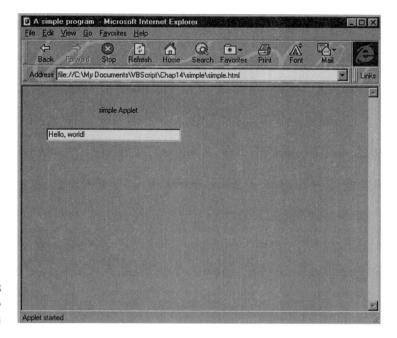

Figure 14-18
Displaying some
text using Java

Next, the init() function is defined. The init() function is called automatically by a Java applet when it begins execution. In this particular init() function, we simply resize the applet, add a label and a text field, and place the text "Hello, world!" in the text field.

The handleEvent function is used to respond to user events, but our particular program does no event handling, so this function is quite short. The call to super.handleEvent executes the handleEvent function of the parent class (which in this case is Applet).

Summary

Java is the new programming language created by Sun Microsystems as a cross-platform solution to executable content on the World Wide Web. You can use Java to create an entire application or to create a Java applet, which is a small Java program designed specifically to be embedded in a Web document. You will need a Java compiler to convert your Java source code (typically a file ending with the ".java" extension) into Java bytecodes (typically contained in a file ending with a ".class" extension).

To insert a Java applet into your Web document, use the **<APPLET>** tag and set **CODE** parameter equal to the name of the Java class file to execute.

QUIZ 5

1. Which of the following is the typical extension for a file containing Java source code?
   a. .source
   b. .class
   c. .java
   d. none of the above

2. What is the term used to represent small Java programs which are designed to be embedded in a Web document?
   a. weblets
   b. applets
   c. applications
   d. none of the above

3. Which of the following is the typical extension of a file containing Java byte-codes to execute?
   a. .exec
   b. .class
   c. .java
   d. none of the above

4. Which of the following Java statements is used to indicate that your Java program will use a specific library of Java functions?
   a. #INCLUDE
   b. include
   c. import
   d. none of the above

5. Which of the following snippets of Java code indicates that the program is an applet?
   a. extends Applet
   b. is Applet
   c. type=Applet
   d. none of the above

EXERCISE 5

Difficulty: Intermediate

1. Create a Java program to display "Hello, world!" within the Java drawing area as opposed to within a textbox. (Hint: Use the DrawText function).

Difficulty: Intermediate

2. Create a Java program which responds to user events such as clicking on a button contained in the Java applet.

SESSION 6

USING JAVA APPLETS WITH VBSCRIPT

The previous section introduced you to Java and explained how a Java applet could be embedded in a Web document. This session builds on that knowledge to explore ways that you can communicate between VBScript and Java applets.

Controlling Applets with VBScript

In order to use VBScript to control your Java applets, there must be a mechanism to pass information to the Java applets. This mechanism is the use of the **PARAM** tag. You can use the **PARAM** tag to pass a variety of information to a Java applet. The **PARAM** tag must appear between the **<APPLET>** and **</APPLET>** tags of the applet to which you want to pass information as shown in Listing 14-11.

Listing 14-11 Using the PARAM tag to pass information to a Java applet

```
<HTML>
<HEAD>
<TITLE> A simple program </TITLE>
</HEAD>
<BODY>

<APPLET CODE="vbstest.class" WIDTH=283 HEIGHT=190>
<PARAM NAME="X" VALUE="100">
<PARAM NAME="X" VALUE="50">
<PARAM NAME="USER" VALUE="Michael">
</APPLET>

</BODY>
</HTML>
```

Within the **PARAM** tag, **NAME="parametername"** specifies the name you will use to refer to this parameter within your applet, and **VALUE="parametervalue"** is the actual value of this parameter. You can then retrieve these values from your Java applet using the Java getParameter function. The general syntax of the getParameter function is as follows:

```
getParameter("parametername")
```

The *parametername* is the name you assigned using the **NAME="parametername"** property of the **PARAM** tag. The getParameter function returns a **String** object, so you might use code similar to the following within your Java applet:

```
String firstName = getParameter("FIRSTNAME");
```

Within your HTML file, you would need to set the value of the **FIRSTNAME** parameter as follows:

```
<APPLET CODE="somecode.class" WIDTH=200 HEIGHT=200>
<PARAM NAME="FIRSTNAME" VALUE="John">
</APPLET>
```

Listings 14-12 and 14-13 contain the code for a Java applet and an HTML file, respectively. The HTML code in Listing 14-13 sets the value of the **DISPLAYTEXT** parameter for the Java applet in Listing 14-12. The Java applet then retrieves this **DISPLAYTEXT** parameter with the getParameter function and displays it in a textbox. The results are shown in Figure 14-19.

Listing 14-12 Java code demonstrating the getParameter function

```java
import java.awt.*;
import java.applet.*;

public class vbstest extends Applet {

    public void init() {

        super.init();

        //{{INIT_CONTROLS
        setLayout(null);
        resize(283,133);
        label1=new Label("VBScript Test", Label.CENTER);
        add(label1);
        label1.reshape(63,15,147,15);
        button1=new Button("Click Me");
        add(button1);
        button1.reshape(91,90,91,30);
        edit1=new TextField(28);
        add(edit1);
        edit1.reshape(14,45,231,22);
        //}}
    }

    public boolean handleEvent(Event event) {
        if (event.id == Event.ACTION_EVENT && event.target == button1) {
                clickedButton1();
                return true;
        }

        return super.handleEvent(event);
    }
```

```
    //{{DECLARE_CONTROLS
    Label label1;
    Button button1;
    TextField edit1;
    //}}
    public void clickedButton1() {
        // to do: put event handler code here.
        String sDisplay = getParameter("DISPLAYTEXT");
        edit1.setText(sDisplay);
    }
}
```

Listing 14-13 HTML that sets the value of a Java applet parameter

```
<HTML>
<HEAD>
<TITLE> A simple program </TITLE>
</HEAD>
<BODY>

<APPLET CODE="vbstest.class" WIDTH=283 HEIGHT=190>
<PARAM NAME="DISPLAYTEXT" VALUE="Hello, world!">
</APPLET>

</BODY>
</HTML>
```

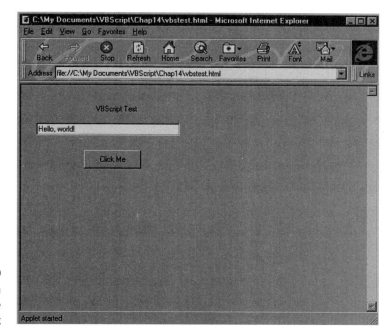

Figure 14-19
Displaying a
parameter value
in a textbox

Passing values from your HTML to a Java applet is a powerful technique, but it can be even more powerful if you use VBScript to construct the **PARAM** values. As we have seen in previous chapters, `document.write` can be used to generate HTML code on the fly. We will use this technique to display either "Good morning!", "Good afternoon!", or "Good evening!" depending on the time of day. Listing 14-14 is the HTML and VBScript code to set the parameters for our Java applet depending on the time of day. The output is shown in Figure 14-20.

Listing 14-14 Revised HTML with VBScript to display different messages

```
<HTML>
<HEAD>
<TITLE> A simple program </TITLE>
</HEAD>
<BODY>

<SCRIPT LANGUAGE="VBScript">
document.write "<APPLET CODE='vbstest.class' WIDTH=283 HEIGHT=190>"
if hour(now) < 12 then
      document.write "<PARAM NAME='DISPLAYTEXT' VALUE='Good morning!'>"
else if hour(now) < 18 then
      document.write "<PARAM NAME='DISPLAYTEXT' VALUE='Good afternoon!'>"
else
      document.write "<PARAM NAME='DISPLAYTEXT' VALUE='Good night!'>"
end if
document.write "</APPLET>"
</SCRIPT>

</BODY>
</HTML>
```

Summary

You can pass values from standard HTML to a Java applet using the **PARAM** tag. The **PARAM** tag must be located between the **<APPLET>** and **</APPLET>** tags for the Java applet to which you are passing values. Within each **PARAM** tag, use **NAME="parametername"** and **VALUE="parametervalue"** to set the name and value, respectively, of each parameter. Within your Java applet, use the getParameter function to retrieve the parameter values. Finally, you can use VBScript to modify the **PARAM** tags in order to achieve a variety of effects.

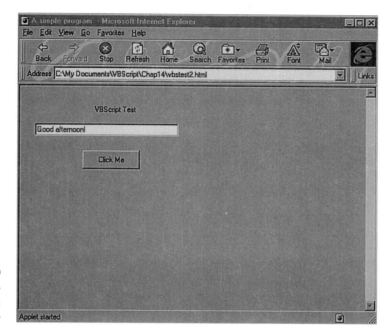

Figure 14-20
Displaying a greeting depending on the time of day

1. Which of the following tags is used to set parameters for a Java applet?
   a. **<VALUE>**
   b. **<PARAM>**
   c. **<APPLET>**
   d. None of the above

2. Which of the following Java functions is used to retrieve a parameter value?
   a. getParameter
   b. getValue
   c. getProperty
   d. none of the above

3. Which of the following parameters of the **PARAM** tag is used to specify the name that will be used within the Java applet to retrieve the parameter value?
   a. **NAME="parametername"**
   b. **CODE="parametername"**
   c. **VALUE="parametername"**
   d. None of the above

4. Which of the following parameters of the **PARAM** tag is used to specify the actual value that will be passed to a Java applet?
   a. `NAME="parametervalue"`
   b. `CODE="parametervalue"`
   c. `VALUE="parametervalue"`
   d. None of the above

5. Where must the **PARAM** tags be located within your HTML source file to pass information to a Java applet?
   a. Between the `<PARAM>` and `</PARAM>` tags
   b. Between the `<APPLET>` and `</APPLET>` tags
   c. After the `</APPLET>` tag
   d. None of the above

Difficulty: Intermediate

1. Create a Java applet to which you pass a first and last name using parameters. Display the first and last names within textboxes in your Java applet.

Difficulty: Advanced

2. Modify the previous lab so that the user can specify a first and last name within VBScript textboxes. Then pass these values to a Java applet for display.

CHAPTER SUMMARY

Although it was designed with simplicity in mind, VBScript can be used to achieve a variety of advanced effects. The ActiveX Control Pad and the HTML Layout Control are two of the tools that are currently available to help you develop advanced VBScript applications, but many more are on the way. You can mix VBScript programming with style sheets to create advanced style effects within your Web documents and with Java applets to create cross-platform solutions.

APPENDIX A

FUNCTIONS

This appendix provides a quick reference to each Visual Basic Script function. It provides the function name, a short description, syntax, and an argument overview.

ABS

Description

Returns the absolute value of a number.

Syntax

`ABS(number)`

The **number** argument can be any valid numeric expression.

Asc

Description

Returns the ANSI character code corresponding to the first letter of a string.

Syntax

`Asc(string)`

The `string` argument is any valid string expression—the string must contain characters.

Atn

Description

Returns the arc tangent of a number.

Syntax

`Atn(number)`

The `number` argument can be any valid numeric expression.

CBool

Description

Returns an expression that has been converted to a variant of subtype **Boolean** (1 or 0).

Syntax

`CBool(expression)`

The `expression` argument is any valid expression.

CByte

Description

Returns an expression that has been converted to a variant of subtype **Byte**.

Syntax

`CByte(expression)`

The `expression` argument is any valid expression.

CDate

Description

Returns an expression that has been converted to a variant of subtype **Date**.

Syntax

CDate(date)

The **date** argument is any valid date expression.

Comments

The IsDate function should be used first to ensure that the expression can be converted to a date.

CDbl

Description

Returns an expression that has been converted to a variant of subtype **Double**.

Syntax

CDbl(expression)

The **expression** argument is any valid expression.

Chr

Description

Returns the character associated with the specified ANSI character code.

Syntax

Chr(charcode)

The **charcode** argument is a number that identifies a character.

Comments

For example Chr(65) would return **A**.

CInt

Description

Returns an expression that has been converted to a variant of subtype `Integer`.

Syntax

`CInt(expression)`

The `expression` argument is any valid expression.

CLng

Description

Returns an expression that has been converted to a variant of subtype `Long`.

Syntax

`CLng(expression)`

The `expression` argument is any valid expression.

Cos

Description

Returns the cosine of an angle.

Syntax

`Cos(number)`

The `number` argument can be any valid numeric expression that expresses an angle in radians.

CSng

Description

Returns an expression that has been converted to a variant of subtype `Single`.

Syntax

`CSng(expression)`

The **expression** argument is any valid expression.

CStr

Description

Returns an expression that has been converted to a variant of subtype **String**.

Syntax

`CStr(expression)`

The **expression** argument is any valid expression.

Comments

The data in **expression** determines what is returned according to the following table:

If expression is	CStr returns
Boolean	A string containing True or False
Date	A string containing a date in the short-date format
Null	A runtime error
Empty	A zero-length string ("")
Error	A string containing the word Error followed by the error number
Other numeric	A string containing the number

Date

Description

Returns the current system date.

Syntax

`Date`

DateSerial

Description

Returns a variant of subtype `Date` for a specified year, month, and day.

Syntax

`DateSerial(year, month, day)`

Argument	Description
year	Number between 100 and 9999, inclusive, or a numeric expression
month	Any valid numeric expression
day	Any valid numeric expression

Comments

For the **year** argument, values between 0 and 99, inclusive, are interpreted as the years 1900–1999. For all other **year** arguments, use a complete four-digit year (for example, 1800).

When any argument exceeds the normally accepted range for that argument (in other words, greater than 12 for **month**), it increments to the next larger unit as appropriate. For example, if you specify 35 days, it is evaluated as one month and some number of days, depending on where in the year it is applied.

DateValue

Description

Returns a variant of subtype `Date`.

Syntax

`DateValue(date)`

The **date** argument is normally a string expression representing a date from January 1, 100, through December 31, 9999.

Day

Description

Returns a whole number between 1 and 31, inclusive, representing the day of the month.

Syntax

`Day(date)`

The **date** argument is any expression that can represent a **date**. If date contains **Null**, **Null** is returned.

Exp

Description

Returns e (the base of natural logarithms) raised to a power.

Syntax

`Exp(number)`

The **number** argument can be any valid numeric expression.

Fix

Description

Returns the integer portion of a number. For negative numbers it returns the first negative integer greater than or equal to the number.

Syntax

`Fix(number)`

The **number** argument can be any valid numeric expression. If **number** contains **Null**, **Null** is returned.

Hex

Description

Returns a string representing the hexadecimal value of a number.

Syntax

`Hex(number)`

The `number` argument is any valid expression.

Comments

You can represent hexadecimal numbers directly by preceding numbers in the proper range with `&H`. For example, `&H10` represents decimal 16 in hexadecimal notation.

Hour

Description

Returns a whole number between 0 and 23, inclusive, representing the hour of the day.

Syntax

`Hour(time)`

The `time` argument is any expression that can represent a time. If `time` contains `Null`, `Null` is returned.

InputBox

Description

Displays a prompt in a dialog box, waits for the user to input text or choose a button, and returns the contents of the textbox entered by the user.

Syntax

`InputBox(prompt[, title][, default][, xpos][, ypos][, helpfile, context])`

Argument

The InputBox function syntax has these arguments:

`prompt`

String expression displayed as the message in the dialog box. The maximum length of `prompt` is approximately 1,024 characters. To separate lines, use the carriage return `CHR(13)` and/or line feed `Chr(10)` characters.

`title`

String expression displayed in the title bar of the dialog box. If no title is used, the application name is defaulted.

`default`

Default response.

`xpos`

Numeric expression that specifies, in twips, the horizontal distance of the left edge of the dialog box from the left edge of the screen. If **xpos** is omitted, the dialog box is horizontally centered.

`ypos`

Numeric expression that specifies, in twips, the vertical distance of the upper edge of the dialog box from the top of the screen. If **ypos** is omitted, the dialog box is vertically positioned approximately one-third of the way down the screen.

`helpfile`

String expression that identifies the Help file to use to provide context-sensitive Help for the dialog box. If **helpfile** is provided, **context** must also be provided.

`context`

Numeric expression that is the Help context number the Help author assigned to the appropriate Help topic. If **context** is provided, **helpfile** must also be provided.

InStr

Description

Returns the position of the first occurrence of one string within another.

Syntax

`InStr([start, ]string1, string2[, compare])`

The InStr function syntax has these arguments:

Argument	Description
start	Starting position of the string to begin the search.
string1	String expression being searched.
string 2	String expression sought.
compare	Can be omitted. 0 specifies a binary comparison, 1 a text comparison.

Int

Description

Returns the integer portion of a number. If the number is negative, Int returns the first negative integer less than or equal to the number.

Syntax

`Int(number)`

The `number` argument can be any valid numeric expression. If `number` contains `Null`, `Null` is returned.

IsArray

Description

Returns a Boolean value indicating whether a variable is an array.

Syntax

`IsArray(varname)`

The `varname` argument can be any variable.

IsDate

Description

Returns a Boolean value indicating whether an expression can be converted to a date.

Syntax

`IsDate(expression)`

The `expression` argument can be any date or string expression recognizable as a date or time.

IsEmpty

Description

Returns a Boolean value indicating whether a variable has been initialized.

Syntax

```
IsEmpty(expression)
```

The **expression** argument can be any expression. However, because IsEmpty is used to determine if individual variables are initialized, the **expression** argument is most often a single variable name.

IsNull

Description

Returns a Boolean value that indicates whether an expression contains no valid data (**Null**).

Syntax

```
IsNull(expression)
```

The **expression** argument can be any expression.

Comments

The **Null** value indicates that the variable contains no valid data. **Null** is not the same as **Empty**, which indicates that a variable has not yet been initialized. It is also not the same as a zero-length string, which is sometimes referred to as a null string.

IsNumeric

Description

Returns a Boolean value indicating whether an expression can be evaluated as a number.

Syntax

```
IsNumeric(expression)
```

The **expression** argument can be any expression.

IsObject

Description

Returns a Boolean value indicating whether an expression references a valid OLE Automation object.

Syntax

```
IsObject(expression)
```

The **expression** argument can be any expression.

LBound

Description

Returns the smallest available subscript for the indicated dimension of an array.

Syntax

```
LBound(arrayname[, dimension])
```

The LBound function syntax has these parts:

Argument	Description
arrayname	Name of the array variable.
dimension	Whole number indicating which dimension's lower bound is returned. Use 1 (default) for the first dimension, 2 for the second, and so on.

LCase

Description

Returns a string that has been converted to lowercase.

Syntax

```
LCase(string)
```

The **string** argument is any valid string expression. If **string** contains **Null**, **Nul** is returned.

Comments

All non-alpha characters remain unchanged.

Left

Description

Returns a specified number of characters from the left side of a string.

Syntax

`Left(string, length)`

The Left function syntax has these arguments:

Argument	Description
string	String expression from which the leftmost characters are returned
length	Numeric expression indicating how many characters to return

Comments

To determine the number of characters in `string`, use the Len function.

Len

Description

Returns the number of characters in a string or the number of bytes required to store a variable.

Syntax

`Len(string | varname)`

The Len function syntax has these parts:

Argument	Description
string	Any valid string expression
varname	Any valid variable name

Log

Description

Returns the natural logarithm of a number.

Syntax

Log(number)

The number argument can be any valid numeric expression greater than 0.

LTrim

Description

Returns a copy of a string without leading spaces.

Syntax

LTrim(string)

The string argument is any valid string expression. If string contains Null, Null is returned.

Mid

Description

Returns a specified number of characters from a string.

Syntax

Mid(string, start[, length])

The Mid function syntax has these arguments:

Argument	Description
string	String expression from which characters are returned
start	Character position in string at which the part to be taken begins
length	Number of characters to return

Minute

Description

Returns a whole number between 0 and 59, inclusive, representing the minute of the hour.

Syntax

Minute(time)

> The **time** argument is any expression that can represent a time. If **time** contains **Null**, **Null** is returned.

Month

Description

> Returns a whole number between 1 and 12, inclusive, representing the month of the year.

Syntax

Month(date)

> The **date** argument is any expression that can represent a date. If **date** contains **Null**, **Null** is returned.

MsgBox

Description

> Displays a message in a dialog box, waits for the user to choose a button, and returns a value indicating which button the user has chosen.

Syntax

MsgBox(prompt[, buttons][, title][, helpfile, context])

Argument

> The MsgBox function syntax has these arguments:

prompt

> String expression displayed as the message in the dialog box. The maximum length of **prompt** is approximately 1,024 characters. To separate lines, use the carriage return **CHR(13)** and/or line feed **Chr(10)** characters.

buttons

> The sum of values specifying the number and type of buttons to display, the icon style to use, the identity of the default button, and the modality of the message box. If omitted, the default value for **buttons** is 0.

title

String expression displayed in the title bar of the dialog box. If no title is supplied, the title defaults to that of the Web page.

helpfile

String expression that identifies the Help file to use to provide context-sensitive Help for the dialog box. If **helpfile** is provided, **context** must also be provided.

context

Numeric expression that is the Help context number the Help author assigned to the appropriate Help topic. If **context** is provided, **helpfile** must also be provided.

Button Values

Value	Description
0	Displays OK button only
1	Displays OK and Cancel buttons
2	Displays Abort, Retry, and Ignore buttons
3	Displays Yes, No, and Cancel buttons
4	Displays Yes and No buttons
5	Display sRetry and Cancel buttons
16	Displays Critical Message icon
32	Displays Warning Query icon
48	Displays Warning Message icon
64	Displays Information Message icon
0	First button is default
256	Second button is default
512	Third button is default
768	Fourth button is default
0	Application modal; the user must respond to the message box before continuing work in the current application
4096	System modal; all applications are suspended until the user responds to the message box

The first group of values (0, 1, 2, 3, 4, 5) describes the number and type of buttons displayed in the dialog box; the second group (16, 32, 48, 64) describes the icon style;

the third group (0, 256, 512, 768) determines which button is the default; and the fourth group (0, 4096) determines the modality of the message box. When adding numbers to create a final value for the argument buttons, use only one number from each group.

Return Values

Value	Button chosen
1	OK
2	Cancel
3	Abort
4	Retry
5	Ignore
6	Yes
7	No

Now

Description

Returns the current date and time according to the setting of your computer's system date and time.

Syntax

`Now`

Oct

Description

Returns a string representing the octal value of a number.

Syntax

`Oct(number)`

The **number** argument is any valid expression.

Comments

You can represent octal numbers directly by preceding numbers in the proper range with **&O**. For example, **&O10** is the octal notation for decimal 8.

Right

Description

Returns a specified number of characters from the right side of a string.

Syntax

Right(string, length)

The Right function syntax has these arguments:

Argument	Description
string	String expression from which the rightmost characters are returned
length	Numeric expression indicating how many characters to return

Comments

To determine the number of characters in a string, use the Len function.

Rnd

Description

Returns a random number.

Syntax

Rnd[(number)]

The **number** argument can be any valid numeric expression.

Comments

The Rnd function returns a value less than 1 but greater than or equal to 0.
The value of the argument determines how Rnd generates a random number:

Argument	Rnd Return Value
Less than zero	The same number every time, using the argument as the seed
Greater than zero	The next random number in the sequence
Equal to zero	The most recently generated number
Not supplied	The next random number in the sequence

Before calling Rnd, use the `Randomize` statement without an argument to initialize the random-number generator with a seed based on the system timer. For any given seed, the same sequence of numbers will be generated.

RTrim

Description

Returns a copy of a string without trailing spaces.

Syntax

`RTrim(string)`

The `string` argument is any valid string expression. If `string` contains `Null`, `Null` is returned.

Second

Description

Returns a whole number between 0 and 59, inclusive, representing the second of the minute.

Syntax

`Second(time)`

The `time` argument is any expression that can represent a time. If `time` contains `Null`, `Null` is returned.

Sgn

Description

Returns an integer indicating the sign of a number.

Syntax

`Sgn(number)`

The `number` argument can be any valid numeric expression.

Return Values

Argument Vaue	Return Value
Greater than zero	1
Equal to zero	0
Less than zero	−1

Sin

Description

Returns the sine of an angle.

Syntax

`Sin(number)`

The `number` argument can be any valid numeric expression that expresses an angle in radians.

Sqr

Description

Returns the square root of a number.

Syntax

`Sqr(number)`

The `number` argument can be any valid numeric expression greater than or equal to 0.

Str

Description

Returns a string representation of a number.

Syntax

`Str(number)`

The **number** argument is any valid numeric expression.

Comments

Note that when numbers are converted to strings, an initial space is always made available for the sign of the number. For positive numbers, the plus sign is represented by the space.

StrComp

Description

Returns a value indicating the result of a string comparison.

Syntax

`StrComp(string1, string2[, compare])`

The StrComp function syntax has these arguments:

Argument	Description
string1	Any valid string expression
string2	Any valid string expression
compare	Specifies the type of string comparison; 0 for binary and 1 for text

Return Values

Comparison	Return Value
string1 is less than string2	−1
string1 is equal to string2	0
string1 is greater than string2	1
string1 or string2 is Null	Null

String

Description

Returns a repeating character string of the length specified.

Syntax

`String(number, character)`

The String function syntax has these arguments:

Argument	Description
`number`	Length of the returned string
`character`	Character to be used to fill the string

Tan

Description

Returns the tangent of an angle.

Syntax

`Tan(number)`

The `number` argument can be any valid numeric expression that expresses an angle in radians.

Time

Description

Returns a variant of subtype `Date` indicating the current system time.

Syntax

`Time`

TimeSerial

Description

Returns a variant of subtype **Date** containing the time for a specific hour, minute, and second.

Syntax

`TimeSerial(hour, minute, second)`

The TimeSerial function syntax has these arguments:

Argument	Description
hour	Number between 0 (12:00 A.M.) and 23 (11:00 P.M.), inclusive
minute	Any numeric expression
second	Any numeric expression

Remarks

When any argument exceeds the normally accepted range for that argument, it increments to the next larger unit as appropriate. For example, if you specify 75 minutes, it is evaluated as one hour and 15 minutes.

TimeValue

Description

Returns a variant of subtype **Date** containing the time.

Syntax

`TimeValue(time)`

The **time** argument is normally a string expression representing a time from 0:00:00 (12:00:00 A.M.) to 23:59:59 (11:59:59 P.M.), inclusive. However, **time** can also be any expression that represents a time in that range.

Remarks

You can enter valid times using a 12- or 24-hour (military) clock.

Trim

Description

Returns a copy of a string without leading and trailing spaces.

Syntax

`Trim(string)`

The **string** argument is any valid string expression. If **string** contains **Null**, **Null** is returned.

UBound

Description

Returns the largest available subscript for the indicated dimension of an array.

Syntax

`UBound(arrayname[, dimension])`

The UBound function syntax has these parts:

Argument	Description
arrayname	Name of the array variable.
dimension	Indicates which dimension's upper bound is returned. Use 1 for the first dimension, 2 for the second, and so on.

UCase

Description

Returns a string that has been converted to uppercase.

Syntax

`UCase(string)`

The **string** argument is any valid string expression. If **string** contains **Null**, **Null** is returned.

Remarks

All non-alpha characters remain unchanged.

Val

Description

Returns the numbers contained in a string.

Syntax

`Val(string)`

The **string** argument is any valid string expression.

VarType

Description

Returns a value indicating the subtype of a variable.

Syntax

`VarType(varname)`

The **varname** argument can be any variable.

Return Values

Value	Variable type description
0	Empty (uninitialized)
1	Null (no valid data)
2	Integer
3	Long integer
4	Single-precision floating-point number
5	Double-precision floating-point number
6	Currency
7	Date
8	String
9	OLE Automation object

continued on next page

continued from previous page

Value	Variable type description
10	Error
11	Boolean
12	Variant (used only with arrays of variants)
13	Non-OLE Automation object
17	Byte
8192	Array

Remarks

For arrays, the 8192 will be added to the value of the variant type of the array. For example, an array of dates would return 8192 + 7 or 8197.

Weekday

Description

Returns a whole number representing the day of the week.

Syntax

`Weekday(date, [firstdayofweek])`

The Weekday function syntax has these arguments:

Value	Variable type description
`date`	Any expression that can represent a date
`firstdayofweek`	A value that specifies the first day of the week, as described in Settings. If not supplied, 1 is defaulted.

`firstdayofweek` *Argument Values*

Value	Variable type description
0	Use NLS API setting
1	Sunday
2	Monday

Value	Variable type description
3	Tuesday
4	Wednesday
5	Thursday
6	Friday
7	Saturday

Return Values

Value	Variable type description
1	Sunday
2	Monday
3	Tuesday
4	Wednesday
5	Thursday
6	Friday
7	Saturday

Year

Description

Returns a whole number representing the year.

Syntax

`Year(date)`

The **date** argument is any expression that can represent a **date** If date contains **Null**, **Null** is returned.

APPENDIX B

METHODS

This appendix provides a brief reference to the methods provided by Visual Basic, Scripting Edition. Note that these specifically relate to error handling.

Clear

Description

Clears all property settings of the `Err` object.

Syntax

```
object.Clear
```

The object is always the `Err` object (in other words, `Err.clear`).

Comments

The error object should be cleared after an error has been handled. There are several cases where the `Clear` method is automatically called by Visual Basic Script:

```
On Error Resume Next
Exit Sub
Exit Function
```

Raise

Description

Generates a runtime error.

Syntax

```
object.Raise(number, source, description, helpfile, helpcontext)
```

Argument

The **Raise** method has these arguments:

object

Always the **Err** object (in other words, **Err.Raise**).

number

Required. A **Long** integer subtype that identifies the type of error. Visual Basic Script errors are in the range 0–65535.

source

Optional. A string expression naming the object or application that originally generated the error.

description

Optional. A string expression describing the error. If not supplied, Visual Basic Script will look up the error code and supply the appropriate message if one is defined.

helpfile

Optional. The fully qualified path to the Help file in which help on this error can be found. If unspecified, VBScript uses the fully qualified drive, path, and filename of the Visual Basic Script Help file.

helpcontext

Optional. The context ID identifying a topic within **helpfile** that provides help for the error.

APPENDIX C

OBJECTS

This appendix provides a brief overview of the only object provided in Visual Basic, Scripting Edition–**Err**.

Err

Description

Contains information about runtime errors. Accepts the **Raise** and **Clear** methods for generating and clearing runtime errors.

Syntax

```
Err[.{property | method}]
```

The two methods are **Clear** and **Raise**, (see Appendix B, "Methods," for more information). For information on the various error object properties, see Appendix F, "Statements."

Comments

The properties of the **Err** object are set by the generator of an error. Note that the default property of the **Err** object is **Number**.

When a runtime error occurs, the properties of the **Err** object are filled with information that uniquely identifies the error and information that can be used to handle it. To generate a runtime error in your code, use the **Raise** method.

The **Err** object's properties are reset to zero or zero-length strings (**""**) after an **On Error Resume Next** statement and after an **Exit Sub** or **Exit Function** statement within an error-handling routine. The **Clear** method can be used to explicitly reset **Err**.

APPENDIX D

OPERATORS

This appendix reviews the operators provided in Visual Basic, Scripting Edition. Most relate to mathematical and logical operations.

+

Description

Used to sum two numbers.

Syntax

```
result = expression1+expression2
```

The + operator syntax has these parts:

Part	Description
result	Any numeric variable
expression1	Any expression
expression2	Any expression

Comments

You can use the **+** operator to concatenate two strings together, but the preferred operator for this is **&**. Also, the **+** operator can be used to add two date variables together.

And

Description

Used to perform a logical conjunction on two expressions.

Syntax

```
result = expression1 And expression2
```

Comments

If, and only if, both expressions evaluate to **True**, the result is **True**. If either expression evaluates to **False**, the result is **False**.

&

Description

Used to force string concatenation of two expressions.

Syntax

```
result = expression1 & expression2
```

Comments

Whenever an expression is not a string, it is converted to a **String** subtype.

/

Description

Used to divide two numbers and return a floating-point result.

Syntax

```
result = number1/number2
```

Eqv

Description

Used to perform a logical equivalence on two expressions.

Syntax

```
result = expression1 Eqv expression2
```

Remarks

The **result** is determined according to the following table:

Expression1	Expression2	**Return Value**
True (1)	True (1)	True (1)
True (1)	False (0)	False (0)
False (0)	True (1)	False (0)
False (0)	False (0)	True (1)

Description

Used to raise a number to the power of an exponent.

Syntax

```
result = number ^ exponent
```

Imp

Description

Used to perform a logical implication on two expressions.

Syntax

```
result = expression1 Imp expression2
```

Comments

The following table illustrates how **result** is determined:

Expression1	Expression2	Return Value
True	True	True
True	False	False
True	Null	Null
False	True	True
False	False	True
False	Null	True
Null	True	True
Null	False	Null
Null	Null	Null

The **Imp** operator performs a bitwise comparison of identically positioned bits in two numeric expressions and sets the corresponding bit in **result** according to the following truth table:

Expression1	Expression2	Return Value
0	0	1
0	1	1
1	0	0
1	1	1

\

Description

Used to divide two numbers and return an integer result.

Syntax

```
result = number1 \ number2
```

Remarks

Before division is performed, numeric expressions are rounded to **Byte**, **Integer**, or **Long** subtype expressions.

Is

Description

Used to compare two object reference variables.

Syntax

```
result = object1 Is object2
```

Remarks

If **object1** and **object2** both refer to the same object, the result is **True**; if they do not, the result is **False**.

Mod

Description

Used to divide two numbers and return only the remainder.

Syntax

```
result = number1 Mod number2
```

#

Description

Used to multiply two numbers.

Syntax

```
result = number1 * number2
```

–

Description

Used to find the difference between two numbers or to indicate the negative value of a numeric expression.

Syntax 1

```
result = number1 - number2
```

Syntax 2

```
-number
```

Not

Description

Used to perform logical negation on an expression.

Syntax

```
result = Not expression
```

Comments

The following table illustrates how **result** is determined:

Expression	Return Value
True (1)	False (0)
False (0)	True (1)
Null	Null

Or

Description

Used to perform a logical disjunction on two expressions.

Syntax

```
result = expression1 Or expression2
```

Comments

If either or both expressions evaluate to `True`, the result is `True`. The following table illustrates how **result** is determined:

Expression1	Expression2	Return Value
True	True	True
True	False	True
True	Null	True
False	True	True
False	False	False
False	Null	Null
Null	True	True
Null	False	Null
Null	Null	Null

The **Or** operator also performs a bitwise comparison of identically positioned bits in two numeric expressions and sets the corresponding bit in **result** according to the following truth table:

Expression1	Expression2	Return Value
0	0	0
0	1	1
1	0	1
1	1	1

Xor

Description

Used to perform a logical exclusion on two expressions.

Syntax

```
result = expression1 Xor expression2
```

Comments

If one, and only one, of the expressions evaluates to **True**, the result is **True**. When neither expression is **Null**, the result is determined according to the following table:

Expression1	Expression2	**Return Value**
True	True	False
True	False	True
False	True	True
False	False	False

The **Xor** operator also performs a bitwise comparison of identically positioned bits in two numeric expressions and sets the corresponding bit in result according to the following truth table:

Expression1	Expression2	**Return Value**
0	0	0
0	1	1
1	0	1
1	1	0

APPENDIX E

•••••••••••••••••••••••••••••

PROPERTIES

This appendix provides a brief overview of the properties provided in Visual Basic, Scripting Edition.

Description

Description

Returns or sets a descriptive string associated with an error.

Syntax

```
object.Description [= stringexpression]
```

The `Description` property syntax has these arguments:

Argument	Description
object	Required. Always the Err object (in other words, Err.Description).
stringexpression	Optional. A string expression containing a description of the error.

Remarks

The properties provide a description of the error that has been raised. This can be presented to the user or directly utilized in your code.

HelpContext

Description

Returns or sets a context ID for a topic in a Help file.

Syntax

```
object.HelpContext [= ContextID]
```

The **HelpContext** property syntax has these arguments:

Argument	Description
object	Required. Always the Err object.
ContextID	Optional. A valid identifier for a Help topic within the Help file.

HelpFile

Description

Returns or sets a fully qualified path to a Help file.

Syntax

```
object.HelpFile [= pathspec]
```

The **HelpFile** property syntax has these arguments:

Argument	Description
object	Required. Always the Err object.
pathspec	Optional. Fully qualified path to the Help file.

Number

Description

Returns or sets a numeric value specifying an error. **Number** is the Err object's default property.

Syntax

`object.Number [= errornumber]`

The **Number** property syntax has these arguments:

Argument	Description
object	Required. Always the Err object (i.e., Err.Number).
errornumber	Optional. An integer representing a VBScript errornumber.

SOURCE

Description

Returns or sets the name of the object or application that originally generated the error.

Syntax

`object.Source [= stringexpression]`

The **Source** property syntax has these arguments:

Argument	Description
objectRequired	Always the Err object.
stringexpression	Optional. A string expression representing the application that generated the error.

APPENDIX F

STATEMENTS

This appendix will briefly review the statements provided in Visual Basic, Scripting Edition such as the `If...Then...Else` and the `Do...Loop`.

Call

Description

Transfers control to a `Sub` procedure or a `Function` procedure.

Syntax

`[Call] name [argumentlist]`

The `Call` statement syntax has these arguments:

Argument	Description
Call	Optional keyword—if specified, you must enclose `argumentlist` in parentheses
name	Name of the procedure to call
argumentlist	Variables, arrays, and expressions to pass into the procedure

Comments

You are not required to use the `Call` keyword when calling a procedure.

Dim

Description

Declares variables and allocates storage space.

Syntax

```
Dim varname[([subscripts])][, varname[([subscripts])]] . . .
```

The `Dim` statement syntax has these parts:

Part	Description
varname	Name of the variable
subscripts	Dimensions of an array variable; up to 60 multiple dimensions may be declared

Remarks

You also can use the `Dim` statement with empty parentheses to declare a dynamic array. After declaring a dynamic array, use the `ReDim` statement within a procedure to define the number of dimensions and elements in the array.

Do...Loop

Description

Repeats a block of statements while a condition is `True` or until a condition becomes `True`.

Syntax

```
Do [{While | Until} condition]
[statements]
[Exit Do]
[statements]
Loop
```

Or, you can use this equally valid syntax:

```
Do
    [statements]
    [Exit Do]
    [statements]
Loop [{While | Until} condition]
```

The `Do...Loop` statement syntax has these parts:

Part	Description
condition	Numeric or string expression that is True or False. Null is treated as False.
statements	One or more statements that are repeated while or until condition is True.

Comments

The `Exit Do` can only be used within a `Do...Loop` control structure to provide an alternate way to exit a `Do...Loop`. Any number of `Exit Do` statements may be placed anywhere in the `Do...Loop`. Often used with the evaluation of some condition (for example, `If...Then`), `Exit Do` transfers control to the statement immediately following the `Loop`.

Erase

Description

Reinitializes the elements of fixed-size arrays and de-allocates dynamic-array storage space.

Syntax

```
Erase array
```

The **array** argument is the name of the array variable to be erased.

Remarks

It is important to know whether an array is fixed-size (ordinary) or dynamic because **Erase** behaves differently depending on the type of array. **Erase** recovers no memory for fixed-size arrays. **Erase** sets the elements of a fixed array as follows:

Type of array	Effect of `Erase`
Fixed numeric array	Sets each element to zero
Fixed string array	Sets each element to zero-length ("")
Array of objects	Sets each element to the special value `Nothing`

For dynamic arrays, the memory is freed.

Exit

Description

Exits a block of `Do...Loop`, `For...Next`, `Function`, or `Sub` code.

Syntax

```
Exit Do

Exit For

Exit Function

Exit Sub
```

The `Exit` statement syntax has these forms:

`Exit Do`

Provides a way to exit a `Do...Loop` statement. `Exit Do` transfers control to the statement following the `Loop` statement.

`Exit For`

Provides a way to exit a `For` loop. `Exit For` transfers control to the statement following the `Next` statement.

`Exit Function`

Immediately exits the `Function` procedure in which it appears. Execution continues with the statement following the statement that called `Function`.

`Exit Sub`

Immediately exits the `Sub` procedure in which it appears. Execution continues with the statement following the statement that called `Sub`.

For...Next

Description

Repeats a group of statements a specified number of times.

Syntax

```
For counter = start To end [Step step]
[statements]
[Exit For]
[statements]
Next
```

The For...Next statement syntax has these parts:

Part	Description
counter	Numeric variable used as a loop counter
start	Initial value of counter
end	Final value of counter
step	Amount counter is changed each time through the loop—default is one
statements	One or more statements between For and Next that are executed with each iteration

Remarks

The step argument can be either positive or negative.

Function

Description

Declares the name, arguments, and code that form the body of a Function procedure.

Syntax

```
Function name [(arglist)]
[statements]
[name = expression]
[Exit Function]
[statements]
[name = expression]
End Function
```

The `Function` statement syntax has these parts:

Part	Description
name	Name of the `Function`
arglist	Variables separated by commas passed to the `Function`
statements	Any group of statements to be executed within the body of the `Function`
expression	Return value of the `Function`

Comments

To return a value from a function, assign the value to the function name. Any number of such assignments can appear anywhere within the procedure.

If...Then...Else

Description

Conditionally executes a group of statements, depending on the value of an expression.

Syntax 1

```
If condition Then statements [Else elsestatements ]
```

Syntax 2

```
If condition Then
[statements]
[ElseIf condition-n Then
[elseifstatements]] . . .
[Else
[elsestatements]]
End If
```

The `If...Then...Else` statement syntax has these parts:

Part	Description
condition	One or more of the following two types of expressions: A numeric or string expression that evaluates to `True` or `False`. If condition is `Null`, condition is treated as `False`.
statements	One or more statements separated by colons; executed if condition is `True`.
condition-n	Same as condition.

Part	Description
elseifstatements	One or more statements executed if the associated condition-n is True.
elsestatements	One or more statements executed if no previous condition or condition-n expression is True.

On Error

Description

Enables an error-handling routine and specifies the location of the routine within a procedure; can also be used to disable an error-handling routine.

Syntax

On Error Resume Next

Comments

If you don't use an **On Error Resume Next** statement, any runtime error that occurs is fatal; that is, an error message is displayed and execution stops.

On Error Resume Next causes execution to continue with the statement immediately following the statement that caused the runtime error. This allows execution to continue despite a runtime error. You then can build the error-handling routine in-line within the procedure. An **On Error Resume Next** statement becomes inactive when another procedure is called, so you should execute an **On Error Resume Next** statement in each called routine if you want in-line error handling within that routine.

Randomize

Description

Initializes the random-number generator.

Syntax

Randomize [number]

The **number** argument can be any valid numeric expression.

Comments

Randomize uses **number** to initialize the Rnd function's random-number generator, giving it a new seed value. If you provide no argument, the value returned by the system timer is used as the new seed value.

If **Randomize** is not used, the Rnd function (with no arguments) uses the same number as a seed the first time it is called, and thereafter uses the last generated number as a seed value.

ReDim

Description

Used at procedure level to declare dynamic-array variables and allocate or reallocate storage space.

Syntax

ReDim [Preserve] varname(subscripts) [, varname(subscripts)] . . .

The **ReDim** statement syntax has these parts:

Part	Description
Preserve	Keeps the data in an existing array when you change the size of the last dimension
varname	Name of the variable
subscripts	Dimensions of an array variable

Comments

If you use the **Preserve** keyword, you can resize only the last array dimension and you can't change the number of dimensions at all.

Rem

Description

Used to include explanatory remarks in a program.

Syntax

```
Rem comment
```

or

```
' comment
```

Select Case

Description

Executes one of several groups of statements, depending on the value of an expression.

Syntax

```
Select Case testexpression
[Case expressionlist-n
[statements-n]] . . .
[Case Else expressionlist-n
[elsestatements-n]]
End Select
```

The **Select Case** statement syntax has these parts:

Part	Description
testexpression	Any numeric or string expression.
expressionlist-n	Required if Case appears. Delimited list of one or more expressions.
statements-n	One or more statements executed if testexpression matches any part of expressionlist-n.
elsestatements	One or more statements executed if testexpression doesn't match any of the Case clauses.

Set

Description

Assigns an object reference to a variable or property.

Syntax

```
Set objectvar = { objectexpression | Nothing}
```

The **Set** statement syntax has these parts:

Part	Description
objectvar	Name of the variable or property.
objectexpression	Expression consisting of the name of an object, another declared variable of the same object type, or a function or method that returns an object of the same object type.
Nothing	Discontinues association of objectvar with any specific object. Assigning objectvar to Nothing releases all the system and memory resources associated with the previously referenced object when no other variable refers to it.

Sub

Description

Declares the name, arguments, and code that form the body of a **Sub** procedure.

Syntax

```
Sub name [(arglist)]
[statements]
[Exit Sub]
[statements]
End Sub
```

The **Sub** statement syntax has these parts:

Part	Description
name	Name of the sub; follows standard variable naming conventions
arglist	List of comma-separated variables that are passed to the sub procedure
statements	Any group of statements to be executed within the body of the sub procedure

While...Wend

Description

Executes a series of statements as long as a given condition is `True`.

Syntax

```
While condition
[statements]
Wend
```

The `While...Wend` statement syntax has these parts:

Part	Description
condition	Numeric or string expression that evaluates to `True` or `False` (`NULL` is `False`)
statements	One or more statements executed while `condition` is `True`

APPENDIX G

HTML 3.2 QUICK REFERENCE

This appendix lists the tags used in various versions of HTML, divided by subject, for quick reference when you're working on a page. Tags available only in HTML 3/3.2 and/or Netscape are noted in the definition; otherwise, the tag is from HTML 2.0. If a tag has an attribute that can be included in the tag, it is shown in an indented list below the tag. An ellipsis (...) is used to indicate where text can be placed between tags. Text in italics indicates a variable that should be replaced with the appropriate filename, keyword, or number.

DOCUMENT BASICS

These tags provide the basic structure for an HTML document.

Element	Definition
`<BODY>...</BODY>`	Marks the beginning and end of the body of an HTML document
`BACKGROUND = URL`	Specifies image to be used as background
`BGCOLOR = color`	Specifies color for background (`color` can be a name or a hexidecimal number)
`TEXT = color`	Specifies color for the text

continued on next page

continued from previous page

Element	Definition
`LINK = color`	Specifies color for links on a page
`ALINK = color`	Specifies color for active links on a page
`VLINK = color`	Specifies color for visited links on a page
`LEFTMARGIN = n`	Specifies the distance between the left side of the document and the left edge of the browser window (Microsoft)
`TOPMARGIN = n`	Specifies the distance between the top of the document and the top of the browser window (Microsoft)
`BGPROPERTIES = FIXED`	Fixes the location of the background image (in other words, doesn't let it scroll)
`<HEAD>...</HEAD>`	Marks the beginning and end of the header of an HTML document
`<HTML>...</HTML>`	Marks the beginning and end of an HTML document
`<TITLE>...</TITLE>`	Identifies the title of an HTML document (used in the heading)
`<!-- ... -->`	Makes a comment in an HTML document
`<!DOCTYPE HTML info>`	Defines the DTD used for this document (`info` is the name of the DTD)
`<META>`	Provides meta-information about a document
`HTTP-EQUIV = name`	The header of the HTTP file relevant to the data in the `<META>` document
`CONTENT = name`	The data associated with the named HTTP header
`NAME = name`	A description of the document
`URL = URL`	An URL associated with the meta-information

PHYSICAL TEXT STYLES

These tags allow you to change the physical style of text in your document; that is, change how the text is displayed for the user.

Element	Definition
`<B>...</B>`	Makes text bold
`<BIG>...</BIG>`	Puts text in a large-size font
`<BASEFONT SIZE=n>`	Sets the default font size for the document
`<BLINK>...</BLINK>`	Makes blinking text (Netscape)
`<FONT >...</FONT>`	
`SIZE = n`	Changes the font size by a value n (n can be any number from 1 to 7, or a positive or negative number to indicate an offset from the base font size)
`COLOR = color`	Changes the font color (color can be a name or a hexadecimal number)
`FACE = font name`	Changes the font style to the fonts named, provided the fonts exist on the local system (Microsoft/Netscape)
`<I>...</I>`	Italicizes text
`<MARQUEE>`	Inserts a marquee of moving text (Microsoft)
`ALIGN = align`	The alignment of text surrounding the marquee (LEFT, CENTER, RIGHT, TOP, MIDDLE, BOTTOM)
`BEHAVIOR = behavior`	How the text moves (SCROLL, SLIDE, ALTERNATE)
`BGCOLOR = color`	Background color of the marquee (color can be a name or a hexadecimal value)
`DIRECTION = direction`	Direction the text scrolls (LEFT, RIGHT)
`HEIGHT = n`	Height of marquee (pixels)
`WIDTH = n`	Width of marquee (pixels)
`HSPACE = n`	Amount of horizontal space around marquee
`VSPACE = n`	Amount of vertical space around marquee
`LOOP = n`	Scrolls the marquee n times
`SCROLLDELAY = n`	Number of milliseconds between each update
`SCROLLAMOUNT = n`	Amount text has moved in one update

continued on next page

continued from previous page

Element	Definiton
`<S>...</S>`	Puts text in a strikethrough font (HTML 3) (also `<STRIKE>...</STRIKE>` (Netscape))
`<SMALL>...</SMALL>`	Puts text in a small-size font (HTML 3)
`<SUB>...</SUB>`	Puts text in subscript (HTML 3)
`<SUP>...</SUP>`	Puts text in superscript (HTML 3)
`<TT>...</TT>`	Puts text in a teletype (fixed-width) font
`<U>...</U>`	Underlines text

CONTENT TEXT STYLES

These tags allow you to change the content style of the text in your document; that is, change the implied meaning of the text.

Element	Definiton
`<ADDRESS>...</ADDRESS>`	Specifies the author, contact information, and so on of the page
`<CITE>...</CITE>`	Specifies a citation
`<CODE>...</CODE>`	Includes code (from a computer program)
`<DFN>...</DFN>`	Specifies a definition
`<EM>`	Emphasizes text
`<Hn>...</Hn>`	Identifies heading for a document (n is a whole number between 1 [largest heading] and 6 [smallest heading])
`ALIGN=alignment`	Sets the alignment of the heading (`alignment` can be LEFT, CENTER, RIGHT, or JUSTIFY) (HTML 3/Netscape)
`SRC = graphic filename`	Includes a graphic as a bullet for the header document (HTML 3)
`<KBD>...</KBD>`	Identifies input or output from a computer
`<SAMP>...</SAMP>`	Specifies a sample of literal characters
`<STRONG>...</STRONG>`	Strongly emphasizes text
`<VAR>...</VAR>`	Specifies a variable

DOCUMENT SPACING

These tags control the spacing in your document.

Element	Definition
`<BLOCKQUOTE>...</BLOCKQUOTE>`	Creates a quotation block
` `	Inserts a line break
`CLEAR = alignment`	Clears text wrap (*alignment* can be LEFT, RIGHT, or ALL)
`<CENTER>...</CENTER>`	Centers text (same as `<DIV ALIGN= CENTER>`)
`<DIV>...</DIV>`	Marks a division in a Web page
`ALIGN = alignment`	Alignment of division (LEFT, CENTER, RIGHT)
`<HR>`	Adds a horizontal line
`ALIGN = alignment`	Alignment of the line (`alignment` can be LEFT, RIGHT, or CENTER)
`SIZE = n`	Specifies the thickness of the line
`NOSHADE`	Makes the line black
`WIDTH = n%`	Specifies the width of the line (`n` can be any number from 0 to 100)
`COLOR = color`	Specifies the color of the line (`color` can be a name or a hexidecimal number) (Microsoft)
`<MULTICOL> ...</MULTICOL>`	Creates multicolumn text (Netscape 3)
`COLS = n`	Number of columns
`GUTTER = n`	Number of pixels between columns
`WIDTH = n`	Width of each column
`<NOBR>...</NOBR>`	Indicates no line break should be included (Microsoft/Netscape)
`<P>...</P>`	Creates a paragraph
`ALIGN = alignment`	Alignment of the paragraph (`alignment` can be LEFT, CENTER, or RIGHT)
`<PRE>...</PRE>`	Identifies preformatted text
`WIDTH = n`	Width of text in characters
`<SPACER>`	Creates horizontal or vertical space (Netscape 3)

continued on next page

continued from previous page

Element	Definition
TYPE = type	Type of spacer to use (type can be HORIZONTAL, VERTICAL, or BLOCK)
SIZE = n	Size of hortizontal or vertical spacer
WIDTH = n	Width of block spacer
HEIGHT = n	Height of block spacer
ALIGN = alignment	Alignment of block spacer (alignment can be LEFT, CENTER, or RIGHT)
<WBR>	Includes a soft line break within a non-breaking line

TABLES

These tags allow you to create tables in HTML 3 or Netscape.

Element	Definition
<CAPTION>...</CAPTION>	Identifies the table caption
ALIGN = alignment	Alignment of the caption (alignment can be TOP or BOTTOM)
<TABLE>...</TABLE>	Defines a table
BORDER=n	Shows the lines of the table to the specified thickness
ALIGN = alignment	The alignment of the table (alignment can be BLEEDLEFT, LEFT, CENTER, RIGHT, BLEEDRIGHT, or JUSTIFY)
WIDTH = n	A fixed width of the entire table (n is any number)
BGCOLOR = color	Defines the color of the background of the table (color can be a name or a hexadecimal number) (Microsoft/Netscape)
BORDERCOLOR = color	Defines the color of a table border (Microsoft)
BORDERCOLORLIGHT = color	Defines the color of the light portion of a 3-D table border (Microsoft)
BORDERCOLORDARK = color	Defines the color of the dark portion of a 3-D table border (Microsoft)

Element	Definition
BACKGROUND = URL	Defines the location of the background image for a table (Microsoft)
CELLSPACING = n	Sets the spacing between cells in a table
CELLPADDING = n	Sets the spacing between cell contents and borders
COLS = n	Sets the number of columns in a table (Microsoft)
FRAME = frame	Defines the type of outside table border to show (frame can be VOID, ABOVE, BELOW, HSIDES, LHS, RHS, VSIDES, BOX, or BORDER) (Microsoft)
RULES = rule	Defines the type of inside table border to show (rule can be NONE, GROUPS, ROWS, COLS, or ALL) (Microsoft)
<TH>...</TH>, <TD>...</TD>	Defines a table heading <TH> or a data table entry <TD>
ALIGN = alignment	The alignment of entries in the row (alignment can be LEFT, CENTER, or RIGHT)
VALIGN = alignment	The vertical alignment of table row entries (alignment can be TOP, MIDDLE, BOTTOM, or BASELINE)
ROWSPAN = n	Number of table rows the cell should cover
COLSPAN = n	Number of table columns the cell should cover
NOWRAP	Turns off word wrapping in the table cell
WIDTH = n	Width of the cell, in pixels or percent
HEIGHT = n	Height of the cell, in pixels
BGCOLOR = color	Defines the color of the background of the table (color can be a name or a hexadecimal number) (Microsoft/Netscape)
BORDERCOLOR = color	Defines the color of a table border (Microsoft)
BORDERCOLORLIGHT = color	Defines the color of the light portion of a 3-D table border (Microsoft)

continued on next page

continued from previous page

Element	Definition
BORDERCOLORDARK = color	Defines the color of the dark portion of a 3-D table border (Microsoft)
BACKGROUND = URL	Defines the location of the background image for a table (Microsoft)
<TR>...</TR>	Starts a new row in the table
ALIGN = alignment	The alignment of entries in the row (alignment can be LEFT, CENTER, RIGHT, JUSTIFY, or DECIMAL)
VALIGN = alignment	The vertical alignment of table row entries (alignment can be TOP, MIDDLE, BOTTOM, or BASELINE)
BGCOLOR = color	Defines the color of the background of the table (color can be a name or a hexadecimal number) (Microsoft/Netscape)
BORDERCOLOR = color	Defines the color of a table border (Microsoft)
BORDERCOLORLIGHT = color	Defines the color of the light portion of a 3-D table border (Microsoft)
BORDERCOLORDARK = color	Defines the color of the dark portion of a 3-D table border (Microsoft)
BACKGROUND = URL	Defines the location of the background image for a table (Microsoft)
<TBODY>...</TBODY>	Defines the table body (Microsoft)
<THEAD>...</THEAD>	Defines the table head (Microsoft)
<TFOOT>...</TFOOT>	Defines the table foot (Microsoft)

LISTS

These tags allow you to create a number of different types of lists in your document.

Element	Definition
<OL>...</OL>	Creates an ordered (numbered) list
COMPACT	Displays a compacted version of the list

Element	Definition
TYPE = type	Specifies the type of numbering used (type can be "A," "a," "I," "i," or "1")
START = n	The starting number of the list
<UL>...</UL>	Creates an unordered (bulleted) list
COMPACT	Displays a compacted version of the list
TYPE = type	Specifies the type of bullet to use (type can be CIRCLE, DISC, or SQUARE)
<DL>...</DL>	Creates a glossary list
COMPACT	Displays a compacted version of the list
<MENU>...</MENU>	Creates a menu list
COMPACT	Displays a compacted version of the list
<DIR>...</DIR>	Creates a directory list
COMPACT	Displays a compacted version of the list
<DT>	Identifies a defined term in a glossary list
<DD>	Identifies a definition in a glossary list
<LI>	Identifies a list item in <OL>, <UL>, <MENU>, or <DIRECTORY>
TYPE = bullet type	Specifies the type of bullet to use for this and subsequent list entries in a bulleted list (bullet type can be CIRCLE, DISC, or SQUARE)
TYPE = number type	Specifies the type of numbering used for this and subsequent list entries in an ordered list (number type can be "A," "a," "I," "i," or "1")
VALUE = n	The starting number of this and later entries in a numbered list (n is any integer)

LINKS

These tags allow you to create links to a Web pages, FTP and Gopher sites, and other Internet resources.

Element	Definition
`<A>...</A>`	Defines an anchor for a link
`HREF = URL`	Specifies the destination of the link, using its URL
`NAME = name`	Specifies the name of a section of a document for later use in links
`SHAPE = shape`	The shape of a link embedded in a figure (`shape` can be "circle x,y,r"; "rect x,y,r,h"; "polygon x1,y1,x2,y2,... , xn,yn"; or "default") (HTML 3)
`TARGET = target`	Specifies the target window for a link
`TITLE = title`	Title that appears when a link is selected
`<BASE HREF=URL>`	Defines the base URL of the relative links in a document (located in the header of the document)
`<LINK>`	Defines the relationship between the current document and other documents
`REL`	The type of relationship between the current document and other documents
`REV`	The reverse relationship between other documents and the current one
`HREF = URL`	The URL of the reference

IMAGES

These tags allow you to incorporate images into your pages.

Element	Definition
`<IMG>`	Includes an inline image
`ALIGN = alignment`	The alignment of the image (`alignment` can be TOP, MIDDLE, BOTTOM, LEFT, or RIGHT)
`ALIGN = alignment`	The alignment of the image (`alignment` can be LEFT, RIGHT, TEXTTOP, ABSMIDDLE, BASELINE, or BOTTOM) (Netscape)

Element	Definition
ALT = "text"	A text decription of the image
BORDER = n	Size of the picture border, in pixels
HEIGHT = n	Fixed height of the image
WIDTH = n	Fixed width of the image
HSPACE = n	The horizontal runaround space, in pixels
VSPACE = n	The vertical runaround space, in pixels
ISMAP	Declares the image to be an image map
SRC = graphic filename	The filename of the image
LOWSRC = graphic filename	The filename of a low-resolution version of the image (Netscape)
USEMAP = URL	The URL of a client-side image map for the image
<MAP>...</MAP>	Collection of links for a client-side image map
NAME = name	Name of the image map
<AREA>	A link in a client-side image map
COORDS = coords	Coordinates defining the location of the link
HREF = URL	Destination of the link
NOHREF	Makes the region inactive in the image map
SHAPE = shape	Type of shape for the link (shape can be RECT, CIRC, POLY, or DEFAULT)
ALT = "text"	Alternative text for the link
TARGET = target	Destination window of the link (Microsoft)

FORMS

These tags allow you to create forms that include different types of inputs; they also specify what to do with the results of the form when submitted.

Element	Definition
<FORM>...</FORM>	Defines a form
ACTION = URL	The location (URL) of the script that will process the form results
METHOD = method	Method of sending the form input (method can be GET or POST)
ENCTYPE = enctype	Encoding type for the form data
<INPUT>	Creates an input area of the form
TYPE =	Type of form input
CHECKBOX	A check box
FILE	Allows user to attach a file
ACCEPT = "text"	Limits the range of acceptable files
HIDDEN	An invisible input
IMAGE	Returns information on where the user clicked on the image
RADIO	A radio button
PASSWORD	A password
TEXT	A single-line text input
SUBMIT	A button to submit the form input
RESET	A button to reset the form input
NAME = name	The name of this input variable, as seen by the script (but not displayed in the form)
SIZE = n	Defines the size of the text display for a TEXT form
MAXLENGTH = n	The maxiumum length of a TEXT input item
VALUE = "text"	Value used to initialize HIDDEN and TEXT fields
DISABLED	Disables the field to prevent text from being entered
CHECKED	Initializes a field in a CHECKBOX or RADIO to be selected
SRC = graphic filename	Specifies the image filename for IMAGE, SUBMIT, and RESET

Element	Definition
ALIGN = align	Alignment of form element (align can be TOP, MIDDLE, BOTTOM, LEFT, or RIGHT)
<ISINDEX>	Defines a searchable index
ACTION = URL	Specifies the gateway program to be used (Microsoft)
PROMPT = "text"	Specifies the text to be shown before the prompt (Microsoft)
<OPTION>	Specifies an option in a <SELECT> menu form
DISABLED	Disables the entry to prevent its selection
SELECTED	Initializes the entry to be selected
<SELECT>...</SELECT>	Creates a menu of selections
NAME = name	The name of the input variable, as seen by the script (but not displayed in the form)
MULTIPLE	Permits multiple selections to be made from the menu
DISABLED	Disables the menu to prevent selections
WIDTH = n	Fixed width of the menu (Netscape)
HEIGHT = n	Fixed height of the menu (Netscape)
SIZE = n	Height of menu
<TEXTAREA>...</TEXTAREA>	Creates a multiline text input area for a form: Any text located between the tags becomes the initial value for the form
NAME = name	The name of the input variable, as seen by the script (but not displayed in the form)
ROWS = n	Number of rows down the text area should be
COLS = n	Number of columns across the text area should be
DISABLED	Disables the menu to prevent input

FRAMES

These tags let you create a variety of different types of frames in a document.

Element	Definition
`<FRAMESET>...</FRAMESET>`	Defines a set of frames in a document (Microsoft/Netscape)
`COLS = n`	Creates column-oriented frames (n is a set of pixel widths or percentages)
`ROWS = n`	Creates row-oriented frames (n is a set of pixel widths or percentages)
`FRAMEBORDER = 0,1`	Turns on (1) or off (0) frame borders (Microsoft)
`FRAMEBORDER = YES,NO`	Turns on or off frame borders (Netscape)
`BORDER = n`	Thickness of frame borders (Netscape)
`BORDERCOLOR = color`	Color of border (color can be a name or hexadecimal number) (Netscape)
`FRAMESPACING = n`	Defines space between frames (Microsoft)
`<FRAME>`	Defines a frame (Microsoft/Netscape)
`ALIGN = align`	Alignment of frame or surrounding text (align can be LEFT, CENTER, RIGHT, TOP, or BOTTOM) (Microsoft)
`FRAMEBORDER = 0,1`	Turns on (1) or off (0) frame borders (Microsoft)
`FRAMEBORDER = YES,NO`	Turns on or off frame borders (Netscape)
`MARGINHEIGHT = n`	Defines the margin height of frame, in pixels (Microsoft)
`MARGINWIDTH = n`	Defines the margin width of frame, in pixels (Microsoft)
`NAME = name`	Defines target name for the frame
`SCROLLING = YES,NO`	Turns scrolling on or off
`SRC = URL`	Defines the URL for the frame
`<IFRAME>...</IFRAME>`	Defines a floating frame (Microsoft)
`ALIGN = align`	Alignment of frame or surrounding text (align can be LEFT, CENTER, RIGHT, TOP, or BOTTOM)
`FRAMEBORDER = 0,1`	Turns on (1) or off (0) frame borders

Element	Definition
`MARGINHEIGHT = n`	Defines the margin height of the frame, in pixels (Microsoft)
`MARGINWIDTH = n`	Defines the margin width of the frame, in pixels (Microsoft)
`NAME = name`	Defines target name for the frame
`SCROLLING = YES,NO`	Turns scrolling on or off
`SRC = URL`	Defines the URL for the frame
`HEIGHT = n`	Defines height of floating frame
`WIDTH = n`	Defines width of floating frame
`<NOFRAMES> </NOFRAMES>`	Defines alternative text for those not using frames-enabled browsers

MULTIMEDIA

These tags allow you to include Java applets, VBScript and JavaScript scripts, and other multimedia elements into your Web pages.

Element	Definition
`<APPLET>...</APPLET>`	Includes a Java applet
`ALIGN = align`	Defines the alignment of the applet (`align` can be LEFT, CENTER, or RIGHT)
`CODE = file`	Defines the filename of the applet
`CODEBASE = URL`	Defines the URL to the applet
`HEIGHT = n`	Defines the height of applet
`WIDTH = n`	Defines the width of applet
`HSPACE = n`	Defines the horizontal space around the applet
`VSPACE = n`	Defines the vertical space around the applet
`NAME = name`	Defines the name of the applet to identify it to other applets on the page
`PARAM NAME = name`	Defines an applet-specific argument from an HTML page (Microsoft)

continued on next page

continued from previous page

Element	Definition
`<EMBED>`	Includes a multimedia object (Microsoft/Netscape)
`HEIGHT = n`	Defines the height of the object
`WIDTH = n`	Defines the width of the object
`NAME = name`	Defines the name of the object to identify it to other objects on the page
`SRC = URL`	Defines the URL of the object
`<NOEMBED>...</NOEMBED>`	Defines alternative text for browsers that don't support embedded objects (Netscape)
`<OBJECT>...</OBJECT>`	Includes a multimedia object (Microsoft)
`ALIGN = align`	Defines the alignment of the object (`align` can be BASELINE, CENTER, LEFT, MIDDLE, RIGHT, TEXTBOTTOM, TEXTMIDDLE, or TEXTTOP)
`BORDER = n`	Defines the width of the object border
`CLASSID = URL`	Defines the class ID for ActiveX controls
`CODEBASE = URL`	Defines the URL for the code base of the object
`CODETYPE = type`	Defines the media type of the object
`DATA = URL`	Defines the location of data for the object
`DECLARE`	Declares an object without starting it
`HEIGHT = n`	Defines the height of the object
`HSPACE = n`	Defines the horizontal space around the object
`NAME = URL`	Defines the name of the object if submitted in a form
`SHAPES`	Specifies that the object has shaped hyperlinks
`STANDBY = "Message"`	Defines a message to display while the object is loading

Element	Definition
TYPE = type	Defines the media type for the object data
USEMAP = URL	Defines a client-side image map to be used
VSPACE = n	Defines the vertical space around the object
WIDTH = n	Defines the width of the object
<PARAM>	Defines parameters to pass to a Java applet
NAME = name	Defines the name of the variable
VALUE = value	Defines the value to pass to the applet
VALUETYPE = type	Specifies how to interpret the data (type can be DATE, REF, OBJECT) (Microsoft)
TYPE = type	Defines the media type (Microsoft)
<BGSOUND>	Includes a sound to play in the background (Microsoft)
SRC = URL	Defines the URL of the sound file
LOOP = n	Defines the number of times to play the sound
<STYLE>...</STYLE>	Includes a style sheet (Microsoft)
<SPAN>...</SPAN>	Applies style information to part of a document (Microsoft)
STYLE = style	Defines the style to be used
<SCRIPT>...</SCRIPT>	Includes a script (Microsoft/Netscape)
LANGUAGE = language	Defines the language of the script
SRC = URL	Defines the URL of the script (Netscape)
<NOSCRIPT>...</NOSCRIPT>	Defines alternative markup for browsers that don't support the script

APPENDIX H

QUIZ ANSWERS

CHAPTER 1
Session 1

1. b

TCP/IP may indeed be a really weird acronym, but in fact it is the set of protocols that handles trafficking data across the Internet.

2. d

The HyperText Transport Protocol is in fact all of these. It is a client-server text transfer protocol for HTML documents. And, in fact, the data transfer can be on the Internet or on an Intranet. Also, as mentioned in the session, HTTP works with CGI for transferring data to and from the client.

3. c

The government ARPA project is where the Internet was developed. While many segments of the computer industry were started in garages (i.e., Apple) the Internet was not one, nor was it a private commercial endeavor. Spontaneous Generation was an old biological theory that life just started *spontaneously* out of common objects.

4. d

The World Wide Web does consist of the HTTP protocol for transferring HTML and data, is not the only protocol on the Internet, and was developed at CERN laboratories in Switzerland.

5. c

TCP/IP breaks down data into packets to be sent across the Internet. The data is then recombined and checked.

Session 2

1. d

There is no formal FOOTER structure in HTML.

2. c

The word **easy** is surrounded by the **<B></B>** tags and will be represented in bold type. The word **question** is surrounded by the **<I></I>** tags and will be represented in italic type.

3. a

The body of an HTML document is surrounded by the two tags. A paragraph is **<P></P>**.

4. a

The text **Working with** is surrounded with the **<B></B>** tags and will be shown in bold type. The text **with the Internet is** is surrounded with the **<I></I>** tags and will be shown in italic type. Note that the word **with** is surrounded by both the bold and italic tags so will be both italic and bold. The word **Internet** is also surrounded with bold tags and will be bold and italic. Finally, **Exciting** will be in italics.

5. a

This is the correct format for the beginning and ending tags.

Session 3

1. c

Visual Basic Script is supported by a browser which runs on the client side. It is not supported on the server side and is specifically designed to be operating system independent.

2. b

ActiveX is a technology by which you can add custom controls such as timers, panels, labels, slider controls, and so on to your HTML documents (not to mention C++ and Visual Basic programs).

3. d

All of these are important uses. We can validate the data a user has entered before sending it off to the server. We can provide a host of different data entry options for a user such as only allowing numeric numbers in a textbox or ensuring that characters entered are all in uppercase. And finally, we can control objects in our Web pages such as ActiveX controls and Java applets.

4. a

One of the primary purposes of being able to do processing on the client side with Visual Basic Script is so that we can minimize transferring data to the server to be processed.

5. c

ActiveX controls and Java applets are run on the local machine as well as downloaded to the local machine. This reduces the amount of processing that takes place across the Internet between the browser/client and the server.

Session 4

1. d

The Internet Explorer supports all of these.

2. d

Visual Basic Script will be supported on different platforms such as the Macintosh. Microsoft has provided free licenses for any browser developers to add Visual Basic Script to their browsers. And, the Internet Explorer fully supports Visual Basic Script.

3. a

Favorites are pointers or references to your favorite Web sites. You, as the user, can set these favorites to any Web locations you desire.

4. c

The Stop button will stop any document from continuing to load.

5. b

Session 5

1. d

Forms are used to retrieve input from the user and, if needed, to send it on to the server. And, you can interact with the user-entered data with Visual Basic Script.

2. c

All are except the button bar.

3. b

The first has an attribute of TEXTBOXSIZE which is not a valid attribute. The third uses TEXTNAME instead of NAME. And, the last uses TEXTTYPE instead of TYPE.

4. a

The **Post** method does send the data in a form to the server. The **Get** method does the opposite. Answer C is incorrect because the *document* is not sent.

5. d

All are correct variations on the tag format.

Session 6

1. c

There are three sets of **<TD></TD>** column tags for each set of **<TR></TR>** row tags.

2. c

Checked is the correct key word.

3 d

The second set of **<TR></TR>** tags indicates the second row. Within that row, the second set of **<TD></TD>** tags indicates the second column. Within that column, the **<FONT></FONT>** tag sets the color to yellow.

4. a

There are two rows in the table with three columns each. The second column of each row has an input type of TEXT.

5. a

There are in fact three columns in the table since the first row has three columns.

Session 7

1. c

The **<BODY>** tag indicates that when the script is loaded, **"AnotherSub"** should be run.

2. d

The two languages supported are Visual Basic Script and JavaScript. You may have picked b. or c., but note that Visual Basic and Java are not supported, just the scripting versions of these languages.

3. d

The second parameter of the **MsgBox** function indicates the type of buttons to be shown. And, a 4 for the parameter indicates Yes and No buttons.

4. c

The third parameter of the **MsgBox** function indicates the title of the dialog box that is shown. Answer c. correctly sets the title to "Hello".

5. b

The end of the subroutine needs to be **End Sub** not just **End**. For answer a., there does not have to be a startup subroutine specified or any language in the **<BODY>** tag.

Session 8

1. a

Visual Basic Script allows you to interact with HTML input elements. HTML cannot interact with Visual Basic Script or ActiveX directly.

2. c

The click event is signified by **OnClick**, not **Click**. So, the code should be as follows:

```
<INPUT TYPE=BUTTON VALUE="Click Here!" NAME="Button">

<SCRIPT LANGUAGE="VBScript">

Sub Button_OnClick
MsgBox "Test"
End Sub

</SCRIPT>
```

3. a

The **<SCRIPT>** tag should be **<SCRIPT LANGUAGE="VBScript">**.

4. d

There needs to be a language identifier; **OnClick** is the event, and the code comments need an **'** character.

5. a

Events are segments of code that run whenever an action happens in the browser. Events don't make an action happen and do not have to just be called through code.

CHAPTER 2

Session 1

1. d

HTML tags indicate to the browser how to display and utilize specified data. They are always surrounded by <> brackets. And, they can have attributes. For example in `<FONT COLOR=RED>`, COLOR is an attribute for the font that we are setting to red.

2. a

The Language attribute indicates what language the browser needs to interpret to execute the following script code.

3. b

To italicize `This` the `<I></I>` tags must be used. The line break tag `<BR>` is used to separate the two lines. And last, the `another line` text is set to bold using the `<B></B>` tags.

4. b

The text will be centered horizontally on the Web page in the browser.

5. d

Each is a true statement about an incorrect tag or attribute.

Session 2

1. d

Each answer is true. For those browsers that do not support graphics, at least a text message will be displayed. A description of the graphic will be shown if the image is still loading, and if the page download is interrupted, the text description of the image may still be visible.

2. b

The graphic will be tiled across the background.

3. b

You need an HREF attribute to indicate what HTML document you want to link to.

4. a

The text will certainly be shown at the top of the graphic because of the ALIGN attribute set to TOP in the image tag. And, since the text is after the image tag, it will show to the right of the image since it will be displayed after the image. To make it show to the left, put the text before the image.

5. d

Color is not an attribute.

Session 3

1. a

There is no need to have two font tags setting each attribute (color and size) in our HTML code. It is easier to simply put both attributes in our `<FONT>` tag.

2. b

Text tags indicate how a browser should display text. But, the Web page author cannot completely control layout or how the text will be displayed. Each browser will implement the tags in different ways. It is up to the browser to determine how the actual formatting will be displayed. Indeed, this will change based on the type of system the browser is running on. The same document displayed on a Windows or a Macintosh system might look different even using the same browser.

3. d

The `<I></I>` tag will make all the text italic. A strike through is just shown on the **S**. The `Text` characters have `<B></B>` tags to indicate that text should be bold. And finally, the `text` characters will be underlined from the `<U></U>` tags.

4. b

We have two ending `</SUP>` tags whereas the first one should be `<SUP>`.

5. a

Session 4

1. d

Since there is no cell padding specified, the value will be the default set by the browser.

2. a

The second set of `<TR></TR>` tags starts the second row. The first column spans two of the table columns. So, the third table column of row two is set up to have an HTML input button element.

3. b

The first column spans two of the table columns, so there will only be two column boxes.

4. a

The `<FONT SIZE=1 COLOR=RED>` tag is used to set the font to red.

5. a

Session 5

1. a

The ROWS attribute indicates that we are setting sizes for frames rows or frames. The '*' character indicates that spacing should be relative and in this case it will be two evenly sized vertical frames.

2. d

The frame tag sets up a single frame.

3. a

SRC indicates the HTML document to be shown in the frame.

4. b

We have two rows of frames. The first row has one frame and the second has three frames for a total of 4.

5. b

Session 6

1. c

For answer a., a text element only inputs one line of text. Hidden textboxes don't allow input. The textarea input element allows for multiple lines of text.

2. c

The Submit button input element will trigger the form action to send or retrieve data from the user.

3. d

The `MaxLength` attribute of a textbox will limit the maximum length of the text entered.

4. a

You simply need to add the `CHECKED` attribute to the INPUT tag and the item will be selected.

5. a

Session 7

1. a

Item 1 falls between the `<DIR></DIR>` tags, but does not also fall between the `<MENU></MENU>` tags.

2. c

The first list item will use alphabetical counting for the list item, the second will use numbers, and the third uses Roman numerals.

3. d

There is no definition tag for **W** since it follows a **<DT>** tag. The **<DT>** tag is used to display definitions, not definition items.

4. d

The first three are true. The TYPE=I tag is only used with an ordered list. So, there will be no Roman numerals shown in this list.

5. b

Session 8

1. d

When using a hyper link, the **<TARGET>** tag will indicate which frame the specified HTML tag will be loaded in.

2. a

The TYPE attribute in the **<LI>** tag will set the counting format and an **I** will indicate Roman numerals.

3. b

In the sample BODY1 HTML document, we set the **super** background by setting the BACKGROUND attribute of the **<BODY>** tag.

4. b

You are not limited to three frames; you can display scroll bars, and using the **<TARGET>** tag on a hyper link, you can dynamically set the HTML document for a frame. And, of course, you can have resizable frames.

5. a

CHAPTER 3
Session 1

1. a

Visual Basic is the most robust and *complete* version.

2. c

Visual Basic Script has been designed to have no negative side effects on the system it will run on.

3. a

4. d

With Visual Basic Script, you can work with HTML in the context of the browser, but you cannot call Windows API functions, do file input and output, or build complete client-server applications.

5. a

Session 2

1. b

The ending comment tag should be before the **</SCRIPT>** tag.

2. c

You need to define that this script code needs to be interpreted as Visual Basic Script. This is done with the LANGUAGE attribute.

3. b

There are many events provided for you by Internet Explorer, but you cannot define your own custom events. For example, there is an **OnClick** event provided for the HTML Button element. You cannot define your own **OnDoubleClick** event for the button.

4. b

Your Web documents can contain Visual Basic and Java script code.

5. d

As discussed in the chapter, each is a valid way of adding script code to your documents.

Session 3

1. d

As our examples clearly demonstrated, we can call the **Write** method as many times as we like from our script code.

2. b

Line three of our example has two **document.write** statements on the same line. This is acceptable if they are separated by a ':' character, but they are not.

3. a

As mentioned in the first session, Visual Basic Script has been specifically designed to not allow your Web pages to interact directly with the end user's system. The other three can be controlled by Visual Basic script.

4. d

Both statements are true about the sample code.

5. d

All are exposed.

Session 4

1. b

ActiveX controls can be developed in a variety of tools including C++, Java, and Visual Basic.

2. c

There are three **PARAM** attributes for the control. This indicates that there are three properties for the control.

3. b

The system registry is where all local controls are registered. The Internet Explorer looks there to find a reference to the control; if it is not there, then it downloads it from your Internet server.

4. b

ActiveX controls can be used in a wide variety of development tools including Microsoft's Visual C++ and Visual Basic.

5. d

The object tag indicates an object has been inserted into the Web document.

Session 5

1. c

Location is an object on the same level as a document and is contained in the **Window** object.

2. d

As our code example showed, **appname** is a property of the **Navigator** object, not the **Window** object. Thus, we must reference the **Navigator** object to retrieve the property.

3. b

The **Location** object provides information about the location of the URL location of the Web page.

4. b

The object model is specifically designed for exposure to your scripts. Thus, each property and method is available to your scripts.

5. a

The **Frame** object in Internet Explorer contains the set of frames that are in the main browser window.

Session 6

1. a

2. a

The timer event is fired off every time the Timer control counts down the amount of time set by the interval property.

3. a

4. c

Each time the timer event is run, the value of X will increase by 2 such that on the third call it will have a value of 6. Note that X is a **global** variable.

5. d

The property is **FontUnderline**.

Session 7

1. b

The second argument to the **InputBox** function will set the title for the input box.

2. c

As shown in all the examples, you need to have parentheses around the arguments you pass into the **InputBox** function. You do not have to specify X and Y positions for the **InputBox** or a default value.

3. c

We have formatted this prompt to have four lines using the **CHR()** function. The first will be "ABCD", the second "ABC", the third "AB", and the fourth "A".

4. c

The third parameter is the default value for the input box. If the user enters nothing, then the default value will be returned from **InputBox** which is "Text3" and will be written to the document.

5. a

Session 8

1. d

All are true. We must have quotes around the two **denvers**, there has to be an '=' sign between **Variable2** and **denver**, and finally an **If** is needed after the **End**.

2. a

In the example question the "" argument after **"Take a Quiz"** is the current default. We simply need to fill in whatever text we would like to have as the default answer.

3. c

4. b

5. a

CHAPTER 4
Session 1

1. a

'A' is globally declared because it is declared at the script level and not inside any subroutine or function.

2. b

'B' is locally declared because it is declared inside the StartSub subroutine.

3. c

'A' is globally declared and is initialized with a value of 0. The first time Work is called, we add 5 to 'A', thus its value is 5.

4. c

Local variables in different procedures have no relation to each other. They can have the same name. Thus, a, b, and d would indicate that they are tied together somehow, which is not true.

5. c

The data type is Integer, and the variable name is Foo. We will take the first three letters of Integer and attach them to the beginning of Foo to indicate that it will hold integer data.

Session 2

1. a

"ABCD" is a valid string. The second answer, 1234, is a number. In order to represent it in a string, it would have to be in quotes. The third answer is missing a double quote in front of the 'P'.

2. b

In the example string equation, the only space to be added is between the 'E' and 'G'. The other answers all place spaces in wrong positions.

3. d

The **Mid** function will parse out three characters starting at the second character in the string **"VBSCRIPT"**. These three characters are "BSC". If we then take the left of "BSC" for two characters, we have the string "BS".

4. b

All basic variables either contain numbers or strings. Answer a. is not true because a variable can, at any time, store any subtype. Answer c. is obviously not false because of the & operator. And, answer d. is not true because we can utilize functions like `Left`, `Right`, and `Mid`.

5. b

Session 3

1. b

Integers are whole numbers; 4.3 is not a whole number. The others all are.

2. a

Fix returns the first negative integer that is greater than the argument to the function.

3. d

First evaluate the result of (1 AND 0). Only (1 AND 1) will return a 1, so the result is 0. Then, 0 OR 0 is going to return 0. The only time OR returns a 0 is when both values are 0.

4. d

The `Mod` function divides numbers, which excludes answers a. and c. `Mod` is specifically designed to return the remainder of a division operation, not the resulting integer portion.

5. a

Session 4

1. a

We set `dtWork1` to be a date using `DateValue`. We then get the day, which is 5 and multiply it by 4 to get 20. Answer b. does not set up `dtWork1` to be a date. Answer c. is close, but the double quotes are missing around the date in the `Day` function.

2. c

The `WeekDay` function returns an integer between 1 and 7 that represents the day of the week in the day.

3. d

The number of days between the two dates is 10.

4. b

We are taking a date and subtracting a larger date. The difference between the two will be a negative number of days. In this case, it is exactly one year, −365 days.

5. a

Session 5

1. c

Remember that position 0 is valid in an array. In this case there is a position for 0, 1, 2, 3, and 4 which totals five elements.

2. c

Because we have the **Preserve** keyword on the **ReDim** statements, the values in the array are not destroyed.

3. c

Using the **ReDim** statements, an array can be resized. Answer a. is not true because an array is not forced to store just one subtype. Answer b. is incorrect because we can have multidimensional arrays.

4. b

UBound in this case checks the first dimension for the upper bound which is 3.

5. a

The first bound will be 0 initially.

Session 6

1. a

The system timer is used to seed the random number generator only when **Randomize** has no parameter passed in.

2. b

The lower bound in our example is 1, and the upper bound is 10. If you add five to each, the range of the random number will be between 6 and 15.

3. b

The first time we call the **Rnd** function, a random number is generated. The second time we send in an argument of 0 to the function. If zero is passed in, the next random number is not generated, and the last number is returned.

4. b

The return value is a decimal value that starts at 0 and is less than 1.

5. c

The next random number in the sequence is returned.

Session 7

1. c

The **Chr** function returns a character based on a passed in ASCII value. Answer a. states that an integer value is returned as well as answer b., which are incorrect.

2. a

The ASCII function returns an ASCII code value for a specified character. Answer b. states that a character string is returned, which is false. The **Chr** function returns a character string which makes answer c. invalid. And, answer d. indicates the **Chr** function returns a character string of a character. It returns a character string of an ASCII code.

3. b

Uppercase 'A' has an ASCII code representation of 65 (97 – 32).

4. a

The **Mid** function will return 'Wor', and the **UCASE** function will return 'WOR'.

5. b

There are three parameters for the **Left** function; there should only be two.

Session 8

1. a

A return value of 1 from **VarType** indicates that the variable contains NULL. The X variable is empty, not NULL. Answer c. checks a nondeclared variable, Y, but it is also empty. And, of course, **VarType** on NULL itself will return a 1.

2. a

Y starts out as an integer value. We then convert it to a string using the **Chr** function. Thus, when we check the variable type, the return value will be 8 to indicate a string.

3. a

The **Mid** of X starting at 7 for a length of 1 is 2. **IsNumeric** will look at this string and report back True, that the string contains a numeric value.

4. a

Cdate takes the string "12/12/96" and returns a date subtype. This is then converted to a string using the **CStr** function. But, the string still contains a valid date, and **IsDate** returns True.

5. d

The value is numeric, and **IsNumeric** would be the appropriate function. The other functions do not exist.

CHAPTER 5
Session 1

1. b

Splitting the code into procedures allows the structure of your code to be built up.

2. c

See the definition for a subroutine.

3. c

Structuring your code may or may not result in faster execution.

4. a

See the definition for **ByVal.**

5. d

See the definition for **ByRef**.

Session 2

1. d

Use functions only when you need to return a value.

2. b

See the definition of a function.

3. c

OncoActive receives the return value from the **X_Ray** function.

4. c

There are many uses for the Exit command, but it always results in the early termination of the procedure.

5. a

A function can receive more values than you will ever need to use, so there is no real limit.

Session 3

1. d

After the dependent code is run, the processor jumps to the **End If** statement.

2. a

If one test fails, then any number of subsequent tests can be applied using **ElsIf**.

3. c

If no other condition is True, then the **Else** statement must be True.

4. d

If statements trigger specific lines of code only when the conditions specified by the programmer are met.

5. c

There is no **If** statement and therefore no dependent code. It cannot be a condition.

Session 4

1. a

See the definition for a loop.

2. c

This is the delimiter for the lower boundary of the loop code.

3. a

Step is used to vary the increment value. It can also be set to a negative value to make decrementing loops.

4. c

The loop runs from one to nine inclusive.

5. d

Going down in blocks of minus five, twenty-five to zero takes six loops. From zero to minus five takes one extra loop.

Session 5

1. d

See the definition of a **Do** loop.

2. c

If the exit condition cannot be met, then the loop will never stop.

3. b

The condition is tested as the first line of the loop block.

4. c

Exit conditions must alway resolve to True.

5. d

Unless you know the starting value of Counter, you cannot tell how many increments of plus one are required to meet the exit condition, or even if it will be met at all.

Session 6

1. b

Only the code dependent on the case conditon that resolves to True will be executed.

2. c

The Select Case does nothing a complex **If** statement cannot do, but it does result in clearer code.

3. d

Else always means "If none of the above conditions are True".

4. c

A case branch can contain as many expressions as you like as long as they are separated by commas.

5. a

No other code is run from within the Select Case after the first matching Case branch has been found.

Session 7

1. c

Event handlers are always subroutines.

2. c

Sub followed by the control name, then an underscore, then the event name.

3. c

The correct event name is **DblClick**, not **DoubleClick**.

4. d

The user/code relationship works both ways.

5. c

The code will always end up back where it first began.

Session 8

1. c

There is no place to hide. Errors in your code are your fault.

2. d.

See the definition for an object.

3. d

There is no information about restarting the code in the **Err** object.

4. a

Generating errors is useful to help debug error trapping routines.

5. c

The local error trapping can be toggled on and off using the `On Error` statements.

CHAPTER 6

Session 1

1. b

First note that we do not have the counter variable globally declared. So, each time the timer is fired off, the counter will be set to 1 and then the label caption is set to 1.

2. b

As mentioned in the text above, the status bar is also generally used by the browser to display status messages. The other statements are, of course, all false.

3. d

To change the text displayed on the button, we need to reference the `Value` property of the button; there is no caption property. The increment in answer a. does not matter, the placement of the script and element do not matter and finally, we can set the text of the button to the value of the `Counter` variable.

4. d

In fact all three can be used to set the point size. For answer a., the label element is not on a form so it is a subobject of the `Window` object in the scripting object model. Of course, you reference the fontsize property directly as in answer b. Answer c. will also work.

5. d

All three are declared globally in the script.

Session 2

1. d

Actually none of the answers is correct. The real problem is that the '&' character should be a '+'. We are adding values, not concatenating strings.

2. c

The first message box will show Yes and No buttons. A return value of 5 is a check for a click on an Ignore button. Thus, the second message box will never be shown.

3. b

Only one icon can be shown.

4. c

We need to have a variable defined to retrieve the return value from the message box. Note that you can call the **MsgBox** function with a return value by dropping the parentheses (i.e., MsgBox "Hello"). Second, to build the prompt and put the string together correctly, we need '&' characters between the different strings in the prompt—"Line 1" & chr(10) & "Line 2".

5. c

Abort, Retry, and Ignore buttons have a value of 2, the Critical Message Icon has a value of 16, and the second button as default has a value of 256. Totaled they have a value of 274.

Session 3

1. b

Any time the mouse moves over the image map, the event is fired off.

2. a

We simply need to provide an HTML document name in the **href** attribute of the link.

3. b

The x coordinate of 34 is not between 90 and 120.

4. b

All four arguments need to be declared, otherwise the browser will error when it tries to run the subroutine.

5. a

A width for the image map needs to be specified.

Session 4

1. a

Just like the **OnFocus** event reviewed in the sample Web page, the implementation of **OnBlur** will be to input the element name then an '_' character and the name of the event.

2. d

Help panels are merely something the Web page designer can implement, if he or she wishes, as a design form.

3. b

In our example, you change the point size, forecolor, bold, italic, and other properties to make the message stand out as you wish. With answer a., you cannot modify a controls methods nor can you change properties of an HTML input text element.

4. d

There is no requirement for where the help panel must be placed. It is purely up to your stylistic consideration.

5. c

Session 5

1. a

You have to remember that the reference to the collection of frames in the document begins with 0. So, `frame(2)` references the third frame and will set its background color to green.

2. d

Each is a valid method for referencing the frame. We can use the actual frame name, the `Window` object is implied in b., and finally, as mentioned in the text, we can reference the parent document and any frames contained in it. The parent document is the one where the script resides.

3. c

The only way we would know that this statement is True is if Foo were the timer event of a timer control or was called by a timer event.

4. b

There are seven images provided on the CD-ROM. Once the counter is incremented and if it has reached 8, then we have moved beyond the last image and need to set the counter back to 1. If we check for 7, the last image will never be displayed because the counter will be reset to 1 before the eighth image can be displayed.

5. b

The document should be closed.

Session 6

1. d

Remember that you must use forward slashes and not back slashes when referencing the location of a file on your system. For answer a., the window object does not have to be specified, and, for answer b., the wave files can be in any location.

2. d

Any one of these will work to have a sound file launched when the document is first loaded in the browser.

3. d

The current document location will be searched for the media file.

4. a

There is no **HREF** attribute to define the file location.

5. c

Session 7

1. d

There will be three menu items left. We start out with two and then add three for a total of five. Then the loop executes twice to remove two menu items, thus leaving three.

2. a

RemoveItem does remove the menu item indicated by the argument sent to the method. The **AddItem** statement is not True because the determination is not made on the value of the menu text, and **PopUp** and **Click** are events, not methods.

3. d

You can ignore the first menu item added because it is removed immediately. Then five menus items are added, and finally the first one is removed. That leaves four menu items with the last one being "Menu 5".

4. b

You can call the **PopUp** method of the control at any point in your code, regardless of the user's action.

5 d

In essence, you control it by calling it from anywhere in your code.

6. a

The **PopUp** event displays the menu for the control.

Session 8

1. d

Since the timer is not stopped when **SizeCount** reaches 25, the code will continue to try and increase the font size of the label control. But, when **SizeCount** does reach 25, the caption of the label will read "DONE".

2. a

Remember that in our example, **SizeCount** was declared globally and not initialized with a value. Thus it started out with a value of 0, and when incremented by 1 in the timer event and then checked, it will have a value of 1. Thus, the font size of the label is set to 50, the timer is disabled, and the subroutine is exited.

3. b

The timer will actually execute 26 times, but the last time the label angle will not be incremented by 3. So, if the angle is starting with a value of 0 and is incremented by a value of 3 for 25 timer ticks, its final value will be 75.

4. d

Note that the `SizeCount` variable has not been incremented with each timer tick. So, the timer event will never stop firing off, and the font size will continue to be incremented.

5. a

If the font size starts out at a large point size and is decreased to 0, then the effect will be reversed.

CHAPTER 7
Session 1

1. a

2. c

3. b

4. b

5. c

A `Frame` object is a `Window` object for all practical purposes.

Session 2

1. d

2. a

3. c

Actually, the `length` property does not function correctly in version 3.0 of Internet Explorer.

4. b

5. a

The `Window` object contains all other objects, either directly or indirectly.

Session 3

1. c

2. c

3. b

4. b

5. a

Session 4

1. b

2. b

3. b

4. d

The `length` property is often used in VBScript to determine the number of items in a collection.

5. b

Session 5

1. a

2. a

3. b

4. d

Microsoft Internet Explorer supports both VBScript and JavaScript.

5. b

Session 6

1. c

2. d

`Writeln` outputs a carriage return at the end of the output.

3. d

4. d

5. a

Session 7

1. d

2. b

3. d

4. d

The correct way to establish an anchor is `<A NAME="anchorname">` (no "#" sign).

5. b

Session 8

1. a

Remember, the `forms` collection begins with zero, so `forms(0)` represents the first form.

2. b

3. d

4. d

5. c

CHAPTER 8

Session 1

1. b

`write` is a method of the document object and is not a subobject of document.

2. c

You do not have to have a `window` tag because Visual Basic Script will assume this reference. But, the `frames` collection is not appropriately referenced. It should be `frames(x)` to indicate which frame should be referenced out of all the frames on the Web page.

3. c

Answer a. describes an `object` property, and b. describes an `object` event. A method is something that you can invoke from your scripts to perform a specific function provided by the object.

4. a

The frames collection will only hold a reference for any frames created on the current document.

5. c

A property describes an object. It defines attributes and characteristics of an object.

Session 2

1. b

When the user makes any changes to the text value in the textbox, this event is fired so that you have the ability to be notified to check the changes.

2. c

The **enabled** property determines whether or not input is allowed into the textbox.

3. b

The **OnBlur** event subroutine is run when the user exits the textbox and the focus is given to another part of the document.

4. a

The **Blur** method will take the focus away from the textbox so that the next user keyboard input will not be sent to the textbox.

5. b

DefaultValue defines the value that will be defaulted if there is no other input.

Session 3

1. b

The value starts at 3 then is multiplied by 4 because the value is True. For the second click, the checked value is False so no multiplication takes place. With the next click, it will be checked so the value will be multiplied again and total 48.

2. c

The first time the check box is clicked regardless of the resulting checked status, the value is multiplied by 3.

3. c

The position of the check box cannot be changed through Visual Basic Script.

4. b

The event in script code that is fired off is **OnFocus**. For **Check1** the subroutine would be declared as is shown in answer b.

5. c

Session 4

1. a

The focus event sets the focus of an element. None of the other events set the focus. For c., the **Blur** event does not set the focus of an element; it takes away the focus.

2. d

The first two answers are true, but so is the third answer because there will be an endless loop of mouse clicks until the browser crashes. This happens because each click event fires the other click event which in turn fires the other, and so on.

3. d

Any text placed in the textbox will then be the value or caption of the button. The values are compatible, and in no way is the name of either input element referenced.

4. d

The functionality of the button does change based on its value, and the **OnClick** event is used to control the starting and stopping of the label control.

5. c

Session 5

1. a

The **History** object allows you to navigate through all the Web pages the user has visited.

2. d

You must reference the actual form and button names, **form1** and **button1**.

3. c

The **Window.Document.Form** reference leads to the text element. Then **Var.Text1.Value** provides the correct reference.

4. d

Since there can be many of these objects on a Web page, they are referenced through an indexed array.

5. a

Session 6

1. d

All are true. It does allow the form to be submitted to the server. You can use the **submit** method to submit the form outside of the form. Finally, because you can control the submission of the form, you can perform data validation on the user input before the data is sent to the server.

2. b

The second element in the elements array is **Button1**. Remember that all elements on the form are stored in the elements array which starts at index 0.

3. a

The **target** property indicates the window in which the form results should be shown.

4. d

The **Form** object falls under the **Document** object in the Internet Explorer scripting object model hierarchy.

5. c

Session 7

1. b

As was demonstrated in the last session, the **Form** object does have a **method** property, but we need to reference which form in the **forms** array. Since there is one form, the reference would be index 0.

2. c

Remember that the index starts at 0 in the array. So the indexes would be values 0 through 5 for the 6 forms. Thus, the upper bound of the array is 5.

3. d

The **For...Next** loop will go one too far since the index into the forms starts at 0 and goes through the number of forms minus 1. And, the **MsgBox** statement needs to reference **Document.Forms(N).Method**.

4. a

Although a form can be referenced by name, there is no actual **name** property of the **Form** object.

5. b

Session 8

1. d

The reference is correct. It references the first frame, second form on the frame, and the first element is referenced.

2. c

The check box is the fourth element placed on the form and can be referenced in the elements array as index 3.

3. d

A frame can contain an HTML document that contains any of these objects.

4. a

The **Window** object is the top object in the scripting object model.

5. b

The first frame is referenced by **frames(0)**, and the second form is referenced as **Forms(1)**.

CHAPTER 9

Session 1

1. a

All alpha characters entered in the text are in uppercase. The 1 and space characters do not affect the fact that the text is all in uppercase.

2. d

All of these are true. A check is done to see if a space was entered in the textbox by looping through each character. And the **Flag** variable will be false for answer c. because there is a space in the string.

3. a

We can ignore all text to the right of the first two characters if we wish to check the abbreviation. This can be done by getting the left two characters of the text string and checking them.

4. c

The **Submit** method fires off the form. If all the data has been validated, then the next logical step for processing a form would be to submit it to the server.

5. c

OnBlur is fired when the focus of the textbox is lost.

Session 2

1. b

To round to two decimal places we used 100 to move the two decimals to the left of the decimal point and then move them back to the right. To save four decimal places, 10000 would be used to move four decimal places back and forth.

2. b

We want to check to see if the value falls BETWEEN the two values. Thus, we want to make sure that **VAL1** is greater then **Val2** AND less than **Val3**. And since we want to look between the values, we will not use the = sign since **Val1** cannot be equal to **Val2** and **Val3**.

3. a

The absolute function takes the absolute value of any number, which is to say that it converts it to a positive value.

4. c

The difference between the two is how negative numbers are handled.

5. d

All can be used to ensure that the data subtype is a type of numerical value.

Session 3

1. d

Regardless of the format of the date entered, 1996 is returned in both cases.

2. d

Let's face it, the code in this example is flawed. The **Val1** date is not in a valid format, the **CDate** function is not called correctly, and the **MsgBox** call is not correct.

3. d

There is a slight difference between the **TimeSerial** and **TimeValue** functions. The **TimeSerial** function takes in separate values for the day, month, and year whereas **TimeValue** takes in a complete string containing the time.

4. d

All these functions can be used to retrieve the specified part of a date variable.

5. a

CDate will ensure that the variable subtype is of type **Date**.

Session 4

1. a

The **SelectedIndex** returns the first selected item in the list box. The **Selected** property indicates whether or not a specific option item is selected.

2. d

The **Options** array reference begins at 0 and goes to the length of the list minus 1. The **For...Loop** should start at 0 and go to the length of the list minus 1.

3. c

The **SelectedIndex** is used to reference the text of the option that has been selected by the user.

4. d

The `options` property references all the options of the `Select` element which are stored in an array.

5. d

Session 5

1. a

The Mid section of the string manipulation returns `"String2"`. The left three characters of that string are `"Str"`.

2. b

The loop goes through each letter in the string. The `If...Then` statement checks for any capital letters in the string. But, `Var2` will only contain the last capital letter in the string, "L", since it does not concatenate each capital letter onto `Var2`.

3. c

The `InStr` function will search for one string in another. `CheckIn` and `MidIn` are not Visual Basic Script functions, and `Mid` is used to retrieve part of a string.

4. d

Each one will return the first character in the string.

5. a

Session 6

1. b

The `Exit Sub` should the last part of the `If...Then` statement and come after the `PopObj.PopUp` call. In the scenario, the hint will never be shown.

2. b

The `Click` event would be used to simulate a click on one of the buttons.

3. d

Each is correct. A document needs to be specified for the pop up window, the event is `OnClick`, and the end of the subroutine is `End Sub`.

4. c

There needs to be a class ID, or UUID, for the pop up menu object.

5. b

The name of the document to show is the first, and the second indicates whether or not the window should be expanded.

Session 7

1. a

The event as demonstrated in the code is the **Click** event, not the **OnClick** event.

2. a

This answer provides a general method for how we would need to reference which features were selected. Since any combination of features could be selected, it will be important to know which feature is being referenced when the menu is selected.

3. c

Of course you can have multiple ActiveX controls on one page, and it would be easy to add multiple menus to provide immediate feedback support for user selections for each Select list or to provide for default configuration selections, or both.

4. b

5. d

No parameters have to be defined for the object initially, and the **Id** property identifies the name of the object.

Session 8

1. d

All will return True. The basic value in each string is a numeric number.

2. b

The last set of numbers starts at position 8, not 7.

3. c

Dollar is not a valid Visual Basic Script function.

4. d

Depending on how you implement your program, any one of these could be used. The state abbreviation example used here was easiest to implement with the **Select...Case**.

5. c

CHAPTER 10

Session 1

1. c

The Wizard automatically inserts the **End Sub** into the parent HTML.

2. a

All the others will allow VBScript to be entered, but unformatted text is the default standard.

3. d

The Wizard does not provide any error code information.

4. c

5. d

No object added to an HTML file can have its event handler details changed.

Session 2

1. b

Xpad will automatically insert the **\<OBJECT\>** tags and the layout file information for you.

2. c

All the others are included in the standard.layout toolset.

3. d

All objects are manipulated via properties and methods.

4. c

5. b

Session 3

1. c

The Wizard automatically inserts the **End Sub** into the parent HTML.

2. a

All the others will allow VBScript to be entered but unformatted text is the default standard.

3. d

The Wizard does not provide any error code information.

4. c

5. d

No object added to an HTML file can have its event handler details changed.

Session 4

1. a

The **Timer** object allows programmers to create their own automatic event.

2. c

The **Forecolor** sets the text color. The **FontName** property changes the font. The **fontsize** property will alter the font size to its new value, that's all.

3. d

4. c

The **Value** property is set to True when clicked. The **caption** property is not affected.

5. d

Session 5

1. b

To prevent the same set of random numbers per run, use the **randomize** statement.

2. b

Although both **Click** and **Change** events can be used to set the **ChartType** value, it must always receive a numeric value.

3. d

4. a

The Select Case construct will always be used to determine which code should be run based on the current value of a single test expression.

5. d

Session 6

1. a

The **Window** object is created from the HTML of the parent HTML file. It is displayed in Xpad, not created by it. It is the highest level object.

2. d

The Window contains documents. **Href** is a property of the **Document** object.

3. b

Link tags in a document would create link objects.

4. c

Open is used to prepare a document to receive HTML. **Input** displays a user input dialog. **Write** is used to send HTML, in this case to the Window document.

5. b

Session 7

1. c

Java has been designed to run on as diverse a hardware platform as possible.

2. b

The variant is the VBScript's only data type. Java does not support it.

3. d.

Just like VBScript, JavaScript can access any part of the IE oject model.

4. d

See definition of parsed in Session 7.

5. d

Both VBScript and JavaScript can be embeded into HTML documents by using the **<SCRIPT>** tag.

Session 8

1. a

A container is a software component but is used specifically to contain information on other OLE objects.

2. c

A bitmap is not an OLE object.

3. d

There is service exchange between a mouse and a mouse mat. Option c. can be argued but in theory democratic institutions are client (voters) and server (the politicians) based.

4. d

The correct label depends on your frame of reference.

5. d

OLE allows the freedom to reuse the software components of Windows and its applications. This freedom can and probably will be abused.

CHAPTER 11

Session 1

1. c

2. a

When you do not specify a complete URL, it is assumed that the picture must reside at the current URL location.

3. b

4. d

5. a

Session 2

1. c

2. a

3. c

4. b

5. c

Remember, no x and y coordinates are passed to the `OnClick` subroutine.

Session 3

1. d

Use the BODY tag with the `BACKGROUND` parameter to set the background to a tiled graphic.

2. a

3. c

4. c

5. b

Session 4

1. c

2. a

3. d

You can either specify color as a hexadecimal value or as a string representing the color name.

4. c

5. b

Session 5

1. d

The BGSOUND tag is used to add MIDI music to your Web pages.

2. d

3. a

4. c

5. a

Session 6

1. c

You can rotate text using the label control.

2. a

You can pick a creative font to use the MARQUEE tag to produce animation.

3. a

4. b

5. b

Session 7

1. b

2. b

Some, but not all streamed video requires special server software.

3. c

4. a

5. c

Session 8

1. c

We use a hidden frame and the `document.write` method to play a sound in the memory game.

2. c

You must use `Set` when referring to an object rather than a standard variable.

3. a

4. d

You need to use single quotes in place of double quotes within the string you write.

5. a

CHAPTER 12

Session 1

1. a

2. d

You can use the asterisk (*) to assign the remaining screen space to a column.

3. d

4. b

5. d

Session 2

1. b

2. c

3. c

It is recommended that you always specify a name for each of your frames so you can easily access them elsewhere in your VBScript code.

4. b

5. c

Session 3

1. c

2. d

3. d

4. d

5. d

You can divide your display area into frames in whichever way is easier for you.

Session 4

1. d

2. a

3. d

4. b

5. a

Session 5

1. a

Use the frames collection to reference an individual frame.

2. c

3. a

4 d

The name of the appropriate object collection is "frames," not "frame."

5. c

Session 6

1. c

2. d

Choice a. would be correct if the current window *is* the top-level window.

3. b

Although it looks as if it could not possibly be right, you can nest the frames collections as far down as the level of frames you have created in your document.

4. d

Use the "top" keyword to refer to the top level window.

5. d

Frames and windows are, for all practical purposes, identical objects.

Session 7

1. c

2. b

3. c

4. c

5. b

Session 8

1. c

2. d

3. b

You can save time using the BASE tag if you want a series of frames to target a particular window.

4. c

5. d

The HREF tag is used to display another page when an image is clicked.

CHAPTER 13

Session 1

1. c

Grouping controls allows functionality to be shared.

2. d

The **Set** command must be used to place controls into an array.

3. c

Using a control from an array makes no difference to its capabilities.

4. b

An object's events cannot be changed by VBScript.

5. d

Arrays of controls are useful in conjuction with shared event procedures. They are commonly manipulated by loops to get at each member in turn.

Session 2

1. b

IsNumeric returns True if all the characters are numbers.

2. d

The Interval is measured in thousandths of a second.

3. c

Using *Not* inverses a Boolean value.

4. a

The substring is the first four characters starting from the right.

5. c

The length of the String "123456" is six characters but the loop starts at zero. Zero to six makes seven iterations in all.

Session 3

1. c

Arrays are synchronized by sharing the same index variable.

2. d

These are the three event sources in VBScript.

3. b

The ASCII value for a new line is 13.

4. b

There are two sets of five members making ten in all. Remember the zero indexed members.

5. c

When the same actions need to be applied to all the controls in an array, then looping through the array can be much easier.

Session 4

1. d

The **Interval** property specifies the pause between enabling the control and the running of the **Timer** event procedure.

2. c

All MS-DOS characters have an equivalent ASCII number.

3. b

The ASCII value for a new line is 13.

4. a

"A" = 65 and "H" = 72. The range is inclusive.

5. c

When the same actions need to be applied to all the controls in an array, then looping through the array can be much easier.

Session 5

1. c

When the user clicks on the option, the **Click** event is triggered, and the numerical value of the option selected is passed as a parameter.

2. b

The **OnLoad** event is triggered when the page is first loaded.

3. c

4. b

Floating point integers are not supported by the Long data type, therefore, VBScript will automatically round any number that is recast to a Long.

5. c

The **AddItem** method adds a new menu option. The **RemoveItem** method deletes the specified option from the menu list.

Session 6

1. b

The **Button** parameter indicates which mouse button the user clicked.

2. c

After the **PopUp** method displays the menu options at the current mouse coordinates, the user activates the menu's **Click** event by selecting one of them.

3. d

Using client data buffers reduces the traffic between the client and the server but does not reduce the amount of data transferred.

4. d

This is true of any array regardless of whether it is sharing a common index variable.

5. b

Trying to compare strings like this causes an error. This is prevented by using the Cint function to temporarily convert the string values to integer values.

CHAPTER 14

Session 1

1. a

2. d

3. c

4. d

5. d

Session 2

1. c

2. b

3. a

4. d

5. a

Session 3

1. d

In-line styles are good for quick style changes, but they do not allow you to easily change several styles at once.

2. b

3. b

4. b

5. d

Session 4

1. b

To use an object's methods (such as the `AddItem` method of a button menu control), you must first ensure that the object exists.

2. b

3. c

4. a

5. c

Session 5

1. c

2. b

3. b

4. c

5. a

Session 6

1. b

2. a

3. a

4. c

5. b

APPENDIX I

·············

INTERNET EXPLORER 3.0: A FIELD GUIDE

A new day dawned. The sun reached its fingers over the digital outback. The mighty Navigators (*Netscapus navigatorus*)—a species that reproduced like rabbits and ran nearly as fast—covered the landscape. Yonder, on a cliff that seemed to be beyond the horizon, a trembling new creature looked out over the Internet jungle. This strange new creature, calling itself the Explorer (*Microsoftus interneticus explorus*), sniffed around, considering whether it should enter the fragile ecosystem. Netscape gators gnashed their teeth, but the Explorers were not daunted. Explorer was a formidable beast. It became a part of the jungle and thrived. And even though it began as a mere pup, it evolved, and it evolved and it evolved.

Now the jungle is rife with two intelligent species.

What follows is a guide to domesticating Internet Explorer. You will learn how to care for your Explorer and even how to teach it tricks. Before long, you shall find truth behind the old axiom that the Explorer is man's (and woman's) best friend.

INTRODUCING EXPLORER TO YOUR ECOSYSTEM

Whether you're running Windows NT or Windows 95, installing Explorer is easy. Explorer's own installation program makes setup a breeze, and you need only to select the appropriate file on the CD-ROM to launch this installer. Make sure the CD-ROM included with this book is in the CD-ROM drive; then, depending upon your system, follow the directions below for either Windows 95 or Windows NT.

Windows 95 Installation

1. Click the Start button in the lower left corner of your screen.

2. Click on the Run... option in the Start menu. A dialog box similar to the one shown in Figure I-1 appears.

3. Using the Run dialog box, type in a pathname and specify the location of the Explorer installation program. IE301M95.EXE is in the CD's \Explorer directory, so if your CD-ROM drive is designated as D:, you'd type

   ```
   d:\explorer\ie301m95.exe
   ```

   If your CD-ROM drive has a different designation letter, type in the appropriate drive designation letter in place of d:.

4. After typing the proper pathname, click the OK button to start the Explorer's installation program. Depending upon your system, it may take a moment to load.

5. Once the installation program loads, follow the on-screen prompts to set up Explorer on your computer.

Windows NT 4 Installation

1. Click the Start button in the lower left corner of your screen.

2. Click on the Run... option in the Start menu. A dialog box similar to the one shown in Figure I-2 appears.

Figure I-1
The Windows 95
Run dialog box

Figure I-2
The Windows NT
Run dialog box

3. Using the Run dialog box, type in a pathname and specify the location of the Explorer installation program. MSIE30M.EXE is in the CD's \Explorer directory, so if your CD-ROM drive is designated as D:, you'd type:

```
d:\explorer\ie301mnt.exe
```

If your CD-ROM drive has a different designation letter, type in the appropriate drive designation letter in place of `d:`.

4. After typing the proper pathname, click the OK button to start the Explorer's installation program. Depending upon your system, it may take a moment to load.

5. Once the installation program loads, follow the on-screen prompts to set up Explorer on your computer.

Once you've run the installation, you'll need to restart your system. You can then click on the Internet icon on your desktop. If you've already selected an Internet provider with Windows dial-up networking, you'll be connected. If not, you'll be walked through the dial-in process. You'll need to enter the phone number of your Internet provider, your modem type, and other related information. Ultimately, you'll be taken to Microsoft's home page, where you can register your Explorer and find out about its latest features.

The Explorer is a constantly evolving animal. For the latest updates, plug-ins, and versions, be sure to regularly check out Microsoft's neck of the woods at `http://www.microsoft.com/ie/`.

Explorer Components

Explorer is more than a plain-Jane Web browser. As you work through the installation, you'll be able to choose a variety of components. You can select the following add-ons:

● **Internet Mail**—This is a comprehensive e-mail package. Using simple icons, you can write and read your mail off-line and then log on quickly to send and receive your latest batch of correspondence. See Figure I-3.

● **Internet News**—This is a window that lets you browse through thousands of newsgroups, read through the threads, and post your own messages. The News system is very easy to use. You can easily keep track of your favorite topics and automatically update with the latest news.

● **ActiveMovie**—This feature of Explorer lets you watch all sorts of video clips—MPEG, AVI, and QuickTime formats. It even supports a special streaming version of video that downloads movies as you watch them, letting you view video with little delay. The ActiveMovie system also lets you listen to all popular formats of audio files—AU, WAV, MIDI, MPEG, and AIFF. This makes it easy to add background sound to Web pages.

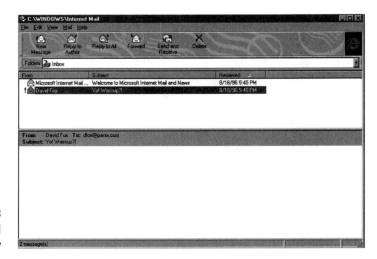

Figure I-3
The Internet Mail
main window

- VRML Support—This feature is a separate module that lets you download and coast through Virtual Reality Modeling Language worlds. This allows you to explore true 3D landscapes and objects.

- NetMeeting—This is a full-featured package that lets you hold entire meetings over the Internet. You can chat with one person or with dozens. If you have a microphone, you can use the Internet phone feature to hold voice conversations with other people. You can share applications. For example, you and a client can edit the same word processing document together. A whiteboard feature lets you draw on a "digital blackboard" that can be updated live across the Internet.

- HTML Layout Control—This tool lets Web page publishers create spiffy versions of HTML pages, the way professional designers would lay out a magazine page or a newspaper. Designers can choose exactly where to place elements within a Web page. You can make objects transparent and layer objects over each other, which helps make a Web page eye-catching yet uncluttered.

THE NATURE OF THE BEAST

Internet Explorer features very up-to-date HTML. It supports HTML 3.2, including the following:

- Frames—These break up the Web page window into several areas. For example, you can keep an unchanging row of navigation controls along the top of the page while constantly updating the bottom. You can use *borderless frames*, which split up the page without making it seem split.

A special type of frame known as the *floating frame* lets you view one Web page within another.

● Cascading Style Sheets—This allows all your Web sites to have the same general look and feel.

● Tables—You can create or view all sorts of fancy tables, with or without graphics, borders, and columns.

● Embedded Objects—Internet Explorer can handle Java applets, ActiveX controls, and even Netscape plug-ins. These objects are discussed later, in the Symbiotic Partners section of this appendix.

● Fonts—Explorer supports many fonts, allowing Web pages to have a variety of exciting designs.

From the get-go, Internet Explorer has included a few special bells and whistles. For example, it's easy to create and view marquees across Web pages. This lets you scroll a long, attention-drawing message, similar to a tickertape, that puts a great deal of information in a very small space.

TRAINING THE EXPLORER

By its very nature, the Explorer is a friendly beast. You can access the full range of the Explorer's talents by pushing its buttons. These buttons, which appear in the toolbar at the top of the screen as depicted in Figure I-4, are as follows:

● Back—Use this to return to the Web page you've just come from. This will help you retrace your steps as you take Explorer through the Internet maze.

● Forward—Use this after you've used the Back button, to jump forward again to the page from which you began.

● Stop—If a Web page is taking too long to load, press this button. Any text and graphics will immediately stop downloading.

● Refresh—If your Web page is missing some graphics, or if you've previously stopped its loading using the Stop button, you can reload it using Refresh.

● Home—This takes you to your pre-set home page. By default, this is Microsoft's main Web page, but you can set your home to any you'd like. See the Taming the Beast section.

● Search—This takes you to a special page that allows you to search for a Web page, using a number of cool search engines. See the Hunting Skills section.

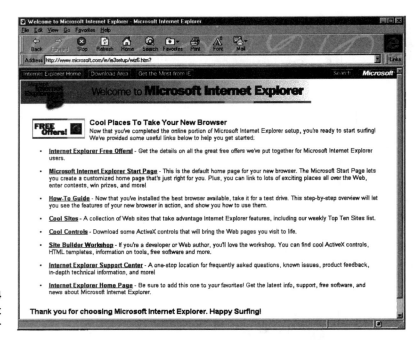

Figure I-4
A cosmetic look at Explorer

- Favorites—This button lets you access a list of your favorite Web sites. See the Favorite Haunts section.

- Print—This allows you to print out the current Web page, allowing you to keep a perfect hard copy of it.

- Font—Find yourself squinting at a Web page? Just click here to zoom in. The font size will grow several degrees. Too big now? Click a few more times and the size will shrink once again.

- Mail—This will launch the Internet Mail program, which allows you to send and receive e-mail and to access newsgroups.

PLAYING FETCH

Your Explorer is a devoted friend. It can scamper anywhere within the Internet, bringing back exactly what you desire.

If you know where you want to go, just type the URL into Explorer's Address box at the top of the screen. If you like, you can omit the `http://` prefix. The Web page will be loaded up. You can also search for a page or load up a previously saved page.

You can now click on any *hyperlink*—an underlined or colored word or picture—to zoom to that associated Web page or Internet resource. Some hyperlinked graphics may not be obvious. Explorer will tell you when you are positioned over a valid hyperlink, because the cursor will change into a pointing finger. Continue following these links as long as you like. It's not uncommon to start researching knitting needles and end up reading about porcupines.

If you're an aspiring Web page writer, you might want to take a peek at the HTML source code to see how that page was created. Just select View, Source.

HUNTING SKILLS

If you want to find Web pages dealing with a specific category, the Explorer makes it easy to find them. Click the Search button. The Search screen will appear, as in Figure I-5. You can search for more than Web pages. With Explorer, it's easy to find

- Phone numbers, ZIP codes, and addresses

- Information on a number of topics—health, home, education, consumer affairs, finance, weather, sports, travel, and so on

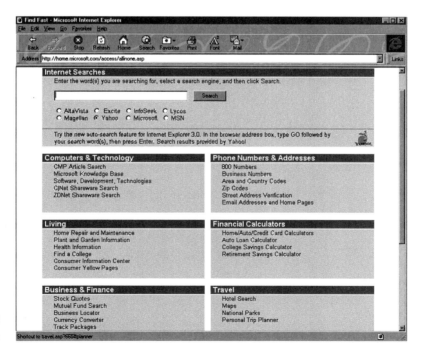

Figure I-5
The Search screen

● References—maps, a dictionary, a thesaurus, quotations, and an encyclopedia

● On-line books, newspapers, and magazines

You can also quickly hunt for any idea, word, or category. Simply type GO in the Address box at the top of the screen, followed by the word or phrase you want to search for.

FAVORITE HAUNTS

It's easy to keep track of the Web pages you visit most. When you want to save a page for future reference, simply click the Favorites button or choose the Favorites menu item. Select the Add To Favorites option. The current Web page will now be added to the list of favorites, which appears each time you click on the Favorites button or menu.

After a while, your list of favorites will get long and cluttered. It's simple to keep track of huge lists of favorites—just put them into separate folders. Organize your favorites, as shown in Figure I-6, by selecting Favorites, Organize Favorites.

To create a new folder, click on the New Folder icon (the folder with the little glint on it) at the top of the window. Now drag and drop your Web page bookmarks into the appropriate folders. You can also move, rename, or delete a folder by selecting it and using the corresponding buttons at the bottom of the screen.

You can even include or attach a favorite Web document within an e-mail message, the way you would attach any other file.

Figure I-6
Organizing the
Favorites list

On Windows systems, the Favorites list is actually a folder within your Windows directory. This reflects a Microsoft trend—treating the entire World Wide Web as just another folder to explore on your desktop. Eventually, you'll be able to drag and drop documents across the Internet as easily as you would within your own hard drive.

MEMORY

Internet Explorer keeps track of every Web page you visit. This is kept in a vast History list. You can view the entire History list, in chronological order, by clicking the View History button. Just click on any page you'd like to revisit.

The History list is cleared every 20 days—you can set this value within the Navigation properties sheets.

TAMING THE BEAST

Now that you and your Explorer are getting acquainted, why not tame it so that it acts and looks exactly like you want? Select View, Options and pick a tab at the top of the window to customize the following properties:

 General—The general properties sheet is illustrated in Figure I-7. Since multimedia content (such as sounds, movies, and graphics) takes longer to load in Web pages, you can choose to not load certain media types. You can also easily customize the color of the text and hyperlinks. Finally, you can decide how little or how much information appears in your toolbar.

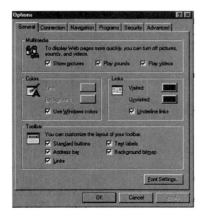

Figure I-7
The general
properties sheet

You can change the size and position of your toolbar simply by clicking on its borders and dragging it to a desired location.

● Connection—You can adjust your connections settings, as shown in Figure I-8, by clicking on this tab. This lets you choose your Internet provider. If you're connecting to the Internet through a network firewall, you can also set your proxy server information here.

● Navigation—You can customize which page you'd like to use as your starting home page. Just enter its URL in the Address box here.

● Programs—This allows you to set which programs you'd like to use for e-mail and for Usenet news. By default, you can use Microsoft's Internet Mail and Internet News, which are included with Explorer. You can also tell Explorer how to handle various types of files by selecting the File Types button. It allows you to designate which program or plug-in should be launched whenever Explorer comes across various unfamiliar file formats.

● Security—You are able to customize how securely documents will be handled by Explorer. If you want to keep your computer extremely safe, you may tell Explorer not to download possible security risks such as ActiveX controls, Java applets, or other plug-ins. Another nice feature is a Content Advisor. Click on Settings; the Content Advisor window will appear as in Figure I-9. You may now decide which Web pages to skip based on Adult Language, Nudity, Sex, or Violence. Many questionable Web pages are written with certain tags so that the pages can be weeded out by people who don't want to see them. This is a great option to use if your kids surf the Internet, or if your sensibilities are easily offended. To turn ratings on, click on the Enable Ratings button. You can also lock this window with a password.

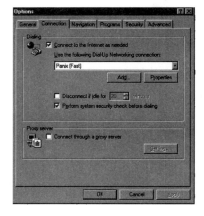

Figure I-8
The connection property sheet.

Figure I-9
The Content
Advisor window

● Advanced—This properties sheet lets you customize when Internet Explorer will issue warnings. This is useful if you deal with sensitive information and want to know which Web pages are secure and which are not. You can also set a number of other advanced Java and Security options here.

SYMBIOTIC PARTNERS

Explorer includes many of the latest Web technologies. These make your Web pages sing, dance, and even act as entire applications. The line between what a computer can do in general and what a computer can do over the Internet is thinning.

ACTIVEX

Microsoft's proprietary ActiveX technology lets you drop controls into your Web pages. Controls are software components such as specialized buttons, input forms, graphics viewers, sound players, and so forth.

When you load a page with an ActiveX control, Explorer will check if you already have that control on your system. If not, you'll be asked whether you'd like to download it. You'll be told whether the control has been authenticated by Microsoft. If the control is secure, it'll automatically be downloaded and installed for you. The resulting Web page may look more like a software program than a Web page. Don't be surprised to find all new types of buttons, such as the up and down arrow controls in Figure I-10.

SCRIPTS

Internet Explorer allows Web page writers to add different types of scripts right into the source code of the Web page itself. This means you can get instantaneous feedback and control of the Web browser, ActiveX controls, Java applets, and other plug-ins. This

Figure I-10
Loading a page
with an ActiveX
control

makes interactivity fast and easy. Internet Explorer supports Visual Basic, Scripting Edition and JavaScript languages.

JAVA

Finally, Explorer fully supports the popular Java language. Java is a programming language that lets you write full applications that run directly within your Web browser. Java is great for writing games, graphics demonstrations, databases, spreadsheets, and much more.

TOTAL MASTERY

Now that you are fully in control of Explorer, you can learn, work, and have fun using it with the greatest of ease. Wandering through the Internet faster than ever, you are ready to investigate new paths of adventure with your trusty, obedient Explorer guiding you every step of the way.

INDEX

G

M

O

Q

T

Books have a substantial influence on the destruction of the forests of the Earth. For example, it takes 17 trees to produce one ton of paper. A first printing of 30,000 copies of a typical 480-page book consumes 108,000 pounds of paper, which will require 918 trees!

Waite Group Press™ is against the clear-cutting of forests and supports reforestation of the Pacific Northwest of the United States and Canada, where most of this paper comes from. As a publisher with several hundred thousand books sold each year, we feel an obligation to give back to the planet. We will therefore support organizations that seek to preserve the forests of planet Earth.

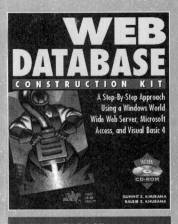

Message from the
Publisher

WELCOME TO OUR NERVOUS SYSTEM

Some people say that the World Wide Web is a graphical extension of the information superhighway, just a network of humans and machines sending each other long lists of the equivalent of digital junk mail.

I think it is much more than that. To me, the Web is nothing less than the nervous system of the entire planet—not just a collection of computer brains connected together, but more like a billion silicon neurons entangled and recirculating electro-chemical signals of information and data, each contributing to the birth of another CPU and another Web site.

Think of each person's hard disk connected at once to every other hard disk on earth, driven by human navigators searching like Columbus for the New World. Seen this way, the Web is more of a super entity, a growing, living thing, controlled by the universal human will to expand, to be more. Yet, unlike a purposeful business plan with rigid rules, the Web expands in a nonlinear, unpredictable, creative way that echoes natural evolution.

We created our Web site not just to extend the reach of our computer book products but to be part of this synaptic neural network, to experience, like a nerve in the body, the flow of ideas and then to pass those ideas up the food chain of the mind. Your mind. Even more, we wanted to pump some of our own creative juices into this rich wine of technology.

TASTE OUR DIGITAL WINE

And so we ask you to taste our wine by visiting the body of our business. Begin by understanding the metaphor we have created for our Web site—a universal learning center, situated in outer space in the form of a space station. A place where you can journey to study any topic from the convenience of your own screen. Right now we are focusing on computer topics, but the stars are the limit on the Web.

If you are interested in discussing this Web site or finding out more about the Waite Group, please send me e-mail with your comments, and I will be happy to respond. Being a programmer myself, I love to talk about technology and find out what our readers are looking for.

Sincerely,

Mitchell Waite

Mitchell Waite, C.E.O. and Publisher

200 Tamal Plaza
Corte Madera, CA 94925
415-924-2575
415-924-2576 fax

Website:
http://www.waite.com/waite

CREATING THE HIGHEST QUALITY COMPUTER BOOKS IN THE INDUSTRY

Waite Group Press

Come Visit
WAITE.COM
Waite Group Press
World Wide Web Site

Now find all the latest information on Waite Group books at our new Web site, **http://www.waite.com/waite.** You'll find an online catalog where you can examine and order any title, review upcoming books, and send e-mail to our authors and editors. Our FTP site has all you need to update your book: the latest program listings, errata sheets, most recent versions of Fractint, POV Ray, Polyray, DMorph, and all the programs featured in our books. So download, talk to us, ask questions, on **http://www.waite.com/waite.**

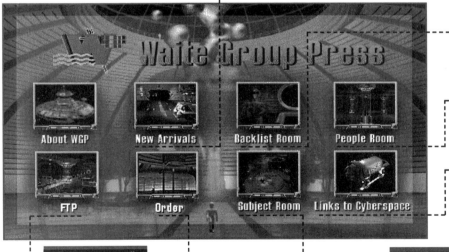

LIMITED WARRANTY

The following warranties shall be effective for 90 days from the date of purchase: (i) The Waite Group, Inc. warrants the enclosed disk to be free of defects in materials and workmanship under normal use; and (ii) The Waite Group, Inc. warrants that the programs, unless modified by the purchaser, will substantially perform the functions described in the documentation provided by The Waite Group, Inc. when operated on the designated hardware and operating system. The Waite Group, Inc. does not warrant that the programs will meet purchaser's requirements or that operation of a program will be uninterrupted or error-free. The program warranty does not cover any program that has been altered or changed in any way by anyone other than The Waite Group, Inc. The Waite Group, Inc. is not responsible for problems caused by changes in the operating characteristics of computer hardware or computer operating systems that are made after the release of the programs, nor for problems in the interaction of the programs with each other or other software.

THESE WARRANTIES ARE EXCLUSIVE AND IN LIEU OF ALL OTHER WARRANTIES OF MERCHANTABILITY OR FITNESS FOR A PARTICULAR PURPOSE OR OF ANY OTHER WARRANTY, WHETHER EXPRESS OR IMPLIED.

EXCLUSIVE REMEDY

The Waite Group, Inc. will replace any defective disk without charge if the defective disk is returned to The Waite Group, Inc. within 90 days from date of purchase.

This is Purchaser's sole and exclusive remedy for any breach of warranty or claim for contract, tort, or damages.

LIMITATION OF LIABILITY

THE WAITE GROUP, INC. AND THE AUTHORS OF THE PROGRAMS SHALL NOT IN ANY CASE BE LIABLE FOR SPECIAL, INCIDENTAL, CONSEQUENTIAL, INDIRECT, OR OTHER SIMILAR DAMAGES ARISING FROM ANY BREACH OF THESE WARRANTIES EVEN IF THE WAITE GROUP, INC. OR ITS AGENT HAS BEEN ADVISED OF THE POSSIBILITY OF SUCH DAMAGES.

THE LIABILITY FOR DAMAGES OF THE WAITE GROUP, INC. AND THE AUTHORS OF THE PROGRAMS UNDER THIS AGREEMENT SHALL IN NO EVENT EXCEED THE PURCHASE PRICE PAID.

COMPLETE AGREEMENT

This Agreement constitutes the complete agreement between The Waite Group, Inc. and the authors of the programs, and you, the purchaser.

Some states do not allow the exclusion or limitation of implied warranties or liability for incidental or consequential damages, so the above exclusions or limitations may not apply to you. This limited warranty gives you specific legal rights; you may have others, which vary from state to state.

SATISFACTION REPORT CARD

Please fill out this card if you wish to know of future updates to *VBScript Interactive Course*, or to receive our catalog.

First Name: _____   **Last Name:** _____

Street Address: _____

City: _____   **State:** _____   **Zip:** _____

E-Mail Address _____

Daytime Telephone: (   ) _____

Date product was acquired: Month _____ **Day** _____ **Year** _____   **Your Occupation:** _____

Overall, how would you rate *VBScript Interactive Course?*

☐ Excellent   ☐ Very Good   ☐ Good
☐ Fair   ☐ Below Average   ☐ Poor

What did you like MOST about this book? _____
_____
_____

What did you like LEAST about this book? _____
_____
_____

Please describe any problems you may have encountered with installing or using the disk: _____
_____

How did you use this book (problem-solver, tutorial, reference...)?
_____

What is your level of computer expertise?

☐ New   ☐ Dabbler   ☐ Hacker
☐ Power User   ☐ Programmer   ☐ Experienced Professional

What computer languages are you familiar with? _____
_____

Please describe your computer hardware:

Computer _____ Hard disk _____
5.25" disk drives _____ 3.5" disk drives _____
Video card _____ Monitor _____
Printer _____ Peripherals _____
Sound Board _____ CD ROM _____

Where did you buy this book?

☐ Bookstore (name): _____
☐ Discount store (name): _____
☐ Computer store (name): _____
☐ Catalog (name): _____
☐ Direct from WGP   ☐ Other _____

What price did you pay for this book? _____

What influenced your purchase of this book?

☐ Recommendation   ☐ Advertisement
☐ Magazine review   ☐ Store display
☐ Mailing   ☐ Book's format
☐ Reputation of Waite Group Press   ☐ Other

How many computer books do you buy each year? _____

How many other Waite Group books do you own? _____

What is your favorite Waite Group book? _____
_____

Is there any program or subject you would like to see Waite Group Press cover in a similar approach? _____
_____

Additional comments? _____
_____
_____

Please send to: **Waite Group Press**
                     200 Tamal Plaza
                     Corte Madera, CA 94925

☐ **Check here for a free Waite Group catalog**

BEFORE YOU OPEN THE DISK OR CD-ROM PACKAGE ON THE FACING PAGE, CAREFULLY READ THE LICENSE AGREEMENT.

Opening this package indicates that you agree to abide by the license agreement found in the back of this book. If you do not agree with it, promptly return the unopened disk package (including the related book) to the place you obtained them for a refund.